WOLVERINE: LOGAN

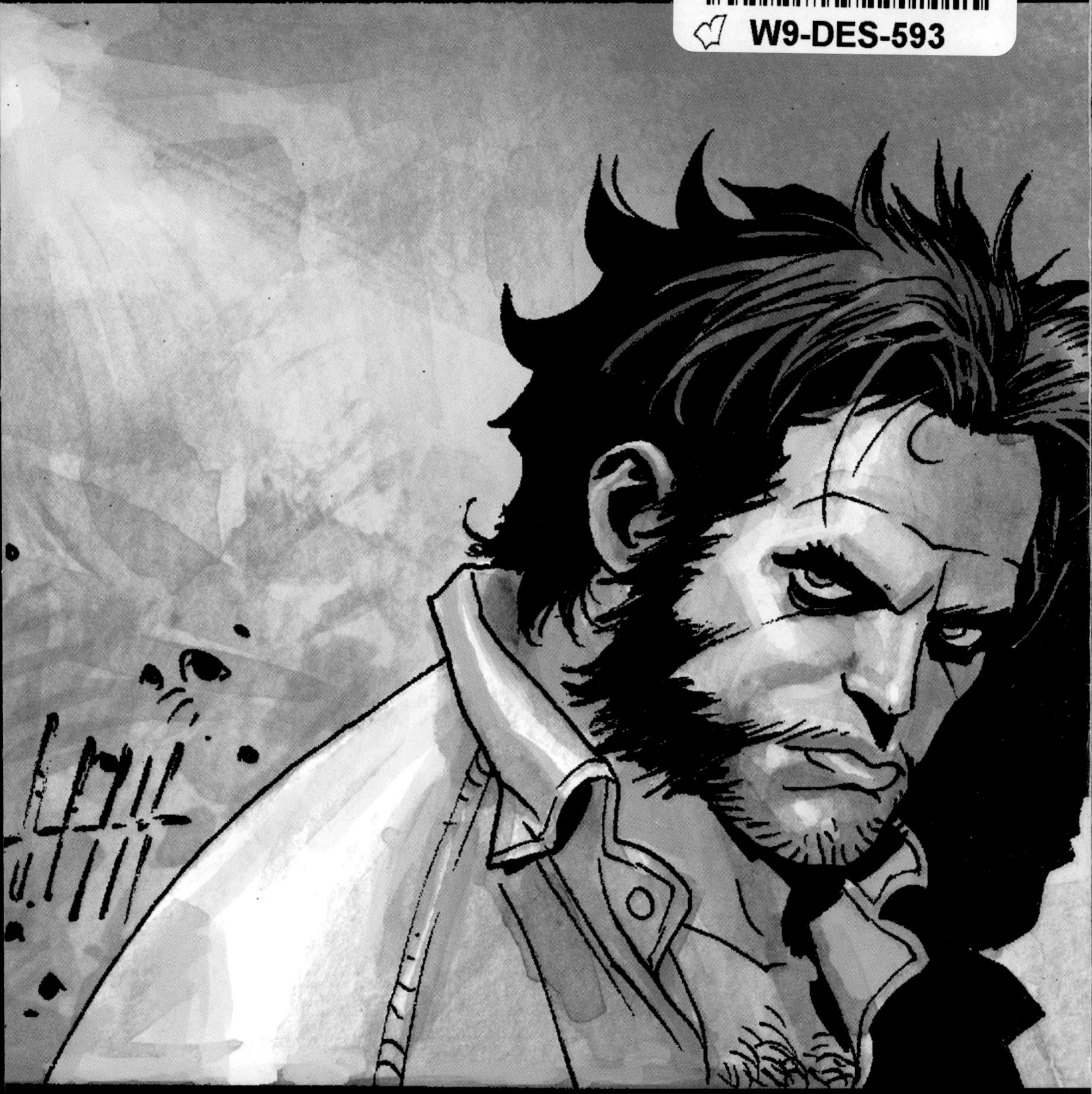

WOLVERINE: LOGAN

WRITER
Brian K. Vaughan

ARTIST
Eduardo Risso

COLORS: Dean White

LETTERS: Virtual Calligraphy's Joe Caramagna

ASSISTANT EDITOR: Daniel Ketchum

EDITOR: Axel Alonso

COLLECTION EDITOR: Jennifer Grünwald

ASSISTANT EDITORS: Jody LeHeup, Cory Levine & John Denning

EDITOR, SPECIAL PROJECTS: Mark D. Beazley

SENIOR EDITOR, SPECIAL PROJECTS: Jeff Youngquist

SENIOR VICE PRESIDENT OF SALES: David Gabriel

BOOK DESIGNER: Spring Hoteling

EDITOR IN CHIEF: Joe Quesada

PUBLISHER: Dan Buckley

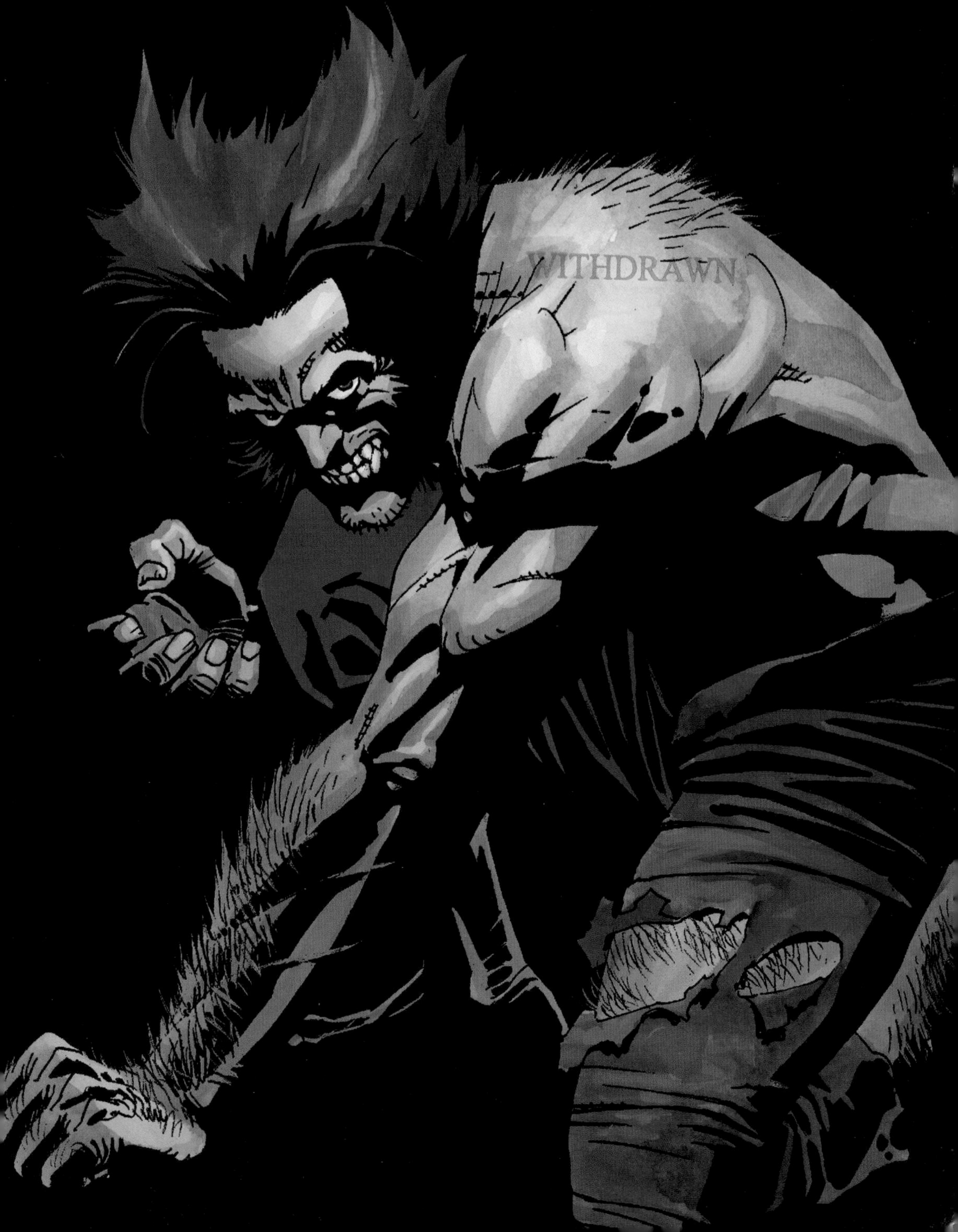

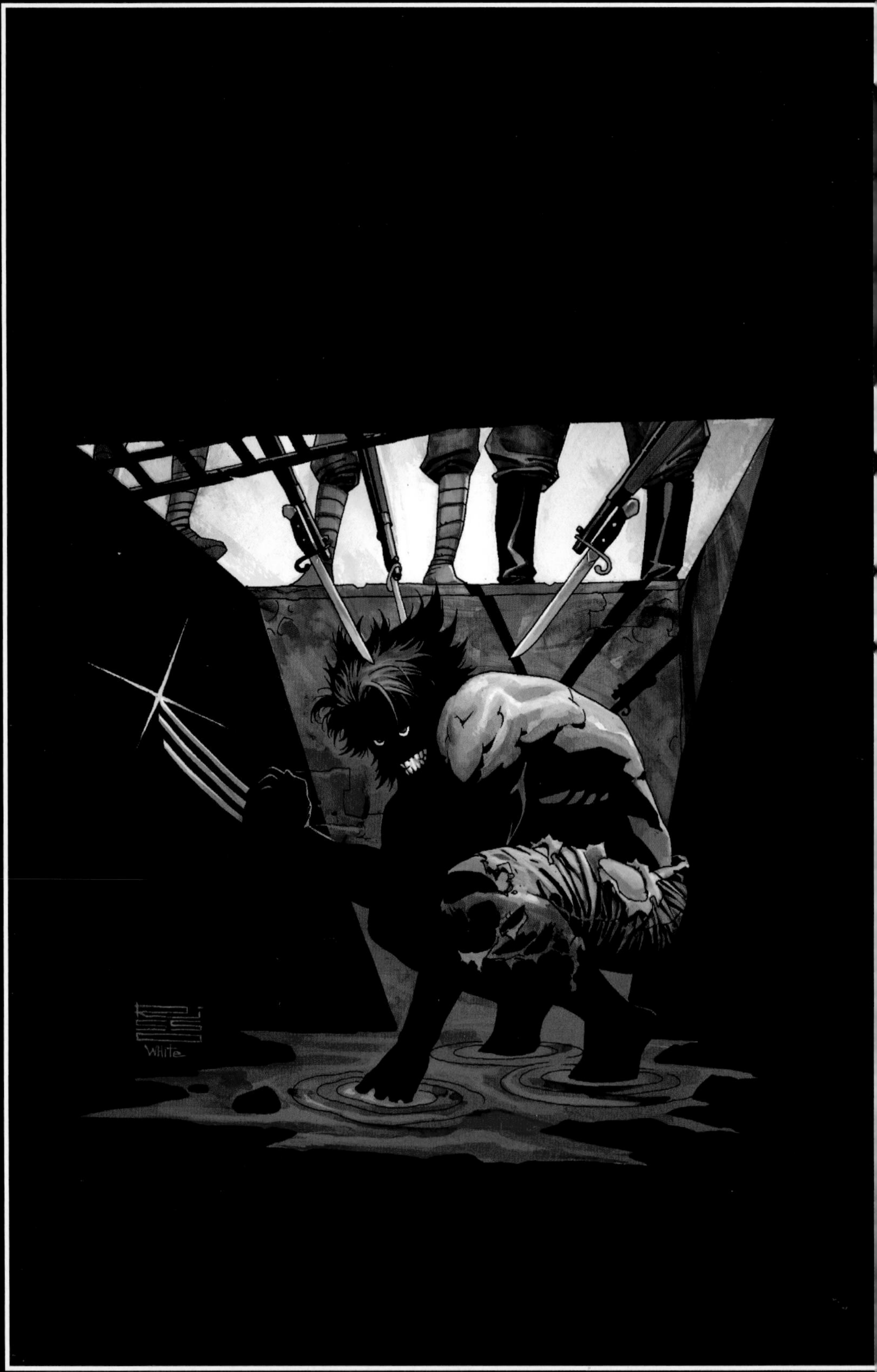
WHITE

issue number one

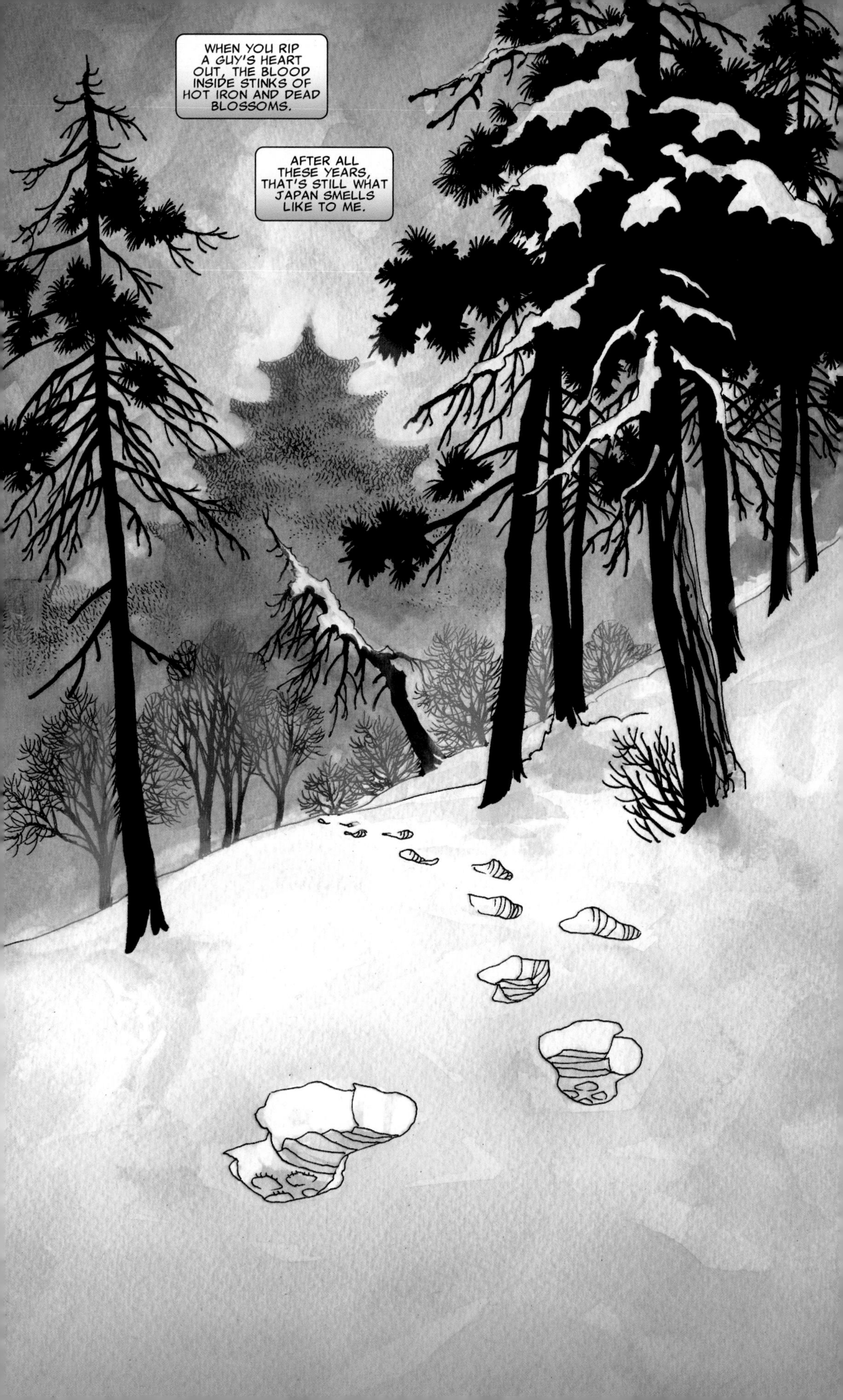
WHEN YOU RIP A GUY'S HEART OUT, THE BLOOD INSIDE STINKS OF HOT IRON AND DEAD BLOSSOMS.
AFTER ALL THESE YEARS, THAT'S STILL WHAT JAPAN SMELLS LIKE TO ME.

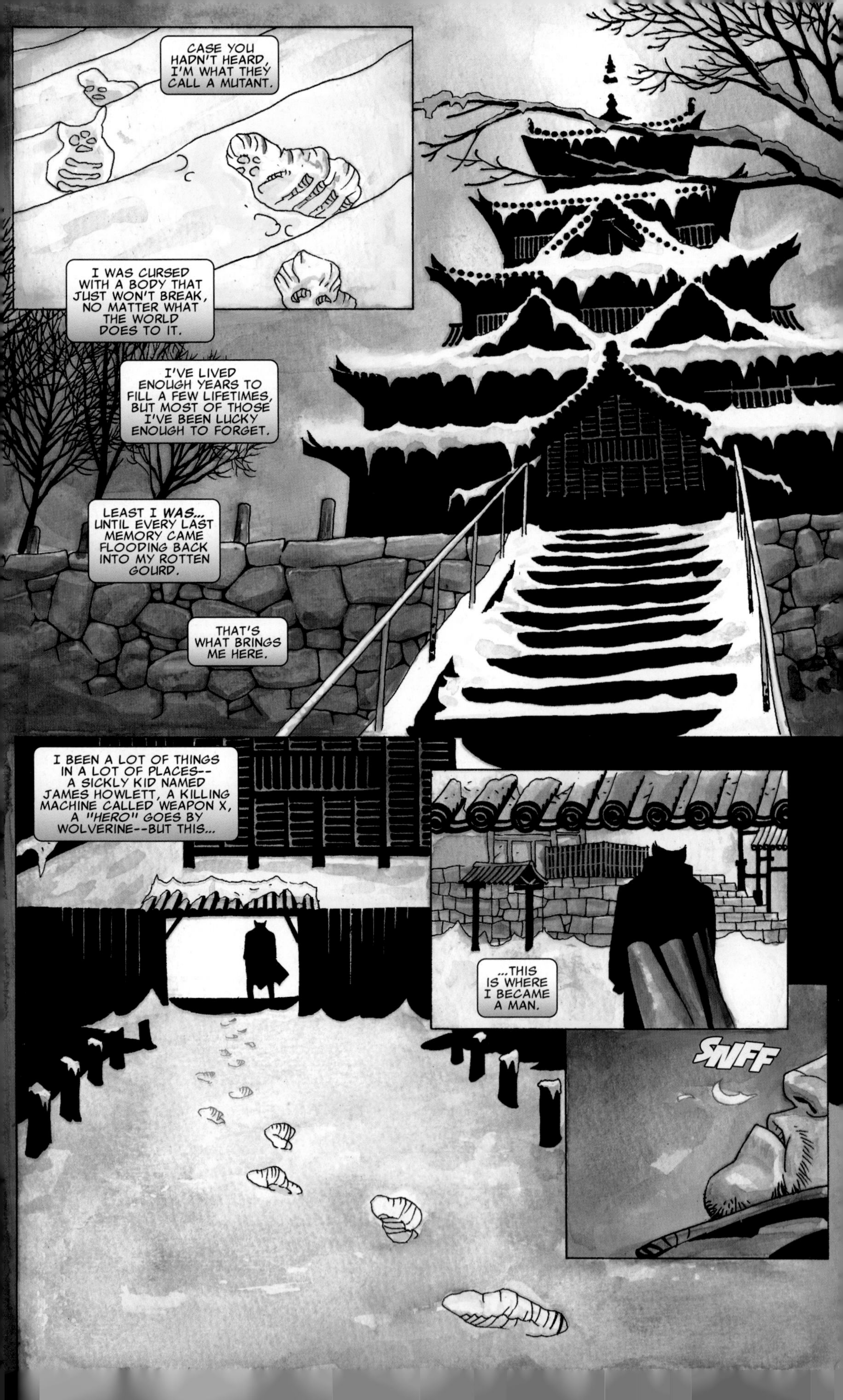
CASE YOU HADN'T HEARD, I'M WHAT THEY CALL A MUTANT.
I WAS CURSED WITH A BODY THAT JUST WON'T BREAK, NO MATTER WHAT THE WORLD DOES TO IT.
I'VE LIVED ENOUGH YEARS TO FILL A FEW LIFETIMES, BUT MOST OF THOSE I'VE BEEN LUCKY ENOUGH TO FORGET.
LEAST I *WAS*... UNTIL EVERY LAST MEMORY CAME FLOODING BACK INTO MY ROTTEN GOURD.
THAT'S WHAT BRINGS ME HERE.
I BEEN A LOT OF THINGS IN A LOT OF PLACES-- A SICKLY KID NAMED JAMES HOWLETT, A KILLING MACHINE CALLED WEAPON X, A "HERO" GOES BY WOLVERINE--BUT THIS...
...THIS IS WHERE I BECAME A MAN.
SNFF

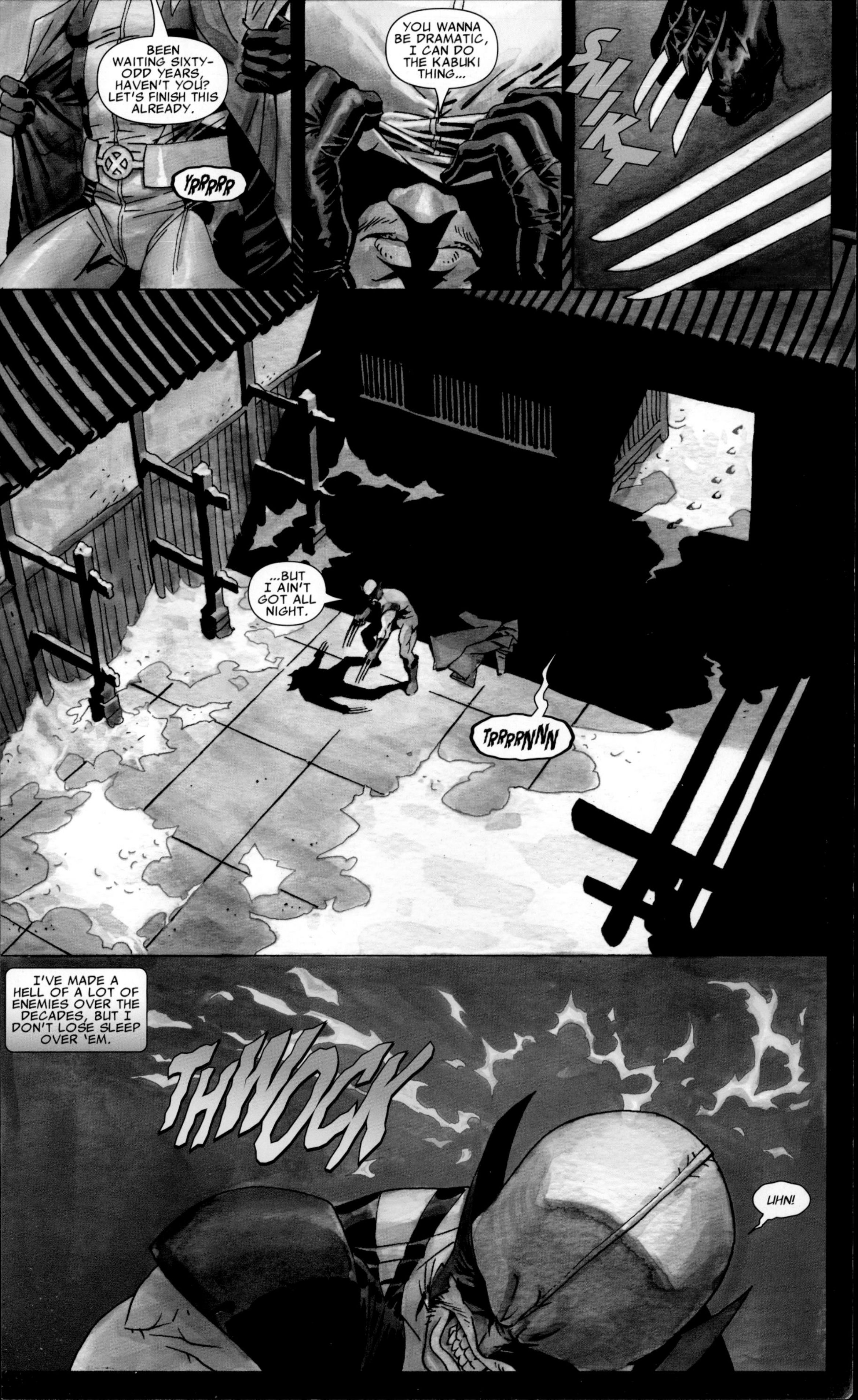
BEEN WAITING SIXTY-ODD YEARS, HAVEN'T YOU? LET'S FINISH THIS ALREADY.
YRRRRR
YOU WANNA BE DRAMATIC, I CAN DO THE KABUKI THING...
SNIKT
...BUT I AIN'T GOT ALL NIGHT.
TRRRRNNN
I'VE MADE A HELL OF A LOT OF ENEMIES OVER THE DECADES, BUT I DON'T LOSE SLEEP OVER 'EM.
THWOCK
UHN!

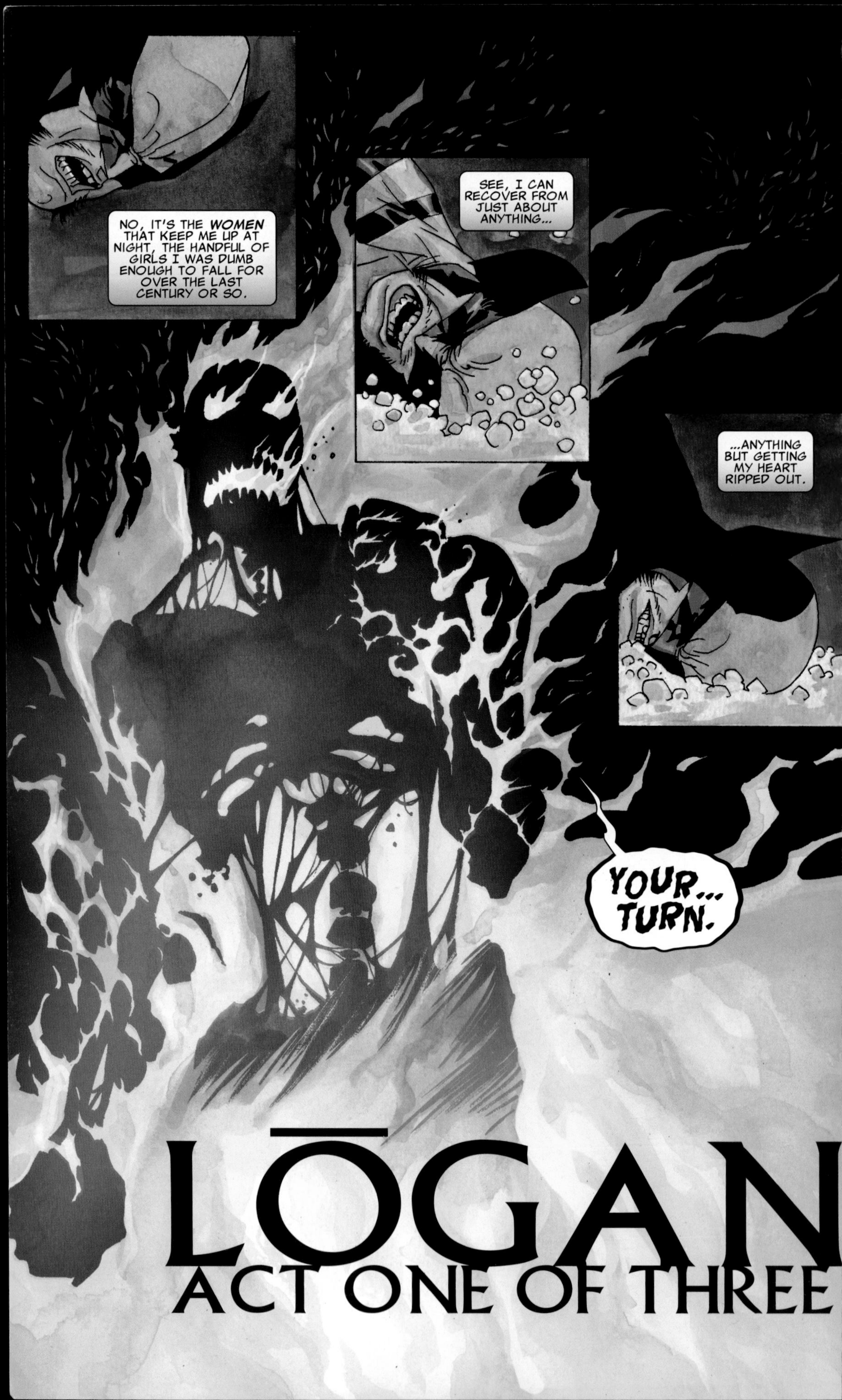
NO, IT'S THE WOMEN THAT KEEP ME UP AT NIGHT, THE HANDFUL OF GIRLS I WAS DUMB ENOUGH TO FALL FOR OVER THE LAST CENTURY OR SO.
SEE, I CAN RECOVER FROM JUST ABOUT ANYTHING...
...ANYTHING BUT GETTING MY HEART RIPPED OUT.
YOUR... TURN.
LŌGAN
ACT ONE OF THREE

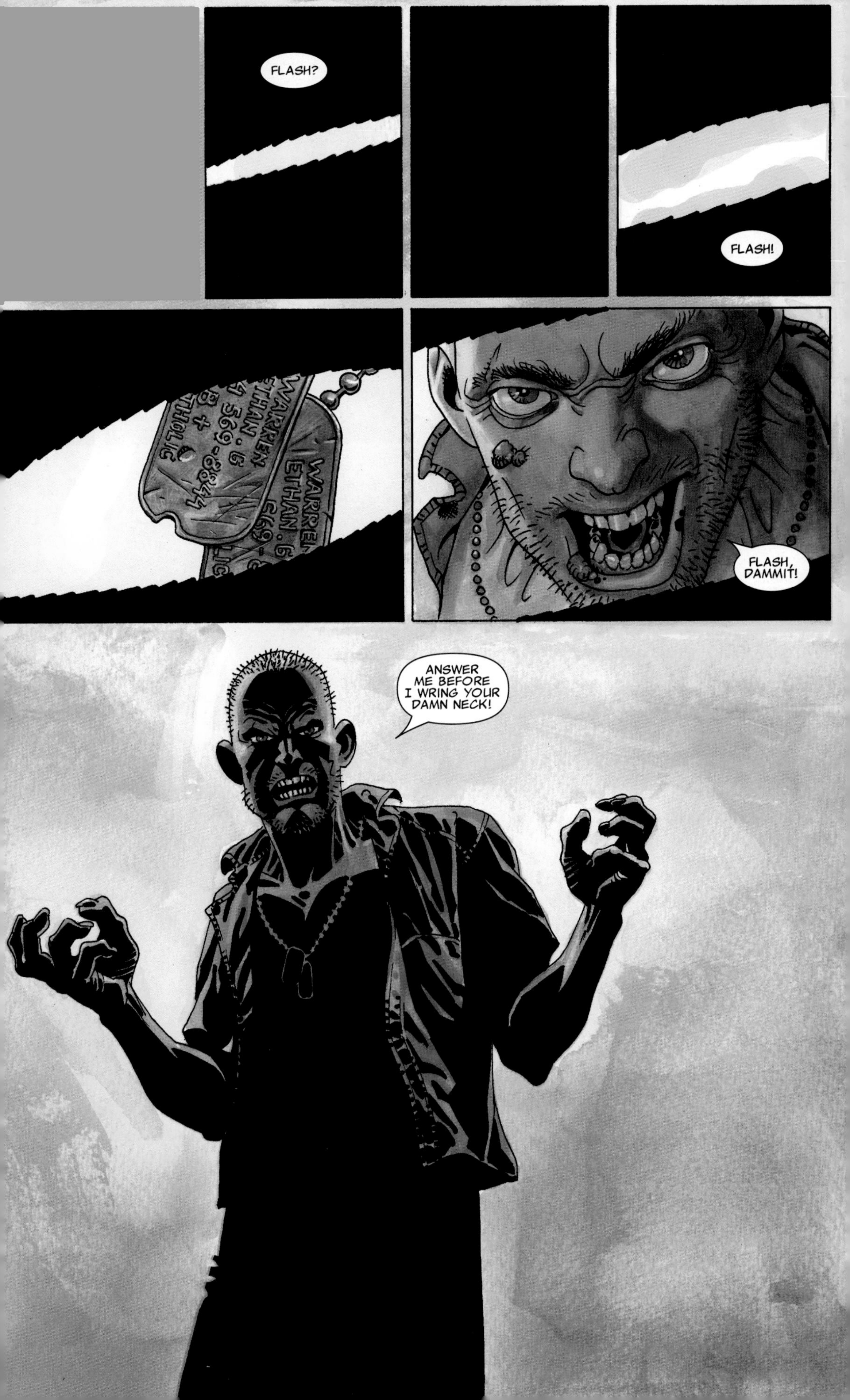
FLASH?
FLASH!
FLASH, DAMMIT!
ANSWER ME BEFORE I WRING YOUR DAMN NECK!

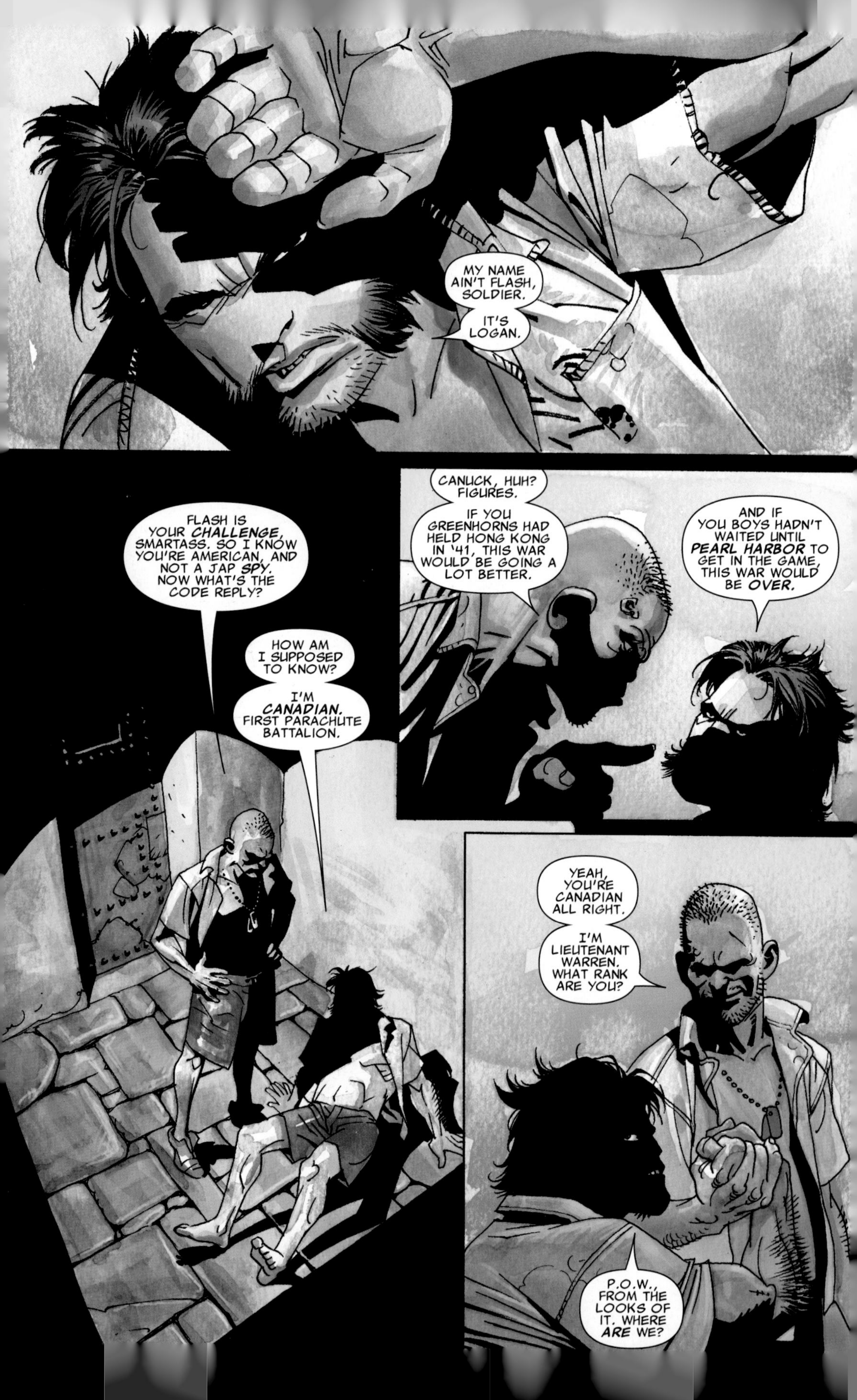
MY NAME AIN'T FLASH, SOLDIER.
IT'S LOGAN.
FLASH IS YOUR CHALLENGE, SMARTASS. SO I KNOW YOU'RE AMERICAN, AND NOT A JAP SPY. NOW WHAT'S THE CODE REPLY?
HOW AM I SUPPOSED TO KNOW?
I'M CANADIAN. FIRST PARACHUTE BATTALION.
CANUCK, HUH? FIGURES.
IF YOU GREENHORNS HAD HELD HONG KONG IN '41, THIS WAR WOULD BE GOING A LOT BETTER.
AND IF YOU BOYS HADN'T WAITED UNTIL PEARL HARBOR TO GET IN THE GAME, THIS WAR WOULD BE OVER.
YEAH, YOU'RE CANADIAN ALL RIGHT.
I'M LIEUTENANT WARREN. WHAT RANK ARE YOU?
P.O.W., FROM THE LOOKS OF IT. WHERE ARE WE?

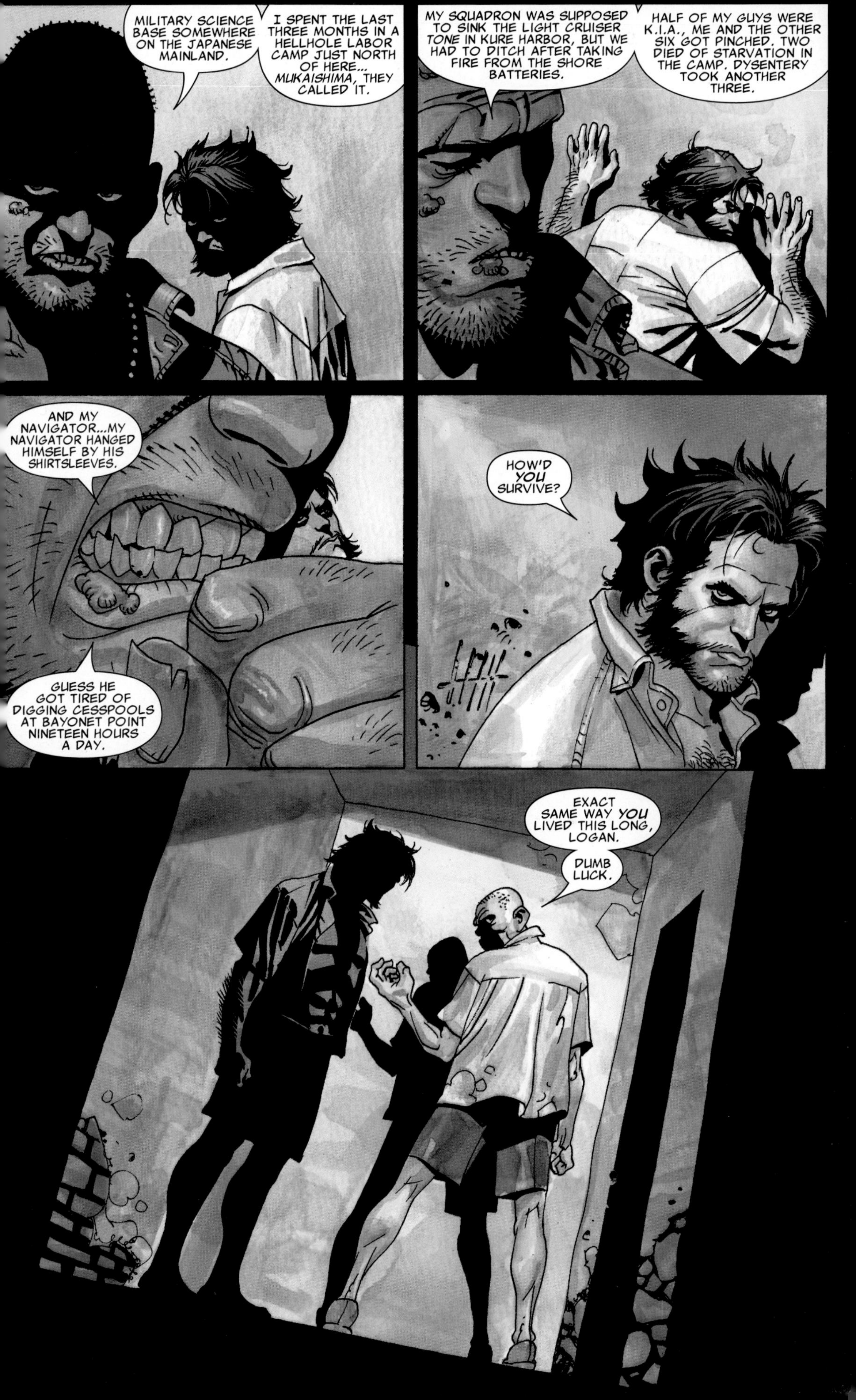
MILITARY SCIENCE BASE SOMEWHERE ON THE JAPANESE MAINLAND.
I SPENT THE LAST THREE MONTHS IN A HELLHOLE LABOR CAMP JUST NORTH OF HERE... MUKAISHIMA, THEY CALLED IT.
MY SQUADRON WAS SUPPOSED TO SINK THE LIGHT CRUISER TONE IN KURE HARBOR, BUT WE HAD TO DITCH AFTER TAKING FIRE FROM THE SHORE BATTERIES.
HALF OF MY GUYS WERE K.I.A., ME AND THE OTHER SIX GOT PINCHED. TWO DIED OF STARVATION IN THE CAMP. DYSENTERY TOOK ANOTHER THREE.
AND MY NAVIGATOR...MY NAVIGATOR HANGED HIMSELF BY HIS SHIRTSLEEVES.
GUESS HE GOT TIRED OF DIGGING CESSPOOLS AT BAYONET POINT NINETEEN HOURS A DAY.
HOW'D YOU SURVIVE?
EXACT SAME WAY YOU LIVED THIS LONG, LOGAN.
DUMB LUCK.

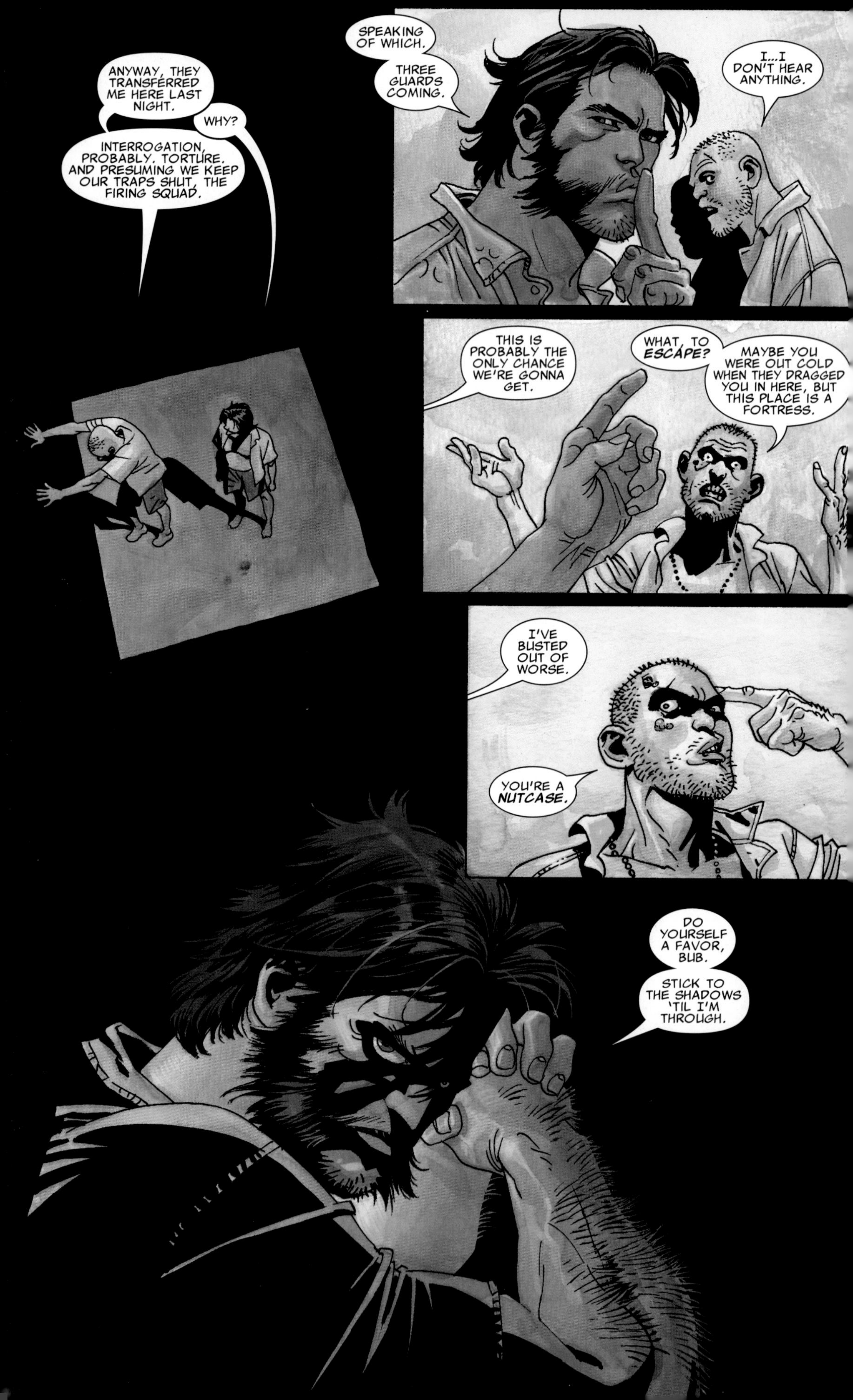
ANYWAY, THEY TRANSFERRED ME HERE LAST NIGHT.
WHY?
INTERROGATION, PROBABLY. TORTURE. AND PRESUMING WE KEEP OUR TRAPS SHUT, THE FIRING SQUAD.
SPEAKING OF WHICH.
THREE GUARDS COMING.
I...I DON'T HEAR ANYTHING.
THIS IS PROBABLY THE ONLY CHANCE WE'RE GONNA GET.
WHAT, TO ESCAPE?
MAYBE YOU WERE OUT COLD WHEN THEY DRAGGED YOU IN HERE, BUT THIS PLACE IS A FORTRESS.
I'VE BUSTED OUT OF WORSE.
YOU'RE A NUTCASE.
DO YOURSELF A FAVOR, BUB.
STICK TO THE SHADOWS 'TIL I'M THROUGH.

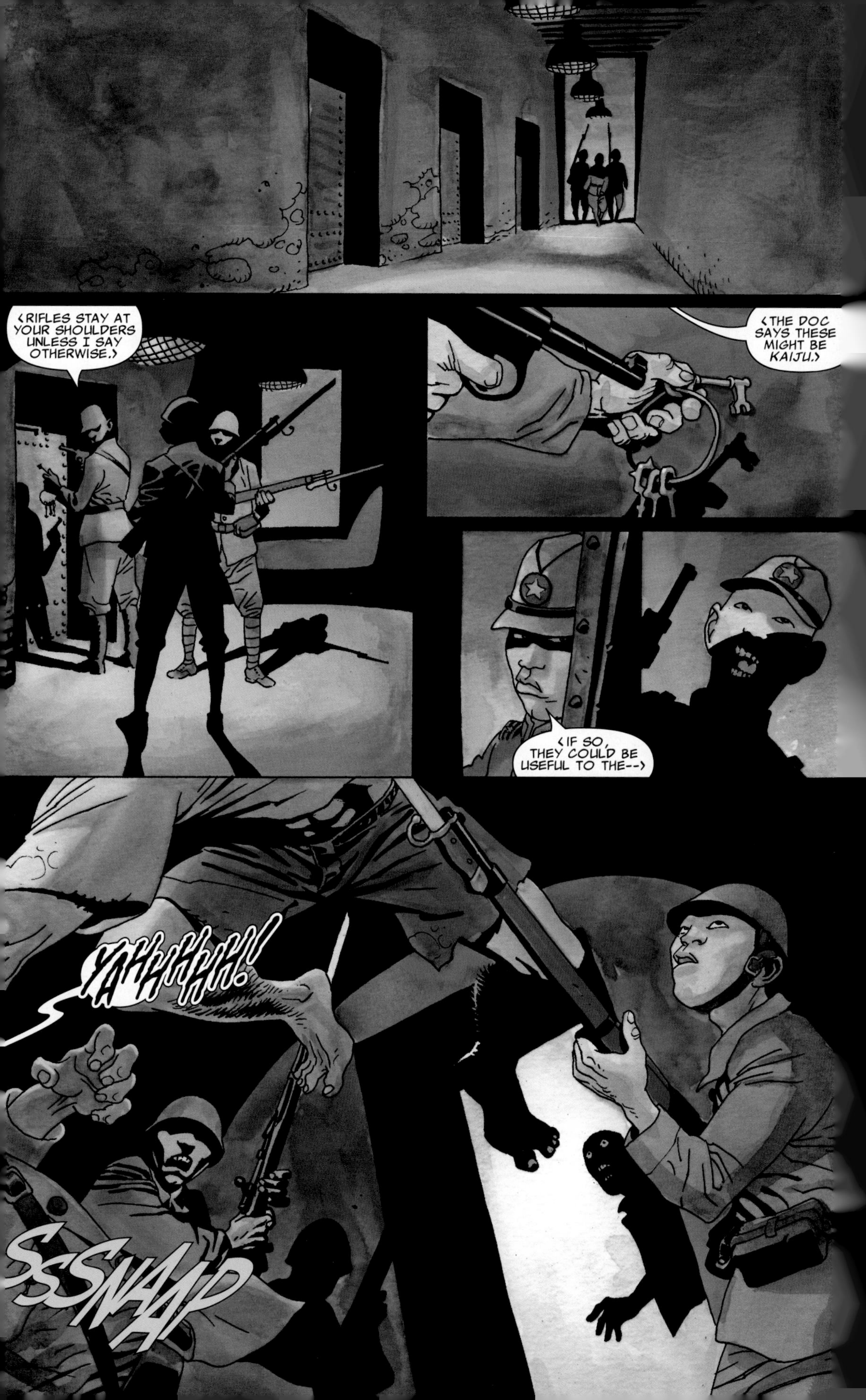
‹RIFLES STAY AT YOUR SHOULDERS UNLESS I SAY OTHERWISE.›
‹THE DOC SAYS THESE MIGHT BE KAIJU.›
‹IF SO, THEY COULD BE USEFUL TO THE--›
YAHHHHH!
SSSNAAP

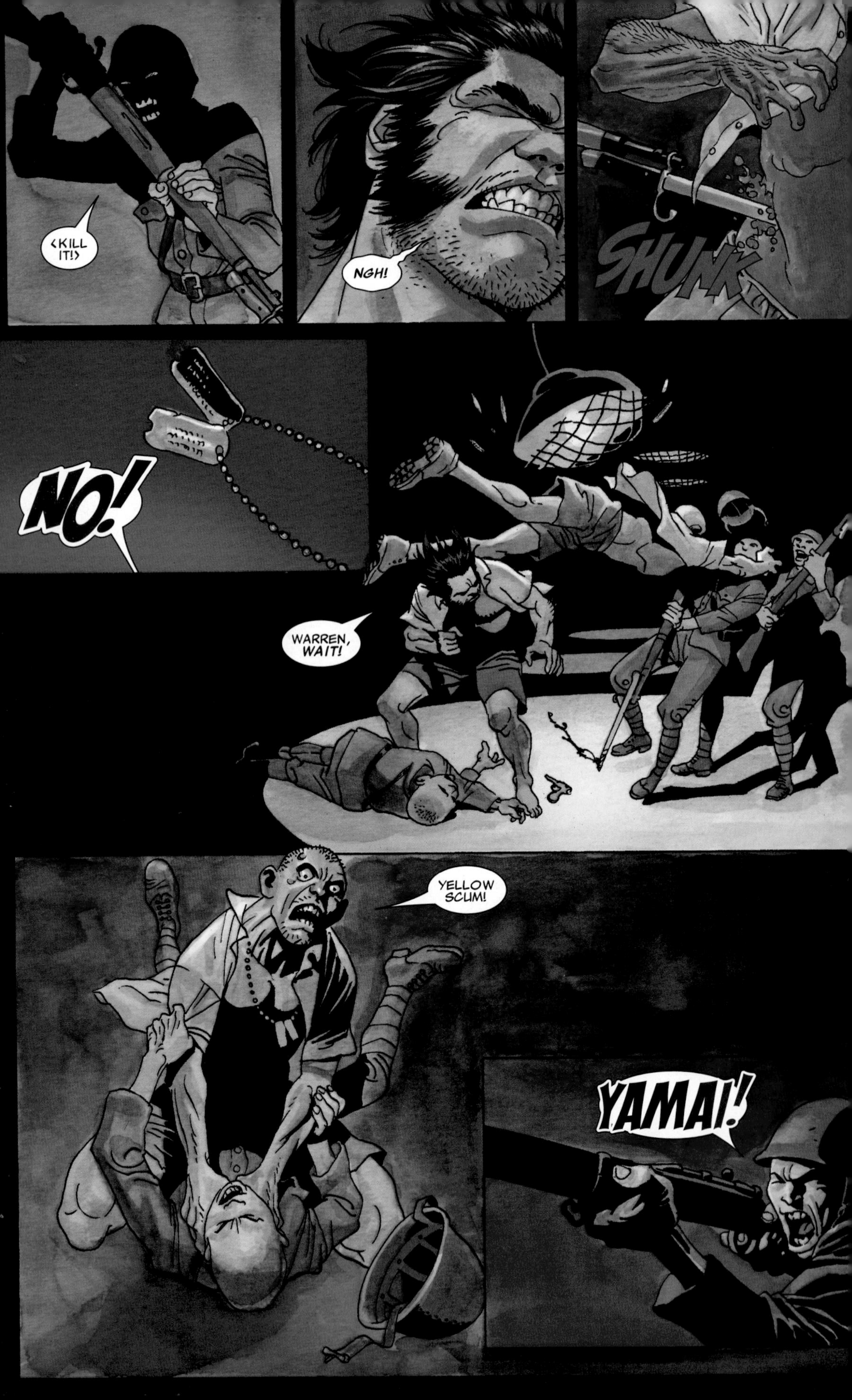

<KILL IT!>
NGH!
SHUNK
NO!
WARREN, WAIT!
YELLOW SCUM!
YAMA!!

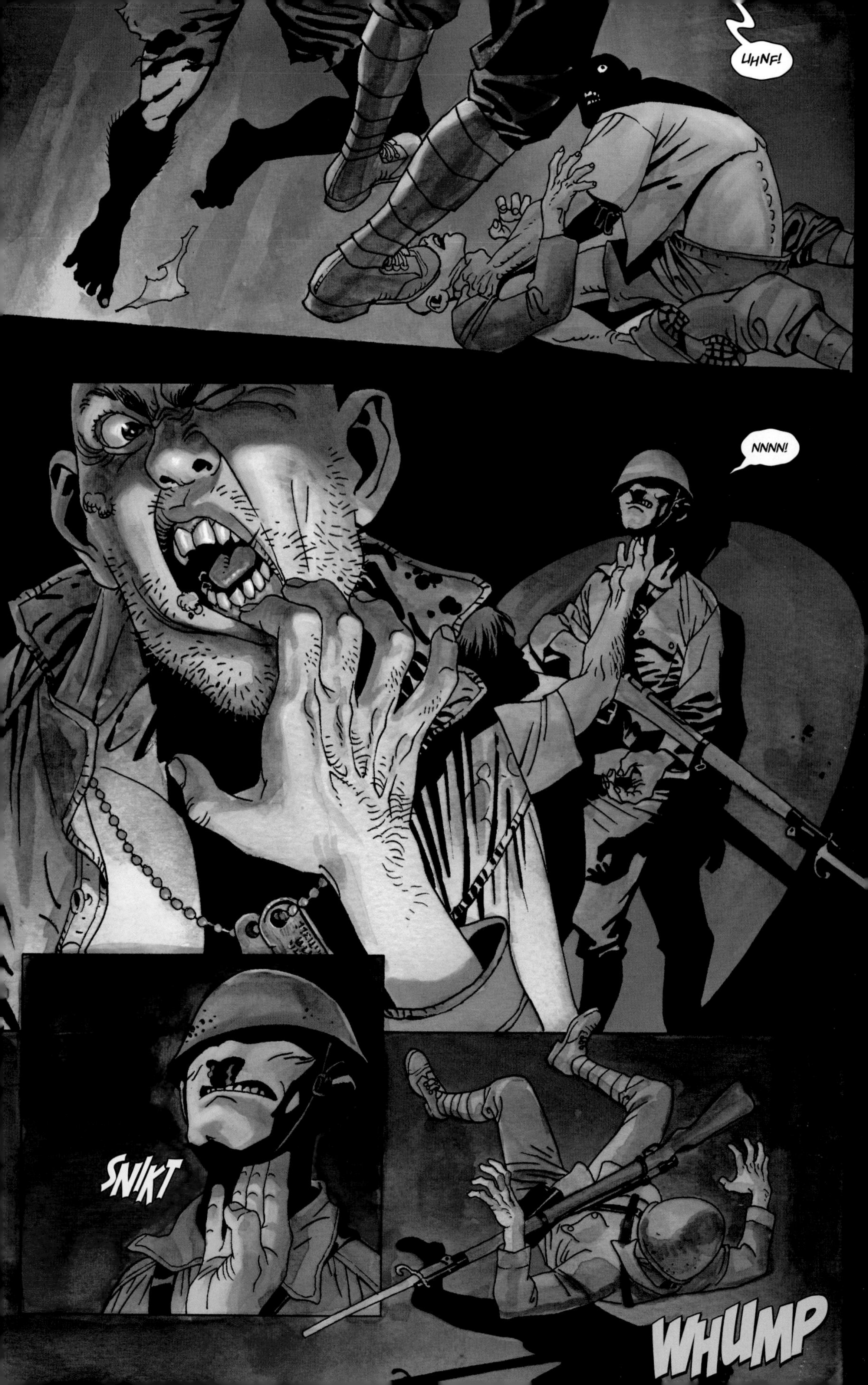
UHNF!
NNNN!
SNIKT
WHUMP

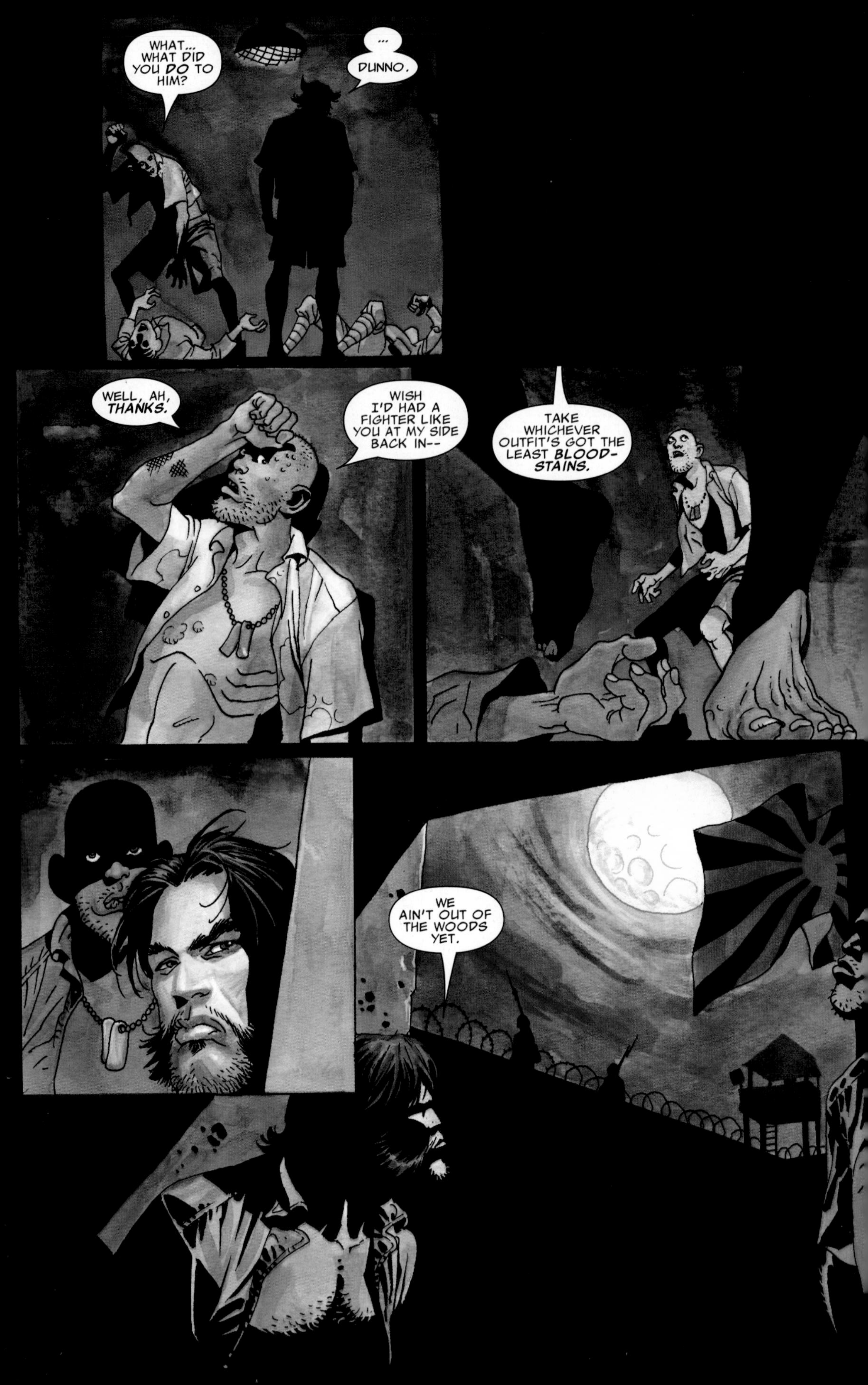
WHAT... WHAT DID YOU **DO** TO HIM?
... DUNNO.
WELL, AH, ***THANKS.***
WISH I'D HAD A FIGHTER LIKE YOU AT MY SIDE BACK IN--
TAKE WHICHEVER OUTFIT'S GOT THE LEAST ***BLOOD-STAINS.***
WE AIN'T OUT OF THE WOODS YET.

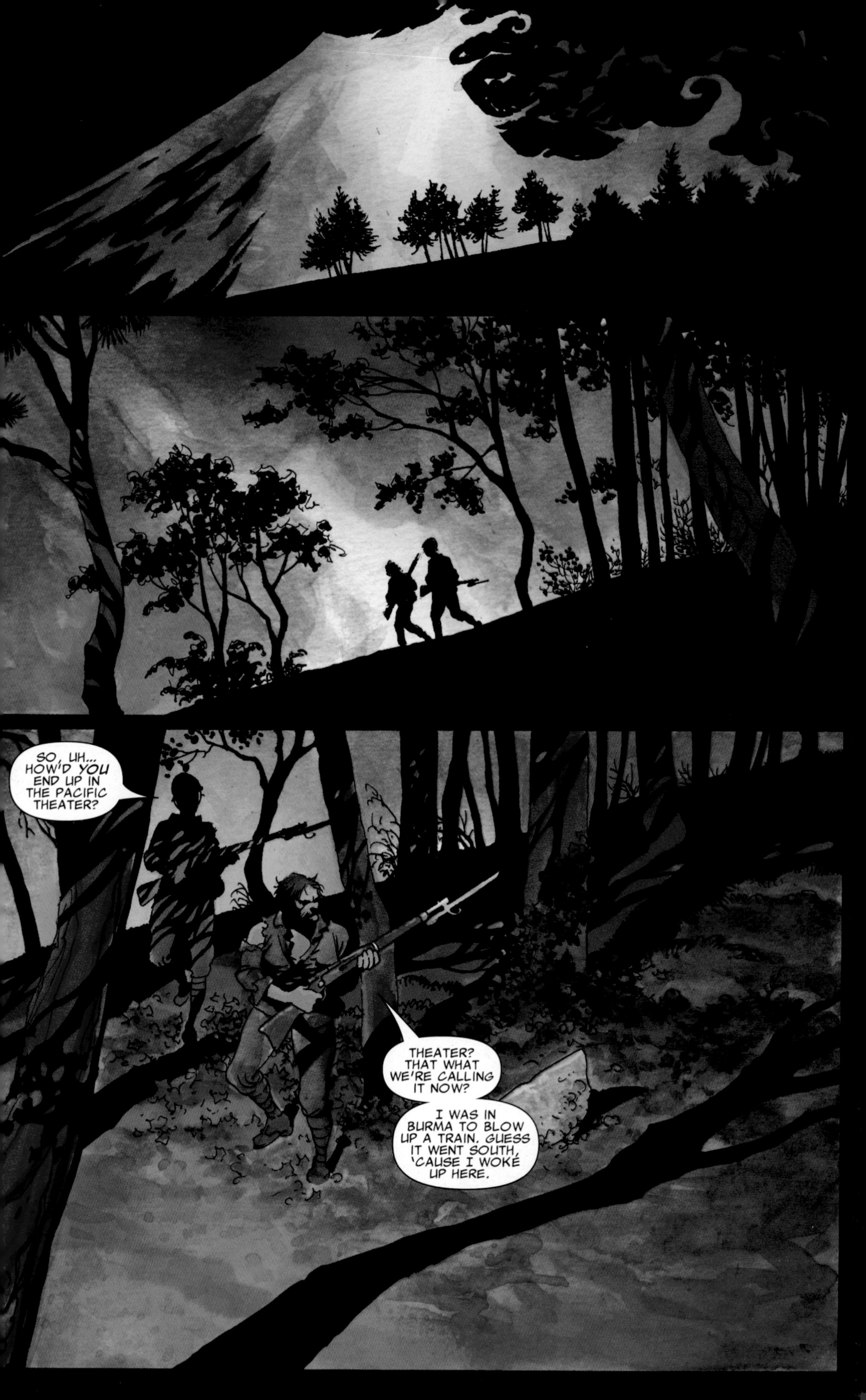
SO, UH... HOW'D YOU END UP IN THE PACIFIC THEATER?
THEATER? THAT WHAT WE'RE CALLING IT NOW?
I WAS IN BURMA TO BLOW UP A TRAIN. GUESS IT WENT SOUTH, 'CAUSE I WOKE UP HERE.

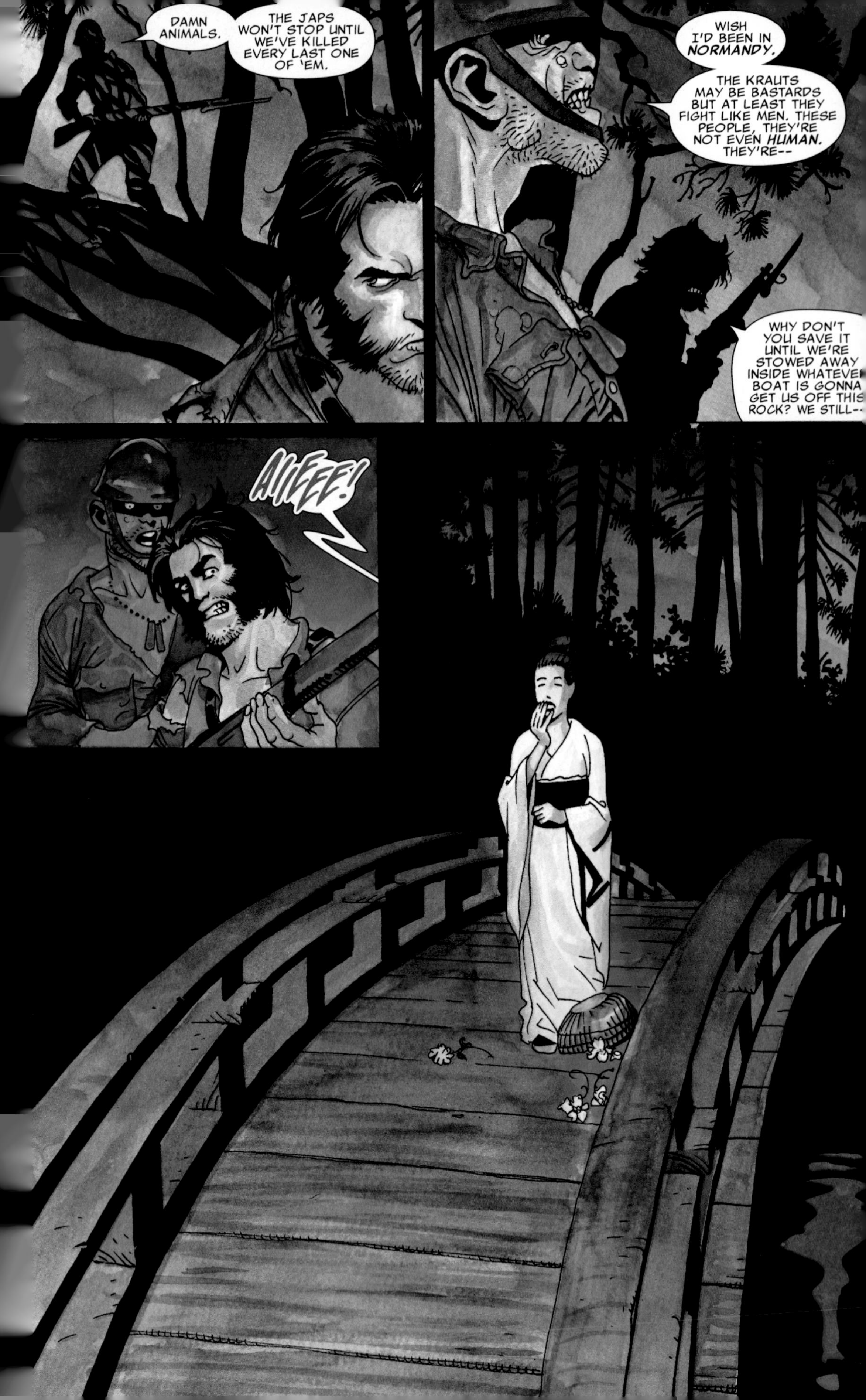
DAMN ANIMALS.
THE JAPS WON'T STOP UNTIL WE'VE KILLED EVERY LAST ONE OF 'EM.
WISH I'D BEEN IN NORMANDY.
THE KRAUTS MAY BE BASTARDS BUT AT LEAST THEY FIGHT LIKE MEN. THESE PEOPLE, THEY'RE NOT EVEN HUMAN. THEY'RE--
WHY DON'T YOU SAVE IT UNTIL WE'RE STOWED AWAY INSIDE WHATEVE BOAT IS GONNA GET US OFF THIS ROCK? WE STILL--
AIIEEE!

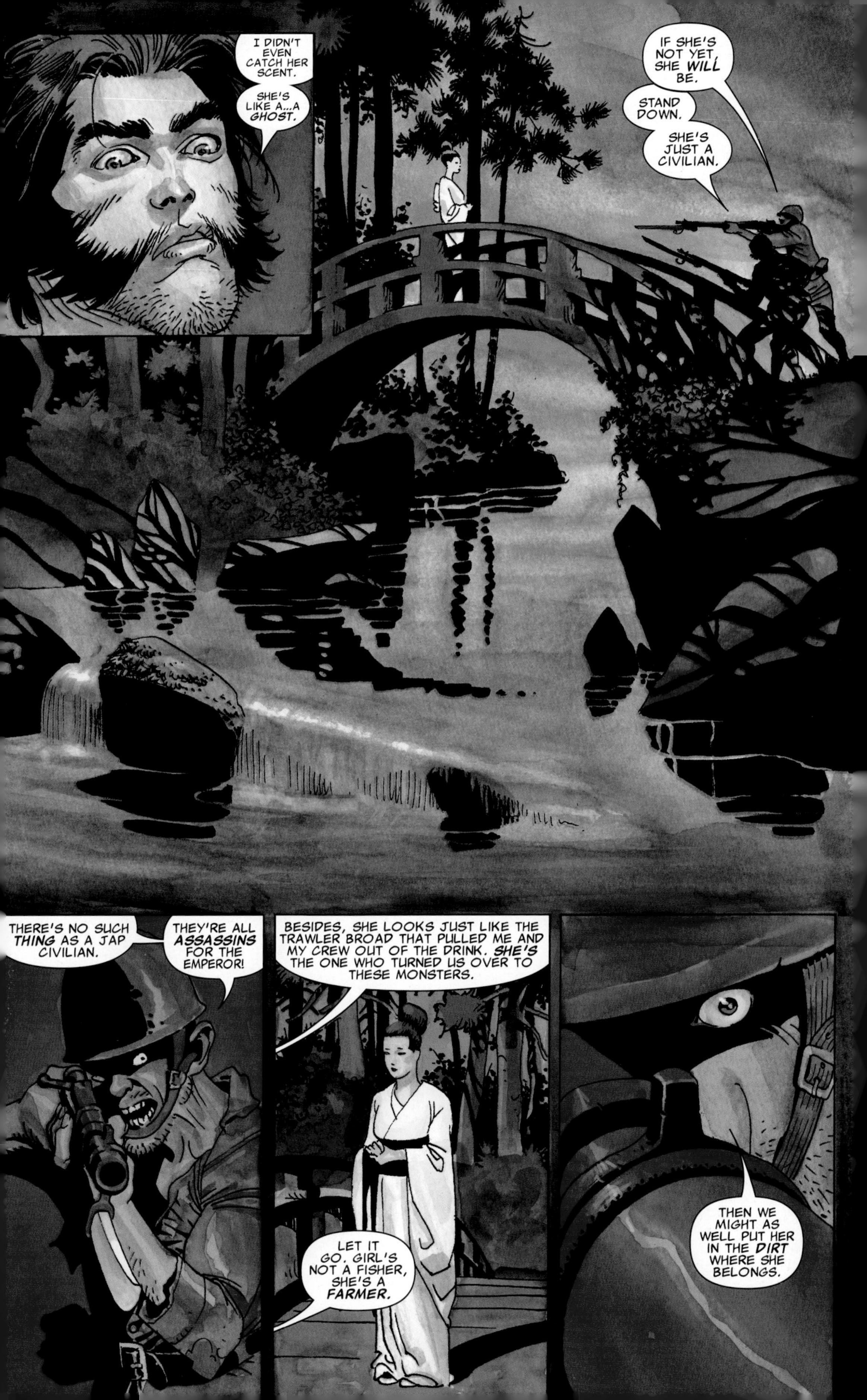
I DIDN'T EVEN CATCH HER SCENT.
SHE'S LIKE A...A GHOST.
IF SHE'S NOT YET, SHE WILL BE.
STAND DOWN.
SHE'S JUST A CIVILIAN.
THERE'S NO SUCH THING AS A JAP CIVILIAN.
THEY'RE ALL ASSASSINS FOR THE EMPEROR!
BESIDES, SHE LOOKS JUST LIKE THE TRAWLER BROAD THAT PULLED ME AND MY CREW OUT OF THE DRINK. SHE'S THE ONE WHO TURNED US OVER TO THESE MONSTERS.
LET IT GO. GIRL'S NOT A FISHER, SHE'S A FARMER.
THEN WE MIGHT AS WELL PUT HER IN THE DIRT WHERE SHE BELONGS.

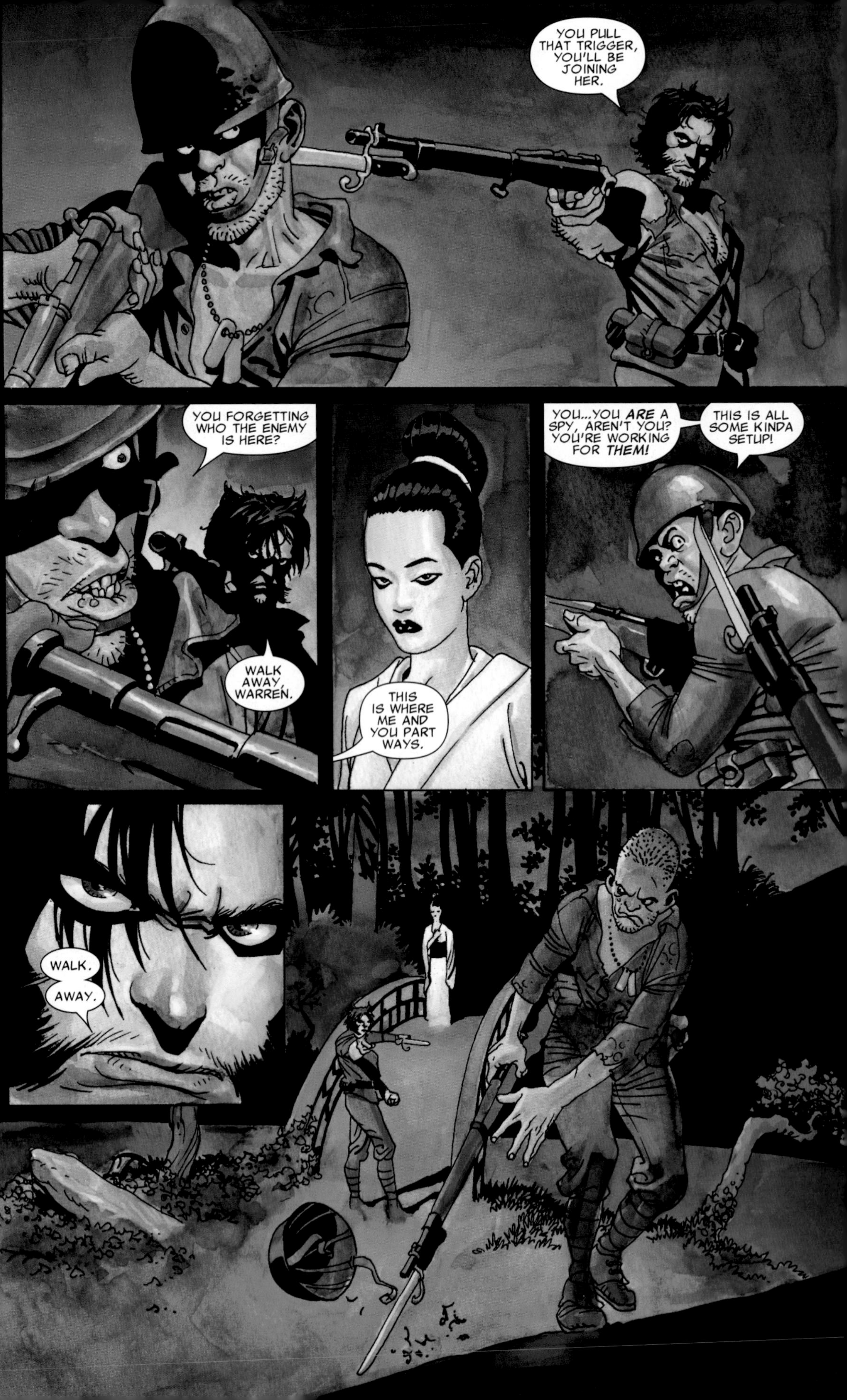

YOU PULL THAT TRIGGER, YOU'LL BE JOINING HER.
YOU FORGETTING WHO THE ENEMY IS HERE?
WALK AWAY, WARREN.
THIS IS WHERE ME AND YOU PART WAYS.
YOU...YOU **ARE** A SPY, AREN'T YOU? YOU'RE WORKING FOR **THEM!**
THIS IS ALL SOME KINDA SETUP!
WALK.
AWAY.

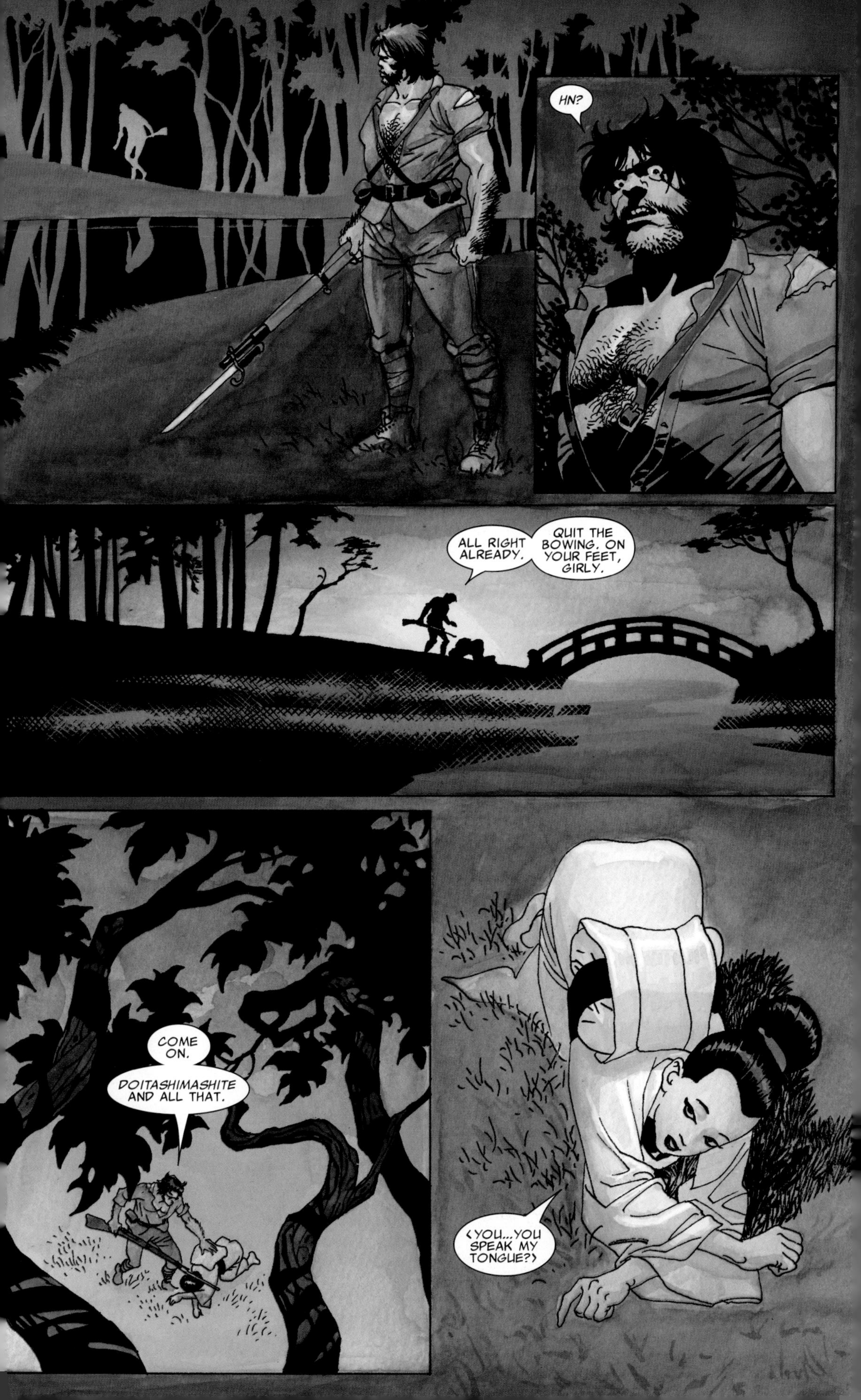
HN?
ALL RIGHT ALREADY.
QUIT THE BOWING. ON YOUR FEET, GIRLY.
COME ON.
DOITASHIMASHITE AND ALL THAT.
‹YOU...YOU SPEAK MY TONGUE?›

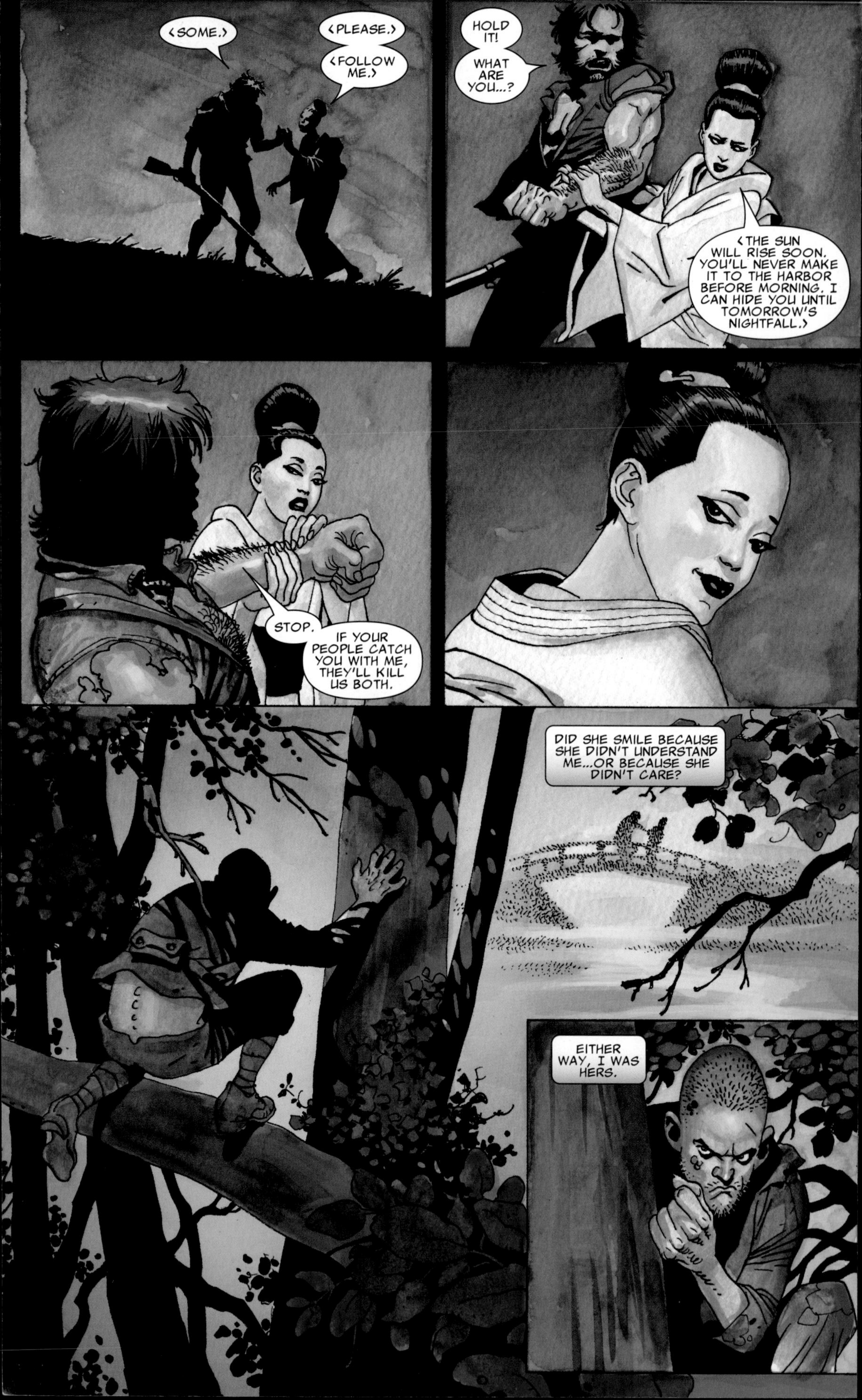
‹SOME.›
‹PLEASE.›
‹FOLLOW ME.›
HOLD IT!
WHAT ARE YOU...?
‹THE SUN WILL RISE SOON. YOU'LL NEVER MAKE IT TO THE HARBOR BEFORE MORNING. I CAN HIDE YOU UNTIL TOMORROW'S NIGHTFALL.›
STOP.
IF YOUR PEOPLE CATCH YOU WITH ME, THEY'LL KILL US BOTH.
DID SHE SMILE BECAUSE SHE DIDN'T UNDERSTAND ME...OR BECAUSE SHE DIDN'T CARE?
EITHER WAY, I WAS HERS.

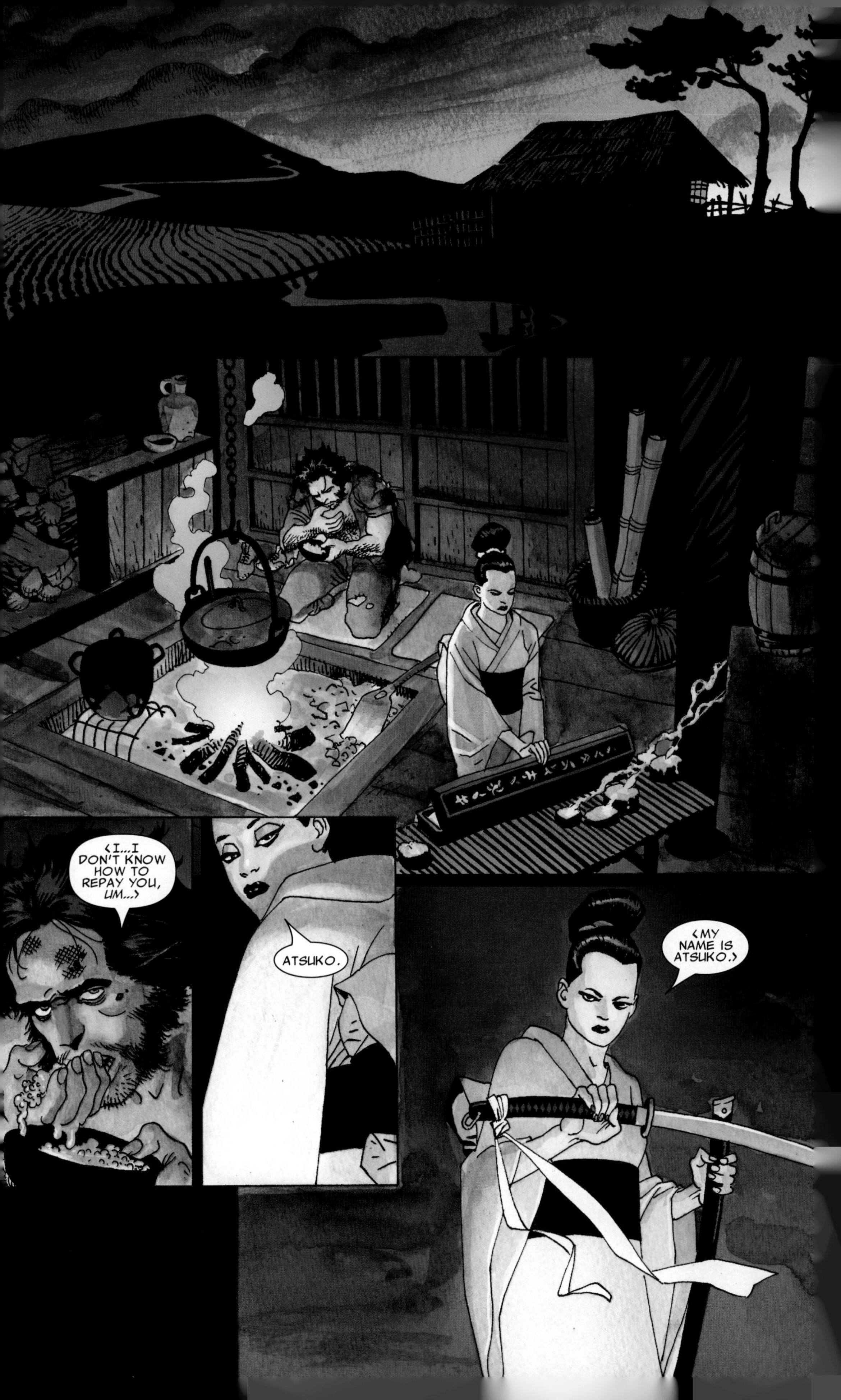

‹I...I DON'T KNOW HOW TO REPAY YOU, UM...›
ATSUKO.
‹MY NAME IS ATSUKO.›

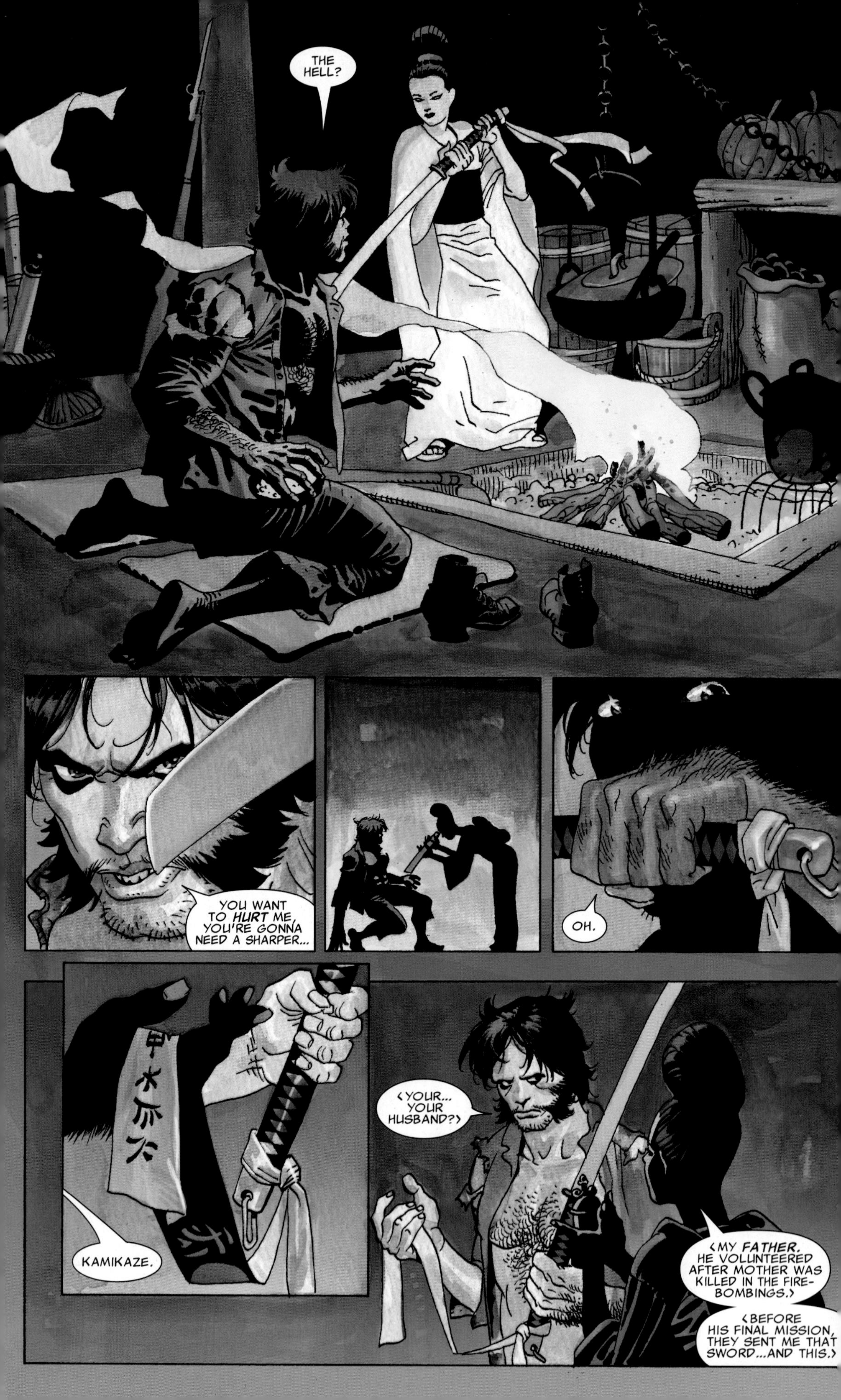

THE HELL?
YOU WANT TO *HURT* ME, YOU'RE GONNA NEED A SHARPER...
OH.
KAMIKAZE.
‹YOUR... YOUR HUSBAND?›
‹MY *FATHER.* HE VOLUNTEERED AFTER MOTHER WAS KILLED IN THE FIRE-BOMBINGS.›
‹BEFORE HIS FINAL MISSION, THEY SENT ME THAT SWORD...AND THIS.›

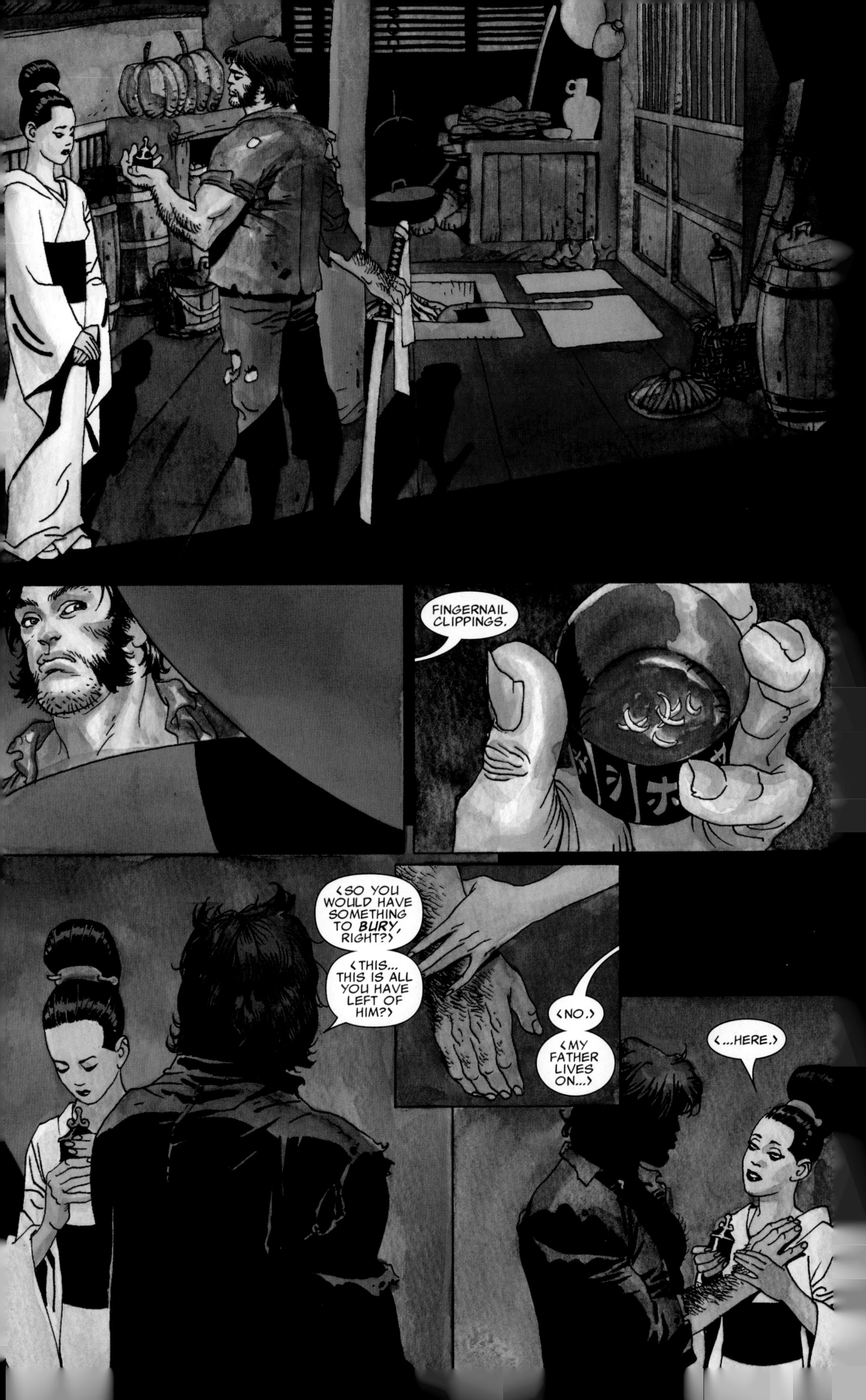
FINGERNAIL CLIPPINGS.
‹SO YOU WOULD HAVE SOMETHING TO BURY, RIGHT?›
‹THIS... THIS IS ALL YOU HAVE LEFT OF HIM?›
‹NO.›
‹MY FATHER LIVES ON...›
‹...HERE.›

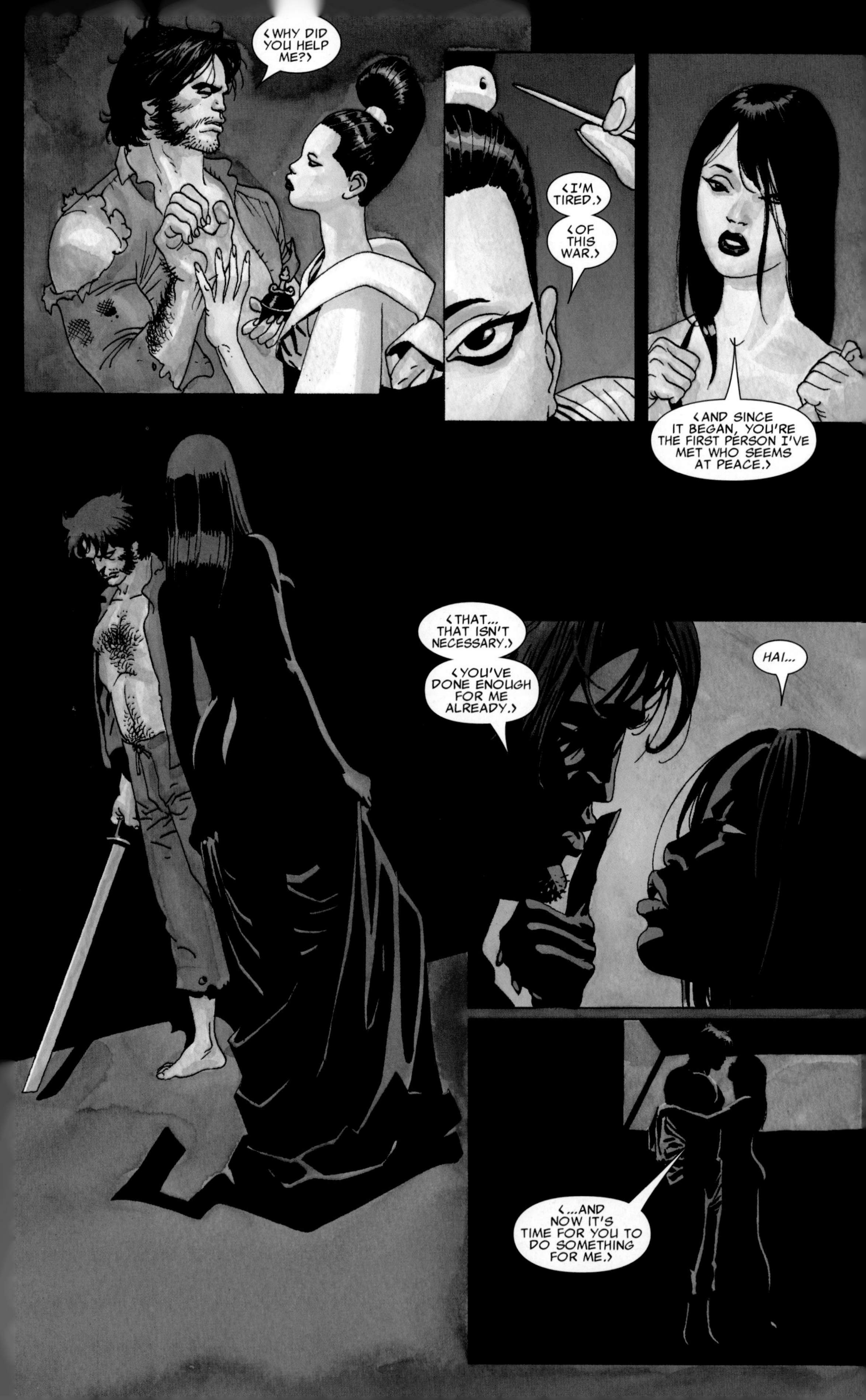
‹WHY DID YOU HELP ME?›
‹I'M TIRED.›
‹OF THIS WAR.›
‹AND SINCE IT BEGAN, YOU'RE THE FIRST PERSON I'VE MET WHO SEEMS AT PEACE.›
‹THAT... THAT ISN'T NECESSARY.›
‹YOU'VE DONE ENOUGH FOR ME ALREADY.›
HAI...
‹...AND NOW IT'S TIME FOR YOU TO DO SOMETHING FOR ME.›

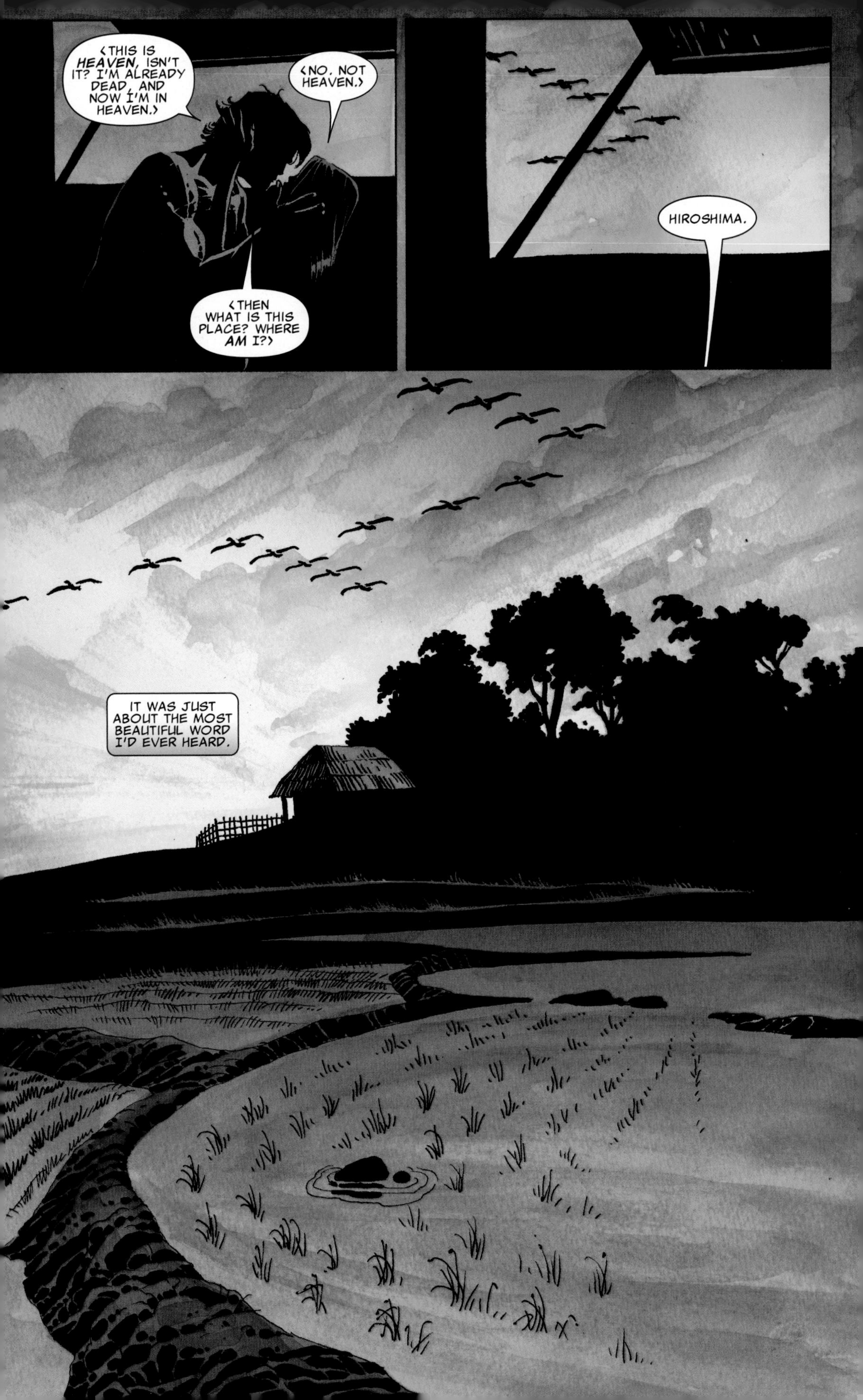
‹THIS IS HEAVEN, ISN'T IT? I'M ALREADY DEAD, AND NOW I'M IN HEAVEN.›
‹NO. NOT HEAVEN.›
‹THEN WHAT IS THIS PLACE? WHERE AM I?›
HIROSHIMA.
IT WAS JUST ABOUT THE MOST BEAUTIFUL WORD I'D EVER HEARD.

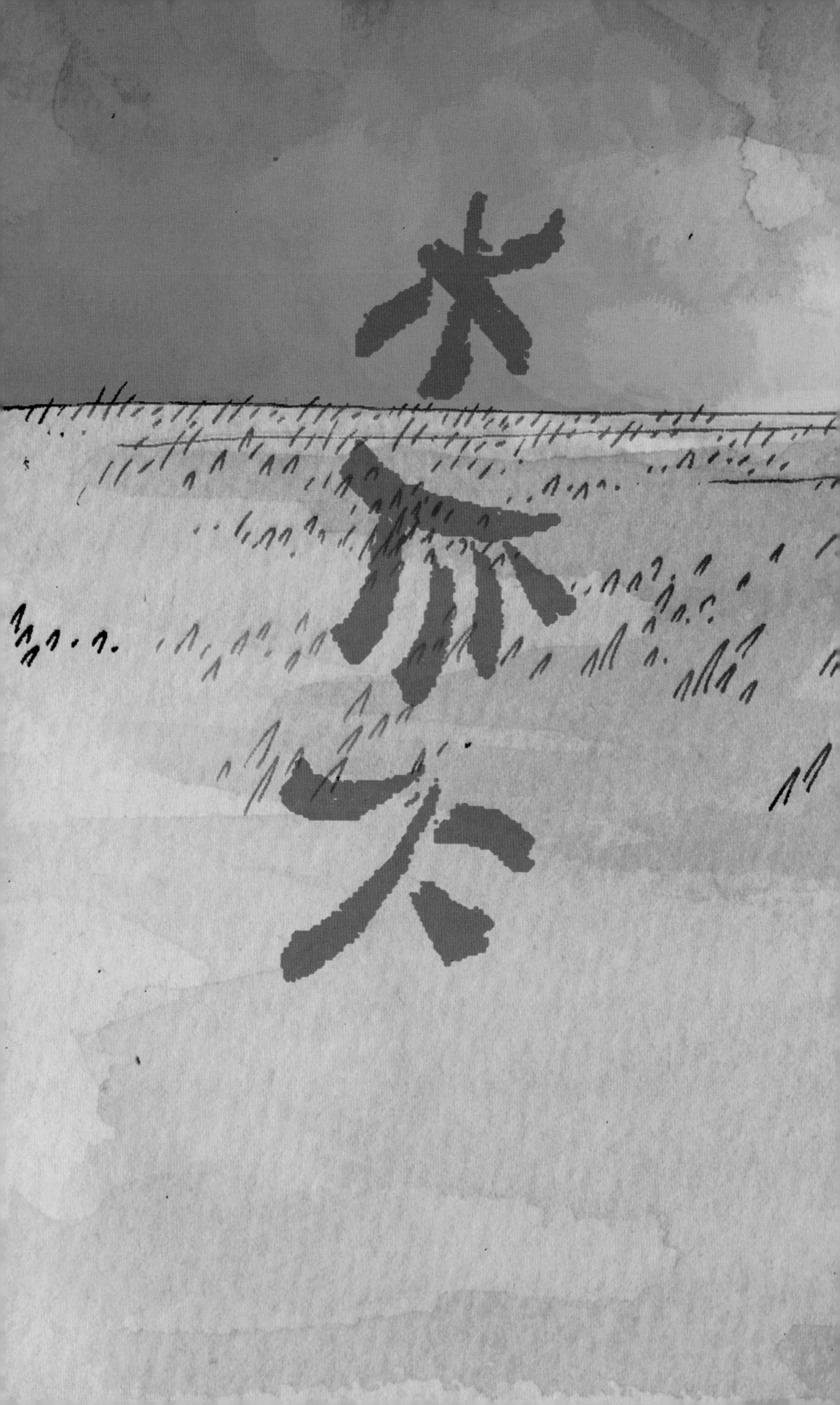

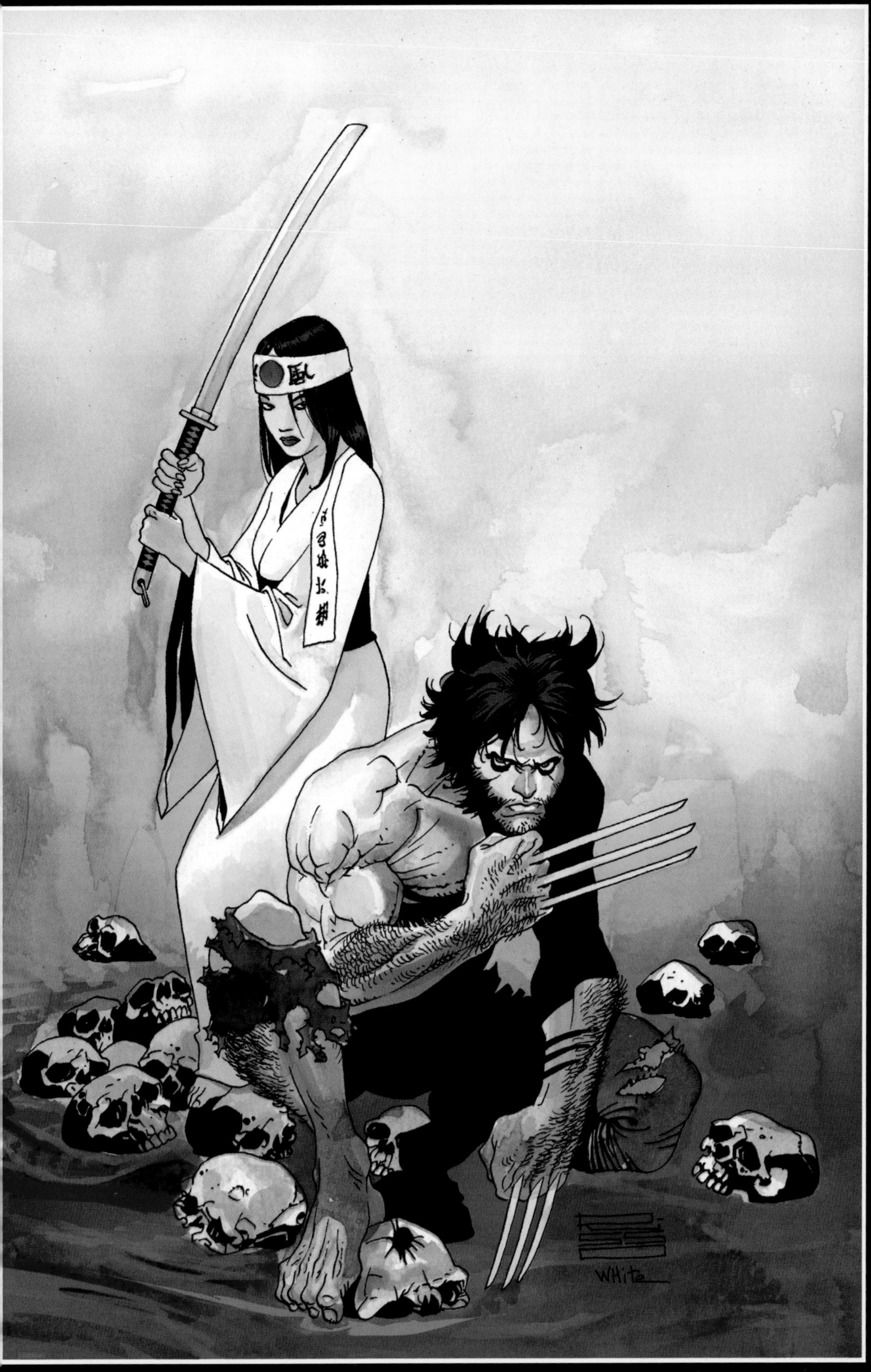

issue number two

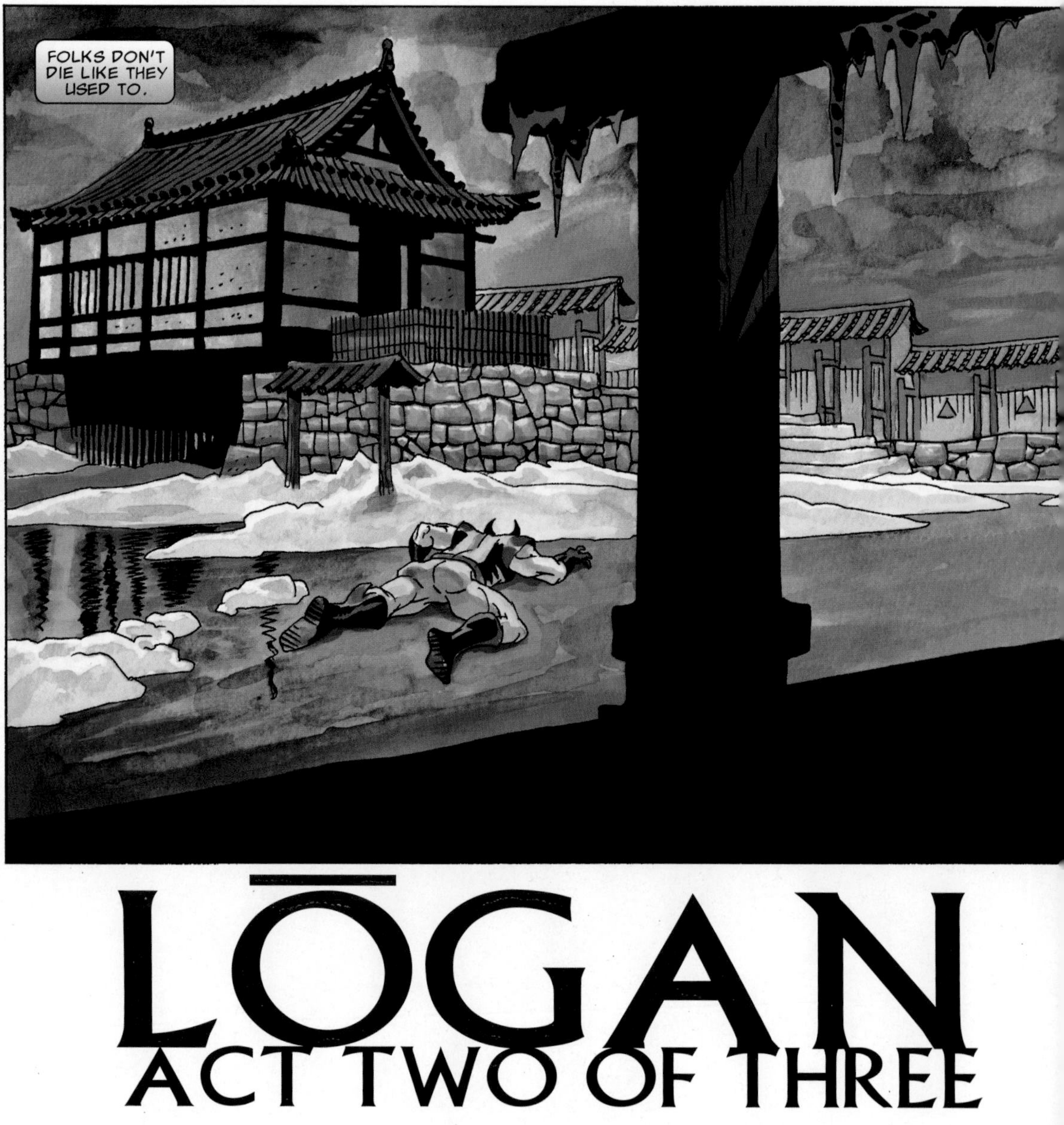
FOLKS DON'T DIE LIKE THEY USED TO.

LŌGAN
ACT TWO OF THREE

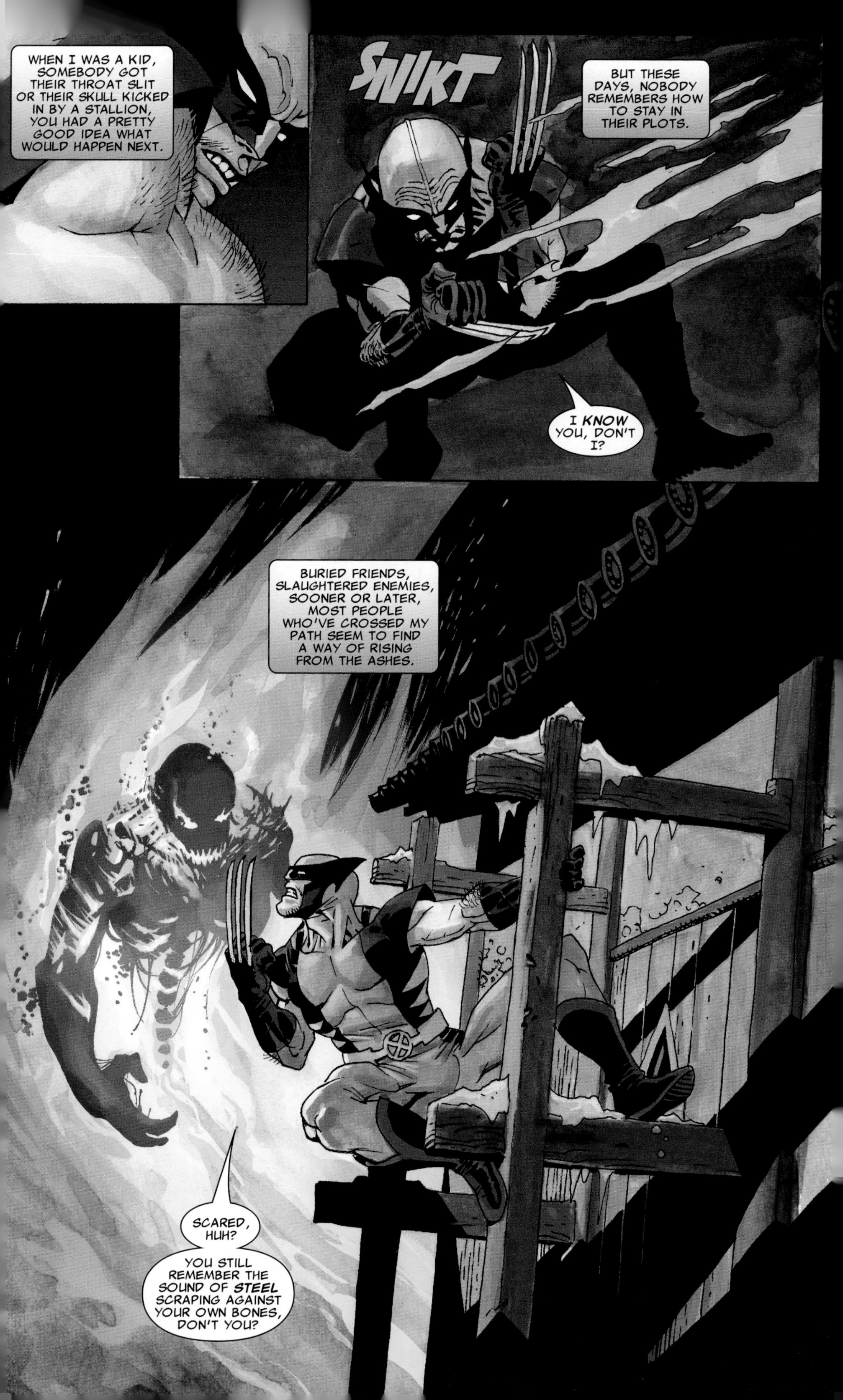

WHEN I WAS A KID, SOMEBODY GOT THEIR THROAT SLIT OR THEIR SKULL KICKED IN BY A STALLION, YOU HAD A PRETTY GOOD IDEA WHAT WOULD HAPPEN NEXT.
SNIKT
BUT THESE DAYS, NOBODY REMEMBERS HOW TO STAY IN THEIR PLOTS.
I KNOW YOU, DON'T I?
BURIED FRIENDS, SLAUGHTERED ENEMIES, SOONER OR LATER, MOST PEOPLE WHO'VE CROSSED MY PATH SEEM TO FIND A WAY OF RISING FROM THE ASHES.
SCARED, HUH?
YOU STILL REMEMBER THE SOUND OF STEEL SCRAPING AGAINST YOUR OWN BONES, DON'T YOU?

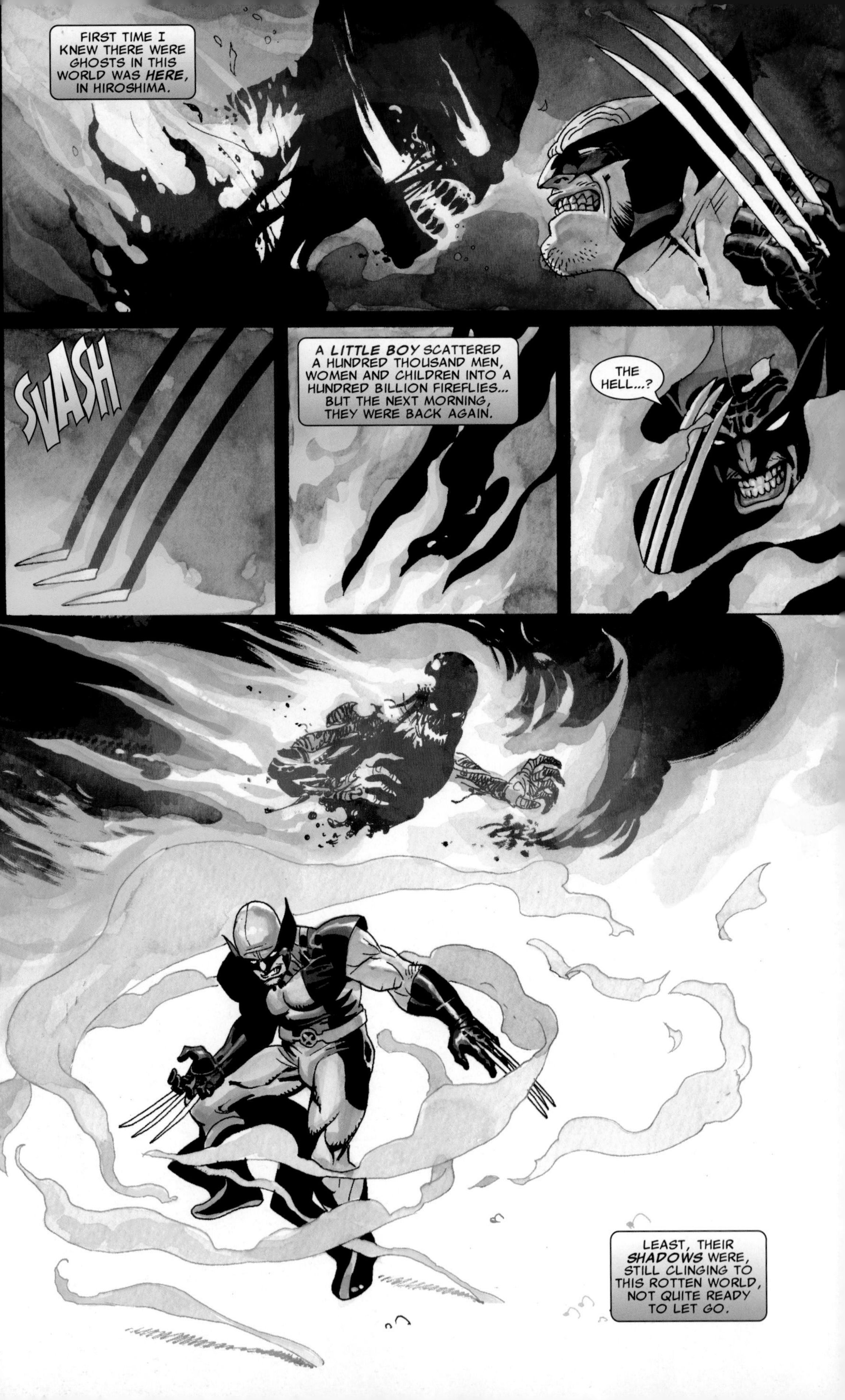
FIRST TIME I KNEW THERE WERE GHOSTS IN THIS WORLD WAS HERE, IN HIROSHIMA.
SVASH
A LITTLE BOY SCATTERED A HUNDRED THOUSAND MEN, WOMEN AND CHILDREN INTO A HUNDRED BILLION FIREFLIES... BUT THE NEXT MORNING, THEY WERE BACK AGAIN.
THE HELL...?
LEAST, THEIR SHADOWS WERE, STILL CLINGING TO THIS ROTTEN WORLD, NOT QUITE READY TO LET GO.

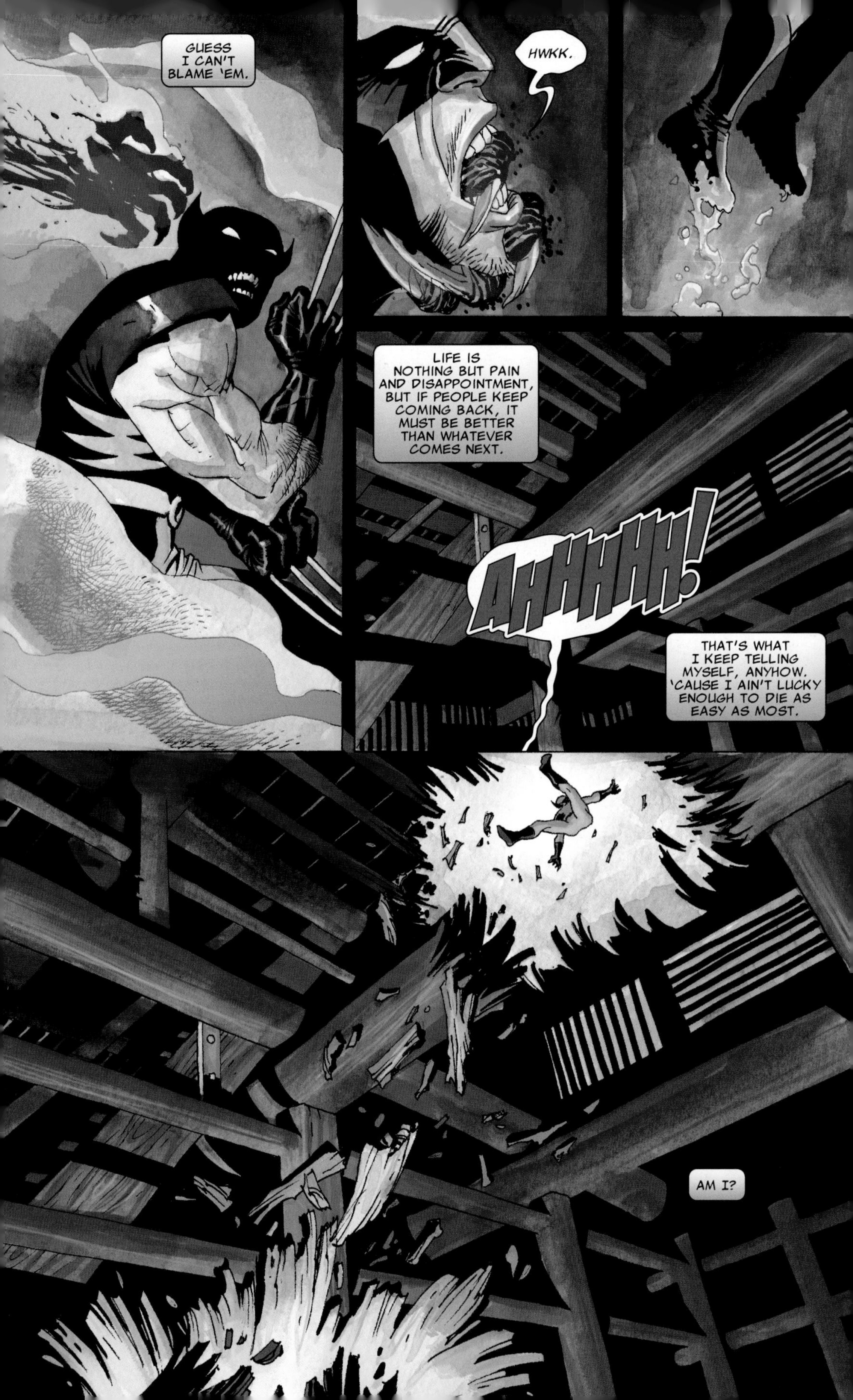
GUESS I CAN'T BLAME 'EM.
HWKK.
LIFE IS NOTHING BUT PAIN AND DISAPPOINTMENT, BUT IF PEOPLE KEEP COMING BACK, IT MUST BE BETTER THAN WHATEVER COMES NEXT.
AHHHHH!
THAT'S WHAT I KEEP TELLING MYSELF, ANYHOW. 'CAUSE I AIN'T LUCKY ENOUGH TO DIE AS EASY AS MOST.
AM I?

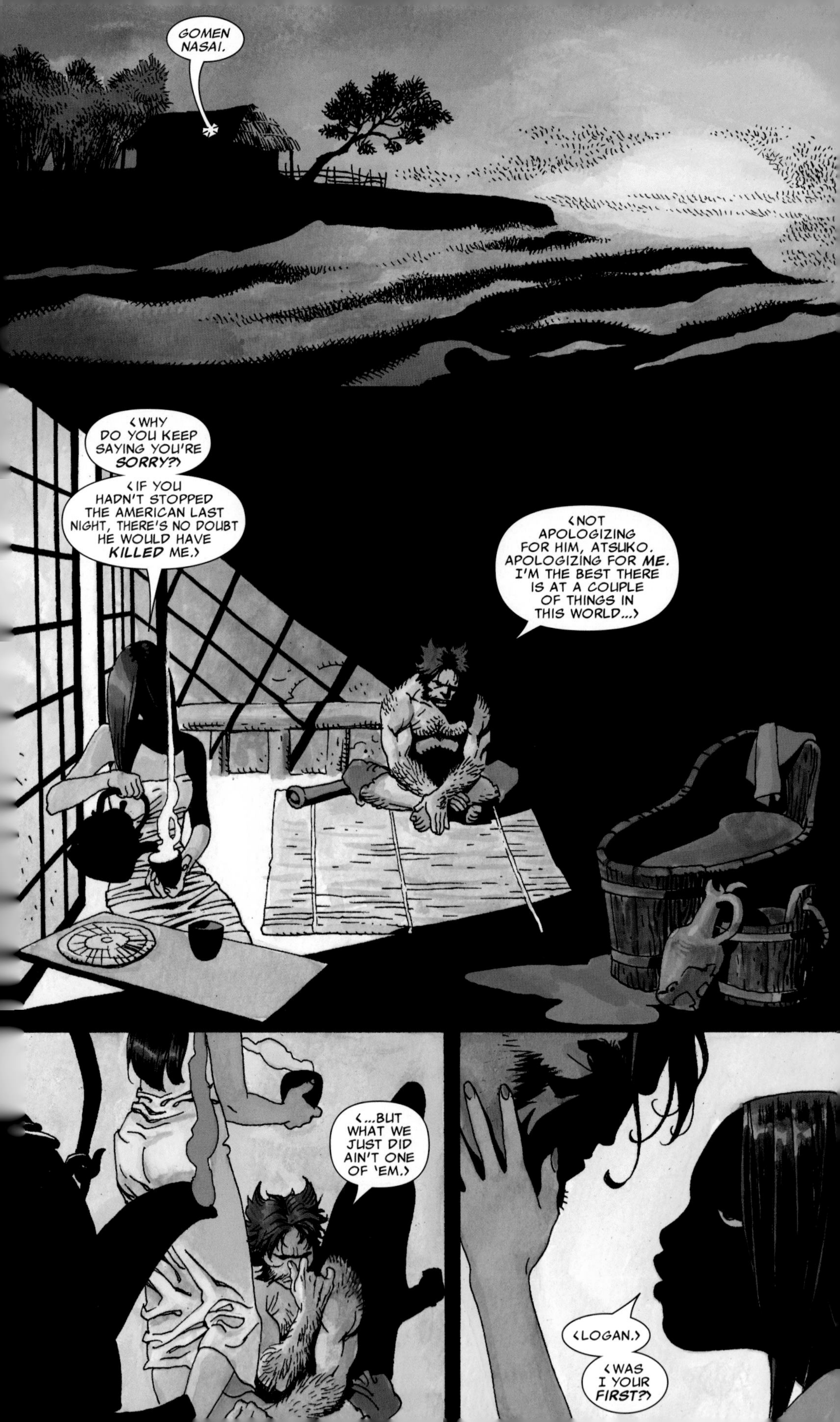
GOMEN NASAI.
‹WHY DO YOU KEEP SAYING YOU'RE SORRY?›
‹IF YOU HADN'T STOPPED THE AMERICAN LAST NIGHT, THERE'S NO DOUBT HE WOULD HAVE KILLED ME.›
‹NOT APOLOGIZING FOR HIM, ATSUKO. APOLOGIZING FOR ME. I'M THE BEST THERE IS AT A COUPLE OF THINGS IN THIS WORLD...›
‹...BUT WHAT WE JUST DID AIN'T ONE OF 'EM.›
‹LOGAN.›
‹WAS I YOUR FIRST?›

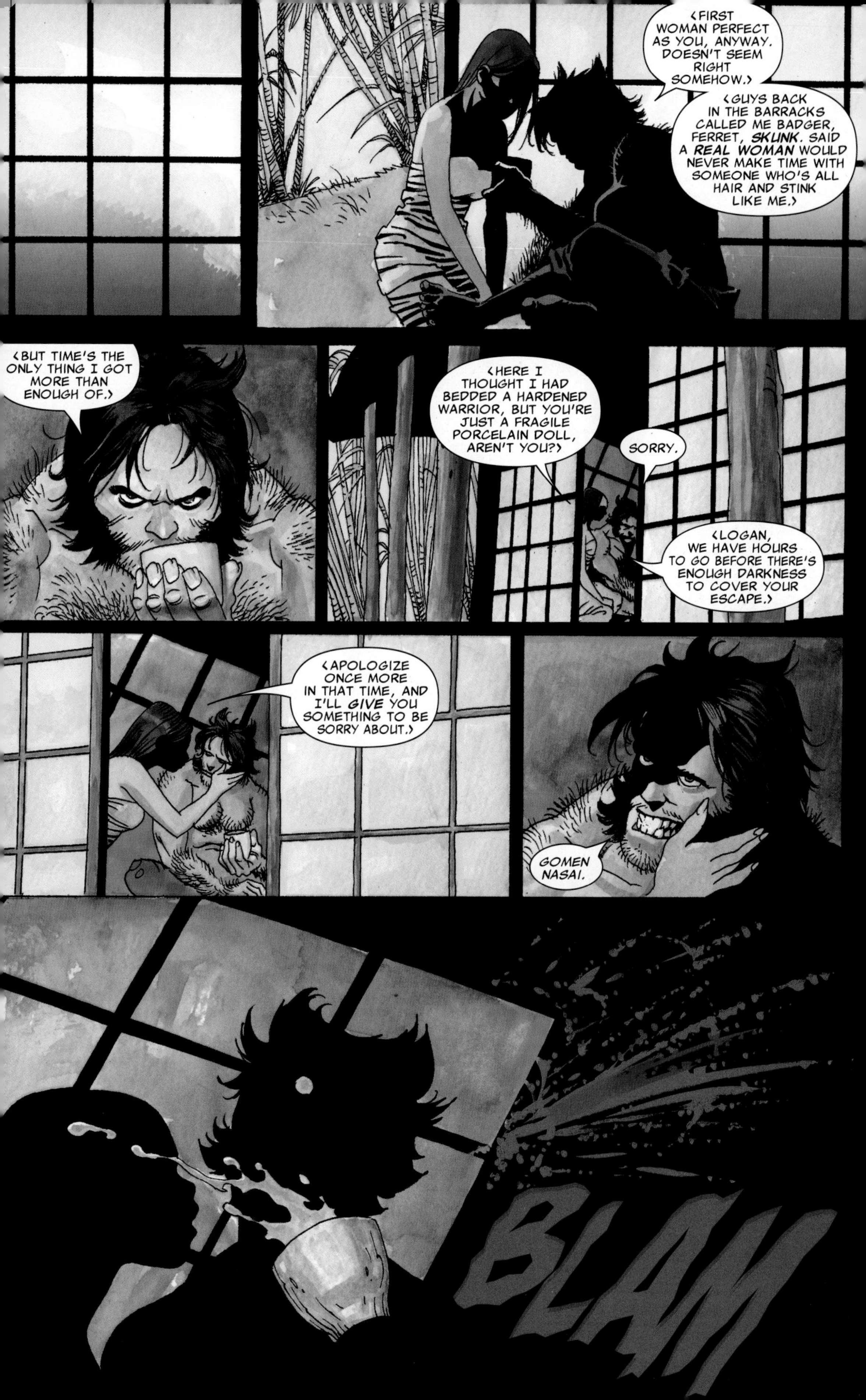
‹FIRST WOMAN PERFECT AS YOU, ANYWAY. DOESN'T SEEM RIGHT SOMEHOW.›
‹GUYS BACK IN THE BARRACKS CALLED ME BADGER, FERRET, SKUNK. SAID A REAL WOMAN WOULD NEVER MAKE TIME WITH SOMEONE WHO'S ALL HAIR AND STINK LIKE ME.›
‹BUT TIME'S THE ONLY THING I GOT MORE THAN ENOUGH OF.›
‹HERE I THOUGHT I HAD BEDDED A HARDENED WARRIOR, BUT YOU'RE JUST A FRAGILE PORCELAIN DOLL, AREN'T YOU?›
SORRY.
‹LOGAN, WE HAVE HOURS TO GO BEFORE THERE'S ENOUGH DARKNESS TO COVER YOUR ESCAPE.›
‹APOLOGIZE ONCE MORE IN THAT TIME, AND I'LL GIVE YOU SOMETHING TO BE SORRY ABOUT.›
GOMEN NASAI.
BLAM

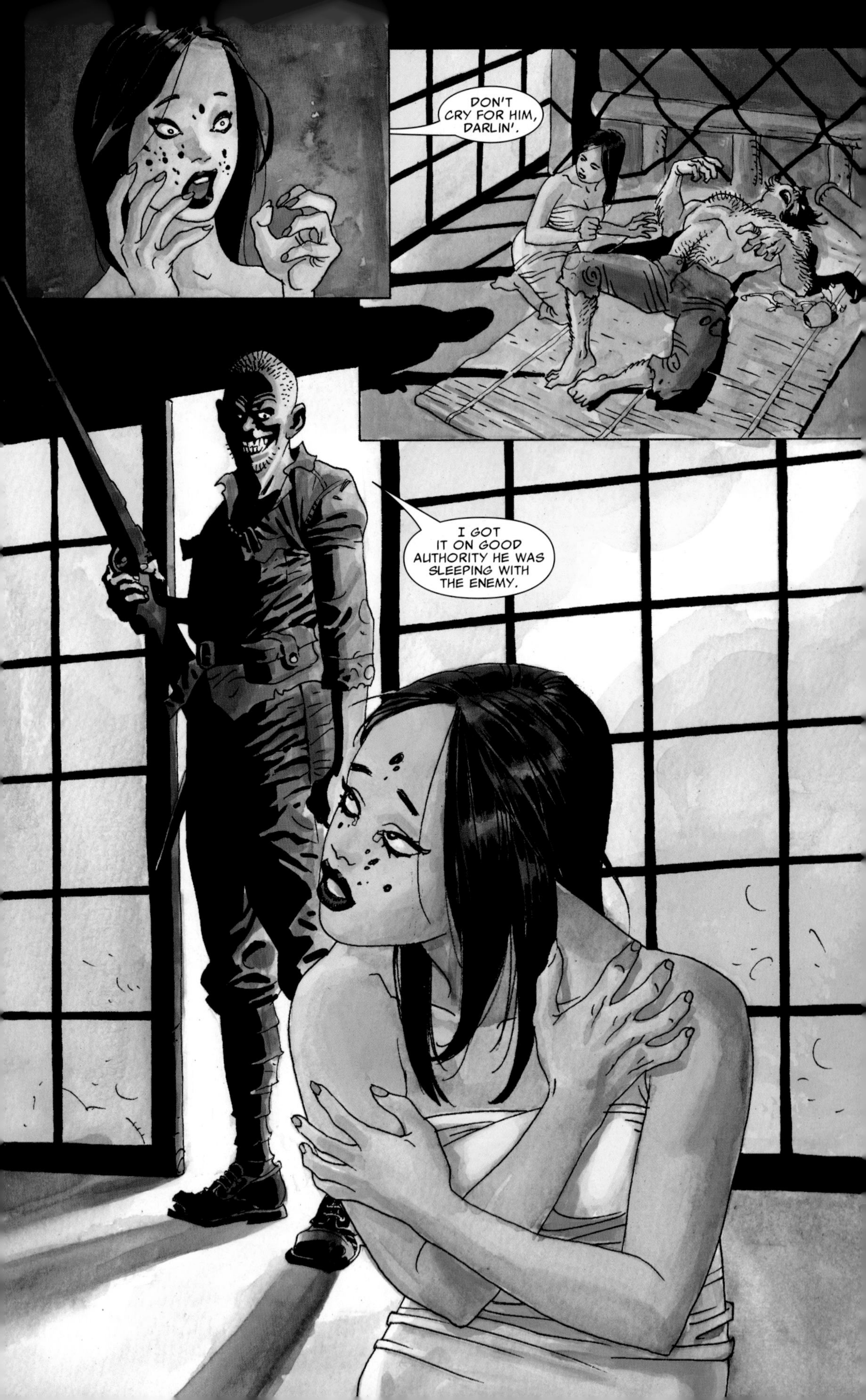
DON'T CRY FOR HIM, DARLIN'.
I GOT IT ON GOOD AUTHORITY HE WAS SLEEPING WITH THE ENEMY.

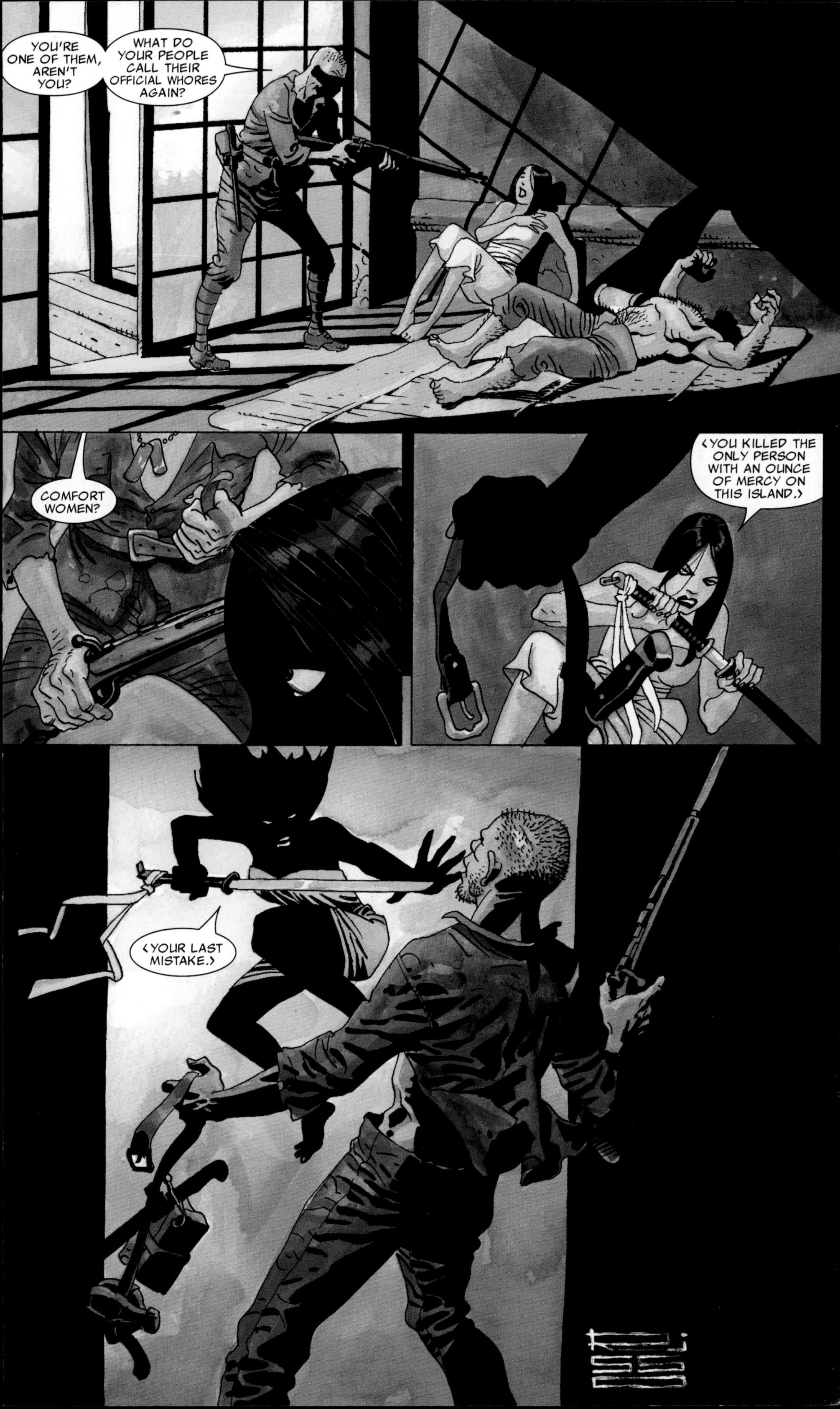
YOU'RE ONE OF THEM, AREN'T YOU?
WHAT DO YOUR PEOPLE CALL THEIR OFFICIAL WHORES AGAIN?
COMFORT WOMEN?
‹YOU KILLED THE ONLY PERSON WITH AN OUNCE OF MERCY ON THIS ISLAND.›
‹YOUR LAST MISTAKE.›

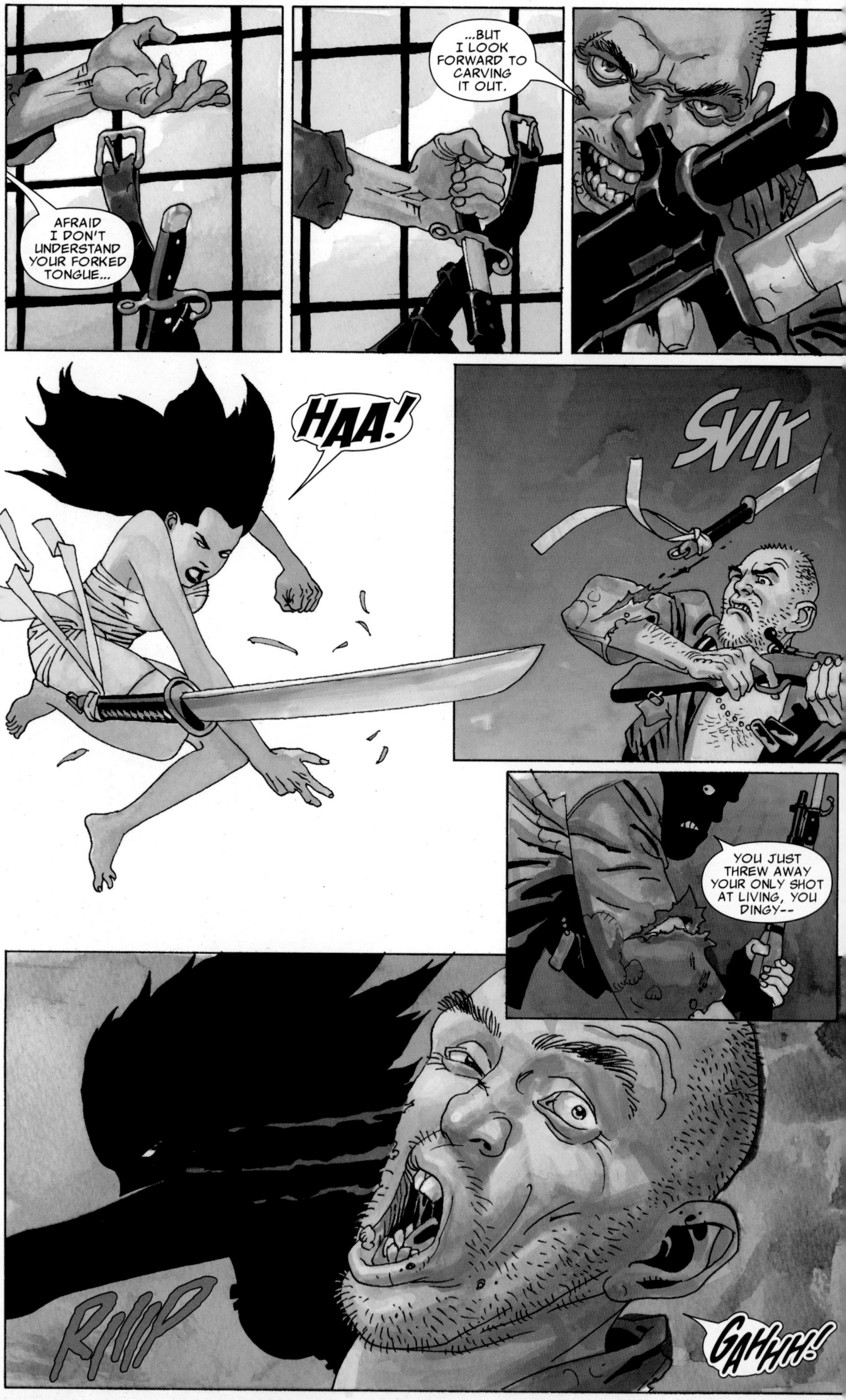
AFRAID I DON'T UNDERSTAND YOUR FORKED TONGUE...
...BUT I LOOK FORWARD TO CARVING IT OUT.
HAA!
SVIK
YOU JUST THREW AWAY YOUR ONLY SHOT AT LIVING, YOU DINGY--
RIIIP
GAHHH!

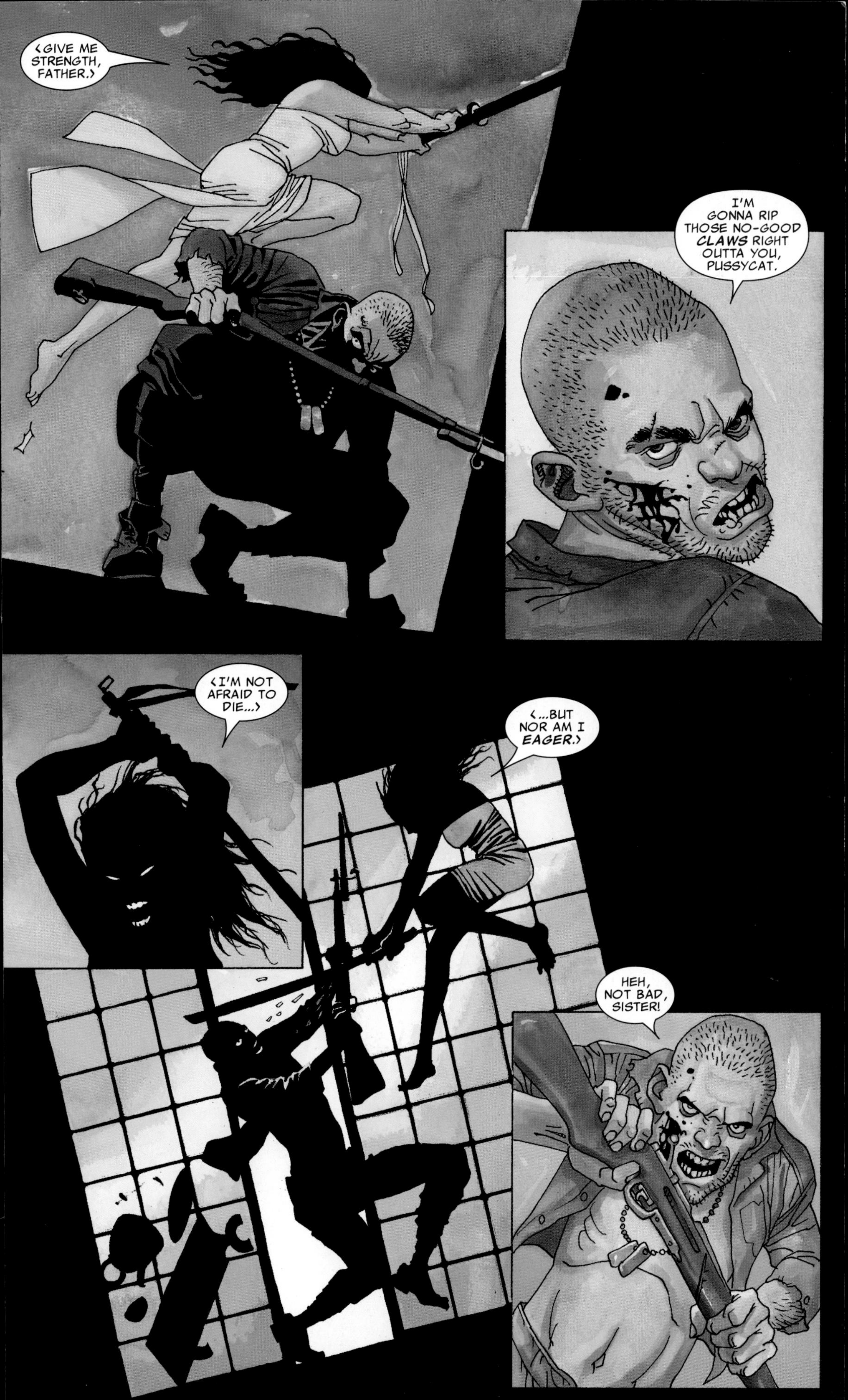
‹GIVE ME STRENGTH, FATHER.›
I'M GONNA RIP THOSE NO-GOOD CLAWS RIGHT OUTTA YOU, PUSSYCAT.
‹I'M NOT AFRAID TO DIE...›
‹...BUT NOR AM I EAGER.›
HEH, NOT BAD, SISTER!

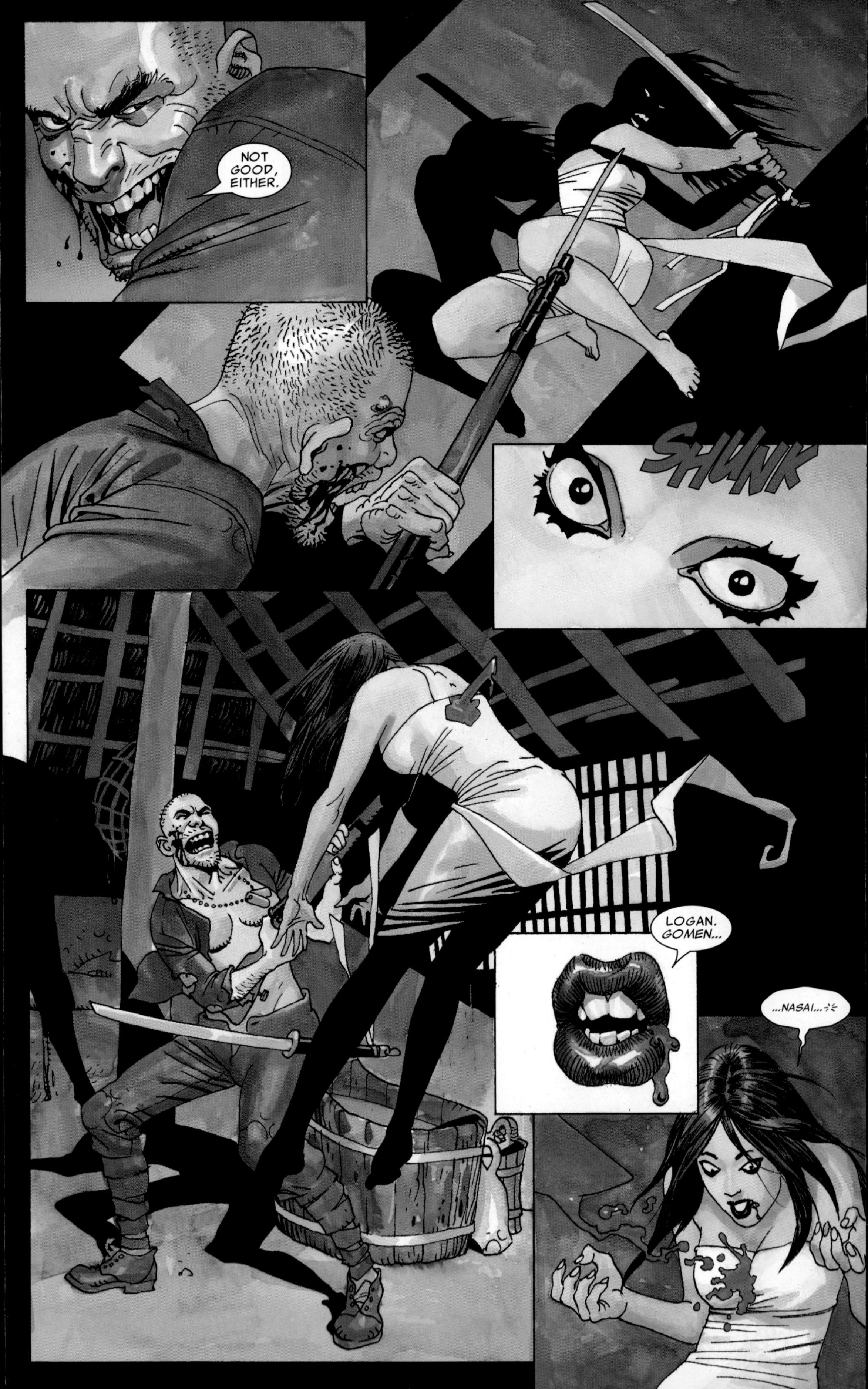
NOT GOOD, EITHER.
SHUNK
LOGAN. GOMEN...
...NASAI...

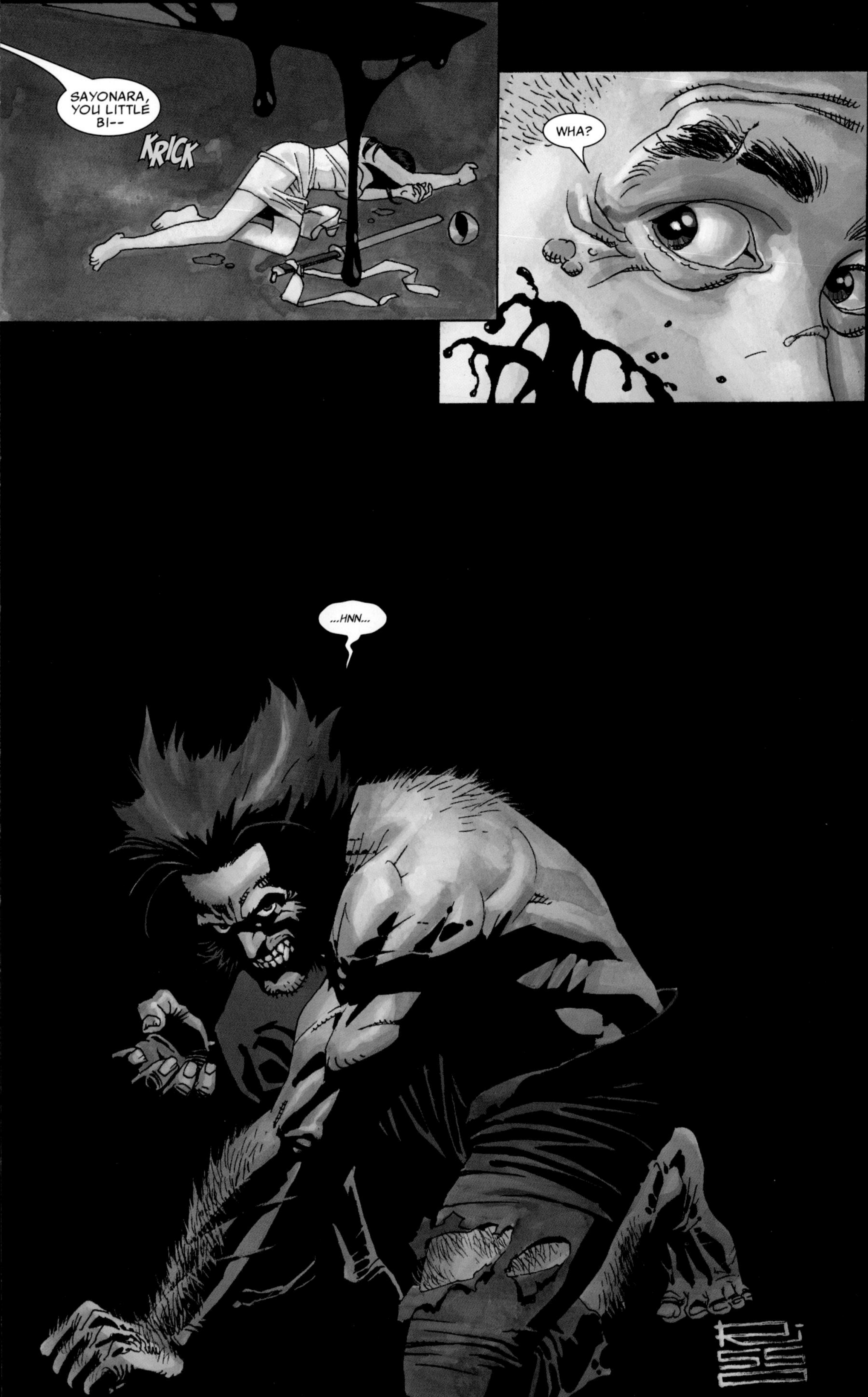
SAYONARA, YOU LITTLE BI--
KRICK
WHA?
...HNN...

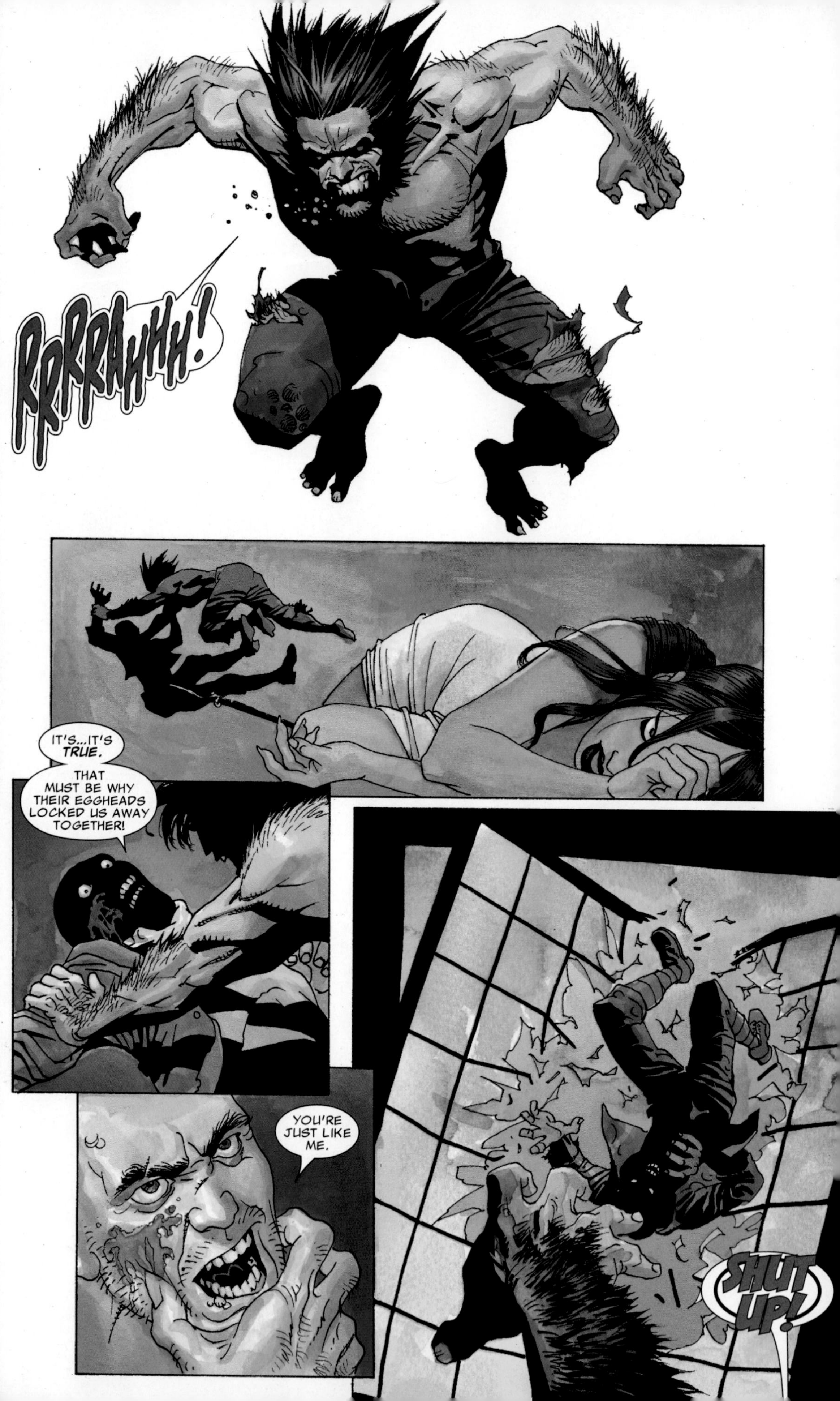
RRRRAHHH!
IT'S...IT'S TRUE.
THAT MUST BE WHY THEIR EGGHEADS LOCKED US AWAY TOGETHER!
YOU'RE JUST LIKE ME.
SHUT UP!

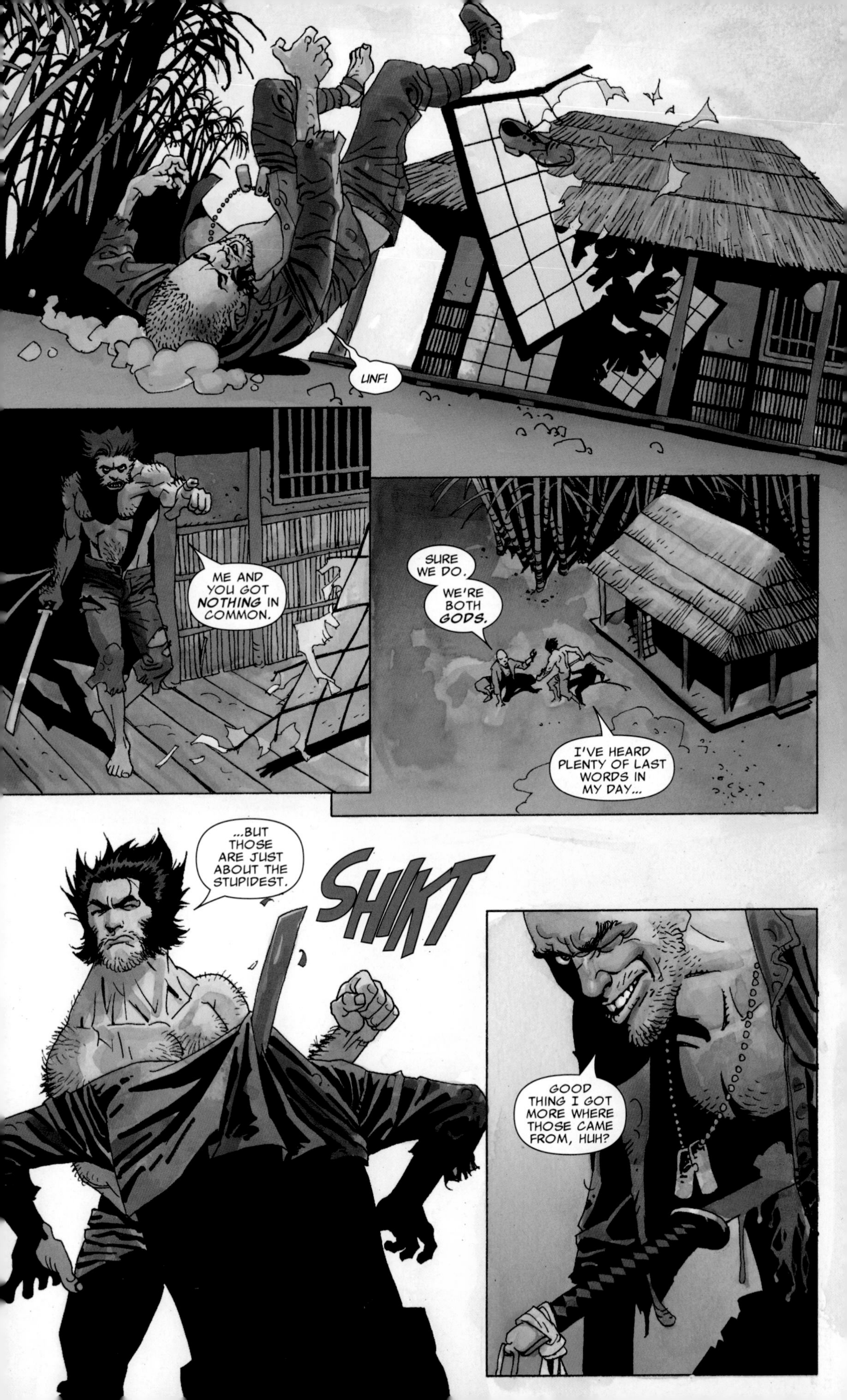
UNF!
ME AND YOU GOT NOTHING IN COMMON.
SURE WE DO.
WE'RE BOTH GODS.
I'VE HEARD PLENTY OF LAST WORDS IN MY DAY...
...BUT THOSE ARE JUST ABOUT THE STUPIDEST.
SHIKT
GOOD THING I GOT MORE WHERE THOSE CAME FROM, HUH?

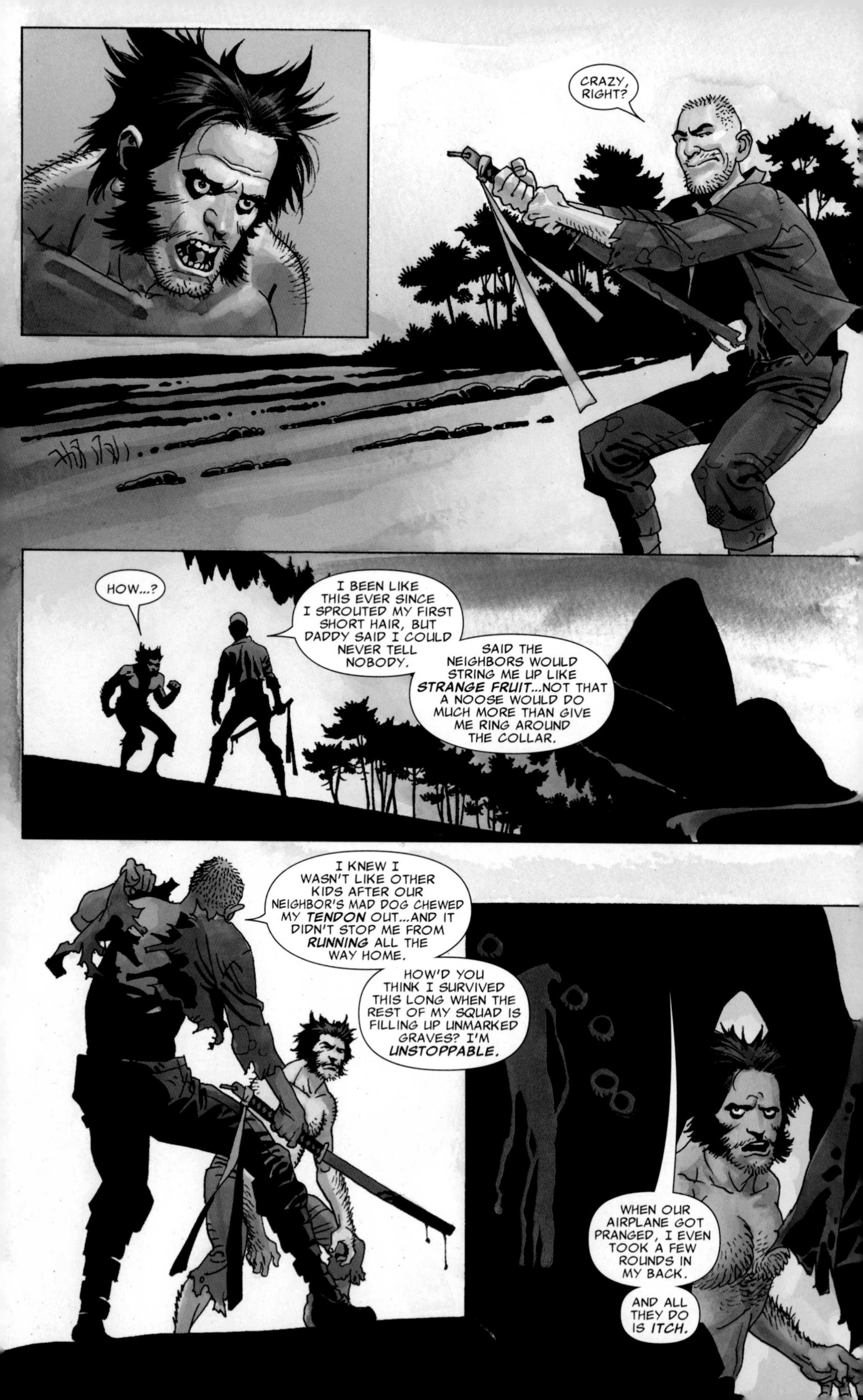
CRAZY, RIGHT?
HOW...?
I BEEN LIKE THIS EVER SINCE I SPROUTED MY FIRST SHORT HAIR, BUT DADDY SAID I COULD NEVER TELL NOBODY.
SAID THE NEIGHBORS WOULD STRING ME UP LIKE STRANGE FRUIT...NOT THAT A NOOSE WOULD DO MUCH MORE THAN GIVE ME RING AROUND THE COLLAR.
I KNEW I WASN'T LIKE OTHER KIDS AFTER OUR NEIGHBOR'S MAD DOG CHEWED MY TENDON OUT...AND IT DIDN'T STOP ME FROM RUNNING ALL THE WAY HOME.
HOW'D YOU THINK I SURVIVED THIS LONG WHEN THE REST OF MY SQUAD IS FILLING UP UNMARKED GRAVES? I'M UNSTOPPABLE.
WHEN OUR AIRPLANE GOT PRANGED, I EVEN TOOK A FEW ROUNDS IN MY BACK.
AND ALL THEY DO IS ITCH.

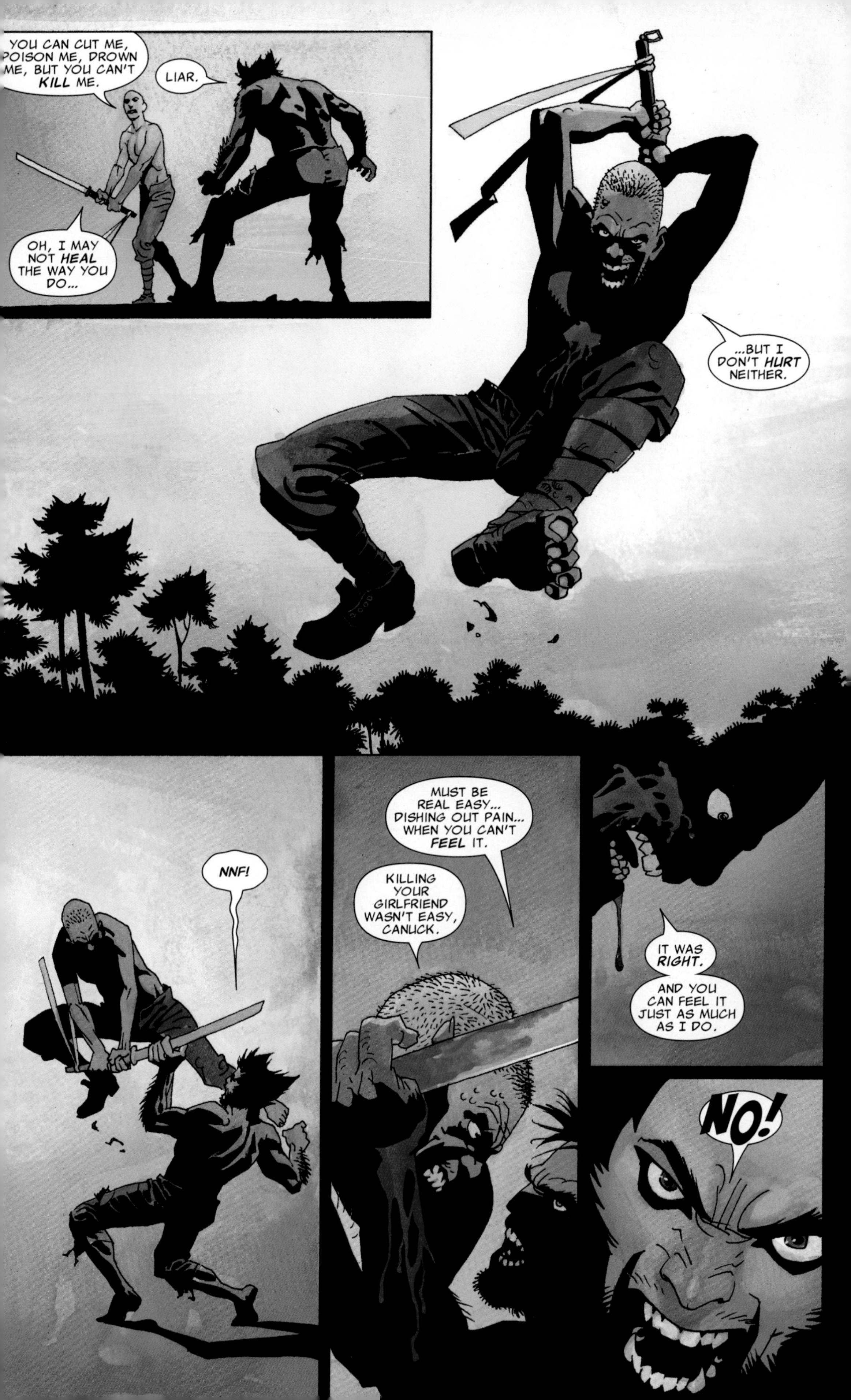
YOU CAN CUT ME, POISON ME, DROWN ME, BUT YOU CAN'T **KILL** ME.
LIAR.
OH, I MAY NOT **HEAL** THE WAY YOU DO...
...BUT I DON'T **HURT** NEITHER.
NNF!
MUST BE REAL EASY... DISHING OUT PAIN... WHEN YOU CAN'T **FEEL** IT.
KILLING YOUR GIRLFRIEND WASN'T EASY, CANUCK.
IT WAS **RIGHT**.
AND YOU CAN FEEL IT JUST AS MUCH AS I DO.
NO!

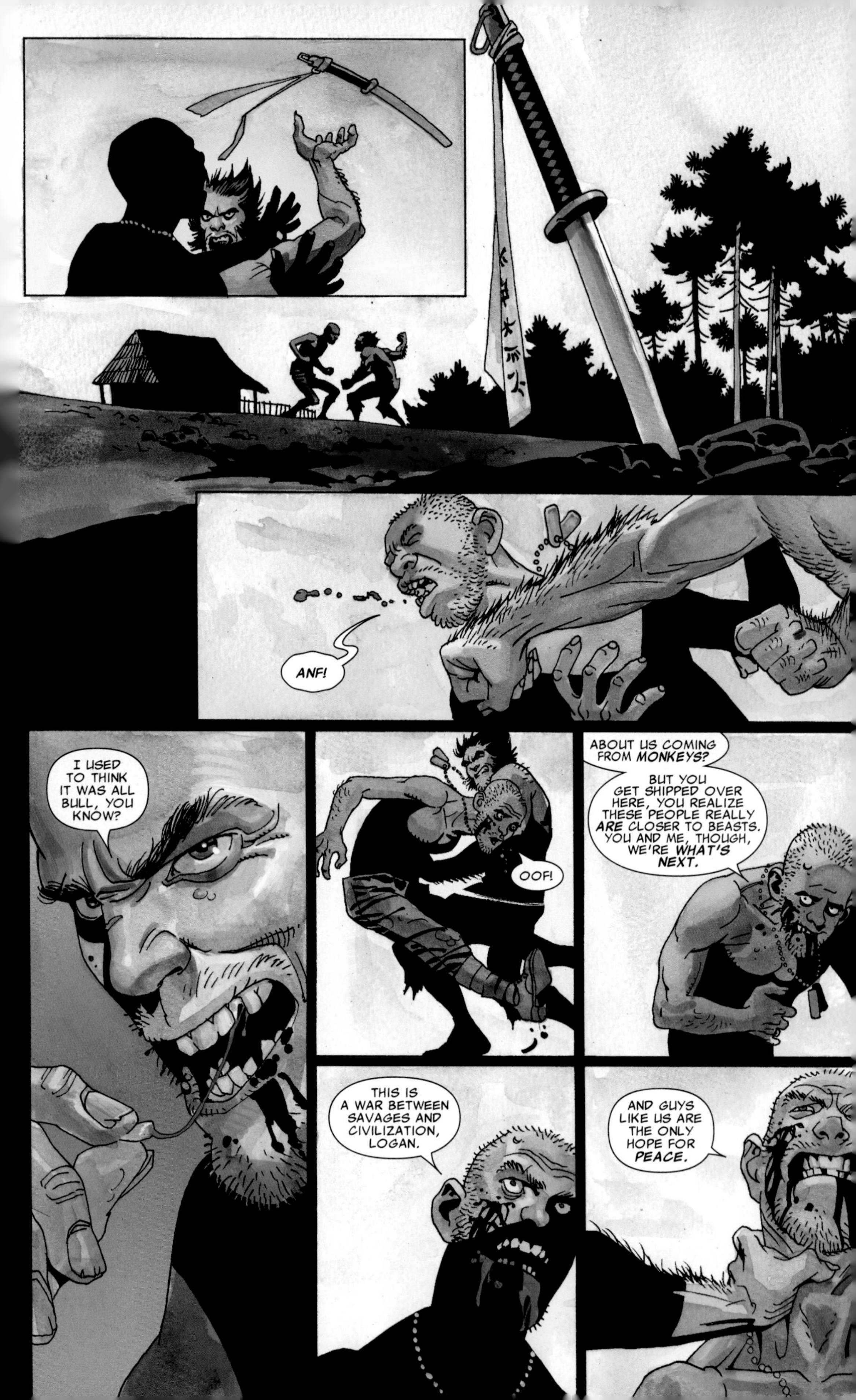
ANF!
I USED TO THINK IT WAS ALL BULL, YOU KNOW?
OOF!
ABOUT US COMING FROM MONKEYS?
BUT YOU GET SHIPPED OVER HERE, YOU REALIZE THESE PEOPLE REALLY ARE CLOSER TO BEASTS. YOU AND ME, THOUGH, WE'RE WHAT'S NEXT.
THIS IS A WAR BETWEEN SAVAGES AND CIVILIZATION, LOGAN.
AND GUYS LIKE US ARE THE ONLY HOPE FOR PEACE.

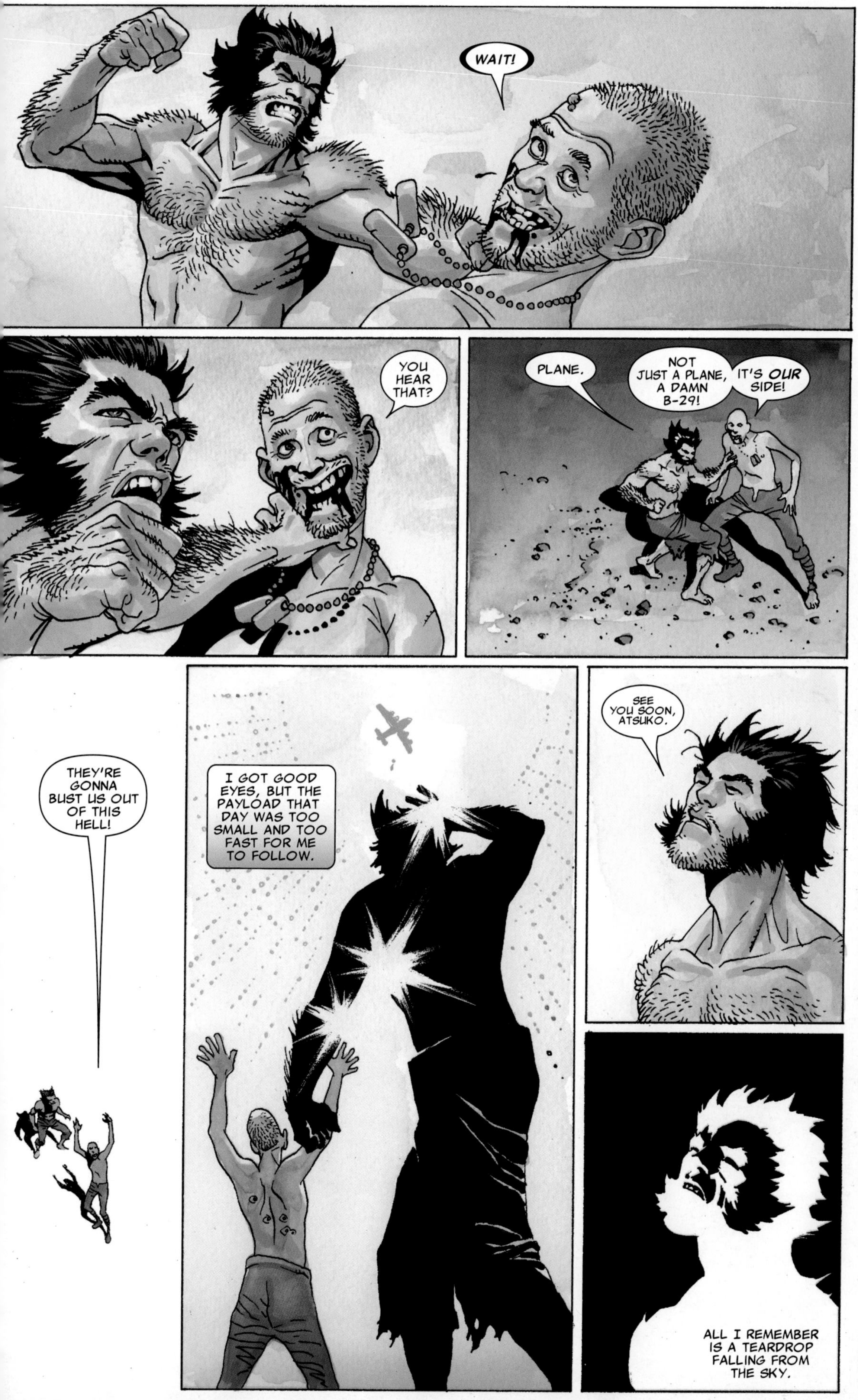
WAIT!
YOU HEAR THAT?
PLANE.
NOT JUST A PLANE, A DAMN B-29!
IT'S OUR SIDE!
THEY'RE GONNA BUST US OUT OF THIS HELL!
I GOT GOOD EYES, BUT THE PAYLOAD THAT DAY WAS TOO SMALL AND TOO FAST FOR ME TO FOLLOW.
SEE YOU SOON, ATSUKO.
ALL I REMEMBER IS A TEARDROP FALLING FROM THE SKY.

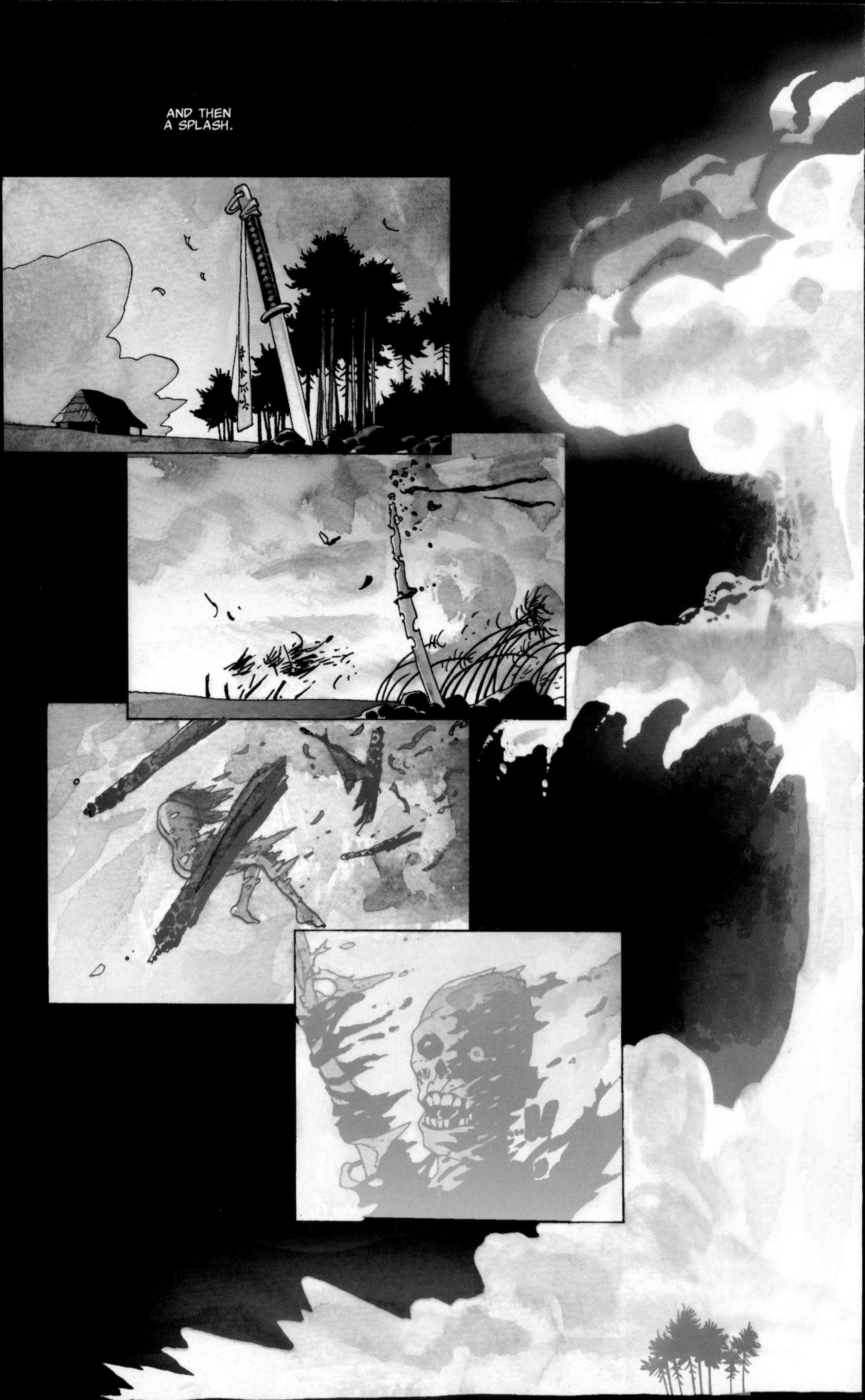
AND THEN
A SPLASH.

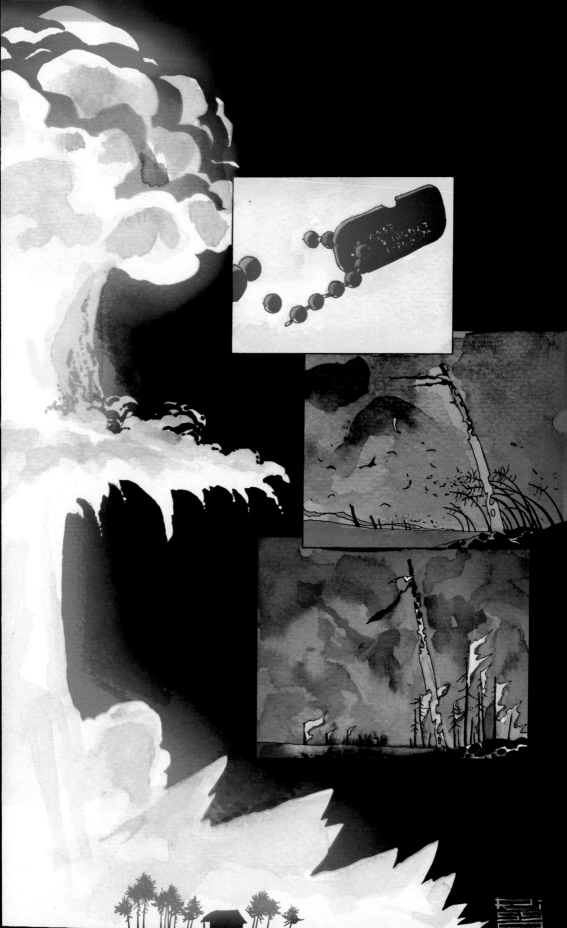

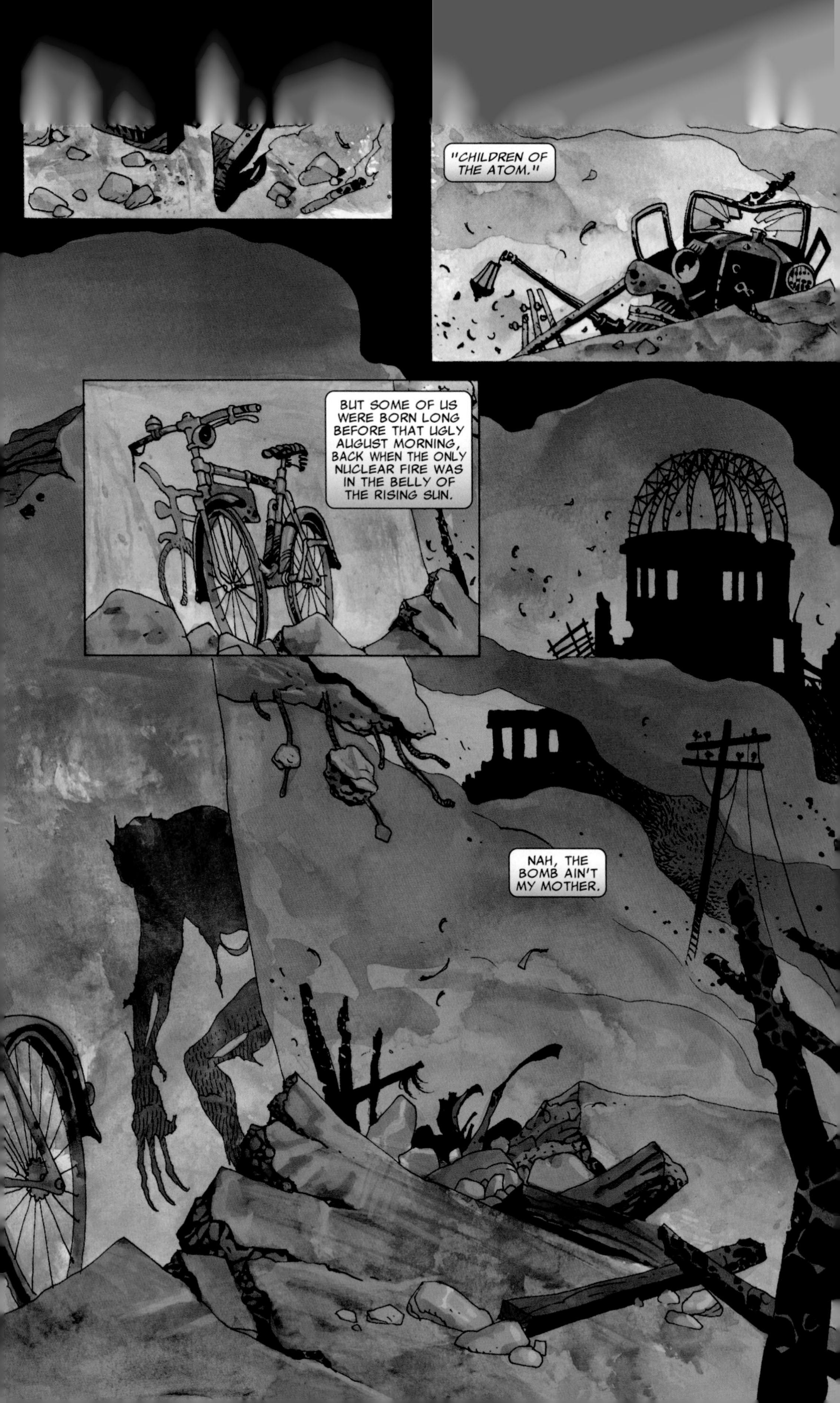
"CHILDREN OF THE ATOM."
BUT SOME OF US WERE BORN LONG BEFORE THAT UGLY AUGUST MORNING, BACK WHEN THE ONLY NUCLEAR FIRE WAS IN THE BELLY OF THE RISING SUN.
NAH, THE BOMB AIN'T MY MOTHER.

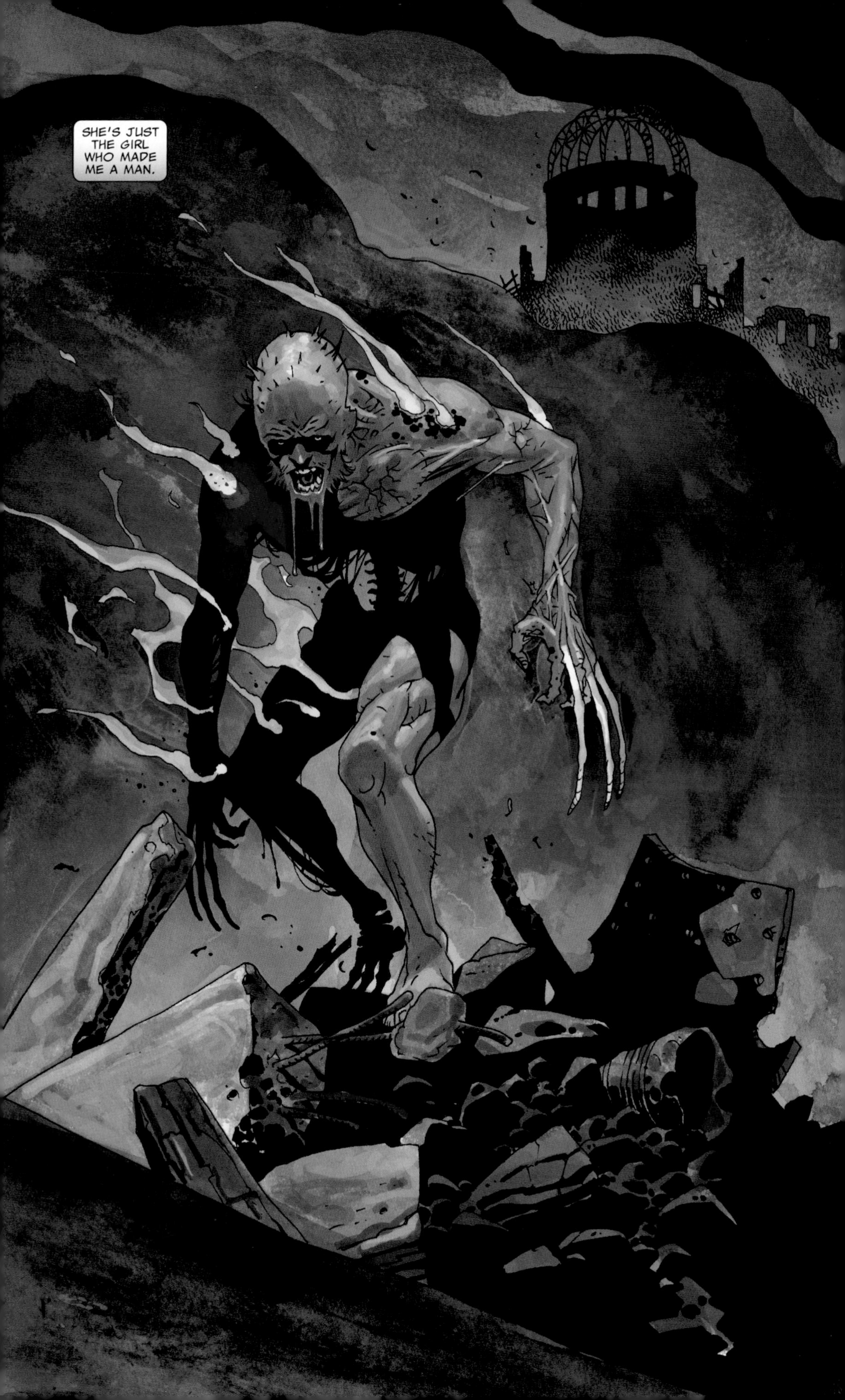
SHE'S JUST THE GIRL WHO MADE ME A MAN.

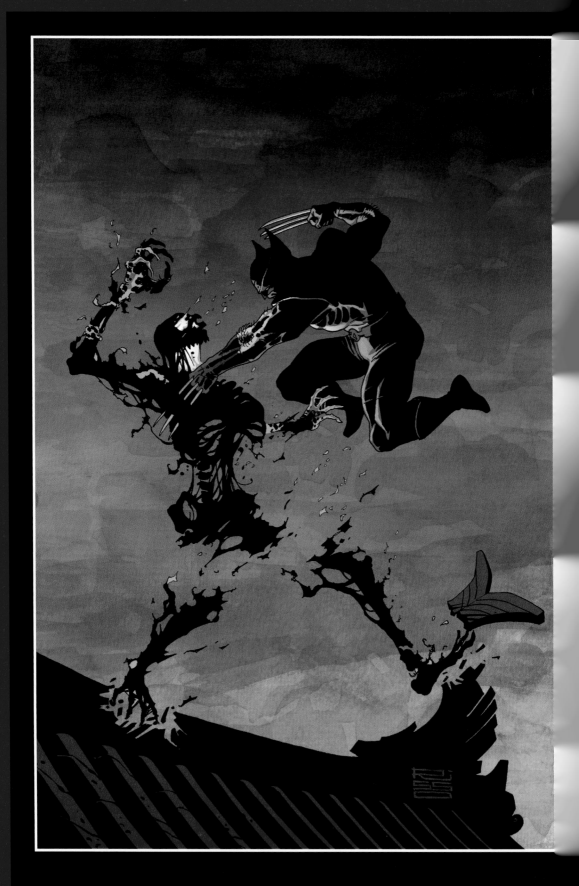

issue number three

IN THE END,
IT'S THE
FALLOUT THAT
GETS YOU.

LŌGAN
CONCLUSION

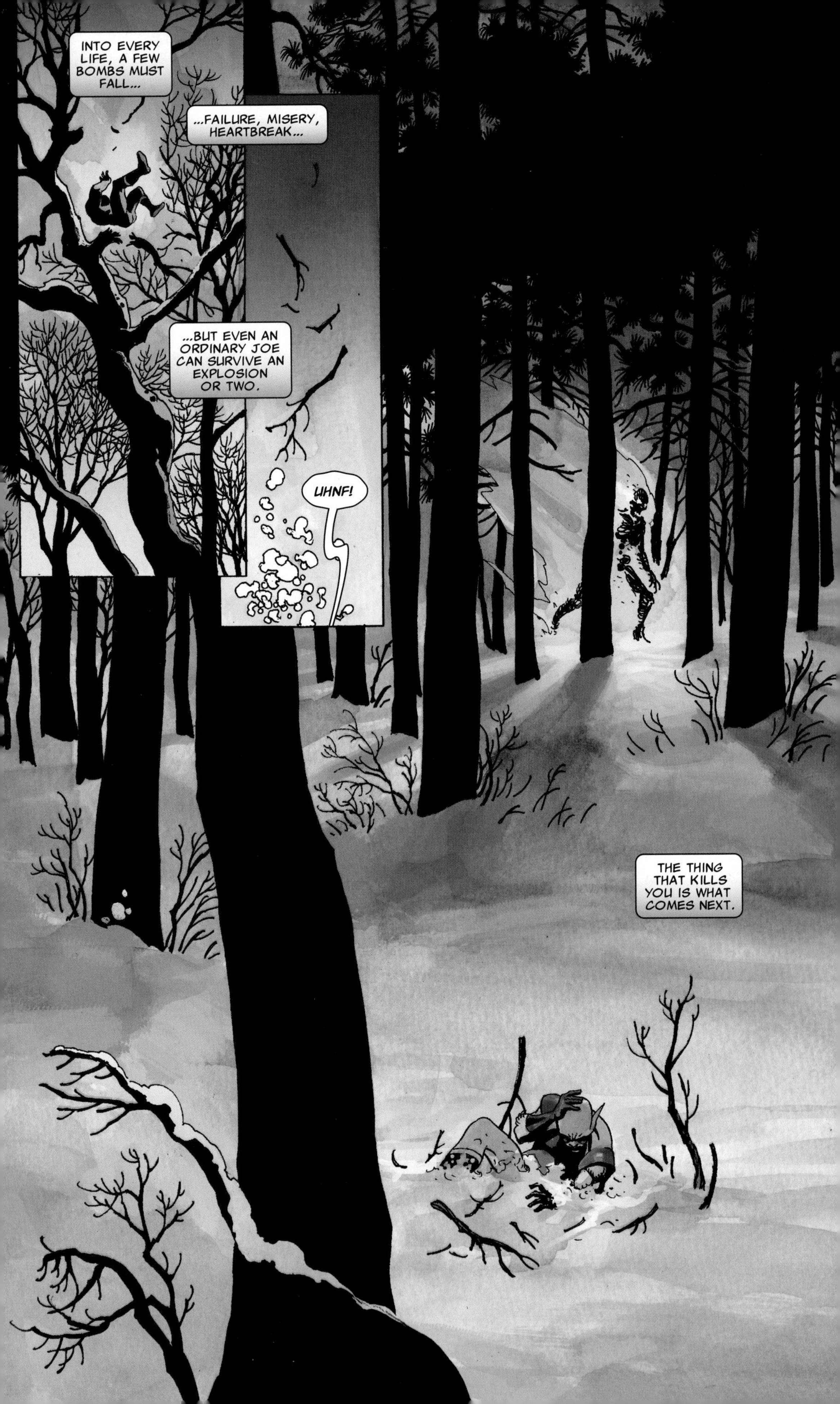
INTO EVERY LIFE, A FEW BOMBS MUST FALL...
...FAILURE, MISERY, HEARTBREAK...
...BUT EVEN AN ORDINARY JOE CAN SURVIVE AN EXPLOSION OR TWO.
UHNF!
THE THING THAT KILLS YOU IS WHAT COMES NEXT.

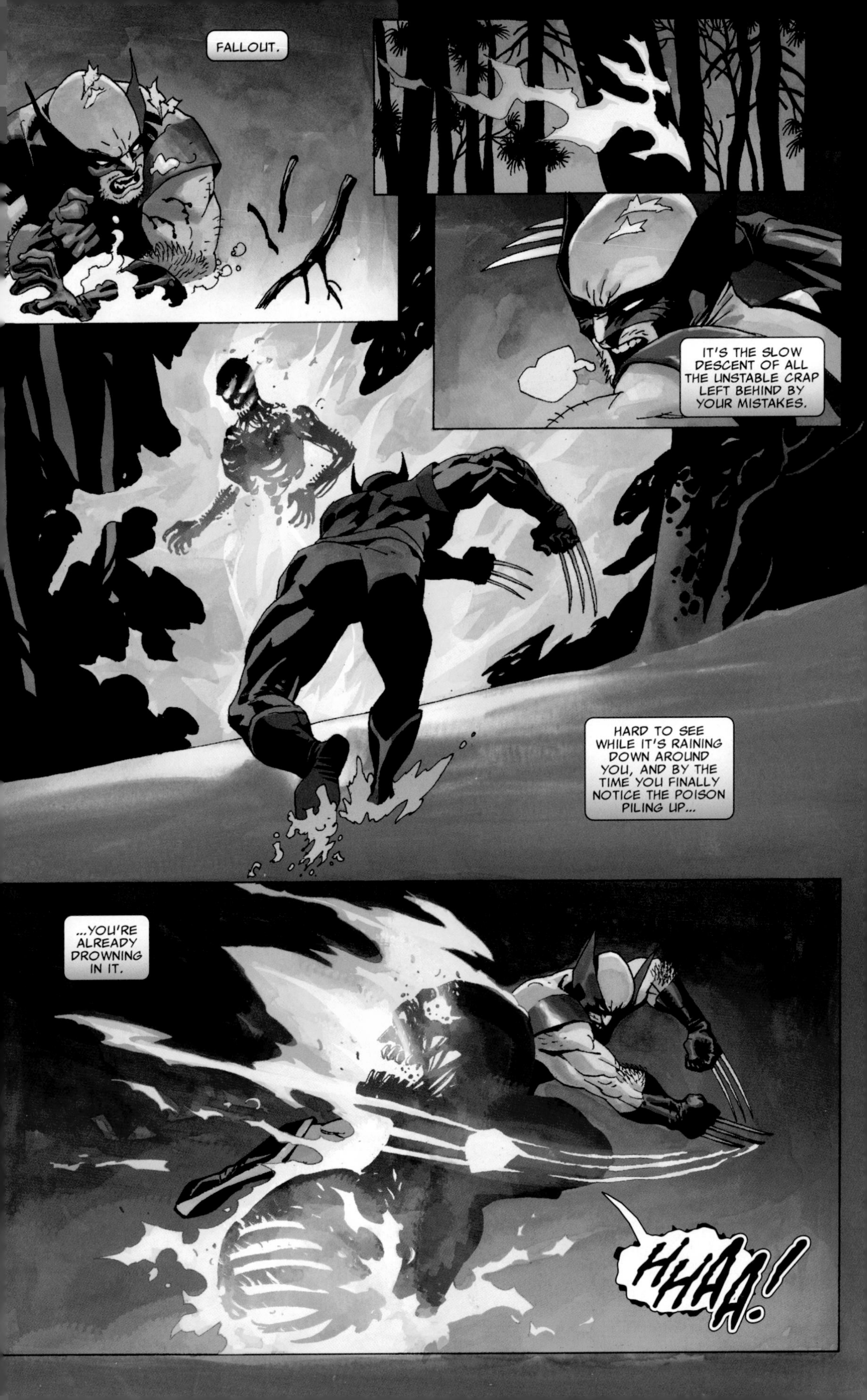
FALLOUT.
IT'S THE SLOW DESCENT OF ALL THE UNSTABLE CRAP LEFT BEHIND BY YOUR MISTAKES.
HARD TO SEE WHILE IT'S RAINING DOWN AROUND YOU, AND BY THE TIME YOU FINALLY NOTICE THE POISON PILING UP...
...YOU'RE ALREADY DROWNING IN IT.
HHAA!

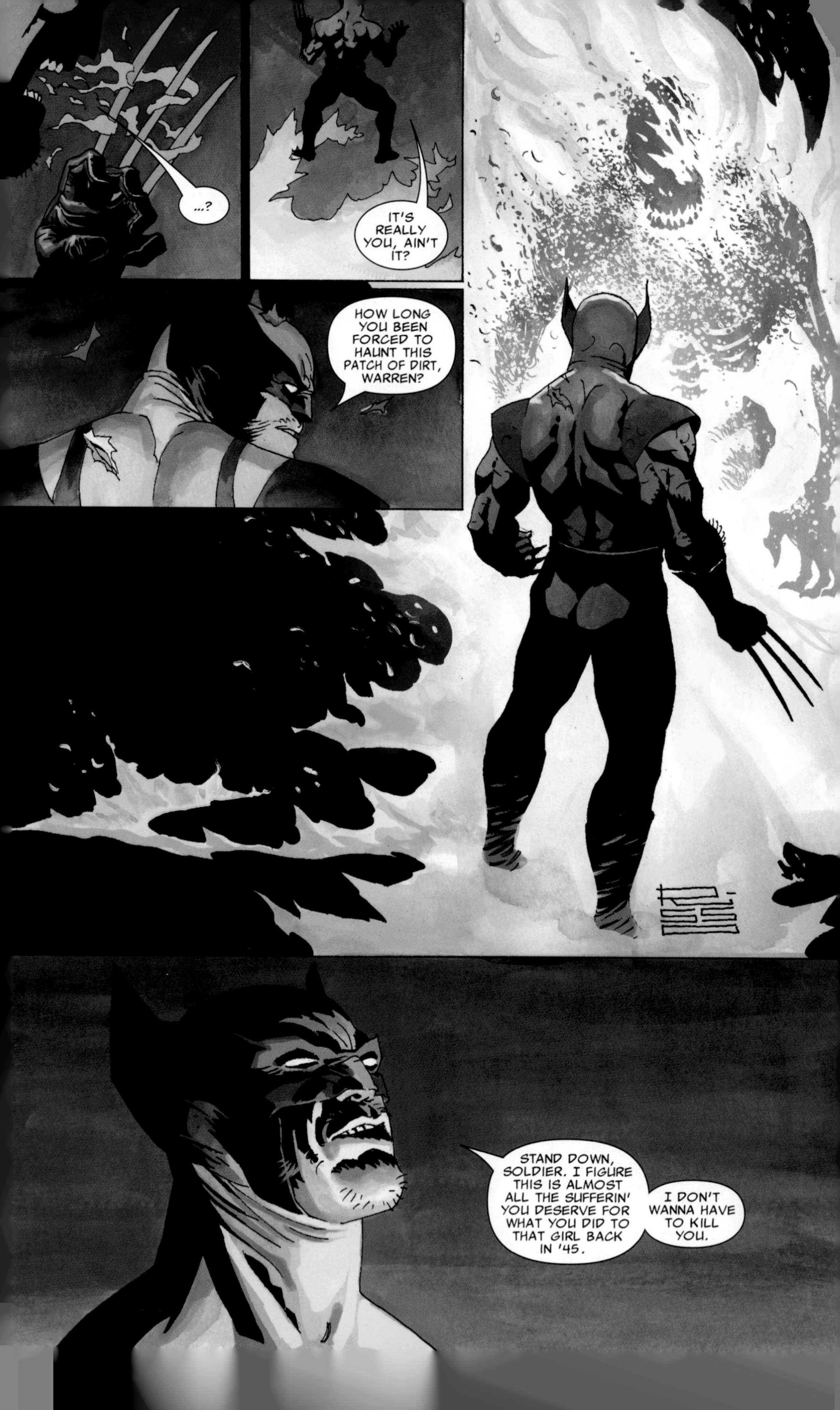
...?
IT'S REALLY YOU, AIN'T IT?
HOW LONG YOU BEEN FORCED TO HAUNT THIS PATCH OF DIRT, WARREN?
STAND DOWN, SOLDIER. I FIGURE THIS IS ALMOST ALL THE SUFFERIN' YOU DESERVE FOR WHAT YOU DID TO THAT GIRL BACK IN '45.
I DON'T WANNA HAVE TO KILL YOU.

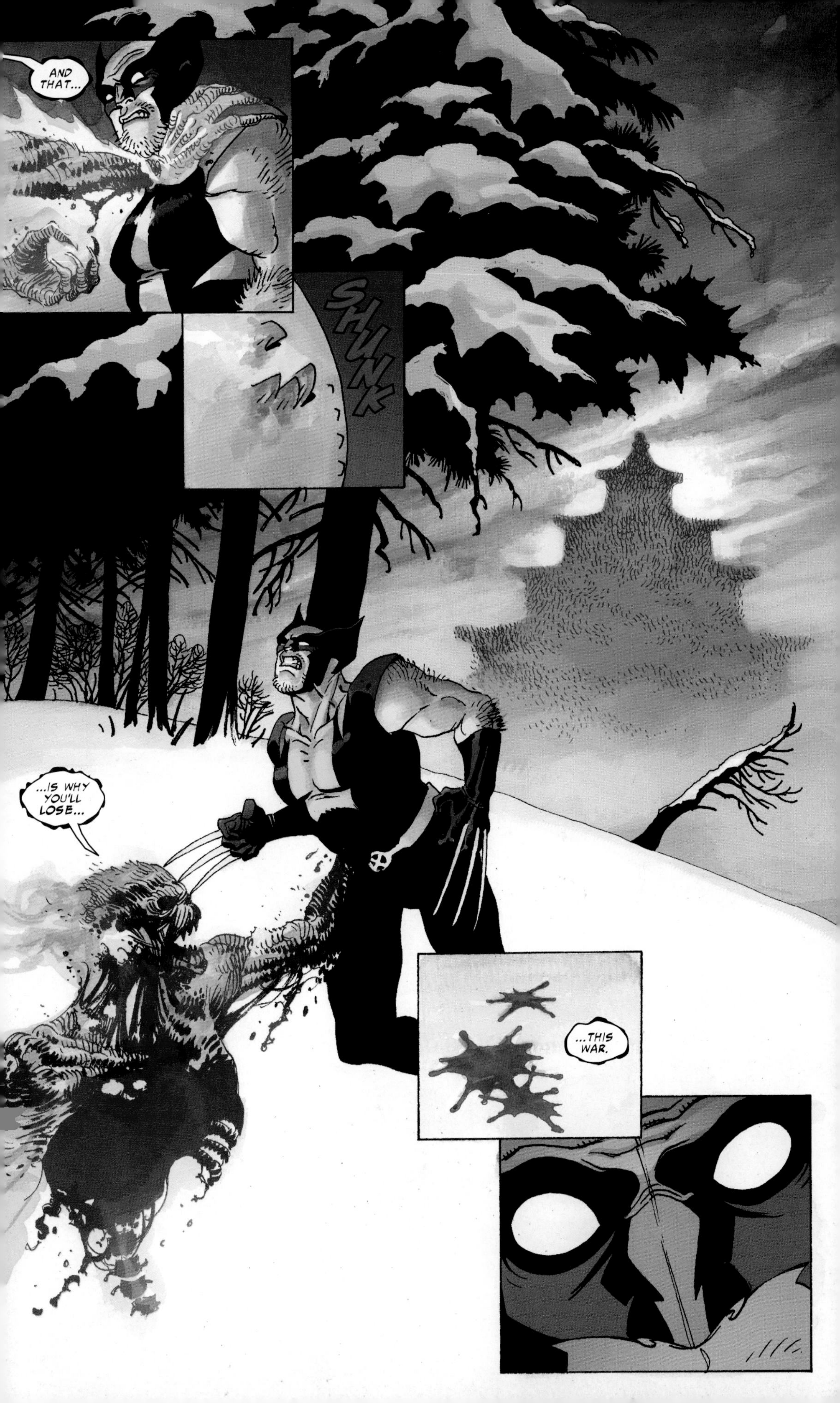
AND THAT...
SHUNK
...IS WHY YOU'LL LOSE...
...THIS WAR.

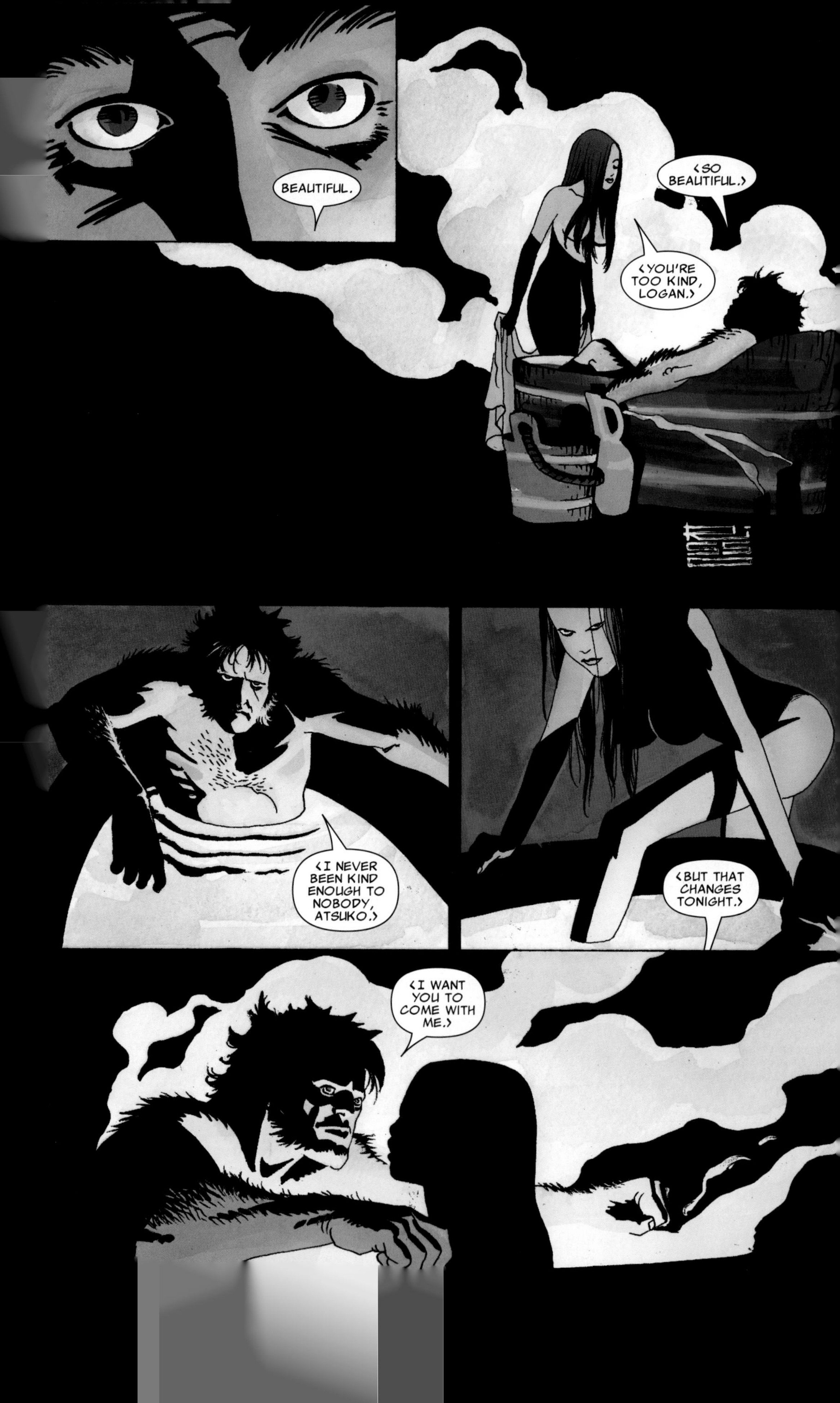
BEAUTIFUL.
‹SO BEAUTIFUL.›
‹YOU'RE TOO KIND, LOGAN.›
‹I NEVER BEEN KIND ENOUGH TO NOBODY, ATSUKO.›
‹BUT THAT CHANGES TONIGHT.›
‹I WANT YOU TO COME WITH ME.›

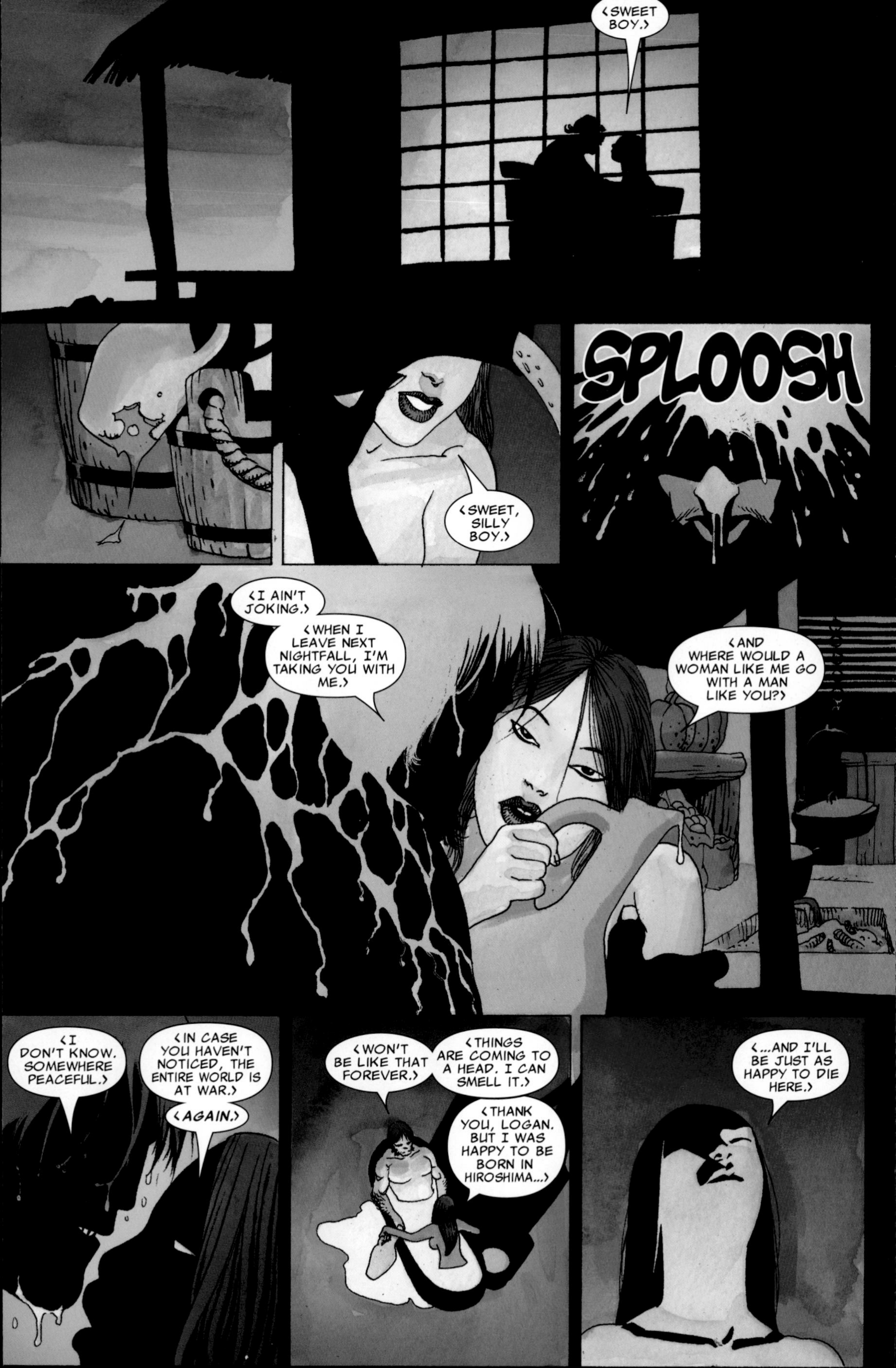
‹SWEET BOY.›
‹SWEET, SILLY BOY.›
SPLOOSH
‹I AIN'T JOKING.›
‹WHEN I LEAVE NEXT NIGHTFALL, I'M TAKING YOU WITH ME.›
‹AND WHERE WOULD A WOMAN LIKE ME GO WITH A MAN LIKE YOU?›
‹I DON'T KNOW. SOMEWHERE PEACEFUL.›
‹IN CASE YOU HAVEN'T NOTICED, THE ENTIRE WORLD IS AT WAR.›
‹AGAIN.›
‹WON'T BE LIKE THAT FOREVER.›
‹THINGS ARE COMING TO A HEAD. I CAN SMELL IT.›
‹THANK YOU, LOGAN. BUT I WAS HAPPY TO BE BORN IN HIROSHIMA...›
‹...AND I'LL BE JUST AS HAPPY TO DIE HERE.›

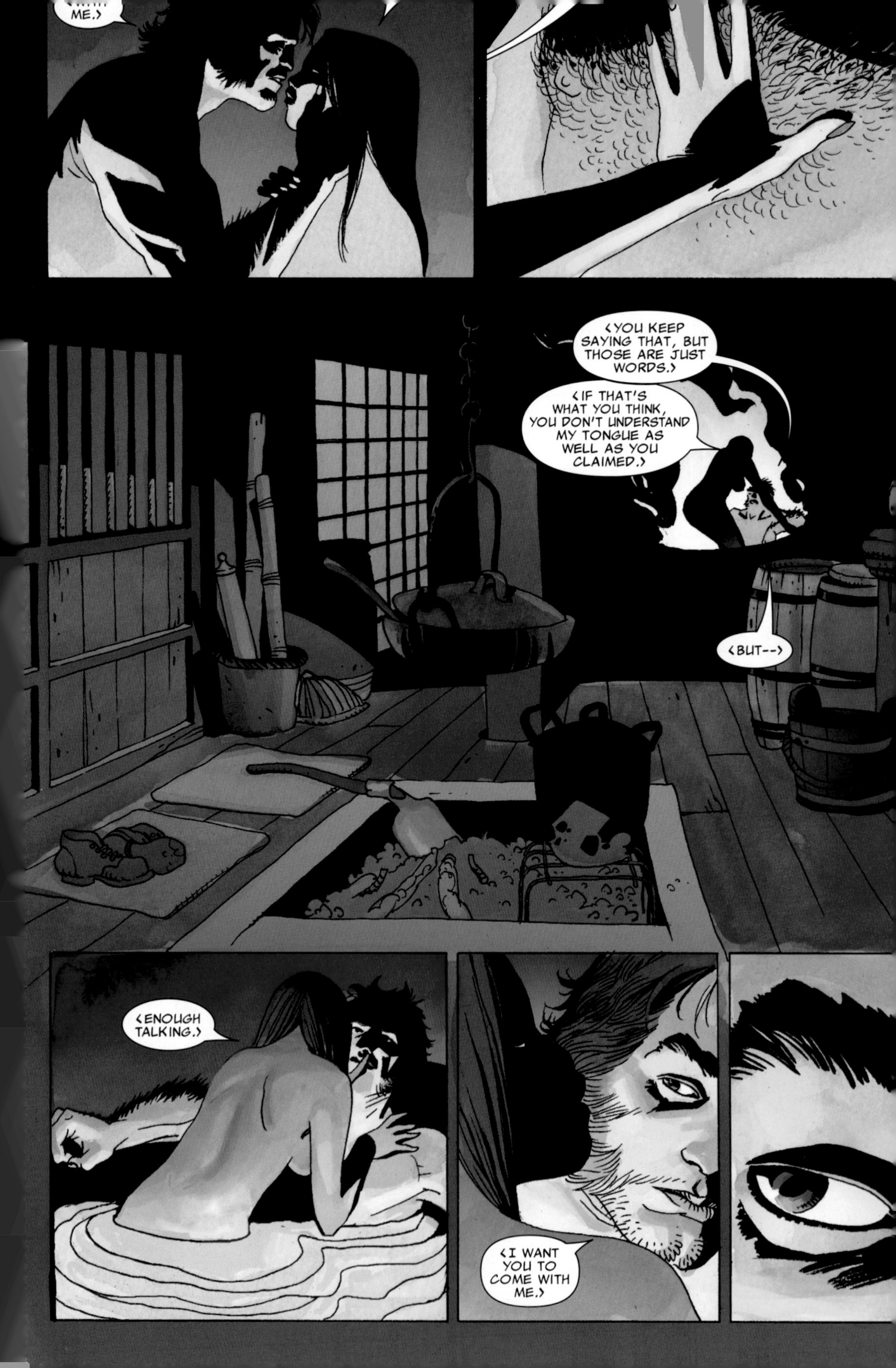
ME.›
‹YOU KEEP SAYING THAT, BUT THOSE ARE JUST WORDS.›
‹IF THAT'S WHAT YOU THINK, YOU DON'T UNDERSTAND MY TONGUE AS WELL AS YOU CLAIMED.›
‹BUT--›
‹ENOUGH TALKING.›
‹I WANT YOU TO COME WITH ME.›

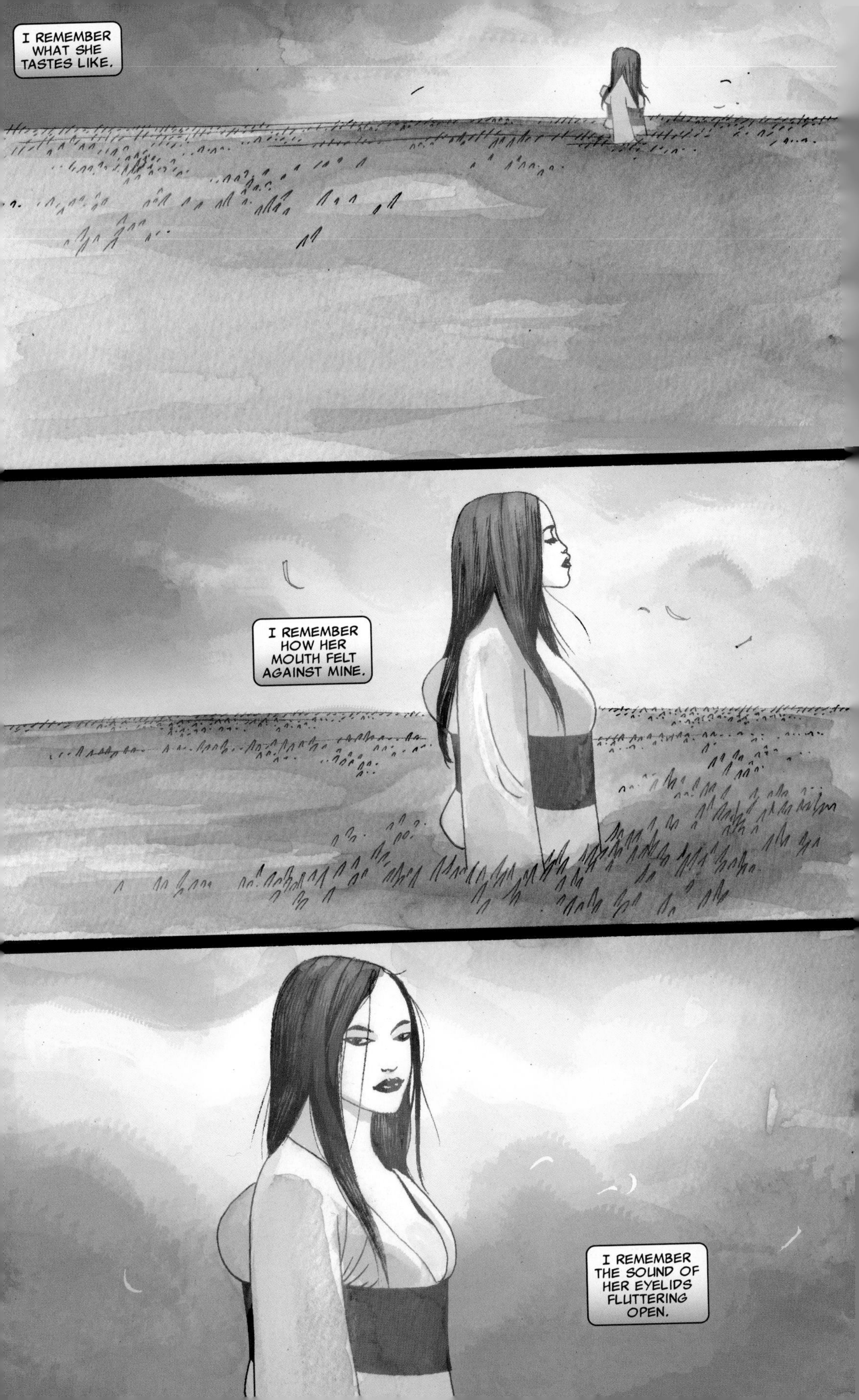
I REMEMBER WHAT SHE TASTES LIKE.
I REMEMBER HOW HER MOUTH FELT AGAINST MINE.
I REMEMBER THE SOUND OF HER EYELIDS FLUTTERING OPEN.

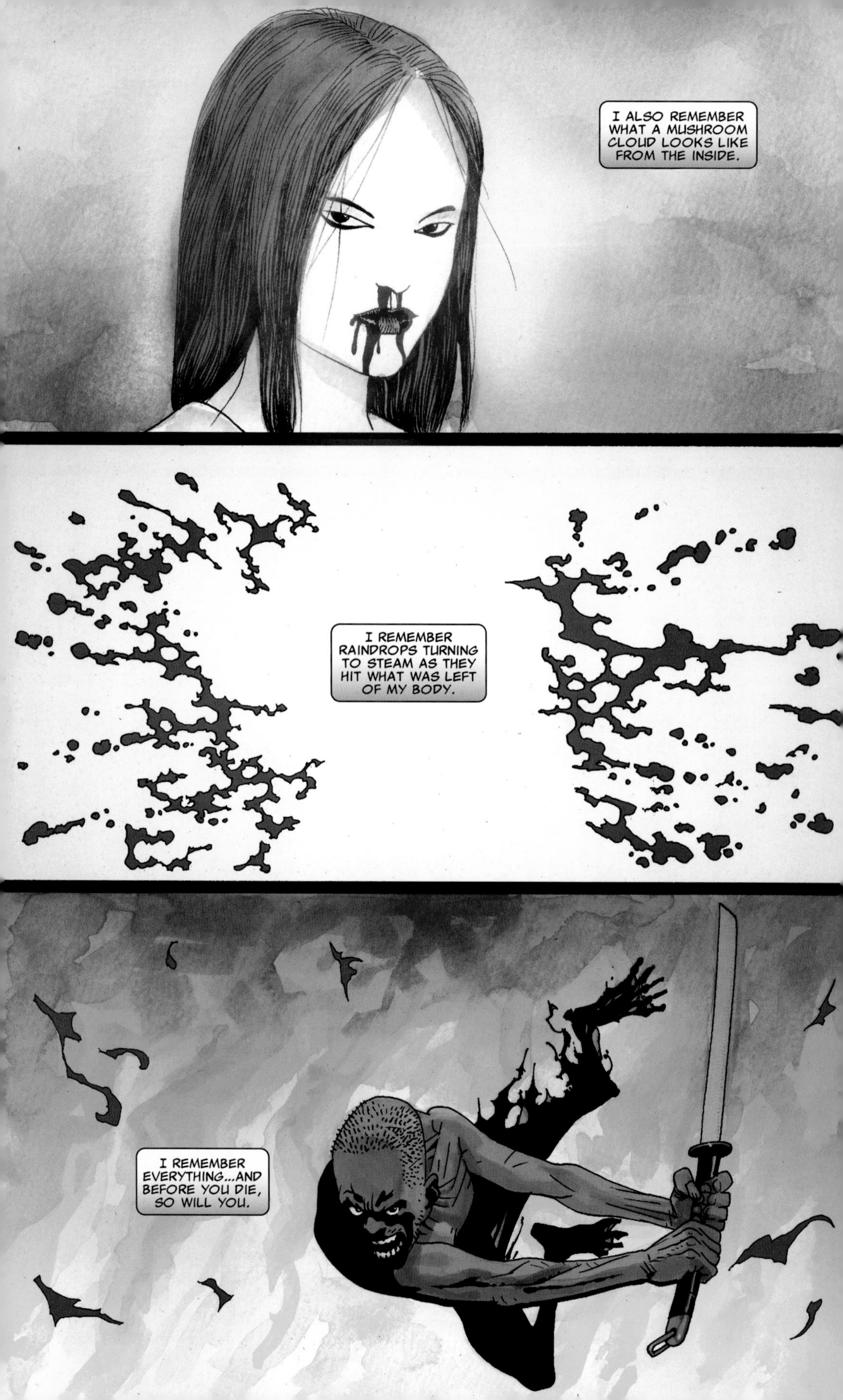
I ALSO REMEMBER WHAT A MUSHROOM CLOUD LOOKS LIKE FROM THE INSIDE.
I REMEMBER RAINDROPS TURNING TO STEAM AS THEY HIT WHAT WAS LEFT OF MY BODY.
I REMEMBER EVERYTHING...AND BEFORE YOU DIE, SO WILL YOU.

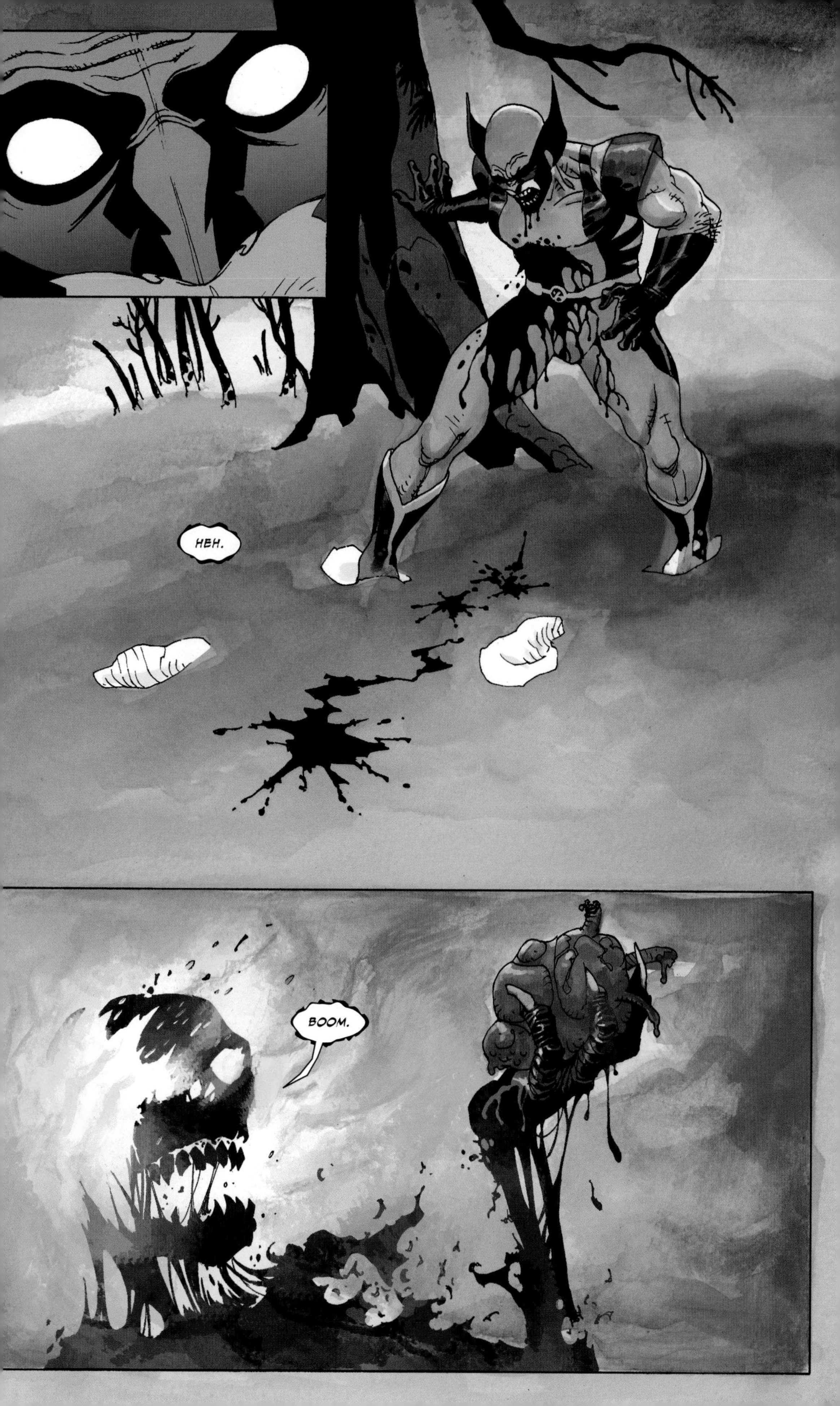
HEH.
BOOM.

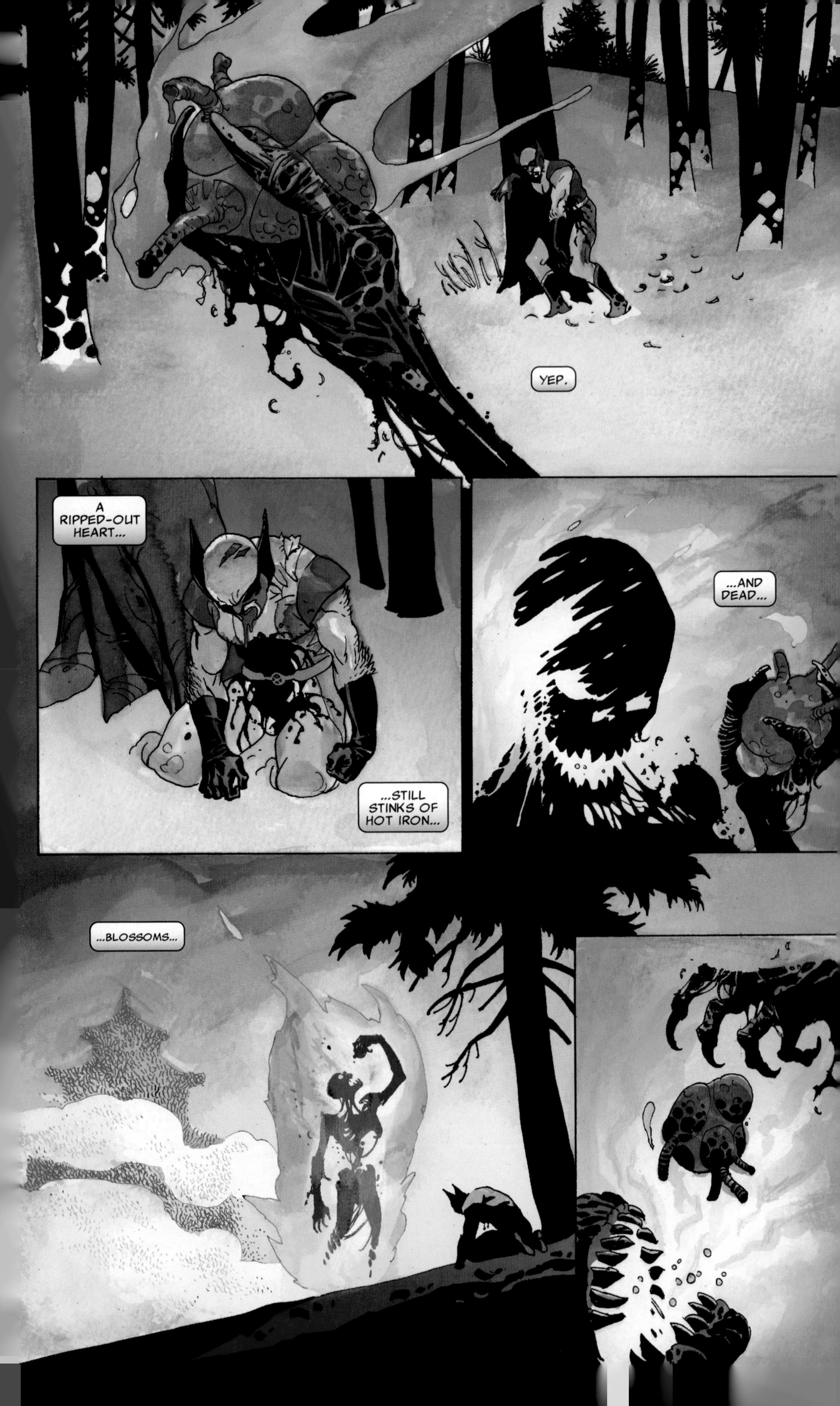

YEP.
A RIPPED-OUT HEART...
...STILL STINKS OF HOT IRON...
...AND DEAD...
...BLOSSOMS...

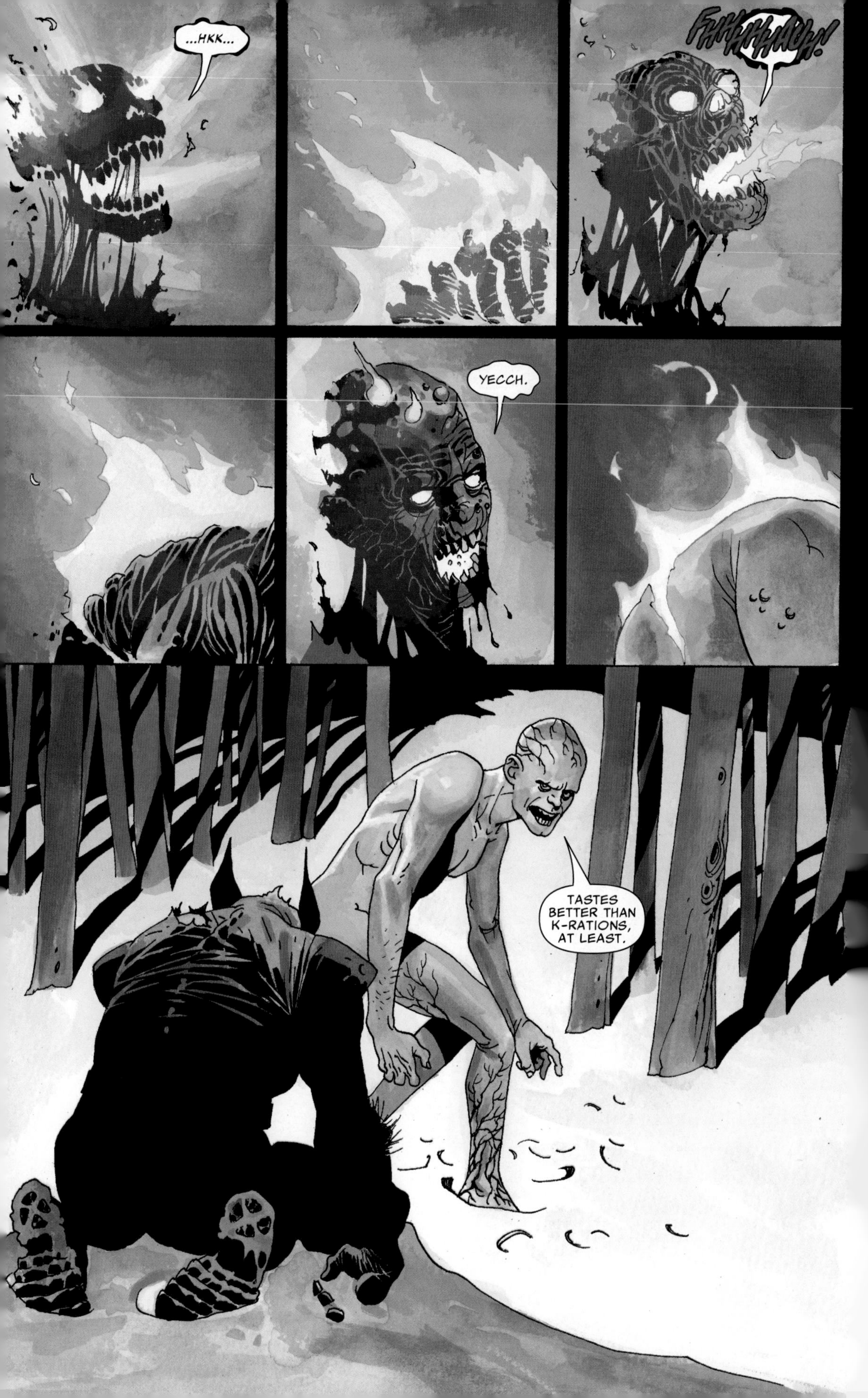
...HKK...
FHHHHHHACH!
YECCH.
TASTES BETTER THAN K-RATIONS, AT LEAST.

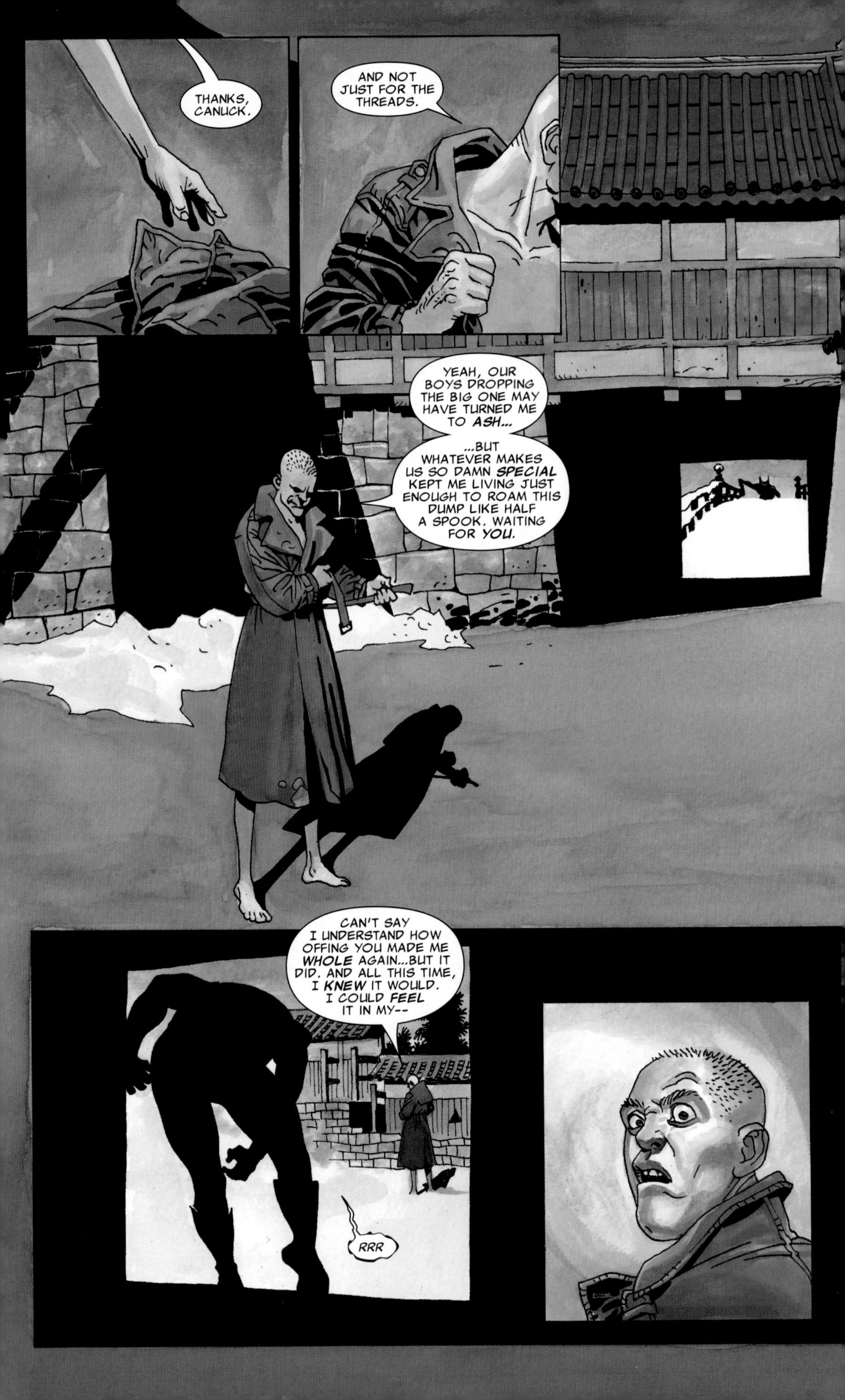
THANKS, CANUCK.
AND NOT JUST FOR THE THREADS.
YEAH, OUR BOYS DROPPING THE BIG ONE MAY HAVE TURNED ME TO ASH...
...BUT WHATEVER MAKES US SO DAMN SPECIAL KEPT ME LIVING JUST ENOUGH TO ROAM THIS DUMP LIKE HALF A SPOOK. WAITING FOR YOU.
CAN'T SAY I UNDERSTAND HOW OFFING YOU MADE ME WHOLE AGAIN...BUT IT DID. AND ALL THIS TIME, I KNEW IT WOULD. I COULD FEEL IT IN MY--
RRR

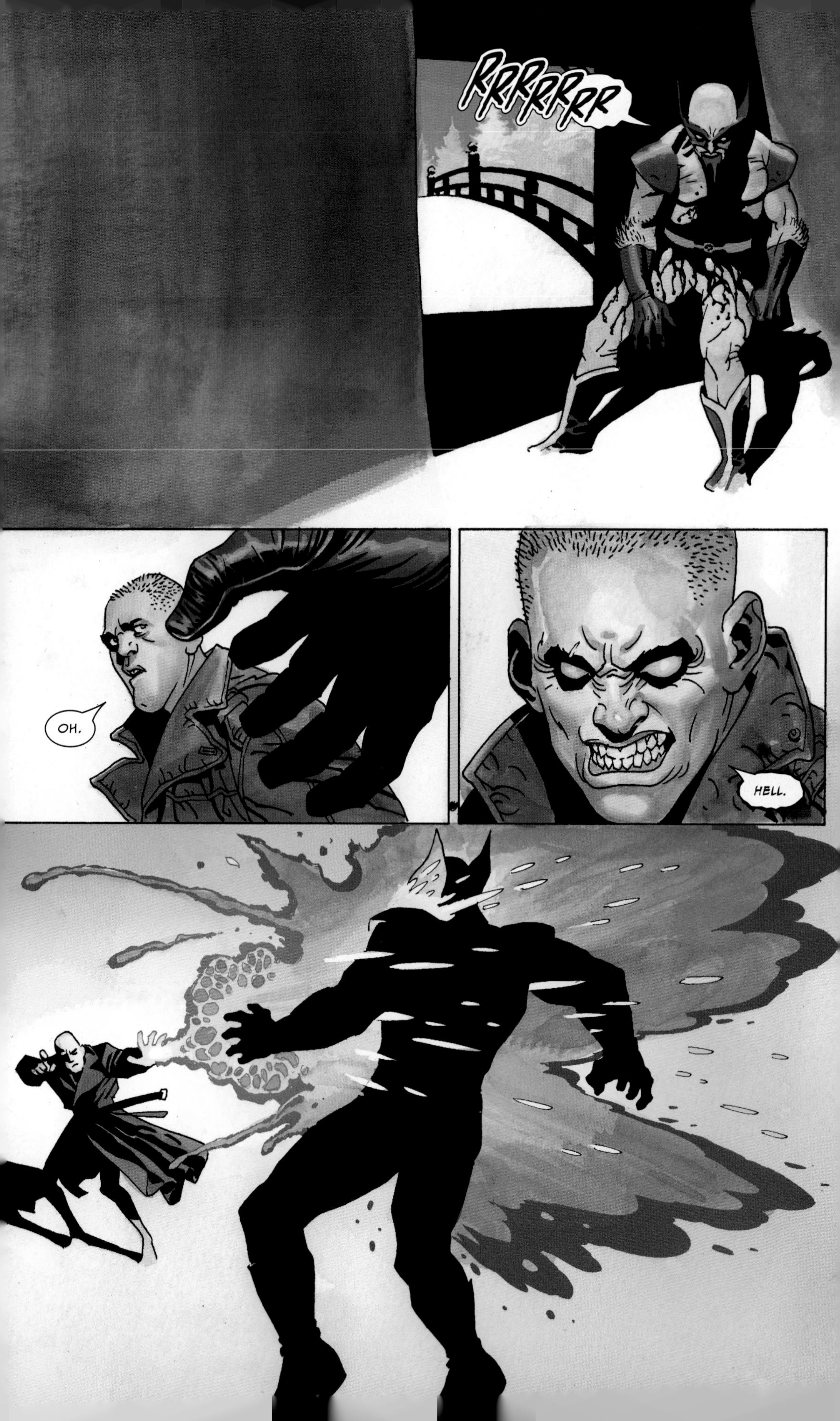
RRRRRRRR
OH.
HELL.

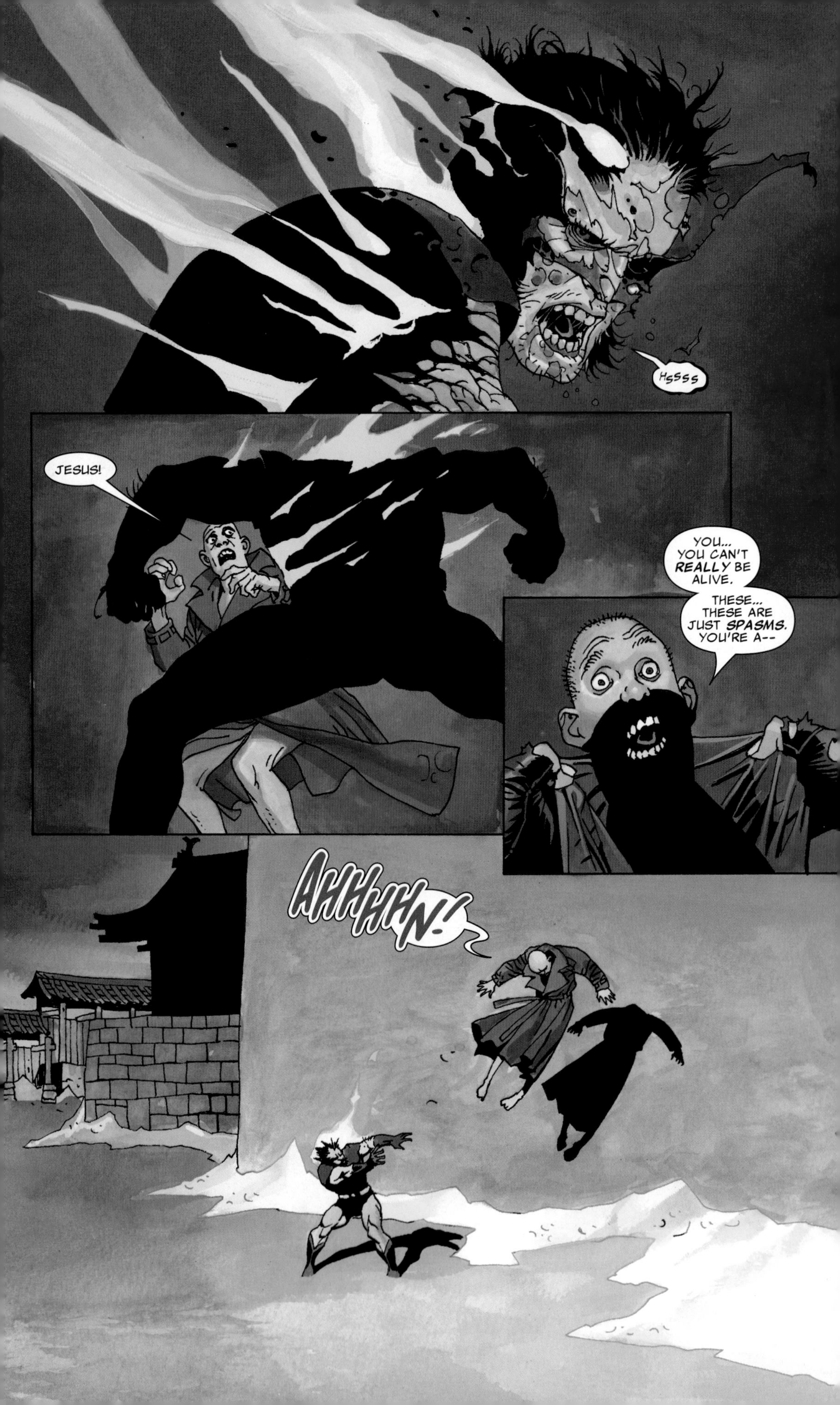
HSSSS
JESUS!
YOU... YOU CAN'T REALLY BE ALIVE.
THESE... THESE ARE JUST SPASMS. YOU'RE A--
AHHHHN!

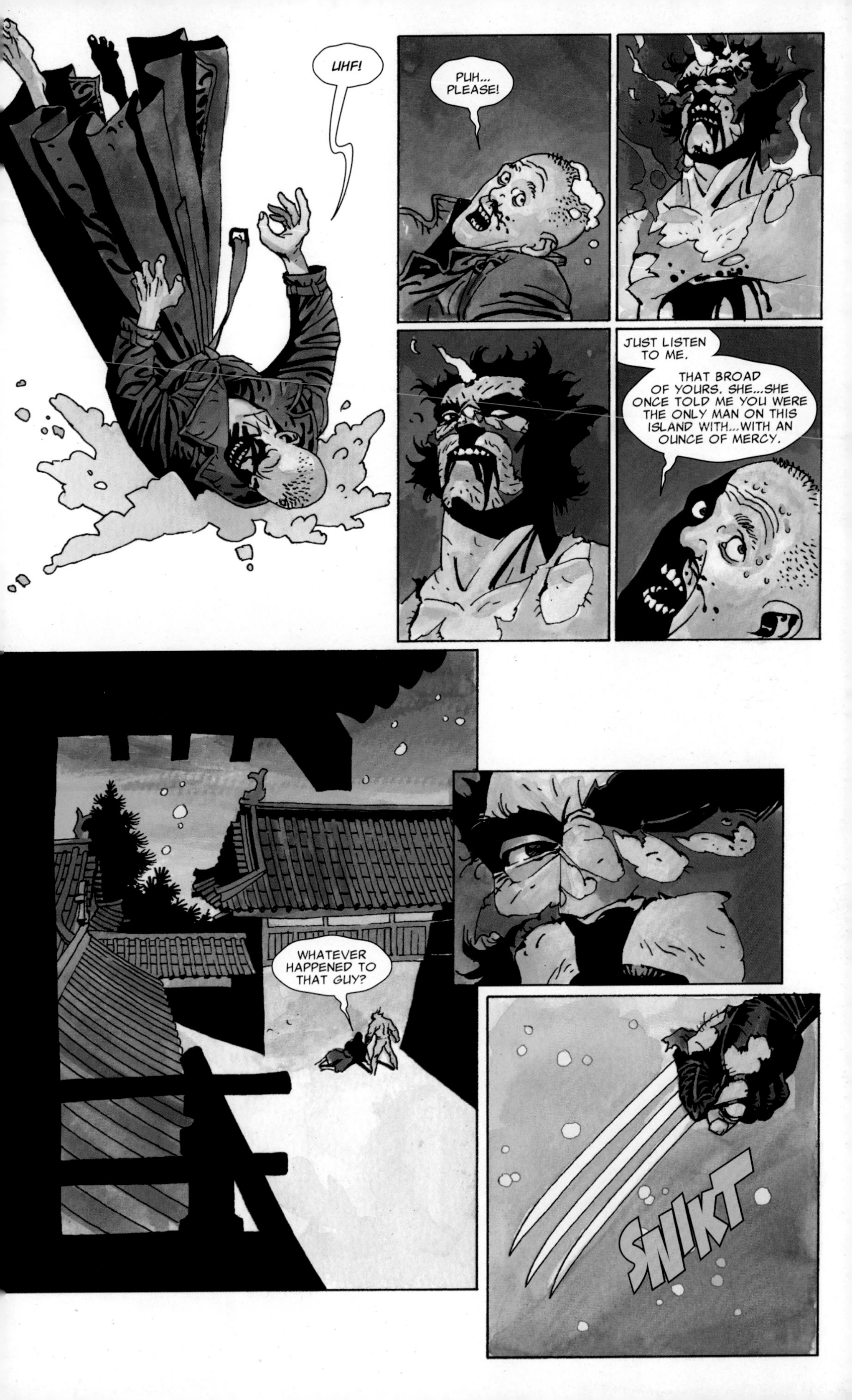
UHF!
PUH... PLEASE!
JUST LISTEN TO ME.
THAT BROAD OF YOURS. SHE...SHE ONCE TOLD ME YOU WERE THE ONLY MAN ON THIS ISLAND WITH...WITH AN OUNCE OF MERCY.
WHATEVER HAPPENED TO THAT GUY?
SNIKT

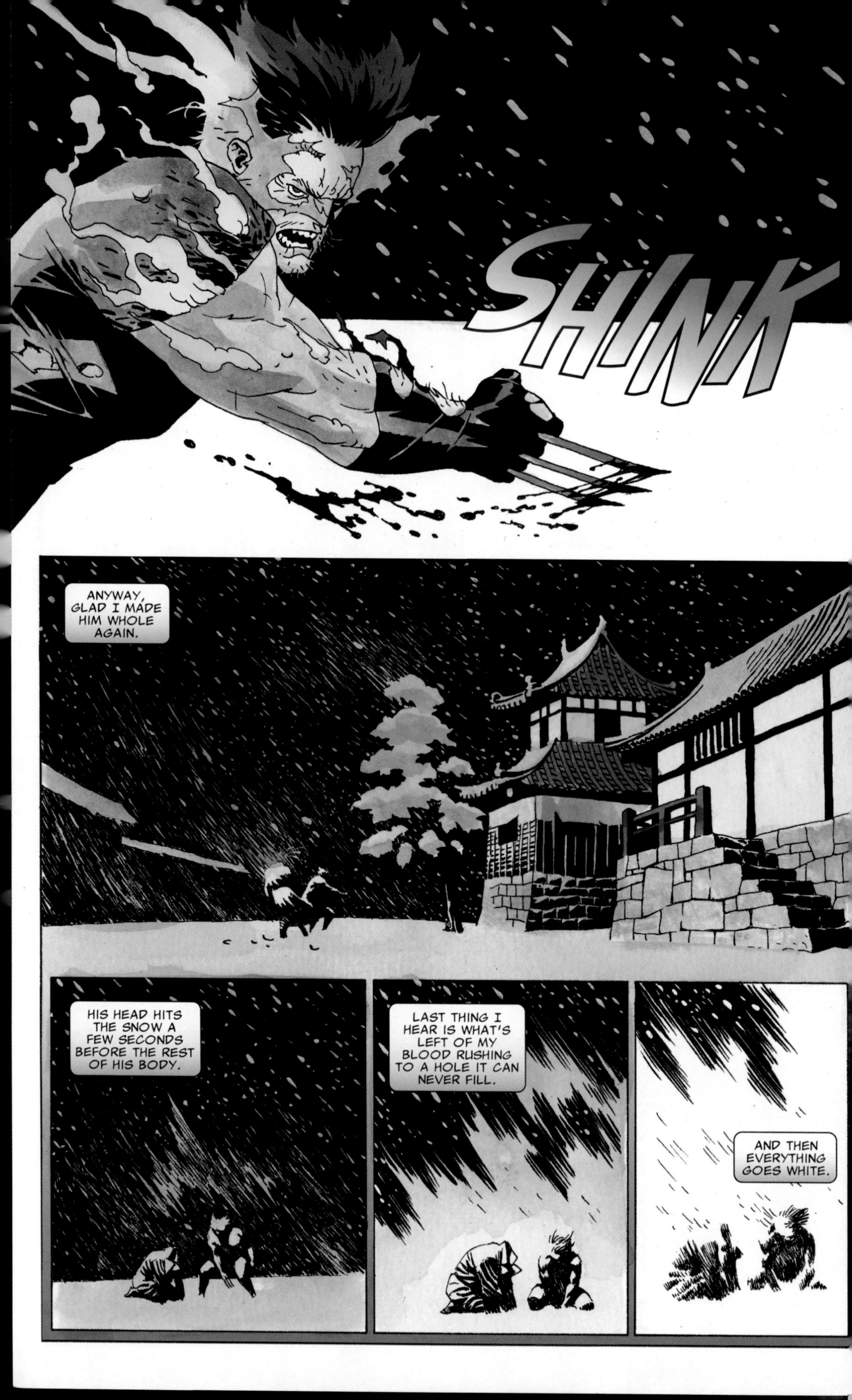
SHINK
ANYWAY, GLAD I MADE HIM WHOLE AGAIN.
HIS HEAD HITS THE SNOW A FEW SECONDS BEFORE THE REST OF HIS BODY.
LAST THING I HEAR IS WHAT'S LEFT OF MY BLOOD RUSHING TO A HOLE IT CAN NEVER FILL.
AND THEN EVERYTHING GOES WHITE.

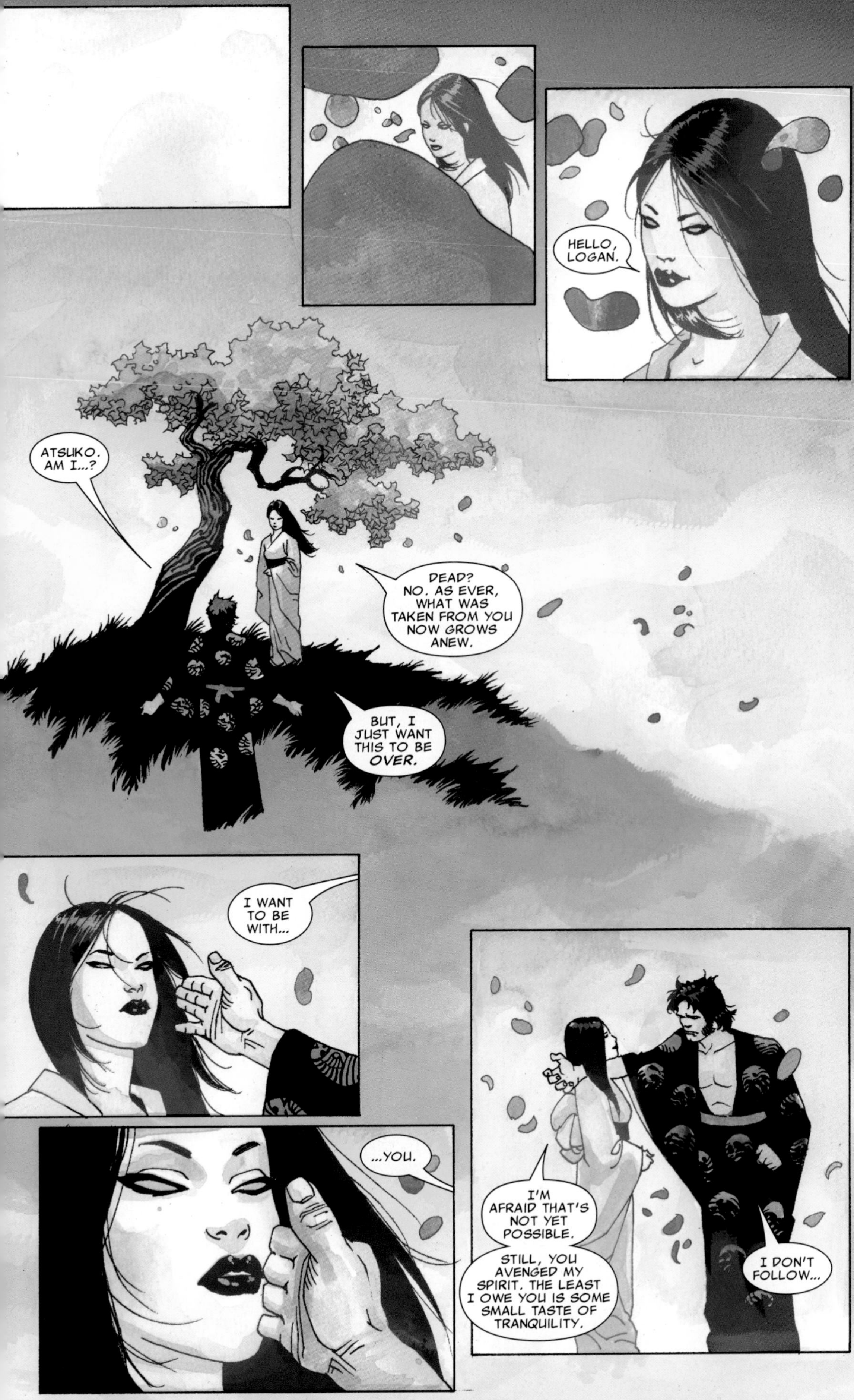
HELLO, LOGAN.
ATSUKO. AM I...?
DEAD? NO. AS EVER, WHAT WAS TAKEN FROM YOU NOW GROWS ANEW.
BUT, I JUST WANT THIS TO BE OVER.
I WANT TO BE WITH...
...YOU.
I'M AFRAID THAT'S NOT YET POSSIBLE.
STILL, YOU AVENGED MY SPIRIT. THE LEAST I OWE YOU IS SOME SMALL TASTE OF TRANQUILITY.
I DON'T FOLLOW...

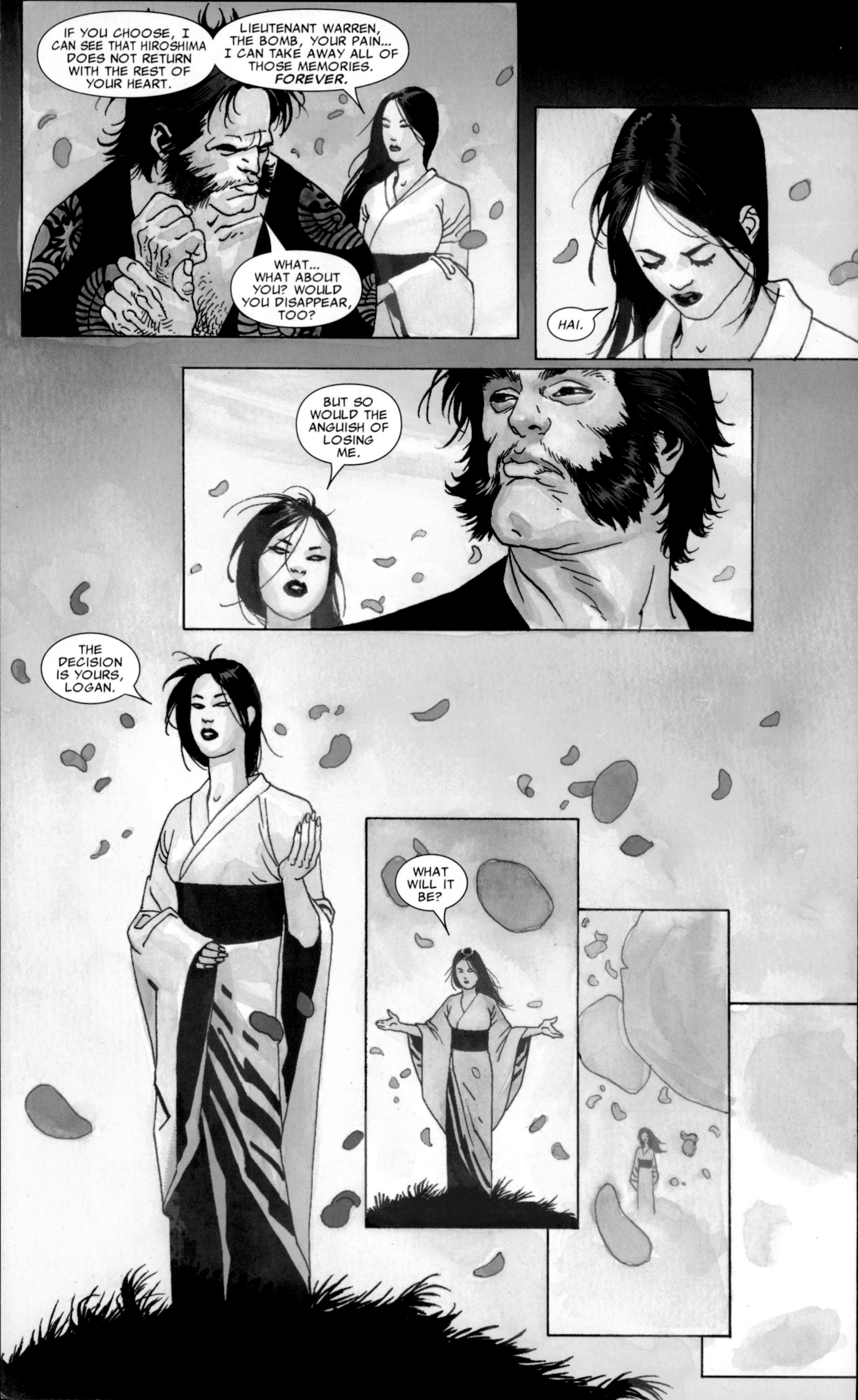
IF YOU CHOOSE, I CAN SEE THAT HIROSHIMA DOES NOT RETURN WITH THE REST OF YOUR HEART.
LIEUTENANT WARREN, THE BOMB, YOUR PAIN... I CAN TAKE AWAY ALL OF THOSE MEMORIES. *FOREVER.*
WHAT... WHAT ABOUT YOU? WOULD YOU DISAPPEAR, TOO?
HAI.
BUT SO WOULD THE ANGUISH OF LOSING ME.
THE DECISION IS YOURS, LOGAN.
WHAT WILL IT BE?

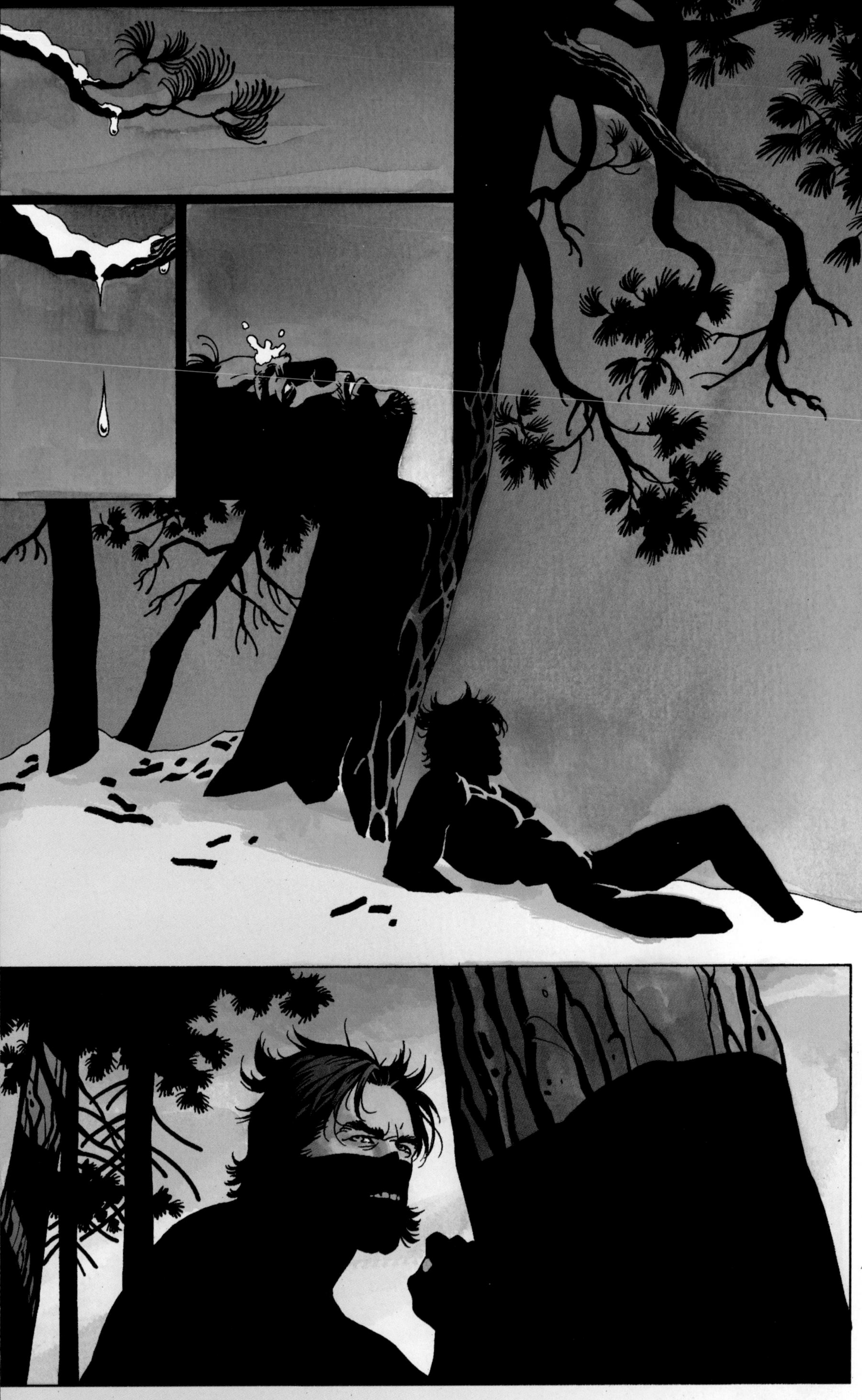

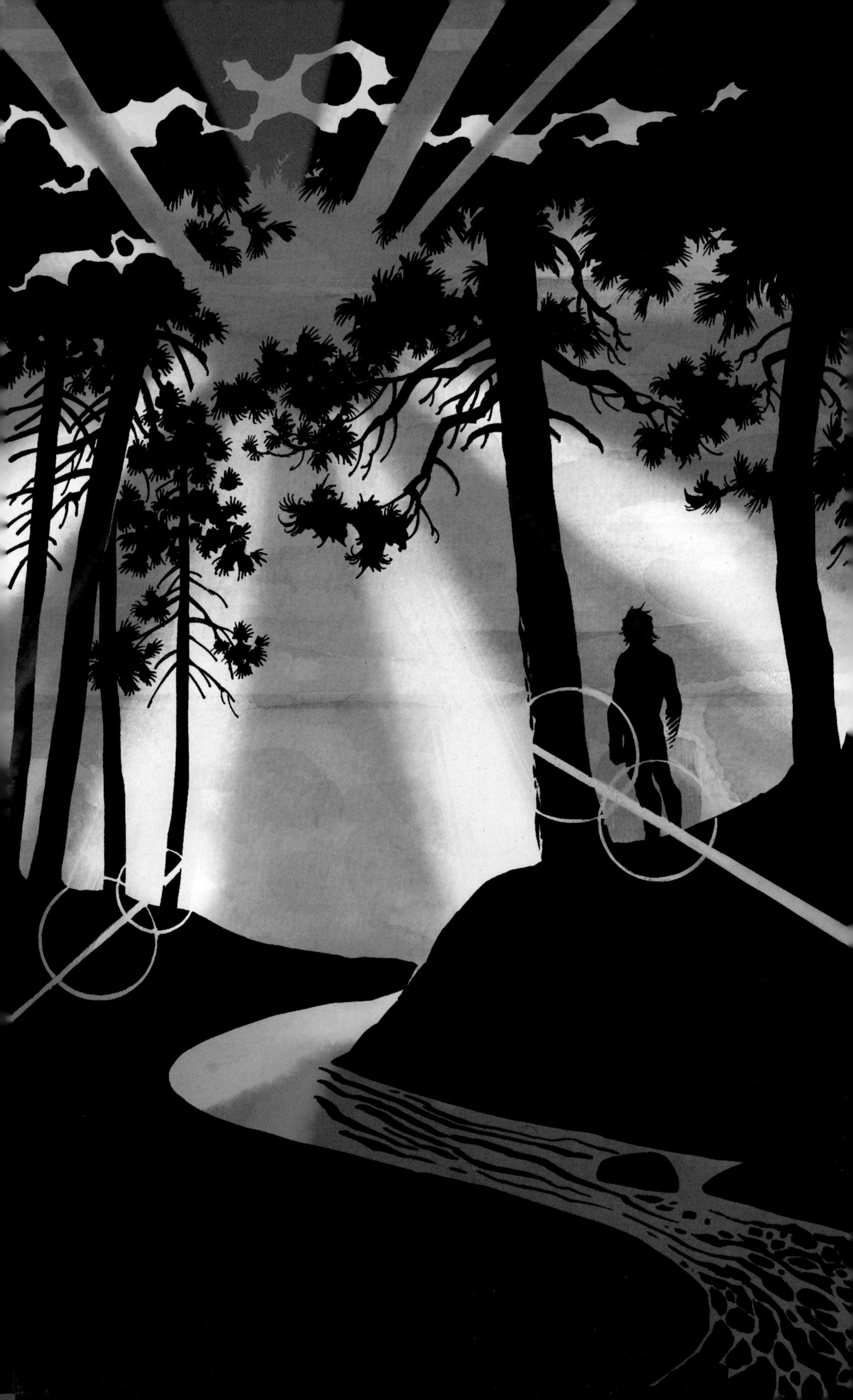

BRIAN K. VAUGHAN
EDUARDO RISSO

—

LOGAN

ORIGIN introduced us to the boy.

X-MEN showed us the hero.

LOGAN finally reveals the day the <u>man</u> was born.

The fates of a young soldier, a beautiful woman, and a vicious monster are forever linked amidst the burning shadows of Nagasaki in this three-part epic, spanning sixty years of the nuclear age.

<u>THE MISSION</u>

There are three things I'd like to accomplish with our three-issue miniseries:

1) Create a story that will showcase the considerable talents of Eduardo Risso, who I've been a huge fan of ever since *Johnny Double*. There are countless Marvel readers who have yet to be exposed to Risso's artwork, and I hope *Logan* will give fans a chance to see what he does best (sophisticated storytelling, visceral action and beautiful women), while also giving Eduardo an opportunity to stretch his muscles and show a whole new side of his work (costumed heroes, misshapen mutants and period drama).

2) Tell a timeless Wolverine story that can stand alongside Miller and Claremont's original miniseries. *Logan* will be a classic, "evergreen" adventure that will appeal to both hardcore fans of the X-Men, and the much larger readership of those only familiar with the character through the movies.

3) Japan and World War II have always been integral parts of Wolverine's shadowy past, but they've usually been shown in a more cartoonish light (with Logan fighting against ninjas or alongside Captain America). With *Logan*, I want to set our hero in a more realistic, relevant version of this time and place. After all, fictional mutants like Wolverine were born in the all-too-real age of atomic paranoia, an era that began in earnest the morning of August 6, 1945.

THE STORY

We'll open in the present, with our modern-day WOLVERINE traveling to Japan after being haunted by nightmares of a beautiful woman from his long-forgotten past.

Flashing back to 1945, we meet up with a young CORPORAL LOGAN of the First Canadian Parachute Battalion, who's being held as a prisoner of war in the terrifying Koyagi Island POW camp in Nagasaki, Japan. Along with a fellow POW, a seemingly indestructible American infantryman (and veteran of several tours of duty) named PRIVATE WARREN, Logan kills his captors before escaping into the night.

On the run, the two fugitives soon encounter a beautiful young Japanese woman named ATSUKO. Eager to punish any member of the race he holds responsible for his brutal treatment in the camps, Private Warren tries to murder this farm girl, only to be beaten down by Logan, who leaves the shamed American to fend for himself.

A grateful Atsuko (orphaned by the war) takes Logan back to her modest farm, where the two wordlessly bond over her family's samurai heirlooms. Fearing that this global war will soon claim them both, Atsuko eventually convinces Logan to join her in one last night of passion.

The next morning, a horrified Logan awakens to find Atsuko's lifeless body lying next to his. A smiling Private Warren is standing over the woman's corpse, chastising a "traitorous" Logan for sleeping with the enemy.

A spectacular clash ensues as Logan uses the ancient samurai weapons to battle his former ally. Ultimately knocking Logan to the ground, Warren prepares to deliver the deathblow… but it's out of the frying pan and into the hellfire, as both men are soon engulfed in the nuclear explosion of an American A-bomb. A nearly skeletonized Logan crawls out of the blast, barely alive and presuming his enemy to be dead.

The rest of our story will take place in the present, as a costumed Wolverine is confronted by a hideous monster (really what's left of Private Warren), who rose from the ashes of Nagasaki after the radiation severely mutated his body. This unstoppable creature is looking to finish a decades-old fight that Wolverine doesn't even remember starting.

But if Logan kills this "son of the atom," he risks destroying his last link to the beautiful young woman who exists only in his dreams.

He's already lived through the war, but now Wolverine will have to survive the fallout.

***

Axel, these are just the very broad strokes of our story, which I'll flesh out in more detail if you and Eduardo feel comfortable with this basic outline. Looking forward to hearing your thoughts!

***

These are some very quick thoughts I had for possible covers, if you want to pass them along to Eduardo. These are all just suggestions, nothing I'm married to at all, and I fully encourage you guys to go in a completely different direction.

Either way, I'm picturing each of these covers featuring one of our three main characters: the man (Wolverine), the woman (a Japanese farm girl named Atsuko), and our monster (Logan's American friend, who will be transformed into a hideous creature):

ISSUE #1: The inspiration for our title (down to the line over the "O" in "Logan") is the novel/movie called SHOGUN.

Like the posters and book covers for that work of fiction, I think our first cover should definitely have clearly Japanese background elements: a temple, a setting red sun, etc. But in the foreground of this shot, because we've seen Wolverine dressed as a samurai/ninja plenty of times before, I think it might be more interesting to see a young Logan dressed in his World War II Canadian soldier outfit (minus the helmet).

Maybe the gun-toting grunt's clothes are torn and dirty, and his silver dog tags are hanging out of his shirt. I think seeing a young Logan in this attire would suggest that this is a story about WAR as much as it is about Japan, and also shows that it's going to reveal an important missing chapter from the character's past.

ISSUE #2: While Logan should definitely be seen somewhere on this cover (maybe we're looking through his metal claws in the foreground?), I think the focus should be Atsuko, Logan's love interest. This beautiful young Japanese woman is a poor farm girl living in Nagasaki during World War II. She was orphaned after her father left her to die for his country as a Kamikaze pilot. On this cover, maybe she's holding his samurai sword (a gift the military sent to pilots' families), and wearing his kamikaze headband.

Families of kamikaze pilots were also given small wooden boxes containing their fingernail clippings (which they cut before their missions, so their families would have a piece of them to bury). That might be a nice touch to incorporate.

Because she's going to die in this issue, maybe Atsuko's wearing a white kimono, and standing in a shallow river (both signs of death/ghosts in Japanese culture).

She should be incredibly sexy (Eduardo's specialty), but also strong.

ISSUE #3: I'm honestly not sure about this cover, and I'd welcome any suggestions from Eduardo. I think this one should feature Wolverine in modern-day Japan (wearing his contemporary costume?), as he battles his nemesis: an American soldier who was mutated by the atomic bomb in Nagasaki.

There are several directions we could go with this villain, and I'm open to any of them. We could make him a shadow creature, to play off the shadows that were burned into the ground by the nuclear explosion in Nagasaki. We could also make him more of a classical demon-type creature. Our third option is to make him a real MONSTER, like Godzilla or the other creatures created by the Japanese in the era of nuclear paranoia. Maybe our villain uses FUSION (like the

A-Bomb) to incorporate aspects of the environment and other living creatures into his massive mutating body, a bit like the Tetsuo character from Akira.

But again, if Eduardo would rather go in a more quiet, grounded direction, I'm fine with that as well. The important thing is that this character represents unchecked American aggression; he possesses all of Wolverine's rage and bloodlust, without being tempered by Logan's sense of mercy.

****

Guys, those are just my really broad initial thoughts. I have the opening of our story pretty well thought out, but the conclusion is still forming in my head. I'm honored to have Eduardo as a collaborator on this project, and I really want him to have a say in our story's direction. I'm open to any and all ideas, so I welcome input from both of you!

More soon,
BKV

The Full Script for

———

LOGAN

Brian K. Vaughan

Prepared for Marvel Comics
August 6, 2005

Eduardo--Once again, it's a tremendous honor to be working with one of my favorite artists. My scripts are somewhat detailed (to help save you time gathering reference, I'll occasionally throw in some annoying web links), but these panel descriptions are only <u>suggestions</u>. You're the best storyteller working in comics, so if you ever see a better way to layout a page or frame a shot, or think of a way to add or subtract panels, please do so with my blessing! And feel free to email me anytime with questions. Many thanks--BKV

PAGE ONE

Page One, SPLASH
We're going to open with a dramatic full-page SPLASH of modern-day Japan, specifically, the rebuilt HIROSHIMA CASTLE. It's night out, so this scene can be lit by moonlight. It's winter, and snowing heavily. We're *behind* WOLVERINE in the foreground of this shot, looking at his back as he stares up at this impressive building. He has a black trenchcoat on, which we'll eventually reveal is covering his current X-Men uniform.

    1)   <u>Caption</u>: When you rip a guy's heart out, the blood inside stinks of hot iron and dead blossoms.

    2)   <u>Caption</u>: After all these years, that's still what Japan smells like to me.

PAGE TWO

Page Two, Panel One
We're looking at Wolverine's face here, as he exhales an icy breath. He's not yet wearing his mask.

    1)   Caption: In case you hadn't heard, I'm a mutant. A

son of the atom ((Save phrase for next issue?)).

2)   Caption: I was cursed with a body that just won't break, no matter what the world does to it.

Page Two, Panel Two
Change angles, as Wolverine walks towards the dark woods that surround this building.

3)   Caption: I've lived enough years to fill a few lifetimes, but most of those I've been lucky enough to forget.

4)   Caption: Least I was…until every last memory came flooding back into my rotten gourd.

5)   Caption: Anyway, that's what brings me here.

Page Two, Panel Three
Pull out to the largest panel of the page, as Wolverine walks through the ominous woods. It continues to snow.

6)   Caption: See, in the Great White North, a sickly kid named James Howlett was born.

7)   Caption: In the backroom butcher shops of evil men, a killer named Weapon X was created.

8)   Caption: And in a little school in Westchester, a "hero" named Wolverine was forged.

Page Two, Panel Four
Push in close on our hero, as he suddenly SNIFFS at the air, having smelled a threat nearby.

9)   Caption: I been a lot of things in a lot of places, but this…this is where I became a man.

10)   SFX: snff

PAGE THREE

Page Three, Panel One
Change angles, as Wolverine looks around.   There's nothing but shadows.

1) Wolverine: You been waiting sixty years, haven't you?

2) Wolverine: Let's finish this already.

Page Three, Panel Two
Wolverine now PULLS ON his mask, and shrugs off his trenchcoat, revealing his yellow and blue uniform.

3)   SFX: aheh heh heh heh

4)   Wolverine: You wanna be dramatic, I can do the kabuki thing…

Page Three, Panel Three
This is a cool, iconic shot of Wolverine as he POPS his glistening metal claws.

5)   Wolverine: …but I ain't got all night.

6)   SFX: SNIKT

7)   Caption: I've made a hell of a lot of enemies over the decades, but I don't lose sleep over 'em.

Page Three, Panel Four
Change angles, as Wolverine is suddenly STRUCK in the back of his head by a MASSIVE FIST OF FIRE belonging to a mysterious creature (more on this creature on the next page).

8)   Wolverine: UHN!

9)   Caption: No, it's the women that keep me up at night, the handful of girls I was dumb enough to fall for over the last century or so.

10)   Caption: After all, I can recover from just about anything…

PAGE FOUR

Page Four, SPLASH
We're with a now *unconscious* Wolverine in the foreground of this shot, as he collapses onto the fresh snow. Standing over him is our MONSTER, a creature whose large body seems to be comprised of BURNING SHADOWS. He or she (we shouldn't be able to tell its sex

yet) is a jet-black monstrosity, whose inky flesh is covered in flames. Maybe a sudden whirlwind of snow partially obscures this strange beast, so we can't yet see it in full detail.

(Eduardo, that's just a suggestion, but feel free to use your imagination. Either way, we'll eventually reveal that this villain is what's left of Lieutenant Warren, an American soldier we're about to meet, who was transformed into this creature by an atomic blast. He's been dormant for sixty years, waiting for Wolverine's return.)

    1)   Caption: …anything but getting my heart ripped out.

    2)   Title (below image):

——

LOGAN
act one of three

    3)   Credits:

Brian K. Vaughan & Eduardo Risso - Storytellers
_____ - Colorist
_____ - Letterer
 Axel Alonso - Editor
Joe Quesada - Chief
Dan Buckley - Publisher

PAGE FIVE

Page Five, Panel One
Our flashback to 1945 begins. I picture this page being made up of four page-wide "letterbox" panels of the same size. This first one is entirely black.

    No Copy

Page Five, Panel Two
This panel is a little brighter, and we can now see the blurry image of a MALE FIGURE standing over us.

    1   Tailless Balloon: Flash?

Page Five, Panel Three
Similar framing, but now the blurry image becomes a little clearer.

2) <u>From Figure</u>: Flash!

Page Five, Panel Four
Same framing one last time, but now we can clearly see the face of LIEUTENANT WARREN, a 29-year-old American prisoner of war. He has blond hair and unshaven blond stubble. We'll eventually see that he's wearing a dirty old white shirt and short black pants (prison attire). He still has his glistening silver DOG TAGS around his neck. He's yelling down at "us" here.

3) Warren: Flash, dammit!

4) Warren: Answer me before I wring your damn neck!

PAGE SIX

Page Six, Panel One
Cut down to LOGAN (who looks slightly younger than when we saw him at the opening of our story). He's squinting up at us as he slowly regains consciousness.

1) Logan: My name ain't Flash, soldier.

2) Logan: It's Logan.

Page Six, Panel Two
Pull out to the largest panel of the page for a shot of both men. We can see that Logan is wearing the same kind of dirty old prison attire as Warren. They're alone inside of a dark, windowless PRISON CELL somewhere inside a Japanese military base. There are no bars, just stone walls and a solid iron door. A single bare bulb lights the scene. Logan looks annoyed with this brash American.

3) Warren: Flash is your challenge, smartass. So I know you're American, and not a Jap spy. Now what's the code reply?

4) Logan: How am I supposed to know?

5) Logan: I'm Canadian. First Parachute Battalion.

Page Six, Panel Three
Push in closer on the two, as Warren frowns at Logan.

6)   Warren: Canuck, huh? Figures.

7)   Warren: If you greenhorns had held Hong Kong in '41, this war would be going a lot better.

8)   Logan: And if you boys hadn't waited until Pearl Harbor to get in the game, this war would be over.

Page Six, Panel Four
Warren smirks a bit, as he holds out a hand and HELPS Logan to his feet.

9)   Warren: Yeah, you're Canadian all right.

10)   Warren: I'm Lieutenant Warren. What rank are you?

11)   Logan: P.O.W., from the looks of it. Where are we?

PAGE SEVEN

Page Seven, Panel One
This is just a close-up of Warren, looking tired and frustrated.

1)   Warren: Military ((science??)) base somewhere on the Japanese mainland.

2)   Warren: I spent the last three months in a hellhole labor camp just north of here… Mukaishima they called it.

Page Seven, Panel Two
Pull out to a shot of both men, as Logan silently listens to Warren's sad tale.

3)   Warren: My squadron was supposed to sink the light cruiser Tone in Kure Harbor, but we had to ditch after taking fire from the shore batteries.

4)   Warren: Half of my guys were K.I.A., me and the other six got pinched.

Page Seven, Panel Three
Push in close on Warren, as he tries to contain his rage over what the

Japanese did to his men.

5) Warren: Two died of starvation in the camp. Dysentery took another three.

6) Warren: And my navigator… my navigator hanged himself by his shirtsleeves. Guess he got tired of digging cesspools at bayonet point twenty hours a day.

Page Seven, Panel Four
This is just a shot of Logan, as he eyes the off-panel Warren suspiciously.

7) Logan: How'd you survive?

Page Seven, Panel Five
This is an ominous shot of Warren, as he stares at the off-panel Logan. Is this American hiding a secret? Is *he* a mutant like Logan?

8) Warren: Exact same way you lived this long, Logan.

9) Warren: Dumb luck

PAGE EIGHT

Page Eight, Panel One
Pull out to another shot of both men.

1) Warren: Anyway, they transferred me here last night.

2) Logan: Why?

3) Warren: Interrogation, probably. Torture. And presuming we keep our traps shut--

Page Eight, Panel Two
Push in closer on the two, as Logan motions for his cellmate to shut up. He's heard something with his heightened senses.

4) Logan: Speaking of which.

5) Logan: Three guards coming.

6) Warren: I… I don't hear anything.

Page Eight, Panel Three
Change angles on the two, as Logan cracks his knuckles.

> 7)　　Logan: This is probably the only chance we're gonna get.

> 8)　　Warren: What, to escape?

> 9)　　Warren: Maybe you were out cold when they dragged you in here, but this place is a fortress.

Page Eight, Panel Four
Push in closer. Warren can't believe what he's hearing.

> 10)　　Logan: I've busted out of worse.

> 11)　　Warren: You're insane.

Page Eight, Panel Five
This is just a cool shot of the deadly serious Logan, as he looks at us and says:

> 12)　　Logan: Do yourself a favor, bub.

> 13)　　Logan: Stick to the shadows 'til I'm through.

PAGE NINE

Page Nine, Panel One
Cut outside this cell for a shot of a brightly lit hallway inside the Japanese military base, which has Japan's old imperial FLAG hanging on one of the walls.

There are some windows in this hallway, too, so we can see that it's late at night out.

Standing outside this cell are THREE JAPANESE IMPERIAL SOLDIERS. The first is unlocking the heavy iron door with an old key, while the other two soldiers keep their rifles and bayonets trained on the door. The soldier with the keys can look like one of these guards.

1) <u>Head Guard</u>: <Keep your safeties on. The doctor says these are *kaiju*, that they're more valuable than-->

Page Nine, Panel Two
As the first soldier opens the door, Logan immediately comes POUNCING out of the cell like a wild animal, LEAPING onto the guard with the keys. (Eduardo, I'm suggesting fight choreography here, but please feel free to add/subtract panels, or to do something entirely different with the action. I trust you completely.)

    2)   <u>Logan</u>: RRRAHH!

Page Nine, Panel Three
Logan quickly and brutally SNAPS this guard's neck, as the two Japanese Infantry soldiers watch with stunned horror.

    3)   <u>SFX</u>: SSNAP

Page Nine, Panel Four
Finally coming to his senses, one of these soldiers STABS Logan in the back with the bayonet at the end of his rifle.

    4)   <u>Infantry Soldier #1</u>: HAAN!

PAGE TEN

Page Ten, Panel One
Cut into the dark cell, as Warren comes CHARGING out at us.

    1)   <u>Warren</u>: NO!

Page Ten, Panel Two
Pull out to the largest panel of the page, as Warren TACKLES the soldier who just stabbed Logan, knocking the bloody bayonet out of Logan's body.

    2)   <u>Infantry Soldier #1</u>: UHF!

Page Ten, Panel Three
Push in on Warren, as he angrily STRANGLES the guard he's just knocked to the ground.

    3)   <u>Warren</u>: Yellow scum!

Page Ten, Panel Four
Cut over to the other infantry soldier, who nervously aims his rifle at the off-panel American, and yells for him to "Stop!" in Japanese.

4) Infantry Soldier #2: Yamai!

PAGE ELEVEN

Page Eleven, Panel One
Pull out, as the wounded Logan SPRINGS forward and GRABS the middle of this soldier's rifle with his left hand, pushing it upwards.

1) Infantry Soldier #2: NAH!

Page Eleven, Panel Two
As Logan and the soldier WRESTLE for control of this rifle, Logan grabs the soldier's shirtfront with his free hand.

2) Infantry Soldier #2: Nnnn…

Page Eleven, Panel Three
Similar framing, but as we hear a familiar sound effect, the soldier Logan is wrestling with suddenly CRINGES in pain. (Eduardo, with the hand grabbing this soldier's shirt, Logan has just plunged his sharp claws--which are still made of bone in this era, not Adamantium--into the soldier's chest, but this should be framed so that we *can't* see the claws at all, please.)

3) SFX: SNIKT

Page Eleven, Panel Four
Push in close on the soldier, who looks stunned. What the hell just happened?

No Copy

Page Eleven, Panel Five
Exact same framing on the Japanese soldier, but now his eyes roll into the back of his head, as a little BLOOD leaks out of the side of his mouth. He's dead.

No Copy

PAGE TWELVE

Page Twelve, Panel One
Cut over to Lieutenant Warren, who is still on top of the first infantry soldier he just strangled to death. Warren's looking at the off-panel Logan with disbelief.

1)   Warren: What…what did you do to him?

Page Twelve, Panel Two
Pull out to the largest panel of the page for a group shot of this carnage, as Logan DROPS the limp soldier he just killed.

2   Logan: What I do best.

Page Twelve, Panel Three
Cut back to a grateful Warren, as he slowly gets to his feet.

3)   Warren: Well, ah, thanks.

4)   Warren: Wish I'd had a fighter like you at my side back in--

Page Twelve, Panel Four
Cut back to Logan, as he looks down at his kill.

5)   Logan: Yeah, yeah.

6)   Logan: Take whichever outfit's got the least bloodstains.

Page Twelve, Panel Five
This is just a dramatic shot of Logan, as he looks out a nearby WINDOW in this hallway at the silver moon outside.

7)   Logan: We ain't out of the woods yet.

PAGE THIRTEEN

Page Thirteen, Panel One
Smash cut to later that night (it's a late August evening) for this establishing shot of a dense area of TREES somewhere in Japan.

No Copy

Page Thirteen, Panel Two
Cut into the woods for this shot of several little wooden bridges, where two DARK FIGURES are walking. Eduardo, the bridges can look like the ones in this photo, but as always, feel free to use other reference you find, or your imagination:

Page Thirteen, Panel Three
Push in on the two dark figures, who we can now tell are Logan and Lieutenant Warren, carrying the rifles and wearing the uniforms of two of the soldiers they just killed. Dark-haired Logan isn't wearing a hat, but maybe Warren is covering up his blond locks with one of those old-fashioned Japanese military hats.

1) Warren: So, uh… how'd you end up in the Pacific Theater?

2) Logan: Theater? That what we're calling it now?

3) Logan: I was in Burma to blow up a train. Guess it went south, 'cause I woke up here.

PAGE FOURTEEN

Page Fourteen, Panel One
This is just a shot of the pissed-off Warren, as he fumes:

1) Warren: Goddamn animals.

2) Warren: The Japs won't stop until we've killed every last one of 'em.

Page Fourteen, Panel Two
Pull out to a shot of both men. Logan clearly doesn't have time for Warren's bull.

3) Warren: Wish I'd been in Normandy.

4) Warren: The Krauts may be bastards but at least they fight like men. These people… they're not even human. They're--

5) Logan: Why don't you save it until we're stowed away inside whatever cargo boat is gonna get us off this rock? We still--

Page Fourteen, Panel Three
Push in close on Logan, who's surprised to hear screaming coming from nearby.

6)   Atsuko (from off): Aiiee!

Page Fourteen, Panel Four

We're *behind* the two men for this largest panel of the page, a big shot of ATSUKO, a gorgeous, twenty-year-old Japanese farm girl wearing sandals and a stark white kimono.

Atsuko is standing on a bridge directly in front of Logan and Warren, and she covers her mouth in horror as she sees the two clearly Caucasian men. Even though she's terrified, we can tell that this young woman is heartbreakingly beautiful.

No Copy

PAGE FIFTEEN

Page Fifteen, Panel One

This is just a close-up of Logan, who looks stunned by the sudden appearance of this girl.

1)   Logan (small, a whisper): I… I didn't even catch her scent.

2)   Logan (small, a whisper): She's like a damn ghost.

Page Fifteen, Panel Two

Pull out to a shot of all three characters, as Warren raises his rifle and aims it at the frozen Atsuko, despite Logan's warning.

3)   Warren: If she's not yet, she will be.

4)   Logan: Stand down.

5)   Logan: She's just a civilian.

Page Fifteen, Panel Three

This is just a shot of Warren (who keeps his rifle trained on the off-panel Atsuko), as he shoots us a dirty look.

6)   Warren: There's no such thing as a Jap civilian.

7)   Warren: They're all spies and… and assassins for the Emperor!

Page Fifteen, Panel Four
Pull out to another shot of all three characters, as Logan begs his companion to lower his rifle.

> 8) Warren: Besides, she looks just like the broad on that trawler that pulled me and my crew out of the drink.

> 9) Warren: She's the one who turned us over to these monsters.

> 10) Logan: Let it go. The girl's not a fisher, she's a farmer.

Page Fifteen, Panel Five
This is just a shot of Warren. We're looking down the barrel of his rifle, which he's aiming *right at us*.

> 11) <u>Warren</u>: Then we might as well put her in the dirt where she belongs.

PAGE SIXTEEN

Page Sixteen, Panel One
Pull out to a shot of both men, as we reveal that Logan now has *his* rifle trained at Warren's head.

> 1) <u>Logan</u>: You pull that trigger, you'll be joining her.

Page Sixteen, Panel Two
Pull out to another shot of all three characters. Atsuko is certain she's about to be executed.

> 2) Warren: You forgetting who the enemy is here?

> 3) Logan: Walk away, Warren.

> 4) Logan: This is where you and me part ways.

Page Sixteen, Panel Three
This is just a shot of Warren, as he angrily lowers his rifle.

> 5) Warren: You…you are a spy, aren't you? You're working for them!
> 6) Warren: This is all some kinda setup!

Page Sixteen, Panel Four
And this is just a shot of Logan, as he gives a stern order.

     7)   Logan: Walk.

     8)   Logan: Away.

Page Sixteen, Panel Five
We're with Logan in the foreground of this shot, as he turns to watch Warren reluctantly retreat into the night.

No Copy

PAGE SEVENTEEN

Page Seventeen, Panel One
Change angles on Logan, as he looks down to discover that Atsuko is now KNEELING in front of him, bowing her head deeply in a sign of gratitude.

No Copy

Page Seventeen, Panel Two
Push in on Logan, who looks a little uncomfortable about this.

     1)   Logan: All right already.

     2)   Logan: On your feet, girly.

Page Seventeen, Panel Three
Pull out to reveal that Atsuko is still on her knees.

     3)   Logan: Come on.

     4)   Logan: Do-itashimashite and all that.

Page Seventeen, Panel Four
This is just a shot of the beautiful Atsuko, as she lifts up her head to look at us.

     5)   Atsuko: <You… you speak my tongue?>

PAGE EIGHTEEN

Page Eighteen, Panel One
Pull out to a shot of both characters, as Atsuko gets to her feet and takes Logan's hand.

   1)   Logan: <Some.>

   2)   Atsuko: <Please.>

   3)   Atsuko: <Follow me.>

Page Eighteen, Panel Two
Change angles on the two, as Atsuko begins PULLING a confused Logan after her.

   4)   Logan: Wait! What are you...?

   5)   Atsuko: <The sun will rise soon. You'll never make it to the harbor before morning. I can hide you until tomorrow's nightfall.>

Page Eighteen, Panel Three
Similar framing, but now Logan stops Atsuko in her tracks.

   6)   Logan: Stop.

   7)   Logan: If your people catch you with me, they'll kill us both.

Page Eighteen, Panel Four
This is just a shot of Atsuko from Logan's point of view, as she looks back at us over her shoulder with a seductive *smile*.

   8)   Caption: Did she smile because she didn't understand me...or because she didn't care?

Page Eighteen, Panel Five
We're in the shadowy woods with Lieutenant Warren in the foreground of this shot, as he watches Logan follow after Atsuko in the background.

   9)   Caption: Either way, I was hers.

PAGE NINETEEN

Page Nineteen, Panel One
Cut to later (the sun is just barely starting to rise in the distance) for this establishing shot of a modest farm somewhere in Hiroshima, perhaps something like this.

No Copy

Page Nineteen, Panel Two
Cut inside this small farm's old-fashioned kitchen, where Logan is kneeling in front of a small table, eating from a bowl of rice. Atsuko is reaching for something inside of an old chest, though we can't see what it is just yet. A small fire lights the scene. For some examples of old Japanese kitchens, check out the three websites:

No Copy

Page Nineteen, Panel Three
Push in close on Logan, as he struggles to find the words in Japanese to thank his hostess.

    1)   Logan: <I… I don't know how to repay you, um…>

Page Nineteen, Panel Four
Cut over to Atsuko, as she menacingly pulls out a glistening SAMURAI SWORD, which has a piece of cloth tied to its handle.

    2)   Atsuko: Atsuko.

Page Nineteen, Panel Five
This is just a shot of Logan, looking betrayed, *reflected* in the blade of the shining sword.

    3)   Atsuko (from just off): <My name is Atsuko.>

PAGE TWENTY

Page Twenty, Panel One
Pull out to a shot of both characters. As Atsuko approaches, Logan slowly puts down his bowl of rice.

    1)   Logan: If you want to hurt me, you're gonna need a sharper…

Page Twenty, Panel Two
Change angles on the two, as Atsuko bows a bit and PRESENTS the sword to Logan, handing it to him handle first.

No Copy

Page Twenty, Panel Three
Logan carefully TAKES the sword from the woman.
      2)   Logan: Hn.

Page Twenty, Panel Four
This shot of the sword can be from Logan's point of view, as he looks down to see a KAMIKAZE HEADBAND tied around the sword's handle.

      3)   Logan: Kamikaze.

Page Twenty, Panel Five
Pull out to another shot of both characters. Logan is still holding the sword, but Atsuko has just produced a small wooden box, which she's holding out here.

      4)   Logan: <Your… your father's?>

      5)   Atsuko: <He volunteered after mother was killed in the fire-bombings.>

      6)   Atsuko: <Before his final mission, father's wretched masters sent me that sword… and this.>

PAGE TWENTY-ONE

Page Twenty-one, Panel One
Push in on Logan, as he sets down the sword and takes the small box.

No Copy

Page Twenty-one, Panel Two
Again, this shot can be from Logan's point of view, as he looks down into the open box, which we can now see contains several FINGERNAIL CLIPPINGS.

      1)   Logan (from off): Fingernail clippings.

Page Twenty-one, Panel Three
Pull out to a shot of both characters, as Logan hands the box back to Atsuko.

> 2)   Logan: <So you would have something to bury, right?>
>
> 3)   Logan: <This… this is all you have left of him?>

Page Twenty-one, Panel Four
Change angles, as Atsuko sets aside the box, and takes Logan's hand with her free hand.

> 4)   Atsuko: <No.>
>
> 5)   Atsuko: <My father lives on…>

Page Twenty-one, Panel Five
Push in closer on the two, as Atsuko romantically PLACES Logan's hand over her heart.

> 6)   Atsuko: <…here.>

PAGE TWENTY-TWO

Page Twenty-two, Panel One
Change angles, as a nervous Logan slowly pulls his hand away.

> 1)   Logan: <Why did you help me?>

Page Twenty-two, Panel Two
This is just an alluring shot of Atsuko, as she begins to UNDO her kimono.

> 2)   Atsuko: <I'm tired of war.>

Page Twenty-two, Panel Three
Change angles, as Atsuko REMOVES her clothing. Obviously, this isn't Vertigo, Eduardo, so please be discreet in how you suggest her nudity!

> 3)   Atsuko: <And since it began, you're the first person I've met who seems at peace.>

Page Twenty-two, Panel Four
Pull out to a shot of both characters, as the naked Atsuko steps closer to

Logan, who looks away. He's trying his best not to give into temptation here.

> 4)   Logan: <That… that isn't necessary.>
>
> 5)   Logan: <You've done enough for me already.>
> 6)   Atsuko: Hai…

Page Twenty-two, Panel Five
Push in on the two. Logan closes his eyes as Atsuko begins to KISS his neck.

> 7)   Atsuko: <…and now it's time for you to do something for me.>

PAGE TWENTY-THREE

Page Twenty-three, Panel One
Change angles on the two, as Logan EMBRACES Atsuko.

> 1)   Logan: This is heaven, ain't it? I'm already dead, and now I'm in heaven.
>
> 2)   Atsuko: No… not heaven…
>
> 3)   Logan: Then what is this place? Where am I?

Page Twenty-three, Panel Two
This largest panel of the page (at least a half-SPLASH) is just a dramatic close-up of Atsuko from Logan's point of view, as she stares directly into our souls, and whispers a single word.

> 4)   Atsuko: Hiroshima.

Page Twenty-three, Panel Three
Finally, this is just an extreme close-up of Logan's emotionless eyes, clearly not realizing the horror that's on its way.

> 5)   Caption: It was just about the most beautiful word I'd ever heard.
>
> 6)   Closing Tag: To Be Continued…

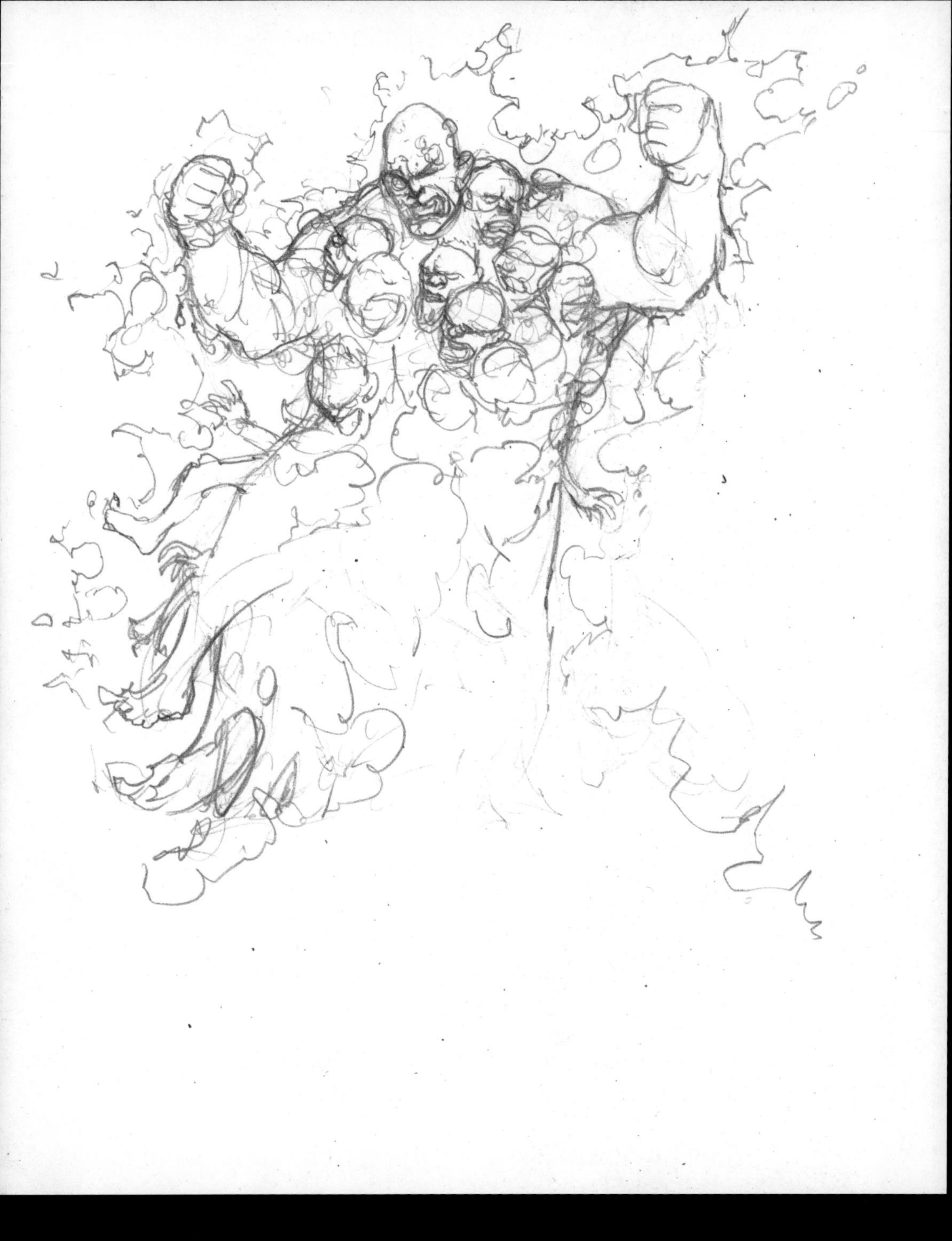

monster conceptual sketch

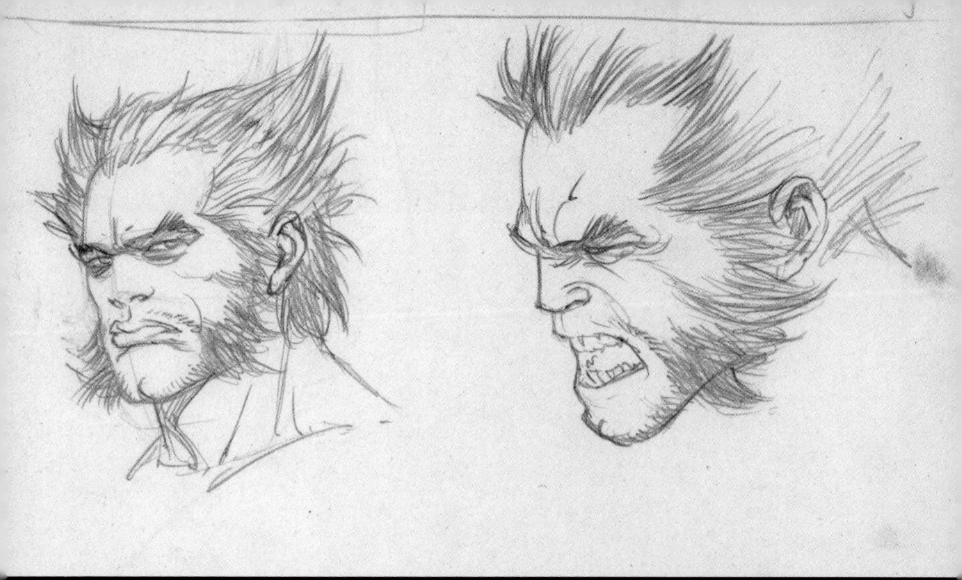
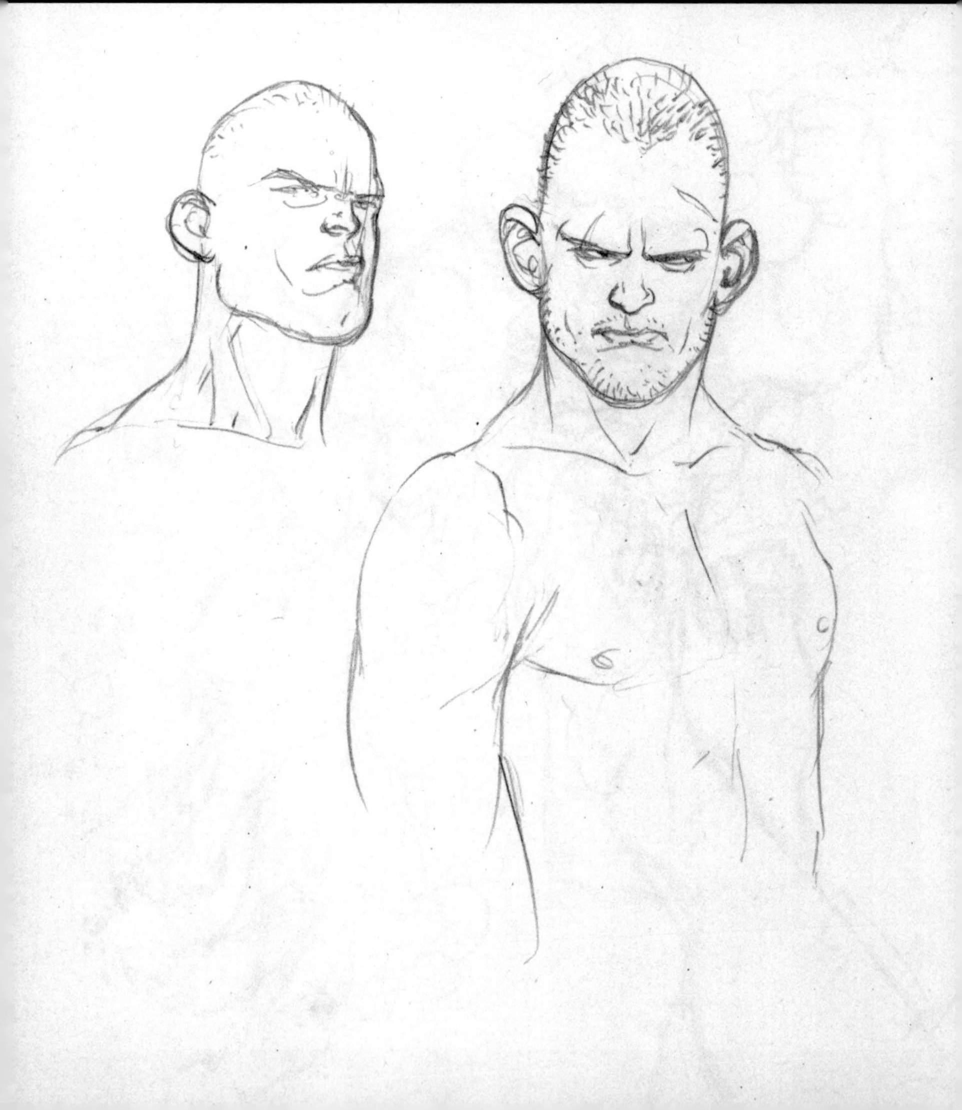

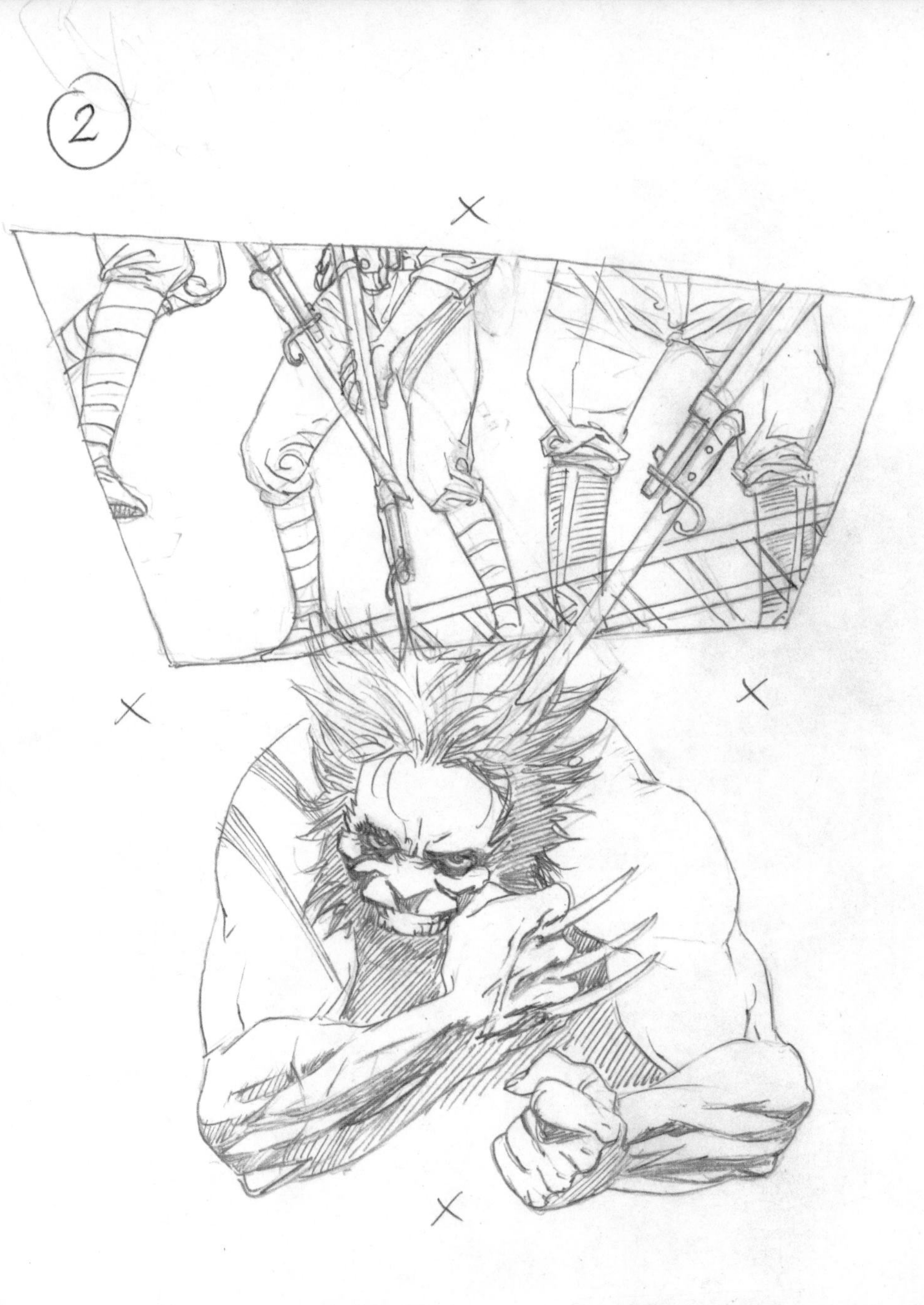

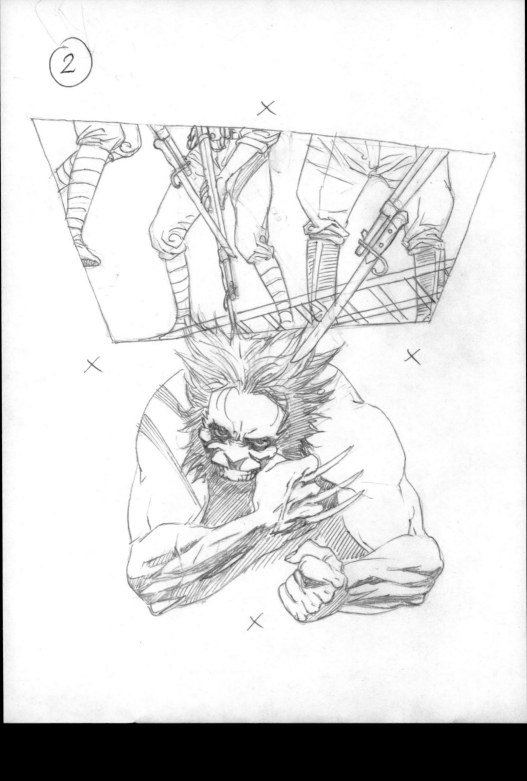

unused issue number one cover sketch

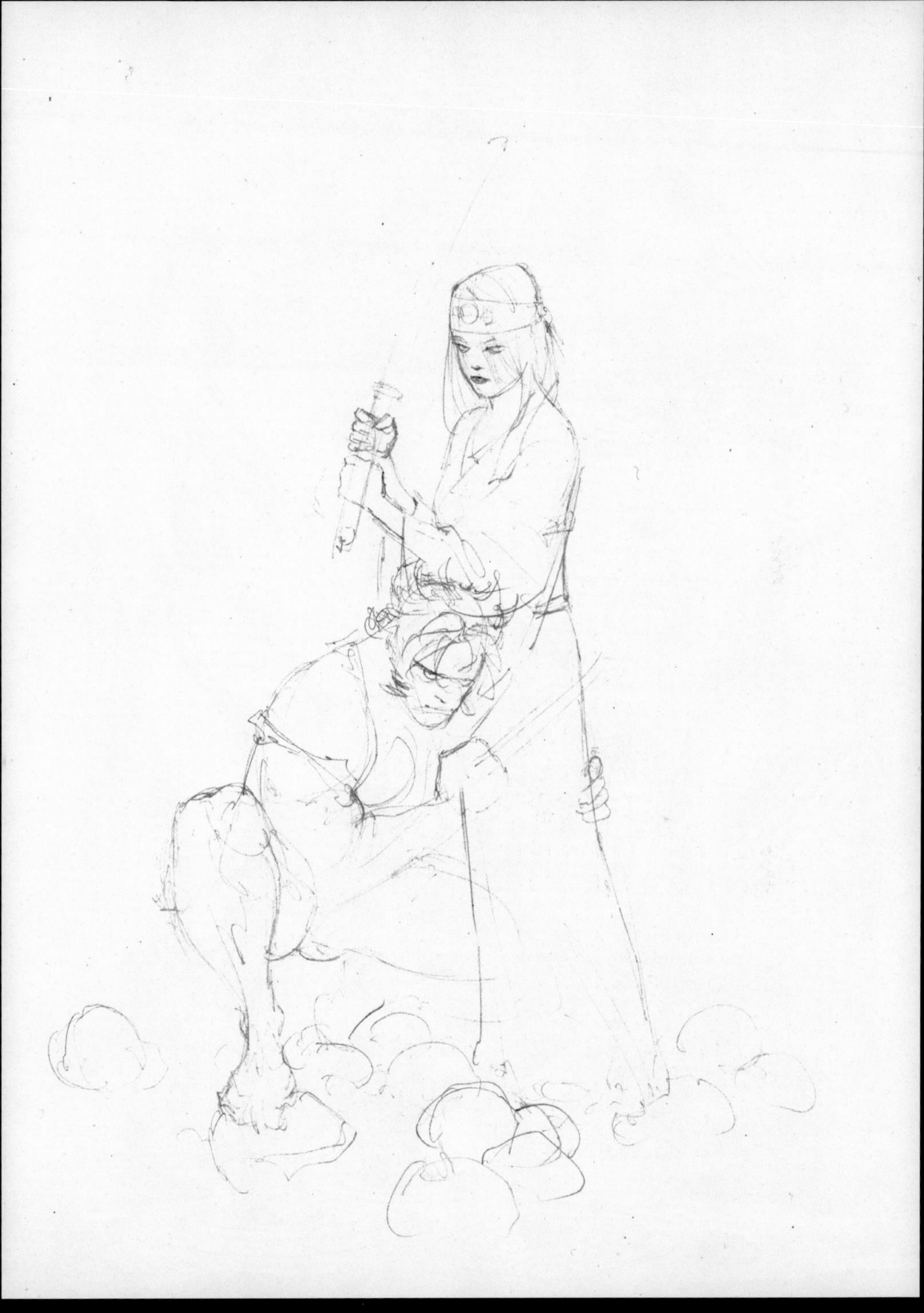

issue number two cover sketch

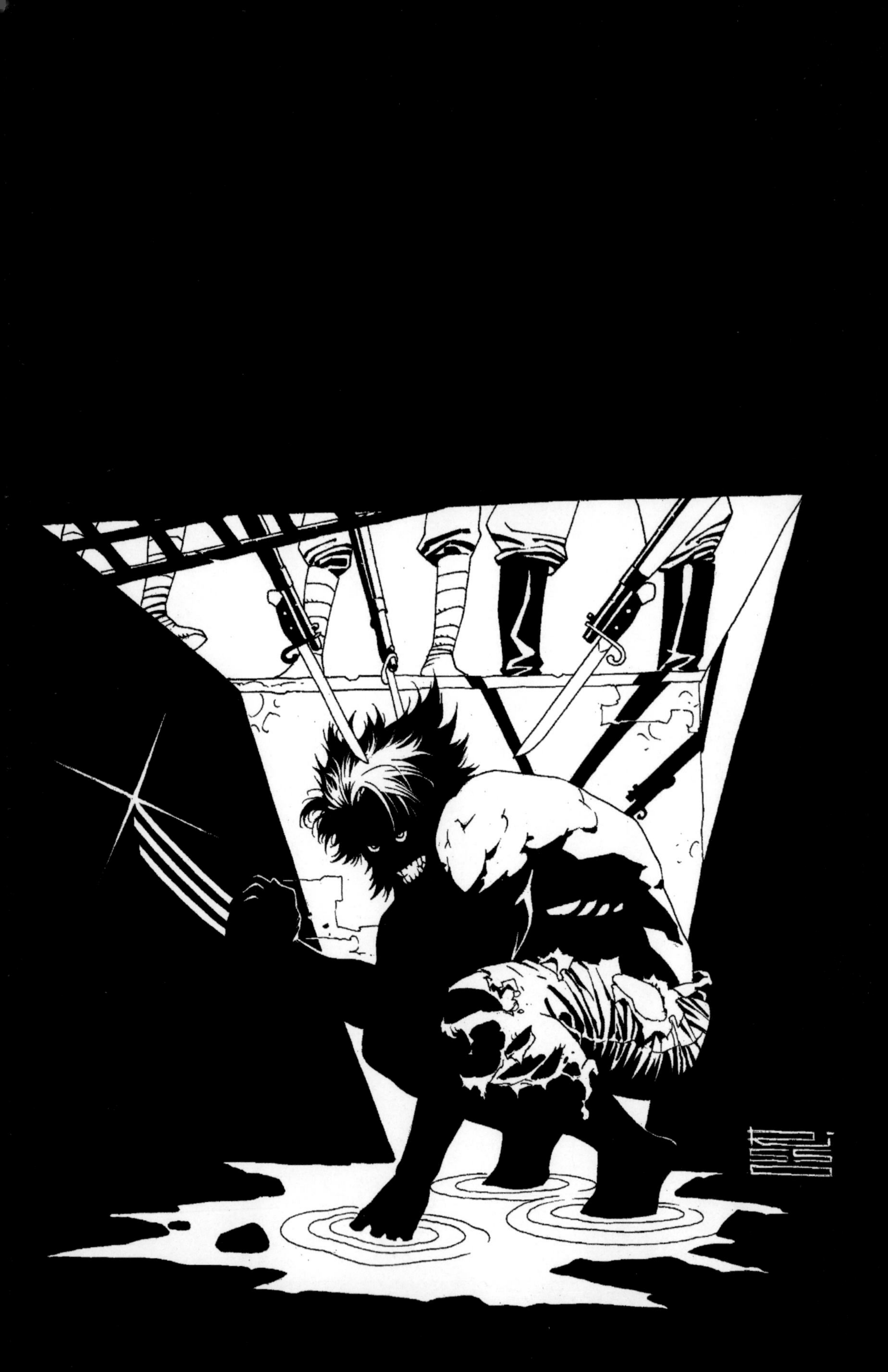

issue number one cover inks

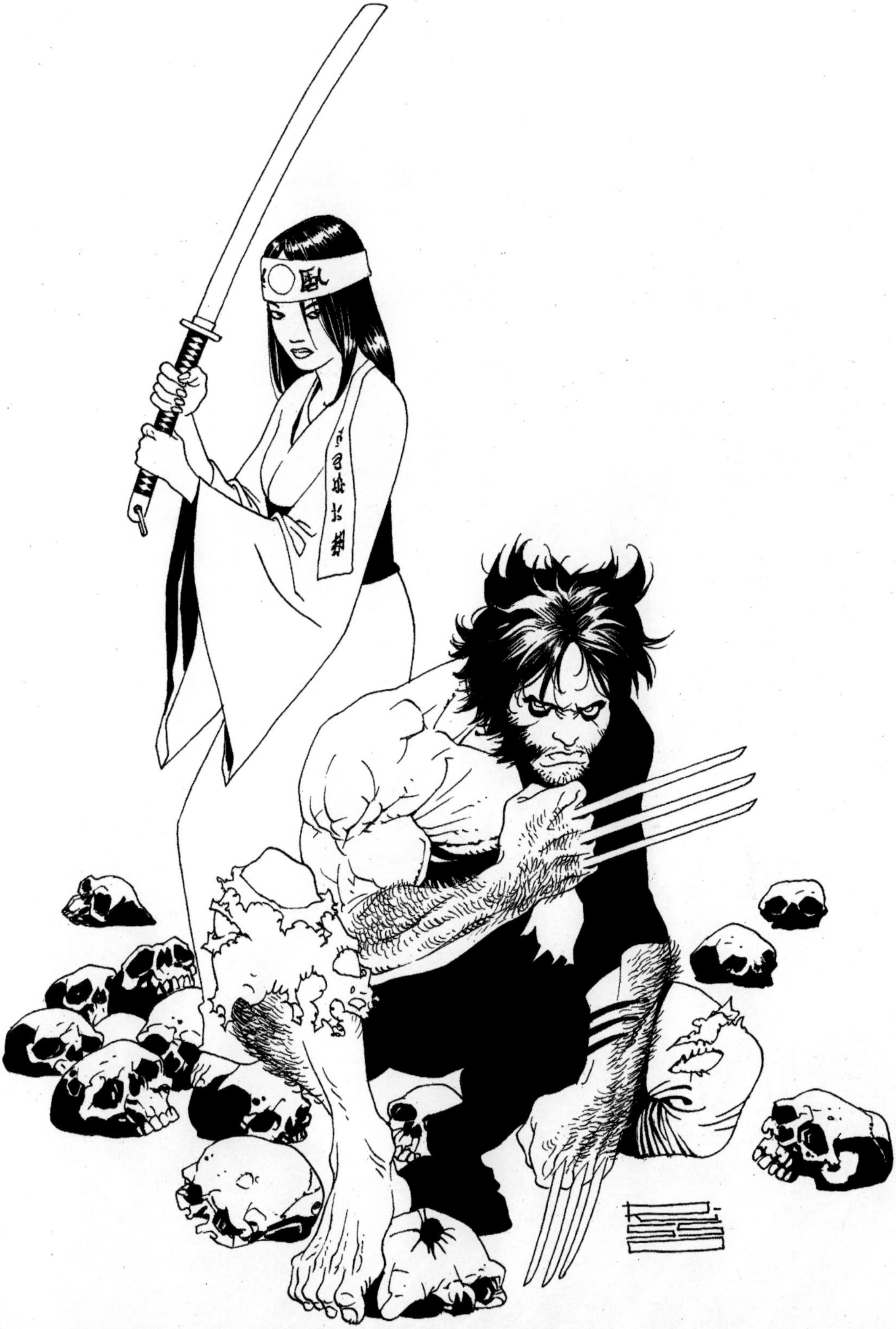

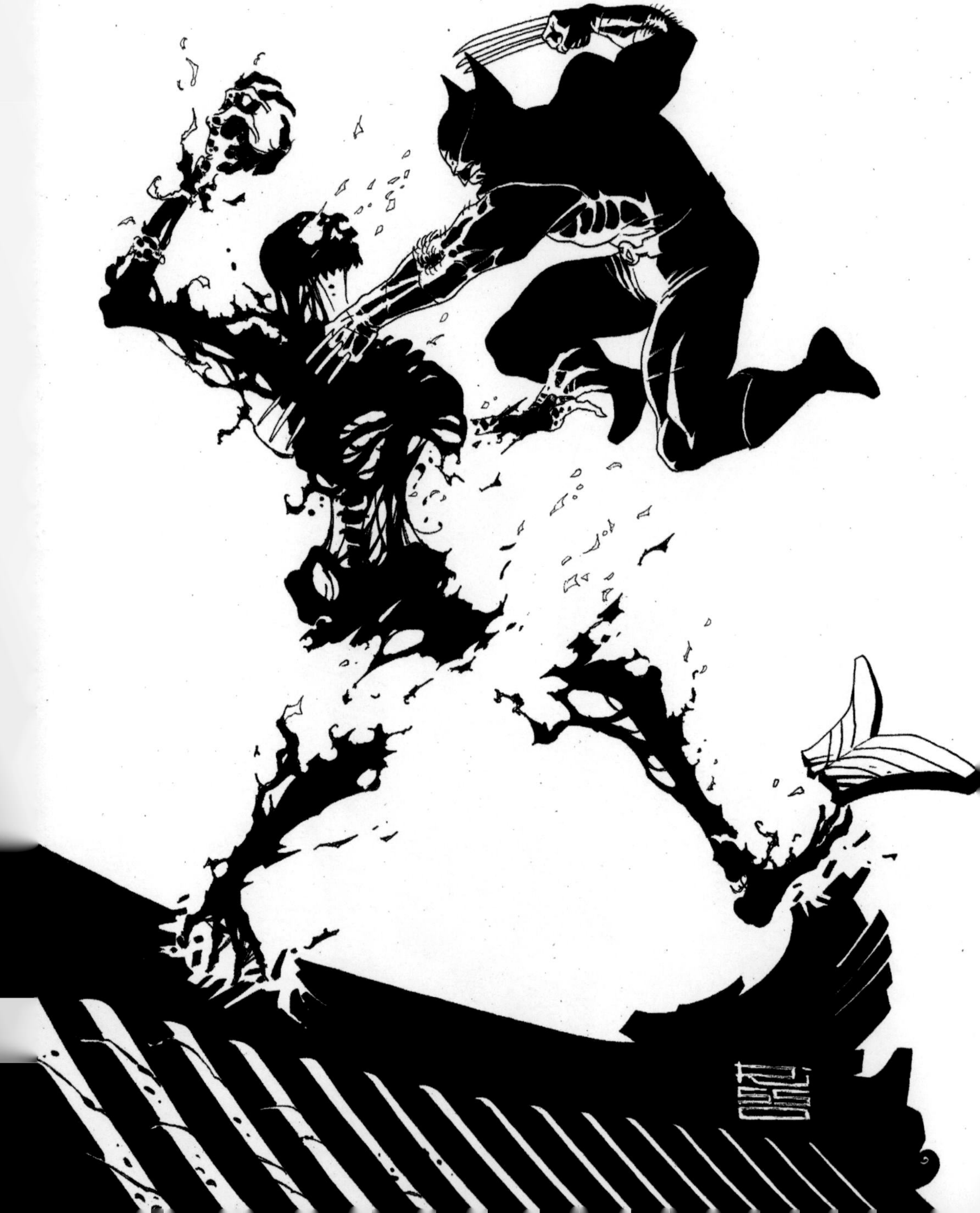

Book LOGAN   Issue 1   Story Page # 4   Line Up Page # 4

Book LOGAN | Issue 1 | Story Page # | Line Up Page # 9

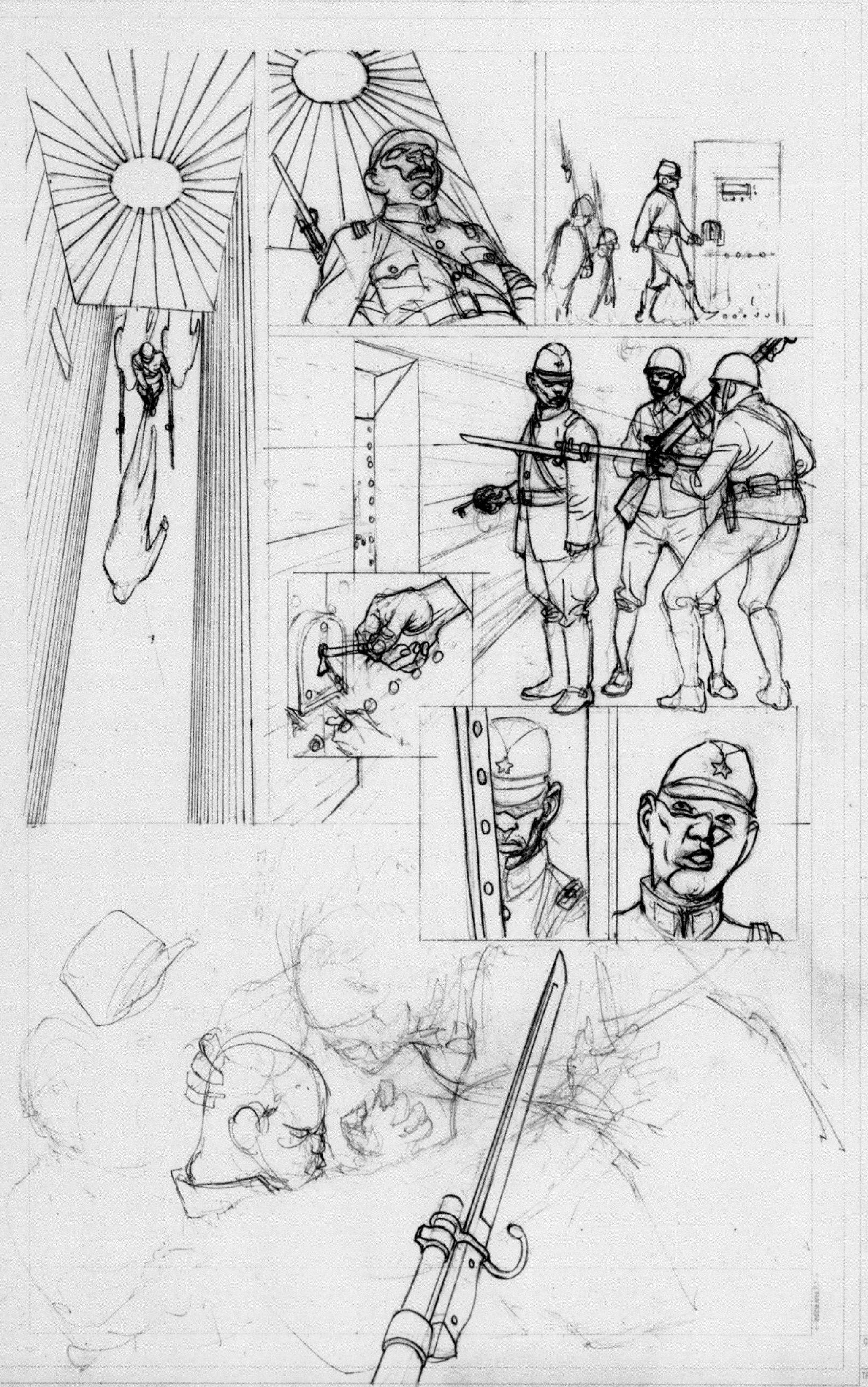

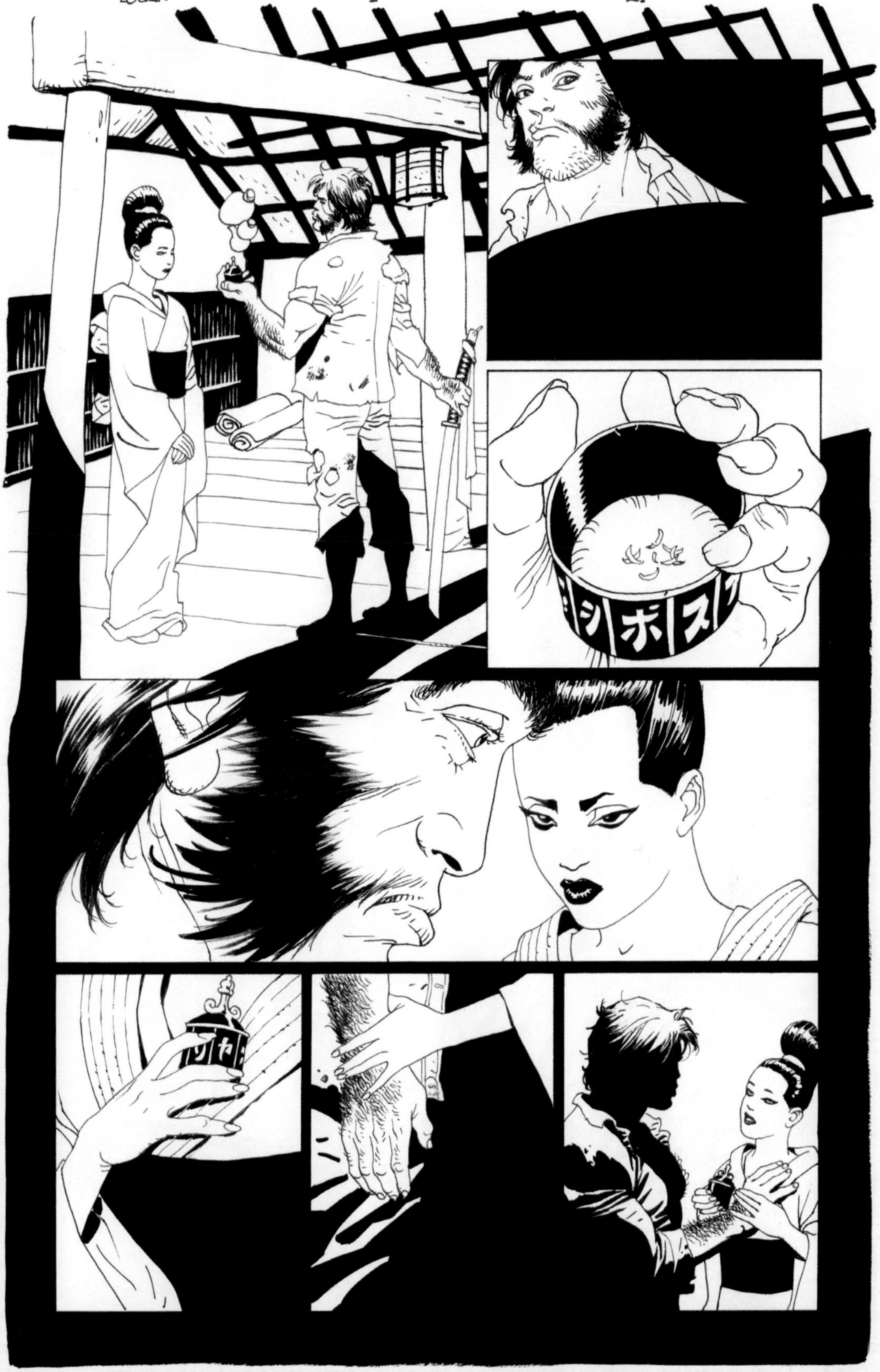

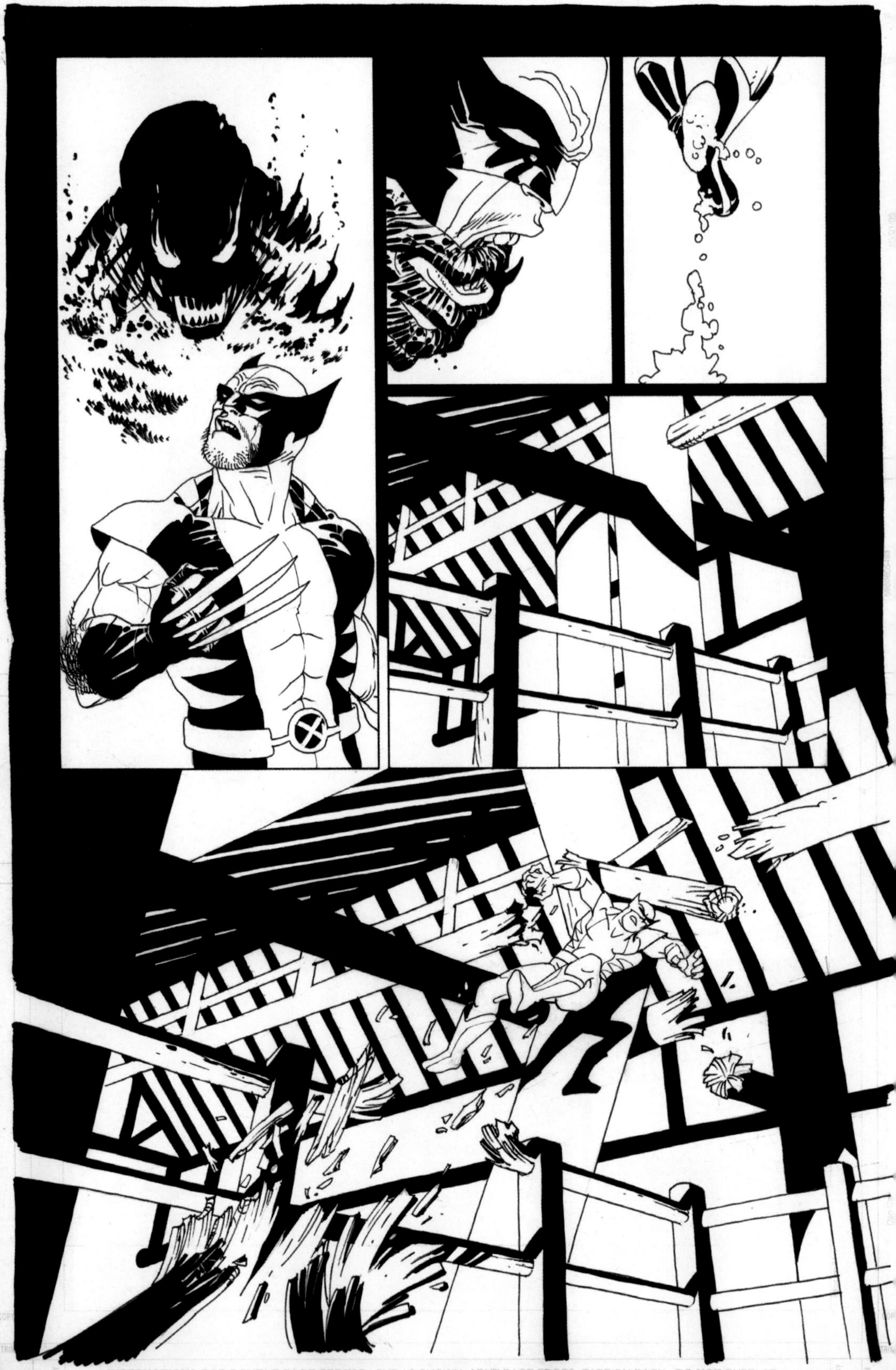

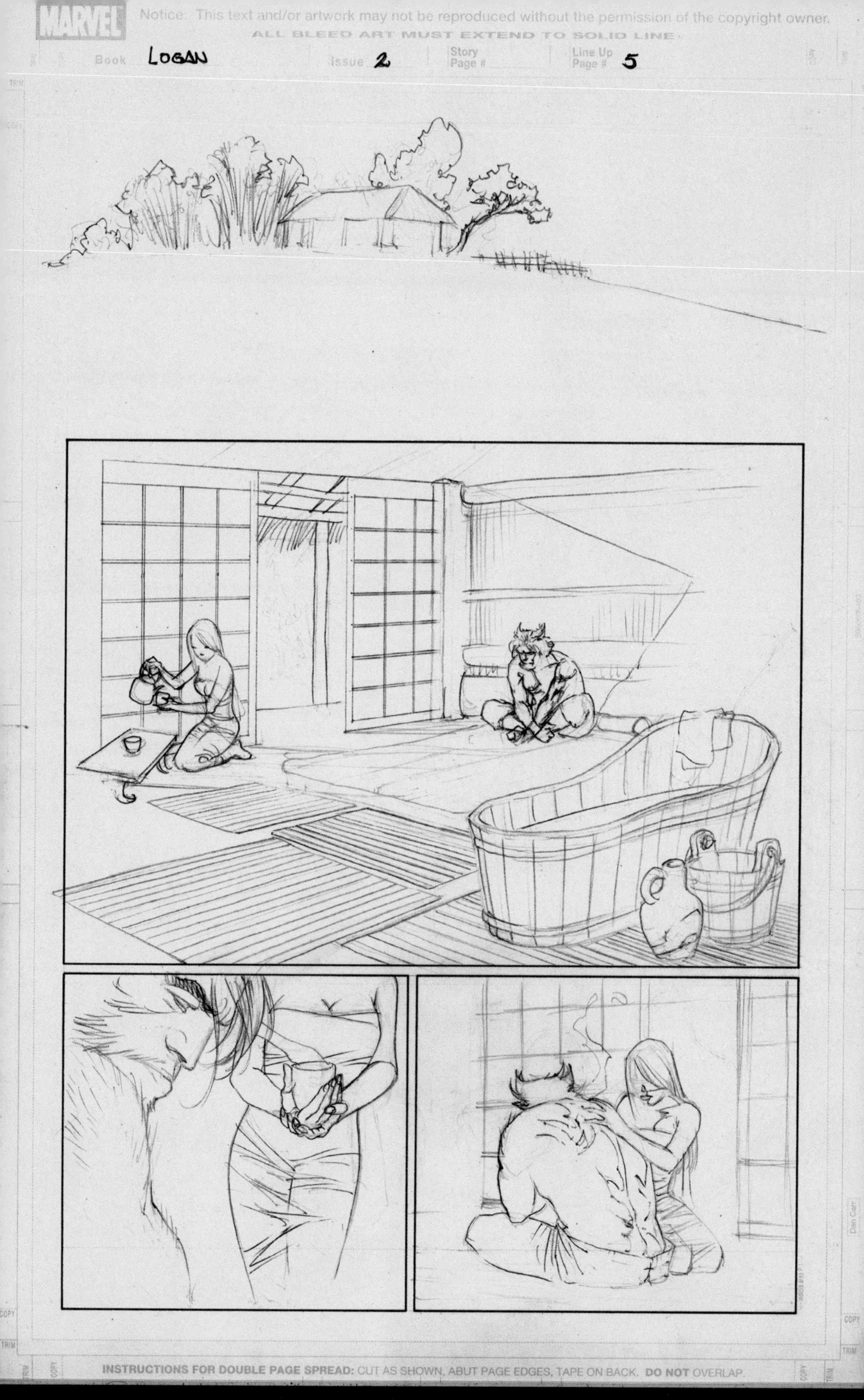

MARVEL
Notice: This text and/or artwork may not be reproduced without the permission of the copyright owner.
ALL BLEED ART MUST EXTEND TO SOLID LINE
Book LOGAN
Issue 2
Story Page #
Line Up Page # 5
INSTRUCTIONS FOR DOUBLE PAGE SPREAD: CUT AS SHOWN, ABUT PAGE EDGES, TAPE ON BACK. DO NOT OVERLAP.

unused pencils for issue number two, page five

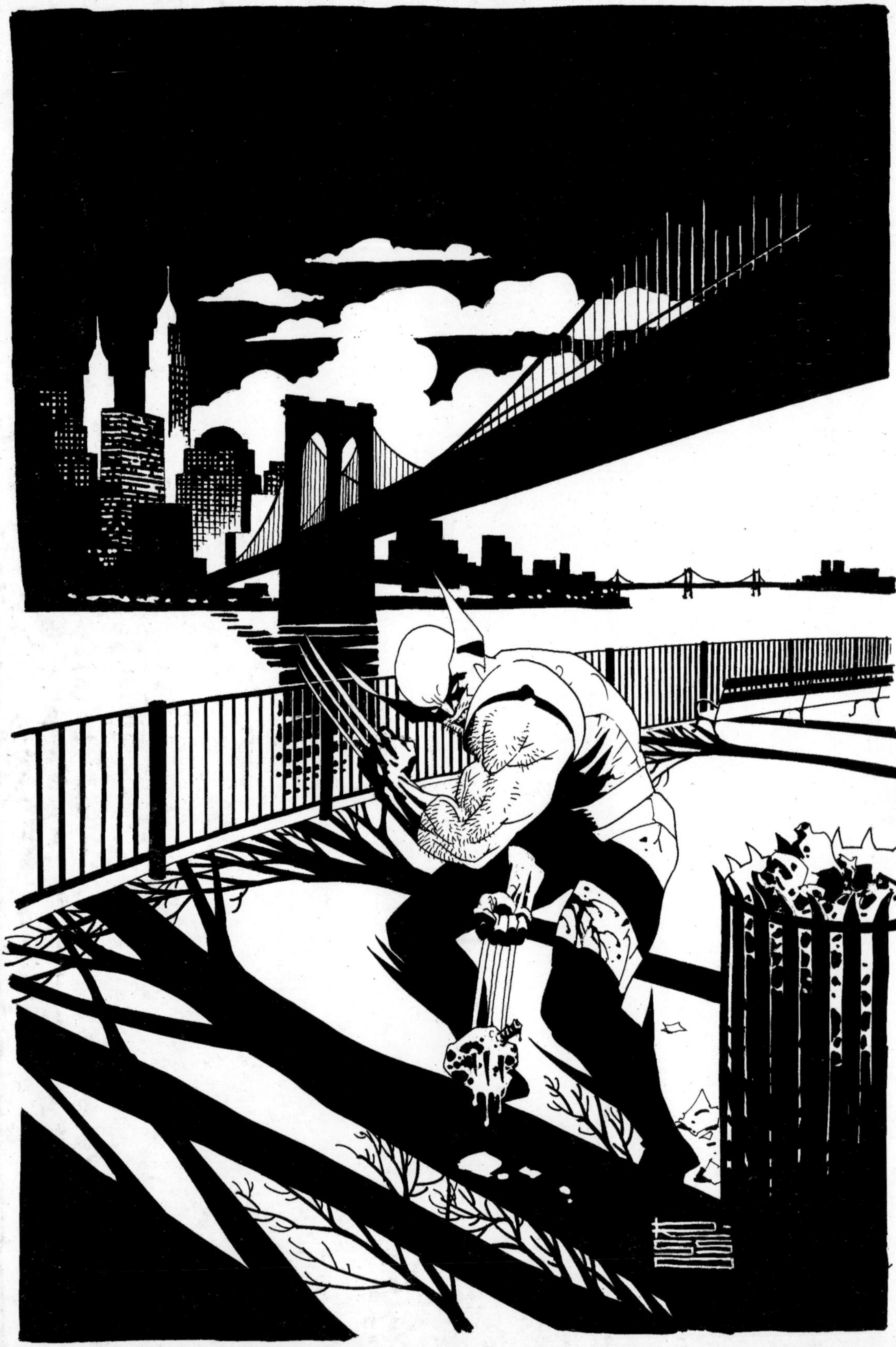

wolverine pin-up by eduardo risso

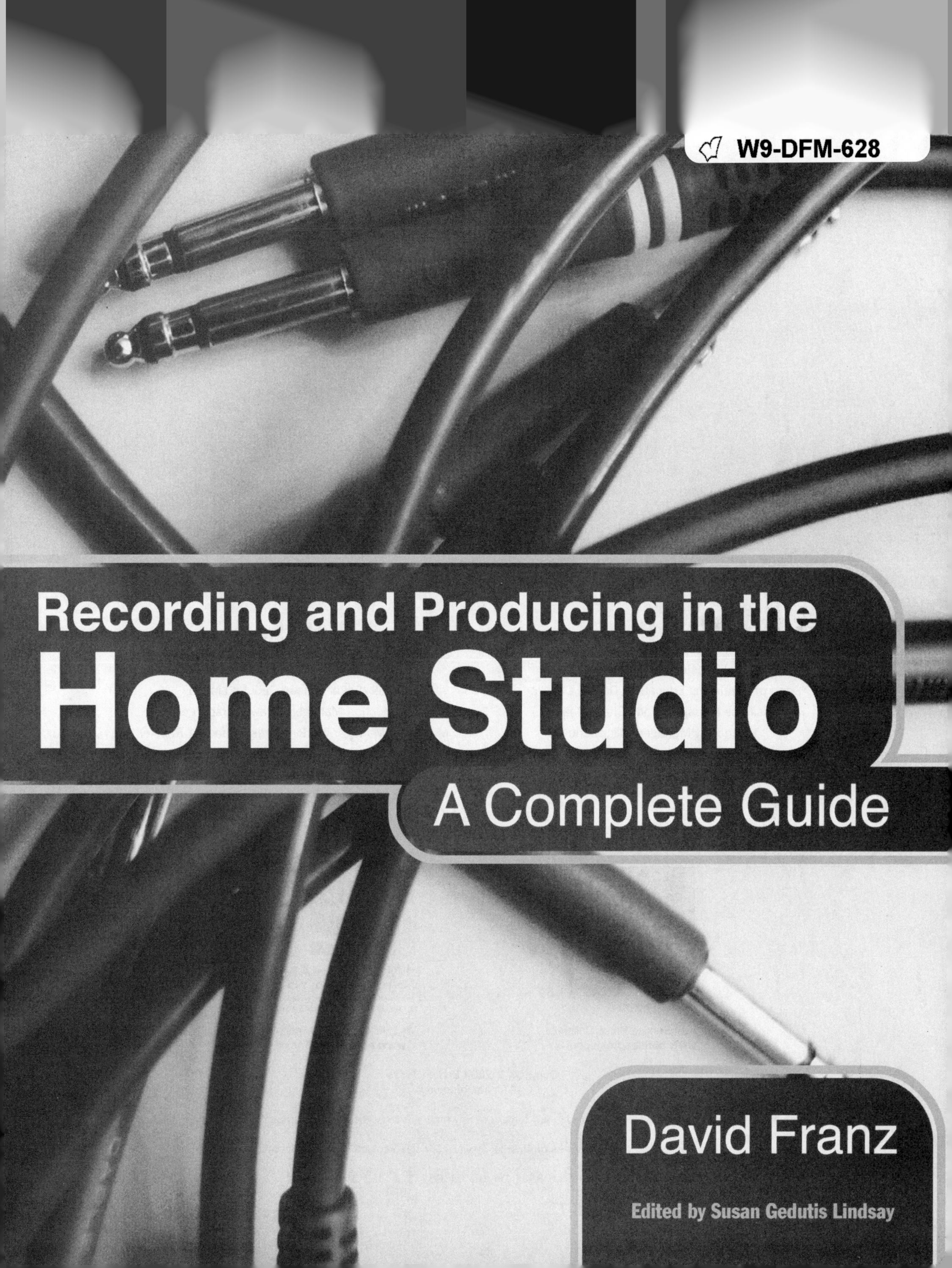

W9-DFM-628
Recording and Producing in the
Home Studio
A Complete Guide
David Franz
Edited by Susan Gedutis Lindsay

Berklee Media

Vice President: Dave Kusek

Dean of Continuing Education: Debbie Cavalier

Business Manager: Linda Chady Chase

Technology Manager: Mike Serio

Marketing Manager, Berkleemusic: Barry Kelly

Senior Graphic Designer: David Ehlers

Berklee Press

Senior Writer/Editor: Jonathan Feist

Writer/Editor: Susan Gedutis Lindsay

Production Manager: Shawn Girsberger

Marketing Manager, Berklee Press: Jennifer Rassler

Product Marketing Manager: David Goldberg

Production Assistant: Louis O'choa

ISBN 0-87639-048-3

1140 Boylston Street
Boston, MA 02215-3693 USA
(617) 747-2146

Visit Berklee Press Online at
www.berkleepress.com

DISTRIBUTED BY

HAL•LEONARD®
CORPORATION
7777 W. BLUEMOUND RD. P.O. BOX 13819
MILWAUKEE, WISCONSIN 53213

Visit Hal Leonard Online at
www.halleonard.com

Printed in the United States of America by Vicks Lithographic and Printing Corporation

10 09 08 07 06 05 04 03   5 4 3 2 1

To my parents, Ken and Phyllis Franz . . . for loving always.

Contents

INTRODUCTION

With the plethora of home and project studio recording gear on the market now, it's easier than ever to create high-quality music at home. Besides the investment in equipment, you only need inspiration, drive, and expertise to make your musical vision a reality. Inspiration and drive are entirely up to you, but this book is your resource for developing the skills you need to create top-notch musical productions—to help you bring out the best in your music or other artists' music.

This book is for artists, songwriters, bands, and aspiring engineers and producers who want to better understand how to engineer and produce their own recordings in a home or project studio. As artists and/or songwriters, it may not be clear what specific functions engineers and producers perform in the creation of music (though you probably already perform many of these functions). For you, the delineation between functions will disappear because you'll learn to do them all at the same time!

In the realm of music, an audio engineer does everything from setting up microphones and pressing Record to mixing and mastering the final tracks of a song. A producer is responsible for nothing less than everything in a project. This means a producer must play many roles. He or she has to facilitate the musical vision, arrange the songs, schedule the rehearsals, lead the recording sessions, and perform many, many other roles as described in the first chapter and throughout the book. The roles and tasks of the engineer and producer are distinctly different from those of the artist or songwriter—but in most cases you can play all of these roles at any given moment in your musical lives.

Knowing that, this book is meant to serve as an all-encompassing home studio self-production guide. The following chapters will demonstrate engineering techniques and production skills necessary to realize the full potential of your (or your client's) songwriting and artistry in your home or project studio.

This book has four sections: Getting Started, Preproduction, Production, and Postproduction. The order of the sections outlines an effective process for bringing projects to completion, and follows the entire musical production process from start to finish. Read the book straight through from front to back, or select individual topics from the index. No matter how you use this book, you will learn something that you can apply to your musical productions today. Enjoy!

ACKNOWLEDGMENTS

Immense thanks to Dave Kusek, Debbie Cavalier, Linda Chase, Jen Rassler, Barry Kelly, Milan Kovacev, and David Goldberg at Berklee Press and Berklee Media. You're all like a family to me. Special thanks to Susan Gedutis Lindsay, Shawn Girsberger, Jim Houston, and Robert Heath in the production of this book. All of you are extremely talented individuals and I've been blessed to work with you.

Special thanks to Will Robertson for your brilliant feedback and technical editing. This book took on new life with your contribution.

I'd like to thank all my teachers and fellow students who I learned from and my current students who I continue to learn from . . . with special thanks to Scott Elson, Will Robertson, Simon Heselev, Alex Wann, Jeff Svatek, Rob Jaczko, Terry Becker, Mitch Benoff, Carl Beatty,

Stephen Webber, and Michael Farquharson. I also owe a large debt of gratitude to the many musicians I've worked with in the past. Special shout outs to Andrew Stern and Fat Little Bastard, Robert Gish and Grey Star Morning, and Barry and Mike, in whatever we're calling ourselves.

And finally, the underlying foundation for anything that I accomplish is rooted in the love and support offered unconditionally by my family—Mom, Dad, Mike, Grandma, Grandpa, Barb, Bert, Kevin, Ruth, Korkut, Marion, John, Peter, and Karen. Thank you for all you've been to me.

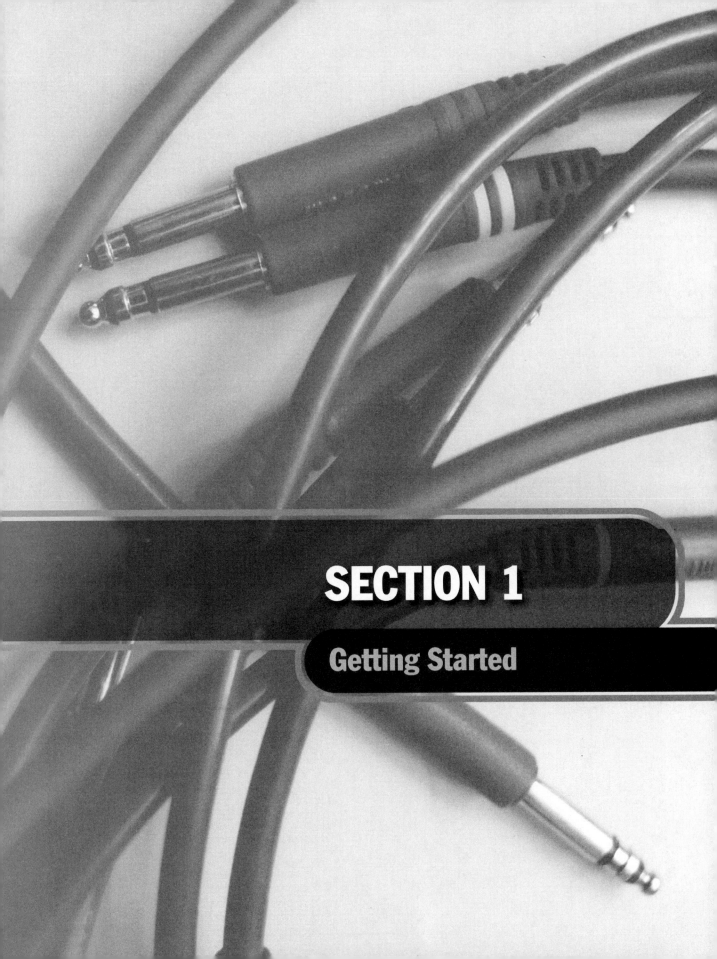

SECTION 1

Getting Started

CHAPTER 1
The Basics of Producing

In this chapter:

• What producers do and why they do it

• Preproduction, production, and postproduction

• Producing your own music

Whether you know it or not, you are a record producer. Anytime you record something and pass judgement on the performance, you're producing. Anytime you change the lyric in the chorus to better fit the song, you're producing. Whenever you edit a drum loop to give the song a better feel, you're producing. You're making music, but you're also making production value decisions.

Being a producer is inherent in creating music. Some people have the natural ability and/or the learned skill to use their production ideas and values to fully produce their own music (like Brian Wilson did for the Beach Boys) or produce and expand on another artist's music (like Sir George Martin did for the Beatles). In this chapter I'll explain the general steps of what a music producer does and you can see how these steps fit into your own music production process.

> *Take Note!*
> For an excellent guide to copyright, licensing, royalties, touring, management, record contracts, and just about anything else that concerns a working musician, check out Donald Passman's classic—but recently revised and updated—*All You Need to Know About the Music Business* (Simon & Schuster, 2003).

Producers play many roles, but no matter what size the recording project is (one song, a multi-song demo, or an entire album), the producer is involved in all three stages of the record production process: preproduction, production, and postproduction.

Generally, **preproduction** consists of all the activities that take place before a recording session, production refers to all of the elements involved in capturing musical performances during a session, and postproduction is anything done to the tracks after the session. Here is an overview of what happens in each stage.

PREPRODUCTION

Preproduction consists of all the activities that take place before a recording session.

Meeting the artist

The first step for a producer is meeting the artist. (For our purposes, the term "artist" can refer to a single person or a group.) The first meeting impacts the type of relationship you'll have with the artist. Like any first impression, this meeting can make or break a project, depending on how everybody gets along.

Listening to the artist's material

Soon after, if not during, the first meeting, the producer must listen to the artist's material (songs), and I mean *all* of the artist's material. It will give the producer some background on the artist's musical development.

Considering the artist's identity

While listening to the artist's material, the producer and artist should discuss the artist's desired identity, image, purpose, and sound. Clarifying them will help create a vision for the project. In the back of the producer's mind during these discussions are demographics: who will buy this music? Demographics are statistical data of a population—in this case, the artist's audience. This can help focus the project and, at the same time, dramatically improve the marketing process after everything is finished.

Choosing the best material to record

Then, the producer and artist should choose which songs to record. Some songs may be ready to record as-is, some songs may need minor improvements, some may need to be completely rearranged or rewritten, and some songs may not even be written yet. Some artists (e.g., Celine Dion and Jennifer Lopez) don't write their own material, instead choosing songs written by professional songwriters. In these cases the producer and artist listen to demos of songs and choose among them, taking into account legal or licensing issues that might come into play when recording third-party material.

The producer might play only a minor role in improving songs by suggesting a few ideas here and there. On the other end of the spectrum, the producer might rewrite entire sections or even write or co-write all of the songs. Regardless, the producer must be very articulate and tactful when discussing any aspect of the song so that the ideas are clear and egos are not damaged. Determining the amount of work that needs to be done on the songs (and whether new ones need to be written) will help when creating project schedules and budgets.

Planning the project—time and money

After the initial meetings, the producer and artist discuss budgets. How much time and money can be spent on this project? When does the project need to be complete? The producer should make a schedule and budget (with the artist's input) to provide a focused plan. This is particularly important when you're working with a record label, because the label will invariably ask for a budget. (Sample budgets and schedules are shown in chapter 4.)

Writing, rewriting, and arranging

In many cases this is where the bulk of real preproduction lies—the producer and artist must create killer arrangements of the songs, including: instrumentation, song form, and attitude. Instrumentation refers to what instruments will be played and what their parts are. Song form refers to the structure and sections of the song (e.g., how many verses and choruses should there be and where will these sections be placed?). Attitude refers to the emotion, feel, and point of view that the song portrays.

Hiring help

A big part of a producer's job is figuring out how to obtain a particular sound on a song or project, and many times this means hiring a specific instrumentalist, vocalist, arranger, orchestrator, programmer, recording engineer, mix engineer, or mastering engineer. For instance, perhaps you want a full choir for background vocals on a particular project. Maybe you need a tight horn arrangement or a clever string part but have never written for those instruments. You'll need to know who to call and how to reach them—quickly. Every producer should develop and maintain a contact list of musicians and recording professionals to call in as necessary.

There will be many times, however, when time and money are constraints. The more

skills you develop in any of these areas, the lower your costs will be, and this makes you more desirable to potential clients. Trying to do things that aren't in your skill set might hurt the project more than it helps. Numerous Web sites are listed in appendix B to help you find freelance musicians for just about any occasion.

Scheduling rehearsals, recording sessions, and mixing sessions

The producer is in charge of determining how much rehearsal is necessary, scheduling the rehearsals, and booking studio time for recording and mixing in your studio or elsewhere. In most cases, the producer should be at all of the rehearsals and studio sessions. It's also the producer's job to see that everyone makes it to the rehearsals and sessions.

Booking Time in a Professional Studio

When booking time in a professional facility, usually at least one recording engineer from the studio is included in the deal. In most cases this is advantageous because that person knows the lay of the land. Sometimes, however, producers hire freelance recording and mixing engineers because they like sounds that those particular folks can get.

In a home studio, the producer often wears recording, mixing, and mastering hats. Nevertheless, bringing in other engineers for recording or mix sessions—even in a home studio—may be helpful because they'll bring new ideas to the project.

With your home setup, you may never need to book time in a pro recording studio, though there are times when you may deem it necessary. Maybe you need to record a drum set for many hours, and your neighbors, spouse, kids, etc. aren't thrilled at the prospect—or you need to record something that's too big or too heavy to move into your home studio (e.g., a set of tympani or a real Hammond B-3 organ). Or, perhaps you want to mix and/or master your recordings in someone else's studio to use their top-of-the-line speakers, console, and outboard effects equipment. These costs should be anticipated and included in your budget at the outset of the project.

Rehearsing

In rehearsals, the producer gets to hear the results of the writing, rewriting, and arranging stages. Rehearsals provide the perfect place to analyze all aspects of the songs, tweak them, and get them into final forms for the upcoming sessions. More time spent rehearsing pays big dividends when the Record button is pushed.

Getting ready for the recording session(s)

When it comes to recording, you (the producer) must make sure *everything* is ready! That means (a) calling the musicians to make sure they'll be at the session on time, (b) checking that you have the necessary equipment and that it's in good working order, (c) creating a plan so everyone knows what's going to happen, and (d) doing whatever else it takes for you to feel confident that the recording session will go off without a hitch.

PRODUCTION

Production refers to all of the elements involved in capturing performances during a recording session.

Directing the session

The production stage is all that most people actually associate with producing—the image of some head honcho sitting behind a big console, passing judgments on performances. But that is only part of the job.

The producer's role includes not only making key project-wide decisions, but also creating a comfortable atmosphere in the studio, making sure the instruments and microphones are set up properly, buying the right foods and beverages for the artist, focusing the artist's energy, evoking and capturing the best performances, recording the best sounds for every instrument and every vocal, providing creative and practical input, listening critically to everything (analyzing both the fine details and the big picture), commending good performances, making difficult but firm decisions, mediating differences of opinion, and many, many more tangible and intangible duties. (See chapter 10 for much more detail on the producer's role during production.)

POSTPRODUCTION

Postproduction includes everything done to the recorded performances after the session.

Directing the mixing and mastering sessions

The mix session is when the tracks from the recording session(s) are mixed together to create a final stereo or surround sound mix. Track levels are adjusted, stereo imaging (panning) is manipulated, and EQ and effects are added. In most cases—though the mix engineer certainly has some creative latitude—the producer directs the session and ultimately has the last word. The producer keeps the original vision for the project in mind, so that the sound of the mix reflects the artist's identity and is accessible by their potential demographic.

Mastering involves getting the final mixes ready for the CD master. The mastering session includes choosing song order, determining how much time there should be between tracks, making the volume of each track similar, and adding EQ and compression/limiting, among many other things. Many professional producers don't perform mastering duties—they send the final mixes off to an experienced mastering engineer, who usually has a fresh set of ears to hear the music, and the experience, knowledge, and special high-end, custom equipment to complete the job. Schedules and budgets might make this impractical in a home studio, so you'll probably play the role of mastering engineer in addition to everything else. (See chapters 12, 13, and 14 for much more information about mixing and mastering.)

Presenting the finished product

This is the moment of truth: The producer delivers copies of the finished project to the artist. If he is working for a record company, he'll also deliver the final masters to the label. Hopefully, both the artist and the label will like the final product, or the project may go back a few steps (e.g., do a remix, write a radio single, or rerecord some tracks). Other provisions—such as creating artwork or providing lyrics for the CD jacket—may also be required when the final master is delivered, depending on the producer's contract.

Other duties

There are many other jobs producers might perform in the line of duty. These aren't heard in the final recordings, but they can certainly influence them.

*   Negotiating contracts with the artist and/or record label

*   Copyrighting the songs

*   Developing and promoting the artist (artist image, stage act, press kit, music videos, Web presence)

*   Building a solid team (finding a good manager, music publisher, accountant, and lawyer)

*   Counseling the artist (helping artists personally, being a friend and confidante)

PRODUCING YOUR OWN MUSIC

You're probably not a professional producer, so you may wonder why I've included a general list of tasks from the perspective of someone who records artists in professional studios. It's because most of the top producers utilize the same techniques and procedures you'll use on your projects.

When you're producing your own music, try to distance yourself from the project and evaluate the music as objectively as you can. Treat yourself as a client and try to act as an independent producer. This can be difficult. However, objectivity is a key trait of successful producers.

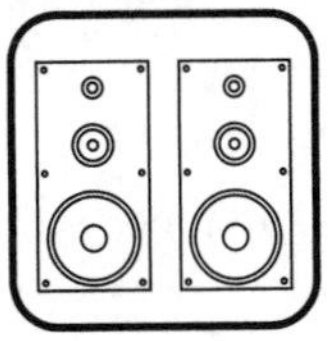

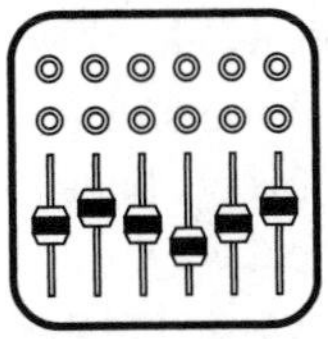

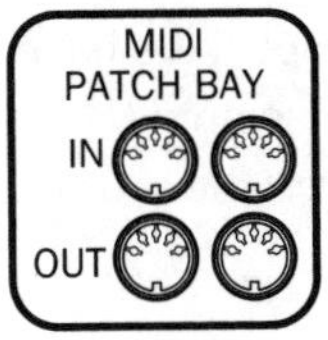
MIDI
PATCH BAY
IN
OUT

CHAPTER 2
Setting Up Your Studio

In this chapter:

- Audio signal flow and gain stages
- Input/output connections
- Signal level, impedance, +4/–10 line levels, and patch bays
- MIDI setups and signal flow
- Smart speaker placement
- Acoustic treatment

With the wide variety of inexpensive recording gear available, recording and mixing at home has never been easier. There are many tools available, including all-in-one analog or digital recording devices, software/hardware combination packages, and more traditional setups with tape machines, mixing boards, and outboard gear. Regardless of your recording gear and medium, setting up your studio to record, edit, mix, and master your recordings efficiently and with high-quality results is critical to your success as a producer or engineer.

Every studio must have some fundamental pieces of gear: microphones, acoustic instruments, electronic line-level instruments, preamplifiers, speakers, and a recording device.

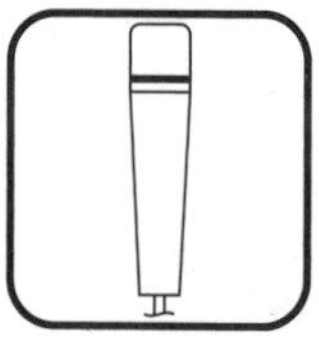

Microphones transform acoustic waveforms into electric current and allow you to record anything that makes sound.

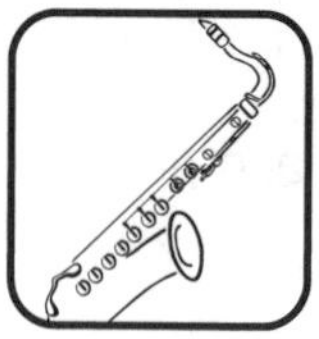

Acoustic instruments (acoustic guitars, drum sets, and any orchestral instrument) require either a microphone or pickup to record them.

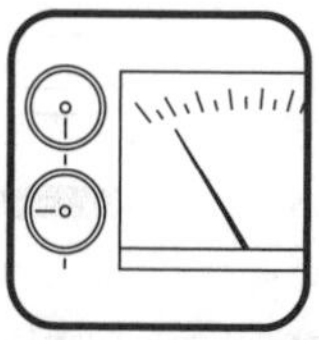

Preamplifiers ("preamps" or "pres") boost a microphone or pickup signal to a good recording level, called "line level" (discussed later in this chapter).

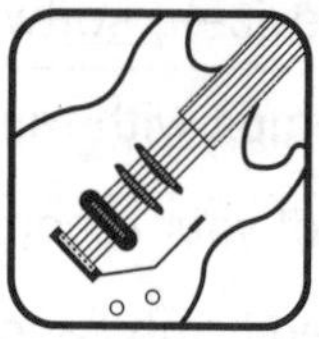

Instruments with pickups (such as electric guitars) output signals between mic and line levels and require amplification for recording.

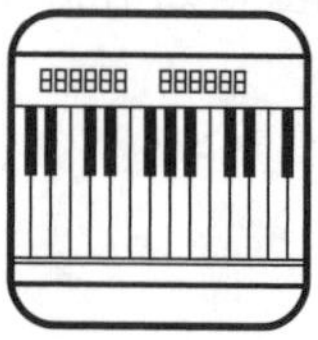

Electronic line-level instruments (such as synthesizers and drum machines) output line-level signals that do not require preamps.

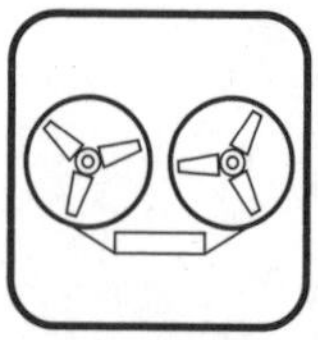

The **recording device** is the centerpiece of the studio. All signals are recorded to and played back from it. Types of recorders include: all-in-one analog or digital recording devices, software/hardware combination packages, and tape machines.

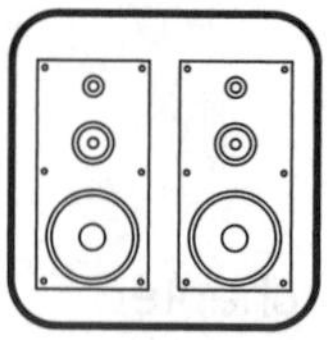

Speakers (including studio monitors and headphones) transform electrical currents back into acoustical waveforms for playing back any recorded material. Passive speakers require an amplifier to power them, while active speakers have amps built in. Unless otherwise noted, we'll use active speakers here.

SIGNAL FLOW

With all this studio gear, you'll need to know where signals are flowing at all times, so that you will know what to tweak to improve the sound. Illustrated in fig. 2.1 and 2.2 are some common signal flow and routing options. In the first example, a microphone is used to record a vocal track. The mic signal is routed into the preamp, where it is amplified to a healthy recording level. Instruments with pickups utilize a similar setup.

Some recording devices have built-in preamps. However, many recording devices only accept line-level signals. Preamps output line-level signals, as do many electronic instruments (fig. 2.2).

VOLTAGE

As you've probably noticed from these brief signal routing explanations, there is a difference between mic-level, instrument-level, and line-level signals. That difference is in the voltage of each type of signal.

Voltage is a measure of power. The voltage of a microphone's output signal is in the range of –60 to –20 dBV. (dBV is the unit of measure for power ratios based on volts.) Instruments with pickups output –30 to –20 dBV signals, while line-level signals are

Instrument with Pickup
Preamp
Vocalist
Microphone
Preamp
Recording Device
Speakers

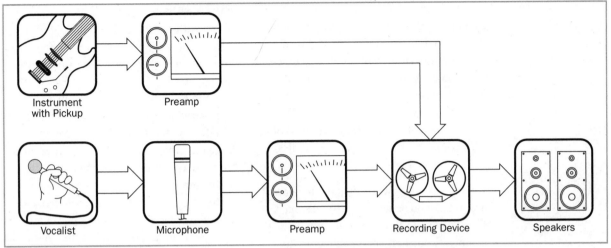

Fig. 2.1. Microphones and instruments with built-in pickups need amplification before being recorded.

either –10 dBV or +4 dBm. (dBm is another unit of measure for power ratios, based on milliwatts.) Mic- and instrument-level signals are lower in power than line-level signals.

SIGNAL LEVEL

In the world of sound, we use the decibel (abbreviated dB) to measure the level of a signal's strength. A decibel is simply a way of expressing level relative to a point of reference. The decibel scale is an exponential or non-linear curving scale, which expresses the huge variation in level that audio signals can have. For instance, a sound level meter on a quiet street may register 60 dB, but holding it in front of a speaker at a rock concert may cause it to read 120 dB. Because we're using the decibel scale, which increases exponentially, this means that the concert isn't twice as loud as the street—it's 1,000 times as loud!

Because the decibel scale just gives us relative level (that is, it can tell us how much stronger x is than y), we can use it to describe the level change in terms of any unit of measure—sonic change (air pressure) or electrical change (volts, watts, etc.), for example. But its relative nature also means that if we want to give signal strength in terms of a single number (to say that something is "60 dB" rather than "60 dB louder than . . . "), we'll have to define a starting point. If you see another

Electric Line-Level Instrument
Recording Device
Speakers

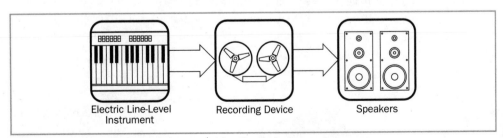

Fig. 2.2. Recording an electronic instrument (synthesizer).

Take Note!

Some newer synths output signals slightly hotter than –10 dBV. If you send this hot signal to an input that's expecting –10 dBV, you might clip the input. Most line-level inputs do have some headroom (space between the optimum and maximum input level), but be careful of distortion.

letter or letters after dB, the measurement is communicating level in terms of a unit of measure relative to a specific starting point. For instance, dBV refers to voltage. A level given in dBV will tell you how much stronger (or weaker, if the dBV value is negative) a voltage (V) is than 0 dBV, which is actually an industry standard of 0.775 volts. To put it another way, 0 dBV = 0.775 volts.

While electrical power is usually measured in watts, sound signals in particular have come to be expressed in volts, which isn't technically correct, but has become the convention. Some devices output stronger signals than others. The output signal of a microphone is in the range of –60 to –20 dBV. Instruments with pickups output –30 to –20 dBV signals, while line-level signals are either –10 dBV or +4 dBm.

Line Levels: +4 dBm and –10 dBV

You may have heard the terms "plus four" and "minus ten" before. These are two different line-level strengths that affect the compatibility of your studio equipment. Most professional gear is +4 dBm and most home recording gear is –10 dBV. There should be no noticeable difference in sound between a piece of gear operating at +4 or –10. However, it's a really good idea to maintain the compatibility of these line levels throughout your studio because +4 gear plays nice with other +4 gear and –10 gear works best with other –10 gear. You can get devices that convert +4 signals to –10 signals and vice versa, if necessary.

IMPEDANCE

Along with level, another consideration when connecting gear in your studio is impedance. In audio and electrical terms, impedance (im-PEED-ance) is the resistance to the flow of electrical current (measured in "ohms"). Just as more water can flow with less resistance through a large pipe than through a thin straw, electrical current flows more easily through a low impedance cable than through a high impedance cable. The impedance of an audio cable is determined by several factors, including the cable's thickness and how it's manufactured.

Low impedance ("lo-Z") = low resistance

High impedance ("hi-Z") = high resistance

Are You Well Balanced?

Balanced cables are made up of two hot leads for the signal and one ground wire. These three connectors work together to reduce or eliminate outside interference (electrostatic and radio) and other noise so that it doesn't affect the audio signal in the cable. Unbalanced cables have only one hot lead and the ground wire, and do not offer the noise blocking features of balanced cables.

Most hi-Z cables are unbalanced and most lo-Z cables are balanced. The main reason we don't use balanced lo-Z cables for every application is that ol' devil, money . . . balanced lo-Z cables are more expensive.

Lo-Z

Balanced low impedance inputs have three-pin connectors (usually XLR, but sometimes TRS).

XLR connector—a three-pinned connector commonly used on microphone cables. X is for the ground wire (connected to the cable's shield to help ground the wire), while L and R stand for the two hot leads that carry signal (fig. 2.3).

Take Note!

Impedance is a type of resistance—specifically, it is frequency-dependent resistance. Impedance causes higher frequency information to deteriorate over some long cable runs.

R
L
2
3
1
Ground
Hot
Cold
2
3
1
Ground

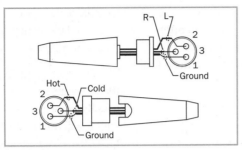

Fig. 2.3. An XLR connector.

TRS connector—a connector with three leads commonly used for stereo headphones (an unbalanced, usually hi-Z application), but also for balanced low impedance cables. T stands for Tip, R stands for Ring, and S stands for Sleeve. The Tip is one of the hot leads carrying signal in a balanced cable or the left side of a stereo signal. The Ring is the other hot lead that carries signal in a balanced cable or the right side of a stereo signal. The Sleeve is connected to the shield (ground) of the cable.

S R T
Ring
Tip (hot)
Sleeve (ground)

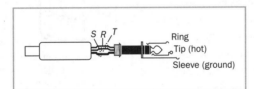

Fig. 2.4. A TRS connector.

Because of their low resistance and good interference prevention, balanced low impedance cables can be up to 1,000 feet long (more than 300 meters) without signal loss. If you're hearing radio interference or other noise from your cables, connect your gear using balanced low impedance cables.

Hi-Z

Unbalanced high impedance inputs (often called "hi-Z") have two-pin connectors and are generally used for instrument cables (like those used for guitars and synthesizers). They are often 1/4" TS connectors, with a tip and a sleeve, but no ring (as in the TRS connectors).

T
Tip = Signal
S
Sleeve = ground

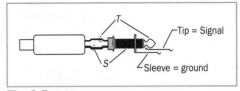

Fig. 2.5. A TS connector.

Hi-Z cables have much higher impedance (remember: they impede the signal) than lo-Z cables, so the signal degrades when the cable is longer than 20 to 30 feet. Hi-Z cables work well for many applications that don't require long cable runs, and their lower cost makes them a popular choice for home studios.

Direct Injection

DI
BOX
HI
Z
LO
Z

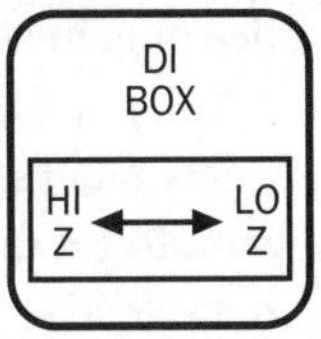

Direct boxes ("DI") are used for converting high impedance signals to low impedance signals, or vice versa. They are used most often for transforming the signal from an electric guitar hi-Z cable into a lo-Z signal for recording into a lo-Z input (preamp).

Summing Up: Level, Impedance, and Your Inputs

How do level and impedance affect the signal flow in your mic-, instrument-, and line-level equipment?

If you plug a high-powered, high impedance instrument (synthesizer) into a low impedance input (preamp), the hi-Z instrument can overdrive (and distort) the input because the synth is expecting a lot of resistance to its powerful signal, but the resistance isn't there. Likewise, if you plug a low-powered, low impedance device (like a microphone) into a high impedance input, the lo-Z signal from the mic might meet too much resistance, and you often won't be able to get enough gain for a healthy recording level, hence the need for preamps.

GAIN STAGES

A gain stage is any device that boosts or cuts the level of an audio signal. This could be an amplifier, such as a microphone preamp or a guitar amp, or an attenuator, like a simple volume knob. An important part of understanding and optimizing the signal flow in your studio is knowing how each piece of gear affects the volume (gain) of an audio signal along the signal's path. To capture the highest quality recordings with your equipment, it's a good idea to know your gain stages.

Examples of gain stages include mic preamp gain pots, guitar volume knobs, and channel faders on a mixer. Often, you'll want to set the level at any gain stage to as close to "unity" as you can get it. "Unity" is the level where what goes in is what comes out . . . such as when a volume fader on a mixer is set to 0. Most musical gear is optimized for the best headroom and signal-to-noise ratio at unity gain. However, the real purpose of any gain stage is to increase or decrease the gain, so keeping all gain stages along the signal path at unity is very uncommon. The best way to optimize your recording levels is to spread out the gain adjustments among the gain stages. (This same approach to spreading out the gain also applies to mixing and mastering.)

The reason to spread the gain is that overloading a gain stage can cause unwanted distortion, and "underloading" a gain stage can introduce unwanted noise into the signal. Your goal is to tweak your gain stages to achieve the optimal settings for each stage, and ultimately get a strong signal into your recording device (see fig. 2.6).

The first gain stage in your signal path is the musician. A good performance will usually involve loud and soft passages, which will affect the gain. When I engineer, I usually set the gain stages to accommodate the player's loudest level for a particular part—and then some. Most folks tend to play harder while recording than while getting initial recording levels.

Look at all the gain stages in fig. 2.6. If one gain stage is under- or overloaded, the negative sonic effects can multiply in the signal path and ultimately ruin the guitar tone before the signal reaches your recording device.

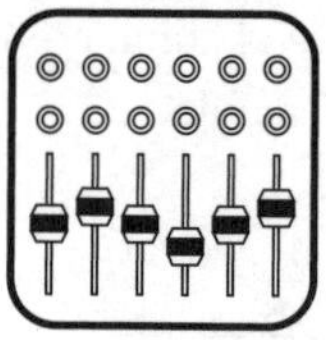

Mixing Board

If an outboard mixer is part of your studio gear, it is important to understand the gain stages on it, too. A mixer has preamp gain controls (usually they are rotary knobs located near the input area) and mixer channel gain controls (usually they are vertical faders located at the bottom of each channel's input/output module). Additionally, a mixer has a master fader and possibly some submix, auxiliary, and control-room gain controls. This is true both for small home studio mixing boards and huge professional studio consoles. Depending on how you set your mixer to interface with your recording device, you may use some or all of these gain stages.

With a complex setup like the one shown in fig. 2.6, you may run into unwanted hum in your input signal . . . even if you optimize your gain structure. What else can you do?

1. Use balanced cables . . . they are designed to cancel out noise.

Signal to noise ratio: The ratio between an audio signal and the amount of inherent noise in a device or recording medium. The larger the signal-to-noise ratio, the better.

your signal path and flip its "ground" switch. (Your amp might have a ground switch, too.)

3. Turn off all dimmer switches. Although the low light from a halogen lamp sets a nice mood, it can ruin your guitar track.

4. Step away from the computer screen. Even with LCD screens, guitars can pick up unwanted hum from your fancy flat-screen monitor.

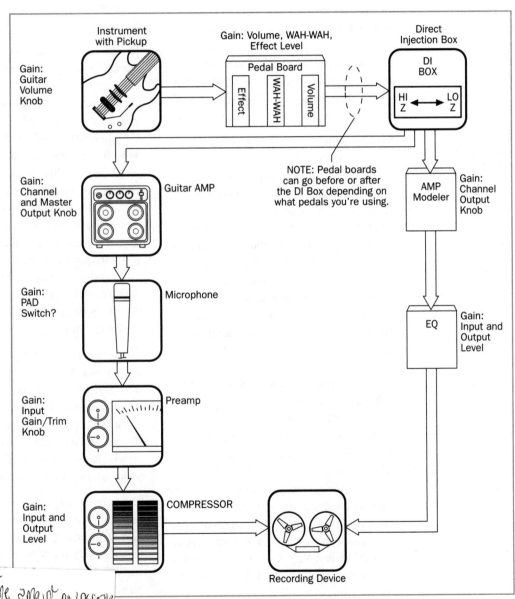

Instrument with Pickup
Gain: Guitar Volume Knob
Gain: Volume, WAH-WAH, Effect Level
Pedal Board
Effect
WAH-WAH
Volume
Direct Injection Box
DI BOX
HI Z
LO Z
NOTE: Pedal boards can go before or after the DI Box depending on what pedals you're using.
Gain: Channel and Master Output Knob
Guitar AMP
AMP Modeler
Gain: Channel Output Knob
Gain: PAD Switch?
Microphone
EQ
Gain: Input and Output Level
Gain: Input Gain/Trim Knob
Preamp
Gain: Input and Output Level
COMPRESSOR
Recording Device

Headroom: The amount of increase in gain that a device can take, above normal working level, before overload distortion occurs.

...gnal flow and gain staging on an electric guitar that is being recorded using an ... preamp, direct box, effects, EQ, and a compressor, all of which come before the ...ches your recording device.

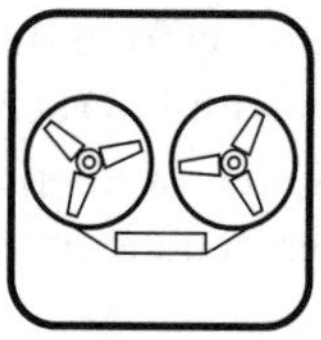

RECORDING DEVICES

From $100 4-track cassette recorders to $2,000 digital recorders to $100,000 2" tape machines, the multi-track recording setup is essentially the same. All have transport controls to control their actions to record, play, rewind, fast-forward, and stop. The biggest difference is that in the analog domain, the recording medium is tape that you can hold in your hand, record linearly and destructively on, and physically splice to edit. With digital recording devices, audio is stored on digital tapes or in hard drives.

A studio with a tape machine as the recording device always has some type of recording/mixing board or console, whether it's built into the tape machine (as in a 4-track cassette recorder) or as a separate piece of gear connected to the tape machine. The recording/mixing board has line-level inputs as well as preamps to record microphones. These inputs are routed into the tape machine or onto a hard drive. Once recorded, the tracks are then returned to the recording/mixing board for playback.

Audio Recording and MIDI Sequencing Software Recorders

Audio and MIDI sequencing software (such as Pro Tools, Logic Audio, Digital Performer, Nuendo, Cubase, Radar, Cakewalk, etc.) enables digital audio and MIDI recording, editing, and mixing on your personal computer. These programs utilize non-linear hard disk recording, non-destructive digital editing, digital signal processing and mixing, and MIDI functionality to help you create your musical masterpieces.

Non-linear Recording

Non-linear recording means your audio files are recorded and stored in chunks on your hard drive and not linearly, as they would be recorded on tape. Non-destructive editing means that any cutting, pasting, trimming, separating, or clearing of audio data occurs virtually . . . the source audio files are not harmed in any way, until you choose to do so.

Recorded audio is edited in a software document, much like words are edited in a word processing file. This document accesses all the data associated with a project, including audio files, MIDI data, sample libraries, edit and mix information, as well as comments and track titles. The program uses this document to perform editing and mixing functions on a map of the actual audio data, rarely touching the recorded source audio tracks. To enable this to happen, most audio and sequencing software packages have separate windows for (1) editing digital audio and MIDI and (2) mixing the tracks. These two windows interact seamlessly and allow you to do anything you want to your digital data.

The window for editing displays audio waveforms, MIDI data, timeline information, and all of the tools for editing the waveforms and data. All other pertinent track data (volume, panning, solo, mute, blocks, and automation data) can also be viewed in this window. Almost all editing tasks are performed in this window.

The window for mixing is designed like a recording/mixing console. Its primary function is for mixing multiple tracks down to a stereo (2-track) or a multi-channel surround sound mix. There are vertical channel strips for each track, with sections for inserts, sends, input/output routing, and volume faders, as well as automation, pan, solo, and mute controls.

All digital audio software programs also have a window, often called the "transport" window, with controls like those on a cassette player or analog tape machine. The controls are used to play, stop, record, fast-forward, and rewind, as well as perform some more advanced functions.

Separate Lives—Partitioning Your Hard Drive

If you're just getting started with a new computer that only has one hard drive, it's a good idea to create two (or more) virtual hard drives from your one existing internal drive. This is called partitioning your hard drive, and is done to separate audio files from all of your other files (system software, applications, documents, etc.) so that your computer (and you) can locate them more easily. It is hard on a computer to have to look all over the place for files, jumping back and forth between areas on an entire hard disk, and the audio playback and recording performance may suffer. If your internal hard drive has 80 GB of total storage, you might create a 20 GB partition (for applications, documents, etc.) and a dedicated 60 GB partition for audio. Partitions are useful for separate physical hard drives, as well. For instance, consider partitioning a 300 GB external drive into five partitions of 60 GB to improve hard drive performance and project organization. Consult your computer's manual to learn more about partitioning, and before doing anything to your hard drive, BACK UP ALL IMPORTANT FILES.

CONNECTING YOUR STUDIO

Regardless of how much gear you own or have access to, your recording device is the centerpiece of your studio. Figs. 2.7–2.9 show several studio setups with their appropriate connections, all based around different types of recording devices. When setting up your studio, be aware of the line levels, impedances, gain stages, and signal flow of your entire setup.

Speakers
Effects
Instrument with Pickup
Line-Level Instrument
Recorder and Mixer Board with Built-in Preamps
Multi-track Tape Machine
Microphone

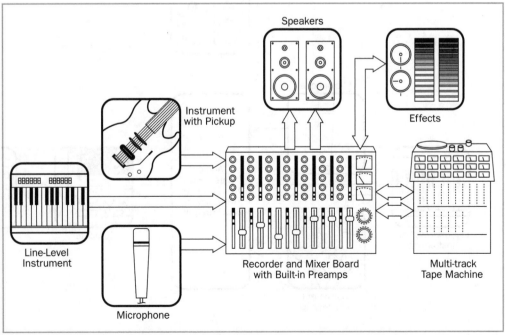

Fig. 2.7. A professional studio setup based around an analog recording/mixing console and a 2" tape machine.

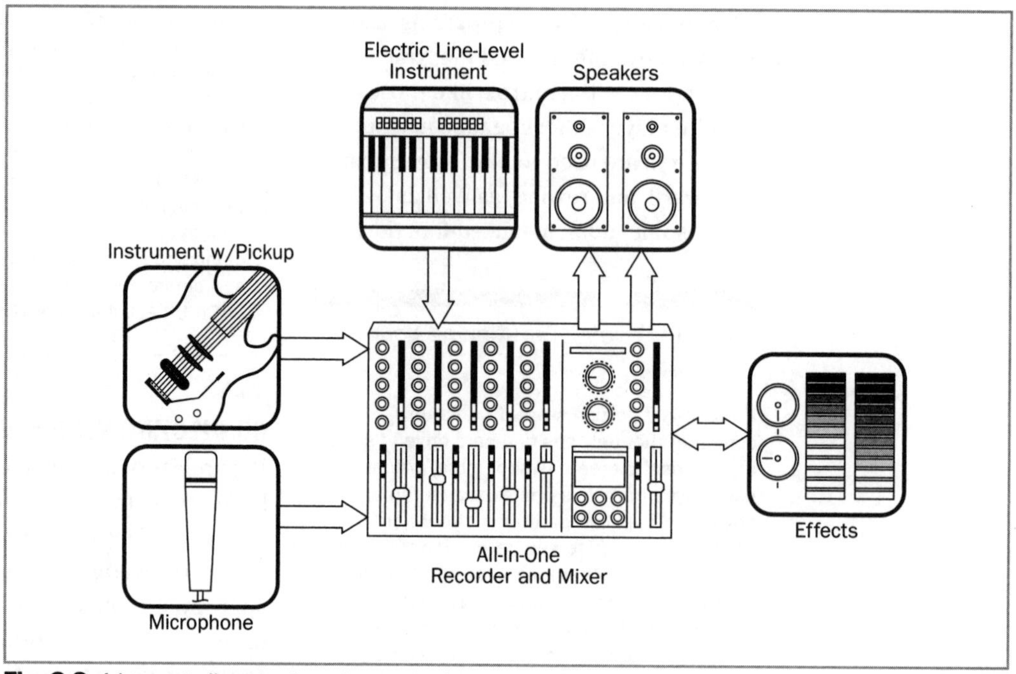
Electric Line-Level Instrument
Speakers
Instrument w/Pickup
Effects
All-In-One Recorder and Mixer
Microphone

Fig. 2.8. A home studio setup based around a 4-track cassette or digital 8-track recorder.

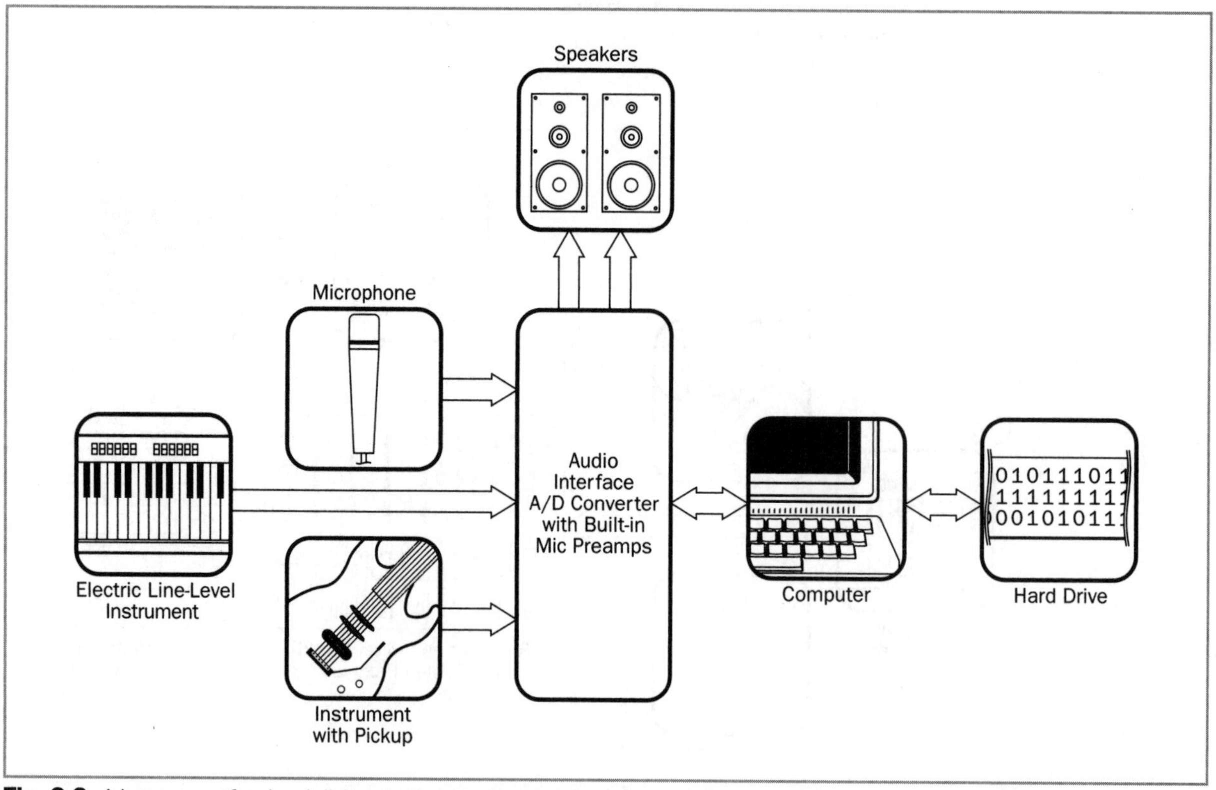
Speakers
Microphone
Audio Interface A/D Converter with Built-in Mic Preamps
Electric Line-Level Instrument
Computer
Hard Drive
Instrument with Pickup

Fig. 2.9. A home or professional digital studio based around an audio recording and MIDI sequencing software/hardware system.

ADDITIONAL HARDWARE: DYNAMICS PROCESSORS, EQS, AND EFFECTS

When integrating additional hardware, such as compressors, equalizers, and effects units, into your studio setup, there are a few issues to consider. For analog gear, make sure you're using the right line level (+4 dBm or –10 dBv). Also check whether the inputs and outputs of the processor are mono or stereo. If your processor has stereo outputs and you'd like to take advantage of that, you'll need to use two inputs on your recording device or patch bay.

When connecting digital gear, be sure that all of the digital gear is synchronized so that the sampling process happens exactly at the same time. All of the digital devices, including reverbs, delays, and other effects, need to be working with the same sampling rate (more in the next chapter on sample rates) and synced to the same sample start time. That is, they all need to be receiving the same word clock, which provides the timing to sync all the digital devices together and controls the playback of every digital audio sample. A master device provides the word clock to one or more slave devices. Most often the sync master should be the recording device, because the signal feeding the processor will often be coming from your recording device. Consult your device's operating manual for information on how to properly connect and synchronize it.

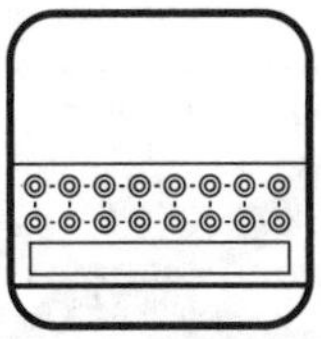

Connecting a Patch Bay

Many of you have enough outboard equipment to warrant the use of a patch bay in your studio setup. What is a patch bay? It is a connection hub for all of your equipment. Patch bays enable you to connect any piece of line-level gear to any other piece of gear quickly and easily, without having to reach behind your gear all the time. Fig. 2.10 is a diagram of a typical 1/4" patch bay.

Plug all the inputs and outputs from all of your line-level gear into the back of the patch bay. For instance, if you want to easily access the input and output of a compressor, run a cable from the input jack on the compressor to the rear of the patch bay into the patch point that you've decided will be labeled "compressor in." Next, run a cable from the compressor's output jack to the "compressor out" patch point.

Now, when you plug a cable from the output of a mic preamp (possibly coming from elsewhere in the patch bay) into the "compressor in" patch point, the signal flows out of the mic preamp, through the patch bay, into the input of the compressor. The compressed preamp signal is available for you at the "compressor out" patch point, as in fig. 2.11.

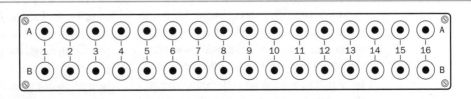

Fig. 2.10. Most patch bays are set up so that a row of input jacks is directly below a row of output jacks. With patch bays, connecting gear is a snap. They can make your life a lot easier when recording and mixing.

MIC PRE 1
MIC PRE 2
COMP OUT
EQ OUT
COMP IN
EQ IN
CHANNEL 1
CHANNEL 2

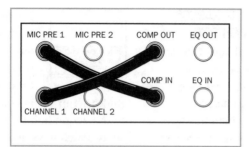

Fig. 2.11. Signal routing made easy with a patch bay.

If you label the front of the patch bay clearly, it will be easy to connect any piece of gear to another using short patch cables.

As I discussed earlier in this chapter, you need to make sure your gear is talking at the same line level—either +4 dBm or –10 dBv. Patch bays will not convert the signals for you. Also, don't use patch bays for powered outputs, like speaker outputs, and rarely for mic- or instrument-level signals. Instead, use them to connect your hardware to line-level gear, such as mixers, mic preamps, sound modules, effects units, and other signal processors.

What makes patch bays so useful is the variety of setups you can create for yourself with a little bit of signal flow knowledge and a few minutes of hands-on tinkering. Most patch bays allow connections (i.e., wiring schemes) of several varieties: full-normalled, half-normalled, split, and isolated. What do these terms mean?

Full-normalled—A wiring scheme inside the patch bay where a signal normally passes from one location to another without the use of any external patch cables. That is, the output signal from one piece of gear passes directly to the input of another device without being routed anywhere else. Fully normalled connections in a patch bay pass the signal from the top jack to the corresponding bottom jack. Inserting a patch cable in the top or bottom jack will interrupt this internal normalling connection. This is called "breaking the normal."

Viewing a patch bay diagram from the side, we can see the signal flow logic a little better. Check out the signal flow with and without a patch cable to interrupt the signal in fig. 2.12.

(a)
Front
Back
A
A
Plug
B
B
(b)
Front
Back
A
A
B
B

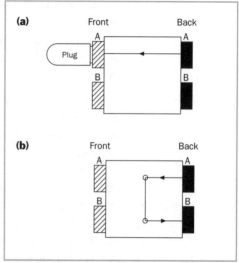

Fig. 2.12. (a) A full-normalled connection with a patch cable to interrupt the signal flow. **(b)** A full-normalled connection without a patch cable, allowing the signal to flow freely.

Although full-normalled connections are an option, half-normalled connections are more prevalent and often much more useful.

Half-normalled—Similar to full-normalled connections, a wiring scheme where a signal normally passes from one location to another without using any external patch cables, but the connection can be interrupted by inserting a patch cable *only in the bottom jack*. Inserting a cable into the top jack sends the signal out *two* places: through the patch cable you've just plugged in to the top jack, and into the bottom, half-normalled jack.

For half-normalled connections, fig. 2.13 demonstrates the signal flow with and without patch cables to interrupt the signal.

(a)
Front
Back
A
A
Plug
B
B
(b)
Front
Back
A
A
B
B

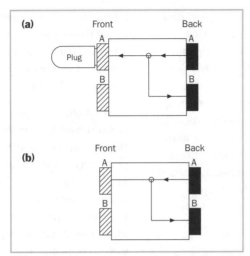

Fig. 2.13. (a) A half-normalled connection with a patch cable to interrupt the signal flow. **(b)** A half-normalled connection without a patch cable, allowing the signal to flow freely.

Consider this example (fig. 2.14). Let's say you have a single mic preamp connected through the patch bay to your recording device using a half-normalled connection. With no interruption, a signal from the preamp will automatically pass right into the recording device without the use of a patch cable. In this configuration, you can listen to the signal from the preamp before it goes into the recording device through the top jack or even send a copy of it to another device.

However, what if you want to insert a compressor between the preamp and the recording device? You would want to break the normal connection between the preamp and the recording device. Insert a patch cable to the input of the compressor from the output of the preamp (the top jack), and a patch cable from the output of the compressor to the input of the recording device (the bottom jack). This ensures that the signal from the preamp is no longer directly routed to the recording device.

If you want the input mic preamp signal to go only to the compressor and not back

(a)
Front
Back
A
A
Headphone Listen
MIC PRE OUT
B
B
REC DEVICE IN
(b)
Front
Back
A
A
To Compressor In
MIC PRE OUT
B
B
From Compressor Out
REC DEVICE IN

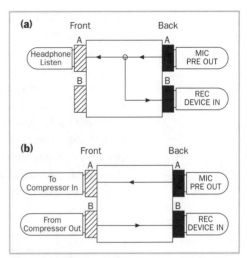

Fig. 2.14. (a) A half-normalled connection with a patch cable on the top jack, which sends a copy of the signal to another device. The original signal still goes straight through the patch bay to the output, because the normal has not been broken. **(b)** A half-normalled connection with a patch cable on the bottom jack that breaks the normal.

to the recording device directly, break the normal by patching the top jack signal to the compressor and then inserting a patch cable into the bottom jack input connected to nothing. This is called "dead patching."

Split—Essentially the opposite of half-normalled, a wiring scheme where one output can feed two inputs. For example, you can route the output of a sampler to two different inputs, such as a reverb effects unit and a separate delay effects unit, as in fig. 2.15.

Front
Back
A
A
To Reverb In
B
B
To Delay In
Sampler Out

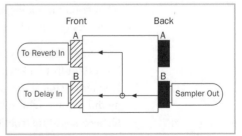

Fig. 2.15. A split connection that routes the output of a sampler to separate reverb and delay effects units.

Isolated (also called "Open")—Based on the split configuration, this wiring scheme completely isolates the top and bottom jacks on the patch bay. There's no normal at all. This is useful when there is no need to split a signal or set up normal connections. It's also very useful when the output of a device is above its input in the patch bay—using a normal connection in this case would create an unpleasant (and possibly damaging) feedback loop!

Front
Back
A
A
REC DEVICE OUT 4
B
B
FROM MIC PRE
REC DEVICE IN 4

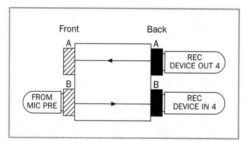

Fig. 2.16. An isolated patch bay wiring scheme.

Now that we've gotten the audio equipment setups taken care of, let's switch gears and talk about MIDI and setting up your MIDI equipment.

THE BASICS OF MIDI

As you may already know, MIDI (Musical Instrument Digital Interface, pronounced MID-dee) data is not audio data. Rather, MIDI is mainly performance data created using a MIDI controller such as a keyboard or drum machine. The MIDI data triggers MIDI sound modules, synthesizers, or samplers that produce audio.

For example, when you play and record MIDI data from a keyboard, the MIDI "sequence" file sends MIDI data to a sound module. You might think of MIDI sequence file as a set of instructions, or data. Let's say you play a few notes on your keyboard, set to a standard piano sound, into a device that captures MIDI data, such as a sequencer. The sequencer records data about the notes you played (e.g., A, C, D, E), when each note started and stopped, how hard you pressed the key for each note, and other data.

Now imagine that you decide that a harpsichord sound would be more suitable for the part. Since the MIDI data exists independently of any sound module, you can just set your keyboard to "Harpsichord" to have your sequencer instruct your keyboard to play your original performance—but with a harpsichord sound instead of piano! You could even have the sequencer send the MIDI data to an entirely different device, like a rack-mounted synthesizer. MIDI opens up loads of possibilities for getting the most out of your musical creations.

Sound modules (also synthesizers and samplers) translate MIDI data and turn it into audio. We can then monitor and/or record that audio from the sound module's audio outputs.

MIDI INTERFACE
IN
OUT

MIDI PATCH BAY
IN
OUT

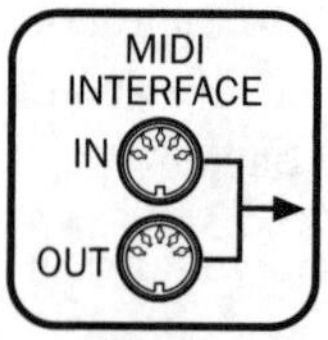

A **MIDI interface** allows quick and easy connections between all your MIDI gear, including your sequencer and/or computer. The interface routes MIDI data to and from your MIDI gear, letting you capture performances as MIDI data into your sequencer, as well as transmit that data to whichever MIDI device you choose. MIDI interfaces vary in size, ranging from a simple one-MIDI-in, one-MIDI-out device to a ten-MIDI-in, ten-MIDI-out unit. The larger units are called **MIDI patch bays** or hubs.

MIDI
IN
MIDI
OUT
MIDI
THRU

MIDI connections are made with **MIDI-in**, **MIDI-out**, and **MIDI-thru** ports. As you might have guessed, MIDI-in ports accept incoming data and MIDI-out ports send MIDI data from a MIDI device. MIDI data travels only in one direction, hence the need for in and out ports. MIDI-thru ports route a copy of all data received at the MIDI-in port directly to another device in the MIDI communication chain; no data produced by that particular unit is transmitted. Not all MIDI devices have all three types of MIDI ports.

MIDI data messages are sent on channels, and each MIDI cable can transmit on 16 *individual* channels. Each channel is used for a distinct instrument sound (e.g., channel 1 for a synth pad, channel 2 for piano, etc.), though channel 10 is often reserved for drums and percussion sounds. Some MIDI devices can only send and receive MIDI data on one channel, but many are multi-timbral, which allows them to send or receive on up to 16 channels or more at a time, and perform all of it using different instrument sounds.

MIDI Studio Setups

There are two basic ways to setup your MIDI devices in your studio: daisy chains and hubs. In a daisy-chain arrangement, a MIDI controller's MIDI-out port feeds another device's MIDI-in port, which feeds a copy of the data from its thru port to the next device's MIDI-in port.

In its simplest form, a daisy-chain MIDI network looks like the one illustrated in fig. 2.17. It is a rudimentary setup with a keyboard controller and a sound module. The hardware connections are as follows:

- Keyboard MIDI-out to MIDI interface in
- MIDI interface out to sound module MIDI-in
- Sound module MIDI-thru to keyboard MIDI-in

With this setup, I can utilize the sounds on the sound module and keyboard (as long as each device is set up to receive MIDI messages on separate channels) while using the keyboard as the controller for both devices. *Don't forget, you need to connect one or both of the audio outs from your MIDI sound module to audio inputs on your recording device to monitor and record your MIDI tracks.*

In a hub-based network, each MIDI device is connected to a MIDI interface, which

MIDI
INTERFACE
IN
OUT
MIDI Controller
MIDI Interface
Sound Module
Sound Module

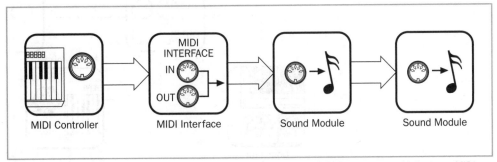

Fig. 2.17. A daisy-chain configuration enables you to use multiple MIDI instruments with just one MIDI-in/out interface connection.

acts as a kind of patch bay. Software in your computer controls the routing of the MIDI signals to and from each MIDI device for the MIDI patch bay. The MIDI interface connects to your computer through a port (e.g., parallel, serial, USB, Firewire, etc.—see fig. 2.18). Regardless of how they're connected or who makes them, MIDI interfaces all work basically the same way, intelligently routing MIDI signals to and from all devices connected to the interface with the help of your computer. Once you've physically connected all of your MIDI devices to your MIDI patch bay, you need to configure your computer to recognize your MIDI devices and route their signals properly. Consult your MIDI interface manual for instructions on how to do this.

Test Your Signal Flow and Gain Stages

Once you've got all your audio and MIDI gear setup, it's a good idea to test your signal flow and gain stages. Start with the outputs. Follow the signal path, starting from the output level from your recording device or software (check the Master Fader or Master Fader track) all the way to the speakers. Adjust any gain stages along the way to optimize the signal. This often means setting all volume faders/knobs to 0 (zero) and adjusting the last gain stage in the chain as your final volume control.

Next test your inputs. Plug an instrument or microphone into the first input of your signal path (e.g., channel 1 of your mixer/mic preamp). If using external mic pres or a mixer, route its output signal into an input on your recording hardware or sound card. Record-enable the input track and check for an input signal. Follow the signal path from the instrument to the mic and examine the levels on all gain stages along the way. Tweak the gain stages so that you can get a good recording level into your

MIDI Controller
Sound Module
Sound Module
MIDI
PATCH BAY
IN
OUT
MIDI Controller
Computer

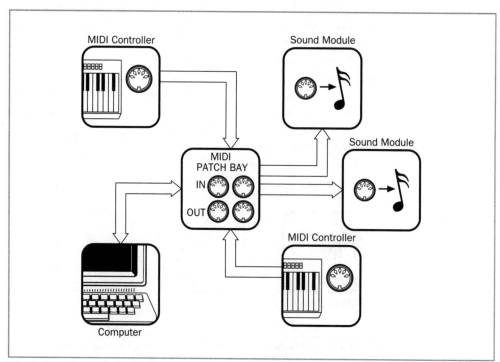

Fig. 2.18. MIDI patch bay configurations make MIDI communications between numerous MIDI devices easy.

recording device without a lot of noise and without distorting any part of the input chain. Do this every time you insert a new piece of gear into the signal path, because the gain structure will change. That way, you'll always be sure to get the highest quality input signal.

Label Your I/O

While you're setting up your gear or even after you've already set everything up, label your inputs and outputs. Make tape labels for each connection on both the cables and the actual gear, so you'll always know where each signal is traveling. You can find good tape for this purpose at any art supply store; simply ask for pH-neutral artist tape, which won't leave a sticky residue when you remove it.

Also, make a customized I/O settings document in your audio software, if possible. For example, edit the software's generic label "Input 1–2" to read "Preamp L–R," if that's what you have connected to inputs 1 and 2 of your audio interface. This will further clarify your studio setup and allow you to make templates to use every time you start a new project. I even recommend drawing up a map of the signal routing in your studio, so you always know what gear and cables are connected to each other, as in fig. 2.19.

SETTING UP YOUR LISTENING ENVIRONMENT

Monitors

Some call them speakers, others call them monitors. Regardless of what you call them, monitors are an essential component of your studio system. Passive monitors (like home stereo speakers) require an amplifier to crank the signal out of them. Self-powered monitors have amplifiers built into them, so you don't need to run them through an amplifier. Connect your passive monitors and amp or self-powered monitors directly to the outputs of your recording device.

An even better idea is to connect the outputs from your recording device into a multi-speaker set splitter, enabling you to listen to your tracks on multiple sets of speakers. Or,

Recording Device Outs
1 2 3 4 5 6 7 8
Recording Device Ins (1–8)
Mic Pre Outs
1 2 3 4 5 6 7 8
Recording Device Ins (9–16)
Outboard Gear Outs
L R L R
COMP1 COMP2 EQ1 EQ2 FX1 FX2
L R L R
Outboard Gear Ins
Isolated
Front
Back
A
B
Half-Normalled
Front
Back
A
B
Isolated
Front
Back
A
B

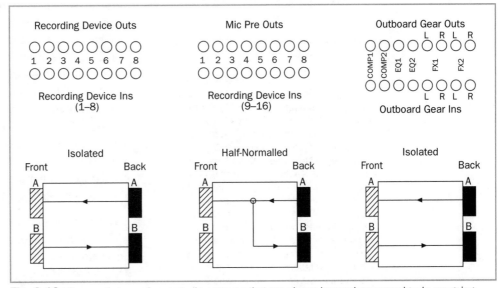

Fig. 2.19. Draw a diagram of your studio setup so that you always know where your signals are going.

you can route your output signal into a mixer that has multiple output options, such as the main outs, tape outs, submix outs, control room outs, direct outs, and a mono output, all of which can send audio to other sets of speakers if configured correctly.

It's also not a bad idea to configure your setup so that you can listen to your tracks through your own home stereo. Because you probably listen to other people's music through that stereo, it might be a good benchmark for listening to your own recordings. Even on your home stereo amplifier, you might have speaker A and B outputs, enabling you to connect a different set of speakers to each of the stereo amp outputs. Listening to your recordings on several pairs of speakers is smart, because one of the key traits of all great mixes is that they sound good on all types of speakers and playback systems. (More information on the importance of using several sets of speakers for mixing can be found in chapter 13.) And make sure you're only listening to one pair of speakers at a time!

What are you listening to?

Using your home stereo for monitoring can work very well, but watch out if you apply a lot of equalization. You may have a graphic EQ built into your amplifier, or even a stand-alone unit. You might consider flattening the settings (by positioning the EQ levels to 0 dB boost/cut) to hear exactly what your mix sounds like on non-equalized systems. Also, home stereos often have preset EQ settings for increased low- and high-end response. In fact, some systems have settings that make your music sound like it's coming from a different ambient space (e.g., a jazz hall or sports arena). I recommend turning off all of these features (bass boost, surround, and EQ presets) and setting everything to normal. This will ensure that you're listening to an accurate representation of your music—the way it really sounds. If you're used to

listening to music with these features activated, your music will probably not sound as good to you at first. Yet, it's worth getting used to listening to the flat and more accurate sound, because you'll ultimately end up creating better final mixes that will translate well to any speaker system.

When setting up your home studio, one of the most important things to consider is monitor placement. Whether you'll be listening through one pair of speakers, switching between multiple pairs, or using a surround-sound setup, there are some standard configurations.

Standard Stereo Systems

When listening to two speakers, your goal is to hear the optimal stereo image. Also called the phantom image, this occurs in the middle of two speakers placed at equal height from the floor. It creates the illusion that sound is emanating from a third speaker between them. To hear the phantom image, your head should be on the median plane, an imaginary line equidistant from each speaker (see fig. 2.20). Ideally your head and the two speakers should form an equilateral triangle—the distance between you and each speaker is the same, and equal to the distance between the two speakers. This ensures that you're hearing the most accurate stereo image from your speakers. In this setup, you'll perceive the sound coming from the area directly between the two speakers. (The way I have my studio set up, it often seems like the sound from my speakers is actually coming from my computer monitor, which is placed directly between them.)

When you are equidistant from the speakers, the sounds from each speaker reach your ears at exactly the same time. Otherwise, you may experience the precedence effect. The precedence effect (or

Phantom Image
Left Speaker
60°
60°
Right Speaker
Median Plane
Listener

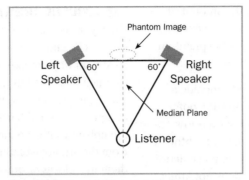

Fig. 2.20. Properly placed stereo monitors should form an equilateral triangle with the listener.

Haas effect) occurs when the listener is off the median plane (by as little as six inches). It shifts the phantom image toward the speaker closest to the listener. As a result, the sound from the closer speaker arrives at the listener's ear first, which may fool them into thinking it's louder. If you're basing a mix on this kind of false imaging, you may have to redo the entire thing!

To create the proper listening setup, I recommend using a tape measure to accurately position your speakers. First, sit down where you'll normally be listening in your studio, then use the tape measure to approximate an equal distance from your head or chest to a spot on your left and right sides where your speakers could be placed. A good distance is 3 to 4 feet, which is the same distance the speakers should be apart from each other.

In fact, the closer you are to your speakers, the less the room acoustics will color the sound. (This is called near-field monitoring, and is the most common approach for mixing.) Additionally, if at all possible, try to keep your speakers away from walls, which (along with the floor and ceiling) have a tendency to magnify bass frequencies.

Next, place your speakers at equal height from the floor in your approximated positions. If possible, the speaker height should correspond to your sitting height (or at least be pointed to that height). Angle the speakers at approximately 60 degrees toward the median plane. Finally, sit down again, use the tape measure, and precisely position the speakers to achieve the equilateral triangle setup. Now listen to some music and find out if you hear the phantom image. Try moving back and forth along the median plane and moving your head side-to-side. Can you hear the difference?

If you think you've placed your speakers correctly but still don't hear the phantom image, first make sure the balance control on your output device is centered. If the sound is "hollow" or strange when you're in the listening position, your speakers may be out of phase. Fortunately, this is an easy fix. If you're running speakers through an amplifier with positive (+) and negative (–) connections, make sure your speaker wire is attached correctly; that is, negative connector on the amp to negative connector on the speaker, and positive to positive. If this doesn't fix the problem, your speaker cables could be wired out-of-phase, so try different wires. Correctly connecting your speakers with properly wired cables should eliminate speaker phase problems.

Surround Sound Systems

Unlike stereo (two-speaker) systems, surround sound systems consist of five or more speakers. However, some of the same principles from two-speaker stereo systems apply. For instance, all speakers should be equidistant from the listener. (The subwoofer is an exception to this; see explanation that follows.) There's also a median plane and a phantom image in a surround sound system; the amount of musical material presented in the front and back speakers can move the phantom image along the median plane.

Most surround sound systems include a subwoofer, though there's no subwoofer shown in fig. 2.21. Because of their low frequencies, bass audio signals are difficult to localize spatially, so precise placement of the subwoofer typically does not affect the phantom image. In most surround sound setups, however, the subwoofer is placed on the floor between the center and one of the front speakers.

Center Speaker
Left Front Speaker
Right Front Speaker
60°
60°
Phantom image
Median Plane
Listener
70°
70°
Left Back Speaker
Right Back Speaker

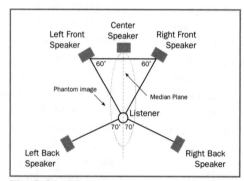

Fig. 2.21. A 5.1 surround speaker configuration (without the subwoofer, which is what the ".1" stands for). In this configuration, notice the back speakers are approximately 70 degrees off the median plane.

This 5.1 setup is used with Dolby Digital and STS surround encoding. There are other surround sound formats with different speaker placements beyond the standard 5.1 setup, such as 4-channel Quadraphonic and LCRS, 7-channel Dolby EX, and 8-channel SDDS. Each of these surround systems has slightly different specs, but many of the concepts behind their setup and sound are the same. (For information on surround mixing techniques, check out chapter 13.)

THE ACOUSTIC TREATMENT

Once your equipment and speakers are set up, you should consider the acoustical treatment of your room(s). First, eliminate as much noise within the studio as you can. Listen for noises such as whirring computer fans and hard drives. Reduce the noise by either removing these devices from the studio, isolating them by putting them in a closet or other enclosure, or by placing solid materials around the objects, making sure not to block any computer or hard drive fans. The most direct path for sound to enter or exit your studio is through a hole, so try double-paning or covering your windows and sealing all door jambs to eliminate outside noise such as traffic or noisy neighbors.

Every room has its own sound, due to its shape, the materials on the walls, floor, and ceiling, and the objects in the space. Each of these factors affects the way sound waves travel and how they're reflected or absorbed. Tiled bathrooms sound more "live" (i.e., they have more sound reflections, or reverb) than "dead" bedrooms with absorptive curtains and carpeting. In fact, the amount of reflected sound is a major factor in a room's overall sound. Hard surfaces are the main culprit for the worst types of sound reflections, such as flutter echoes, low-frequency buildup, and standing waves.

When setting up your studio, test the room where you'll record, and listen to your tracks for the room's acoustical properties. Clap your hands and talk aloud in different areas. (You may want to make sure nobody's around when you do this.) Listen for ringing, hollow sounds, or fluttery-sounding repeats. Play some of your favorite music to listen for any frequency boosts/cuts in different areas, such as low-frequency buildup in the corners.

Standing waves are created when a sound wave and its reflection either add together or cancel each other out. Similar to acoustical phase cancellation (explained in chapter 6), standing waves create unwanted boosts or cuts in certain frequencies in your studio. This isn't as easy to hear as listening for flutter echo or low-frequency buildup and is often performed by professionals. However, eliminating reflections using acoustical treatment materials can help to reduce standing waves, flutter echo, and low-frequency buildup.

There are three types of sound wave reflection:

- axial

- tangential

- oblique

Each of these terms describe the direction of sound reflections within the room. Be aware especially of **axial mode**, in which sound is bouncing between opposing walls or ceiling to floor.

Tangential modes involve reflections that bounce off of two surfaces, like where two walls meet. They aren't as strong as axial reflections.

Oblique modes occur in corners, where three surfaces meet. Even though they are usually weaker than the tangential modes, reflections in room corners cause a lot of problems because they can make it sound like there is up to three times as much bass as there really is.

To combat axial, tangential, and oblique sound wave reflection, there are two methods of controlling sound: **sound absorption** and **sound diffusion**. The best sounding rooms tend to have a good blend of soft and hard surfaces, providing both acoustic absorption and sound diffusion.

A naturally ambient room has a good balance of absorbtive (soft) and reflective (hard) surfaces, but no flutter echoes or false bass buildup. You can get up to four times the acoustic absorption if you spread your absorbent material evenly around a room instead of putting it all on just one wall or ceiling. For example, sound absorption material called "corner bass trapping" is specifically designed to suck up bass frequencies and even out the room's sound.

To achieve a live yet controlled ambience, use corner bass traps, thinner absorbent materials on the walls and ceiling, and extra sound diffusion material. This type of treatment creates a controlled, yet spacious sound. In fact, diffusion, as opposed to absorption, is recommended for live studios and control room rear walls.

In addition to the acoustical benefits within the studio, sound absorbers and diffusors also can help to soundproof your room, minimizing the sound that comes in and gets out. You can also remove or add objects in your room (such as furniture) to change its overall sound. Heck, sometimes just throwing a blanket or hanging a tapestry on a reflecting surface can have significant acoustical benefits.

In most home studios, where you likely did not have an acoustic engineer on hand to design the room, it's best to create a "dead" environment for recording and listening. That way you have control over the sounds you record. You can always *add* "liveness" by inserting effects (reverb, delay, etc.), but it's hard to remove too much liveness from an already recorded track.

Acoustic Treatment Resources

For more information on acoustical treatment products, visit Auralex's Web site (www.auralex.com). For practical guidelines for building a sound studio, download the Acoustics 101 PDF (written by Eric Smith, President of Auralex). Also check out McSquared Web site (www.mcsquared.com), an independent acoustical design consulting firm, for some interesting information on room acoustics, room modes, and even reverberation calculations for your studio.

Okay. Your gear is set up and plugged in, your speakers are placed properly, and your room is acoustically treated . . . your studio is ready for action. ∎

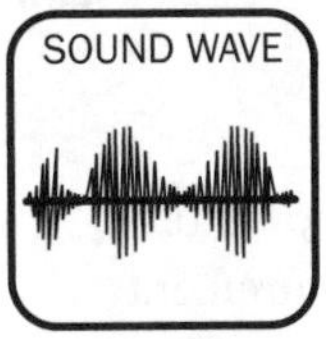
SOUND WAVE

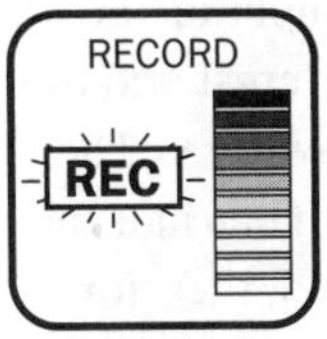
RECORD
REC

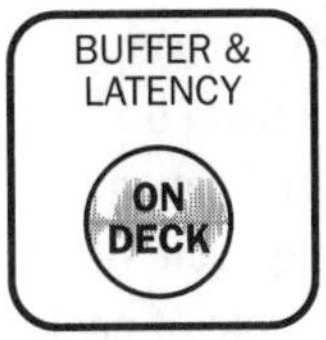
BUFFER &
LATENCY
ON
DECK

CHAPTER 3
The Basics of Recording

In this chapter:

- Analog and digital recording
- Sound wave fundamentals
- Digital memory requirements
- Recording levels
- Digital buffers and latency

The two main recording media used in today's studios are magnetic (analog) tape and digital storage devices (mainly hard drives). Though the media are different, their function is the same: to capture sound waves. In this chapter, I'll briefly explain sound wave fundamentals, then move into how sound waves are recorded onto analog and digital media.

SOUND WAVE FUNDAMENTALS

Sound emanates from a sound source in waves. These waves move through the air and cause vibrations in our eardrums, which our brain interprets as sound.

Fig. 3.1 illustrates a simple sound wave, depicting its hills and valleys intersecting a horizontal axis line. Although it looks like the sound is going up and down, what this graph really represents is how the sound affects air over a period of time. When the line is *above* the horizontal axis, the sound causes the air to compress (become more concentrated); when the line is *below* the axis, the air is "rarified" (thinned out) in response to the sound. For instance, when you see a subwoofer (bass speaker) shake during a loud, low note, what you're actually witnessing is the speaker cone moving rapidly in and out to compress and rarify the air, causing very quick changes in air pressure. Our ears pick up this change in air pressure and send it to our brain, where it is registered as sound.

There are four important characteristics of sound waves: amplitude, frequency, length, and speed.

Amplitude expresses the amount of energy in a waveform, a measurement for the amount of air being moved by the sound wave. In fig. 3.1, the amplitude is indicated by the height of the crest and the depth of the trough of the waveform. The second waveform in the figure has half the amplitude of the first wave and, therefore, moves half the amount of air.

The horizontal line on the graph has 0 amplitude. When a wave progresses from 0 through its crest and trough, and returns to 0 again, this is known as one cycle of the wave. Fig. 3.1 shows one cycle of each wave. **Frequency** describes the number of times the wave completes its cycle in one second. Frequency is expressed as Hertz, abbreviated Hz. A frequency like 10,000 Hz is abbreviated 10 kHz (kiloHertz; 1 kHz = 1,000 Hertz), or more simply as 10 k. Humans can hear sounds from roughly 20 Hz on the low end to 20 kHz on the high end. Our brain's interpretation of frequency is pitch. High frequencies have high pitches and low frequencies have low pitches.

Each frequency has a unique length—the distance the sound travels while

+
crest
Air Pressure
0
trough
–
Time
+
crest
Air Pressure
0
trough
–
Time

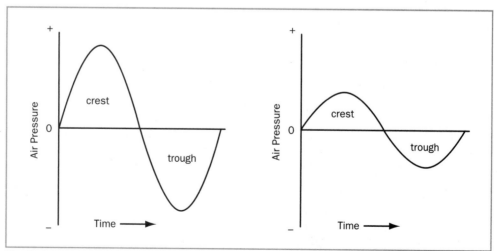

Fig. 3.1. The waveform on the left moves twice the amount of air as the one on the right.

Table 3.1. Common frequencies and their associated wavelenghs

Frequency	Wavelength (feet)	Wavelength (meters)	Comment
28 Hz	40.4	12.3	Lowest note on the piano
440 Hz	2.57	0.784	Concert A tuning note
1 kHZ	1.13	0.345	
4186 Hz	0.27	0.08	Highest note on the piano
20 kHz	0.056	0.017	0.68 inches/1.7 centimeters (highest frequency most humans can hear)

completing one cycle, called a **wavelength**. Wavelength can be mathematically calculated by dividing the speed of sound by the frequency of the waveform in Hz. The **speed of sound** is approximately 1130 feet per second, or 345 meters per second. Thus, the equation is the following:

wavelength = 1130 feet/sec ÷ Hz

= 345 m/sec ÷ Hz

Some common frequencies and their associated wavelengths are listed in table 3.1.

As the table illustrates, the higher the pitch, the faster the frequency, and the shorter the wavelength. Likewise, the lower the pitch, the slower the frequency, and the longer the wavelength. Use the illustrations in fig. 3.2 as a guide.

Let's now explore how sound waves are recorded and played back from analog and digital devices.

THE RECORDING PROCESS

The Analog Recording and Playback Process

Analog tape contains magnetized particles that, when arranged in a certain way, can approximate a sound wave and reproduce a sound. When you record to analog tape, whether it's 2" professional tape or cassette, the record head on the tape machine sends an electromagnetic current

Short Wavelength
High Frequency = High Pitch
+
0
–
Air Pressure
Time
Long Wavelength
Low Frequency = Low Pitch
+
0
–
Air Pressure
Time

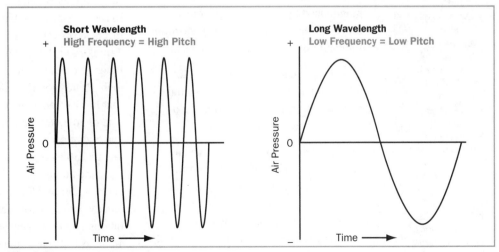

Fig. 3.2. Short wavelength vs. long wavelength.

Take Note!

Any device that transforms one kind of energy into another (like a microphone or speaker) is called a **transducer**.

Take Note!

Two issues can arise in analog recording if there is a problem with the tape movement or the tape tension in the tape machine's transport system—wow and flutter. **Wow** is slight frequency changes in the playback due to variations in the speed of the tape transport. **Flutter** is volume fluctuations due to friction between the tape and any part of the tape transport system. Faster recording speeds reduce wow and flutter.

to the tape. This current reorders the magnetic particles on the tape to represent the sound you recorded. Here's what happens when you record and play back sound in the analog domain:

Recording

1. The vocalist makes a sound with her vocal cords, which creates acoustical sound waves that vary the air pressure.

2. A microphone's diaphragm (a thin metal plate) moves in response to the changes in air pressure and produces an electrical current.

3. The electrical current from the mic travels into the analog tape machine (by way of a microphone pre-amplifier to boost its signal strength).

4. The record head on the tape machine mimics the varying mic signal and converts it into a varying magnetic current.

5. Changes in this magnetic current are recorded on the magnetic recording tape. The vocal performance is recorded.

Playback

1. The tape machine's playback head is magnetized by the tape and "reads" the magnetic data on the tape, transforming the data into an electrical signal.

2. The electrical signal is then sent to an amplifier, which boosts the signal so that it's strong enough to move a speaker cone back and forth.

3. The speaker converts the electrical current from the tape machine into sound pressure waves by moving its cone back and forth. If everything works right, these sound waves precisely reproduce the original sound made by the vocalist.

Tape Speed and Width

Tape speed is measured in inches per second, or "ips." The three standard recording speeds for professional analog tape are 7.5 ips, 15 ips, and 30 ips, while most pros use either 15 ips or 30 ips. Tape speed noticeably affects sound. Using faster recording speeds means that more tape is available to hold the audio information, resulting in improved sound quality. Faster recording speeds also operate with less noise, and thus have a lower signal-to-noise ratio. With a high-quality noise reduction system in the setup, recording at 15 ips yields a subjectively better low-end sound whereas recording at 30 ips captures the high frequencies more accurately. However, faster recording speeds also consume more tape . . . which can be quite expensive.

Recording Speed	Amount of Recording Time on a Reel of Analog Tape
7.5 ips	66 minutes
15 ips	33 minutes
30 ips	16.5 minutes

The tape width and the track count also affect the recording quality. The wider the track, the more magnetic particles available to represent the analog audio signal, which offers improved sound quality. A portable 4-track recorder that uses 1/4"-wide cassette tapes gives each track roughly 1/16 of an inch. Professional studios often use 2" tape that has 24 tracks on it, making each track 1/12 of an inch wide. However, they usually use higher speed recording, so longer areas are available on the tape for audio information, and sound quality does not suffer. In short, wider and longer tracks yield higher quality analog recordings. That's why some mixing and mastering engineers now use 1/2" and 1" 2-track tape machines at 15 or 30 ips for their final mixes or masters. For example, a track recorded on a 2-track, 1" tape at 30 ips has twelve times the area of magnetic material available to represent its waveform, compared to a track recorded on a 24-track, 2" tape at 15 ips. The same formula applies to cassette tape. A simple 2-track recorder that uses half of the tape width for each track will record at a higher fidelity than a 4-track recorder, given the same recording mechanisms.

Although not the same, the effect that each track width and tape speed have on the quality of an analog recording is similar to how bit depth and sampling rate affect the quality of digital recordings.

THE DIGITAL RECORDING AND PLAYBACK PROCESS

The digital recording process is similar to the analog process, though the recording devices work differently. Instead of transforming electrical currents into magnetic currents, digital recording devices transform electrical currents into binary digital data stored on hard drives as massive streams of 0s and 1s. Computers use the simple, binary language of 0s and 1s for all the complex things they do. Before getting into the language of 0s and 1s, let's explore the digital recording process.

Digital recording works by transforming electrical currents into 0s and 1s for recording and back into electrical currents for playback. This conversion process is known as analog-to-digital (or "A to D," written "A/D") conversion. The A/D conversion from analog electrical signals to digital data happens in several steps, as seen in fig. 3.3.

Sampling Rate

In order to capture continuous analog sound waves and save them on our computer hard drive, we have to digitally **sample** the waveforms. To reproduce the sound accurately, we have to sample very quickly so we can construct a digital version of the sound.

Think of the sampling rate in terms of photography. If you set up a camera to take a picture of the sky once every hour, you can follow weather patterns in a very rough way. With this low "sample rate" you would probably miss many significant events. However, if you took pictures every second, you would see much more detail, like the moment rain began to fall or when sun broke through the clouds.

Digital recording is like taking pictures of music at a speed determined by the sample rate. In order to reconstruct an accurate continuous analog sound from digital samples, we need to take over 40,000 samples per second. That is referred to as the sample rate. If the

Analog signal
Anti-aliasing
A/D conversion
(sampling, quantizing, coding)
Digital

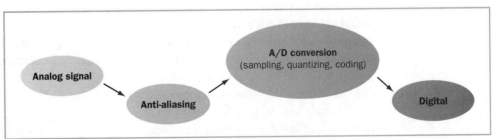

Fig. 3.3. The analog-to-digital conversion process. An analog signal goes through anti-aliasing and A/D conversion (sampling, quantizing, coding), transforming it into digital data.

Take Note!

How can Hz refer to both the frequency of a sound (pitch) and the sample rate? That because hertz is simply a measure of frequency—how many times something happens per second. In sample rate, Hz expresses the number of samples per second, while in frequency, Hz refers to the number of full cycles that the sound compresses and rarifies the air per second.

sample rate is set to 44.1 kHz, your digital recording device takes 44,100 "pictures" of your input audio signal every second. Each picture—each sample—captures the amplitude (level) of the audio signal at that moment. So, when even one second of an analog signal is recorded digitally, there are thousands of samples to represent it as digital information.

To send the digital representation of the sound back through the speakers, an analog version of it must be reconstructed from the digital version. When digital audio information is converted back into analog sound, the thousands of digital samples are played back so quickly that our brains "mush" the samples together and interpret a continuous analog signal. Scientifically speaking, I say "mushed" because we hear continuous audio, even though it's being reproduced from tiny, discrete samples. It's just like watching a movie. We are really watching 24 frames per second of still photos (which are samples), but our brain interprets these images as fluid motion.

So, going back to the 40,000 samples per second, how did we arrive at that magic number? If that's all we need, why would we use the common 44.1 kHz, 48 kHz, or even higher sample rates?

The American engineer Harry Nyquist figured out that the sample rate must at least double the frequency (pitch) that we want to represent in order for it to sound accurate to our ears. That is, our sound "camera" has to snap at least twice as fast as the wave is cycling in order for us to get a good picture of its waveform. Because we can only hear sounds up to 20 kHz, we only need to sample at twice that frequency, 40 kHz. This formula is known as the **Nyquist theorem**.

So what happens if the sampling rate is not twice the frequency we want to record? Suppose we're trying to capture a 16 kHz sound, but our sample rate is only 20 kHz. It might map the sound wave as represented in the image below. (Figures 3.4–3.11 are simplifications of the actual process.)

16 kHz signal
Sample rate = 20 kHz

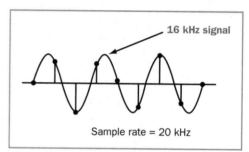

Fig. 3.4. A 16 kHz sound sampled at 20 kHz.

The computer would then store its samples like this.

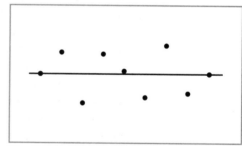

Fig. 3.5. Samples from the 16 kHz sound.

When the computer reconstructs the signal, we get an inaccurate waveform.

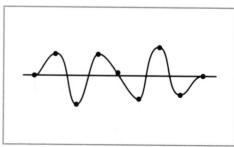

Fig. 3.6. The computer reconstructs the signal inaccurately.

When the sampling occurs at twice the rate of the waveform, we get a better picture of the way the wave is moving, as shown in the pictures below.

16 kHz signal
Sample rate = 32 kHz

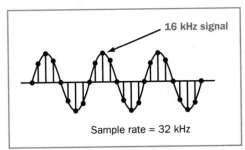

Fig. 3.7. A 16 kHz sound sampled at 32 kHz.

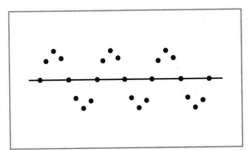

Fig. 3.8. Samples from the 16 kHz sound.

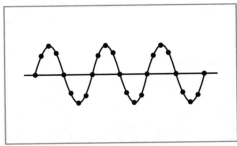

Fig. 3.9. Sampling at twice the rate of the waveform produces a more accurate result.

Anti-Aliasing

What happens when there are pitches in our original sound that are above the range of human hearing—the sounds that your howling dog might hear—such as the overtones on a cymbal? Suppose the cymbal emits a ringing at 30 kHz, as illustrated in fig. 3.10. If the sampling rate is set at 44.1 kHz, you will record sound at the dots on the waveform shown in fig. 3.11.

30-kHz signal

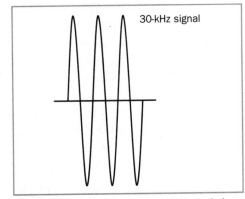

Fig. 3.10. The waveform created by a cymbal ringing at 30 kHz.

Sample rate = 44.1 kHz

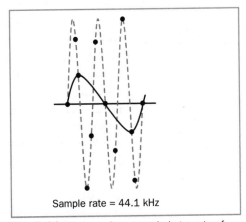

Fig. 3.11. The waveform sampled at a rate of 44.1 kHz.

Unfortunately, the sampled sound creates a new waveform (unlike the original waveform) with a completely new pitch. The resulting pitch is actually 44.1 kHz–30 kHz, or 14.1 kHz. 14.1 kHz is the 30 kHz tone's **alias**, its false identity. This alias frequency creates an audio artifact (distortion) in your recording if left in there. To fix the problem, we need to filter out any frequencies above 20 kHz so that they don't get aliased. This is called **anti-aliasing**.

A **low-pass filter** (which allows only frequencies below a certain amount to pass through) is placed in the signal path before the analog signal is sampled and converted to digital. Because the filter cannot cut off all of the analog signal right at 20 kHz, there is a margin of several thousand hertz for the filter to kick in totally, hence the extra 4.1 or 8 kHz above the 40 kHz mark. We won't miss the sound of the filtered-out frequencies (above 20 kHz), because most of us can't hear them anyway. And it makes your howlin' dog happy!

Incidentally, 44.1 kHz is such a common sampling rate because CD manufacturers chose it based on CD disk size, playing time, cost, and the technological limitations that existed in the early 1980s when the CD was developed. Higher sampling rates are available and are being used in newer technology (e.g., DVDs and SACDs), yet higher sampling rates require more computer processing power, more disk space, and thus more money to create. In any case, the 44.1 kHz sample rate remains the de facto standard for your final stereo mix.

Quantizing

Once an analog audio signal has been filtered (anti-aliased) and sampled, each sample is then quantized. That is, each sample is digitally mapped to an exact digital value (or quantization level). How does that work?

As the samples of analog audio are quantized, the electrical voltages that make up the analog audio signal are converted into a value. The computer expresses values in **binary digits** (or **bits**). Each bit can be either 0 or 1. The number of bits in the system is referred to as **bit depth**.

A quantity expressed as a binary number is called a **digital word**. The size of a

digital word depends on the bit depth. The higher the bit depth, the more information you can include about the sound, and thus, the more accurately you represent an analog sound digitally. In a 16-bit system, each digital word is 16 bits long (e.g., 0110111000101100).

In a 1-bit system, there are two quantization levels, represented digitally as 0 or 1. If you sampled and quantized audio with a 1-bit system, all you could represent is whether there was a signal (1) or not (0).

In 2-bit systems, you have four possibilities, as in fig. 3.12(a). A quantity expressed as a 2-bit word can take on one of four values: 00 (silence), 01 (a little louder), 10 (louder still), and 11 (loudest). A 3-bit word can quantify eight levels: 000, 001, 010, 011, 100, 101, 110, and 111, as seen in fig. 3.12(b).

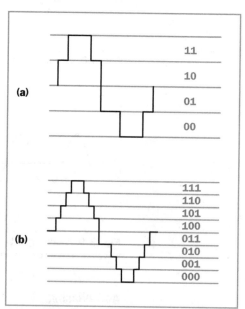

Fig. 3.12. (a) 2-bit system with four quantizing levels **(b)** 3-bit system with eight quantizing levels.

As the bit depth increases, the number of quantization levels increases exponentially. For example, $2^4 = 16$ and $2^5 = 32$. Common bit depths are 16 and 24; 16-bit resolution offers 65,536 (or 2^{16}) quantization levels and 24-bit resolution offers 16,777,216 (or 2^{24}). 24-bit resolution can represent analog audio as digital information more accurately, because it has more quantization levels, and thus offers more detail about the sound.

Back to our photography example: In color photography, a photo taken with a bit depth of 4 bits (2^4) would only allow 16 different colors ($2^4 = 2 \times 2 \times 2 \times 2 = 16$). If the color of a photographed object is not precisely one of the 16 colors allowed, the closest color would be assigned to it. Obviously, 16 colors can't possibly describe all of the shades and hues found in our colorful world. The same logic applies when describing the myriad nuances of sound with an audio signal—the more bits, the better. With bit depths up to 16 or 24, it's like having thousands (or millions) of colors to choose from, instead of only 16.

Coding

The final step in A/D conversion is coding. That's when the anti-aliased, sampled, and quantized audio gets coded into binary digital information (0s and 1s). Each quantization step for each sample is turned into digital data and stored on your hard drive. This data is a stream of billions of 0s and 1s compiled and organized by your digital recording device on a hard drive. Pretty amazing stuff!

The D/A Process

To play back this digital data, the A/D process is reversed, with a few twists. The data must be retrieved from the proper location on the digital tape or hard drive, then errors in the digital data transmission are corrected. The data is then decoded and converted from 0s and 1s back into electrical currents, and sent through a low-pass filter to remove unwanted high-frequency audio information.

Error Correction

The error correction process is necessary because it helps to avoid potentially devastating errors in the digital data flow from bit errors and burst errors. Bit errors are noise pulses that inadvertently get placed into the digital data stream, causing unwanted pops or clicks. Burst errors are often larger scale errors due to imperfections in the recording medium and can cause dropouts (empty spots) in the digital data stream.

Error correction schemes add extra data into the digital audio data stream to help identify errors and create redundant data. The redundant data can be used for reconstructing errant data. If some of the original data is completely lost, error correction will use an educated guess to approximate what the data should be, using data before and after the error point. (This process is called "interpolation.") Even though the interpolated data may not be exactly right, it's usually pretty close to the original data.

Digital
D/A conversion
(decoding, error correction,
D/A conversion)
Low-pass
filtering
Analog signal

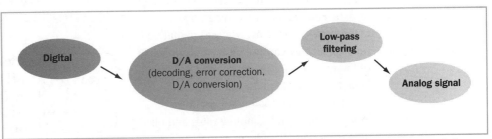

Fig. 3.13. The digital-to-analog conversion process. A digital signal goes through error correction, D/A conversion, and low-pass filtering, transforming it into digital data.

Microphone
Vocalist
Computer
Preamp
Recording Device
Hard Drive
010111011
111111111
001010111
Speakers
Recording Device
Computer

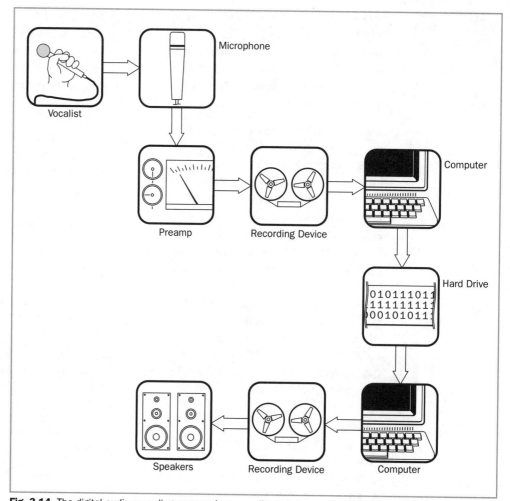

Fig. 3.14. The digital audio recording process is a complicated process, yet it happens in just a split second.

Recording Process Wrap-Up

Digital recording is becoming more popular every day, though analog has a few clear advantages. Analog recordings are technically more accurate than digital recordings, because analog recordings capture continuous waveforms, whereas digital recordings only capture discrete samples of the waveform. Digital recordings do, in fact, miss some of the sonic information. However, as computers become more powerful and sampling rates and bit depths increase, the distinction in accuracy between analog and digital recordings will significantly diminish. Truthfully, even now most people cannot tell the difference between songs that were recorded digitally or on analog tape—but even audiophiles have a tough time telling analog from 24-bit, 96 kHz digital recordings!

010111011
111111111
001010111

DIGITAL RECORDING AND HARD DISK SPACE REQUIREMENTS

CDs are recorded with 16-bit resolution and a sample rate of 44.1 kHz. However,

Number of tracks and length	16-bit at 44.1 kHz	16-bit at 48 kHz	24-bit at 44.1 kHz	24-bit at 48 kHz	16-bit at 88.2 kHz	16-bit at 96 kHz	24-bit at 88.2 kHz	24-bit at 96 kHz
1 track, 1 minute	5MB	5.5 MB	7.5 MB	8.2 MB	10 MB	11 MB	15 MB	16.4 MB
2 tracks (stereo), 5 minutes	50 MB	55 MB	75 MB	83 MB	100 MB	110 MB	150 MB	165 MB
2 tracks (stereo), 60 minutes	600 MB	662 MB	900 MB	991 MB	1.2 GB	1.3 GB	1.8 GB	1.9 GB
24 tracks, 1 minute	120 MB	132 MB	180 MB	198 MB	240 MB	164 MB	360 MB	396 MB
24 tracks, 5 minutes	600 MB	662 MB	900 MB	991 MB	1.2 GB	1.3 GB	1.8 GB	1.9 GB
24 tracks, 60 minutes	7 GB	7.8 GB	10.5 GB	11.6 GB	14 GB	15.6 GB	21 GB	23.2 GB

Fig. 3.15. Hard disk space requirements for different sampling rates and bit depths. If you plan to do a lot of hi-res recording, you may need to stock up on hard drives.

Take Note!

Regardless of the 16/44.1 kHz CD standard, many people record at the highest resolution possible, simply to have a hi-res archive to remaster from, if or when the standard moves to a higher bit depth and/or sample rate. Also, digital compressors, equalizers, and effects work better with high-resolution digital audio than they do with lower res material.

recording in your studio with faster sample rates and higher bit depths yields more detailed audio representations and more accurate recordings. High-resolution recording also requires more hard disk space. Since the word length of a 24-bit recording is 50% longer than that of a 16-bit recording, recording at 24-bit resolution requires 50% more hard disk space than 16-bit recording. For example, a mono audio track recorded at 16-bit resolution and a 44.1 kHz sample rate requires approximately 5 MB per minute of hard disk space; the same track recorded with 24-bit resolution requires 7.5 MB per minute. Using a sample rate of 48 kHz or higher also increases the disk space needed to store files. If you do a lot of high-resolution recording, you may need an extra hard drive or two.

Use the guide in fig. 3.16 to figure out the hard drive space needed for a project you're working on. Enter the sampling rate, bit depth, number of tracks, and time of the tracks into the equation and convert

bits to megabytes (MB) or gigabytes (GB). You'll notice that a five-minute song with 24 tracks recorded at 24-bit and 44.1 kHz is less than one gigabyte.

But what if you have several takes of each track? Three takes of that five-minute song will take up almost three gigabytes of hard disk space. See how quickly disk space gets eaten up? Think about this when you're starting a new project. You don't want to run out of room halfway through a recording session.

Assigning audio files to be recorded on multiple hard drives can increase your system performance while playing back and/or recording additional tracks. Instead of making one hard drive do all the work of searching for and playing back tracks, the work can be distributed between several drives, allowing each to perform more efficiently.

Despite the bit depth and sample rate you use when recording, you must convert the files to 16-bit/44.1 kHz to burn them to a

Time		Number of Tracks		Sample Rate		Bit Depth		File Size
5 min x 60 sec/min	×	24 tracks	×	44,100/sec	×	24 bits	=	7,620,480,000 bits

Bits		Bytes		Kilobytes (KB)		Megabytes (MB)		Gigabytes (GB)
7,620,480,000 bits	=	952,560,000 bytes	=	930234 KB	=	908 MB	=	0.89 GB

Fig. 3.16. Estimating the size of your project will help you plan for how much hard disk space you need during the recording process. I recommend at least doubling or tripling your final number so that you have room for unexpected tracking and experimentation.

CD. I often record at the highest sampling rate and bit depth available to ensure the highest recording quality, then apply dither during the mastering process to convert tracks to 16-bit files, or even MP3s. More on file conversion and dithering is found in chapter 14.

SETTING RECORDING LEVELS

When recording to professional analog tape, most people try to push the recording level to the highest point they can without distorting the sound. This is done to maximize the **signal-to-noise ratio**—in this case, the ratio of audio signal recorded to the amount of inherent noise on the analog tape medium. Recording at high levels on analog tape increases the clarity of the recording and keeps the inherent noise as low as possible in comparison. And in fact, many people even like the sound of slight analog **distortion.** This occurs when the tape is overloaded with audio signal (often called "tape saturation"), and can create a pleasingly "warm" sound. This ability is one reason that some people are still partial to analog recordings over digital ones. (However, don't try overloading a cassette-based, 4-track recorder. You'll most likely create ugly unwanted distortion.)

There's very little noise associated with digital recording, and it has a much higher signal-to-noise ratio than analog. Most people push digital recording levels to allow for the use of greater bit depth. Utilizing the entire bit depth provides the most accurate picture of the analog waveform. However, overloading a digital track causes digital clipping—the audio signal is literally cut off at 0 dB, often creating a decidedly nasty sound. Digital distortion isn't pleasing like analog distortion can be, so digital levels should always remain below 0 dB, the digital clipping point . . . unless you're going for a distorted effect.

When recording, your input levels will fluctuate with the dynamics of the input signal. In digital recording, your goal is to get the input level as high as you can without having the signal clip, causing digital distortion. Here are some examples of recording levels (figs. 3.17–3.20).

Even if you see the red peak indicator on one or several of your tracks, your signal may not be clipped. Your recording device has a certain amount of **headroom** between the level at which the red peak light is activated and the level at which the audio is clipped. Watch the meters, but also use your ears to experiment with recording levels and find what works well for your system. In general, it's usually

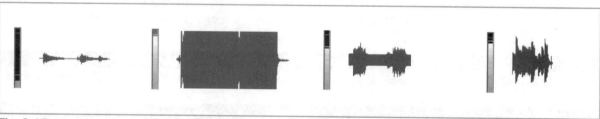

Fig. 3.17. Low recording level and resulting waveform.

Fig. 3.18. Recording too "hot" (with high input levels) causes the meter to peak and the waveform to clip.

Fig. 3.19. Even with good recording levels, noise on the track can be heard and even seen on the waveform.

Fig. 3.20. Good level with no noise. Ahhh . . . doesn't that sound better?

fine if a signal peaks very occasionally. However, if the signal peaks often or always, then decrease the input level.

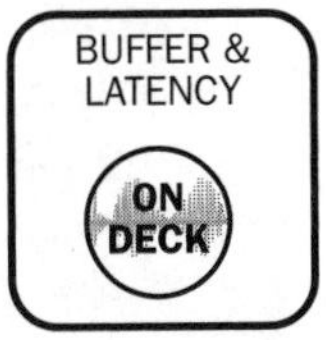
BUFFER &
LATENCY
ON
DECK

BUFFER SIZE AND LATENCY TIMES

One other consideration to make when recording digitally is your recording buffer and the latency time of your system. Your digital recording device has a buffer, a place where a fluctuating amount of data is held in its RAM (Random Access Memory) before the data is played back. It's like an "on-deck circle" in baseball. As digital data is recalled for playback, it is moved into the buffer, where each digital sample is then governed by the master word clock. The word clock controls the exact time each sample is played back, so that every sample is in sync with anything else that is connected to and controlled by the master word clock. In other words, the buffer holds the digital data until the word clock determines when to play it.

Through the process of digital recording, analog audio signals are converted into digital data, the data is recorded, and then the data is converted back into an analog signal for playback. Although very fast, this conversion process is not instantaneous. The time it takes your computer to receive an input signal, process it, and send it to an output is called **latency**. Latency values can be as low as 3.0 milliseconds (essentially unnoticeable) or higher than 50 millisec-onds (quite noticeable). These times vary depending on the buffer size in your digital recording device, which you can probably adjust. The buffer size is measured in digital samples and can be translated into "time" using the equation in fig. 3.21.

Anytime you convert an analog signal to digital or vice versa, the analog-to-digital (A/D) or digital-to-analog (D/A) converter delays the signal by about 1.5 millisec-onds. When a signal is converted on the way in to your computer (A/D) and then converted as it's played back out of the computer (D/A), the conversion delay adds up to 3.0 milliseconds. Your computer also takes some time to process the audio (depending on the buffer size set in your digital audio recording device) as it comes and goes, which means the total latency of your system equals the conversion delay (3.0 milliseconds) plus double the latency amount given in the chart in fig. 3.22. For example, recording with a sample rate of 44.1 kHz and a buffer size of 128 samples, the total latency is 2.9 ms * 2 plus 3.0 ms, equaling 8.8 ms. Check out the chart in fig. 3.22. You can extrapolate the numbers when using higher buffer settings.

While recording, you'll often want to operate with the lowest possible level of latency. Why is latency a factor when recording? Because latency affects the timing between the actual performance and the playback of the performance in the headphones or speakers while recording. For example, if you record with a buffer size of 128 samples at 44.1 kHz sampling rate, you will experience 5.9 milliseconds of delay between what you play and what you hear back from your digital recording device (unless your device has low or no latency monitoring). 5.9 milliseconds of

Buffer Size (samples) ÷ Sampling Rate (samples/sec) 1000 ms/sec = Latency of the buffer

Fig. 3.21. Buffer-size time equation. If the buffer size is 128 samples at 44.1 kHz sampling rate, the latency caused by the buffer is 2.9 ms. 128 ÷ 44, 100 x 1000 = 2.9 ms

Buffer Size (samples)	Sample Rate (kHz)	Delay Time (ms)	D/A/D Conversion	TOTAL DELAY (ms)
128	44.1	2.9	+ 3 ms	5.9
	48	2.7	+ 3 ms	5.7
	88.2	1.5	+ 3 ms	4.5
	96	1.4	+ 3 ms	4.4
256	44.1	5.8	+ 3 ms	8.8
	48	5.4	+ 3 ms	8.4
	88.2	2.9	+ 3 ms	5.9
	96	2.7	+ 3 ms	5.7

Fig. 3.22. Larger buffer sizes increase latency, while higher sampling rates decrease latency.

delay is not that noticeable, so it shouldn't be a problem. However, if for some reason you need to record with a larger buffer size, you may experience latency large enough that it might negatively affect your ability to record your performance. Thus, it's best to record with the lowest latency possible. When mixing, the buffer size and latency can also be an issue if you're using outboard analog gear with your digital recording device . . . but we'll get into that topic in chapter 7. For now, let's move away from the technical to discuss the early stages of project development: preproduction. ■

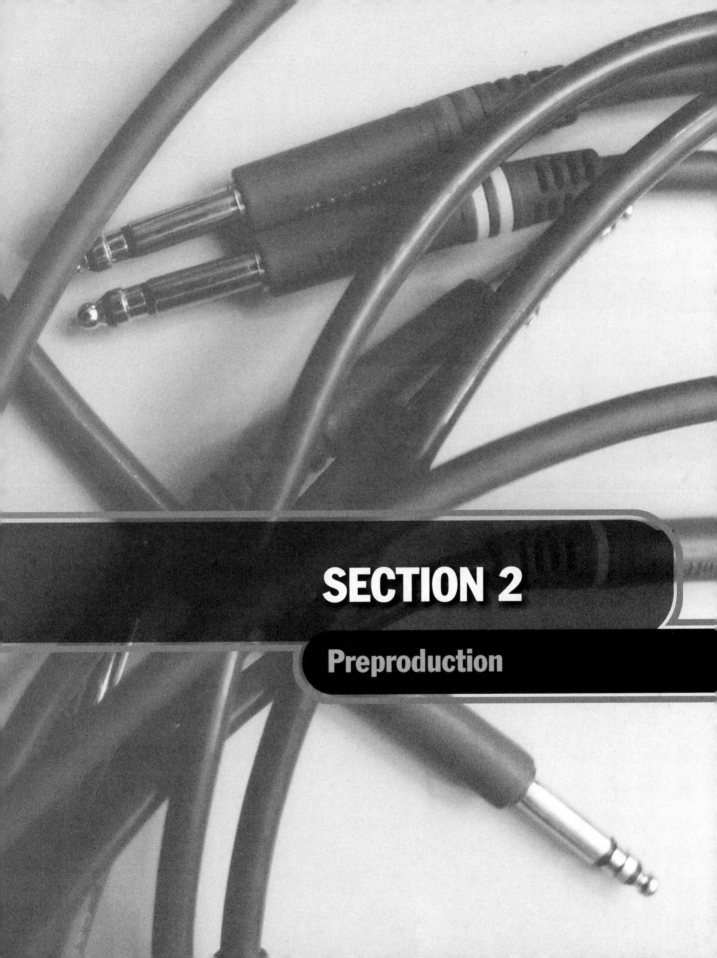

SECTION 2

Preproduction

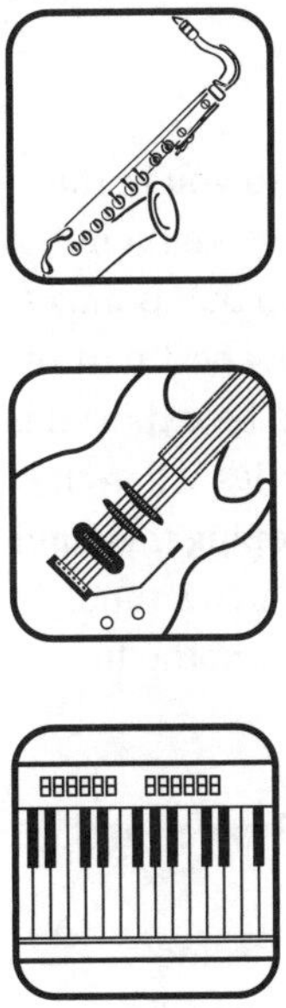

CHAPTER 4
The Producer's Role in Preproduction Part I

In this chapter:

- Working with artists
- Helping an artist define their artistic vision
- Finding the artist's potential marketing demographics
- Choosing the artist's best material to record
- Planning and budgeting your project

Terry Becker, a professional producer and engineer for artists such as Bonnie Raitt and Taj Majal, says, "Three primary elements predict whether a producer will help create a successful project: organization, preparation, and documentation." The preproduction phase is the time that you lay the groundwork for that success. So, it's time to get very specific about what the producer does during preproduction . . . probably the most time-consuming and arguably the most important phase of the production process.

Preproduction consists of all the activities that take place before a recording session. Getting songs ready to record can take much more time than actually recording and mixing them, but the time is well spent because the recording session will go a lot smoother and the final product will be much better.

Take Note!

When I engineer and/or produce music for friends, I sometimes rely on a handshake as a contract, but only with close friends. Having a lawyer draft a contract for a project—or at least using a boilerplate from a music business book—may save you a lot of headaches (as well as time and money) if things don't turn out as all parties expected.

Whether you're working on your own music or someone else's, these ten elements are the foundations of preproduction:

1. Meeting the artist
2. Listening to the artist's material
3. Considering the artist's identity
4. Choosing the best material to record
5. Planning the project: time and money
6. Writing, rewriting, and arranging
7. Hiring help
8. Scheduling rehearsals, recording sessions, and mixing sessions
9. Rehearsing
10. Getting ready for the recording sessions

In this chapter, I'll cover how to implement the first five steps in this list in your productions, enhancing the descriptions from chapter 1. This is the planning part of preproduction. (Remember, for our purposes the term "artist" can refer to a single person or a group.) Here we go . . . .

1. MEETING THE ARTIST

If you're producing your own music you're obviously familiar with your material and work ethic. However, if you're producing someone else's music, you have to develop an **artist/producer relationship**. In the first meeting, this involves listening to the artist's ideas, asking questions about the project, and sharing experiences. Subsequent meetings and "hang" time will help you to get to know each other better and establish trust. The goal is to connect with the artist and make them feel comfortable with you.

They'll be spilling their guts to you in the form of music, and that can make them feel vulnerable. But getting to that point where the artist allows the deepest part of their heart, mind, and soul to be exposed is right where you want to be—it's when the best music is created. Developing this kind of relationship with an artist takes time, but the foundation for it is set in the first meeting.

Defining the Scope of the Project and Your Role

At the beginning of every recording project, define its scope. This usually happens when you first meet the artist, or when you decide you're going to record something serious for yourself. The project may be a single song, a three-song demo, or a full-length album. It might require you to be the engineer only or it may also include the duties of engineer and producer (as well as artist and songwriter). If you're producing someone else's music you might be asked to act only as an opinion-giver or you might take part in every aspect of the song's development (writing, rewriting, arranging, etc.). Understanding your role in the recording process is imperative and will influence your every action during a project.

If you're producing an artist, create a contract to outline the scope of your duties. This should include a schedule and a budget (see "Planning the Project: Time and Money" later in this chapter), as well as royalty agreements and other clauses to be mutually approved. Read other books on the music business for details on contracts, and, as much as you may not want to, consult a lawyer to make sure the contract you're creating is good. (I'm sure you've heard of people unknowingly signing severely binding contracts—even ones that they've created themselves—so be careful!)

2. LISTENING TO THE ARTIST'S MATERIAL

If you're working with a new client and you're not familiar with their music, you should listen to everything they have available—previous CDs, live shows, old demos, tapes of random guitar licks, etc. This will give you an idea about (a) the style of music they want to make, (b) the direction their most recent music is going, and (c) the sound they want to have. It will also help you decide what you think is their best material. Sometimes artists get bored with their older material . . . if they only bring you recent music they might bypass great tunes for the project.

Even if you're producing your own music, consider playing through all your material (new and old song ideas). You may stumble across a song (or even a song fragment) you haven't heard for a while and discover that it's really good. Or you may see that your best material is your latest material. In any case, try to evaluate your ideas objectively; that is, try to listen like it's the first time you've ever heard the song. Also play your stuff for other people—their feedback can be quite valuable.

3. CONSIDERING THE ARTIST'S IDENTITY

Defining an artist's identity, purpose, sound, and image helps focus your efforts. There are several important questions you should ask about any project you produce:

1. What's the purpose of the recording? For fun, a demo to get gigs, a demo to shop to record labels, a full-length CD to sell?

2. What do you want this recording to sound like? A style similar to a known artist, a conglomeration of styles, something completely different?

3. Who will want to listen to the recording? Your family and friends, most people who like the genre, pop radio listeners?

These questions appear easy to answer. However, if the ultimate goal is to sell the music you're producing, then a lot of effort should go into dealing with these issues. You need to help artists find their current identity, and figure out if it matches their vision of the project (especially if the artist is you). If the artist's image doesn't match the vision of the project, you need to help change either the image or the expectations.

Demographics

Finding detailed answers to the three questions above will help artists define themselves and create a vision for the final recording. And this vision should align with the demographics of the audience they want to buy the music. Demographics are statistical data used to market a product to a specific population. Common demographic data includes age, ethnicity, gender, income, geographic location, tastes, buying habits, and education.

These days, some of the biggest pop acts sell their music primarily to a pre-teen and teen white female population who use their parents' income to buy the recordings. They're located all over the country (within reach of Top-40 radio and MTV), and their tastes, buying habits, and level of education are fairly homogeneous. You wouldn't try to sell an avant-garde jazz album to this population, just as you wouldn't try to sell teen pop music to an avant-garde crowd. This is obvious. However, there are overlaps among audiences—okay, maybe not between the two I mentioned, but there's overlap between other audiences (e.g., people who like blues and jazz, rock and country, hip-hop and reggae, metal and techno). Many people like a variety of music, and finding the overlap or niche where you or the artist you're producing fits in—now, that's the tricky part. Therefore, defining the artist's identity, purpose, sound, and image, as well as the target demographic for the music, will provide long-term benefits.

Being a Visionary . . . and More

A producer must be a visionary. The producer has to have a vision of the final outcome of an artist's music. But that's only part of it. Producers also are involved in the even larger matter of sculpting an artist's entire artistic purpose, image, and identity.

Some artists have already established their identities. They are comfortable with their "act" and their "sound," so all the producer has to do is record them well and not screw it up. However, many young artists or new artists that you record in your home studio may still be looking for their true artistic identity. It's your job as their producer to help them find themselves. How do you do that?

I think the key is asking the right questions, followed by creative suggestions that steer them down a particular path. Producers often need to ask really tough questions to get to the heart of an artist . . . to find out what really inspires them, motivates them, and drives them to create music.

Just by assessing their personality, style, and energy within the first few meetings

with the artist, you should be able to tell if your artist wants to take chances or if they are set in their ways. You can tailor your suggestions accordingly. Ask them leading questions to help them discover their style themselves, and guide them to choose their own musical path. This process is not meant to be manipulative . . . it's merely a technique for achieving a unified artistic goal. Whatever artistic path you and the artist decide to follow, it should include a shared vision. If it doesn't, you and the artist should probably not work together.

Imagine you are working with a new artist that you just recently met. The artist has raw talent and some interesting and original song ideas. However, they don't have a clear artistic vision and their music reflects that fact. What questions would you ask this artist to help define their artistic vision, purpose, image, and identity? Help them answer the following questions:

1. What is the artist's musical style?

2. What are their philosophies on life?

3. What are their personal attributes and style?

4. What is their vision of themselves?

5. What are their goals?

6. What do they think makes them "special?"

Think deeply about the big picture of the artist and their career so that you can then help them develop a plan to realize the shared artistic vision. Now let's go a little more in depth about demographics.

Finding Potential Marketing Demographics

Part of creating the shared musical vision with your artist is determining who will enjoy, and ultimately purchase, the artist's music. These potential fans are part of a demographic. For example, "males aged 20–25 who read car magazines" is a particular demographic of a population. Demographic data will help you create music that appeals to your chosen audience. Common music-related demographic data includes age, ethnicity, income, geographic location, tastes, buying habits, and education. Also, think of products related to music, or other products that people who also buy music might buy.

The idea is to figure out who your artist's music will appeal to. Most companies (including record companies) collect demographic data so that they know who their consumers are. For example, *Billboard* magazine (www.billboard.com) publishes information about its readership online that includes statistical details about the people who read their magazine.

The following Web site has demographic data on a slew of industries, including online music companies: http://cyberatlas.internet.com/big_picture/demographics.

There are a number of organizations and Web sites that collect demographic data independently. Most of this data is probably too general to be helpful to you, but it will definitely give you perspective on some of the potential populations that you could reach with your music. A quick search on the Internet will yield many sites that post demographic data.

Musical Genres

Humans have a need to label and organize things. As with all other forms of art, most music gets codified into categories called genres. A musical genre represents a particular style of music. I've come up with a long list of musical genres, including . . . but not limited to:

Genre
African
Alternative/modern rock
Adult alternative
Adult contemporary
Americana
Ballet
Bluegrass
Blues
Caribbean
Children's
Classical
Classic rock
Contemporary Christian
Country
Electronic
Ethnic & international
Folk & traditional
Gospel
Heavy metal
Hip-hop
Jazz
Latin
Lullabies
Middle Eastern
Military marches
Musicals
New Age
Novelty
Opera
Popular
Punk
Rap
Reggae
Religious & sacred music
Rhythm & blues
Rock
Soft rock
Soul
Theme music
Top-40
World fusion

And even within these genres, there are sub-genres. Take electronic music for example. Here are a few sub-genres of electronic music:

| Ambient |
| Dance |
| Downtempo |
| Drum-n-bass |
| Garage |
| House |
| Jungle |
| Lounge |
| Techno |
| Trance |

All the music you produce will likely fit into one or more of these categories. You should be able to describe your artist's music, because (a) it will force you to be articulate (which is an invaluable skill of successful producers) and (b) it will help you market the music better. How? Your description will lead you to finding the appropriate people (demographics) to market your artist's music to. An accurate description of the music could also steer your artist onto the right Billboard chart . . .

Billboard Charts

In *Billboard* magazine, the top-selling songs/albums are listed on charts based on sales and radio play. Here are all of the current charts that *Billboard* tracks. Notice the limited number of genres that are represented in the charts.

| **ALBUM CHARTS** |
| The Billboard 200 |
| Top R&B/Hip-Hop Albums |
| Top Country Albums |
| Pop Catalog Albums |
| Electronic Albums |
| Top Heatseekers Albums |
| Top Independent Albums |

| Top Internet Album Sales |
| No. 1 In Billboard |
| **SINGLES & AIRPLAY** |
| The Billboard Hot 100 |
| Modern Rock Tracks |
| Hot Rap Singles |
| Hot Country Singles & Tracks |
| Hot Dance Music/Club Play |
| Hot R&B/Hip-Hop Singles & Tracks |
| Adult Top 40 |
| No. 1 in Billboard |
| **LATIN MUSIC** |
| Hot Latin Tracks |
| Billboard Latin 50 |

Many people dream of having a song on the *Billboard* charts. However, it may not be your goal to produce music that appeals to millions of people or that's appropriate for these charts. Regardless, having knowledge of the charts is good for many reasons:

- It makes you, as a producer, more informed in case you or one of your artists is interested in attaining massive popular success.

- It helps you watch some of the trends in music.

- It identifies music that has state-of-the-art production, so you can check it out.

- It gives you ideas for your own music, even if it's nothing like what you do.

Regardless of whether you want to make music for a hundred people or for a hundred million people to enjoy, having a clear vision of who your music is for makes choosing the right songs to record on a project an easier process.

4. CHOOSING THE BEST MATERIAL TO RECORD

This is probably your most important duty as a producer. If you're choosing songs for your own recording, be honest with yourself. Combine your own "objective-as-you-can-be" opinions, feedback from others, and analysis of your identity and potential marketing demographic. Sometimes this can be difficult; sometimes it's quite easy. You don't want to delay the decision, but if it's difficult to choose among several songs, you might record all of them and then decide which one turned out best, or most "on target." Naturally, not everyone has the time and money to take this approach.

If you're producing an artist, helping them choose the songs on their record is a big responsibility. However, *they* came to you, so you could help them decide. If you've developed a close relationship with the artist, they look to you for honesty and will respect your opinions. Remember, they're your client: You're working for them and they want you to do your job. That said, there will be situations where you have to speak with great tact.

Tact and Diplomacy

There will probably be times when your opinions differ from the artist's, and in the music business, differences of opinion can be intense because you're not just quibbling over business decisions. You're dealing with people who have exposed their souls to you and shared their heart-felt creations. Egos are easily hurt with stray negative comments. Therefore, if you need to disagree with an artist, you must be *diplomatic*. It's a true skill to deal with sensitive matters without hurting people . . . while keeping them motivated.

You do this by stating your opinions in honest, yet non-offensive and non-confrontational words. It's best to say something positive first, then follow that with a tactful opinion. For example, instead of saying "Song 3 stinks! Song 4 is better," say something like "I like Song 3. It's got a strong chorus, but Song 4 really gets me. Its lyrics grab me, its melody is so catchy," and so on. With comments like these, you get your point across but keep the artist motivated to do great work.

Also notice that my comments personified the song. By personifying the song you discuss it as its own entity, which allows you to be critical of the song without being critical of the writer. This is a useful strategy because people tend to be less defensive if you point at an object instead of at them. You can also personify the entire recording by saying something like, "This demo only needs one love ballad, not two." By personifying the songs or the record, you create a working environment focused on the music, not the people.

As a producer, you need to be especially tactful when suggesting changes to existing songs. It can be tricky to tell someone that the chorus of their song needs work, but you can handle it using the same method as above. Instead of saying, "The chorus sucks. Write a new one," try "The current chorus is good, but it's not grabbing me like the verse does. Can we try some other ideas just to see what they might sound like?" This technique works better with sensitive artists (who are numerous). Some other artists might prefer a more direct (or "tough love") approach, but they'll respect your tact if you use it without sounding too flattering or wishy-washy.

However, there are certain traits that are common among many good producers, especially tact and diplomacy. Without those traits, you'll have difficulty getting your opinions accepted. All producers have different personalities and use different tactics in their discussions with artists.

I Have a Theory

If you're working with musicians who have some knowledge of music theory, you can make your comments more pointed by "talking shop." For example, you might suggest to the artist that the chord resolution in the chorus might sound stronger with a V-I instead of a IV-I progression. However, making comments like these to musicians without music theory chops will not only be ineffectual; it may also intimidate them or disconnect you from them.

So, after listening to all of the artist's material (even if the artist is you) and considering the artist's vision, identity, and marketing demographic, the producer and artist together should choose which songs to record. Some songs may be completely ready to record and others may need extensive work. Still others might just be ideas that haven't been fully realized. Even after the songs have been chosen, there should be some amount of flexibility because you (or the artist) might write a completely new tune during the project that's better than any you've chosen so far. However, choosing the material to record early in the process is beneficial because it gives you an idea of how much work needs to be done, and helps estimate the time and money needed to complete the project.

5. PLANNING THE PROJECT: TIME AND MONEY

Time and money are constraints on almost any project you'll be producing. Understanding how much of each you have to work with is imperative to a successful recording . . . and running out of time or money can obviously have a detrimental effect. Therefore, you should create a schedule and budget for each project: Schedules and budgets provide organization and documentation and are tools that help focus your energy.

It may be more difficult to create a schedule if you're producing your own music. When working on my material, I tend to set aside specific times, but I also work on it in my spare time—this practice doesn't lend itself to a strict schedule. However, setting a deadline for the project is probably the best motivating factor. I usually pick a date that has some significance, for instance, to meet a festival submission deadline, or a friend's birthday. Otherwise—because it's your music and you're probably somewhat of a perfectionist—you might work on it forever.

Depending on your financial status, creating a budget may also be very important. There are many expenses to take into account: What materials will you need? CDs, DATs, copies, additional equipment? Will you rent, buy, or borrow the equipment? Do you need to hire additional musicians, an arranger, an orchestrator, a lyricist, an engineer, etc.? Do you need to rent a rehearsal space to practice? Will someone else be mixing or mastering the project?

Working with friends, playing most of the parts yourself, practicing at home, borrowing equipment you need, and engineering, mixing, and mastering the project yourself will save tons of money. However, you may not have the time or skills to do this. It may be worth it to spend some money where it either (a) improves the recording, (b) allows you to keep your head in a creative space, or (c) saves time. I recommend figuring out what your budget can handle early on, because it can save you a lot of grief later.

If you're producing (or just recording) an artist or band, it's *imperative* to set a schedule and budget at the beginning of the project. That way you'll know what they expect of you and what you can expect from them. You can charge an hourly rate or set a flat fee for your services.

Engineers often work on hourly rates, whereas producers usually work for a fee. Charge what you feel you (and your studio) are worth. Adding the other expenses mentioned above (i.e., materials, equipment, musicians, etc.) to your rate or fee will give you an estimated recording budget. Creating a budget before the project begins will prepare you and the artist for what to expect—if the artist you're working with has been signed by a record label, the label will invariably provide a budget.

PROJECT BUDGET | EXPENSES

Date: 1/18/2004
Artist: Go Figure
Project Title: Three Song Demo
Producer(s): Andrew Stern/David Franz
Engineer(s): David Franz

MATERIALS/EQUIPMENT (CDs, copies, food, strings, drum heads, new and rental gear, etc.)

Item	Cost	Number Needed	Total Cost
Hard drive	$300	1	$300
CD-Rs	$1	30	$30
Food & Drink	$100	—	$100
		SUBTOTAL	$430

REHEARSAL SPACE AND STUDIO TIME

Item	Cost/hour	Hours Needed	Total Cost
Studio Time (Rehearsal)	—	10	—
Studio Time (Recording)	$40	24	$960
		SUBTOTAL	$960

MUSICIANS (rehearsals and recording sessions, including AFM and AFTRA payments, if applicable)

Name	Instrument	Session #	Hours	Rate	Other Expenses	Total Cost
Andrew	Guitar/Banjo					—
Michael	Clarinet					—
Rushad	Cello					—
Noah	Bass					—
Eric	Drums					—
Vin	Turntables					—
Maria	Vocals					—
					SUBTOTAL	—

PRODUCER/ENGINEER (recording, mix, remix, and mastering – fee or hourly rate)

Engineer	Cost/hour	Hours Needed	Total Cost
David Franz – recording	$40	24	included
David Franz – mixing & editing	$40	24	$960
David Franz – mastering	$40	6	$240
		SUBTOTAL	$1200

OTHER EXPENSES

Item	Cost	Number Needed	Total Cost
Mic preamp rental	$100/day	3	$300
		SUBTOTAL	$300

PRODUCER'S SIGNATURE | GRAND TOTAL | $2890

Fig. 4.1. A sample project budget. The old carpenter axiom "measure twice, cut once" definitely applies here. Plan your budget carefully, as running out of time or money can put a damper on your dreams of becoming famous . . . much less finishing your CD.

Take Note!

If you're producing a band that sells a lot of their own recordings, you might want to ask for a percentage of sales. Big-name producers working with big-name acts usually get 3%, and up to 5% on rare occasions. However, this may be difficult to keep track of if the artist isn't affiliated with a record label or some other sort of accounting service.

As you know, a budget is an estimate. Coming in under budget at the end of a project is always welcome, but being over budget isn't good. Many times the amount over budget is paid by the producer, so consider yourself warned. Because of this, it's usually a good idea to include some sort of "slush fund" to cover unexpected costs. (I'll let you figure out how to incorporate the "slush fund" into your budget.)

Creating a schedule can help a project stay on budget. It will also help organize the work and focus the artist's and your energy. Here's a sample schedule for a band you might produce or engineer. The band wants to record a three-song demo.

If you're engineering but not producing the project, then you might only need to be present for the last six or seven events on the schedule in fig. 4.2. If you're

PROJECT SCHEDULE

Artist: *Go Figure* — Project Title: *Three Song Demo*

Producer(s): *Andrew Stern/David Franz* — Engineer(s): *David Franz*

DATE	TIME	EVENT	NOTES
1/10	6 pm	Band meeting	Meet everyone, talk about music
1/12	7 pm	Rehearsal	Play through all potential songs to record
1/15	7 pm	Band meeting	Hang, talk about recording songs, budget
1/17	7 pm	Rehearsal	Tighten up three songs
1/18	8 pm	Rehearsal	Work out final song arrangements
1/20	2 pm	Recording session	Tracking the basics (drums, bass, guitar, vocals)
1/21	8 pm	Editing	Editing the basic tracks
1/22	8 pm	Overdubs	Overdubbing
1/24	2 pm	Overdubs	More overdubs
1/25	8 pm	Editing	Editing the overdubs
1/26	8 pm	Overdubs	Final O/D session
1/30	6 pm	Editing	Final edits
2/1	6 pm	Mixing	Mix Song #1
2/2	6 pm	Mixing	Mix Song #2
2/4	6 pm	Mixing	Mix Song #3
2/5	2 pm	Check mixes	Tweak as necessary and give to artist
2/8	8 pm	Meeting	Discuss mixes and tweak
2/10	6 pm	Mastering	Master the 3 songs
2/11	8 pm	Meeting	Check masters, discuss with artist, and tweak
2/12	2 pm	BURN FINAL MASTER CD	Give to artist

Fig. 4.2. A possible schedule for a three-song demo; notice the events are primarily in the evening. Besides the fact that some musicians actually have day jobs, remember that most musicians tend to shy away from morning gigs.

working on a project that requires writing new material, rewriting old material, and arranging and/or orchestrating the material, you should also create a schedule for those activities. I know . . . scheduling time to write a new song might sound strange, contradictory to your artistic/creative flow, or even impossible. As a good friend of mine once said, "There is no timetable on inspiration." However, you'll find that once you do sit down with a handful of ideas, you just might be able to create new songs on a schedule—this is actually a skill that develops with practice. I'm not suggesting you try to force creativity. I'm simply saying that focused work toward a specific goal usually pays off.

AFTRA and AFM

Many producers hire professional musicians and singers to record on their projects. These professional musicians are often part of a union and are paid at pre-determined session rates. Producers fill out contracts with the unions and hire the musicians through the unions. The two main unions you might deal with if you want to hire professional musicians are AFTRA and AFM.

AFTRA: The American Federation of Television and Radio Artists (AFTRA) is a national labor union affiliated with the AFL-CIO. Its headquarters are in New York City and there are 36 local offices throughout the country. AFTRA represents its members in four major areas: 1) news and broadcasting, 2) entertainment programming, 3) the recording business, and 4) commercials and non-broadcast, industrial, and educational media. AFTRA's 80,000 members are seen or heard on television, radio, and sound recordings and include actors, announcers, news broadcasters, singers (including royalty artists and background singers), dancers, sportscasters, disc jockeys, talk show hosts, and others. According to the AFTRA Web site (www.aftra.org), talent payments under AFTRA contract total more than $1 billion a year.

AFM: The American Federation of Musicians (AFM) is the largest entertainment labor organization in the world and is also affiliated with the AFL-CIO. AFM represents professional musicians similarly to the way in which AFTRA represents its members. AFM has over 120,000 members throughout the United States and Canada.

Producers deal with AFTRA for hiring vocal talent and AFM for hiring musicians. The national AFTRA organization determines the payment rates for singers; the information can be found on their Web site. In contrast, local chapters of AFM set their own rates. For example, AFM Chapter #47 sets rates for recording in the Los Angeles area (see their Web site at http://promusic47.org). But if current AFM rates aren't posted on a Web site for your area, you'll have to call the local chapter.

With all the "planning" part taken care of, we can now move on to the "doing" part of preproduction. Go forward to chapter 5 for the next stages in the preproduction process. ∎

CHAPTER 5
The Producer's Role in Preproduction
Part II

In this chapter:

- Writing, rewriting, and arranging

- Songwriting concepts and techniques

- Hiring help

- Scheduling the sessions

- Session preparation

The planning part of preproduction is done. Time to move on to the second half of the producer's role in preproduction, the "doing" part. This is often the most creative time of any project, when ideas are flowing and excitement is building.

To recap, whether you're working on your own music or someone else's, these ten elements are the **foundations** of preproduction:

✔ 1. Meeting the artist

✔ 2. Listening to the artist's material

✔ 3. Considering the artist's identity

✔ 4. Choosing the best material to record

✔ 5. Planning the project: time and money

6. Writing, rewriting, and arranging

7. Hiring help

8. Scheduling rehearsals, recording sessions, and mixing sessions

9. Rehearsing

10. Getting ready for the recording sessions

6. WRITING, REWRITING, AND ARRANGING

Writing, rewriting, and arranging the artist's material may be the most important step in the entire production process. This is when you transfer your (or your artist's) musical identity, purpose, and image into sound. You iron out most of the details in each song by making important decisions about the effect of the music on the listener. This is when new material is written, older material is rewritten, and all material is arranged.

Your primary job as a producer during this step of preproduction is to rework each song (if the song needs alterations) by adjusting the music, lyrics, and arrangement. Here are some general questions to ask yourself about the content of the songs.

Music: Does the music match the mood of the lyrics? Does that matter? Do the dynamic changes (loud vs. soft parts) work? Are the feel and tempo right? Do all the parts fit together well? Is the music too busy or not busy enough? If it's a pop song, do you make the listener wait too long for the chorus? Are you working in the best key for (a) the tune itself, and (b) your vocalists or instrumentalists? Or, is the music too difficult for the players/singers you have access to?

Lyrics: Do the lyrics make sense? Are they supposed to make sense? Do they flow? Do they capture the emotion, image, or event in the song? Are they easy to sing? Do they have a good rhythm? Are they too hokey? Does it matter if they are?

Arrangement: Does the current instrumentation work or does the song need additional (or fewer) instrumental parts? Does the song's form match its emotion? Does the form need to be rearranged to create a better flow? Does the arrangement capture the attitude of the song? Overall, does it feel like anything is missing from the song? Do you have access to the musicians or gear to really carry this arrangement off?

If you're working on your own music, try to remain objective. Often we get tied to our original ideas so much so that we can't look past them. On the other hand, overthinking and reworking a song too much can do more harm than good. The real emotion or spirit of the original idea may be processed too much and ultimately lost. It's a fine line that producers have to walk everyday, in helping artists craft the best songs they are capable of.

Craftsmanship

What does it mean to craft a song? It means creating a story or mood in which every piece of the song fits together somehow in the way you want the story told or the mood experienced. Each part, from the lead vocal to the bass drum, should be right for the song. This comes from a collaboration of the artist's and producer's creativity in music and lyric writing, arrangement, and production planning, and from a unified idea of how the song should sound when it's complete.

To achieve this, the producer must specifically analyze all aspects of the song including key, tempo, length, lyrics, arrangement (instrumentation, song form, and attitude), and its overall meaning and intent.

Key: The key is the principle tonality found in the song or the scale on which the song is based (e.g., the key of C major). It can help set the mood for the song because certain keys have particular sounds (e.g., Spinal Tap's usage of D minor—the saddest of all keys). It's also very important to choose a key in which the singer (or lead instrumentalist) can perform well. Choosing a key that's out of range (too high or too low) for the vocalist (or lead instrument) can ruin a recording. If you don't want to change the key, you should probably change the melody to accommodate the vocalist's range or choose another vocalist/lead instrument to perform the part.

Change the Key of a MIDI-Driven Song

The vocalist is usually the centerpiece of any song, so the producer must take special care to make them sound their best. Because of this, many songs written in one key end up in a different key during preproduction to better suit the singer's range. Changing the key (transposing) in MIDI-based songs in most sequencers is quite easy.

In your MIDI sequence, select the MIDI track(s) you want to transpose. Be careful not to select drum tracks to transpose. There are 12 semitones in an octave. To move the key up a perfect fifth interval, use 8 semi-tones, like from the note C4 to G4. To move the key down a minor third interval, use −4 semi-tones, from C4 to A3.

Tempo: A song that's recorded when the tempo is too slow will drag on and bore the listener. A song recorded at a tempo that's too fast will lose its groove and may sound rushed. Use a metronome to evaluate the tempo at which your song sounds best. You can have a range ($\quarternote$ = 118–120 BPM) or you can get very specific ($\quarternote$ = 84.5 BPM). You'd be surprised how a small change in tempo (sometimes even just a fraction of a beat per minute) can make all the difference in the feel of a song.

Beats Per Minute

The acronym BPM stands for "beats per minute" and is usually written as: $\quarternote$ = 120. This means a quarter note gets one beat at a tempo of 120 beats per minute. You can have other note values or resolutions (e.g., half notes) as the basis for your tempo, but the quarter note is the most frequently used.

Length: When considering the length of the song you should consider the song's purpose. If you and the artist want the song to be "radio-friendly," you should think about what radio stations will play it and how long their songs usually are. These days, it seems that most major pop radio stations play songs that are two and a half to four minutes long, with five minutes being the maximum. You can record a longer version of the song for the album version, but edit it to comply with other radio material. Of course, if you're not worried about radio airplay, a song can be any length you want.

Music: You can analyze the music by simply listening and getting in touch with how it makes you feel. Does the music express the intended emotion of the song? Do the harmony and melody interact well? Is the music catchy? Does the melody have a hook—something that you find yourself singing when you wake up in the morning?

Lyrics: As a producer, you should know all the lyrics to every song you produce. You should also be able to sing them, even if you're not a good singer; this will give you increased understanding of their "singability." You'll learn the spots where the singer might struggle with the melody, syllables, or overall rhythm of the vocal part. When you sing the lyrics, you'll also absorb its meaning and become more involved with the song emotionally.

Having a lyric sheet is imperative when recording the vocal tracks. Keep a copy of the lyrics with you at all times, for reference. Ask the artist to give you a copy early on during preproduction, or write or type the lyrics yourself. (See chapter 10 for more information on vocal production.)

Arrangement

In my view, a great song arrangement consists of three main components: instrumentation, song form, and attitude. Instrumentation refers to the instruments that are played and their parts, including vocals. Song form refers to the structure and sections of the song (how many verses and choruses there should be and where they'll be placed). Attitude refers to the emotion, feel, and point of view that the song should portray. The intended attitude of the song will greatly influence instrumentation and song form. In fact, all three of the components of song arrangement affect each other, so if one is altered, the

producer must consider the effects on the other two components. Like any facet of songwriting, arranging is a skill that's honed with practice.

Instrumentation: Part of a producer's job when arranging is adding vocal or instrumental parts to augment the song. When arranging these parts, be mindful of leaving space for every element of the song. For example, most times you don't want an intricate horn line to interfere with the lead vocal. Likewise, multiple guitar tracks can really fill out a song, but if they're all playing something different at the same time, the song can sound cluttered. Placing each part in the right place in a song is an important production duty.

Listen to the basic tracks (e.g., guitar/vocal or piano/bass/drums/vocal, etc.) to determine (a) where you might want more or less instrumental support, (b) where the open spaces in the song are, and (c) whether you want to fill the open spaces. (Just because there's an open space doesn't mean it needs to be filled!) Discuss your ideas with the artist and get feedback. Sketch out the ideas and play them along with the basic tracks.

If you're going to create parts for instruments you don't usually write for, be aware of each instrument's range. I've included range charts for many instruments in appendix A; refer to them when you're coming up with the parts, whether you're going to be recording real instruments or synthesized/sampled versions. That way your parts will actually be playable by real musicians or at least sound more realistic when played by your MIDI instruments. If you have little time or experience writing for particular instruments, consider hiring someone else to do the parts for the arrangement.

> *Take Note!*
> Musicians often refer to arrangements as "charts" (e.g., "the horn chart"). There are professional arrangers who specialize in writing charts for all types of instrumental groupings, including horns, strings, and percussion sections.

Song form: The form establishes a structure that helps guide the listener through the song. Skillful arrangement of the pieces of a song (verses, choruses, bridge, etc.) creates a natural musical flow. The song form can help establish imagery, story line, prosody (explained in the next section), and repetition. There are no rules for the form of a song, but several forms are prevalent in music today. One of the most common is: intro, verse, chorus, verse, chorus, bridge, chorus, chorus.

It's easy to try different song forms using a digital audio editing program; you can order sections any way you want. By cutting and pasting different sections together, you can test basic arrangements without actually recording new tracks.

Attitude: There are no rules for this aspect of arranging, either. Simply consider whether the emotion and feel of each instrument fits with the others and solidifies the meaning and intent of the song. The point of view should be consistent, unless you intentionally change it.

Songwriting Concepts

As a producer and a songwriter, you know there are many ways to write songs. You might start with a great lyric, a strong melody idea, a cool chord progression, or a tasty drum beat. Building that one idea into an entire song is a challenge for both the songwriter and the producer. There are some principles that hold true in a great majority of songs, regardless of genre or approach. Understanding and applying the principles below may improve your creative process. Consider these in your role as producer:

Imagery: Many songs evoke images in the listener's mind. Imagery can be created verbally and sonically through descriptive lyrics and expressive music. Images help connect the listener to the song in a way that allows them to imagine the setting for the music, be it the state of mind of the narrator and singer, or the location in which the song's story takes place. The stronger the image, the deeper the listener can connect with the meaning of the song.

Story line: Songs with stories also pull the listener in to the music, and the lyrics are the most important part of a song. But just as there are many ways to write a song, there are many ways to tell a story. Most stories have some sort of character introduction, plot development, and then build to a climax, resolution, or surprise. When crafting a story with music, consider how the story unfolds and try to match the story line with the emotion of the music.

Prosody: Prosody occurs when the mood of the music (expressed primarily in the harmony and rhythm) matches the mood of the lyrics and melody of the song, and all parts of the song fit together. Prosody is entirely subjective. It is impossible to measure, but you'll know it when you hear it. For example, if the tune "Happy Birthday" were played in a minor key, the melody wouldn't fit the celebratory mood of the lyrics, and would lack prosody. You may strive to produce music with prosody or you may intentionally avoid it, but you should always evaluate songs for prosody before the recording is complete.

Hook: A hook is a small piece of a song that's considered catchy. Usually repeated several times, a hook can be a unique lyric, melody, chord progression, sound effect, or rhythmic figure. Consider the frequency and placement of hooks in the music because, if done well, they will make the listener want to hear the song again.

Repetition: Another device to help listeners follow your songs is repetition. Repetition is found mainly in song form (Verse > Chorus > Verse > Chorus), harmony (recurring chord progressions), and lyric structure (repeated words or phrases). Repetition helps the listener remember the song and creates a sense of predictability that makes them feel more comfortable.

Creating Lead Sheets

At some point in your musical life, you'll have a recording session and will need to organize players who don't already know the song. A great way to get those players up to speed is to provide them with a demo tape and lead sheet beforehand. The demo tape can be a simple recording of just the chords and melody. Or, you may create a lead sheet. In its most basic form, a lead sheet shows the song's structure, key, tempo, time signature, and chord progression. More detailed lead sheets show the melody, lyrics, and rhythmic hits.

Once the song is down on paper, you (the producer) can analyze it from a different perspective—especially helpful if a song doesn't seem quite right but you can't figure out why. You might notice that a chord progression doesn't resolve, or that a melody doesn't have enough tonal variety. By looking at the lead sheet, you can tell if a rhythm is off or if the melody is too high or low for a vocalist's or instrumentalist's range. Additionally, a producer (and engineer) can use the lead sheet as a road map of the song when recording and mixing. While looking at the lead sheet in a recording session, a producer might say to the artist, "That whole guitar take was great . . . we just need to punch in bars 3 and 4 of the bridge." Besides providing organization and documentation, a lead sheet helps a producer offer explicit comments and helps musicians find specific measures in the song much faster.

Writing out lead sheets on staff paper can be convenient, but it can also be time consuming. Learning how to use a music notation program can be a real asset to your musical career. The software programs print out neater parts than handwritten ones, and will play your music so you can hear if there are any mistakes, ahead of time. Creating lead sheets early in the preproduction phase can eliminate many problems, and will ultimately lead to improved efficiency in later phases. Although not a necessary skill for producers and engineers, knowing how to create a lead sheet is a very useful production tool.

Producer's Perspective—Interacting with an Artist

At any time during the preproduction process, if you find that any part of a song has to be reworked, you must to be articulate about what needs to be changed and why—and you must be tactful about it. You'll also need to gain trust and respect from artists. First and foremost, artists need to feel comfortable around you. You need to gain their confidence as a counselor and a confidant. To do this, you should cultivate an open relationship by not being judgmental and by allowing them to be themselves. You should be open-minded and flexible. Most artists are afraid that people won't like their music. Fear prevents people from doing a lot of things—it certainly prevents artists from opening up and exposing their souls. You need to use all of your power as a producer to quell this fear. In an environment where artists are comfortable, special things happen.

Try to be a catalyst for ideas, and a stimulus for creativity. Build on the artist's ideas and provide encouragement. Artists look to the producer to provide a different point of view. You're also expected to have a tremendous amount of patience. You need to mediate and moderate any tricky situations and protect the democratic process when dealing with a group of artists or a band.

The artist wants to create the best recording of their life with you. Thus, you must support their music, provide translations of their musical visions, and offer camaraderie. You need to develop your psychology skills to deal with the many moods, egos, and personalities of artists. And develop your management chops to help focus the artist's attention while following the budget and schedule, without making them feel pressured.

Likewise, when working on your own music, allow the producer in you (as best you can) to be a non-judgmental, flexible, and open-minded objective source. That way the artist in you can truly express itself.

Artist's Perspective—Interacting with a Producer

Collaborating with a producer can be a tricky thing for an artist. It may be difficult to completely open up to someone new. If you (the artist) want to have a close relationship with a producer, you've got to spend time breaking down any barriers the two of you might have. And you've got to be as articulate as you can when describing your musical ideas and overall vision.

Ideally you and your producer will create a relationship based on honesty, trust, and respect. Both of your opinions on where the music should go should be relatively mutual. However, there will be times when

you disagree. Maybe the producer wants to change a lyric or a chord progression. Or maybe the producer wants to change a song of yours more drastically than you'd like. Comments about changes, if worded poorly, can sound like criticisms of your musical ideas. However, the producer is only giving his opinion. You should try to keep an open mind, because ultimately he's only trying to help improve your songs. Listening to and validating the producer's ideas will connect the two of you in a collaborative way, even if you decide that you disagree.

There's something to be said for uncompromising artistic expression, but you (the artist) need to be clear with the producer about why you don't want to change part of the song. For example, if you feel a producer's change would lose what you're trying to state as an artist, then you should stand up for your original idea. In doing so, however, you might also want to suggest a smaller or similar change that addresses the producer's concerns but stays true to your intent. That way you'll satisfy the producer and maintain your artistic expression at the same time.

There's also something to be said for connecting with your audience. If these two concerns (artist expression and audience connection) clash, it's the producer's job to inform you. Just try not to shoot the messenger—you hired the producer for his or her honest opinion and guidance.

The relationship you create with your producer will determine how well your musical vision comes across in the final product. If you spend time cultivating a solid relationship based on trust and honesty, you'll usually get much in return.

The Preproduction Process—Examples

Although there are many common themes, the process of preproduction will probably be different for each project that you work on. You'll usually need to alter your preproduction techniques to match (a) the type of music you are producing and (b) the writing/rewriting processes of the artist.

For instance, if you are producing a pop or rock band that has already written a bunch of tunes and you simply want to sift through them to find the best ones, try this technique:

1. Have the band play through every song they've written.

2. Collectively choose the best ones to record . . . that is, pick out the "singles," the must-haves, and the ones for which the band has some special attachment to or specific reason to record.

3. Sometimes, bands have songs with some great sections (e.g., an excellent chorus), but the song as a whole is not great. In this case, it's often a good strategy to have the band rework the song by building a new song around the great section. Bands do this all the time. For an example, listen to how some songs progress on the *Beatles Anthology*.

4. For each song, play through all of the instrumental parts one at a time and gradually add instruments. This process double-checks that the parts work together cohesively (melodically, harmonically, and rhythmically). For example, start with guitar and vocals, then guitar and bass, then bass and vocals, then bass and drums, then guitar and drums, then vocals and drums, then guitar, bass, and drums, and then all instruments together. Add vocal harmonies and any other instruments. Rewrite parts if there are any clashes.

Let's consider an r&b, rap, hip-hop, or electronica production. In these cases, you're often not dealing with a band in which each person plays their own instrument and creates their own part. Instead, you're working with one to three people who create most (if not all) of the tracks using their voice, matched with beats, samples, various MIDI performances, sound effects, DJs, etc. Because the writing process is different, you'll need a different preproduction technique. In this case, I recommend this technique:

1. Identify the hook, then solidify the beat. Get a great feel for each track. Rhythm is king in these styles of music. Make sure the beats work with the proposed rhythm of the lyrics or rap.

2. Add the bass groove, lyrics, or rap, and melody line or hook. Make sure these all work together tightly. As you might do with a pop or rock band, check each part against all of the others individually. Rewrite parts if there are any clashes.

3. Add vocal harmonies and any other instruments that will fill out the songs, but be careful to ensure that those additional parts don't step on any of the core instruments (drums, bass, melody, and lyrics/rap).

Even though the writing process is different in this second example, many of the same principles from the first example apply that should help open up your minds to the similarities and differences between preproduction in various musical genres.

7. HIRING HELP

In many regards, a producer acts as a project manager. Like project managers, producers create budgets and schedules, and generally make sure things are moving ahead as planned. Good managers also delegate duties in order to get things done more effectively. Hiring good help is a form of skillful delegation. If you (or the artist) can't or don't know how to do something needed for your project, consider bringing in outside talent.

As the producer, one of your primary jobs is to create a certain sound for the recording. Hiring someone for their specific vocal or instrumental ability is a very common practice in the music business. The same goes for arrangers, orchestrators, programmers, recording engineers, mix engineers, and mastering engineers. Most producers aren't capable of competently performing all of these functions by themselves, so they hire experts.

The more skills you have in these areas (e.g., instrumental abilities, arranging, or drum programming), the more you'll be able to get done on your own, which will make you more desirable to artists looking for a well-rounded producer. And there are times when you may want to try something new. For example, maybe you've never written a horn chart, but you'd really like some horn stabs in a song. Try it out when you're working on a small assignment. Starting small and working your way up to more involved projects is the way to go.

However, biting off more than you can chew might come back to hurt you in several ways. First, it might take your focus away from your other duties as a producer. Second, it might take you too long to do what you thought you could do, pushing your project off schedule. Third, what you do might not turn out very well because you didn't take the time to really learn the skill. Fourth, you may overextend yourself, causing a number of side effects (stress, tiredness, irritability) that could negatively impact the project. Any of these reasons provide additional justification to hire some help for your project.

But who should you hire? Do they have the necessary skills? Do they feel comfortable with the musical style? Have they done projects like this before? Are they easy to work with? When choosing players and singers, also consider their range and whether they can read music.

Where can you find help? Through friends, friends of friends, the *Yellow Pages*, the Internet, and local chapters of the professional unions (AFTRA and AFM). Mostly I try to use my friends or other acquaintances. Sometimes I just search the 'Net for musicians, arrangers, or other artists. The 'Net is also useful for finding bandmates, used gear or instruments, and musical services. Better yet, some Web sites list their entries by geographical location, making it easier to find people close by. A non-exhaustive list of Web sites I've found to be helpful is located in appendix B.

If you're thinking of working with someone you've never worked with before, I recommend getting demos. If they have a good demo, meet them in person to see what they're like. Play them demos of your project to give them an idea of where you're heading and to get a feel for what they think of the music. It always helps to hire folks who will enjoy the music they'll be making.

8. SCHEDULING REHEARSAL, RECORDING, AND MIXING SESSIONS

At some point you'll need to book time in a professional studio. Maybe you'll need to record a full drum set but your neighbors or roommates won't be cool with hearing death metal grooves for hours. Or maybe you'll go all-out and record a full orchestra! Whatever your needs, book your time well in advance and at a reputable studio. Call around to compare rates and available times. You should also visit potential studios to meet the people you'd be working with and see their equipment and recording room.

Be sure that the recording studio has the right equipment for your recording needs. Most professional studios have a variety of equipment . . . everything that you need to capture your brilliance. But don't assume that. Call the studio and make sure all the equipment you need is there and in working order.

Finally, as a producer you're responsible for everyone showing up to rehearsals, recording sessions, and mixing sessions. When scheduling the dates and times for these events, be sure to verify that those who need to be are available before you set the date in stone. This seems obvious, but you'll never need to be reminded again after the first time you have to make twenty-five calls to reschedule a session, because you wrongly assumed the drummer could make it.

9. REHEARSING

It is a given that rehearsing songs before the sessions will improve the recordings. One of my drum teachers once told me that practice makes permanent; rehearsals serve to solidify the song's arrangement (feel, form, and attitude) in the artist's memory. The better the artist knows the song, the easier it will be to record. However, too much time spent rehearsing a song can kill its freshness and energy. To capture the best recordings, you must find the balance between rehearsing too little and too much.

I recommend recording all rehearsals, even if only on cassette. In so doing, you can separate yourself from the energy of the rehearsal and listen carefully, without being influenced by the live performance. You can gain a lot of information by listening back to these recordings before the actual session. It may also be useful to play rehearsal tapes for other people (friends, family, other musicians) to get their feedback. I often record rehearsals digitally, then create MP3s of the recordings and send them to the members of the group the day after the rehearsal. Here are some other reasons to record rehearsals:

- You can figure out if the agreed upon arrangements are working. For example, maybe you'll hear that the four extra bars you added after the bridge interrupt the flow of the song.

- You can analyze the parts individually. For example, maybe you'll find that the bass line is too busy.

- You can identify areas where "ear candy" can be added. For example, maybe you'll hear a small section of the song that needs an additional guitar lick to fill a space. Or maybe you'll imagine a sound effect panning back and forth through the stereo field during a particular section. This kind of work can be the most exciting and satisfying part of being a producer.

> *Take Note!*
> Even in free-form jazz recordings—where spontaneity and improvisation are fundamental elements of the music—it's beneficial for the musicians to play together before the recording sessions to get a feel for the energy of the songs, and to create group synergy.

- Or . . . you may find you're happy with the work you did prior to the rehearsal and are satisfied with everything. This means you are ready to record!

If you're rehearsing in your studio, it's a good idea to record directly into the recording device. Sometimes rehearsals have the best energy, because everyone's relaxed and not worried about performing perfectly, as they might have to for a recording session. The performances are often quite good, and if you mic everything well but keep the pressure of recording to a minimum, you might capture a performance you can keep. Even if you grab just a small section of "keeper" material (like a cool drum loop or guitar lick), it still can be very valuable.

10. GETTING READY FOR THE RECORDING SESSIONS

The producer has several concerns in the final days before a recording session. The first is connecting with everyone who's a part of the session: This means calling, e-mailing, paging, faxing, writing a message in the sky . . . anything it takes to make contact with the participants, remind them of the session, and confirm that they'll be there. Musicians—maybe even more so than other people—forget things. They lose messages, phone numbers, and directions. They get distracted and lose track of time. If you haven't experienced this, then consider yourself lucky. . . . I've worked with several fantastic musicians who don't wear a watch or carry a planner or Palm Pilot. Multiple calls to these types of folks are a necessity. When you're working with a close-knit bunch of musicians, this may not be as much of an issue because they'll talk to each other often. However, if you're working with folks who spread themselves pretty thin (like most talented people) communication about scheduled events is imperative.

The second main concern in the final days is that you discuss the upcoming session with the recording engineer ahead of time. Talking about the session beforehand will greatly improve the efficiency of the session because the engineer can prepare everything before you arrive. If you're the producer and engineer for the session, then discussion may not be necessary (unless you like talking to yourself)—but planning is still a must.

Your third concern as producer is creating a plan of action for the recording session. This plan begins with the three items you discussed with the engineer (see previous paragraph and chapter 6). It also includes creating a rough timetable for what you'd like to get done and how you'd like to do it. For example:

6:00	Set up instruments and mics
7:00	Begin to get sounds
7:30	Run through Song 1 to warm up
8:00	Have first take of Song 1 . . . and so on

This plan should be as flexible as possible. Flexibility allows for new ideas and mistakes—both of which are common occurrences in a fertile and imperfect recording environment.

If you do all of the preproduction steps suggested above, you'll definitely be prepared for a great recording session. ■

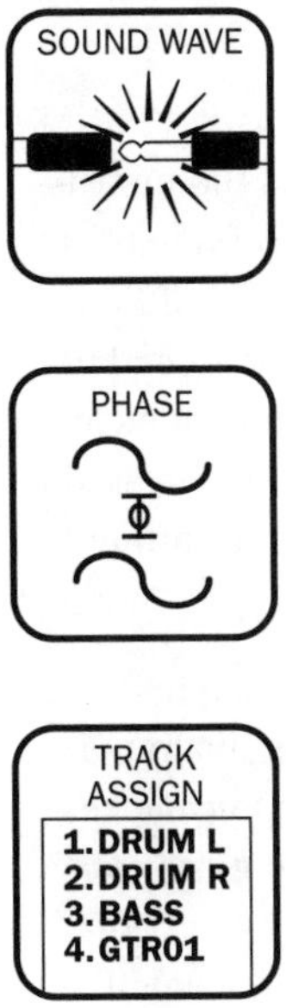
SOUND WAVE
PHASE
TRACK ASSIGN
1. DRUM L
2. DRUM R
3. BASS
4. GTR01

CHAPTER 6
The Engineer's Role in Preproduction

In this chapter:

- Studio and equipment setup
- Microphone basics and phase cancellation
- Making track assignments
- Additional engineering duties

Now that you know what goes into preproduction from a producer's standpoint, let's look at things from a more tangible and technical perspective—as an engineer.

During production, an engineer's responsibilities are about preparation: studio setup, equipment setup, and track assignments.

Studio setup involves decisions about where instruments will be placed and where the players will be situated in your recording space. Equipment setup includes choosing microphones, amps, headphones, and effects, and checking that the equipment is in good working order. Track assignments refers to determining how many tracks you're going to record and how you want to record them. The number of tracks may be limited by the number of mics you have, the number of physical inputs, or the number of tracks you can use.

Studio Setup

The first step when preparing for a recording session is to plan how you'll use your studio space. Some questions to ask yourself include: What is the instrumentation of the session? Do I need sound separation, isolation, or baffling of some sort? Do the musicians need to see each other? Where can the musicians stand or sit comfortably? Does the studio need some special acoustical treatment for the session?

While you're considering these questions you might try sketching diagrams of possible setups to help you visualize how the studio will look with everyone in it. I've included a sketch (fig. 6.1) of a session I engineered once in a small apartment . . . we recorded drums, electric guitar, acoustic bass, keyboards, and scratch vocals all at once in my home studio at the time.

Scratch Lead Vocals
L out
R out
KEYS
Recording Device
Closet
Blankets
GOBO
GOBO
Guitar Amp
GUITAR
DRUMS
Snare
Overhead L
Kick
Overhead R
Blanket on door (to absorb drum reflections)
Door
GOBO
Hallway
ACOUSTIC BASS
= microphone

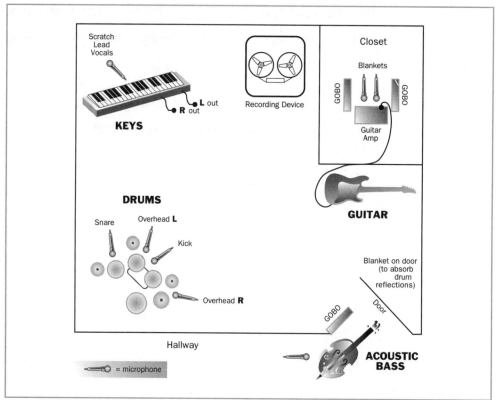

Fig. 6.1. A small one-room studio setup with the guitar amp in the closet, the standup bass in the hallway, the drums in one corner, and the keys/vocals in the adjacent corner. This setup facilitated eye contact among members of the band and provided enough sound separation to record great tracks.

Sound Separation

In multi-track recording, we usually try to isolate sounds as best we can to have more control over the mix. That is, if the guitar is isolated from the drums, we can put effects on the guitar track without changing the drum sound. But if there's a lot of leakage from the drums into the guitar track, then whatever effect we put on the guitar will show up to some degree on the drums. There are several techniques engineers use to achieve sound separation, often utilized in combination.

The first technique is microphone placement—aiming mics at only one source is the key. For example, if you're recording a drum kit, pointing the hi-hat mic away from the snare drum will decrease the amount of snare leakage on the hi-hat track.

The second technique is physical separation of the instruments from each other, which provides greater isolation for their tracks. For example, as you see in fig. 6.1, I put the guitar amp in the closet. This physically separated the loud amp so its mics picked up far less of the other instruments, and vice versa.

Engineers also use a variety of devices to achieve sound separation and isolation. One such device is a moveable wall called a "gobo," which is usually smooth on one side and carpeted on the other. The smooth side provides reflections, while the carpeted side absorbs sound. You can make your own gobos using common items: I have used the front and back covers from my equipment rack and some large pieces of wood, and sometimes even my mattress! Plexiglas shields/walls are also used, but they can cause a lot of reflections. On the plus side, they're transparent—so people can see through them. Blankets can be used to cover reflective surfaces as well as isolate instruments. They're good for absorbing sound, and I often use them on pianos and around guitar amps.

Ideally, multi-track recording captures the best sound of instruments playing together while keeping those great sounds (tracks) separate from each other.

You also need to consider how many mic/line cables, microphones, mic stands, headphones, and headphone extension cables you'll need for the session, because your access to these items may influence the setup. For those of us on tight budgets, creative setups are the only way to maximize our equipment while minimizing expenses. Regardless, when it comes right down to it, you may have to buy some extra equipment to make sure sessions go smoothly and sound good.

Even with planning, there are still many last-minute contingencies that will require a flexible setup. The musical lineup may change, and you'll have to record unexpected instruments. Or the band may have a particular requirement. For example, the bass player and the drummer may ask to be next to each other, even though it would work better for you if they were across the room. To help accommodate sudden changes like these, you might want to sketch several scenarios ahead of time. Because the fundamental role of the engineer is to capture a great performance, you need to do everything in your power not to impede the performance. It's like the Hippocratic oath doctors have to take: "First, do no harm."

If you're only recording yourself, one instrument at a time, then you won't need to worry about sound separation at all. However, once you start recording multiple instruments at one time in the same room, studio setups and mic placement become important.

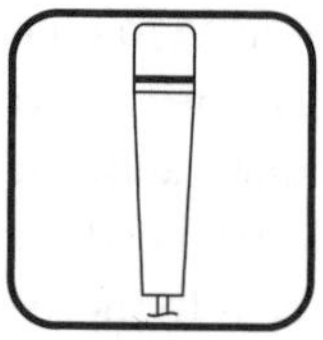

Equipment Setup: Microphones

Once you've considered your studio setup, you'll need to think about what equipment you'll use during the session—many engineers start with microphones. If you have a limited number of mics, your choices might be out of necessity, or you may have mics you always use for specific applications (for example, a Shure SM57 on the guitar amp). Either way, the more mics you have, the more interesting and creative the decision-making process becomes.

Microphone Basics

When choosing a mic, consider its polar pickup pattern(s), frequency response, whether it has a pad or rolloff, its mic type, and whether it needs phantom power. Some mics are better suited, or at least more commonly used, for certain applications. Knowing this information will help you choose wisely. Ultimately it will help you record better sounds.

Microphone polar patterns range from omni-directional to super-cardioid (very uni-directional). The patterns (shown in fig. 6.2) indicate from what direction the mic receives audio signals.

An omni-directional mic receives audio signals from all directions, whereas cardioid microphones (including hyper-cardioid and super-cardioid) receive the majority of their signal from one direction only. Bi-directional (or figure-8) mics pick up audio signal from the front and back of the mic while rejecting sounds from the side. In addition, if you look at the specifications of any mic you own you'll notice that the polar pattern is slightly altered at different frequencies. For example, all mics, even omni-directional mics, tend to become more directional when picking up high frequencies (see example in fig. 6.3). Consult your

0°
0 dB
10 dB
20 dB
30°
60°
90°
120°
150°
180°
210°
240°
270°
300°
330°
Omni-Directional
Figure-8
Cardioid
Supercardioid
Hypercardioid

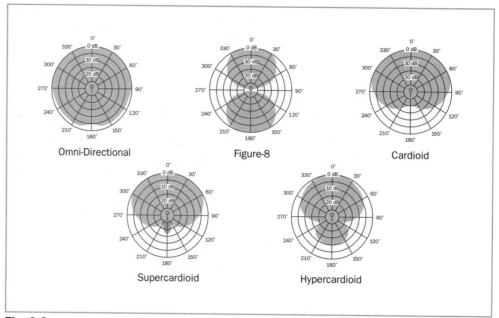

Fig. 6.2. Microphone pickup patterns. A mic's pickup pattern affects how much "clean" sound, room ambience, and bleed from other instruments are captured by the mics.

microphone's user guide for more information about its polar pattern.

The directionality of a microphone can help determine its use in a recording session. Typically, directional mics are used to pick up one sound source at a time, whereas omni-directional mics are often used as room mics—to pick up everything. Most mics have only one pattern, however some allow you to switch between several.

Condenser, dynamic, ribbon, and electret are the most common types of mics. And of those, you'll use condenser and dynamic mics for most applications. Condenser mics require phantom power and are fragile, whereas dynamic mics are more rugged and don't need phantom power. Phantom power is a 48 V current that powers condenser mics, but it won't hurt dynamic mics. Ribbon mics—which use ribbons to pick up acoustic audio signals— are the most fragile and can be destroyed if given phantom power, so be careful! Your recording device may actually provide phantom power to its microphone inputs. Otherwise, phantom power can be supplied by a mixer or, in few cases, by a battery pack that comes with the microphone.

Knowing the frequency response of a mic will help you choose the right application for it, as well. In this case, frequency response refers to a microphone's ability to pick up a certain frequency range. Some mics are designed to primarily pick up bass frequencies (20 Hz to 800 Hz), while others are better for middle frequencies (800 Hz to 8 kHz) or high frequencies (8 kHz to 20 kHz). For example, the Shure Beta 52 is specifically designed to capture bass frequencies, but the Shure SM57 has a boost in its mid range. So you see, it's no coincidence that professional engineers use the Beta 52 on kick drums and the SM57 on snare—the frequencies those drums produce align with the best areas of response for those mics. Condenser mics usually have flat response curves, whereas dynamic mics have some peaks and valleys. Check out the frequency response curves for the KSM44 (condenser) and the SM57 (dynamic) in fig. 6.4.

Some mics have bass rolloff, bass cutoff, and pad switches. A bass rolloff switch is a low-frequency filter that can help reduce unwanted background noise (such as the low hum of an air conditioner) or counteract proximity effect. A cutoff switch is just an extreme version of a rolloff switch;

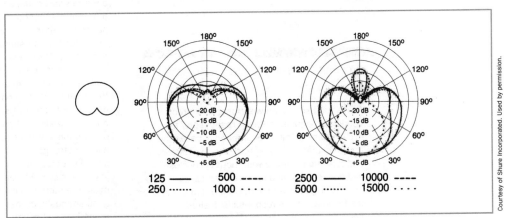

Courtesy of Shure Incorporated. Used by permission.

Fig. 6.3. The cardioid polar pattern at different frequencies for Shure's KSM44. This microphone also has settings for omni-directional and figure-8 patterns.

KSM44
+10
15 cm.
dB
0
60 cm.
-10
20 50 100 1000 10000 20000
Hz
SM57
RELATIVE RESPONSE IN dB
+10
0
-10
20 50 100 1000 10000 20000
FREQUENCY IN HERTZ
TYPICAL FREQUENCY RESPONSE

Courtesy of Shure Incorporated. Used by permission.

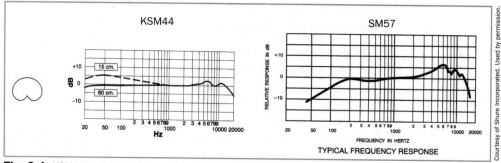

Fig. 6.4. KSM44 and SM57 frequency response curves.

it tries to eliminate lower frequencies. For example, the KSM44 has a three-position bass rolloff switch: you can choose flat response (no rolloff), low-frequency cutoff, which provides an 18 dB-per-octave cutoff at 80 Hz, or low-frequency rolloff, which provides a 6 dB-per-octave rolloff filter at 115 Hz. (See fig. 6.5.)

+5
0
dB
-10
20 50 100 2 3 4 5 6 789 1000
Hz
Flat Response
Low-Frequency Cutoff
Low-Frequency Rolloff

Courtesy of Shure Incorporated. Used by permission.

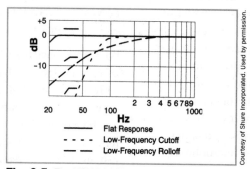

Fig. 6.5. The KSM44 offers three bass rolloff settings.

Proximity Effect: Please Stand Too Close to Me

As a sound source moves closer to a directional microphone, the bass response of the mic increases. This phenomenon is called the proximity effect. To hear this, set up a mic and talk into it—move your mouth very close and notice the sound is more bass heavy than when you're off the mic a bit. Sometimes the increased bass response is desired, however, a mic's bass rolloff switch can help reduce the proximity effect if you don't want it. Another way to get rid of proximity effect is to lower the EQ gain at around 200 Hz.

A pad switch attenuates the incoming signal, preventing extremely high signals from overloading and damaging the microphone. For example, the KSM44's pad is –15 dB. This reduces signal level at the mic by 15 dB without altering frequency response. Most mixers have pads too. Press the pad button to help reduce the incoming signal strength so that the input signal doesn't overload the preamp.

Experiment with Mic Placements and Mic Choices

Probably the best way to learn how to capture great sounds is to experiment with different microphones and placements on several different instruments. Try putting mics close to the sound source, then move them away. Record new sounds and note the sonic differences. Angle the mics differently and point them at different parts of the instrument. Try combinations of mics on a sound source. Use the different polar patterns, pads, and bass rolloff settings on your mics, if they have them. Try putting mics in strange places, away from the sound source, even behind a barrier or inside of a box. The better you know your mics, the more you'll know how to capture good sounds with them, and the better your recordings will sound.

Take Note!

Every time you record a track with a microphone, phase interaction occurs between the direct and the reflected sound from the room. This phase interaction gives your studio its own distinctive sonic vibe.

Acoustical Phase Cancellation

Microphone frequency response can depend on the mic's surroundings and its relationship with a closely positioned mic. When two or more sound waves of the same frequency arrive at a point in space at the same time, an effect called phase cancellation can occur. If the sound waves are out of phase, some frequencies will be cut or even completely lost. How does this happen?

Acoustical phase refers to the time relationship between two or more sound waves and where those waves are in their wavelength cycles. This means that when two sound waves of the same frequency come together at the exact same time, the amplitudes of the waves will add to each other. Depending on the phase of each wave, you will hear either a boost or a cut in the frequency. Figs. 6.6 and 6.7 show the results of two sine waves added together that are in phase and out of phase.

Amplitude
+
Amplitude
=
Amplitude
Time
Time
Time

Fig. 6.6. When two sound waves are in phase, the amplitude (or sound output) is boosted. If they're perfectly in phase, the amplitude is doubled.

Amplitude
+
Amplitude
=
Amplitude
Time
Time
Time

Fig. 6.7. Phase cancellation occurs when a particular frequency arrives at a mic at the same time as the out-of-phase version of the same frequency. Here, we see that the sound wave has been completely cancelled out.

Fortunately, most sound waves are much more complex than sine waves and thus aren't as easy to eliminate. However, partial phase cancellation does occur more often than complete phase cancellation and is more difficult to hear. To detect phase cancellation on an input, listen for unequal low- and low-mid frequency response or an unstable or washy quality to the sound.

Phase cancellation can also occur with a single mic in a reverberant environment. The mic will pick up the original signal, plus a quick reflection of the signal from the wall, floor, or ceiling. If you find that a mic is picking up less low end than expected, cover the reverberant surface with some sort of absorptive material, such as blankets or carpet.

Phase cancellation happens more often between two microphones. To rectify this situation, be sure to follow the three-to-one (3:1) rule. That is, microphones should be placed no closer together than three times the distance between one of them and the sound source. For example, if a mic is one foot from a sound source, another mic shouldn't be placed within three feet of the first microphone. A common application of the 3:1 rule is shown in fig. 6.8 for a pair of overhead mics used on cymbals.

3'
microphone
1'
1'

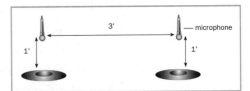

Fig. 6.8. Follow the 3:1 rule to avoid phase cancellation between two mics.

Phase cancellation can also be an issue when miking the top and bottom head of a drum. I often use a top and bottom mic on snare drums and find that, depending on their positioning, I usually need to flip the phase of the bottom mic. Flipping the

Take Note!

Phase cancellation may not be apparent when listening in stereo. Listening in mono—that is, merging the left and right channel into a single signal—sums the stereo sound waves and helps identify the problem . . . often a good idea to try while mixing.

phase inverts the amplitude of the sound wave, as seen in fig. 6.9. You may also find phase cancellation due to improper wiring in the microphone itself or in the mic cable.

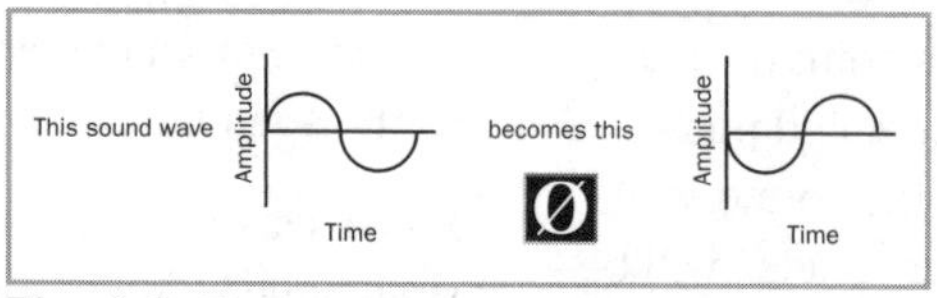
This sound wave
Amplitude
Time
becomes this
Ø
Amplitude
Time

Fig. 6.9. Flipping the phase. Phase flip buttons come standard on many recording devices and mixers.

Regardless of mic specifications, you should experiment with your microphones. Try using them in different positions, on different instruments, and with different effects and EQ settings. You'll learn much more about the nuances of each mic and how unique it sounds, as well as develop some new techniques that will become part of your "sound."

Equipment Setup: Other Gear

You'll also need to choose which amplifiers, outboard effects units, compressors, and other tools to use in the session. This might be easy if you don't have any of this gear, but if you do have choices, plan it out just as you would with microphones and the rest of your studio setup.

You'll need the right cables, and you'll want to be clear on the routing of the audio signals. I recommend labeling everything—put tape labels on all cables, effects units, etc., and on your inputs and outputs. Then, if you have to change something midway through a session, it will be much faster to find what you're looking for. This can really save you when you're in the middle of a recording session and the artist or producer unexpectedly asks you to route a signal through a new piece of gear he bought today (see fig. 6.10).

You should also create a list of everything you'll need for the session, as in fig. 6.11. This includes mics, mic stands, mic cables, pop filters, instrument cables, headphones, headphone extension cables, and instrument stands and music stands. Also included are any instruments and instrument supplies (guitar strings, drum sticks, etc.) as well as other hardware you'll need, such as amplifiers, monitors, and outboard effects processors. The artist, producer, and engineer need to work together on the list so that everyone has what they need.

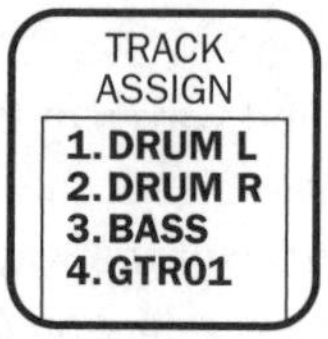
TRACK
ASSIGN
1. DRUM L
2. DRUM R
3. BASS
4. GTR01

Track Assignments

When recording using a finite number of inputs and tracks, you and the producer need to think about how you're going to allocate these to the instruments. For example, you may have a recording device that only allows a maximum of four inputs. If you want to record an entire drum set on those four tracks, how do you do it? One track for the kick, one for the snare, and two for the overheads (including cymbals and toms)? What if you also want to record an electric guitar and bass at the same time? You might create a submix of the drums on your mixer, then use one track for the guitar, one for the bass, and two tracks (panned left and right) for the drums.

Even if you're using a large multi-track recorder or a software package with many inputs and almost unlimited tracks, you're still often limited to a certain input amount due to physical track space constraints or computer processing power. Track "real estate" and processing power gets eaten up fast if you're not careful. I recommend creating a track sheet that lists all the tracks you intend to record on the song (see fig. 6.12).

I/O CONNECTIONS
In
Out
L R
Mic/Line/Gear/Instrument
S/PDIF
In
Out
Inputs
Mon
Outputs
Optical
1 3 5 7
2 4 6 8
L 1 3 5 7
R 2 4 6 8
8 7 6 5 4 3 2 1
Inputs
Outputs

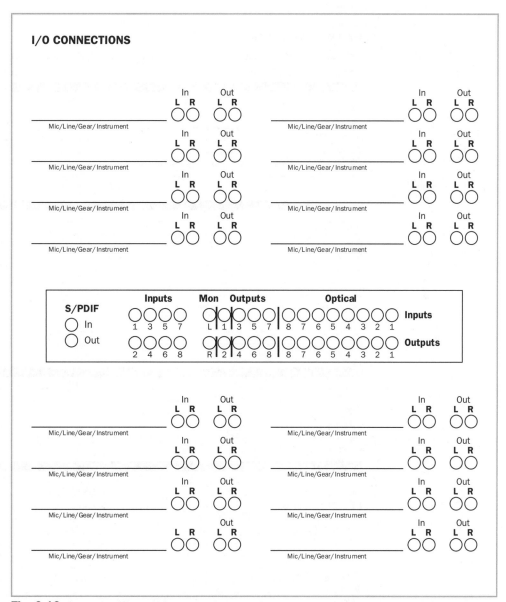

Fig. 6.10. A sample I/O connection sheet. Make a template like this for your gear to keep track of your equipment setup.

EQUIPMENT NEEDED LIST

Date	1/18/2004

Artist	Go Figure	Project Title	Three Song Demo
Producer(s)	Andrew Stern/David Franz	Engineer(s)	David Franz

CABLES

Type	# Needed	Notes
Mic cables	14	
Mic cable snakes	2	8 cables each
Guitar/instrument cables	6	
RCA cables	2	For turntables
Headphone extension cables	8	

MICROPHONES

Type	# Needed	Notes
All studio mics	All	
AKG 535	1	For bass (borrow)
Neumann U87	1	For vocals (borrow)
AT 4050	1	For vocals (borrow)

STANDS

Type	# Needed	Notes
Regular	6	
Boom	10	
Mini	4	

ADDITIONAL EQUIPMENT AND SUPPLIES

Item	# Needed	Notes
Pop filters	3	
Guitar & banjo strings	3 pairs	
Drum sticks	5 pairs	
Turntable needles	2	
Clarinet reeds	1 box	
Mic preamp	3	Rental
Headphones (studio)	all	
Guitar amp (special)	1	Borrow
DI boxes	3	

Fig. 6.11. Equipment Needed List. Planning ahead helps you make sure you've got what you need for a recording session.

TRACK ASSIGNMENTS

Song Title: Come N' Get It   Artist: The Cool Grape Goodness

Producer: David Franz   Engineer: Simon Heselev

Track Name	#	Intro	Verse 1	Chorus 1	V2	C2	Bridge	B2	C3	C4	Outro	#
Kick	1	Kick →										1
Snare Top	2	Snare Top →										2
Snare Bot	3	Snare Bot →										3
Hihat	4	Hihat →										4
Hi Tom	5	Hi Tom →										5
Mid Tom	6	Mid Tom →										6
Lo Tom	7	Lo Tom →										7
Overhead L	8	Overhead L →										8
Overhead R	9	Overhead R →										9
Room L	10	Room L →										10
Room R	11	Room R →										11
Bass	12	Bass →										12
B-3 L	13	B-3 L →										13
B-3 R	14	B-3 R →										14
Guitar L	15	Guitar L →										15
Guitar R	16	Guitar R →										16
Gtr Riff	17	Intro Riff								Main Riff	Outro Lick	17
Grt Solo	18	Lead Vox →								Riff harm	Gtr Solo	18
Lead Vox	19											19
Back Vox	20		Back Vox			Back Vox				Yeahs		20
Rap	21						Rap			Yells		21
Rap Backs	22						Rap Backs			Yells		22
DJ L	23	Sample	Loop	Sample	Loop	Sample						23
DJ R	24	Sample	Loop	Sample	Loop	Sample						24

Fig. 6.12. A track sheet for "Come'N Get It." Documentation is an important part of an engineer's role in the production process.

If you think you might come close to filling all of your available tracks, consider submixing and bouncing logical instrument groupings to free up tracks for additional overdubs. This subject is fully explained in chapters 7 and 13.

Additional Engineering Duties

There are several other duties an engineer should perform in preparation for a recording session. If you're recording material that's unfamiliar to you, consider going to a rehearsal or live show—that way, you'll understand what the music sounds like before you mic it. Also consider recording the rehearsal or show as a reference. (If the artist is rehearsing in your studio, it's especially good to record. You might get lucky and be able to keep a great take.) If you can't do any of this, try to get your hands on previous recordings of the music or other material from the artist.

The Recording Medium

There are also some clerical things to take care of before engineering a session. Make sure you have an adequate amount of the necessary recording medium, be that analog tape, cassettes, digital storage devices, or hard drive space. With analog and digital tape, the only option outside

Take Note!

VU stands for Volume Units. A VU meter measures average signal levels.

Take Note!

Always make backups! Tapes get lost or erased, computers crash, and hard drives die. As the engineer, backups are your responsibility. Clients and musicians aren't fond of "the dog ate my files" excuse, nor do they care if the latest version of your OS is buggy, or if there was a freak electrical storm in your studio during the session. If the files are lost, it's your fault. (Ok, I'll get off my soapbox now.)

of buying more tape is to record over old recordings. However, if you don't have enough hard drive space, there are several things you can do to increase the space on the drives you already have:

1. Defragment your hard drive to eliminate holes in its storage. Defragmenting is like compacting trash: All of your files are pushed together, making room for more. Consult your computer's operating system manual or the specific defragmenting software's manual for instructions on how to do this and understand any risks to your files.
2. Eliminate unneeded files from your hard drive. Instead of trashing them outright, you should probably write them onto another storage medium (CD-R, CD-RW, DVD-RAM, DAT, tape backup systems, etc.), especially if you haven't made backup copies yet.
3. If the two options above aren't available, you can either use fewer tracks than you intended or purchase another hard drive. This isn't desirable if you're on a budget, but it may be necessary to get the job done (and external hard drives are increasingly affordable).

If you're working with a tape machine (any tape machine—analog or digital), it's a really good idea to perform the necessary maintenance on the recording device. For analog tape machines, demagnetize (degauss) and then clean the tape transport mechanisms. For cassette recorders and digital recorders, use the proper cleaning tapes for these devices . . . but not too often. The cleaning tapes contain abrasive material that, if overused, can damage the tape mechanisms.

Recording reference tones to your analog or digital tape is also a smart idea. A reference tone is a sine wave used to calibrate the levels in your studio equipment and recording device. Your recording device or mixer may have an oscillator to produce these tones, or you can pick up an inexpensive tone oscillator at your local electronics store. The idea is to play a reference tone at nominal level through the entire signal path on all tracks and make sure the levels all register the same level. Then you adjust the tape recorder input accordingly so that they receive the optimal signal level. For analog gear, we can use a level of 0 Volume Units (always abbreviated VU) for this calibration. In the digital realm, a level of –12 dB is usually used for calibration, since 0 in the digital scale is at the very top and would sound rather nasty. Then, record about 30 seconds of 1 kHz tone and play the tape back to observe whether the output levels come back at the same nominal level. For analog tape, also record 30 seconds of 100 Hz and 10 kHz (separately) to check the accuracy of the low- and high-frequency playback. These extra two tones are not necessary to record on digital tape, because the frequency on digital tape is usually very accurate and doesn't need to be calibrated. The whole point of calibration is to make sure your inputs and outputs are operating at good and consistent levels. It is also helpful if you want to take your tape to another studio. That studio can be calibrated from the tones on your tape to ensure the most accurate reproduction of your recorded material.

Finally, you should know whom to contact if you have problems with your system. Be ready with the technical support phone numbers for any important piece of gear in your studio. Make friends with local music store salesmen who handle studio problems regularly. Seek out people with systems similar to yours, ask each other questions, and if necessary, get immediate help in times of need (like when you're "on the clock" during a session). Some people find it rewarding to start local user groups for their recording devices. Also, find resources on the Internet that cover your specific gear. There's tons of information out there.

If you plan your studio setup, equipment setup, and track assignments, and perform additional engineering duties before the recording session, you'll be prepared for a smooth recording experience. Your producer (or the producer in you) will be very pleased . . . it never hurts to impress the boss! ■

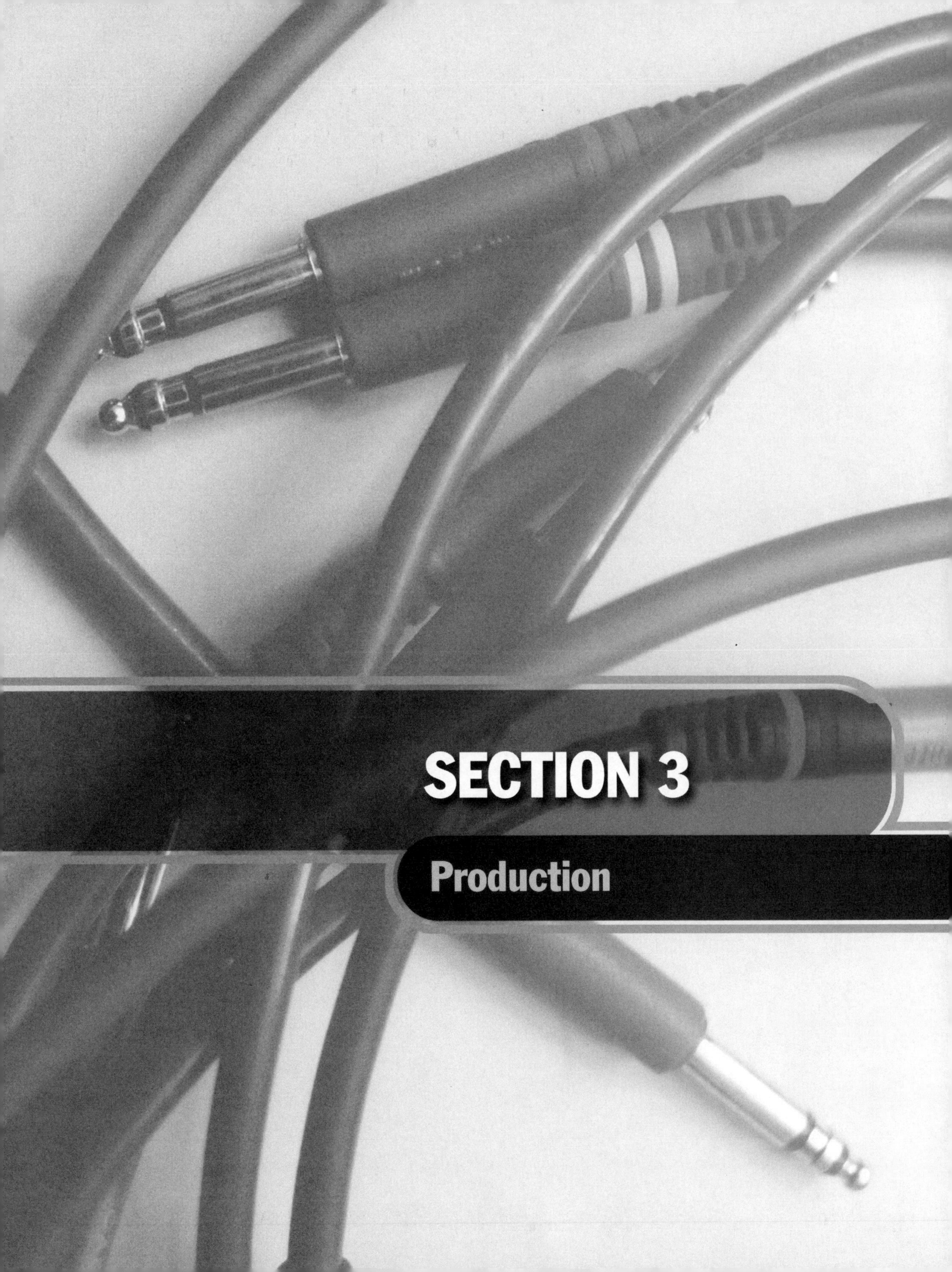

SECTION 3

Production

CHAPTER 7
Recording and Engineering Techniques, Part I

In this chapter:

- Duties of the recording engineer during a recording session

- Types of recording sessions

- Microphones

- Essential recording techniques

- Advanced recording techniques

Here we start the "production" stage of the production process—all of the elements involved in capturing musical performances during recording sessions. Now is the time to see if all the preproduction work pays off.

Most people consider the engineer's primary responsibilities during a recording session to be technical in nature, however, engineers must also deal with musical issues (e.g., listening to the tuning of the guitar) and personal issues (e.g., making the vocalist feel comfortable) in the session. In this chapter and the following one, I'll discuss in detail what an engineer does in a recording session, describing many of the concepts and techniques fundamental to having a successful session. I'll start with explaining the types of recording sessions and then give an example that demonstrates many of the things that happen in a typical session. Then I'll delve into specifics about how to do each part of an engineer's job during a recording session, focusing on recording techniques here and covering the other engineering duties in chapter 8.

The engineer has many responsibilities during a recording session:

1. Setting up microphones: choice, placement, and adjustments

2. Establishing sound separation: setting up gobos, baffles, and blankets for isolation

3. Setting up and working with the recording device and medium

4. Routing signals and getting good recording levels

5. Recording the artist

6. Troubleshooting: computer, equipment, signal path, etc.

7. Creating and adjusting the headphone mix and click track

8. Managing outboard equipment and syncing gear when necessary

9. Setting up effects and printing effects on tracks

10. Constantly attending to the artist's and producer's needs

11. Overdubbing and submixing

12. Creating a good rough mix

TYPES OF RECORDING SESSIONS

Typically, several recording sessions are needed to capture all of the tracks for a song. The first tracking session, often called the "basics session," is commonly used to record rhythm section instruments, such as drums, bass, and guitar. This creates a rhythmic and harmonic foundation and helps the rhythm section build a dynamic groove. The other instruments (including voice) might play or sing along with the rhythm section, but they're usually recorded later. Loop-based music often follows this convention, as well, building songs from drum loops and bass grooves first, then adding other tracks, such as lead vocals and instrumental solos, in overdub sessions. Often, overdubs are recorded one at a time and can take as long or longer than recording the basic tracks, especially if you're recording lead vocals.

Once the overdubs are finished, "sweetening" tracks are recorded to fill out the song or add a special sound. Horns, strings, and backing vocals are examples of sweetening and are called this because they're not the main instrumental or vocal parts. Sweetening tracks shouldn't interfere with the main tracks—especially the lead vocal or instrument—but can augment them in a number of ways.

Of course, you don't need to record your projects in this order. Sometimes I build my songs around an acoustic guitar played to a click track, then overdub drums and bass. I've even built tracks starting with just an *a cappella* vocal with no click track. Regardless of how you build a song in the recording sessions, you (as the engineer) perform many of the same tasks in any type of recording session.

An Example Recording Session

Let's say you're working with a four-piece band made up of drums, bass, guitar, and vocals. The first recording session is tonight in your studio. You've done all the preproduction preparation, making sure your equipment is working, and the studio is set up as much as possible before the musicians arrive.

The band arrives at 6:00 P.M. You greet everyone, offer them a beverage, and suggest locations for their instruments. While the drummer is getting set up, you arrange the room and construct temporary sound separation for the guitar and bass amps. Then, you start setting up mics, placing a mic in front of the each bass and guitar amp, and setting up a mic and stand for the vocalist.

Once the drummer is set up, you place all the mics around the drums . . . making sure all of the mic signals for all instruments are routed to the right places. You begin to check the incoming recording levels and sounds by having each musician play their instrument, testing one mic at a time. Then, you record a little of the band, play it back, and listen to the quality of the sounds. If anything isn't sounding good, you adjust the mic, alter the input signal path, or add or replace gear.

Once you have all instruments sounding good, you create a headphone mix for everyone, running headphone cables to each musician. You might decide to add effects to the headphone mix, such as putting reverb on the vocal track, or add inline processing to an instrument's signal path, such as putting the bass signal through a compressor before it's recorded. Then, you set up the click track if necessary. You ask the band to play again with the click, so you can tweak the headphone mix. After asking for and acting on the band member's feedback about the headphone mix and their instrument sounds, you're ready to record.

Once you've recorded some material, the band or producer might want to go back and overdub a part. That is, you either fix something that was already recorded or add something that hasn't been recorded yet. After you've finished recording for the night, you might make a rough mix of the songs and give it to the band and the producer to take home and evaluate.

This is a common example of a "basics" recording session. Let's delve into some of the methods an engineer uses to capture great sounds during a recording session. We'll start with microphone recording techniques.

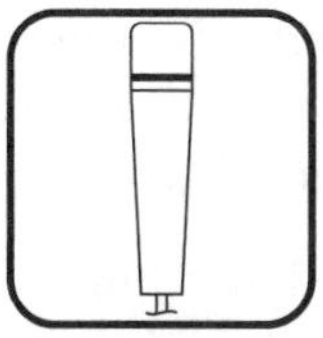

Mic Choice and Placement

Choosing the right mic and putting it in the right place to capture a great sound is an art in itself. There are no recipes for doing this, and many times you have to improvise or compromise, depending on your mic selection and available space. However, if the source sounds great before you even put the mic up, more than half of your work is already done. It's then your job to not screw it up.

There is an infinite number of ways to mic instruments. Everyone has their own techniques and you'll develop yours over time. The techniques I describe below are simply a few that I've learned or created—none of them should be considered the only approach.

Microphones in Digital Recording

When recording to analog tape, engineers often choose microphones that have increased high-frequency response to help deal with the loss of those frequencies during analog reproduction—particularly during mastering and duplication. Digital recording doesn't automatically lose high frequencies on playback, so using microphones with boosted highs could make your recordings biting and shrill. I recommend using mics with smooth high-frequency response when recording to a digital recording device.

Recording Drums

Regardless of what you're recording, I recommend listening to the sound source before you put up a single mic—to see what you have to work with. With drums, some of the issues to consider include: drum heads, tuning, dampening, noises such as rattles, squeaks, and buzzes, cymbal choice, and the drummer's playing style and genre of music.

First, listen to the drum's heads. Are they new heads or do they sound dead? New heads can substantially improve the sound of almost any drum, and are usually a good investment before important sessions.

Second, listen to the drum tuning. Is the snare tight (or loose) enough for the sound you want? Is the kick sound deep enough? Are the toms (and kick) tuned to specific pitches that correlate with the key of the song? Try to tune drums so they fit with the particular song you're recording. For example, when recording a song in the key of E, I often tune my high tom to B, my middle tom to A, and my floor tom to E. (If the key of the song is E and the kick is inadvertently tuned to E-flat, the results can be ugly.) The tighter the snare is tuned, the crisper it will sound when recorded. Or, you might prefer a deeper sound from a snare head that's a little looser. As an engineer you should own a drum key in case the drummer forgets theirs, because tuning can make all the difference when recording percussion. The sad fact is that many drummers don't even know how to tune their kits. It is an art and is not easy. Knowing how to tune drums is a very valuable engineering skill. There are resources online about tuning techniques. Check them out and practice the art . . . and your value as an engineer will increase dramatically!

When I record drums I also put a weight in the kick drum. You can use something like a brick or a weight from that old bench-press set you bought ten years'ago. The weight anchors the kick drum, which gives it an unexplainable solidity and seems to add depth and strength to the sound. It also holds dampening material in place.

Third, consider dampening any drum that's producing an ugly ring or that decays too slowly. Use a little tape, a cotton pad with some tape, a Zeroring plastic head ring strip (from Noble and Cooley), Moongel Damper Pads (from RTOM), a cloth strip, or even your wallet, on any toms or snare, and use a pillow or blanket that touches the head(s) of the kick. Be careful, though. Dampening a drum can take away a lot of its character and easily make it sound worse than it did before you tried to fix the problem. Often you'll find that the ringing of a particular drum may not even be noticeable when the entire kit is played or when other instruments are added to the mix.

Fourth on the list is getting rid of any rattles, squeaks, and buzzes that shouldn't be present. Drummers are notorious for having squeaky kick drum pedals and various rattles coming from their rack-mounted toms. Use a little oil (WD-40 is always handy) to lube up a squeaky kick pedal. Also make sure all lugs, wing nuts, and screws are tightened, even if they're not being used to hold anything in place. Remember, hitting one drum in the kit can cause sympathetic vibrations in other drums (and sometimes in other instruments or objects across the room).

Fifth, listen to the cymbals. Do they ring forever? Do they sound similar in frequency to each other? Does the ride cymbal have enough of a "ping" sound to cut through a mix? Does the hi-hat have the right sound for the song (high and tight, low and rumbly)?

For stereo imaging purposes, consider having two different-sounding crash cymbals near the overhead mics. When you pan the overheads you'll create a cool stereo image of the two crashes. Cymbals with long decays can make a mix sound washy, so you might consider using cymbals with shorter decays for recording. For instance, washy ride cymbals can lose their ability to cut through a mix if they have long decays—not only a sonic problem, but also a potential groove- killer. Also consider the sound of the hi-hat and how it fits with the snare drum sound. These two instruments must work well together to create a unified rhythmic palette.

Finally, all drum miking decisions should include considerations of the drummer's playing style. Hard-hitting players may require different mics and techniques than lighter players. Sticks can dictate mic choices, as well: Different sounds come from nylon-tip vs. wood-tip sticks and thick vs. thin sticks. Also, different types of music are often recorded different ways. For example, I usually mic jazz drum kits differently than rock kits due to (a) the sounds distinctive to each genre of music, (b) the characteristics of the drums and cymbals used in each genre, and (c) the amount of control I want over the sounds during mixing.

There are two basic methods of miking drums: ambient and close miking. Ambient miking uses a minimal number of mics (e.g., two overheads and a kick mic) to capture the full drum kit sound—usually better for jazz. Close miking means putting one (or more) mics on each drum and cymbal, and this is the technique often

used for rock. Using a combination of these two techniques is common, but which one you choose could be dependent on the number of mics you own. I'll list a number of options that cover most drum miking possibilities.

Mic Types and Pickup Patterns on Drums

Generally, condenser mics are best used for ambient miking applications (e.g., overhead mics) because they're better at reproducing transients and usually have a more even frequency response. Dynamic mics are best used for close-miking drums, because they can handle large amounts of volume before distorting and often have frequency responses tailored to accentuate a drum's attack.

Typical Ambient Drum Mic Setups

OPTION 1: two overhead mics + one kick drum mic (three mics total)

OPTION 2: two overhead mics + one kick drum mic + one snare mic (four mics total)

In these setups, the overhead mics are placed above the drums and cymbals and are used to pick up everything but the kick drum (hence the need to mic the kick separately). Be sure to listen to the balance between toms, snare, and cymbals in the overhead mics. Moving the cymbals higher or lower can improve this balance. The overhead mics can be placed anywhere from about one foot to ten feet above the drum kit. However, be aware that the farther away you move the overheads, the more room ambience you'll capture.

There are different ways to position over-head mics. I usually use a spread pair; that is, two mics that are spread apart from each other using the 3:1 rule, so there's no phase cancellation. You can also use an

Spread Pair
X/Y Configurations
3'
microphone
or
1'
1'
cymbals

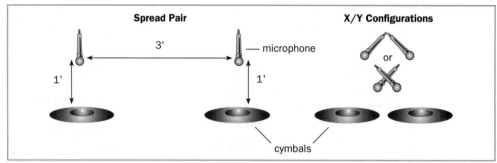

Fig. 7.1. Spread pair and X/Y mic configurations are often used for drum overheads.

X/Y configuration. To make an X/Y configuration, put the two overhead mics (with cardioid patterns) together at a 90-degree angle, making an X shape (see fig. 7.1).

When using an ambient miking technique, the sound of the room can make all the difference in the overall drum tone—the natural room reverb will be captured. If you record in a deadened room, this isn't as much of an issue, as you can add reverb to the tracks later in the mix. However, if you record in a very reverberant room, the room reverb will be recorded on the tracks forever. That's not all bad, though: The late John Bonham (of Led Zeppelin) was recorded several times in a castle using three mics on his drum kit, and it sounds incredible!

Kick: A kick drum mic can be put in several different places. It may be put inside the drum an inch or two away from the beater head, right where the beater strikes the head. This will capture the most attack. Or, it can be placed just *outside* the drum in the hole of the resonant head (the back drum head, if the drum has one). In this position, the mic will pick up a good amount of the air movement from inside the drum. The sound is powerful but has less attack. Placing the mic somewhere between these two extremes also works and combines the effects of both aforementioned techniques.

beater head
resonant head
kick drum
OPTION 1
OPTION 2
microphone
kick drum pedal

Fig. 7.2. Typical kick drum mic configurations.

Snare: The snare mic is usually placed between the hi-hat and the first rack-mounted tom, located roughly two inches above the drum, peeking over the outer rim. You can also put the mic higher (6–8 inches) above the snare for a more roomy sound. The mic should face the center of the top head if you want to capture the most attack. To hear more of the drum tone, aim the mic just inside the rim. (There is more on drum miking later in this chapter.)

Recording a Drum Set with One or Two Mics

Most of us don't have the money to buy a whole closet full of microphones. If you're limited to using one or two mics to record a drum kit, you can still capture excellent sounds. If you only have one mic, try one of these options:

- Place a condenser mic (cardioid pattern) about a foot or two in front of the drum kit, at about six feet from the floor, pointed at the kit.

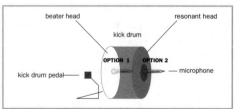

- Place a condenser mic (cardioid pattern) just above the drummer's head, pointed at the kit.
- Place a condenser mic (cardioid pattern) about four feet directly above the cymbals, pointed at the kit.
- Place a condenser mic (cardioid or omni pattern) about six to ten feet in front of the drumset, pointed at the kit.
- If you're desperate you can also use a dynamic mic placed above and to the side of the kick on the opposite side of the snare drum. I used this technique early in my 4-track recording days.

If you can spare two mics:

- Create "earrings." That is, put one mic next to each of the drummer's ears, about a drumstick's length away from each ear, and point the two mics at the kit (more about this technique later in this chapter).
- Place one in the kick drum and one directly over the entire kit.

Minimal Close Miking Drum Setups

OPTION 3: option 2 (above) + one mic for each pair of toms (five+ mics total)

OPTION 4: option 3 + one mic for each individual tom (six+ mics total)

OPTION 5: option 4 + one mic for the hi-hat (seven+ mics total)

Toms: If you use one mic to capture two toms, try to use a mic with a wide cardioid pattern in order to get the most attack from both drums. It should be placed directly between the toms. However, having mics on each tom gives you more control over capturing the right sound. As with snare mics on the top head, these mics should be aimed at the center of the drum for more attack and less ring. Also, try to keep them out of the way of the drummer's stick motion. Sometimes I like to use Shure Beta 98s, because they're so small that they never impede a drummer's tom fills.

Like snare drums, toms have a propensity to produce large transients, so engineers use both dynamic and condenser mics on them. Condenser mics on toms add more air to the sound and often reproduce a more realistic representation of the actual drum's sound due to the flat frequency response of most condenser mics. Position condensers carefully around the drums . . . they can't take the beatings that dynamic mics can.

Hi-hat: In close-miking applications, the hi-hat mic is usually aimed at the middle or center (bell) of the top hi-hat cymbal. For more sound separation, I recommend pointing the mic away from the snare drum. That way, if you want to bring the hi-hat up in the mix, the snare level won't rise, as well.

Miking a Kick Drum and Building a Tunnel

A technique often used with good results is building a "tunnel" for the kick drum. What on Earth does that mean? First you need to take the resonant (front) head off the kick. Then you set up two mic stands and extend the booms about three or four feet perpendicular to the ground, at the height of the drum. Place a condenser mic just inside of the mic stands at the far end of the drum, about a foot off the floor, aimed at the kick. Cover the mic stands with thick blankets, creating a tunnel for the kick drum sound to travel through the mic. (The blankets isolate the mic from the other drums and cymbals.) Why is the tunnel cool? It gives you a more distant and roomy kick sound, but without picking up any other drums in the room.

beater head
kick drum
Hang blankets over the mic stands to make a tunnel
microphone
kick drum pedal
mic stands

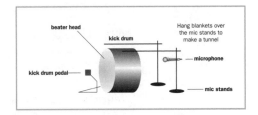

Take Note!

When using electronic drums, you may want to overdub real cymbals for a more realistic cymbal sound. Although electronic drums are sounding better each year, electronic cymbals are lagging behind and still sound rather fake. If you can't use real cymbals, get some high-quality samples instead of using electronically made sounds.

In recording sessions where I am at liberty to use as many mics for as many tracks as I can, I sometimes use up to four mics on the kick drum. Each mic captures a specific part of the kick drum sound. They can be mixed together or used individually for different songs or even specific sections in a song. What can I say? I like to have options. Here's one example:

The first mic is a dedicated kick drum mic—the Shure Beta 52—placed inside the drum within two inches of the beater head. I place the mic near where the pedal strikes the head to maximize the amount of attack that the mic picks up. Because of the frequency response of this mic, it also picks up a good bit of low end.

The second mic—a Shure Beta 91—is placed inside the drum as well, resting on a brick, concrete block, sand bag, or some other implement used to weigh down the drum and hold absorbtive material in place. This mic picks up a lot of attack, but also some resonance of the drum.

The third mic (no particular kind, but often a dynamic mic) is placed in front of the kick drum on the beater side, right next to where the pedal hits the drum. This mic picks up a lot of the "click" sound of the beater against the drum head.

The fourth mic—a nice condenser mic—is placed in a drum tunnel, as described earlier. This gets more of the tone of the drum, as well as the air moved by the drum. By being farther from the drum than all of the other mics, it can pick up more of the low end because the longer wavelengths of the bass frequencies have more of a chance to propagate before reaching the mic.

When using multiple microphones like this to record one source, especially a bass-heavy instrument, you may run into acoustical phase cancellation. The low end of the kick drum sound can simply disappear due to phase cancellation, so be careful.

More Extravagant Drum Mic Setups

OPTION 6: option 5 (above) + room mics (nine+ mics total)

OPTION 7: option 6 + multiple mics on drums (ten+ mics total)

Cymbals: There are many ways to mic the cymbals, from X/Y pairs to spaced pairs to earrings. These techniques are discussed in detail later in this chapter in the "Advanced Miking Techniques" section.

Room: Room mics are often omni-directional, to capture as much of the room's sound as possible. They can be placed close to the drums for less room ambience or very far from the drums for more. Often these mics are pointed at the snare drum, no matter where they are in the room, and are used in pairs to create a stereo image.

As I've gotten deeper into the art of miking drums, I've found I like certain sounds from different mics and enjoy using mics together on one source. Yes, using multiple microphones on one drum can be extravagant—especially if you have limited mics to choose from or a limited track count—but the sounds you capture can be worth it. For example, I like using two (or more) mics on my kick drum . . . a Shure Beta 52 to pick up the meaty bass boom and a Beta 91 to capture the upper attack frequencies. For my snare, I like combining the sound of the Shure Beta 56 and SM57 (or Sennheiser MD 441). Usually I put the Beta 56 on the top head and the SM57 on the bottom head, but sometimes I use the 56 and 57 on the top alone, or with another 57 on the bottom. (Often, I'll flip the phase on the bottom snare mic.) To save track real estate you can bus these multiple mics to record on just one track, or simply bounce to one track after you've already recorded them on separate tracks (so you can really be sure of the mix and their sound relationship).

Everyone has their own way of miking drums and there are many techniques I haven't listed here. I've included these because they're some of the common techniques taught at the Berklee College

Take Note!
Microphone spec sheets are fountains of knowledge when it comes to figuring out the best uses for a mic. Most mic manufacturers publish their mic specs, as well as uses for their mics, on their Web sites. Shure has an extensive collection of information on microphones for you to check out for free on *www.shure.com.*

of Music. Regardless, you can use these miking options as foundations for your own sonic experiments.

Miking the Whole Kit—An Example

Here's one possible multi-mic setup for a drum set utilizing many of the techniques described here:

Kick Drum: Beta 52 placed either at the beater head inside the drum or in the hole of the resonant head. Beta 91 placed inside the drum, lying on a weight and a pillow. KSM44 placed in a tunnel and a Beta 56 on the front of the beater head.

Snare Drum: Beta 56 placed at the top head about two inches above the head, aimed at its center. SM57 (or Sennheiser MD 441) on the bottom head (polarity reversed), facing the snares, about eight inches away.

Hi-hat: Shure SM81 (or AKG 535) on the top cymbal, pointed away from the snare.

Toms: Beta 98 mics with drum mounts (or Sennheiser MD 421 mics) on each tom, about an inch or two from the head, aimed at the center of the drum. Many condenser mics also sound great on toms.

Cymbals: A pair of Shure KSM32 mics (or AKG 535 mics) about a foot above the cymbals, placed strategically to capture all of the cymbals, implementing the 3:1 rule.

Room Mics: A pair of omni-directional condenser mics (like the Earthworks TC40) placed away and equidistant from the kit, usually pointed at the snare drum.

Note: The Shure mics mentioned in the examples here have a proven record in the recording industry and provide great starting points for capturing excellent sounds without spending tens of thousands of dollars on mics. Your budget and sonic preferences will dictate your mic choices. Top-drawer mics can often yield superior sounds—but proper mic technique allows

Room Mics
Overhead Mics
Individual Tom Mic
Hi-hat Mic
Top and Bottom Snare Mic
Three Mics: On Kick – Front and Back of Beaterhead Plus Mic in Tunnel

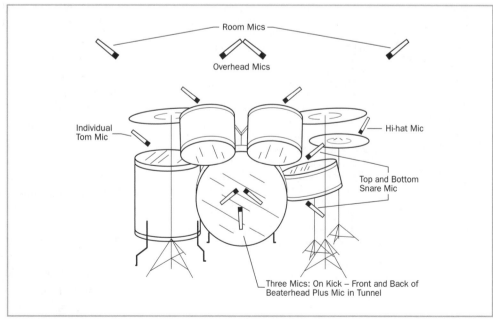

Fig. 7.3. A rather extravagant drum set miking configuration.

Take Note!

I recommend using new or fairly new strings for recording sessions—I've found this to be particularly important on acoustic guitars. Strings tend to lose their brightness and attack quickly, which can make the guitar tracks sound muddy. Dead strings can easily take the life out of an exciting performance. Plus, new strings are less likely to break mid-session (theoretically). Boiling bass strings in water for about ten minutes can extend the life of old strings by cleansing them of ground-in oil and dirt. However, this is a very short-term fix that may only add a few takes' worth of life to the strings. Restringing with new strings is the real fix for better sounding tracks.

you to capture high-quality sounds with almost any mic.

I've recorded drums using twenty-two microphones and I've recorded drums using one microphone. However, if the drums sound bad and the player isn't very good, it really doesn't make a difference how many or what kind of mics you put up. Likewise, if the player is killin' and the drum kit sounds great, then you just have to avoid screwing it up . . . any of the miking techniques in this chapter will help you capture good sounds.

Fun With Mic Techniques

Experimentation with mic placement and usage is a fun learning experience. Each time you try something new you can learn whether the technique works or not, and you'll soon develop recording tricks that contribute to your unique sound. For example, one time a friend and I were recording drums for some loops and had a whole slew of mics on the kit . . . several on the kick, snare, and hi-hat, one for each tom, and a number of overhead and room mics. Just for the heck of it, we set up one Shure SM81 far behind the drummer's chair. In fact, the mic was head-high in a corner of the room, with a gobo in front of it.

When we finally listened to the SM81, we found that it sounded terrible, by usual standards. The frequency response due to the mic's placement behind a gobo in the corner of the room was really bizarre, giving the track a totally gnarled and distorted tone. But at the same time, it was so cool . . . it captured the sound of the kick and snare in a very unusual way. It was naturally lo-fi, but with a sound that we might have never thought to create using EQ. In the end, we made more drum loops with the signal from that one SM81 than from all of the other mics we used on the drums.

RECORDING ELECTRIC GUITARS AND BASSES

As with drums, there are several issues to consider before you start recording a guitar or bass, including tuning, strings, intonation, pickups, rattles/hums/buzzes, the genre of the music, and the guitarist's or bassist's playing style. In this section you can assume, unless stated otherwise, that any references I make to guitar also apply to bass.

The first aspect of getting good guitar and bass sounds is recording an instrument that is (a) in tune with itself and (b) in tune with the rest of the instruments on the track. Tuners are cheap and you should own one, but you can also tune to other instruments with fixed pitches (like synths) or to instruments that are difficult to tune on your own (like pianos). However, it's usually a good idea to tune with a tuner, so that when you have to go back and do overdubs later you'll have a common reference pitch to match. Also, guitars and basses can go out of tune quickly! Have the player retune often during a session so you avoid a situation in which you've gotten the perfect performance, only to find that the guitar was out of tune. Retune even more frequently if the player put new strings on before the session. (If recording on analog tape, it's a good idea to record a tuning note at the beginning of the tape as a reference pitch to tune to later . . . in case you work on another tape machine that is calibrated differently and runs at a slightly different speed.)

Second, check the intonation of the guitar. After tuning the open strings of the guitar, test the 12th fret tuning of each string. If the 12th fret tones are in tune with the open strings, you're usually all set. If not, take the guitar to your favorite guitar

Take Note!

Some guitar effects processors act as direct boxes because they have both line- and mic-level outputs. Some even have digital outputs that you can plug directly into a digital recording device.

repair person . . . unless you really know how to intonate a guitar yourself.

Third, listen to the guitarist play and have him cycle through all of the pickups. Listen for noisy pickups and for any irregularities in the sounds. If you notice one pickup is getting more of the low strings than the high strings, the pickup might not be level (it's angled slightly toward the low strings). With a couple twists of a screwdriver, you can make the pickup parallel with the strings and even out the response.

Fourth, as the player is warming up, listen for any rattles, hums, and buzzes. These noises can come from a variety of places. Check that the input is secure in the body of the instrument. Check the instrument cable and its connections—guitar cables are notorious for giving out in sessions. Hums and buzzes often come from electrical grounding problems; if the guitar is going through a direct box, flip the ground switch, or if you're using an amp, get the amp up off of the floor. Active pickups require batteries, and batteries low on power often make noise. (It's a good idea to replace all batteries before the session, anyway.) Also watch for interference from your computer screen. Finally, if you're still getting unexplained noise, try having the guitar player face a different direction or move to a different location in the room. This will often get rid of the problem.

Finally, consider the guitarist's playing style and the genre of the music you are recording before putting up any microphones. Will the guitarist be playing with a pick, fingers, a slide, or some other device? Will the bassist be slapping, popping, tapping, or using some other non-standard technique? Will the guitarist be using an amp, a direct box, a combination of these two, or will the guitar be miked? Is

the guitarist playing through any pedals, effects units, or other devices? As with drums, mic techniques differ for different genres of music and playing styles.

There are several ways to record electric guitars: direct, mics on an amplified speaker, or a combination of both.

Direct: Plugging a guitar or bass directly into an instrument- or line-level input jack usually provides the most noise-free input signal and zero leakage from other instruments being recorded at the same time. To record direct you need a preamplifier to boost the signal.

You can also record direct using a direct box (commonly called a "DI" for "direct injection"). A **direct box** transforms line-level input signals into mic-level signals so you can plug the cable into a mic preamp. To use a DI, plug the 1/4" cable from the guitar or bass into the direct box and connect a mic (XLR) cable from the direct box to a mic preamp on your mixer. Signal processors can be inserted between the guitar and the DI.

Bass parts are frequently recorded direct. However, guitar parts are often written using a particular sound from an amp and/or signal processors, making it better to use amps and processors to capture the part, even if the signal isn't as clean as a direct in. Plus, recording without the effects can negatively affect the guitarist's performance because the guitarist is used to hearing the amped or effected sound. Always try to capture the best performance as well as the best sound.

Miking an amplified speaker: There are several ways to mic an amplified speaker. Close miking is the most common technique and, as the term implies, consists of putting a mic within a foot of a speaker

Take Note!
Each guitar and bass amp has its own sound. Although not impossible to fix, bad amp sounds are a pain to work with and can ultimately bring your entire recording down. A simple gear switch can make all the difference in finding the right sound for a song. Regardless of what amp you choose, it's often good practice to turn the amp up as loud as possible when recording (without overloading the microphone or mic preamp) to get better tone from the amp. As discussed in chapter 6, some mics (and even preamps) have pads to reduce incoming volume and allow the mic to handle louder levels.

cabinet. To capture the sound right at its source, I often put a dynamic mic up against, but not touching, the grill of the speaker. With electric guitars, the Shure SM57 is a popular mic for this application, as is the Sennheiser MD 421. The Shure Beta 52 works well on bass cabinets. Some engineers like to use a combination of close mics and EQ them differently to create a thicker or more exciting tone. Experiment with different mics to see which ones sound best together.

GUITAR
AMP
SPEAKER CABINET

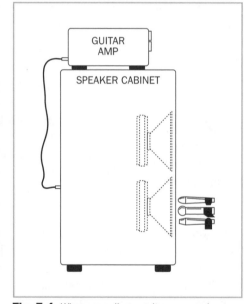

Fig. 7.4. When recording a guitar amp and speaker cabinet with multiple close mics, make sure the diaphragms of all the mics are exactly the same distance from the speaker so they are all in phase.

Where you point the mic will determine the type of sound you'll get. If you want an edgy sound, point the mic at the center of the speaker to pick up more of the high frequencies. If you want more of a warm and smooth tone, point the mic toward the outer edge of the speaker cone. If the cabinet has more than one speaker, make sure to put the mic in front of the one that sounds best. Have the guitarist play and listen to each speaker to find the one with the most impact, cleanest signal, and least amount of rattle and buzz.

Natural ambience can add a lot of character to a guitar sound. Placing a condenser mic several feet back from the speaker will give you a detailed recording of the amp sound interacting with the room ambience. Blending this distant mic with the close mic(s) can produce a fuller overall guitar track. Experiment with different rooms or spaces . . . you may find that recording in the bathroom or the kitchen could add a cool vibe to your track!

If you're recording everyone at once, it's a good idea to separate the speaker cabinet from the rest of the band, since guitar amps generally sound better the louder they are. If you have the space, put the cabinet in a different room than the drums. If your studio consists of only one room, put the cabinet in the closet and deaden all the space around it. That is, set up the mics the way you want them, then put absorptive materials (like blankets or pillows) all around the amp. Although not as clean as going direct, this technique will sufficiently isolate the guitar signal from the other instruments. Also don't forget to deaden the floor so you don't encounter reflections that might cause phase cancellation. I sometimes use laundry for this purpose (and of course, it gets picked up immediately after the session).

Combining direct and miked signals: An effective way to make a more interesting guitar or bass sound is to combine the direct input with the miked signal. If you have the track real estate, use two or more tracks for different guitar inputs and mix them down later. You may want to add a special effect to the dry direct signal and

> **Take Note!**
> An upright bass can also be called a double bass, string bass, or contrabass.

then combine it with the close-miked and distant-miked speaker tracks.

Current amp modelers allow you to combine (or keep separate) the direct signal and the amp model signal. It's very cool to have the direct signal available on a track during the mix session, because later you can add different effects that you might not have thought of during recording.

RECORDING ACOUSTIC GUITARS AND UPRIGHT BASSES

Although some acoustic guitars and upright basses have electric pickups, I often find that miking these instruments with condensers sounds better than recording them using their built-in pickups. I've gotten great sounds using Shure KSM32s and SM81s on acoustic guitars and KSM44s on upright basses, as well as other condenser microphones like AKG 414s. I also like combining the direct signal with the miked signal to add character to the overall sound—even just a small amount of the DI signal can provide additional clarity, presence, and bass to make the track sound incredible.

Assuming the guitar or bass sounds good, mic placement is the key to getting good acoustic recordings. For acoustic guitars you'll get more high frequencies the closer the mic is to the neck, more mids the closer the mic is to the bridge, and more low frequencies the closer the mic is to the sound hole (avoid pointing the mic directly at the sound hole though). I like using two mics, one placed above the sound hole toward the bridge and one placed below the sound hole toward the neck. When panned left and right they create a nice

Head
Tuning Knobs
Nut
Neck
Fretboard
Body
Sound Hole
Bridge
Tuning Knobs
Head
Neck
Body
Bridge
F Holes

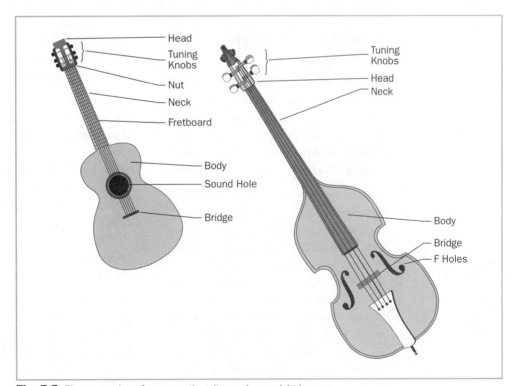

Fig. 7.5. The anatomies of an acoustic guitar and an upright bass.

stereo image, since each mic is picking up slightly different frequencies. But this setup is only the technique I've been using lately. I've tried many others and there are numerous positions in which you can capture great acoustic guitar sounds. Experiment, and try rolling off the low end if it gets too boomy.

There are three main ways to mic an acoustic bass. The first is to place a condenser mic anywhere from 6 to 30 inches away from the strings, just above the bridge where the strings are being plucked. The distance will determine how much room ambience is included in the sound, as well as how much isolation you'll have on the track. This technique will capture a good amount of the attack on the strings when they're plucked and is also good for bowed parts.

The second technique is miking the F hole at anywhere from 6 to 30 inches away. This technique will provide increased bass and low-mid frequencies, but will lose some of the attack.

The last technique is wrapping a mic in padding and wedging it between the ebony tailpiece and the body. I've gotten the best results using this technique. It simultaneously captures the attack and a wide frequency range in a crisp yet bassy blend.

A note on bass compression: Most bass parts need compression to even out the volume of the notes so that the bass track sounds more constant in the mix and provides a solid foundation for the recording. Compression also allows the softer nuances of the bass track to be heard. You can compress bass on the way in to your recording device using an external compressor; this technique is described in chapter 8. You can also compress the bass signal once it's been recorded during the mix session; this technique is described in chapter 12. Both techniques have their advantages.

RECORDING PIANO

Although most home studios aren't likely to have a grand piano, I'll briefly touch on recording techniques for those that do, for those who might have an upright or console piano, or for those who will record pianos in a pro studio with a piano.

One basic technique for recording piano is using two condenser mics, one aimed at the low strings and the other aimed at the high strings, both about six inches or more from the strings. When panned left and right these two mics will create a large and pleasing sound that captures almost all of the piano's frequency range. To use only one mic, center it at the opening of the piano's lid. Consider deadening the underside of the piano lid, which can cause unwanted reflections, with foam or a blanket. And to make your piano sound even better, try to write parts for it in its best-sounding range(s).

Experiment with other miking techniques, such as putting the mics close to the hammers or using an X/Y configuration. Listen to the differences when you move mics closer or farther away from the piano, and note how the lid height interacts with the sound. If you need to isolate the piano, put blankets over it so that little outside noise gets into the mics. (Additional stereo mic techniques are discussed later in this chapter.)

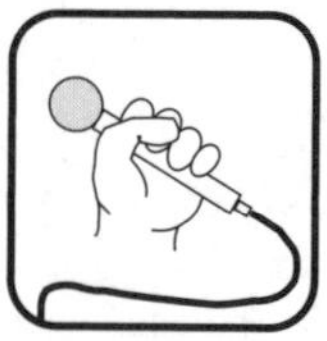

RECORDING VOCALS

Technically speaking, recording vocals seems like it should be one of the easiest jobs in the

Take Note!

The diaphragm of a condenser microphone is a micro-thin metal plate that moves in response to air flow, generating an electric signal that represents the sound it's recording.

recording process. Just put a mic in front of the singer and let the singer do his or her thing. Right? Well, this couldn't be further from the truth. Vocals are often the most important tracks you'll record as an engineer, and they require more attention to detail than all other instrumental tracks.

To capture an emotional and energetic vocal performance, several factors must be considered in addition to mic choice and placement. The physical environment should be to the vocalist's liking. Adjust the lights, temperature, and decor to suit the mood of the song or the personality of the singer. Your goal is to make singers feel comfortable in their surroundings. The environment and *your* mood will help set the tone. Remember, energy is contagious, whether positive or negative, and the energy you give off will have an impact on the artist, the producer, and everyone else.

A good overall vibe for the session is extremely important, and creating an excellent headphone mix with a flattering vocal sound enhances that good vibe. Be sure to listen to the mix that the *vocalist* is listening to as you're creating and tweaking it—that way you'll know of any problems immediately. I recommend boosting the keyboard or guitar tracks in the headphone mix so the vocalist has a solid pitch reference. To further enhance this, keep the effects on those tracks to a minimum.

Interact with the singers as you're adjusting the level of their voices in the mix. Have them sing along with the track at full volume to accurately assess levels, and ask them how they feel about the sound. Note that vocalists tend to go flat if their voices are too high in the headphones and sharp (because they try to push their voices) if they're too low in the mix. Also be aware that most vocalists like hearing some reverb on their voices when recording, so use a reverb plug-in or an external unit on their track solely for this purpose. Very subtle adjustments can have huge benefits, and a good headphone mix might make the difference between an average and an outstanding recorded performance. (We'll discuss setting up headphone mixes and adding effects to the headphone mix in more detail in chapter 8.)

As with all other instruments, the voice interacts with the acoustics of its environment. The size and shape of the space, as well as the reflections from the material on the walls, floor, and ceiling, will influence the overall sound of the vocal track. Listen carefully to the sound of the space where you'll be recording your vocals.

Condenser mics often yield the best vocal recordings because of their flat frequency response and ability to capture sonic detail. Since they are recording in a cardioid pattern, these mics should be placed about six inches to two feet from the vocalist, depending on how much ambience you want to include in the track. Close miking a vocalist with a condenser often creates proximity effect (bass boost). Sometimes used for effect or to indicate intimacy, this bass boost can also create a muddy vocal sound. If you really need to close-mic a vocalist with a condenser, you can use the bass rolloff to eliminate some of the boomy low frequencies. If the vocalist is very loud, use the microphone's pad so you won't get distortion and so that you protect the mic's diaphragm.

Don't rule out dynamic microphones for vocals. Some voices sound great recorded utilizing the non-flat frequency response of a particular dynamic mic. It might accentuate the best part of the vocalist's sound or may boost a frequency that's lacking in their natural tone. However, experimentation is the only way to find engineering gems like these. Dynamic mics are also useful for creating vintage vocal tones or other interesting sounds. When using a dynamic mic keep the vocalist within six inches of the mic, otherwise the signal will sound thin because low frequencies will be lost.

There are many possible positions for a vocal microphone, but I'll recommend only two here. The first is directly in front of the vocalist's mouth, when the vocalist is standing up straight. This position provides the most natural vocal sound but might pick up more breathing and plosives than desired. The second and probably more useful mic position is to place it slightly above (2–4 inches) the singer, pointed down at their mouth. This forces a vocalist to really open up his or her throat, which is useful when they have to hit some high notes, and also decreases the amount of breathing and plosive sounds on the recording. This position can be uncomfortable to some singers, however.

Notice that for all vocal mic positions, the mic should be placed so that the vocalist is required to stand fully erect. Standing while singing helps expand the chest and elongate the throat, which most times creates a better vocal sound. It also ensures that the singer isn't bending their neck downward, which can block air passage though the throat. Sometimes singers can achieve this same effect by lying on their backs. Although not recommended, sitting while singing can work, as long as the singer is sitting up straight without having to bend their neck down.

Vocal parts are often very dynamic—the volume of a singer's voice can vary greatly within a single recording. As you're setting up the mic, creating a headphone mix, and getting sound, ask the vocalist to sing as loud as they think they'll sing during the loudest part of the song. Make sure you're not peaking on the input meters at any stage in the signal path. (Be aware that although the singer thinks that's the loudest they will sing, they'll usually sing even louder once they get into the emotion and energy of the song, so make sure you have some headroom for the additional volume.)

Veteran studio singers know how to back off the mic for loud notes and get closer for softer parts. You might be able to coach amateur singers to do this, too. However, volume riding and compression may still be needed on charismatic vocal parts, especially if the vocalist has little recording experience or underdeveloped microphone technique. If you know the song well and are familiar with the vocalist's interpretation, you can adjust the input levels by riding the input volume level from the mic at the preamp's Gain knob, the mixer's mic trim and/or channel fader, or the input gain of the recording device.

Pop Those Plosives

You can cut down on plosive ("pop") sounds with a pop filter. A pop filter is a device placed in front of a microphone to reduce the plosives. Plosives can be described as explosions of air from the mouth, and they often occur when using the consonants P, T, K, B, D, and G.

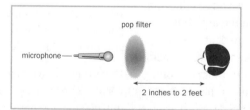

pop filter

microphone

2 inches to 2 feet

Properly placed pop filters perpetuate punchy but pretty tracks.

Riding the volume of a track can even out the input level, and is beneficial because it reduces the amount of compression you'll need to control the dynamic range of that track in the mix. However, many times you may need compression on the track anyway, so if you aren't *extremely* familiar with a track, I recommend against volume-riding the input signal. (Chapter 8 has more information about adding compression onto a vocal track while recording.)

Your goal as an engineer, producer, and artist should be to get the best vocal take possible—one that includes style, emotion, inspiration, and a great sound. There's much more to it than just recording clean audio.

I recommend recording every take of the vocal, whether you're recording line by line, or an entire run-through of the song. The early takes might be rough around the edges, but the energy is often the best. By later takes, the singer usually gets into the flow of the song and sings more evenly, but the energy might start to fade. At any rate, there's usually some part of every take that's worth keeping. You and the producer should take notes about the location of the keeper words, phrases, or sentences, so you can find them later. Use a take sheet for this purpose (see chapter 9). It's also a good idea to have the lyric sheet on hand, so that you always know where you are in the song. If the singer says they want to redo the second line of the third verse, you should know what that line is and where to find it. (Note: Many of the vocal takes you hear on pop radio are pieced together, phrase by phrase, word by word, or even syllable by syllable, in some cases!)

Be constantly aware of the vocalist's energy level (even if you're the one singing). Take breaks to rest the singer's vocal cords and to relax from the stress of tracking. Some vocalists can sing for hours, while others need frequent breaks. Be ready for either of these types or anyone in-between.

Background Vocals

If you're recording one backing vocal track at a time, use the same microphone techniques as you did for lead vocals. However, if you want to record more than one backing vocalist simultaneously, there are several effective techniques you can use.

First, I recommend using no more than two mics at one time—regardless of how many background singers there are—to avoid phase problems. One mic with an omni-directional pattern works well for a group of singers positioned in a circle around the mic. Here, creating a good vocal blend is the key. If you want the background voices to be in stereo, you can record two tracks like this and pan them as wide as you'd like—on the second track, try moving the singers around for a slightly different sound that will give more dimension to the stereo image. Or, if you want to use two mics to capture a stereo image, try putting two condensers in cardioid patterns back to back (a foot or more away from each other). Split the

Back vox group 1
1' or more
Back vox group 2
microphone

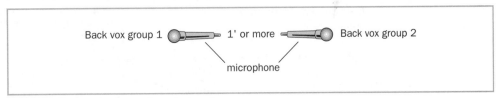

Fig. 7.6. A stereo background vocal mic setup.

vocalists into two groups and have them face each other.

Experiment with your own techniques as well, but watch out for phase problems and stay focused on getting a good blend of voices.

RECORDING OTHER INSTRUMENTS

Here are some general principles for several main families of instruments that you might record in a session.

Synths: Although recording direct from your synthesizer is the easiest and most effective way to track synth parts, experiment with running synth tracks through miked amplifiers or speakers. Combining the direct and miked signals might create some interesting timbres.

Horns: Most woodwind instruments (e.g., saxophones) usually sound best when recorded with dynamic microphones such as the Electro-Voice RE20 or the Shure SM57, whereas brass instruments (e.g., trumpets and trombones) are often recorded with condenser microphones such as the Shure KSM32 or AKG 535. Be careful not to put condenser mics too close to brass instruments, though. Keep the mic at least ten inches away from the bell of the horn, so that the mic's diaphragm isn't destroyed by a stray triple-forte note. Sometimes it's a even a good idea to have the brass player point the bell 15 degrees to one side of the mic. A pair of condensers works well for a stereo horn section, or a section with many players to capture. You just need to be sure you're getting an even blend of the different instruments.

Strings: To record strings, use condenser mics. Position the mics close to the players if you want little room tone or further away if you want more. Be careful with close miking, though . . . it can sound a bit strange and might make the players a little uncomfortable. Ambient miking is more common than close miking.

Also, consider double-, triple-, or quadruple-tracking the string parts to make them sound more full. Double-tracking often sounds artificial, so I recommend at least triple-tracking if you want a more natural sound.

Percussion instruments: As with the drum kit, use dynamic mics if close miking and condenser mics if ambient miking.

Turntables: Recording turntables through a DJ mixer is really straightforward. Just connect the mixer to any two line-level inputs to your recording device. Often, there are a number of ways to adjust the output volume on a DJ mixer. Just be aware of the signal flow, and don't overload any part of the signal path.

Take Note!

Some newer synths output signals slightly hotter than –10 dBV. If you send this hot signal to an input that's expecting –10 dBV, you might clip the input. Most line-level inputs do have some headroom (space between the optimum and maximum input level), but be careful of distortion.

Troubleshooting the Signal Path

If a signal from an input isn't getting into your recording device or is excessively noisy, check all points along the signal path. Start with the mic or the instrument input. Check to see if the cable is plugged in properly, and try giving it a jiggle. If the connection seems fine, it could be a bad cable. Try a different cable. Then move on to the input on your mixer, your outboard mic preamps, and your recording device. Is the connection good between the cable and the input? Is the input gain high enough? Is phantom power on? Check any other connections that route your signal to your computer. Finally, make sure your recording device is configured properly. Is the correct track record-enabled? Are the right input and output paths chosen?

mic/instrument
cable
input device (hardware, mixer, outboard mic preamps]
recording software

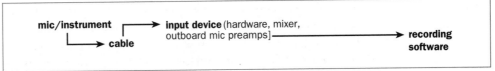

Always follow the signal path when you're trying to track down a problem.

ADVANCED MIKING TECHNIQUES

Utilizing some of the techniques already discussed in this chapter and some of the sonic principles covered in chapter 6, here I want to cover some more advanced mic techniques. However, before we jump into specific mic placements, let's talk about some concepts that affect all mic techniques: stereo imaging, ambience, and mono compatibility.

Most often, we listen to recordings from two speakers and call it "stereo." Yet, the stereo signal coming from the two speakers often creates a sound that is beyond two-dimensional, which makes it more real and interesting. Our ears can perceive this three-dimensional sound so well that we can actually tell where an individual sound is coming from—behind or in front of us, left or right of us, and above or below us, as well as how close or far the sound is from us in any direction. Because of our innate ability to perceive the direction and distance of a sound, we can identify the location of each ingredient in a stereo recording. Each sound we hear has its own **stereo image** and when sounds are combined, the combination has its own stereo image, made up of the individual images.

A sound's stereo image consists of its distance and direction from the listener, as well as the ambience surrounding the sound. For example, if on a recording, an electric guitar sounds like it's coming from the stage of a small jazz club, ten feet away, two feet off the ground, and slightly to the right, that's its stereo image. When miking any instrument, always consider the stereo image that you want to achieve in the final mix.

Where's the bass?

Low frequencies, from about 150 Hz and below, are omni-directional. That is, unlike frequencies above 150 Hz, we can't perceive which direction they're coming from. Thus, creating a specific stereo image for a low-frequency instrument is often pointless—you should usually just place it in the center.

As you read earlier in this chapter, you can set up a mic right next to the sound source (called "close miking") or you can setup mics farther away from the source to capture more of the **ambience** around the instrument. Whichever method you choose, be aware of how it will affect the stereo image. When close miking, you will not record much of the ambience and will have to add the desired amount of ambience in the mix. When ambient miking, the ambience of the recording space around the sound source is often an obvious addition to the raw sound source and will affect the sound's stereo image.

Another thing to think about when recording (and mixing) is **mono compatibility**. What's mono compatibility? Basically, it's when the two sides of a stereo signal are summed to one and that one (mono) signal accurately reproduces the stereo signal:

stereo left + stereo right = mono

Remember the discussion on phase and acoustical phase cancellation in chapter 6? If so, you'll understand why in-phase stereo signals add when summed to mono, but out-of-phase stereo signals cancel each other out when summed to mono. What does that mean? Well, if you listen to your recording through a device with a mono speaker (like a clock radio or mono TV set), you may notice some sonic problems with your tracks. Unless the phase relationships in your stereo signals are mono compatible, phase-induced additions can increase the level of some or all frequencies by as much as 6 dB, and phase-induced cancellations can decrease or even destroy some or all frequencies of a signal. When both addition and cancellation occur at once, this is referred to as *comb filtering* because some frequencies are more pronounced than others and some are eliminated, creating a frequency response curve that resembles a hair comb.

Thus, check your tracks in mono when you're recording them for mono compatibility. You can do this by simply panning all the tracks to the center and listening for comb filtering.

Stereo Miking Techniques

When recording, we often strive to capture the true sound of an instrument and the environment in which the recording is taking place. A good way to do this is to use two microphones and create a stereo pair: two microphones set up to capture a sound source on two tracks. This preserves the distance and directionality characteristics of the sound. In many cases, the mics are setup so that they capture a sound similar to what we might hear with our two ears at some location around the instrument being recorded.

There are innumerable applications for recording using a stereo pair of microphones, from recording a horn section to capturing the room sound while recording a drumset. And there are many varieties of stereo pairs, including coincident pairs, near-coincident pairs, spaced pairs, Mid-Side matrices, earrings, and binaural heads. We'll cover most of these here, starting with coincident pairs.

Coincident Pairs

Coincident miking techniques are those in which two mics are very close to each other, essentially occupying the same position. More specifically, the diaphragms of the two mics are in the same vertical plane and placed very closely to each other. This results in a very phase-coherent, mono-compatible signal that also picks up the stereo ambience of the physical space.

- X/Y

The first of two coincident pairs we'll cover is the X/Y setup. The X/Y setup consists of two cardioid mics placed at 90° angles to each other and 45° from the center of the object being recorded. The mics should overlap, almost touching each other. This ensures that the mics receive audio information nearly simultaneously so that their signals will be in phase.

An X/Y pair usually yields a focused stereo image. However, it may not sound as wide as other stereo pairs due to the fact that this setup picks up an increased amount of signal (up to 6 dB) in the center where the polar patterns of the cardioid mics overlap and the mics receive common audio information. This overlap can be decreased by widening the angle between the two mics from 90° to 110° or 120°. Another way to combat this is to use mics with hypercardioid pickup patterns. X/Y setups are commonly used when miking pianos, drums, and cymbals (as drum overhead mics).

90° – 120°
Center of
Sound Source

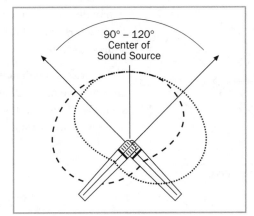

Fig. 7.7. An X/Y mic configuration.

• Blumlein

Another coincident miking technique is called Blumlein. Named after prolific inventor and EMI sound engineer Alan Blumlein, the Blumlein configuration consists of two bi-directional (figure-8) mics placed at a 90° angle to each other. The overlap of their polar pattern occurs where the bi-directional mics' sensitivity decreases (on the outer edges) by about 3 dB. This ensures that the signal at the center of the image has a good level relative to the sides.

This setup actually works well for capturing a very accurate impression of width and depth because the rear-facing diaphragms pick up a lot of the room's ambience. And, the stereo image transfers well to mono. However, the sonic information that appears at the sides of this setup will be picked up by both the front and rear lobe of the bi-directional mics and will not have a proper position in the stereo field. Considering this, the Blumlein technique should be used for central line on-axis plus rear sonic information only. That is, try this technique when miking one centralized sound source and its sonic relationship with the room, such as drums or piano. (It is also a good technique for recording ensembles like choirs and orchestras, if placed at the right distance from the ensemble.)

90°
0°
0° on-axis
L Mic
0° on-axis
R Mic

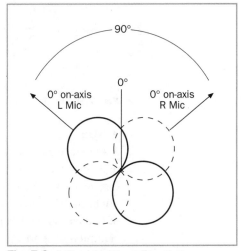

Fig. 7.8. A Blumlein mic configuration.

Near-Coincident Pairs

Near-coincident pairs use two mics spaced no more than 30 centimeters apart horizontally. Offering many of the same benefits as coincident pairs like close placement and mono compatibility, they also add a wider sense of space to the stereo image, due to the fact that each mic receives the same audio information at slightly different times.

• ORTF

The ORTF (named after the company that developed the technique—Office de Radiodiffusion-Television Francaise) configuration consists of two cardioid microphones spaced 17 centimeters apart at a 110° angle. It's no coincidence that the spacing and angle of these mics in this configuration is similar to the positioning of our own ears.

110° Center of
Sound Source
0°
17 cm

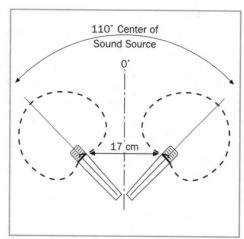

Fig. 7.9. The ORTF mic configuration.

- NOS

A similar technique is called NOS (a standard approved by the Dutch Broadcasting Organization—Nederlanshe Omroep Stichting). The NOS configuration consists of two cardioid microphones spaced 30 centimeters apart at a 90° angle. Because of the spacing, this configuration also has a properly balanced center signal, just like the Blumlein and ORTF configurations. However, when summed to mono, the NOS system yields an attenuated low-frequency response due to phase differences induced by the increased distance between the mics.

90° Center of
Sound Source
0°
30 cm

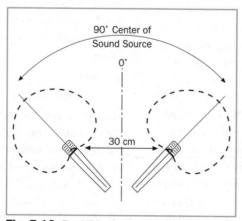

Fig. 7.10. The NOS mic configuration.

- FAULKNER

Another near-coincident miking technique you may want to experiment with is called the Faulkner configuration. In this system, two bi-directional mics are placed 20 centimeters apart, both facing the sound source, as in fig.7.11.

These near-coincident mic configurations are effective on small ensembles, horn sections, choirs, orchestras, and even solo acoustic instruments.

Center of
Sound Source
0°
[+]
[+]
[–]
[–]
20 cm

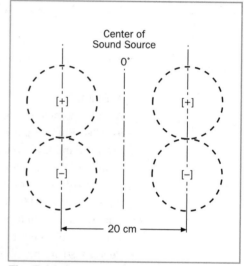

Fig. 7.11. The Faulkner mic configuration.

- Earrings

In an even more realistic representation of what our ears hear than the ORTF configuration, the earring configuration consists of two cardioid mics positioned right next to a drummer's ears, pointing at the drum kit. Because drummers don't usually keep their heads completely still while playing, make sure there's at least 4 inches between the drummer's head and the mics. This technique captures a great stereo image, and also uses the drummer's head as a baffle to separate the two mics. (In fact, some call this a "head baffle.")

> *Take Note!*
> By adding an extra kick and snare mic to an earring setup, you can augment the sound of the kick and snare in the drum mix. That is, you can boost their relative volumes, alter their sounds with separate EQs, add reverb to only the snare, etc. Basically, the more mics you use on a drum kit, the more control you can have over the sound when you're mixing.

This earring technique is particularly effective for miking jazz drummers, because they play with more attention to dynamics and often want to record exactly what they hear while they're playing. When augmented with a mic on the kick drum and one on the snare, the earring technique can yield incredible sounds.

Let's discuss some more advanced stereo miking techniques: spaced pairs, MS matrices, and binaural heads. Particularly useful when you've got limited numbers of mic preamps, these techniques can help you capture great sounds with only two or three mics.

- Spaced Pairs

Spaced pairs are useful for capturing a wide stereo spread as well as more of the acoustical environment than the coincident and near-coincident pairs. Often, engineers use spaced pairs as room mics. The key to success in getting good room sound using a spaced pair is to set up the mics where you hear the best sound. Sounds simple enough, eh? While the artist is playing, walk around the room/space, listening for a spot with a good balance of the instrument(s) and room ambience that you want to record. Listen carefully to the frequencies and watch out for areas that have a build-up of a particular frequency. Remember, bass frequencies often build up in corners, so you may want to avoid placing mics in the corners of your studio. Trust your ears. If you like what you hear, put a mic there and record it.

> *Take Note!*
> Spaced pairs using omni-patterned mics may not have very mono-compatible signals, however the sense of space that they provide, as well as their tonal accuracy, will often outweigh the need for mono-compatibility.

It's usually a good idea to place the mics at an equal distance from the main sound source (so the signal levels are relatively equal) or in a place that picks up a nice blend when listening to the two mics by themselves. For example, when setting up room mics on a drum kit, place the room mics at an equal distance from the middle of the snare drum. Use a tape measure for accuracy.

For spaced pairs, I recommend condenser mics because their frequency response is flatter than dynamic mics. This will help to pick up all of the room tone equally and will present a more accurate aural picture of the recording space. The polar pattern also plays a big part in the quality of sound for a spaced pair. Use cardioid patterns if you want directionality, however, omnidirectional mics are often more desirable because they can be placed closer to the sound source without sacrificing ambience. Also, they will not color the ambient sound as much as the off-axis frequency response of a cardioid mic. Omni mics will pick up sound from the entire recording environment, including reflections from behind the mic, and this often leads to sonically pleasing results.

If you haven't the luxury of a large space to move the mics apart in, you can also try another technique: Move the omni mics closer together, but put a partition (a baffle) between the two mics. That way, you may achieve nice stereo separation and a different sound than you would have using two cardioid mics.

Center of
Sound Source
0°
BAFFLE

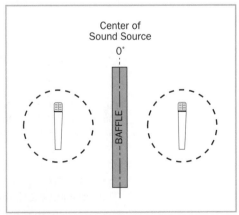

Fig. 7.12. A spaced pair and baffle mic configuration.

In the near-coincident techniques we discussed earlier, you may have noticed that as the mics got further from each other, the less the angle between the mics had to be to maintain the overlap of polar patterns and capture the right amount of signal from the center of the sound source. For example, in the ORTF technique, the cardioid mics are placed 17 centimeters apart with an angle of 110° between their diaphragms. In the NOS technique, the cardioid mics are placed 30 centimeters apart with an angle of 90° between their diaphragms.

As we move mics farther apart from each other into spaced pairs, we can capture a wider stereo spread, however we may run into the problem of not capturing the right amount of signal from the center of the sound source. This can create a hole in the middle of the stereo image. To combat this, place a third mic in the middle, as in fig. 7.13.

Center of
Sound Source
0°
Left
Center
Right

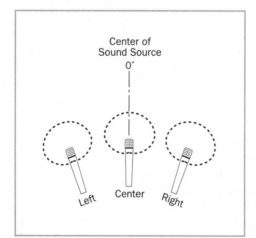

Fig. 7.13. This three-mic technique requires some extra care in keeping the levels of the left, right, and center in balance with each other.

• MS Matrix

The MS matrix technique yields an exceptionally accurate stereo image that is also completely mono-compatible. Here, M stands for "MID" and S stands for "SIDE" and each refers to one mic in the pair. The MID mic is a cardioid or omni condenser mic and the SIDE mic is a figure-8 (bi-directional) condenser mic. Aim the MID mic directly at the source and the SIDE mic perpendicular to the mid mic, as in fig. 7.14.

Center of
Sound Source
0°
[+]
[–]

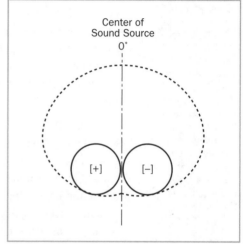

Fig. 7.14. When you combine a cardioid mic pattern and a bi-directional mic pattern, you can capture a very accurate stereo image.

In an MS Matrix, the MID signal is centered and each side of the figure-8 mic is sent to opposite sides in the stereo field (left and right). The phase of one of the sides of the figure-8 mic is then inverted. To get this mic setup working, it takes a bit of trickery. But, it's not impossible; you just need to know how to do it.

To make an MS matrix, you will need:

1x bi-directional mic (figure 8)—the SIDE mic

1x cardioid or omni mic—the MID mic

1x polarity reversal switch

3x audio tracks

1x aux track

Instructions:

1) Using three new mono audio tracks, assign the signal from the MID mic to the input on your first track. Assign the signal from the SIDE mic to **both** the second and third tracks.

2) Reverse the polarity (also called "invert the phase") on the third track, which is the second input of the SIDE mic. (Many mixers have a button for this and software recording programs have plug-ins that can do this. You can also buy or make a device to do this.)

Now for the magic step . . .

3) Find the Null Point. What's that? The null point is the point where the signals from both sides of the SIDE mic are equal and, when you invert the phase of one of the signals, they cancel each other out. However, when recording a figure-8 mic, you only have one gain control for the mic (on the mic pre), so you'll need to adjust the levels of the two sides while monitoring them from your recording device.

To find the null point, first mute the MID mic (Track 1) and listen only to the input signals on tracks 2 and 3. Pan both track 2 and 3 to the center and set the track 2 channel level to 0 on the fader. Adjust the level of track 3 until the sound drops substantially in volume and essentially cancels itself out. This is the Null Point: the place where the two signals from either side of the mic cancel each other out completely. (Remember the section in chapter 6 on phase cancellation? Here it is—in all its glory!)

4) Set up a "group" for tracks 2 and 3 so that the relative level of those tracks will be the same always (otherwise you may lose your null point). A **group**

is when multiple tracks are linked together so that an action on one of the tracks (e.g., volume adjustment) affects all of the tracks in the group equally.

5) Pan track 2 to the left and track 3 to the right. You should now have a nice stereo image.

6) Un-mute and bring up the MID signal on track 1 (panned center) to taste. Get a nice balance between the MID and SIDE signals.

7) Assign the outputs of all three tracks to a stereo bus and use that bus as the input to a stereo aux track. That will let you control the signal of all three tracks on one fader as well as ensure that you don't mess with the balance of the three signals. (Busses and aux tracks are explained in chapter 8.)

You now have a MS signal! The MS mic technique is great, because it creates an awesome stereo image, it uses the science of acoustics in an interesting way, and it is totally mono-compatible (because the SIDE mic cancels itself out in mono leaving only the MID mic signal). And . . . it will impress your clients—even the audio geeks.

- Binaural Head

A binaural head is a device that is shaped like a human head and uses two small condenser mics placed in the head where our eardrums would be. With accurate size, shape, and density, the binaural head captures a sound very much like what a human hears.

These devices record incredible stereo imaging. Listening through headphones to recordings made with a binaural head is a particularly cool experience, because you can detect the location and direction of motion of any sound.

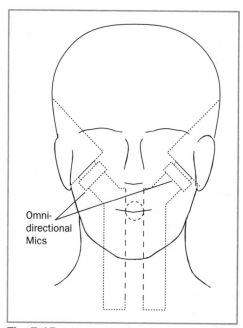

Omni-
directional
Mics

Fig. 7.15. A binaural head captures sound like a real human head does.

pleasing way. Although you could try to predict what mics might sound good together by evaluating their frequency response curves, what fun is that? The true test is how they sound together. Experiment with the techniques presented here and develop your own techniques. Most of all, have fun!

Okay. So now you know more about mic techniques than you thought you'd ever know. Let's move on to some of the other more advanced duties an engineer performs during a recording session. ■

You can simulate a binaural head without actually buying one by putting two small condenser mics close to your own ears (or someone else's) and record what you (they) hear. Listen back in headphones and check out the 3-D sound.

Recordings made with a binaural head sound best when listened to with headphones. Unfortunately, they don't translate well to speakers, so the technique is not used often in music recording.

MICROPHONE WRAP-UP

As you can see, there are thousands of methods to use microphones to capture great sounds. As you experiment with mic placement and technique, compare the sounds of different mics on one sound source. Sometimes using multiple microphones to record one sound source will yield a better overall recording, because the frequency response curves of each individual mic combine in a sonically

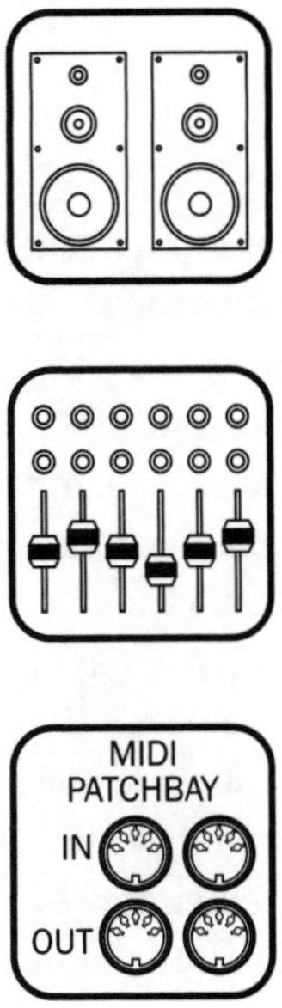
MIDI
PATCHBAY
IN
OUT

CHAPTER 8
Recording and Engineering Techniques, Part II

In this chapter:

- Headphone mixes and click tracks
- Inserts and effects loops
- Sends, returns, and busses
- Overdubbing and submixing
- Rough mixes

With all the mic techniques from the last chapter in your trick bag, let's add some more skills and style to your engineering magic act. In the previous chapter I listed the main responsibilities of the engineer in a recording session. So far, we've covered the first six in chapters 6 and 7 . . . now let's move on to the rest of the list.

- ✔ 1. Setting up microphones: choice, placement, and adjustments
- ✔ 2. Establishing sound separation: setting up gobos, baffles, and blankets for isolation
- ✔ 3. Setting up and working with the recording device and medium
- ✔ 4. Routing signals and getting good recording levels
- ✔ 5. Recording the artist
- ✔ 6. Troubleshooting: computer, equipment, signal path, etc.
- 7. Creating and adjusting the headphone mix and click track
- 8. Managing outboard equipment and syncing gear when necessary
- 9. Setting up effects and printing effects on tracks
- 10. Constantly attending to the artist's and producer's needs
- 11. Overdubbing and submixing
- 12. Creating a good rough mix

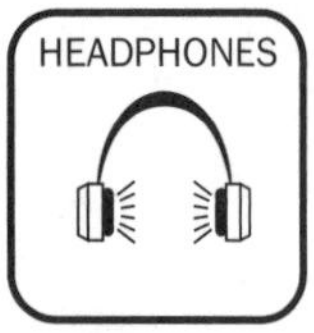
HEADPHONES

HEADPHONES AND HEADPHONE MIXES

A large proportion of recording in professional and home studios is done with headphones on to avoid feedback, create sound separation, and allow separate headphone mixes for individual musicians (if needed). The engineer must be constantly aware of the recording and playback levels of the headphone mix, the routing of audio signals, the hardware it's routed through, and the sound of the overall mix.

Creating a Headphone Mix

A good headphone mix (sometimes called a "cue mix" or "foldback") allows the performer to clearly hear their part along with the other instruments and voices while recording. Often you can use the mix you're already listening to (i.e., the main stereo mix) and simply plug everyone into that signal, depending on where you have your headphone feed in your home studio, as discussed in chapter 2. Usually you can adjust the levels of each track in that one headphone mix so it's good enough for everyone. This gets more difficult the more people you're trying to record at once.

When creating a headphone mix, first be sure that the main rhythm instrument is always audible and somewhat prominent. This instrument is often the drums, percussion, or even a click track, but can also be a bass, an acoustic guitar, a piano, or whatever is leading the rhythmic feel of the song. Any recorded performances that lose the rhythm will be essentially useless (unless that was the point, or if you feel like editing for days).

Most instrumentalists like to hear a lot of themselves in the headphone mix. When recording with several musicians at once, this can become a problem. If you cannot provide a variety of headphone mixes, it's your job to create a mix that everyone can live with. Listen carefully as the musicians play through the song, and adjust the levels so that all of the instruments can be heard at once. Ask them what they want more or less of in the mix. And don't be afraid to use EQ to accentuate certain frequencies in the mix that will help each musician to hear their instrument better. If you have the time and ability, you can create several different headphone mixes using sends or multiple outputs from your recording device, and tailor each mix to an individual's liking.

Creating a good headphone mix for a vocalist is of the utmost importance; it can mean the difference between capturing a mediocre performance and a fantastic performance. If the vocal level in the headphones is too low, the vocalist will tend to sing sharp because they are trying to sing above the music. If the level is too high, they have a tendency to sing flat, because they don't have to try as hard. Listen carefully to the vocalist's headphone mix as well as to what the vocalist is saying about the mix and about how they're singing. They will often tell you what they need, whether it's in the form of blatant opinions, subtle comments, or pitch clues. Minor tweaks in the mix can make all the difference!

Also, consider getting creative with the headphone mix . . . like sending the drummer a compressed and/or distorted version of the drum sound. It might inspire him to play better or create cooler parts.

Multiple Headphone Mixes

There are several ways to get multiple feeds to different sets of headphones in your studio. Here are some ideas:

- If you're using your home stereo as the monitor output, plug a Y-splitter into the headphone jack and run your headphones from there.

- If your recording device has a headphone output, you can split that output.

- If you're using a mixer, there are probably several stereo outputs that can feed headphones.

- If you're using a home stereo and a mixer together, you can utilize the headphone jacks from both units (as well as the one from your recording device), giving you a total of at least three direct headphone outputs (or six if you split all three). However, using all of these different headphones with separate level controls might get confusing.

A better solution is to buy a headphone amplifier specifically made to supply multiple sets of "cans." Simply plug any of the monitor outputs (home stereo headphone out, recording device headphone out, or mixer out) to the input of a headphone amp. Each amp supplies multiple pairs of headphones with the stereo signal, and every pair has its own volume control, allowing each person to adjust their own overall level. Headphone amps may also accept multiple input signals, so technically you could supply some headphones with one mix and the other with a different mix. There are also more advanced headphone amps that accept submixes so the recording artist can essentially make their own headphone mixes by adjusting the levels of each submix to their liking. They could choose to boost the submixed guitar tracks over the submixed drums, etc.

Keep Feedback in Check

Except when they want Jimi Hendrix–like guitar feedback, most people try to avoid feedback in studio environments. Acoustic feedback is created when two magnetic pickups (e.g., microphone and speaker) feed each other the same audio signal. An audio signal going into the mic comes out of the speaker back into the mic and so forth, creating a loop. This feedback loop is the result of the signal building upon itself and creates a sometimes painful and injurious noise. Feedback at high decibel levels can cause hearing loss—not to mention damage to equipment—so be careful! It's a good idea to keep your monitor level down or *preferably off* when recording using microphones that are in the same room. Create a headphone mix instead.

Choosing Headphones

Let's continue with the headphone topic. When buying headphones for your home studio, it's most important to consider how they'll be used. Will you be using them during recording sessions? Consider buying closed-ear headphones so there's minimal sound leakage while tracking. Will you be using them as a reference when mixing? Consider choosing headphones with a flat frequency response so you're sure of their accuracy. Will clients be using these headphones for extended periods of time during sessions? Consider comfort as an important factor in the equation.

There are three types of headphones: open-air, semi-open, and closed-ear (or sealed). These terms refer to how much sound isolation the headphones provide. Often the open-air or semi-open are more comfortable than closed-ear headphones because they don't fit so tightly. However, open-air and semi-open headphones allow some amount of sound to escape into the room. That means the sound could leak into microphones in the recording studio—particularly important to consider if you'll be recording with a click track. Sealed headphones allow very little leakage, so click tracks and other loud signals won't be picked up by mics in the room.

There are other factors to consider when choosing headphones:

- Long-term wearing comfort: People might have to wear them for many hours at a time.

- Spatially accurate sound field: That is, they accurately reproduce the stereo image you've created.

- Extended, smooth frequency response: At least 20 Hz to 20 kHz.

- Reliability and durability: People tend to toss around headphones like they're indestructible.

- The ability to produce high levels with very low distortion: Some people like their headphones loud. (See sidebar on noise levels later in this section).

Before buying headphones, compare models to find the ones that suit you best . . . you'll be wearing them a lot so you better like them. And, being aware of the characteristics of your specific headphones will provide useful information during recording, critical listening, mixing, and mastering. (I'm not advocating using headphones only to mix or master, but sometimes that might be the only option if your roommates, family, landlord, or neighbors are sleeping or otherwise sensitive to volume.)

For example, the headphones I use for recording sessions in my home studio are closed-ear, comfortable, loud, and bass-heavy. This information tells me that (a) I don't need to worry about leakage into microphones, (b) I should be careful of the overall volume of the headphone mix, (c) I don't need to pump the bass in the headphone mix, but I may need to bump up the mid and high frequencies in the headphones to compensate for the bass response, and (d) if I'm recording a bass part, I'll know that what I record isn't as boomy as it sounds in the phones. For critical listening, I use a separate pair of headphones that are closed-ear, extremely comfortable, and have a softer volume and flat frequency response.

[Don't] Stick It in Your Ear

Listening to high levels of any type of sound (whether it's music, jackhammers, or jet engines) can be dangerous if done even for short periods of time. OSHA (Occupational

Beatles producer Sir George Martin has said that the tempo of the song should be felt in the heart . . . with the beating of the heart. If the chorus is more exciting and has more energy, a person's heart will speed up just as a song might speed up. Tempo fluctuations are natural to our human existence as well as our listening experience.

Safety and Health Act, 1970) provides the following data:

SPL (A-weighted)	Daily Exposure
90 dB	8 hours
92	6
95	4
97	3
100	2
102	1.5
105	1
110	0.5
115 dB	0.25 hours

Decibels (dB) are the units used to measure the ratio of sound pressure level (SPL) of an audio source to the lower threshold of human hearing. An SPL of 130 dB is the upper threshold of human tolerance; a noisy factory might have an SPL of 90 dB; your house or apartment has an SPL of approximately 45 dB. (Apparently some Who concerts reached a noise level of 120 dB . . . it's no wonder Pete Townsend is having difficulties hearing these days!)

Please be careful with listening levels and be sure to give your ears a break from time to time—allow them to recover from loud levels. If you *must* listen at loud levels, try to protect your ears (using plugs, etc.), because permanent damage to your hearing could mean permanent damage not only to your career, but also to your basic enjoyment of music.

CLICK TRACKS

Often, as part of the headphone mix, the engineer has to set up the click track for each song that's being recorded. A click track is a steady beat or pulse used to help musicians keep a consistent tempo while recording. The producer should have already established the tempos and meter changes (or time signatures) with the band during the preproduction process or, more specifically, during the writing and rehearsing stage. However, that doesn't mean that the artist or producer won't change the tempo (or, less frequently, the

meter) during the recording session. With creativity comes the flexibility to try new ideas.

When recording, it's often helpful to have a steady beat to follow, whether you're recording yourself or your artist. Even when recording your own fresh new ideas, consider playing to a click track, because who knows . . . you may want to use the initial tracks later in the production process. This is especially important if you've captured the raw emotion or right feel on early performances; many times it's impossible to recreate everything that went into getting that dynamite first pass. And, if you think that you might need to edit together two different takes of a song later, using a click ensures that all of the recorded takes will be at the same tempo. (For more about editing, see chapter 11.)

To get a click happening, set the tempo on a metronome. Better yet, program a drum machine or software-based click track as your guide. With the latter options, you can program changes in tempo and meter that are not feasible on your standard metronome. You can use audio or MIDI clicks. Once you've set the final tempo and meter changes, it's often a good idea to record the click track as a permanent audio guide. Do this for each song on which a click is appropriate.

Be careful with using clicks, though. There are times when the feel of a song can be destroyed by a click, especially if a band is not used to playing with a click or if a song needs the push and pull of slight tempo adjustments. Many songs do not need to be confined by tempo; they need to "breathe." Yet, musicians who have practiced with a metronome usually can play naturally around the confines of click track and still allow the track to breathe.

Here are some additional things to think about when using a click track:

Tap it: Don't know what tempo you want? Try tapping it in. Most drum machines and software-based clicks allow you to tap in the tempo you want and they'll figure it out the beat-per-minute (BPM) for you automatically. As an engineer in a recording session, you should be able to change the tempo and meter for a track quickly, and tapping is a good tool for this.

Practice with a click: You or your artist might not be used to playing with a click track. However, practicing with a click can greatly improve your timing and rhythm. After a few weeks of playing with a click, it should be much more natural to play and record with one.

Overdub parts: One of the main benefits of recording with a click is you can overdub other parts later and not have to guess about the tempo. For example: If you record a guitar part today, two weeks from now your drummer friend can lay down some tracks without worrying about tempo fluctuations.

Choose the right subdivision: Experiment with the subdivisions of the click beat. Try every downbeat (1, 2, 3, 4), beats 2 and 4, eighth notes, etc. Depending on the type of song and its tempo, more pulses might help the musicians play the rhythms tighter, while less pulses might make the song breathe more.

Choose the right sound: Experiment with the sound of the click. Try anything percussive, like sidesticks, cowbells, tambourines, shakers, or even counting "1, 2, 3, 4." Or, instead of using a simple click sound, program a beat (loop) to play along with. This can make it more interesting for the musicians and possibly improve the feel of the entire song because they're playing along with a groove instead of beeps and blips.

Watch out for bleed: Musicians should wear closed headphones so that the click doesn't bleed into the mics while recording. Playing along with a loop instead of a loud click can also lessen the bleed. Also consider turning the click off at the last note so that there's no bleed on the last note's sustain or fade out. If you're recording a click track to analog tape, record it at low levels because it can bleed onto adjacent tracks on the tape.

Experiment with the tempo: Try speeding up the click by one or two beats per minute (1–2 BPM) before the chorus to build excitement. If recording a band, sometimes just starting with the click at the beginning of the song is enough, if the band can keep good time or if the song has rubato sections.

Setting delay times: Clicks can also be helpful to set delay times (e.g., tempo-based guitar delays) as well as to trigger gated effects during recording and mixing. (More about delays and gates can be found in chapter 13.)

USING EFFECTS WHILE RECORDING

As you gain experience and confidence in engineering recording sessions, you will find it appropriate to utilize effects during the recording session. Sometimes you may want to record (or "print") effects to a track. For example, you might want to compress the electric bass track on its way into your recording device. Or, you might find a cool guitar effect that you're sure you want to keep for the final mix. To do these things, you often need to use *inserts* to create an effects loop.

Other times, you may just want to add an effect during the session without recording it, such as when adding reverb to the vocal track so the singer feels more comfortable with his or her voice while recording. To do this, you need to utilize *sends*, *returns*, and *busses* to create an effects loop. In the following section, I'll explain how to set up these two types of effects loops to use in a recording session.

INSERTS
FX

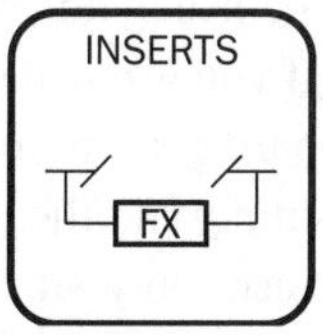

PRINTING EFFECTS TO TRACKS USING INSERTS

To record an effect on a track (e.g., to print compression on a bass track, etc.), you need to route your input signal through the effects unit before it reaches the recording device. That's obvious. However, the process is slightly different if using outboard gear (hardware) versus software effects.

For example, to record compression using an outboard compressor, you first need to connect the vocal mic to a preamp (as usual), then patch the output of the preamp to a compressor, which then feeds the recording device, as in fig. 8.1.

If you're recording through a mixer, you'll need to set this up in a slightly different way, using inserts.

Hardware Inserts

Mixers have insert patch points so you can utilize the mixer's preamp, then route the signal out of the mixer via the insert patch point to another device . . . ultimately sending the signal to the recording device. Often this requires a "Y" insert cable for sending the uneffected ("dry") signal and returning the effected signal.

On one end, there's a TRS (Tip-Ring-Sleeve) plug that splits out into two TS (Tip-Sleeve) plugs for the send and return signals, as in fig. 8.2. The tip of the TRS plug feeds the tip of the send plug, which goes to the input of the external device (e.g., compressor in). The signal then returns from the output of the external device (e.g., the compressor out) through the return TS cable and feeds the ring part of the TRS plug . . . which goes back into the mixer. This is called an effects loop. See fig. 8.3.

COMPRESSOR
Microphone
Preamp
Compressor
Recording Device

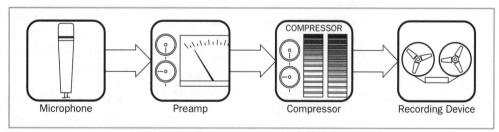

Fig. 8.1. Recording serially through an outboard compressor is fairly straightforward.

Send
Return
Return
Send

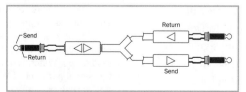

Fig. 8.2. A "Y" insert cable.

INSERT
COMPRESSOR
OUT
IN

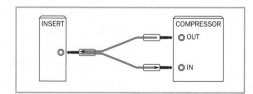

Fig. 8.3. An effects loop at an insert patch point.

If, instead of using a TRS cable to create an effects loop, you use a TS cable, you've got some other options. On most mixers, if you connect a TS plug into the Insert patch point but only push it in to the first click, the signal will split. One copy of the signal will go through the mixer like it wasn't touched, and a copy of the signal will be sent on the TS cable. If you push the TS cable all the way in and hear the second click, the signal will be sent completely out of the mixer and cannot return along that TS cable. See figs. 8.4(a) and 8.4(b).

Fig. 8.4(a). A TS cable plugged in only one click.

Fig. 8.4(b). A TS cable plugged in all the way—two clicks.

What if you're recording directly into your recording software (without using a mixer), but you want to use a piece of outboard gear as an insert? You'll need to set up your recording device to receive the input, use the software to send it back out another output (not the main output) to the piece of gear, and then return the processed final to another input on your recording device and record that signal. With this signal flow, you need to be aware of the possibility of higher latency.

If you are using an analog piece of outboard gear with a digital recording device for an effects loop, there will be some additional delay due to D/A/D conversion. Once the original signal has been converted to digital, it's sent back out and reconverted to analog for the outboard gear, then finally returned, where

it's converted back into digital. However, the delay is not much. If you remember from the section on buffer size and latency times in chapter 3, converter delay is around 1.5 milliseconds. For the extra D/A/D conversion that occurs in an effects loop with analog gear, 3.0 milliseconds of delay is added to the signal from the conversion process. That doesn't seem like much, but when added in with high buffer settings, it might create phasing problems while you're recording and/or mixing.

NOTE: If you are using a digital piece of outboard gear, there is no conversion delay; simply run the appropriate digital cables between your recording device and the effects processor. Likewise, if your signal path is all analog, there is no delay. If you need to convert an analog signal to digital to route it through a digital-only processor, the A/D/A conversion will also take three milliseconds.

Software Inserts

If you're using a software plug-in as the compressor, in most cases, you'll need to set this up a little differently. Send the signal from the mic preamp into your computer and software program. Bring this signal up on an auxiliary track and insert the plug-in on that track. Then, route the output of that aux track to the input of an audio track to record the effected signal, as in fig. 8.5.

Watch Your Levels

When printing effects, be sure you're not overloading the signal path at any point. For example, if you're recording vocals through an outboard compressor, you might not see clipping at your recording device, but the mic preamp or compressor could be distorting on loud notes. Watch your levels at all points in the signal path and use your ears to detect any worrisome sounds.

Computer
Audio Interface A/D Converter with Built-in Mic Preamps
Microphone
Preamp
AUX TRACK
COMPRESSOR
AUDIO TRACK
Compressor
Hard Drive

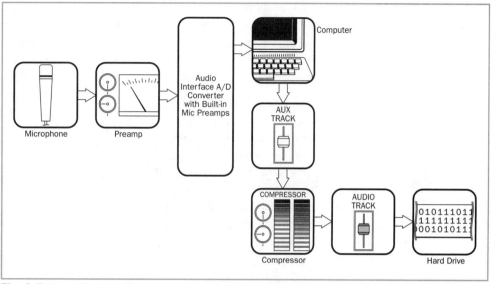

Fig. 8.5. Recording through a compressor software plug-in is really the same process as with hardware, but the signal flow is a little more complicated. NOTE: If you simply insert the plug-in on the audio track instead of routing through the aux track first, the signal will not be recorded with compression; the compressor plug-in will be affecting the already-recorded uncompressed audio signal.

EFFECTS LOOP
FX

Effects Loops with Sends, Returns, and Busses

Another method of setting up an effects loop is using busses, sends, and auxiliary track returns. Those may be new terms to you, but don't let the jargon scare you. Once you understand the terms and the signal flow, setting up an effects loop this way will be a very powerful engineering tool.

Effects loops that make use of sends, returns, and busses have a variety of uses during recording and mixing sessions. For example, they can be used to apply one effect (like reverb) on multiple tracks, distribute multiple different headphone mixes, or submix tracks. Applying one effect to one or more tracks is the most common usage, and I'll explain the terms, setup, and signal flow as they relate to that usage. Let's start with the terminology:

A **bus** combines or sums signals together and then carries that combined signal somewhere else . . . often out to one mono or stereo input. It is a means of combination and transportation for one or more audio signals. To visualize it, think of it literally as an automotive, passenger-carrying bus traveling from one location to another. Alternatively, I usually think of a bus as a physical or virtual cable that carries multiple signals from one place to another.

A **send** is a routing mechanism that tells an audio signal where to go (i.e., which bus to travel on). This is the "bus station" at the start of the trip, or the beginning of the effect loop's signal path. I think of the send as one end of the physical or virtual "bus cable."

An **auxiliary (aux) track** is the destination of the bus, the input where the bussed signals are sent to be processed (e.g., by a reverb plug-in). I think of the aux track as the other end of the physical or virtual bus cable.

Take Note!

Mixing boards often call their sends and returns "aux sends" and "aux returns."

A **return** is the output of the aux track. This output often travels directly to the main outputs (to your speakers). The return allows us to hear and adjust the sound of the processed audio signals.

So how does an effects loop that utilizes sends, returns, and busses work? Let's say we're recording a vocalist. Vocalists often like to hear reverb on their voice while recording. However, we don't want to record that reverb on the track with the vocal performance (as we might do with an insert). We want to simply listen to the effected vocal while recording the uneffected "dry" signal. So, we set up an effects loop with a send, return, and bus.

What really happens is that the send makes a duplicate of the vocal track so that there are two identical versions of the vocal track—the original and the copy. The original signal flows out to the main outputs as usual. That's our "dry" signal. The copy is routed out of the send on a bus to the effects unit (a reverb on the aux track) and is processed by the effects unit. The effected copy (the "wet" signal) is then sent out of the return to the main outputs, too. So, both the dry and the wet signals are routed to the main outputs, and it's up to us to determine how much of both we want to mix together for the overall vocal sound. Check out fig. 8.6. for a graphical representation.

In most situations, we can tweak all of the same parameters of the original track as we can on the copied track. We can adjust the volume, mute, solo, and panning of the copied track that is sent on the bus using the send controls. Also, once the copied track has reached the aux track, we can adjust the same parameters on the aux track, as well as add additional inserts or effects loops onto the aux track, if desired. For example, the send controls regulate the volume of the copied signal that is sent on the bus to the reverb effects unit. The aux track fader controls how much of the reverb effect on those tracks is added to the overall mix. If you add an EQ insert on the aux track, you can change the EQ of the "wet" signal without affecting the "dry" signal.

Wet/Dry Mix

There's an additional parameter within most effects units called the "wet/dry mix." This parameter determines how much of the effect should be added to the incoming signal. In almost all cases, when setting up effects loops, this parameter should be set for 100% wet. This ensures that you're maximizing the usage of the effect. Besides, you already have control of the wet/dry mix because you can tweak the mix of dry original track and wet-effected track yourself.

Pre and Post

There's one more aspect of effects loops that we need to discuss . . . pre-fader and post-fader sends. "Pre" and "post" are short for pre-fader and post-fader. Deceptively simple, these two functions are quite useful in any recording and mixing environment. But, to use them effectively, you need to understand signal flow.

When a signal is sent from a track on a bus pre-fader, it means that the track's volume fader does not affect the volume level of signal that is sent on the bus. In fact, the *pre-fader* signal is not affected by the solo or mute buttons on the track, either. If a signal is sent post-fader, it means that the volume fader *does* affect the overall volume level of signal that is sent on the bus, as do the mute and solo buttons. Thus, when signals are sent post-fader, any adjustments made to the channel's volume

Microphone
Preamp
Electric Line-Level Instrument
AUDIO TRACK
AUDIO TRACK
AUX TRACK
Reverb
BUS 1
MAIN OUTPUT
DRY SIGNAL
WET SIGNAL
Main Output
Speakers

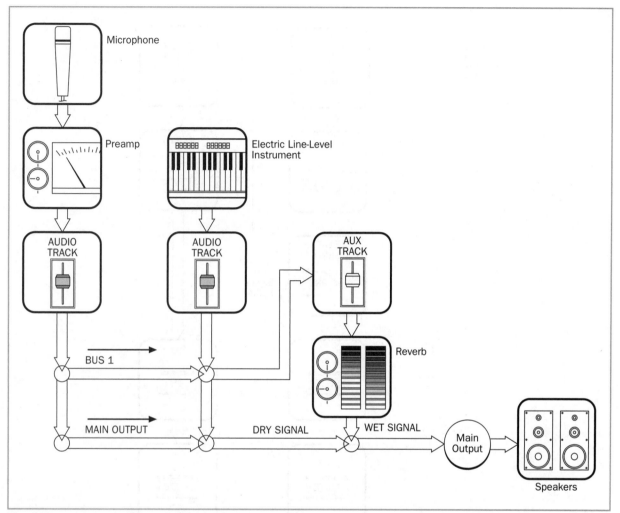

Fig. 8.6. Understanding the signal flow of an effects loop will open up your mind to many creative signal routing options while recording and mixing.

fader (or mute and solo status) affect the send level. Note: Inserts (plug-ins and/or hardware inserts) affect both pre-fader and post-fader signals.

Pre-fader sends are great when you want a copy of a track going out of the send, no matter what happens with the volume fader, mute button, and solo button of the original track.

Let's say you want to create a special effect in a song, in which the lead vocal slowly disappears into the background. You route a copy of the lead vocal track out of a pre-fader send to a reverb effect. As you pull down the fader on the vocal track (decreasing the level), the reverbed vocal stays at the same level. As the dry vocal track fades, you can start fading the wet version to create the illusion of the vocal slowly disappearing into the distance.

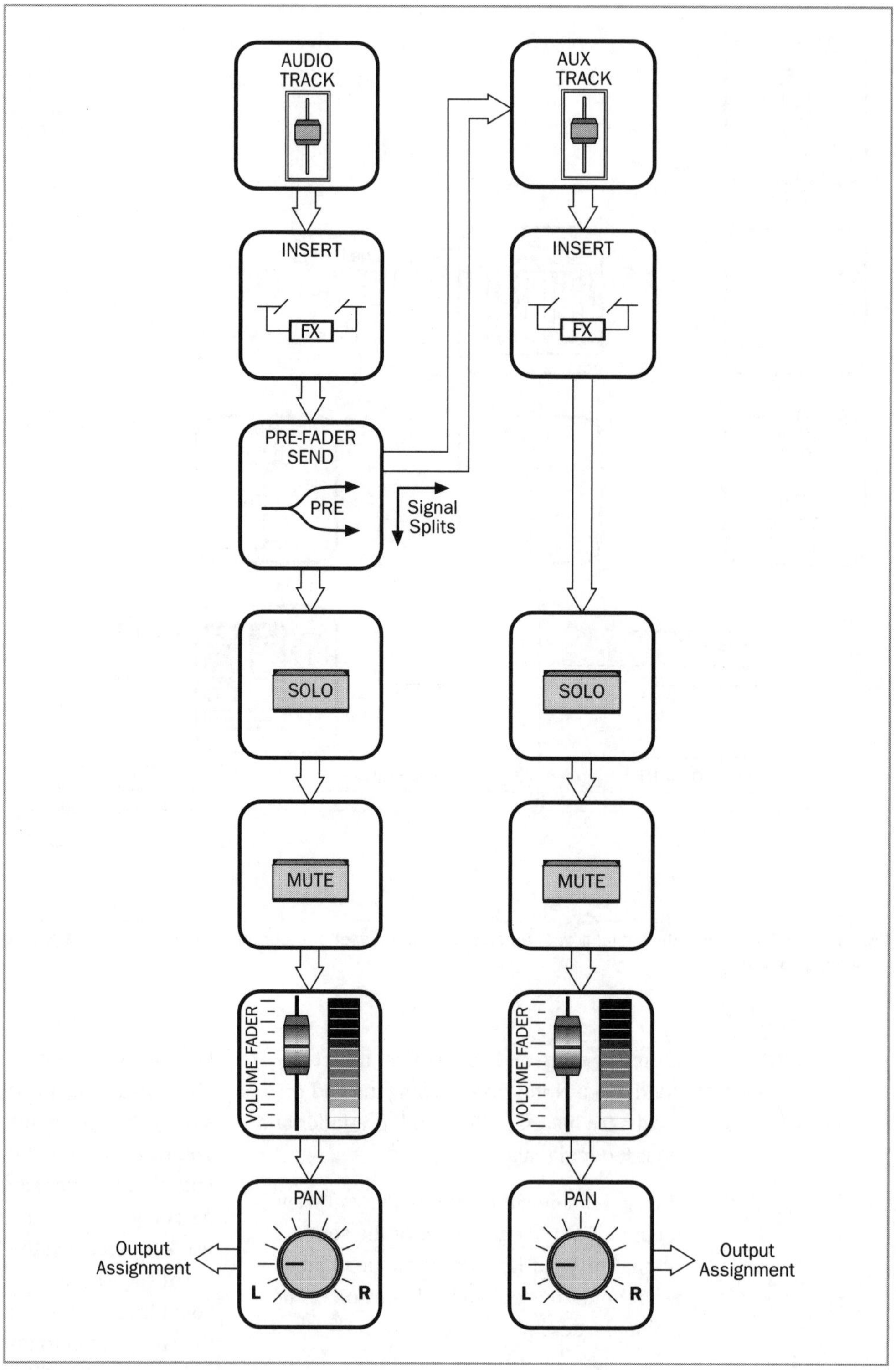
AUDIO TRACK
AUX TRACK
INSERT
FX
INSERT
FX
PRE-FADER SEND
PRE
Signal Splits
SOLO
SOLO
MUTE
MUTE
VOLUME FADER
VOLUME FADER
PAN
Output Assignment
L
R
PAN
L
R
Output Assignment

Fig. 8.7(a). Pre-fader signal flow.

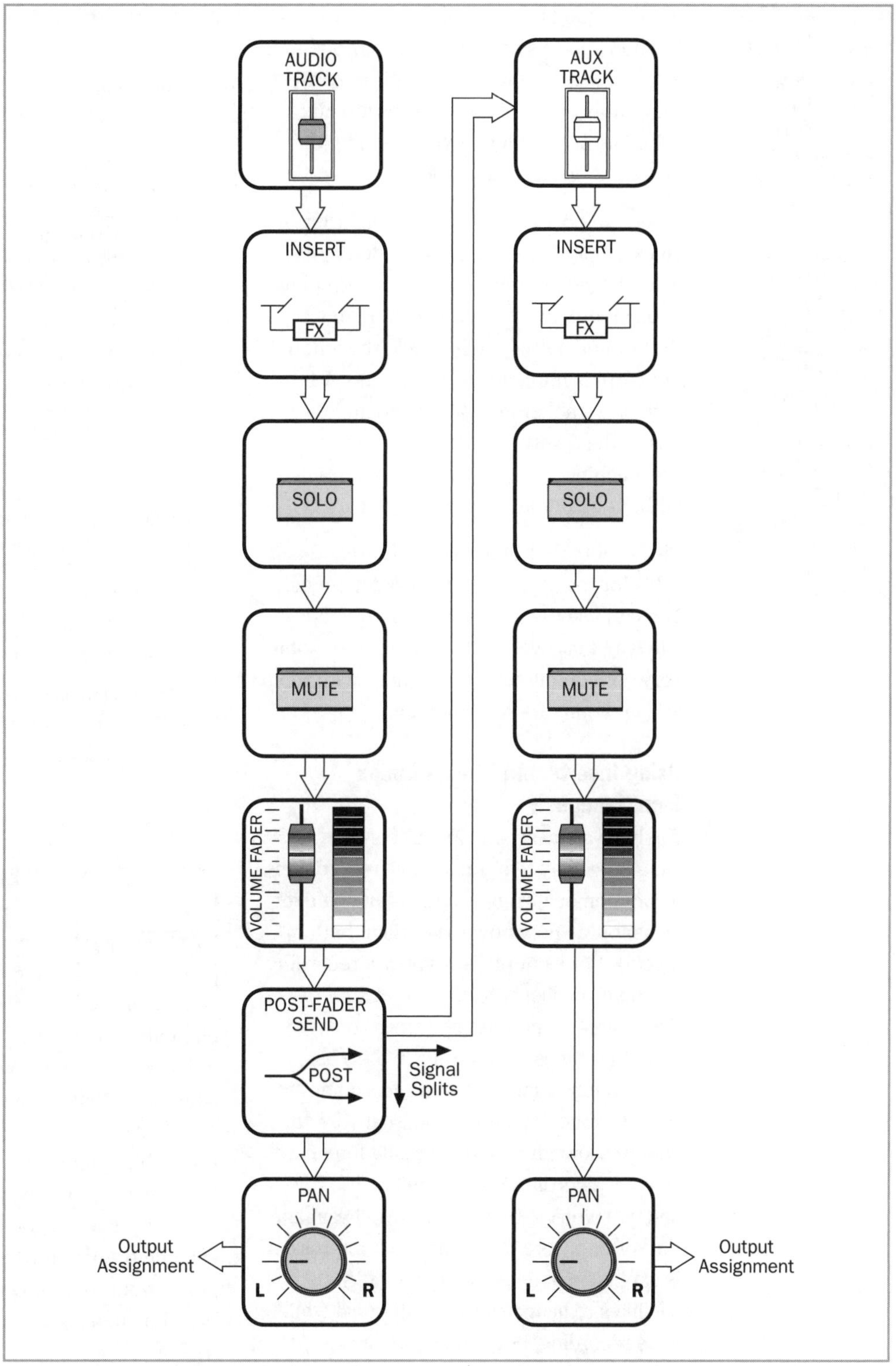
AUDIO TRACK
AUX TRACK
INSERT
FX
INSERT
FX
SOLO
SOLO
MUTE
MUTE
VOLUME FADER
VOLUME FADER
POST-FADER SEND
POST
Signal Splits
PAN
L
R
Output Assignment
PAN
L
R
Output Assignment

Fig. 8.7(b). Post-fader signal flow.

Take Note!

If you find an effect that you really like while recording but don't want to commit it to the track directly, record the output of the effects unit onto a separate audio track while recording the uneffected track, too. That way you have both the "dry" track and the "wet" track, and can decide what to do with them later in the mix.

Another good time to use pre-fader sends is when you're setting up a headphone mix with sends. Use pre-fader sends because they allow you to create a separate mix using the send faders, while keeping the main mix on the track faders.

When are post fader sends useful? Here's an example. I often use post-fader sends when I send audio tracks to a reverb plug-in on an aux track. That way, if I adjust the volume on the audio track, the amount of reverb is impacted in kind. Also, if I mute the track, the send has no audio to bus to the reverb so I don't get a ghost in the machine . . . an extra reverbed track without its dry audio counterpart.

Please note that there are no hard and fast rules for using pre- and post-fader sends. You can use them creatively in the opposite way that I've mentioned here for some very cool outcomes. Experiment with them and let your ears be the judge.

Using Inserts and Effects Loops Simultaneously

Applying an insert and an effects loop simultaneously to a track while recording is a common occurrence, and, as an engineer, you should know how to set them both up quickly. For example, say you are recording a female vocalist who sings with a lot of dynamics—sometimes she sings softly and other times very loudly. In this case, it's probably a smart idea to record her track through a compressor. That way, the compressor can lessen the really loud parts, so your recording levels won't be too hot and you won't get clipping, as well as make the softer parts a little louder. (Compression is explained in detail in chapter 12.) Also, she likes to hear reverb on her vocal while she's recording, but you don't want to record that reverb on the vocal track. This setup is demonstrated in fig. 8.8.

Learn the Lingo

Using the effects loop lingo in a recording session, a producer might say, "Send the electric and acoustic guitar tracks on a bus to the Reverb effects unit and return it to an aux track named Reverb Return." However, many people combine the functions of the aux tracks and returns as described above and use the terms interchangeably to represent both. For example, a producer might say, "Send the guitars to the Reverb and return it on track 24," or even simpler, "Set up a reverb effects loop for the guitars." Some producers might just say, "Throw a reverb on that track," and will leave it up to the engineer to set it up in whatever way makes the most sense.

As a rule of thumb, compressors, limiters, and EQ are often set up as inserts on a specific track, whereas reverbs and delays are usually set up on sends. So, if a producer says to you (the engineer):

- "Compress this track." Add a compressor as an insert on the track.
- "There's too much low end on this track." Add an EQ as an insert on that track.
- "Wow—that track is dry." Send that track to a reverb.

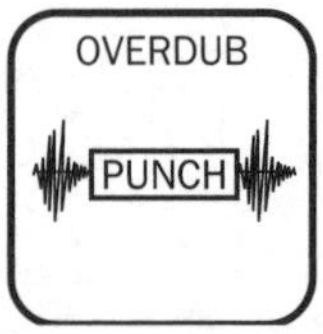
OVERDUB
PUNCH

OVERDUBBING

Having the click track, a good headphone mix, and effects loops under control are three key elements for successfully performing overdubs. An overdub is when you record over something that has already been recorded, whether you record onto a brand new track (like recording vocals for the first time over top of the pre-recorded rhythm section) or when you're fixing spots on specific tracks on which you've already done some recording (like re-recording the bass line in a song's second chorus).

Vocalist
Microphone
Preamp
INSERT
FX
Compressor
Mixing board
AUDIO
TRACK
POSTFADER
SEND
POST
AUX
TRACK
INSERT
FX
Reverb
Speakers
Recording Device

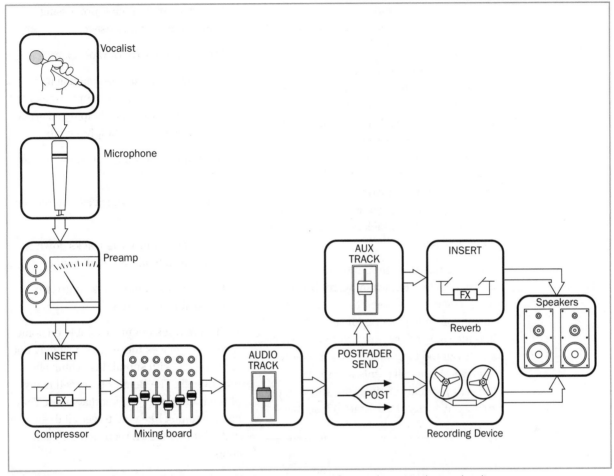

Fig. 8.8. Here, the vocal signal is recorded through the compressor and a copy is sent to the reverb unit.

Often, overdubs require punching in and out of a track. Punching means "to drop a track into record." In other words, you pick and choose spots to record new material, and "punch" the record button at those exact moments. For example, say the bass player played several wrong notes at the end of the second chorus. After cueing up that spot in the song and pressing Play, the bass player plays the part again. The engineer punches in to record over the wrong notes, and then punches out of Record mode (back into Play mode), once the new correct notes have been recorded. Ideally, no one will be able to tell that the punched part of the track was from a different recording take than the original.

With overdubbing on analog tape, punching is an art—almost a sport—where impeccable timing and a musical ear are the difference between a punch-in superstar and a tape machine outcast. With digital recording systems, the sport of punching in and out has lost a lot of its pizzazz and even its necessity, because punching can now be automated. Regardless, knowing how to quickly punch in and out can make your recording sessions go much more smoothly. Your tracks will sound better, and ultimately the producer and artist will be happy.

Two tools that make punching in and out easier are pre-roll and post-roll. Pre-roll is the amount of playback time before punching in to record an overdub. Often it's only several seconds or a couple of measures of the song. Post-roll is the amount of playback time after the punch recording has been made (i.e., the time after the punch out). Sometimes, only pre-roll is used and the track is stopped at the end of the punch.

Choosing the right amount of pre-roll is a key consideration when overdubbing. As an engineer, you need to give the artist enough pre-roll to get comfortably back into the song, but not enough to make the artist wait too long and lose their energy. Also, get the punch points and pre/post roll set up quickly so the artist stays "in the zone" and doesn't have time to lose focus.

Punch
IN
Punch
OUT
Pre-Roll
- - - Recording - - -
Post-Roll
2 Bars
8 Bars
2 Bars

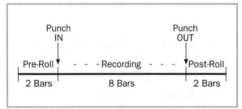

Fig. 8.9. Overdubbing on a track: pre-roll, punch in, record, punch out, post-roll.

SUBMIX

COMBINING TRACKS—SUBMIXES

A submix is a combination of several tracks, such as three harmony vocal tracks, or groups of several tracks, such as all drum, bass, and guitar tracks. There are a few reasons to combine several tracks into a mono or stereo submix:

- To reduce track count, processing power, and memory usage
- To save hard drive or tape space
- To create stem mixes—making it easier to manipulate multiple tracks at once while mixing, or helping an artist control their own headphone mix

Here are a few examples of what you can do with submixing:

- Record eight drum mics as a stereo pair onto two tracks
- Mix twenty-four vocal tracks down to four tracks to lessen track count
- Combine six guitar tracks onto two tracks for monitoring

With large track counts available on some recording devices these days, you may not have to deal with submixing. Think about this, though: The Beatles recorded many of their albums on 4-track machines. They had to submix like mad to get all their widely-varied tracks recorded for each song.

To submix while recording or mixing, all you need to do is route all the signals you want to combine together onto a bus. You can then record (or just listen to) the output of the bus. But be careful of the effects you use—if you record the submix, the effects will be permanently printed on the submixed tracks! Depending on the tracks that you're combining, you might want to wait to add effects until the mixdown. Or, you may chose to record a separate track for just the printed effects. If you're submixing during the mixing process, make backup copies of the original unsubmixed files in case you're later not happy with the submix and want to bring back the original tracks.

ROUGH MIXES

Most musicians (including artists, producers, and engineers) like to take something home to listen to after they've recorded all day and night. The engineer is in charge of making rough mixes for this purpose. Record rough mixes onto CDs, DATs, cassette tapes, or whatever format the artist and producer want to listen to.

Many engineers like to do some amount of mixing for their "roughs." That is, they like to add EQ, effects, and other processing to make the best sounding tracks in a short amount of time. That makes the producer and artist happy and adds value to the recording they're taking home. If the artist sounds good, the engineer (you) looks good.

AT THE END OF THE SESSION

Once you're done with the session, be sure to save your files and make backups! Nothing is worse than losing files you worked on all day—or worse, an artist's once-in-a-lifetime performance. And finally, cleaning up the studio after the session and doing any preventative maintenance on equipment, from dusting to defragmenting, keeps your studio in good working order, making it more pleasant to come back to the next day.

Personality Matters: The Engineer's Other Side

I saved one of the most important topics for the end of this chapter . . .

The engineer often plays a service role during a recording session, and a big part of the job—in addition to all of the engineering tasks—is to constantly attend to the artist's and producer's needs. Regardless of all the technical skills that are required, this means the engineer must first and foremost be a good listener. Being an engineer requires a flexible demeanor to accommodate input from many people and instruments at one time.

Good recording engineers capture high-quality sounds with creative recording technique and are responsive to the needs of the artist and producer. Great engineers have these qualities plus a deep understanding of the signal flow of the studio and all of its gear . . . *and* are generally fun to be around.

Now let's look at what the producer does . . . in the next chapter. ■

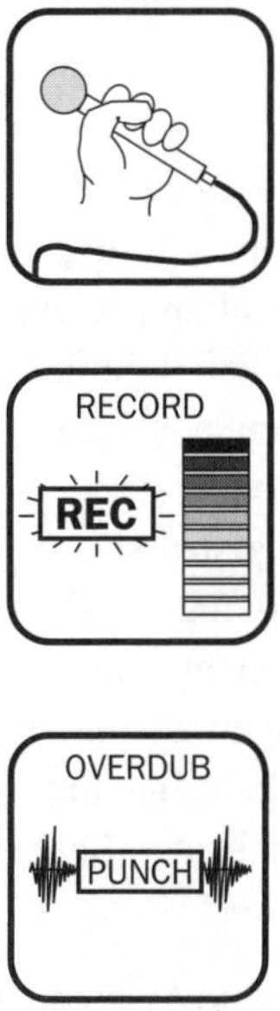
RECORD
REC
OVERDUB
PUNCH

CHAPTER 9
The Producer's Role While Recording

In this chapter:

- The ins and outs of producing a recording session
- Interacting with the artist and the engineer
- Vocal production
- Producing your own music

After all the preproduction that you've done, the recording session is where you, the producer, transform the artistic vision into reality . . . by encouraging the best performances possible from yourself or your artist. But before the session starts, there are several things you can to help ensure a smooth session.

RIGHT BEFORE THE RECORDING SESSION

Preparation is a key element of any successful recording session, even if you're recording your own playing. First, make sure you have all the equipment you need. You and the engineer (probably one and the same) should have already filled out the "Equipment Needed List" (chapter 6). Double-check that you have the right number of mic stands, mic cables, pop filters, instrument cables, headphones, headphone extension cables, and instrument and music stands. Also check for mic selections and any instruments and instrument supplies (e.g., guitar strings, drum sticks, etc.), as well as hardware such as amplifiers, monitors, and outboard effects processors. Don't forget to check the space available on your hard drive(s), and to defragment the drives, if necessary. Also, be sure you have enough CD-Rs, DATs, cassettes, and other media, to make rough mixes for the artist after the session.

Check the studio diagram you made to see where each player and piece of equipment should be set up, and always be aware of maintaining the line-of-sight between players and sound separation between instruments. Arrange the studio as best you can before the players arrive. (Even though the engineer is usually responsible for all of these things, the producer is ultimately responsible for everything . . . so it can't hurt to double check.)

Studio Ambience

Before the session, assess your studio environment: Is it clean? Is it conducive to creativity and an emotional performance? Will it make the artist comfortable? Does it make you feel relaxed? How is the temperature and lighting? Consider changing your light sources from direct to indirect lighting, from fluorescent to halogen, or even use candles or other mood lighting. Ask the artist, too. He or she might prefer a different environment than you'd think. At the beginning of the session, ask them about the temperature, lighting, and the placement of equipment and instruments. Do everything that you can to make the environment favorable to musical expression. Little things can pay big dividends in the long run. This also includes having food and beverages available, preferably items and brands the artist likes.

Professional studios spend a lot of effort (time and money) to create a good vibe. Recording at home, the best any of us can do is work with the space we have and make it comfortable for ourselves and the other musicians. It's your job as the producer to make the artist feel comfortable, and if you're not comfortable in your own studio, then no one else will be, either. Make your studio a place where you enjoy creating music, and that creative vibe will rub off on other people.

Producing a Recording Session

If there was an exact procedure for running a recording session as a producer, I'd include it here. However, there's no single "right" way, so you're going to have to plan it out as you see fit. I can tell you that the usual flow is:

1. Setting up the studio (mics, environment, etc.)

2. Getting sounds (making sure the mics work, that they're placed well, and that your recording device is getting good recording levels)

3. Doing a warmup and practice take (which you should record anyway)

> **Take Note!**
>
> When working with union musicians, producers have to fill out AFM and AFTRA documentation at the end of every recording session. Consult the AFM and AFTRA Web sites (as listed in chapter 4) for more details on this procedure.

4. Recording as many takes as necessary (with breaks in between, when needed)

5. Tearing down the equipment, making a rough mix of what you recorded, saving and backing up the files

No one can tell you how to become a good producer; I can only tell you about some of the things that successful producers do. Producing a recording session is an art, learned from experience. The more sessions you work on, the better producer you'll become.

A Producer's Style and Energy

All producers have their own style. Some are very hands-on—they get up and dance around, feeding on the energy of performers and bouncing energy back at them. Some stay detached, letting the artist simply do their thing. The really good producers can do *both* of these things when called for. They do whatever it takes to get the best performances from their artists.

The ability to figure out what an artist needs in order to evoke their best effort is one of the most (if not *the* most) important skills a producer can have. It requires the producer to really understand the artist. (And if you're producing yourself, you need to figure what motivates you to draw out your best performances.) All of the work you did building a relationship with the artist during preproduction pays off in the production phase.

The energy you display in each recording session is incredibly important. Other people will feed off of your enthusiasm or negativity. Often the producer must act as the inspirer when artists are down, tired, or nervous. A producer's energy has a huge effect on not only the performances in the sessions, but also on the entire project.

What an Artist Wants from a Producer

Artists want a number of things from their producers. They want someone who supports their music, who provides camaraderie, and who can translate (or at least interpret) their musical vision. They want a creative ally who will help them make the best music of their lives. To provide all of this for the artist, you need to do many things, including:

- Making them feel comfortable enough to be really open and expressive

- Focusing their attention on the work that must be done

- Helping to spur their creativity . . . being a catalyst for new ideas

- Keeping an open mind and being flexible about new ideas

- Knowing when to make suggestions and when to keep your mouth shut

- Providing a different point of view

- Offering articulate and constructive criticism, even when it's something that you know the artist doesn't necessarily want to hear

- Being prepared to accommodate anything they need

- Mediating and protecting the democratic process (when dealing with a group)

- Knowing when the democratic process isn't working, and making a decision

- Creating an atmosphere where special musical moments can happen

There are few constants for producers, from session to session. Every session is different. However, the real pros are known for their abilities to do all these things in one way or another.

DURING THE SESSION

Whether you're producing your own music or someone else's, it is beneficial to think and act like a professional record producer during your recording sessions. Philosophically, you need to be aware of the big picture but focused on the small details of each part. Psychologically, you need to be critical of the performances yet comforting to the performers. Physically, you need be aware of your own energy as well as that of the performer.

Seeing the Forest AND the Trees

Always be aware of the overall sound and each part, separate from the whole—this requires a very attentive ear and the ability to hone in on specific parts, while also looking at the big picture of the song. For example, when recording a guitar part, listen on three different levels:

- *Listen to the details of each track.* Does the guitar part groove by itself? Is it in tune? Is it creating a good sound/ tone? Is the player into the song and is that energy being captured? Could the part stand on its own? Is the rhythm tight? Are the chord voicings good? Does the phrasing create the right feel?

- *Listen to how certain tracks interact with each other.* Are the guitarist and drummer locking up? Do their parts fit together? Are the bassist and guitarist playing well together? Does the tone of the guitar clash with the bass? How does this guitar part sound with the other guitar track? Do the rhythms and chord voicings of the keyboard and guitar fit together, or do they step on each other? Are the bass and drums tight?

- *Listen to how the entire song sounds as one unit.* Do all the parts fit together well? Does each part have its place in the mix? Do any parts stick out? What's the intended overall vibe of the tune? Is it actually being captured? Is the tempo right? How does this song make you feel? Does the song represent part of the artistic vision of the project?

Critical and Comforting at the Same Time

Critical and comforting . . . these two terms aren't often used together. However, as a producer you must become skilled at melding both terms into comments you make about your artists' performances. Remember the discussion in chapter 4 on tact and diplomacy during preproduction? Tact and diplomacy are just as important during the production phase. Develop methods for giving critical opinions without hurting the artist's feelings—they'll appreciate your honest opinion, but not if it's given in a harsh way.

I recommend using positive feedback first, then making any critical comments. Also make sure your comments are specific and directed at a particular thing the performer can improve. Let's look at some responses to a typical recording session situation. For example, let's say the bass player is overdubbing a part that was good in some spots, but not so good in others.

1. The producer says, "Let's do it again." This gives the bass player no feedback whatsoever. He doesn't know what was right or wrong, plus it does nothing for his self-esteem.

2. The producer says, "That sucks. Let's do it again." This is even worse than the first response because not only does it provide no specific feedback about the part, it also demeans the performer. This shows little respect for the musi-

> *Take Note!*
> I've found energy and performance are like intersecting lines on a graph—earlier takes are a little sloppier, but have better energy; later takes are usually tighter but the energy declines. The intersection point when the best performances happen are different for each artist, so pay close attention to this in each recording session. When you get to that optimal point with the artist in a session, capitalize on it.

cian. (You might wonder if people actually say stuff like this in sessions, but I've seen it happen.)

3. The producer says, "That was good, but I think you can do it better." The best response of the first three, but still it lacks concrete feedback.

4. The producer says, "That was really good. I liked the lick you played in the fifth bar and the feel you had in the last chorus. Try to get that feel for the entire song and put that cool lick in there . . . it really makes the song. Let's roll it again." This is what I'm talking about. Pointed comments, positive feedback. Apply your knowledge of music to the specific comments you make. The musicians you work with will really appreciate your attention to detail and positive energy.

All that said, you have to go with it artist by artist, relationship by relationship, and moment by moment. If you and the artist are in the zone, and you each know exactly what you're going for, sometimes "again" or "one more time" is all you need to say; anything more would break the flow. In certain circumstances, like when it's an angry song and you know the artist like your brother, yelling, "That sucked! Do it again!" might just give the artist the kick in the pants he needs. Just learn to read the artist and the mood.

Energy vs. Performance

In any recording session you need to be aware of the energy vs. performance curve. The energy level of each person involved in a recording fluctuates, which affects their performance. Some people are best on the first take, therefore, you'd better be ready to record when they're ready to lay it down. Others need a number of takes to warm up. In this case, be wary of the performer's energy level—once you've crossed a certain threshold the performances will start to degrade. If you notice this happening, take a break. This is particularly important for vocalists, whose voices can tire after just a few takes of a demanding song.

The same things apply when you're producing yourself. If you feel you're losing energy, take a break and come back after some rest and relaxation. Your performances will be better after you recharge your battery.

Taking a break is also an effective method for easing the nerves of musicians who have little recording experience, or who generally get freaked out when the Record button is lit. People get nervous, they try too hard, they forget parts, or they lose the groove. It's your job to ease the stress of studio recording. After a few takes, let the musicians "take five." When they return they'll be more relaxed and will probably perform much better.

It's also up to you to help the artist focus their energy so you can capture the best performances. You must understand that your words and actions in the studio directly influence their playing or singing—you need to say or do whatever it takes to elicit their best. If you inspire them to turn in killer tracks, they'll want you to produce on their next project.

Making Decisions

While in a recording session, the producer must make creative decisions about performances, as well as field new ideas that come up. I recommend recording every take, from the warmups to the last licks to any impromptu jam in the middle. That doesn't mean you need to keep every take.

Make creative decisions so that your hard drive or tape isn't cluttered with a thousand takes of the same thing. Commit to some ideas and go with them. If new ideas are flowing, keep the juices flowing by recording, but also stay focused on the plan you created in the preproduction phase.

Adding Ear Candy

Adding "ear candy" to a song can be one of the most fulfilling jobs of the producer. The term refers to any special little bit placed in a song that adds extra interest for the listener. Ear candy often comes about by experimenting, mutating an existing idea, and creating "happy accidents" (as Bob Ross would say) during the recording and mixing processes. Some examples include adding sound effects, reversed tracks, extra back vocals and hooks, and numerous mix techniques like imaginative panning, EQ, and effects.

Interacting with an Engineer During a Session

In professional studios, a producer usually has at least one engineer, and possibly multiple assistant engineers, working during the session. In your home studio you most likely won't have that luxury. You'll probably be the engineer and producer simultaneously (and possibly the artist as well). In the event you're lucky enough to be working with an engineer, you can focus all of your energy on producing. In fact, I recommend using an engineer if you can . . . it will free your mind of the technical aspects of recording and allow you to concentrate entirely on listening and evaluating performances.

Communication between the engineer and producer is extremely important for a successful session. The producer needs to be clear with his ideas and requests. This means being explicit and confident about what you want, including the type of sound you want on a track, how much preroll to give the artist, and where to punch in and out of tracks. I've found that it's also good to keep the mood light by joking around with the engineer.

Remember that communication is a two-way street. While it's great to be confident, check your ego at the door. Good engineers are often a great source of information on recording techniques, the latest sounds, and new styles. Keep in mind that some engineers may have been in—and produced—many more sessions than you. When they talk, it's worth listening. That said, never forget this is your show and the final call is yours to make.

Vocal Production

One of the most important skills you can learn is how to produce a vocal recording session. Because vocals are often the focal point of a song, they need to be the track(s) you spend a lot of time getting just right. In fact, it's a good idea to spend 30 to 40% of your recording time on vocals alone.

There are many things you can do as producer to elicit great vocal performances. First, get yourself or your singer into the right psychological space. For a believable vocal performance, the artist needs to feel the emotion of the song. Talk to the artist, help them get inside the song, have them read the lyrics aloud (or slowly to themselves), and delve into the feeling and meaning of the song. You're halfway to a good performance if you can get the vocalist into the right state of mind.

I cannot stress enough the importance of a good headphone mix! When the singer is comfortable with their headphone mix, they'll just plain sing better. Get the

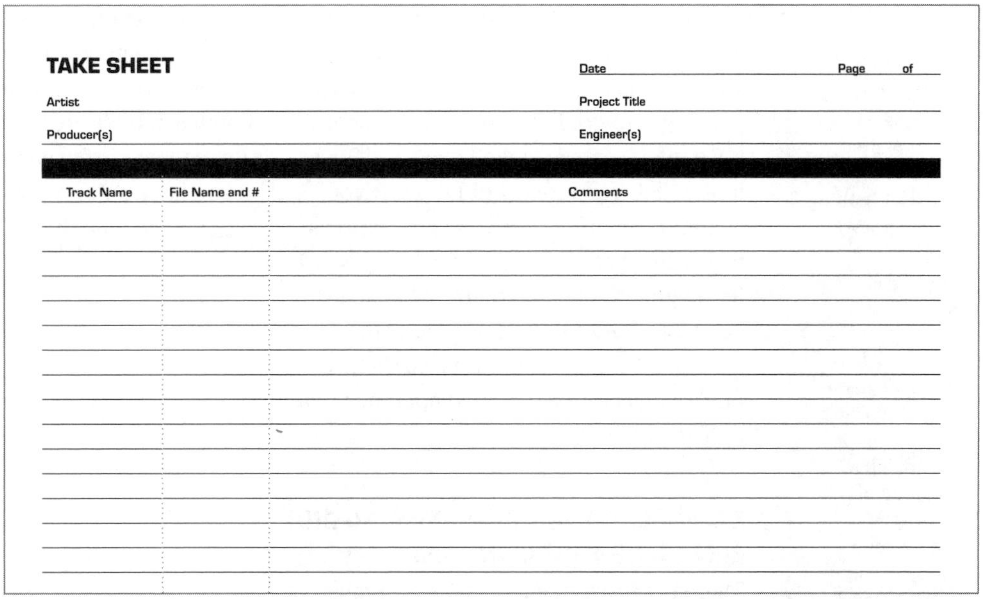

TAKE SHEET

Date _____ Page _____ of _____

Artist _____ Project Title _____

Producer(s) _____ Engineer(s) _____

Track Name	File Name and #	Comments

Fig. 9.1. As a producer in a recording session, you've got to constantly evaluate musical performances. This involves making judgments and taking notes quickly to keep the energy of the session moving forward. Take sheets help you keep track of your assessments for each recorded take as they happen so when you listen back later, you know what you've got.

Take Note!

I recommend recording vocal takes on several different, physically separate tracks in your software or on tape. You can also utilize virtual tracks with digital recording devices, which can really come in handy while tracking and editing vocals. Regardless, I wouldn't use more than four or five physical tracks so that you can manage all the takes relatively easily.

levels right, put complimentary effects on the vocal track, and tailor the mix to the artist's liking. (See chapter 8 for more on headphone mixes.)

As you're tracking the lead vocals, there will be many opportunities to practice punching in and out. When you're performing punch-ins, pick a good pre-roll amount. Vocalists usually like short pre-rolls, so that they can jump right in on the vocal line and not have to wait too long to record. You (and your engineer) should be aware of this to keep the session moving and help the vocalist stay focused.

In any vocal recording session, you should have the lyric sheet in front of you when tracking vocals, so you can make comments as you record. Once you start tracking, mark the good spots on your lyric sheet and constantly evaluate the interpretation and pitch of every word—even every syllable—because the smallest vocal inflec-

tions can make or break a song. Make sure you get at least one good take of each line.

When tracking vocals, record notes about each take on a take sheet. Vocal take sheets consist of the lyrics with large spaces (or grids) between each line for performance notes. Make a new vocal take sheet for each vocal session. On the take sheet, be specific about what you like about each performance. Write descriptive notes. Although several word phrases may be small enough chunks for you to evaluate at one time, don't be afraid to get down to the details of each word and syllable. Sometimes, you might even need to take it down to the specific letter, zooming in on an important consonant or vowel sound.

As a producer, you should also *know* the words to the song you're recording. In fact, you should know how to sing it. Knowing the words (and their meaning) as well as

> *Take Note!*
> Unless you're working with a very gifted "one-take" vocalist, getting the best overall performance usually involves cutting and pasting parts together from multiple takes. This is called "comping." (Comping is covered in chapter 11.) Thus, keeping track of the best parts of each take using a Take Sheet is often imperative to your success in creating a great vocal performance.

the melody, puts you inside the song right along with the singer. Be as articulate as you can when describing what you want the singer to do. Point to sections where the singer performed well and say, "Sing it like that. You already did it once; you can do it again." And if you can't express how you want a part to sound using words, try singing it. Even if you're not a singer, don't be afraid to sing the melody to get your point across. All of this will help you inspire an emotional and compelling vocal performance.

BALANCE: THE ART OF PRODUCING AND RECORDING YOUR OWN MUSIC

There is a progression from being a musician, engineer, or songwriter to also being a producer. It requires a change in your perspective about recording. In your recordings from now on, you'll probably be thinking like a producer, at least in the back of your mind. You'll think about the big picture and how each part fits into that grand view. You'll think about the overall vibe of the song and how each individual part either contributes or detracts from that.

As you progress from your musician shoes into your producer shoes, be careful not to turn your back on the powers of musical inspiration. If you're trying too hard to make a hit, you can suck the life out of the music. The performance will not have the magic that can make it a great recording. In producing and engineering your own music, it is important to maintain a balance: be both an artist and a technician. Reaching the point where you can see the big picture but remain in the moment is the key.

Okay, you're armed with many of the techniques that make producers successful. It's now up to you to utilize them. The goal is to translate the musical vision into reality by connecting with the artist through mutual trust and respect, helping the artist unleash their creativity, and capturing excellent performances. If you can do that, you have achieved your primary purpose as a producer. ■

CHAPTER 10
MIDI Production Techniques

In this chapter:

- MIDI recording techniques

- MIDI editing techniques

- MIDI production techniques

- Other useful MIDI production topics

Projects in almost every genre of music utilize MIDI, whether it's to trigger samples, make beats, add synth lines, score string parts, or create loops. To be an effective producer and engineer, you need MIDI production, recording, and editing skills in your production toolbox.

In chapter 2, I explained the basics of setting up your MIDI gear and helping it communicate correctly with your recording device or sequencer. In this chapter, I will assume your MIDI devices are all hooked up and you're ready to make some music with your MIDI controllers and sound modules.

Take Note!

For more info about setting up MIDI instruments, the MIDI protocol, MIDI tutorials, and other useful MIDI information, check out *www.midi.org*.

Before we get started, I want to lay down some fundamental definitions so that we're all on the same page. You will see these terms used in our discussions on MIDI production techniques later in this chapter.

Sequencer. A sequencer is a hardware- or software-based tool that enables you to record, play back, and edit MIDI data.

MIDI controller. A MIDI controller is an instrument or device that interprets, codes, and sends MIDI note and performance data. Controllers can be one of three varieties: instruments (e.g., MIDI keyboard); continuous controllers (e.g., modulation wheel); or switches (e.g., a sustain pedal that's either on or off).

MIDI sound module. A MIDI sound module is a device that receives and interprets MIDI instructions and produces audio waveforms according to those instructions. Sound modules can be *synthesizers* that physically make sounds (patches) in their internal circuitry or *samplers* that play back prerecorded sounds from their memory.

Patch. A patch is a particular instrument sound, e.g., a piano sound. The term patch is synonymous with "program," "voice," "sound," "instrument," "timbre," or "part," depending on the sound module's manufacturer.

Multi-timbral. Multi-timbral MIDI devices can send and/or receive MIDI data on up to 16 channels or more at a time. A multi-timbral sound module can listen to all 16 MIDI channels at once, and play any 16 of its patches simultaneously, with each of the 16 patches set to a different MIDI channel.

Polyphonic. Polyphonic devices can output several MIDI notes at once, such as in a four-note piano chord. Most modern MIDI devices have at least 32-voice polyphony.

Continuous controller. A continuous controller is a device such as a modulation wheel or foot pedal that sends a steady stream of controller data, rather than a single command.

Sysex. Short for "system exclusive," sysex refers to any data that is unique to a particular manufacturer or model of MIDI instrument.

MIDI data dump. A MIDI data dump is a transmission of MIDI data, either from a MIDI device to a sequencer or from a sequencer to a MIDI device.

Loop. A loop is a repeated musical phrase, often one, two, four, or eight measures long. It is a commonly used building block in hip-hop, electronica, and other sample-based music.

Volume. Volume is the amplitude or loudness of a sound.

Mute. Muting a track or instrument means making the track or instrument silent.

Pan. Panning is the virtual placement from left to right of instruments in the stereo spectrum.

MIDI note parameters (a.k.a. Channel Voice Messages)

Note On/Note Off. A Note On message is created when a note is activated, such as when a key is pressed on a MIDI keyboard. A Note Off message is created when that note is released.

Velocity. Velocity is a measure of how hard a key on a MIDI keyboard or other MIDI controller is pressed. The possible values are 0 (softest) to 127 (hardest).

Aftertouch. Aftertouch is a measurement of pressure put on a MIDI controller while it's being depressed (e.g., the pressure on the keys, or single key, of a MIDI keyboard). Mono aftertouch refers to the pressure on one key, while polyphonic aftertouch refers to the strongest overall pressure on all the keys at one time.

Pitch bend. Pitch bend is an effect triggered by a *continuous controller* device (like a pitch bend wheel) that either raises or lowers the pitch of a note.

Program change. A program change is a MIDI message that indicates what sound (patch) is to be used on a given MIDI channel.

Controller data. Controller data refers to the data created by continuous or switched MIDI controllers. It may also refer to channel mode messages and (as of yet) undefined parameters.

MIDI RECORDING TECHNIQUES

The data created when you play a MIDI controller and record it in a sequencer is called performance data. This data consists of long streams of channel voice messages that tell the sequencer exactly how you played the part, including articulation and dynamics. The MIDI language models your performance with note on, note off, velocity, aftertouch, pitch bend, program change, and continuous controller data.

Monitoring Your MIDI Performance

As long as your sequencer and your MIDI controller are communicating with each other correctly, you can record MIDI performance data and then edit it in the sequencer. While recording the performance data, you'll probably want to listen to the part you're playing. To do this, first route the recorded MIDI material out to a sound module. Second, route the audio

output from the sound module to a place where you can hear it . . . such as an auxiliary or audio track in your sequencer or one/two inputs on your mixer or recording device. (See fig. 10.1.)

Recording MIDI and Audio at the Same Time

Once you have the audio signal and the MIDI data flowing, you can record both at the same time. I often record both the audio and MIDI versions of the performance at the same time. Why? The audio track gives me a reference (a scratch track) for the sound and feel of the performance. Like most scratch tracks, it doesn't have to be a keeper track; it's just there to give a rough idea of the part. Having the MIDI performance data recorded alongside the audio allows me to go back later and edit the performance and then re-record the audio version with the edited MIDI data. Recording both audio and MIDI at the same time offers me the best of both worlds: an audio scratch track and a totally editable MIDI performance.

MIDI Signal Delay and Recording Audio While Playing Back MIDI

If you try to record audio while playing back MIDI tracks, you may find that the two signals are slightly out of sync due to latency. (See chapter 3 for info on latency.) If you're monitoring your MIDI sound source through your recording device, your MIDI tracks will usually play back slightly later than the audio tracks—the larger the setting for the hardware buffer size in your sequencer, the larger the latency.

Also, because it takes about three milliseconds for a note to be played and received by another device, the more MIDI devices you run serially (daisy-chained together), the longer the delay times get. For instance, if you have a MIDI keyboard attached to four sound modules in a daisy chain, by the time the original MIDI message reaches the last

MIDI
MIDI Controller
MIDI
MIDI PATCHBAY
IN
OUT
MIDI
Computer
MIDI
Sound Module
AUDIO
Mixing Board
AUDIO
Speakers

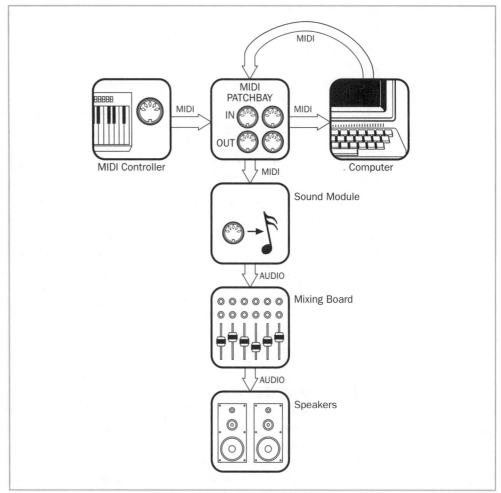

Fig. 10.1. Signal routing to monitor your MIDI tracks.

sound module in the chain, the message will be delayed by 12 milliseconds. This delay will be apparent on percussive sounds, but may not be noticeable on sounds with slower attacks, such as string pad sounds.

To compensate for this latency, you can configure an offset, which can make *all* of your MIDI tracks play back slightly earlier by a specified number of samples or milliseconds. This offset affects playback only; it doesn't actually move the recorded MIDI data. In some sequencers, you can actually combat this delay by shifting the playback time of *each* track forward by multiples of three milliseconds, depending on which sound module is playing each track. Or, you can actually move the MIDI data in the track so that it aligns with the incoming audio. Personally, I often just record the MIDI tracks as audio to avoid this issue.

Overdubbing MIDI data

When you want to edit your performance data by re-recording parts or punching in and out, most sequencers have two ways to perform overdubs. You can either completely overwrite the data on the track or you can add new MIDI data to the data that's already recorded. In the latter case, each time you record over the same

Take Note!
Due to the MIDI spec, MIDI data cannot be transmitted any faster than 31,250 bits per second. This equals just over 1040 MIDI messages a second. That means songs with faster tempos can transmit *less data per beat*. So, folks making Drum&Bass music, beware. You are more limited in the amount of MIDI data you can have flowing at one time.

section of the track, new data is added to the track. Let's learn how to build a drum loop.

Building a Drum Loop

There are several features on many sequencers that make recording MIDI more efficient and even more creative. First, sequencers often have a function that lets you build loops one instrument or sound at a time. For instance, say you want to build a simple drum loop with a kick, snare, and hi-hat. In your sequencer, choose a tempo and meter, then select the length of the loop (e.g., two bars) and start recording. The sequencer will start looping the selected amount of time while playing to a click track. Record your hi-hat part on the first pass, play the snare on the second pass, and the kick on the third. Voila! You've got a loop. You can even just play sections of each part, like one kick note at a time for each pass through the loop.

Using Input Quantize

I'm a drummer, and consider myself to have pretty good timing and feel. However, when recording MIDI notes on a keyboard instead of drum pads, I sometimes have trouble getting the right feel. Input Quantize helps with this problem by auto-matically quantizing all incoming MIDI notes while you play them. Quantizing aligns MIDI notes to a rhythmic grid, helping/forcing them to be more in time or simulating a particular rhythmic feel. (More information on quantization is presented later in this chapter.)

Recording Edited MIDI Performances as Audio

Once you've created and edited a MIDI track, it's common to record the MIDI track as audio so that you can mix it with other audio tracks and apply additional

effects to it during the mixing process. Unless you have limited track space, it's usually a good idea to record each MIDI track individually to its own audio track. This even includes drums . . . a track for the kick drum (or one for each sound, if layering several samples), one for the snare, one for the hi-hat, etc. That way you have more control when you want to mix.

When recording MIDI tracks as audio, the main things you should be concerned with are recording levels. Getting strong recording levels out of your MIDI sound module is important to recording good sounds. Most times you can record directly out of the line outs of your sound module right into your recording device. If you can't get high enough levels out of your sound module, you should probably use a direct box (DI) to change the output of the sound module into mic level. Then you can plug the DI into a mic preamp and boost the signal that way.

Avoiding MIDI Congestion

If you've got a good number of MIDI events all happening at once (like on the first beat of a measure), you might need to space them out by just a few milliseconds. Why? MIDI is a serial communication format. Each MIDI message is sent one at a time through each MIDI interface and cable. If too much data is trying to pass all at the exact same time, some of the data will get delayed, and you don't have control over which pieces of data are delayed.

To combat this, you may need to adjust some of the MIDI performance data in your sequence. First, make sure the percussion instrument data is playing back exactly when it should. Then, move data on tracks where timing is not quite as important or noticeable to the overall feel of the track.

Inserting Program Changes

A cool way to make sure the right sounds play on your MIDI tracks is to insert a program change MIDI message. Place a program change message at the beginning of your track (before the track starts to play) to automatically assign the right patch (a.k.a. "program") to your MIDI sound module for that MIDI channel. You can also insert program changes at any point within the track to change the patch along the way.

Personally, I usually just make a new MIDI track for any new sound that I want on a track instead of using program changes. For me, having one sound per track makes the MIDI tracks easier to remember as well as control in the mix. Often each sound has its own volume level (as well as other settings like EQ and compression) that can make mixing a track with multiple program changes more difficult.

Drawing in MIDI Data

In many sequencing programs, there's another method to "record" MIDI data; you can draw it in without actually playing a single note on a MIDI controller. For example, you can create a bass line by drawing in the pitches and rhythm. However, this functionality is used most often for creating drum loops and editing pre-existing MIDI tracks. And speaking of editing . . .

EDITING MIDI DATA

Typical Sequencer Editing Functions

All aspects of a recorded MIDI note can be edited, including start and end points, duration, pitch, and velocity. You can select one MIDI note or multiple notes, change their start and end points, move the notes horizontally (in time) or verti-

cally (in pitch), and edit their velocity values. You can insert, trim, and delete notes, as well as draw velocity curves for entire phrases.

More specifically, you can select a single note or group of notes, and move them forward or back in time horizontally. You can change the pitch of (transpose) the notes by moving them vertically. You can also transpose a *copy* of a note, leaving the original note where it is; this is an easy way to make one-note riffs into chord progressions or add harmonies to melody lines.

You can also change any MIDI note's attack velocity. A common way to represent each MIDI note's velocity value is as a "stalk"—the taller the stalk, the higher the value (from 0 to 127). When viewing the velocity of a MIDI note (as in fig. 10.2), drag the top of a velocity stalk up or down to increase or decrease the value.

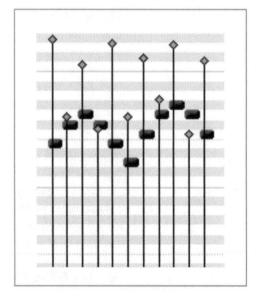

Fig. 10.2. Edit the velocity stalks on your MIDI data to alter the dynamics of your recorded performance.

Transposing a track means to move all of the notes together up or down in pitch. Most sequencers allow you to make absolute transpositions, where the exact MIDI data is moved to a different key. Some sequencers also allow you to make relative transpositions— in which you can retain the same key while moving the MIDI data to a different pitch position within the key. Performing a relative transposition on a melody part is an easy way to create harmony parts that match the melody exactly.

To insert new MIDI notes, click in the MIDI track at the desired pitch and location. If you want to insert particular types of notes (e.g., all eighth notes), use a grid and choose "1/8 note." To erase MIDI notes, you can select, clear, or cut them, just as you would delete text in a word processing document. Continuous controller data can also be inserted and edited in your sequencer, including volume, pan, pitch bend, aftertouch (mono), and any other MIDI controllers (0–127).

The MIDI Event List

Most sequencers have a MIDI Event List . . . a list of all MIDI data in a sequence. When you *really* want to fine tune your MIDI data, use the MIDI Event list to precisely edit any parameters of a MIDI event as well as copy, paste, and delete individual parameters, events, or phrases.

In the MIDI Event list in fig. 10.3, you see the start time of the event, the type of event (e.g., the quarter-note symbols indicate note data), the note's pitch, the note's attack and release velocity, and length of the note, or other information such as an event's end time. Most of this data can be edited by double-clicking on the data you want to change.

start	event			length/info
0:00.000	♩ F#1	100	64	0:00.066
0:00.000	♩ C1	103	64	0:00.291
0:00.250	♩ F#1	92	64	0:00.060
0:00.500	♩ F#1	103	64	0:00.086
0:00.750	♩ F#1	97	64	0:00.064
0:00.750	♩ C1	122	64	0:00.286
0:01.000	♩ F#1	97	64	0:00.066
0:01.000	♩ E1	127	64	0:00.225

Fig. 10.3. The MIDI Event List gives you every detail of your MIDI performance. People have been known to obsess over MIDI event editing to the point where they're completely unable to finish a tune. Don't let this happen to you!

Big-Picture MIDI Editing

In addition to being able to edit the smallest details of your MIDI performances, you can also cut, copy, and paste entire tracks and song sections just as you move text around in a word processing program. This enables you to try out different song forms with a few easy edits. You can also change the tempo of the song without affecting the pitch of the MIDI tracks, or change the key of song (or transpose certain tracks) with a few button pushes or mouse clicks. The ability to do these big-picture edits is one of the strongest reasons to use MIDI in your music productions.

Quantization

Quantizing is the process of aligning MIDI notes to a rhythmic grid to get them more "in time," or to change the rhythmic feel of a performance. Some notes may be moved forward in time while others may be moved back, and some notes will be more drastically affected than others. A quantize grid determines the beat boundaries to which notes are aligned; note values from whole notes to 64th notes with any tuplet divisions can make up the grid.

It's very simple to quantize a MIDI performance so that each note lines up perfectly with the beat. This creates a mechanical-sounding MIDI part. In some cases, the music may call for this. However, most times you'll want your MIDI parts to have some life . . . that is, some inconsistencies, some imperfections, some humanistic elements. The real trick is using quantization is to turn a halfway decent performance into a tight yet slightly imperfect performance with a great feel.

Before quantizing any tracks, you should figure out and describe the rhythmic feel that you want the song (or the specific track) to have. People describe rhythmic feels in a variety of ways, usually using nontechnical adjectives like "driving" or "chilled." Often, feels are expressed as being "ahead of the beat" for a pushed, excited, or driving song, "behind the beat" for a laid-back, relaxed, or even dragging song, or "right on the beat" for a steady song that's "in the pocket."

You can quantize the attack (start point), release (end point), and/or the duration of MIDI notes to the quantization grid. Quantizing attacks means that the start point of each note will be moved so it aligns with the closest rhythmic grid value. Naturally, quantizing release times will move the end point of each note. By quantizing both the attacks and releases, each note will be quantized to the beginning and end of the closest grid value, thus quantizing the note durations as well. There are often other "sensitivity" parameters in sequencer programs that enable you to move MIDI data closer to the grid so that it stays true to some or most of the original performance. Most sequencers also have a "randomize" function that enables you to add random rhythmic inaccuracies (notes away from the grid) into your MIDI data. This will make the track sound more natural. Finally, many sequencers have a "swing" parameter that you can implement to add or remove a triplet-like or shuffle feel from your MIDI data.

(NOTE: Your MIDI sequencers may call these parameters by other names and may have additional parameters for altering MIDI performances. Regardless of the names, knowing how to manipulate these quantize parameters is an important part of tweaking your MIDI performances and creating better MIDI tracks.)

Tick Talk

Sequencers usually use a quarter note as a reference point for timing and quantization grids. Each quarter note is divided into 480 or 960 subdivisions called ticks. The duration of a tick will vary according to tempo. For example, if quarter notes equal 120 BPM, the duration of a tick is 1.041 ms (at 480 ticks/quarter note, or half that at 960 ticks/quarter note). Faster tempos yield shorter tick values, while slower tempos have longer values. If you're the mathematical type, the formula for determining a tick's length is: 1 tick = 60,000/tempo/480 (where 60,000 refers to the number of milliseconds in a minute).

How do you apply quantization to create a particular rhythmic feel that is either ahead of, behind, or right on the beat?

1. Choose the quantize grid value—the rhythmic value that you want to align your MIDI notes with. It's often a good idea to use the most common subdivision of the main beat in the song when selecting the grid value. Here are a few generalized examples: You can probably use eighth notes for many pop, rock, and hip-hop songs, and sixteenth notes for electronica, funk, disco, and fast samba tunes. For swing or shuffle songs, select eighth-note triplets as your grid. Obviously, use your own best judgment, as each song in any style may require a different quantization grid value.

2. Choose whether you want to align the attacks and/or releases of the notes. Aligning the attacks to the grid ensures that your rhythms are lined up with the beat, or subdivision of the beat. Aligning the releases to the grid means your notes will be held out to the end of the beat (or subdivision of the beat). In many cases, I align the attacks and

allow the note durations to remain the same, not aligning the releases. This keeps all of my MIDI performance data intact, but lines up the attacks better with the quantization grid. This is particularly useful for piano tracks, or any other tracks where you want to preserve the player's style while simply improving the timing of the performance. Or, you can turn a staccato part into a more legato part by aligning the release times to ensure that each note gets its full duration. Each new musical part you record may require a different application of quantization.

3. Decide if you want to change the overall rhythmic feel using an offset or the swing parameters. An offset enables you to move the overall MIDI performance data ahead or behind the beat by fractions of the beat (ticks). For example, offset the snare back in time a little so that it sits on the back half of the beat to help create a more laidback feel. The swing parameter actually alters the quantize grid to help you create a triplet-like swing or shuffle feel. The higher the percentage you choose, the more swing added. Using lower or negative swing percentages, you can remove swing from a MIDI performance.

4. Adjust the sensitivity parameters to determine which MIDI notes are to be quantized. In most performances, the notes between the beats (or between the quantize grid) give the performance its style and sometimes even its rhythmic feel. You can use the sensitivity parameters to quantize the notes closest to the grid and leave the notes in between alone. For example, to quantize the notes that are 10% away from the grid (on either side), choose 20%

as the sensitivity value. If you want to include all notes, choose 100%.

Like a magnet, the strength parameter determines how close MIDI notes are pulled to the quantization grid. For example, 100% strength means every note will be pulled all the way to the closest grid value, while a 50% strength value only draws the notes halfway towards the grid. Personally, I think strength should be used on almost every sequenced part that needs to be quantized. This parameter may be the most important one for transforming halfway decent tracks into tight musical performances.

5. Use the randomize function. It's funny that Randomize is a quantization parameter, because it essentially mucks up the work that all the previous quantization parameters performed on a MIDI performance. A value of 100% randomize will move some notes up to 50% away from the quantization grid (on either side). Usually, this will sound terrible! The rhythms will be way off. However, small percentage values are useful for adding a human element to an otherwise mechanical-sounding track. Use this parameter with care.

Experimenting with Quantization

Through experience I've found that, in many cases, using low values on the sensitivity parameters and high values for strength give me good results when trying to preserve the original feel of a MIDI performance. But even with that and other basic knowledge of quantization, I find that quantizing a MIDI part requires experimentation. Because each recorded MIDI performance is different, you'll usually have to play with the parameters when you quantize.

Once you've quantized a track or part of a track, listen carefully to hear if you obtained the feel you were after. If not, undo the edit, adjust the parameters, and try again. If you can't seem to get the right feel using quantization, you may want to just rerecord the track and get a performance that has a better overall feel.

MIDI PRODUCTION TECHNIQUES

Creating Great MIDI Drum Tracks

Each song has a rhythmic feel—a groove. For both audio and MIDI recordings, many hours are often spent trying to establish the right groove for each song. Many facets of a song make up the groove. As your sequencing skills improve, you will begin to hear the benefits of creating realistic MIDI parts that fit into a stylistically accurate groove. The best way to achieve this is to study music from the genre that you're writing in. Analyze all of the components, both individually and collectively. How do you do that? Try this.

- First, listen to the rhythmic importance and placement of beats. For instance, most reggae music is driven by the offbeats (or upbeats), whereas most electronic dance music is driven by a strong downbeat. And, as we covered earlier, rhythms are played either ahead of the beat, right on the beat, or behind the beat. Pay close attention where the rhythms fall in the style of music you're making.

- Second, listen for accents within the groove. Find out where the accents are placed in the groove and how much emphasis is placed on each one of them. Some accents may be stronger than others.

- Third, listen to the durations of notes and chords—that is, how long each note or chord is played. Smooth and flowing music will most likely have longer notes (considered "legato"), whereas excited and uptempo songs will likely have shorter notes ("staccato"). However, each musical style holds particular notes and chords longer than others. Take, for example, jazz and swing music. Eighth notes on the beat are held longer than eighth notes on the offbeat. That is the essence of the swing feel. It has a triplet-like sound, in which straight eighth notes are transformed into some degree of triplet subdivision.

- Fourth, listen to the rhythmic interaction between instruments. For instance, often the rhythmic pattern of the bass will match up with the kick drum. In some styles, harmonic instruments (like guitar or keyboards) will play right along with the bass, yet in other styles they will play in the spaces left by the bass, or something altogether different.

- Fifth, listen to the overall instrumentation within a musical style. What instruments are in the songs? Listen carefully to discern details about the recordings. Ask specific questions like, was that an acoustic guitar with a chorus effect or was it a 12-string guitar? Was that acoustic bass part plucked or bowed? Was that percussion part played on bongos or congas? Did the horn section consist of an alto sax, a trumpet, and a trombone, or was there also a tenor sax or a bass trombone?

- Finally, make note of the emotional intensity. Every style of music has a unique way of expressing emotion. Plus, every instrument has its own way of conveying that emotion. Learning more about each instrument and the techniques used to create emotive performances will infinitely improve your MIDI tracks.

To get more specific, let's start with drum beats. MIDI sequences are driven by the feel in their drum beats. Just like live bands, a MIDI sequence is only as good as the feel of the drums and percussion tracks. In fact, the most important aspects of most MIDI sequences are the drum and percussion tracks. Why do I say this? Simply because if your drum and percussion tracks lack a solid groove and feel, all of your other tracks are forced to follow the un-grooving rhythm tracks, and the entire sequence suffers.

Most of you are probably not drummers. And even if you are a drummer, you may not have had extensive lessons on all of the wide variety of grooves and musical styles that you may find yourself producing someday.

There are an infinite number of drumbeat possibilities, and every genre of music has its own set of stylistic attributes. Thus, to create realistic sounding MIDI drum tracks, you should study music from the genre that you're trying to write in. Listen closely to musical examples and take notes.

A key aspect to making realistic-sounding drum parts is to be sure that a real drummer could actually play the part. For instance, if you create a beat on a MIDI drum set with five or six parts going on at once, it's obvious that a real drummer could not play the beat. It's totally cool to do this if you're not looking for realism, or if you're trying to model multiple percussion players. However, any drummer, upon hearing the beat, will tell you if it's impossible for one person to perform.

Included in writing realistic parts are some important nuances, like the time it takes a drummer to hit a crash cymbal and return to the hi-hat rhythm. Often, this may take as long as a sixteenth note or eighth note, so the hi-hat rhythm will not pick up immediately after the crash cymbal. This is true when drummers come out of fills, as well. The more you understand what it's like to play drums (including the feel and physical limitations), the better your MIDI drum parts will become.

Creating Drum Loops

MIDI makes it easy to create a drum loop as a foundation for your musical ideas. Even if you want to use real drums for your final recordings, creating a MIDI drum part for the demo can help get your ideas across to other people effectively and establish a "feel" to the song.

There are many tools available today that enable you to create great drum tracks without using any "real" miked drum tracks. And while sampling beats is a common practice, there's a more creative (and legal) way to model beats and rhythmic feels in your sequencer. Here, I'm going to take beat sampling several steps further, and use a cool beat as a stepping stone to new ideas while building on some of the skills you've already learned earlier in this chapter.

Sampling vs. Modeling with MIDI

One of the techniques I use to create a new beat is to rework a beat from an old funk or r&b song and transfer some elements of its feel into a hip-hop or electronica groove. The process of modeling a beat goes like this:

1. Listen carefully to the original track. Then transcribe the beat, or at least note where specific snares, kicks, or

Take Note!
"Ghost" notes often fall between accented beats, and fill the spaces while giving the groove continuous motion. In this case, ghost notes occur when the drummer hits the snare drum very softly, creating a sound similar in level to an unaccented hi-hat beat.

other elements are played, and their relationships to the other notes.

2. Find the sounds. Create several MIDI tracks and assign them to drum sounds that are like the original beat.
3. Find the tempo—that is, estimate the original beat's tempo.
4. Input the MIDI notes. You can either play the beat on a MIDI controller and record your performance, or enter the MIDI notes to a grid. You don't have to be a drummer to make this technique work.
5. Alter the MIDI notes to create a "feel." Anybody can plop notes down on a grid and make a drum track. However, without some manipulation, those beats can often sound sterile and mechanical. There are places for those types of beats: $50 toy keyboards. If you want to give your beats a more interesting feel, you've got to tweak some of the MIDI parameters and move the notes around.

Usually I start by tweaking the velocities of almost every note in the groove, adding accents and "ghost" or "grace" notes to give the track more life. Then I mess with some of the quantization parameters—the ones I use most often are swing and randomize. At the same time, I'll move individual notes forward or back in time, offsetting them to adjust the feel. (Don't trust your sequencer to do all this work for you.)

Creating a New Beat from the Modeled Beat

Okay, we've got a cool beat modeled in MIDI. Now the real fun begins. Let's mess with it!

6. Adjust the tempo. For example, transform the modeled beat from old-school funk into hip-hop. Funk is often faster than hip-hop so you'll want to slow the beat down to match the genre.
7. Change the sounds. Now that we're in the genre of hip-hop, our funky drum sounds don't really cut it. Choose sounds that are more current. Consider layering sounds, like having two different samples playing the kick track to thicken the kick sound.
8. Alter the beat. Change anything about it. Tweak the velocities, timing, or quantization. Also consider turning the beat around or starting the loop in a different place.

You're done! You've got a cool new beat modeled on an old beat. If you like a drum groove on an old CD, now you know how to mimic it with MIDI and take it farther by adding different sounds, changing its tempo, and altering the feel. A new beat with old-school influences. More interested in current trends? Make new beats with new influences. Or just make your own from scratch. However you like to create, the techniques presented here can improve any MIDI drum track.

Creating Great MIDI Bass, Guitar, and Keyboard Tracks

Bass

Once you've got a good drum groove, the next important part of the groove is the bass line. Whether acoustic, slapped electric, or synth, the bass sound needs to work with the drum part. Often, the bass part should line up closely with the kick drum of the drum groove, whether playing the identical rhythm or some close variation with similar accent patterns. Thus, the bass line should usually be quantized

Take Note!

Sub-bass:
Frequencies in the very low range of the audible frequency spectrum. Typically below 50 Hz, these frequencies are called sub-bass because they are too low for many speaker systems to reproduce.

in the same way that you quantized your drum groove. In this way, the groove is supported not only by the rhythmic elements of the bass part, but also the harmonic foundation of the song through the individual bass notes.

Because the bass provides this harmonic foundation, you'll often want your MIDI bass lines to consist mainly of the root note of the chord, the third and fifth of the chord, and, more sparingly, other notes from the associated scale for each chord.

Simple bass lines consisting primarily of the root and fifth best solidify the harmony and rhythm of a song. However, there is certainly something to be said for bass lines that stand on their own as melodies. Melodic bass lines will often make use of many notes in the scale, but they will always imply the chord and will hit the root note in important places, such as on beat 1 of a measure. It is also common practice for bass lines to bridge the gap between two different chords by moving stepwise up to the next root.

Once you've decided on the notes in a bass line, the next step is to create a MIDI performance that fits the style of the music. This involves getting the right bass sound, feel, emotion, and playing technique.

Sound: Often based on the style of music, the bass sound is important in establishing the believability of the song. Bass sounds can be edgy with their high frequencies accentuated, low and boomy when they only consist of low frequencies, or anywhere in between. Your MIDI sound module should have many choices of bass sounds; hopefully one will be appropriate to the style of music that you're creating the part for. Regardless of the actual sound you choose, realistic bass parts should have characteristics derived from the design of the instrument.

Four-string bass guitars (with open strings tuned to E, A, D, and G) have a finite note range starting from the low E string (known as E1 on your MIDI keyboard) and stretching up to a high G (G4) on the G string on a 24-fret bass. Five-string basses have a low B (B0) string, and six-string basses have a high C string, on which you can get notes as high as around G4.

If you're working in truly synthesized music genres (e.g., any form of electronica), you are not confined by the limitation of notes on strings. You can go even lower into **sub-bass** tones without worrying about replicating them on authentic bass instruments.

HOW LOW CAN YOU GO?

The low E note on a bass guitar (E1 on a MIDI keyboard) represents approximately 41 Hz. Check out this table of bass note frequencies.

Note	Description
B0 30.9 Hz	Open String on a 5-string bass guitar
E1 41.2 Hz	Open string on a bass guitar
D2 73.4 Hz	Open string on a bass guitar
G2 98.0 Hz	Open string on a bass guitar
C3 130.9 Hz	Open string on a 6-string bass guitar
G4 392.0 Hz	Highest note on a 24-fret, 4-string bass guitar
C5 523.3 Hz	Highest note on a 24-fret, 6-string bass guitar

Feel and emotion: Revisit the discussion on feel in the previous section. Although that section was written with drum parts as the focus, all of it applies to bass parts as well.

Take Note!

Guitars usually have six strings. That means there are only six notes you can possibly play at one time. Even though you've got ten fingers, be sure to only play six notes at a time when trying to create a realistic guitar part on a MIDI keyboard.

Playing style: Bass playing techniques include playing with fingers, playing with a pick, slapping and popping, and using a bow (on an acoustic bass). Often MIDI sound modules will have patches that model these different types of bass sounds. Using velocity-sensitive MIDI controllers, you can even play different sounds on one key, depending on how hard you press the key. For example, if you press a key lightly, a fingered bass note will play. If you hit the key hard, a slapped or popped bass note will play. The playing technique you choose should match the style of music you're creating, so choose your MIDI sound wisely.

Guitar

It's not the easiest thing to create a guitar part on a MIDI keyboard. If you can, get your hands on a guitar MIDI controller and have a guitarist play the part. If that's not possible, there are several considerations to make when creating a guitar part on a keyboard.

Even though many guitar parts are based on chords, keyboardists often play chordal parts differently than guitarists. Guitars are more limited in available notes and playable chord voicings than keyboards. Yet, much of a guitar's signature sound comes from the way a chord is voiced and strummed. In fact, guitar chord voicings are sometimes difficult to play on a keyboard.

To create realistic sounding guitar parts using a keyboard, you need to play authentic guitar chord voicings and imitate the sound of the strum. The notes in a guitar chord are not all played at once; they are strummed, either from the top string in a chord to the bottom one, or vice versa. Even the speed of the strum can affect the overall sound and style of music.

Most guitars have six strings with the pitches E, A, D, G, B, and E, from lowest to highest. Like a bass, the strings on a guitar have intervals of fourths between them, except for the major third interval between the G and B strings.

Open Guitar String	MIDI Note	Frequency
Low E	E2	82.4 Hz
A	A2	110.0 Hz
D	D3	146.8 Hz
G	G3	196.0 Hz
B	B3	246.9 Hz
High E	E4	329.6 Hz

To create realistic-sounding guitar parts using MIDI, you should work closely with a guitar player (if you're not one), or at least buy a guitar chord book to learn how guitar chords are voiced. For example, a keyboardist might voice a CMaj7 chord one way, while a guitarist might voice it differently, as in fig. 10.4 and fig. 10.5.

As with any other instrument, the guitar part in a song has to fit the style of music through its sound, feel, emotion, and playing technique.

Sound: Your MIDI sound module should have a variety of guitar patches for you to choose from, varying in authenticity and quality. Choose one appropriate for the style of music, and alter it if needed.

Guitarists often use bends, slides, hammer-ons, and grace notes to add style, musicality, and individuality to their parts. You can model many of these actions with a keyboard. In fact, the standard pitch-bend setting on a MIDI keyboard is essentially the same thing as a whammy bar on an electric guitar. However, that same pitch bend on a keyboard can sound distinctly different from some types of bends and

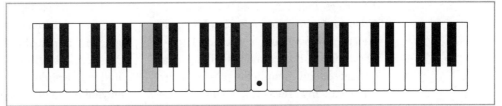

Fig. 10.4. A CMaj7 chord voiced on a piano.

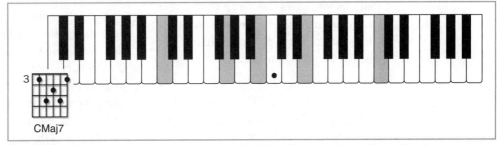

CMaj7

Fig. 10.5. A CMaj7 chord voiced on a guitar and what the guitar voicing looks like on the piano.

slides on a guitar. Like whammy bars, standard keyboard pitch bends usually bend notes or chords continuously and smoothly from one pitch to another, whereas guitarists sometimes bend one note while holding another at the same pitch, or even sliding or hammering-on notes in discrete intervals (from note to note instead of a continuous bend). Thus, to model these types of guitar idiosyncrasies, you'll need to adjust the pitch bend on your MIDI controller so that it bends chromatically (from note to note, e.g., C to C# to D) instead of continuously like the normal pitch bend.

It's also a good idea to factor in strum patterns when creating a MIDI guitar part. Guitarists often strum down a chord on the downbeats and strum upwards on the upbeats. That means that when a chord falls on a downbeat, they'll play the lowest string of a chord first and end with the highest string. In songs where the guitar part is only on the upbeats, the guitarist will often only strum upwards because

they're so used to playing the downbeat while strumming down.

Feel and emotion: Much of what was written about feel in the drum section applies here as well. Being ahead of, behind, or right on the beat is important in creating the right guitar part for a particular style of music. Study the rhythmic relationship of the guitars to the drums and bass to make sure you accurately model the style you're writing for.

Guitars are very expressive instruments. Using longer (legato) notes can express deep passion, heartbreak, longing, etc., while short (staccato) notes often express strong positive or negative energy, whether it's happy and excited energy, nervous and anxious energy, or angry and driven energy.

Playing technique: The emotion of a song, as well as the style, sound, and feel, is directly influenced by the playing technique used by a guitar player. In addition to using their fingers to pluck and strum the strings, guitarists often use picks, slides, and other interesting implements, such as an e-bow (an electric bow), to make sounds. Each playing technique has a unique sound. Couple the playing technique with any effects that a guitarist uses, and you've got an infinite number of sound possibilities. To accurately model all of these factors when creating a MIDI guitar part, you'll need to choose your sounds wisely based on the playing technique suitable for the style of music.

Keyboard Instruments

Piano parts, whether MIDI or audio, can occupy a lot of space in a song. Because pianos have such wide frequency and dynamic ranges, they can often overpower a song if the parts are not well thought out. Plus, many piano players create parts that sound fantastic if they're played solo, but are way too busy when mixed with a full-band arrangement. Unless the song you're creating is entirely piano driven, sculpt piano parts that fit seamlessly into the song and allow space for all of the other instruments.

Be sure to analyze how the piano and bass parts align. Watch out especially for piano parts where the piano plays bass lines. These can really get in the way of each other. Also, check out the relationship between the guitar and piano parts to be sure they're not stepping on each other. Listen to the chord voicings of each instrument to be sure they work together. There is an art to creating interesting instrumental parts that fit tightly with each other, yet leave room for each instrument to be heard.

Like most other instruments, piano parts are based on the style of music. If you're not well-versed in piano styles, it's a good idea to hire a talented piano player

to create the parts, or do some serious research by listening to music in the same style and reading books about the style. Pay close attention to the rhythms associated with a style (the feel) as well as the playing techniques and chord voicings. The piano is as much a rhythmic instrument as is it harmonic and melodic.

Just as with drums, bass, and guitar, some musical styles will require the piano parts to be ahead of, behind, or right on the beat. If necessary, quantize your parts accordingly. However, be careful of over-quantizing them. Try to allow as much of the player's performance as possible into the overall feel of the song; piano parts sound best when the player's natural accents, phrasing, and artistic touch are allowed to shine through. Only quantize the parts of the performance that really need it. That could mean only quantizing one measure (or even just a note) at a time.

Most of these concepts also apply to other keyboard instruments, including electric pianos, Rhodes pianos, and synthesizers. The parts created for these instruments (as well as their sound) are usually style driven. As mentioned in the previous section, you can alter the individual sounds of any piano or synth to best suit the song or to create a completely original sound.

Creating Great MIDI Sweetening Tracks

Once you've got all the rhythm section tracks laid down, arranging and orchestrating additional parts for the song can really sweeten up your songs. Adding strings, synth pads, horns, sound effects, or additional percussion is actually called "sweetening" a track. Sweetening must be done effectively to have the intended impact, however. As your producing and arranging skills improve, you'll be able to hear parts for these new instruments and will be able to quickly determine what level of involvement they should have in the song. That is, you'll understand how to add minimal sweetening to songs that need only a little and more sweetening to those songs where it will be very valuable.

Listen to your pre-existing rhythm tracks closely and locate spots where sweetening could help. Look for places where there is a lull, where you momentarily lose interest in the song, or where there is an unintended drop in energy. In many cases, you should only add sweetening to your song if you find a spot like this.

Try several sweetening methods to see which works the best and then choose one or more to fill the void. While you're writing these new parts, always ask yourself if the new parts are necessary, if they fit the song, and if they make song better. Once you've decided to take the plunge into sweetening a track, go at it full force to create the best track you can.

Strings and Synth Pads

Once you've found the place (or places) to insert your string or synth pad sound into the song, it's important to figure out when it should enter and when it should leave the song. Because these sounds are often pretty massive, you may feel a hole left in the song once the sound is gone. Thus, you might need to accentuate some other instrument while the string or pad part fades. Also, consider starting your string or pad part as a single note and expanding it into chords later in the song. This technique can build up a song nicely.

One of the best ways to get good string and pad sounds—and make your song unique—is to layer sounds together. The main idea is to create a sound that provides the song with a distinctive texture. All you have to do is play the part

through two or more different sounds that combine in an interesting way. You can easily do this using two or more MIDI tracks in your sequencer, each assigned to different patches from your sound modules.

To layer sounds well, choose two sounds that contain aspects of the overall sound you want to create and play them together. The upper harmonics and overtones of each patch will combine in new ways and fill out the complete sound. Combining sampled sounds with patches can also add more realism to your layered sounds. Detuning one or more of the layered patches can further fill out the overall sound by making the harmonic interactions between the patches more noticeable.

Detuning

Detuning can be used to create a chorus-like effect that tends to make an instrument sound more rich and full. Detuning essentially means tuning an instrument up or down a little bit away from actually being "in tune." Often, this means tuning the instrument ±10 cents away from the regular tuning pitch. There are 100 cents between any two adjacent notes, e.g., C and C#. Cents represent gradations of frequency, or pitch. Middle C (C4 on your MIDI keyboard) has a frequency of 261.6 Hz and C#4 has a frequency of 277.2 Hz. If a C# note is detuned by −10 cents, then it is 90 cents away from C, and its frequency is approximately 275.6 Hz.

Some other ideas for layering sounds include EQ'ing the sounds differently, adding effects (reverb, compression, etc.) to one or more of the layers, and doubling the tracks in different octaves. Any or all of these methods might make your layered tracks sound incredible!

Yet, be careful with big, layered string pad sounds. They can add thickness that easily makes a song sound washed out. Single countermelodies that come and go might be more effective, and keeping the melodies simple and low in the mix will add depth but won't distract the listener from the main melody of the song.

Horns

In contrast to creating string and synth pad parts where you don't need much experience or crazy chops, creating a cool horn section part can be much more difficult. To get a horn section part sounding really good using MIDI, you'll need to study horn arranging techniques and listen to examples of great horn charts. To do it right, you should learn the ranges of each instrument and write their parts accordingly. (Check out appendix A for these ranges.) You should also learn how to voice the instruments for the type of sound and musical style appropriate for the song.

Horn charts often contain chords, either short stabs or long notes, that are voiced in a certain way to create a particular sound. For example, close voicings are chords in which the notes of each instrument are very close to each other, often with all the notes being within one octave. Alternatively, spread voicings are chords in which the notes for each instrument are spread apart more than an octave. Spread voicings yield very rich and full harmonic sounds and are often useful for percussive and relatively short melody lines.

This is just a small taste of the many facets of horn arranging. There is much more you can learn about this subject. To look for more information on horn arranging techniques, check out *Modern Jazz Voicings* by Ted Pease and Ken Pullig (Boston: Berklee Press, 2001).

If you've never arranged for horns before, I recommend starting simple. Create

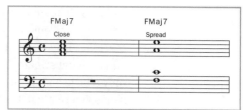

Fig. 10.6 (a & b). Close vs. spread voicings.

single melody or harmony lines for one or more horns playing in unison or on octaves. Branch out from there into two-voice harmonies, always making sure that the horn parts don't conflict with vocals or other melodic instruments. Two-voice harmonies can actually support a song like string or synth pad parts do. Move on gradually from there into three- and four-part writing.

If you don't have the time to experiment or learn about horn arranging and you're feeling that it sounds rather daunting, get someone else to help you write a part (or at least teach you how to do it). Utilizing someone else's expertise and delegating work to others are two valuable skills you should have as a producer.

OTHER USEFUL MIDI PRODUCTION TOPICS

Importing and Exporting MIDI Files

Another cool thing you can do with MIDI is import and export MIDI files between different MIDI applications. To do this, the files must first be saved as Standard MIDI Files (SMFs). SMFs are great for transferring MIDI data between different sequencers or between a sequencer and a music notation program to make a lead sheet or score. You can also create music in a music notation program, save it as a SMF, and then import it into your sequencer. The music itself will often be exactly right on the beat (100% quantized), so you'll probably have to make it less mechanical-sounding in your sequencer to adjust its feel for playback, using the methods explained earlier in this chapter.

Among other data, SMFs include notes, controller events, program changes, system exclusive data, tempo, and meter information. There are two main types of SMFs—type 0 and type 1—both of which are supported by most MIDI applications. Type 0 MIDI files store data for all MIDI channels on one track. When importing these files, your sequencer separates the data by channel and places the channels in separate regions and tracks. Type 1 MIDI files, sometimes referred to as multi-track MIDI files, contain multiple tracks of MIDI data. When importing these files, each track's data is placed on its own new MIDI track in your sequence.

Using System-Exclusive Data

Manufacturers of MIDI hardware create their own MIDI messages customized for their products, called system-exclusive (or "sysex") data. Sysex data is MIDI data, specific to an instrument or piece of hardware, that enables manufacturers to define MIDI messages that address parameters unique to a MIDI device. Sysex can be used to store patch and configuration data for a MIDI device and record real-time changes for non-standard parameters (such as filter cutoff frequency). You can store sysex data messages in your sequencer so that it can recall edited sounds, presets, data dumps, and any other special parameters specific to a MIDI device.

For example, some people like to edit the parameters of the preset sounds in their MIDI sound modules to make the sounds "better" or "different and cool." These edits are often saved as part of the sysex data. Use sysex data to back up these edited sounds by placing the sysex data in a sequence. In fact, the most common reason for inserting sysex data in your sequence is to "dump" a sound module's patches onto the beginning of a MIDI track. This way, no matter how many changes you've made in the module since the last time you worked on your sequence, your sequencer and your sound module will communicate so that the right sounds will be loaded back into your sequence every time.

Once you've recorded sysex data on a MIDI track, it is sent from your sequencer to the MIDI device each time you play the track (from any point before the sysex data occurs). Just be sure that your MIDI device is set to receive sysex and that the output of your MIDI track is properly assigned. Also keep in mind that sysex can take a few seconds (or longer) to transmit and be received—you may need to leave some blank measures at the beginning of your song to allow for this.

Often, sysex messages will be MIDI **data dumps** from a MIDI device into your sequencer, or vice versa. Usually these dumps have no MIDI channel assignment, so if you are daisy-chaining MIDI devices together, all of the devices will receive the MIDI data dump. This is not an issue if the devices in the daisy chain are from different manufacturers, because they won't recognize each other's sysex data. However, if you have devices from the same manufacturer on the daisy chain, these devices will receive the data whether you want them to or not. This could erase presets, edited sounds, and other parameters in the devices that were not supposed to receive the sysex data.

Fortunately, MIDI devices usually have some sort of default settings that you can restore. And, if you have a MIDI interface (hub or patch bay), this sysex data flow is not an issue; the data is only sent to the device it's meant for because the MIDI interface routes it to the right place.

To be safe, you can create a special sequence and dump all of your sysex data from each device to a MIDI track for storage. Then, if for some reason, your sysex data on any of your MIDI devices is lost, you can restore it from that sequence.

Because MIDI data dumps can take a few moments, it's a good idea to place your sysex events at the beginning of your sequence, several seconds (or measures) before the song actually starts. This will allow enough time for the data to be transferred into your sequence without affecting playback.

General MIDI

General MIDI (GM) is a specification that standardizes locations and MIDI channels for synthesizers and sound modules. This allows musicians with GM instruments to share sequences with each other and have some faith that the sequences can be played back easily and the sounds are at least similar to those used in the original recording, if not exactly the same.

Utilizing all 16 MIDI channels and having at least 24-note polyphony and 16-voice multi-timbral output, GM synthesizers have at least one voice open for each MIDI channel. Channel 10 is reserved for percussion parts and the percussion instrument set has at least 47 drum and percussion sounds. These sounds are mapped according to the GM standard and are shown in the following figure.

GENERAL MIDI DRUM SOUNDS

MIDI Note #	Drum Sound	MIDI Note #	Drum Sound
35	Acoustic Bass Drum	59	Ride Cymbal 2
36	Bass Drum 1	60	Hi Bongo
37	Side Stick	61	Low Bongo
38	Acoustic Snare	62	Mute Hi Conga
39	Hand Clap	63	Open Hi Conga
40	Electric Snare	64	Low Conga
41	Low Floor Tom	65	High Timbale
42	Closed Hi-Hat	66	Low Timbale
43	High Floor Tom	67	High Agogo
44	Pedal Hi-Hat	68	Low Agogo
45	Low Tom	69	Cabasa
46	Open Hi-Hat	70	Maracas
47	Low-Mid Tom	71	Short Whistle
48	Hi-Mid Tom	72	Long Whistle
49	Crash Cymbal 1	73	Short Guiro
50	High Tom	74	Long Guiro
51	Ride Cymbal 1	75	Claves
52	Chinese Cymbal	76	Hi Wood Block
53	Ride Bell	77	Low Wood Block
54	Tambourine	78	Mute Cuica
55	Splash Cymbal	79	Open Cuica
56	Cowbell	80	Mute Triangle
57	Crash Cymbal 2	81	Open Triangle
58	Vibraslap		

General MIDI also has a set list of 128 program sounds. They are defined by their type and patch location, as seen on the following page.

GM devices also respond to all the same MIDI controller data mentioned previously. So, even though there are a multitude of synthesizer and sound module manufacturers, MIDI instruments with GM capabilities provide a convenient and solid foundation for sharing musical ideas.

GENERAL MIDI PATCHES

Prog#	Instrument	Prog#	Instrument
	PIANO		**CHROMATIC PERCUSSION**
1	Acoustic Grand	9	Celesta
2	Bright Acoustic	10	Glockenspiel
3	Electric Grand	11	Music Box
4	Honky-Tonk	12	Vibraphone
5	Electric Piano 1	13	Marimba
6	Electric Piano 2	14	Xylophone
7	Harpsichord	15	Tubular Bells
8	Clavinet	16	Dulcimer
	ORGAN		**GUITAR**
17	Drawbar Organ	25	Nylon String Guitar
18	Percussive Organ	26	Steel String Guitar
19	Rock Organ	27	Electric Jazz Guitar
20	Church Organ	28	Electric Clean Guitar
21	Reed Organ	29	Electric Muted Guitar
22	Accordion	30	Overdriven Guitar
23	Harmonica	31	Distortion Guitar
24	Tango Accordion	32	Guitar Harmonics
	BASS		**SOLO STRINGS**
33	Acoustic Bass	41	Violin
34	Electric Bass (finger)	42	Viola
35	Electric Bass (pick)	43	Cello
36	Fretless Bass	44	Contrabass
37	Slap Bass 1	45	Tremolo Strings
38	Slap Bass 2	46	Pizzicato Strings
39	Synth Bass 1	47	Orchestral Strings
40	Synth Bass 2	48	Timpani
	ENSEMBLE		**BRASS**
49	String Ensemble 1	57	Trumpet
50	String Ensemble 2	58	Trombone
51	SynthStrings 1	59	Tuba
52	SynthStrings 2	60	Muted Trumpet
53	Choir Aahs	61	French Horn
54	Voice Oohs	62	Brass Section
55	Synth Voice	63	SynthBrass 1
56	Orchestra Hit	64	SynthBrass 2
	REED		**PIPE**
65	Soprano Sax	73	Piccolo
66	Alto Sax	74	Flute
67	Tenor Sax	75	Recorder
68	Baritone Sax	76	Pan Flute
69	Oboe	77	Blown Bottle
70	English Horn	78	Shakuhachi

---

sors or utilizing a MIDI control surface. Being able to effectively use the MIDI recording, editing, and production techniques discussed in this chapter will not only make you a better producer and engineer, it will also open your productions to new sounds that could take them to a whole new level. ■

Using MIDI can be helpful all the way through the production process. In preproduction, you can use MIDI tracks to sketch out basic song ideas—from drum loops to chord progressions. In the production stage, you can turn these ideas into full-blown tracks and fine-tune them. Even in postproduction, you can use MIDI in your mixes by automating outboard MIDI effects proces-

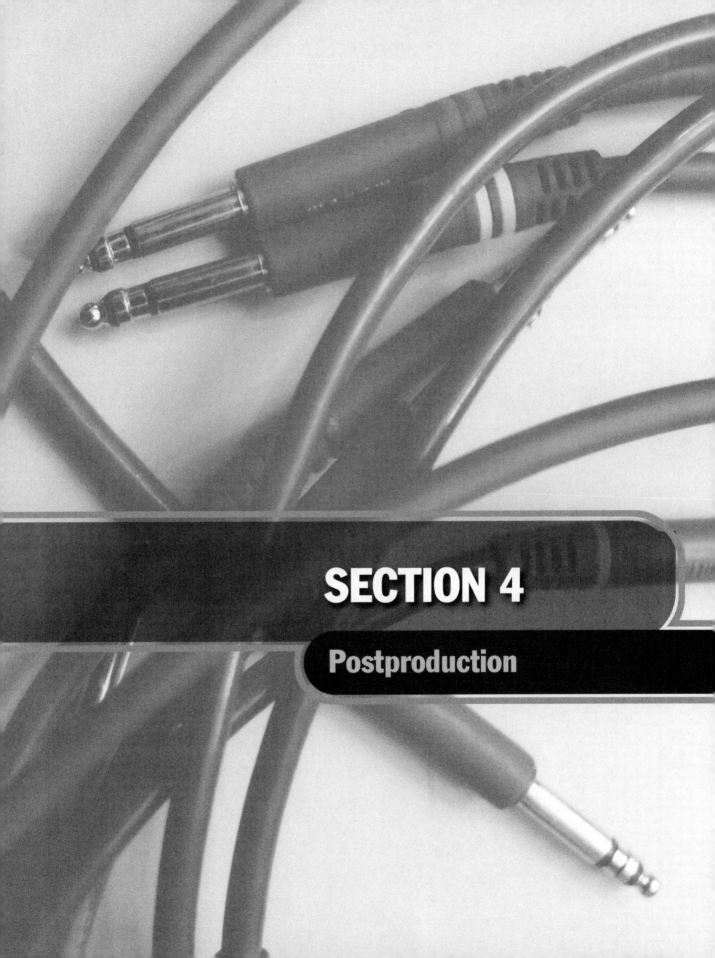

SECTION 4

Postproduction

CHAPTER 11
Editing Techniques

In this chapter:

• Analog and digital editing techniques

• Comping tracks, fades, and crossfades

• Vocal track editing and auto-tuning

• Making loops and other creative editing practices

• Getting tracks ready to mix

At this stage in the production process, you have recorded some or all of your tracks and now you want to begin editing those tracks. In this chapter I'll present a number of editing techniques you can use to improve your productions. Editing fits into all three stages of the production process, depending on the project. For example:

In preproduction, you can edit **rough tracks** and create new arrangement ideas. Rough tracks are unfinished and unperfected tracks recorded for the purposes of getting an idea down and hearing it back. Used in the stages of preproduction and production, rough tracks are a good way to see if a musical idea works within a song, without wasting time on elaborate engineering and production setups.

In production, you can **comp** multiple takes into a final master take and edit the final individual tracks to perfection. To comp is to edit (or compile) the best parts from multiple takes of a track into one master "keeper" take.

In postproduction, you can edit the final tracks for a different song form or **remix**. A remix is a completely new mix of a song that makes use of some of the original tracks but also adds new elements to transform the song into something new, usually with an altered feel and a different style.

ANALOG AND DIGITAL EDITING

Most studios perform digital editing these days. Professional producers and engineers, even if they record tracks onto analog tape, will dump the analog recordings into a digital editing program for quicker, easier, and more accurate editing. That being so, I'll focus most of the information in this chapter on digital editing concepts and techniques.

The reason that editing digital audio is so powerful is that most editing functions are non-destructive. What does that really mean? Non-destructive editing means that any cutting, pasting, trimming, separating, or clearing of audio data occurs virtually . . . the source audio files are not harmed in any way. These editing functions are performed on a map of the actual audio data, never touching the recorded source data. All edits that you perform simply help your digital editing program tell your hard drive where to look for data and how to arrange it for playback. More specifically, the edits tell your hard drive at which point to start and stop playing each audio file.

When you first record a track, it usually consists of just one entire whole-file audio region, as in the guitar track in fig. 11.1. Say you like some parts of the track and not others, plus you want to get a bit creative with the track. So, you cut out some parts and move other parts so the track sounds good and ultimately looks like fig. 11.2.

Editing a track creates many distinct audio regions. Yet, instead of creating brand new audio files for each small part of the track shown, your editing program simply directs the hard drive to the place where each part of the audio track is located on the original source audio file, in the order determined by the onscreen edits.

> **Take Note!**
> Almost every song you hear on the radio has been edited in one way or another—even live recordings. In fact, most of the songs have been edited heavily.

El Gtr 1_25

Fig. 11.1. One whole take of a guitar track. Your digital editing program draws this waveform to represent the source audio file for the track.

El Gtr 1_26-07
solo cool section-01
El Gtr 1_09-04

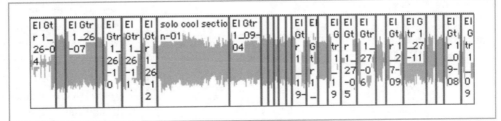

Fig. 11.2. If you were recording with analog tape and had to chop up the file like this, the edit would take forever!

Having a large number of edits on your tracks requires the hard drive to do a lot of locating. For example, the track edits may first direct the hard drive to read the first two seconds of the source audio file. Then an edit occurs that tells the hard drive to read the last four seconds of audio on the source file. The next edit instructs the hard drive to read a different section, and so on. The original audio file is not actually cut apart and spliced together; it only appears that way on your computer screen. In reality, the source audio file is completely intact and untouched.

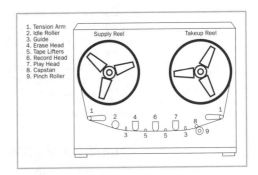

Analog Tape Editing Concepts and Techniques

Analog editing is another animal. Editing analog tape requires physically cutting ("splicing") the tape with a razor blade at the appropriate place, taking out a section of tape, and then reattaching the spliced tape. This requires the engineer to keep track of each piece of tape that is cut. Labeling each piece is imperative.

A technique called scrubbing is used in all analog edits to locate edit points. When scrubbing, engineers roll the tape back and forth over the tape machine's playhead at slow speeds by manually turning the supply and takeup reels with their hands to find a particular location on the tape . . . the location for an edit. Once the edit location is found, it is marked with a pencil and then cut.

1. Tension Arm
2. Idle Roller
3. Guide
4. Erase Head
5. Tape Lifters
6. Record Head
7. Play Head
8. Capstan
9. Pinch Roller
Supply Reel
Takeup Reel

Finding the right edit location is quite a skill because it requires the engineer to identify edits while listening to the audio at very slow speeds. It takes practice to hear what certain instruments sound like at slow speeds and where good edit locations should fall. Often, it means searching for a specific noticeable transient, like a snare hit or the attack on a guitar track.

Take Note!

Scrubbing is a valuable editing technique with digital audio too. By scrubbing over a digital audio edit point, you can listen in closely to find the exact edit point, which may not be obvious just by looking at the waveform.

If the tape is spliced perpendicularly (straight down), this is called a "butt splice." This type of splice is used for abrupt edits. However, many analog tape edits are performed at an angle. You can create automatic **crossfades** of several lengths, depending on the angle of the cut. *Crossfading* is the process of blending two regions of audio together to avoid obvious changes in sound or pops and clicks at the edit point. There are usually several different splicing angles available on the tape machine, and each yields different crossfade lengths.

Splicing Block
7.5° 15° 30° 45°

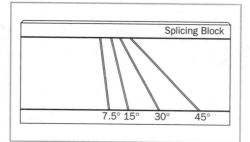

When cutting and splicing analog tape, you rely solely on your ears to find musical edit points. There are often hundreds of pieces of tape to keep track of and all razor-cut edits are destructive. It is an exacting and exhaustive process that yielded good results for several decades. However, it's fast becoming a dead art since digital editing has forever changed the way we think about production.

Engineers have been performing analog editing for many years but most have now made the switch to digital. Regardless, there are many concepts and techniques used in analog editing that exist in digital editing, such as scrubbing, cutting, pasting, and creating crossfades.

DIGITAL EDITING CONCEPTS

One of the best features of editing digital audio is that you actually see the waveform you're trying to edit. For visually oriented people like me, being able to see what I'm listening to helps me find accurate edit points much faster. In fact, most people rely on sight as their primary sense . . . even musicians.

Identifying Waveforms

When you get more familiar with hearing and *seeing* waveforms, you'll get to a point where you'll be able to interpret the waveforms, even without hearing them. Different types of instruments produce different types of waveforms. Some have more distinct short peaks and valleys, while others have long, continuous sounds without many peaks or valleys. The first way you'll be able to interpret waveforms is to tell what type of instrument made the waveform; then, how it was played and/or recorded. All of this interpretative data will help you (1) make judgments about how the sound was recorded and how best to edit it, (2) edit the right part of the sound without having to listen to it over and over, and (3) choose good points to edit the waveform.

Fig. 11.3(a). Snare drum waveform.

Fig. 11.3(b). Electric bass guitar waveform.

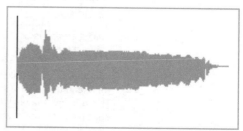

Fig. 11.3(c). Voice waveform.

When editing audio, it's usually a good idea to create regions precisely before a volume peak and end it immediately before another volume peak, as in fig. 11.4. This technique will help you capture the complete sound of the instrument and makes for smoother transitions between parts when cutting and pasting.

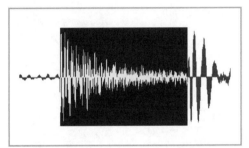

Fig. 11.4. Capturing one entire note—from the initial attack to the end of the decay before the next attack.

If possible, select a region that starts and ends on exactly the same part of the beat (e.g., beat 1). That way, it's easier to make repeatable loops (or regions of differing lengths that can be pasted together) and keep a steady beat. This is easy to do when editing on a grid, as in fig. 11.5.

Recall the discussion in chapter 2 about the peaks and troughs of waveforms. If possible, try to arrange your edits so that the peaks and troughs of the waveforms flow naturally throughout the edit. That is, try to edit so that the troughs follow peaks and vice versa, as in fig. 11.6. Try to avoid having two consecutive peaks or troughs. Pay more attention to this on monophonic (single-note) parts such as bass lines or synth leads, because it could seriously affect the sound of the track and make the edit obvious.

peak-trough_2

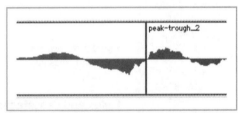

Fig. 11.6. Try to make edits so that the peaks follow troughs, and vice versa.

12|1|000
13|1|000
14|1|000
15|1|000
16|1|000
0:24
0:25
0:26
0:27
0:28
0:29
0:30
0:31
0:32
0:33
1100000
1200000
1300000
1400000
Manual Tempo: ♩110.00
Default: 4/4

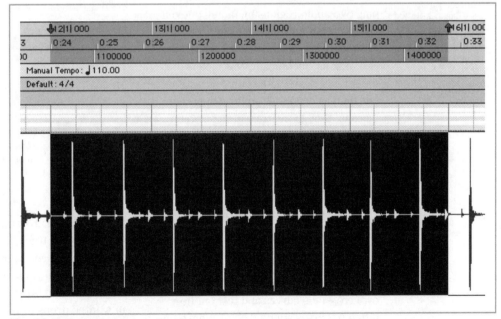

Fig. 11.5. Selecting a loop on the grid.

Take Note!

Expanding a track's height and width on your computer screen can be a very useful tool for examining the fine details of waveforms or automation data. Sometimes, you'll want to zoom in closely to one track's waveform so that it occupies your entire computer screen. At other times, you'll often need to view all the tracks on your screen at once (for large-scale edits across many tracks). Using keyboard shortcuts to quickly change your editing view will greatly improve your editing efficiency.

Ideally, you can create your edits at zero amplitude crossings, as in fig. 11.7. If the sound wave's amplitude is zero at the edit point, you will not hear audible clicks or pops between two adjacent regions. However, if the sound quality or background noise is different, you still may hear a sonic difference at the edit point if you don't have a crossfade between the two audio regions. (We'll cover crossfades in the next section.)

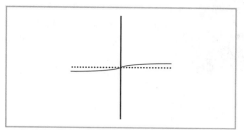

Fig. 11.7. Two regions edited together at 0 amplitude crossings.

Fades and Crossfades

A huge part of making your edits sound natural is your ability to use crossfades. Crossfading is the process of overlapping two audio regions by fading one out and the other in to prevent pops, clicks, or sudden changes in sound between the two regions. Technically, this means that the listener hears both tracks playing at one time as one fades out and the other fades in, though the transition between the two audio regions is often quite short. Crossfades have many applications, from smoothing transitions between regions to creating special audio effects.

For those who've edited analog tape, you know you're basically limited to choosing one of a few different angles of tape cuts to create crossfades. But with digital editing, you are able to draw your own crossfade curves and test out how different curves sound. You also have the option of placing a crossfade before the splice point, right on the splice point, or after the splice point.

Splice Point
Audio Region #1
Audio Region #2
Pre Crossfade
Splice Point
Audio Region #1
Audio Region #2
Centered Crossfade
Splice Point
Audio Region #1
Audio Region #2
Post Crossfade

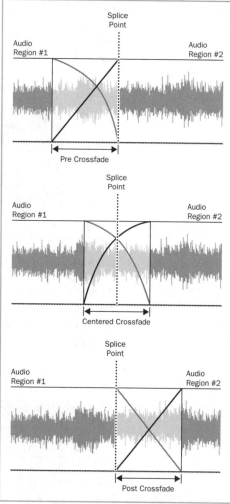

Fig. 11.8. With analog angle splices, you are limited to creating crossfades of several different lengths. In digital editing, you can choose the length as well as the type of curve for your crossfade.

When creating crossfades, be careful not to overload your track. If you create a crossfade that happens to overlap two powerful waveforms, they might sum together to create clipping. Also, crossfades can cause unwanted drops in volume if the fade-out

> **Take Note!**
> Personally, I often try to make my crossfades as short as I can while still achieving a natural transition between audio regions. With longer crossfades, you may find that notes overlap too much and the crossfade becomes very obvious.

and fade-in curves don't overlap enough. For crossfading between two completely different types of audio material, I recommend using a crossfade curve similar to the "Equal Power" crossfade shown in fig. 11.9(a). This will ensure there's no noticeable drop in volume at the edit point. For crossfading between two regions of similar audio material (like when creating loops), I recommend using a crossfade curve similar to the "Equal Gain" crossfade shown in fig. 11.9(b), to create a smooth and even transition between regions and make sure the overlapping signals don't clip. (I've found that the opposite works well in certain circumstances, too, so experiment!)

Audio
Region #1
Fades Out
Audio
Region #2
Fades In

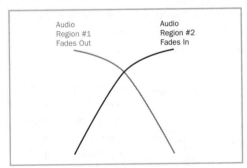

Fig. 11.9(a). An Equal Power crossfade.

Audio
Region #1
Fades Out
Audio
Region #2
Fades In

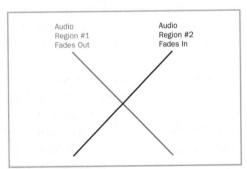

Fig. 11.9(b). An Equal Gain crossfade.

DIGITAL EDITING TECHNIQUES

With its variety of functions, there's really little you can't do when editing audio or MIDI. In fact, because there are so many ways to digitally edit your music, every digital audio editor seems to utilize different techniques and functions to get their work done—an entire book could be written on editing techniques alone. I'll cover just a few of the functions I use regularly. Try these out for yourself. I also recommend getting together with other folks and exchanging editing tips—you'll be surprised how much you can learn when sharing secrets.

In its most basic forms, digital editing includes cutting, pasting, copying, and clearing regions and files; being familiar with these commands is imperative. Editing also involves dexterity in creating audio regions, capturing regions, placing regions in tracks, working with regions on a rhythmic grid, and sliding regions freely around in your tracks. Most editing programs have keyboard shortcuts for these actions. I highly recommend learning them so you can manipulate your audio regions comfortably and quickly. Shortcuts can help to make editing a more creative and enjoyable task.

COMPING: Real vs. Virtual

Comping is the process of combining (compiling) all the best parts from multiple takes into one master take. For example, say you have three vocal takes of the first verse of a song. If you edit together the first line from take #2, the second line from take #3, and the third and fourth line from take #1 into one "keeper" take, that's comping.

You will comp in two primary ways: real and virtual comping. Real comping occurs when you combine parts of *different* tracks into one new track. In virtual comping, you combine parts from different takes that are stored on the same track, into a single "virtual" track.

Take Note!

If you want to record a double of a vocal track (i.e., having the lead vocalist sing exactly the same part on a separate track), you'll need to comp the lead vocal track first before recording the double track.

Line 4
Line 3
Line 2
Line 1
1.4
1.3
1.2
1.1
2.4
2.3
2.2
2.1
3.4
3.3
3.2
3.1
1.4
2.3
3.2
2.1
VOX TAKE 1
VOX TAKE 2
VOX TAKE 3
COMP
Separate Audio Tracks
2.1 3.2 2.3 1.4 COMP
3.1 3.2 3.3 3.4 VOX PLAYLIST 3
2.1 2.2 2.3 2.4 VOX PLAYLIST 2
1.1 1.2 1.3 1.4 VOX PLAYLIST 1
Line 1
Line 2
Line 3
Line 4
One Audio Track with Multiple Playlists

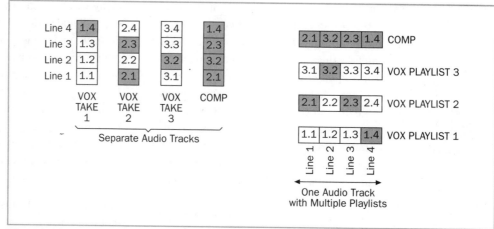

Fig. 11.10. It's just as easy comping takes together from multiple "real" tracks or from virtual tracks (a.k.a., playlists) on one track stored on top of each other.

NOTE: I use "virtual tracks" and playlists interchangeably in this book. In your software program, these two terms may mean different things, but I'm not making any distinctions between them here.

Whether you use multiple "real" tracks or "virtual" tracks, there are advantages to each in the editing process. By working with different takes on multiple "real" tracks you always have access to each track, you can see each track all the time, and you have a dedicated fader for each take. However, you need to make sure the levels and the effects on each track are the same. In fact, it's a good idea to bus them all to one separate aux track so you only have to control one fader and one set of effects. Also, performances are not always recorded at a consistent volume. Quieter passages may not sound as "good" as louder passages simply because they're not as loud—but you should still consider boosting their levels and using them in your comp.

With virtual tracks, only one "real" track is used (which is beneficial if you have limited track counts). Because the different takes reside "on top" of each other on separate virtual tracks, it's quick and easy to switch between the takes, and cut, copy, and paste to make a comp. As opposed to using multiple "real" tracks, this means you only need to adjust one volume fader and one set of effects on the track. Each virtual track will make use of the same volume level and effects on the one "real" track.

Regardless of which recording and editing process you prefer, it's best to limit the number of takes of the track that you're comping together to 5 or 6, and keep good track of them. Otherwise, you can easily be overwhelmed by the sheer number, and lose track of the good takes. If you were organized enough to use a take sheet while recording multiple takes of a track, then you should have notes about what parts of each take are "keepers."

Although being able to record many takes of a track is a great feature of digital audio, it can also be a curse. Having too many files to sift through can make your editing task much more difficult and time consuming. I recommend trashing takes that you know have no useful performances on them and limiting the number of keepers to a manageable size.

Take Note!

Another huge benefit to editing digital audio is the ability to undo an edit. The editing program keeps track of the undoable operations that you perform in a queue. This gives you the freedom to try any edits and undo them if you don't like them, and even go back and undo previous edits that are stored in the undo queue.

Cut, Copy, Paste, and Clear

Essential to the comping process are the cut, copy, paste, and clear functions. In your digital editing program, you are cutting, pasting, copying, and clearing audio or MIDI data instead of text or numbers. If you've used word processing or spreadsheet software before, you will be familiar with these commands. These commands are very useful for editing and can be used to edit any type of track material.

The Copy command temporarily stores a copy of the selected material on what is referred to as the clipboard. The Cut command chops out the selected material and places it on the clipboard. The Paste command inserts the data from the clipboard to the location you tell your editing software to place the data. The Clear command removes a selection from a track without placing it on the clipboard.

Editing Between Virtual Tracks/ Playlists on Multiple Drum Tracks

In my opinion, one of the coolest functions in digital audio editing is the playlist. I often record multiple takes of a multi-miked/multi-tracked drum part on separate playlists, literally right on top of each other, so that it's *really* easy to edit the drum part by pulling pieces from each take into a master take on a new playlist. This works particularly well when recording with a click track. If the drummer can stay with the click, you can copy and paste regions between playlists in seconds, and create the edited master drum track in just a few minutes.

Try this method: Listen to the different takes and choose the best overall take. Use that take as the starting point and make a copy of it on a new playlist. After determining where you want to edit that take, evaluate the other takes in those spots by switching between playlists and listening. Then simply cut and paste replacement sections from other takes onto the master take. Make sure that the edited sections work timing-wise. If they don't, slightly move them so that they do. (We'll get into techniques on how to do this in the next section.) After you've positioned your edits correctly, draw crossfades at the edit point across all the tracks and there you go . . . a master drum track in minutes.

Nudging

When editing, you will probably encounter many circumstances where you want to slightly push an audio or MIDI region (or even one audio or MIDI note) just a small amount so that it lines up with the beat or with a specific rhythmic hit. You may also want to fix an entire rhythmic feel ("groove") or create a different rhythmic feel by slightly adjusting the timing of the part. This is called nudging, and many digital software programs have this capability built-in.

For instance, let's say you have a great take, but the bass player hits a downbeat slightly ahead of when the drummer hits the kick drum. To align the timing, you can nudge the bass note slightly later in time to match the kick downbeat.

To nudge a note or several notes, first find the note(s) in the waveform. Zoom in close enough so you can see where the note begins and ends. Separate the note into its own audio region, then move it slightly later in time. I recommend trying 10 ms as a starting nudge value and adjusting from there. Be careful using the nudge editing technique, though. You can go crazy trying to align every note, killing way too much time and taking away from the real performance—the vibe—of the part. If the part needs that much fixing, re-record it!

> **Take Note!**
>
> A **group** is a collection of several linked tracks that have some relationship to each other, such as all of the drum tracks for a drum set or all of the backup vocal tracks. Groups allow you to apply an edit to one member of the group and have it be mirrored on all of the tracks in the group.

Using Markers for Editing Audio

Markers can assist you in easily and quickly locating specific parts of a song for edits. Among their many other uses, markers are particularly beneficial when you are editing groups of audio tracks, because they can help to expedite moving large amounts of audio around quickly. For example, say you've recorded the rhythm section (guitar, bass, keys, and drums) for an entire song. After listening to the song several times, you realize that you'd like to try doubling the length of the second verse. If you've got markers set up at the exact beginning and ending of a verse, you can easily select that portion of audio on all of the tracks, copy it, and paste it in a matter of seconds. (Try that with analog tape!)

When making large scale edits like this, you may need to extend or shorten the beginning or end of each individual track to smooth out the edits. Obviously, crossfades will help with this, too. Just be careful . . . once you get the regions into the right places, be sure not to nudge any individual track or you could screw up the feel during the rest of the song!

Drum Editing: A Case Study

Here is a case study on digitally editing drums. It applies and summarizes many of the techniques you've learned so far in this chapter and puts them into a real-world context. You can utilize these same techniques on all types of tracks . . .

In my opinion, editing is an art form, particularly when it comes to drums. Without good edits, drum tracks can inadvertently lose power and feel, as well as create some nasty digital pops and clicks that you definitely don't want in the final mix.

V1b
PC
Chorus
Gt...
V2
V2
PC 2
Chorus 2
BR a
Gtr Solo 2
Kick 1 B52-0
Kick 1 B52-05-00-DE4A-04
Kick 2 B91-0
Kick 2 B91-05-00-DE4A-0-04
Snare-05-00
Snare-05-00-DE4A-00-ADC-04
Hi Tom-05-0
Hi Tom-05-00-ADCL-04
Lo Tom-05-0
Lo Tom-05-00-ADCL-04
OH-05-02 L
OH-05-04 L
OH-05-02 R
OH-05-04 R
GTR Close-05
GTR Close-05-04
GTR Far-05-0
GTR Far-05-04
Bass DI-05-0
Bass DI-05-04
Bass Mic-05-
Bass Mic-05-04
Gtr Overdubs-04-00 L
Gtr Overdubs-05-00 L
Gtr Overdubs-04-00 R
Gtr Overdubs-05-00 R
Gtr Solo 2
Gtr Solo 2
Gtr Solo 2-05-0
Gtr Solo 2-05-0
Lead Vox
Le
Le
Lead
Lead Vox 2-0
Lead Vox 2-01-04
A Vox-04
A Vox 2-

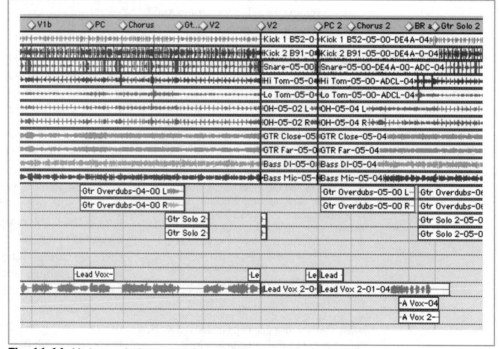

Fig. 11.11. Markers make it easy to quickly rearrange the form of a song.

In most situations, the best place to edit a drum track is right before a large transient. What's a transient? In this case, it's the initial attack in the sound wave when the drummer strikes the drum. Transients in drum tracks are easy to find. In fig. 11.12, you'll see an edit placed right before a transient.

Kick.03_04-02

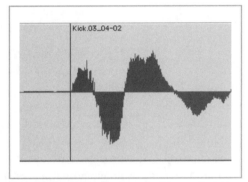

Fig. 11.12. A kick drum track with an edit right before the attack transient.

The reason to put the edit here is twofold. First, the decay from the last drumbeat on that track is usually as small as it's going to get. With so little digital information at that point, you might not even need to create a crossfade between the two regions. If you do need to use one, try using an equal gain crossfade.

Second, when editing multiple drum tracks, placing edits across all tracks at one spot before a transient will often make the entire drum kit edit less obvious. Often I'll put an edit right before the downbeat of a measure, or at a place where either the kick drum or the snare has an accented note. Even better, place your edit right before a big cymbal crash. Fig. 11.13 demonstrates an edit placed right before the beginning of a new measure.

Speaking of cymbal crashes, sometimes you'll want to place an edit on a downbeat, but sounds between the two edited regions don't quite match up. For instance, the drummer played a different cymbal,

Kick.03_04-04
Snare.03_04-04
Hat.03_04-04
Tom 1.03_04-04
Tom 2.03_04-04
Tom 3.03_04-04
OH.03_04-04 L
OH.03_04-04 R
Room.03_04-04 L
Room.03_04-04 R

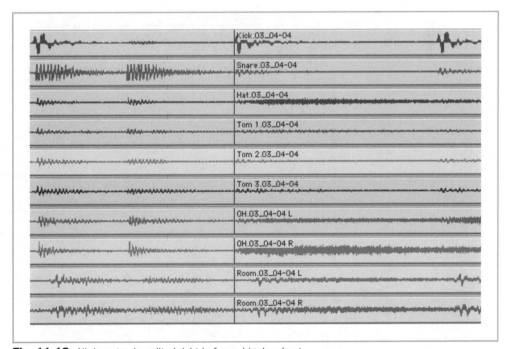

Fig. 11.13. All drum tracks edited right before a big downbeat.

Take Note!

Don't be afraid to edit between syllables. In singing (and speech) there is sometimes less amplitude in the signal in the middle of a word than there is between words. Many times, bringing out the best syllables and creating words with them can really improve the impact of a performance.

or a different tom is resonating from the previous region. When editing across all drum tracks at once, listen closely for these nuances. To avoid problems like this, you can extend the cymbal tracks (usually the overhead mic tracks) or tom tracks into the next measure to allow the previous sound to fully decay. Fig. 11.14 shows an example of this.

Vocal Editing Techniques

Comping the Lead Vocal Track

Comping the lead vocal comp is no different that any other comp, except that it often requires much more time than any other edit. Often, the goal in creating a vocal comp is to get the most emotive performance possible—to capture the appropriate emotion that the artist intends for the song. We need to keep this in mind as we're editing . . . to think of the song first and choose performances that are best for the song. Often, the best vocal performances are not technically perfect. There might be slight pitch issues, slight mispronunciations, mic level issues, or even noise and distortion on the track. Yet, as a whole, the performance is perfect in delivering the emotion of the song. So, don't get caught up in finding the best technical performance by sacrificing the emotion in the editing process.

If you used a take sheet, follow the notes you made on the take sheets to steer your vocal edits. Without the take sheets or other comments on your recorded tracks, you'll probably need to listen to each take and make notes now during the editing process. This makes the editing process much more time consuming.

For vocal tracks, I analyze the delivery of every phrase, every word, and even every syllable. Although you probably didn't get

Kick.03_04-04
Snare.03_04-04
Hat.03_04-04
Tom 1.03_04-04
Tom 2.03_04-04
Tom 3.03_04-04
OH.03_04-04 L
OH.03_04-04 R
Room.03_04-04 L
Room.03_04-04 R

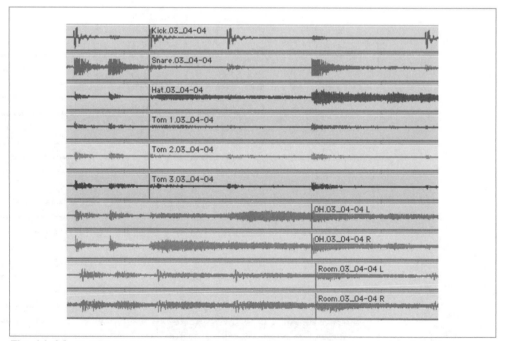

Fig. 11.14. All drum tracks are edited right before a big downbeat, but the overhead mic tracks are extended into the next measure to allow the cymbal crash to decay.

that detailed when recording the vocal tracks, it's good to get that detailed now. Write down additional notes on the take sheet or lyric sheet about edit points. Pick and choose each part of the vocal performance carefully when creating your master comp. Professional producers go to this level of detail. Will you?

Tuning a Vocal Track

After you've comped your vocal tracks, it's common to tune them using an auto-tuning program. These programs can automatically tune the track for you, but often result in decent, yet imperfect tuning performances. I recommend taking control of the tuning process and tuning the vocal track manually. To perfect the tuning of your vocal track, you should analyze and tune each vocal phrase separately.

The program enables you to see the pitches of each vocal note plotted against the notes in the song's key (the scale). You can then manually alter the pitch of each note by drawing new pitch lines/curves. Finally, you can re-record each newly tuned vocal phrase onto a new track, eventually making a completely tuned vocal track.

NOTE: Some artists make it a point *not* to use auto-tuning. This is noteworthy. If the singer on your project can sing totally in tune (or in tune enough), don't bother with auto-tuning and leave the raw performances. Often, the "realness" of these raw performances creates a better overall feel on the recording than processed vocals.

Aligning vocal melodies and harmonies

After comping the lead vocal track, it's a good idea to tighten up the rhythms of the harmony vocal tracks to match the lead vocals. The point is to get the start and end point of each harmony note tightly aligned with the lead vocal. If the harmony note is too long, shorten it by cutting some of the middle of the note out, creating crossfades between the remaining regions, as in fig. 11.15. You may need to use equal power crossfades here, and the crossfades may have to be a little longer than usual to make this sound natural.

Lead Vox_1
Back Vox_1
Back Vox_2

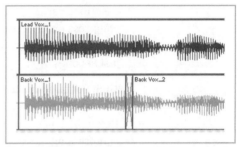

Fig. 11.15. Cut down the size of a harmony note to match the length of the lead line.

If the harmony note is too short, then you should copy a part of the middle of the harmony note, and paste it into the middle of the note to make it longer. Then apply crossfades to smooth it out, as in fig. 11.16. In this case, too, you may need to use equal power crossfades, and the crossfades may have to be a little longer than usual to make this sound natural.

Lead vox_3
back vox_3.1
bv n
ote3
-01
bv no
te3-0
1
back vox_3.2

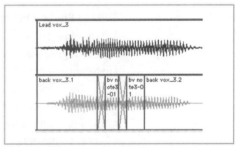

Fig. 11.16. Insert a copied piece of the harmony note to match the length of the lead line.

Also, trim the starts and ends of the notes so that they are rhythmically tight.

Time Compression/Expansion

Another technique you can use here is time compression and/or expansion. Some digital audio editing programs enable you to expand or compress an audio region without affecting its pitch. Thus, instead of performing the somewhat complicated editing on the harmony vocal lines described earlier, you can apply time compression or expansion to the particular notes and align them with the lead part in just seconds.

Time compression and expansion is a powerful yet somewhat limited tool. Depending on the program you use, compressing or expanding an audio region too much may create audible digital audio artifacts (distortion) in your tracks. You may only be able to compress an audio region by 5% while keeping the pitch the same and producing no audio artifacts. However, there are some products that can perform this process very well at much higher percentages away from the original region length. Explore the options and limitations of these programs, especially if time compression and expansion is something you might use regularly.

Editing Spoken Word

When editing speech (for a voice over, a monologue, lead vocals, etc.), it's customary to edit the words so that there is no stuttering, stammering, hesitation, or mistakes in the reading or performing of the material (unless, of course, those effects are desired). Many times it's also beneficial in voiceovers to eliminate unnecessary pauses and open spaces between words and sentences. This will increase the pace of the performance and is often done when there are a lot of breathing pauses, or when you want to intensify the impact of the delivery (e.g., a fast-talking radio DJ). The idea is to create a "perfect" performance.

When you are editing speech or vocals, it's always a good idea to have the script, text, or lyrics as a printed guide for making notes about where to place your edits. Having the words in front of you while editing can also help if you want to remove parts of the text while keeping the overall meaning.

A tricky yet interesting part of editing speech or vocals is figuring out the best edit points. Because language possesses such complex sounds and sound patterns, figuring out where words start and end can be challenging—but you need to be aware of how sounds look as waveforms. Parts of words each have distinctive sounds and often sound totally different from each other, once you listen to them more closely and analyze their waveforms. As you get better at identifying waveforms, you will begin to not only hear, but also see, the differences between consonants and vowels, as well as differences within these categories of sounds.

Editing Spoken Word—Learning the Technique

Try this technique: First, listen to the track at full speed to get a feel for it. Then, listen to the track at half-speed, if possible. Try scrubbing on some sections of the track. Listen to consonants and vowels, and look at the differences between the shapes of their waveforms. Spend a minute or two scrubbing over different consonants and vowels to get a feel for where each word starts and finishes. Listen closely for the **sibilant** sounds of the letter "s" and also to the larger spaces left for commas and periods, as well as the smaller spaces between words.

Once you've gotten a feel for the track, edit out the mistakes by cutting and pasting syllables, words, and phrases together.

Then, smooth out the timing of the track so that you create a near-perfect performance. If desired, shorten the open spaces between some of the words and sentences to increase the pace of the performance. You can use time compression here, too, to increase the speed without affecting the pitch of the performance.

Between your edits, you might have some open (noise-free) space. It's common to fill these empty spaces with "room tone." Room tone is the sound of the room where you're recording the voiceover. The tone of the room includes any unintended noise from computer fans, A/C units, or other equipment. I recommend recording around 30 seconds to a minute of room tone, just in case you need it to fill in gaps between edited phrases in the voiceover track.

Repairing Waveforms

Your editing program may allow you to redraw waveforms. That is, you can alter audio files on the sample level. This is particularly useful for repairing vocal plosives and pops or clicks that might randomly occur. Be careful when using this tool though; redrawing a waveform permanently alters the audio file on your hard drive once it's saved (i.e., destructive editing), so it's a good idea to make a backup of the original file before editing.

When repairing a waveform by redrawing, try to keep the same basic form of the sound wave or you might create an even nastier sound than the pop or click you were trying to fix. On the other hand, you can create some wacky effects editing on the sample level. Experiment with your waveform drawing technique . . . remember, you can always undo your edits before you save.

CREATIVE EDITING

Creating Loops

So much of music today is based on loops. Drum loops, bass line loops, synth chord progression loops, vocal loops, etc. One of the most common applications of editing is creating loops. You can make a loop out of any audio clip. Here's the technique that I use to make a drum loop, however this technique applies to making almost any other type of audio loop.

First, find and select a section of music that you'd like to loop, such as one measure of a drum beat. Play the section back, looping the playback. Adjust the selection length so that the loop doesn't lose the beat. That is, make sure the rhythm, timing, and feel are not altered when the end of the loop goes back to the beginning and starts playing again.

Next, separate the regions in each track so you can manipulate them. To do this on multiple tracks at once, highlight the section on all the tracks, then separate them. If you want to make the loop faster or slower, apply time compression or expansion to the loop material. Now make several copies of the loop, and paste them together. You may need to put crossfades between each loop to ensure there are no pops or other sonic inconsistencies between the end of one loop and the start of the next loop.

Creating Samples

Another common editing application is creating samples to be triggered by a sampler. Samples are easier to edit because you often don't have to worry about the timing; you only need to worry about capturing the whole sound.

For instance, say you really like the sound of a snare drum that you recorded in a session in your studio. During the session, the drummer played really well, hit the snare hard, and had it tuned up nicely. You even managed to get good separation on the snare track with minimal leakage from the hi-hat. (It's not uncommon for people to record samples off of CDs, etc. in a similar fashion.)

Once you've chosen the audio to sample, record or import it into your editing program. Then, all you need to do is clean it up. I recommend using the same technique as demonstrated in fig. 11.4, where you capture the note right at the beginning of the transient and then cut it off right before the next transient to ensure you get the entire decay of the note.

However, it's even more important to make your edits tight when sampling. Make sure you edit right up close to the beginning of the transient, but don't cut off so much that you lose part of the attack. If you don't make your edit tight, the note will always be "late" when you trigger it with your sampler, due to the extra space at the beginning of the audio sample. It's a good idea to fade out the sample as well as add a tiny fade-in so that there are no digital clicks or pops when the sample is triggered.

Kick sample edit (bad)

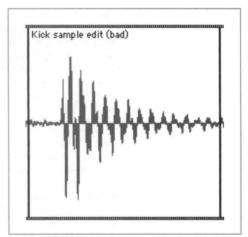

Fig. 11.17(a). A poor sample edit. There's too much space at the beginning of the sample and the end is not faded out. When triggered by a sampler, this sample will playback later that expected and will likely have a nasty click sound at the end of it.

Kick sample edit (good)

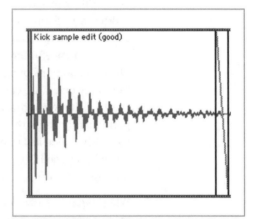

Fig. 11.17(b). A good sample edit. Notice there is little space at the beginning of the sample (with a tiny fade in) and the end is faded out. When triggered by a sampler, this sample will playback on time without any editing artifacts.

Special Effects

Editing is one of the times during the production process when you can add special effects to your music. You can reverse tracks, slow down, speed up, and change the pitch of entire tracks or parts of tracks, create alternative arrangements within a track (like altering the flow of a guitar solo), and use plug-ins or effects units to permanently add distortion, modulation, phasing, or any other crazy effect to your tracks. You're limited only by your editing tools and your imagination.

POST-EDITING CLEANUP AND MANAGING REGIONS

Once your track edits are complete, there are several things you can do to clean up your tracks and get them ready for mixdown. Stripping out the extraneous noise from tracks can really clean up the sound of your tracks. Also, consolidating each track will reduce the number of edits, which is very beneficial because every individual edit consumes precious processing power from your computer. Having fewer edits at mix time will help your hard drive find files faster.

Consolidating

By the time you're satisfied with an edited track, you most likely have a whole bunch of edits on it. Your tracks may contain many regions, like the messy track shown in fig. 11.18.

You can clean up your files and make them easier to mix by consolidating your tracks. Consolidating combines multiple regions into a single region (and a single new audio file), making the track much easier for you to work with, and easier for your hard drive to locate and process.

When you consolidate an audio track, your digital editing program writes a whole new audio file that combines selected material on a track, including blank space. Fig. 11.19 shows what the same track looks like after it's been consolidated.

When I consolidate tracks, I usually copy (or duplicate) the track material to another playlist first, then I consolidate the copy. Using this technique, I still have the original unconsolidated track on another playlist that I can easily get back to without having to undo the consolidate selection command. Check your edits one last time before consolidating. Be sure there are no pops or clicks, because they will be there on the consolidated tracks and will rear their ugly heads in the mix.

Cleaning Up

While editing a session, you will probably create many unneeded audio regions. When it comes time to mix the session, you may not want so much clutter. There are three main options that can help you tidy up your sessions before mixing them. You can hide, remove, or delete unused audio regions. Hiding simply puts the audio regions out of view. Removing them makes them unavailable for the mix (yet they can still be imported if needed because the audio is still on your hard drive). Deleting audio regions permanently erases the audio files.

cool bass loop-06
Last lick
Bass End

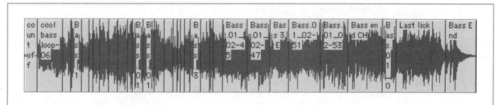

Fig. 11.18. A track with many edits.

Bass DI_01

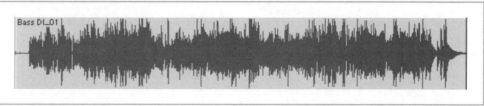

Fig. 11.19. A consolidated file. As you can see, the track is now one region and is a new audio file.

If you are mixing your own music, then you may not worry too much about cleaning up before the mix. However, if you are passing your songs on to someone else to mix, then making your files uncluttered is a smart and considerate action.

By consolidating and then deleting the unused audio files from your hard drive, you can make transferring and archiving your songs much more manageable. For instance, you can consolidate a four-minute, 24-track song recorded in three takes plus overdubs—7 GB worth of hard drive space —to under one GB. That's massive storage savings!

THE FLOW AND BALANCE OF EDITING

Time

There are a million ways to change any recorded audio performance and each has the potential to be tedious. This reality will continually call into question how much editing you should do on any given project. You could spend months perfecting a track by editing every bit of it, or you could allow the track to have imperfections that make it more human. Or, you could even re-record the track a month later after the performer has practiced the part more, saving you a month's worth of editing work. There are several issues at work here.

On each project you work on, you will need to find a balance between how much time you spend editing and how much time you spend trying to record better performances that require less editing. You should be thinking about editing in the preproduction phase of the production process. Consider this: If you plan for more practice time, or even writing easier parts, in the preproduction phase, your editing timeline can be drastically reduced. As Thoreau once wrote, "Our lives are frittered away by detail . . . Simplify. Simplify. Simplify." Do your best not to get sucked into a project with never-ending edits.

Practice

Although it's a good idea to not get bogged down with too much editing, some of the techniques you've learned here are not easy to master. You will need time to practice these techniques to become skilled at using them and you may experience difficult situations along the way. But keep at it, and look at any mistakes you make as learning opportunities. ■

EQ

INSERTS

CHAPTER 12
Mixing, Part I

In this chapter:

• Mix preparation and process

• Applying EQ

• Using filters

• Frequency tweaks on specific instruments

Mixing is an art and a science. Ultimately, it is a sonic and musical interpretation of sound, combined with a collection of techniques that, when used well together, result in neither art nor science, but magic . . . a sound that is greater than the sum of its parts and that gives an indescribable "life" to musical performances.

In the following two chapters, I will cover many of the techniques and skill sets that you'll need to mix your music well. I'll start with the core values of good mixing and finish up with the final little tweaks that can push your mix over the edge so that it "sounds like a record."

Take Note!

"Sounds like a record" is a phrase engineers and producers often use to describe a song or, most often, a mix that is record-quality; that is, it sounds so good that it should be on a major-label released record.

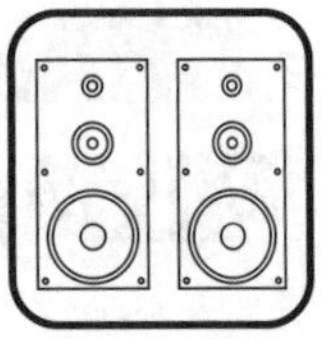

PREPARING FOR THE MIX

A mix is the combination of all your recorded tracks reduced to two tracks (for stereo playback) or six to eight tracks (for surround playback). The goal of mixing is to create an overall sound that helps support the purpose of the song. You want to put the listener in an appealing acoustical space by tweaking individual sounds (volume levels, panning, EQ, and effects) in a creative way to enhance the overall impact of the final recording, making sure that every element of the soundscape has its place. There are many ways to approach mixing, but before we jump into them, there are a few things you should do before digging into a mix.

First, make sure your listening environment is set up right. Most of you will probably be mixing using *near-field monitors*, that is, speakers that are placed within a few feet of your ears. Reread the section on "Setting Up Your Listening Environment" in chapter 2 to ensure the proper setup.

Your Listening Environment and Monitoring Levels

It is important to have good speaker placement, but ideally your listening environment for mixing should have a flat frequency response. What does that mean? It means that there should be no frequencies that are unintentionally boosted or cut due to the acoustics of the environment (the room). Unless acoustically treated, many rooms have "modes"—certain frequencies that are accentuated or swallowed up due to the room dimensions and sound reflections that take place between the walls, floor, and ceiling.

These frequencies may become very apparent when you take a mix that you made in your studio and listen to it in environments other than your studio. For example, because your studio may naturally boost 200 Hz, you may leave out too much of this frequency when you mix. Thus, when you play it in your friend's car, some of the low end is missing.

Also, check out your mixes at different volume levels. Do this throughout the mixing process, as well as in other listening environments, to make sure you can hear everything you want to hear at all playback volumes. Getting all your levels to work in every listening environment is tricky. I'll tell you why.

Humans are designed to hear certain frequency ranges better than others. Findings by the famed researchers Fletcher and Munson show that humans are more attuned to sounds between 1 and 4 kHz (mids) and are less sensitive to lows and highs at low volumes than at high volumes. Why is that so? Because most of the important frequencies for speech recognition are in the middle. Over time, our ears have evolved to be more sensitive to those frequencies. What does that mean in terms of mixing music?

The apparent loudness of those frequencies affects mixing in several ways. Because our ears are less sensitive to low and high frequencies and more sensitive to mid frequencies, if we mix at low volumes, we tend to boost the low and high frequencies because we can't hear them as well. Then, if we play that mix back at a high volume, it will be too bassy and too trebly. Also, at low mixing volumes, we tend to put the lead instrument (or voice) very high in the mix. This will come back to haunt us if the mix is turned up loud. The lead instrument will probably stick out too far above the rest of the mix.

If we mix at high volumes, we tend to reduce the lows and highs because we can hear them fine. But, when we listen back at low volume, the mix will sound mid-rangey. And, if we bury the lead instrument (or voice) while mixing at high volumes, it will be lost when listening back at low volumes.

There is a balance that you must strike when mixing and listening back to your mixes. In this case, there are two things that should influence your actions: the style of music and what volume level the music will most often be played at. For example, rock and dance music are often listened to at loud levels, so they should be mixed appropriately—often with slightly less bass and treble frequencies. However, that does not mean that you need to mix them at loud levels. As long as you understand the concepts presented here, you can mix at lower volumes (which is much better for your ears) and still create killer mixes that sound great when turned up loud.

Next, listen to some of your favorite mixes. . . . the ones that sound really good to you. This will get your ears ready for mixing towards the great sounds on those recordings. Also, listen to recordings in the same genre of the music you're mixing for reference. It's useful to identify some key characteristics of the mixes from particular genres. For example, listen to the levels of certain instruments, e.g., where the vocals sit (on top of the instruments or in the mix), and particular stylistic effects, like how much reverb is used on the snare drum.

Finally, get your songs ready for mixing. That is,

1. Make sure all of your editing is complete. For example, check your edits for unwanted clicks and pops, etc.

2. Organize your hardware mixer or mixing software so that your tracks are in a logical order and that they're easier to work with. For example, put all the drum tracks next to each other, all the vocal tracks near each other, etc.

3. Group your tracks, if possible.

4. Set up any inserts and effects sends that you're sure you want to use in the mixing session.

Let's look at these four in a little more detail:

1) Checking the Edits

It's a good idea to check the quality of your edits before you start mixing. We all make mistakes and accidentally let sub-par edits slip by. Sometimes, these edits can create clicks and pops that, if not caught before the mixing process, can rear their ugly heads in strange ways. For example, if you have a "clicky" edit on a keyboard part that has delay on it (in the mix), that edit click can be multiplied as it's repeated with the delay effect. To be really anal, check each track in solo . . . especially if someone else did the editing and you're in charge of mixing.

2) Organizing Your Mixer

Whether you're mixing with a hardware analog mixer, a digital mixer, a "control surface" for your software recorder, or your mouse, it's extremely beneficial to descriptively label your tracks. Use tape by the faders, type names into your software, and organize the tracks in meaningful groups by physically moving or routing them to the appropriate locations.

3) Grouping Tracks

It's a good idea to group tracks to improve your efficiency while mixing. I usually set up both small and large groups of tracks. Here's an example. The number of tracks that are grouped together is shown in parentheses.

Small Groups	Large Groups
Drum overhead mics (2)	All drums (4-12)
Room mics (2)	All guitars (4-12)
All toms (2-4)	All vocals (2-12)
Stereo Rhythm Electric Guitar (2)	

Having both small and large groups makes it easy for you to switch between working with individual instruments or parts and working with macroscopic multi-tracked groups. Having groups simplifies the process of muting or soloing a particular instrument group when checking its sound. It also allows you to adjust the entire group volume level all at once, or add special effects (like muting all of the guitar tracks during a verse) in your final mix.

4) Setting Up Inserts and Effects Sends
Professional mixers often set up effects sends and returns so that they have a variety of effects at their fingertips.

In fig. 12.1, there are two reverbs, two delays, one pitch shifter, and one chorus effect. Why two reverbs? It's a good idea to use multiple reverbs in your mix so that you can put instruments into different acoustical environments, like a medium room and a large hall. Why two delays? Professional mixers often set up two delays—one with an eighth-note delay and one with a sixteenth-note delay—to have rhythmic delays handy just in case. (Delay time calculations and reverbs are explained in chapter 13.) The pitch change effect is effective for making backing vocal tracks sound bigger. The chorus effect does essentially the same thing for guitars.

Other effects to consider using as inserts right at the beginning of your mix are compression and EQ. There are many times when it's appropriate to put a compressor and/or an EQ on the master stereo output. However, be careful. Any plug-in or hardware insert that you put on the master stereo output sonically colors your final mix. That's why it's a good idea to add whatever effect you want to add on the master stereo output (a compressor, an EQ, etc.) right at the beginning of your mix session. If you add the effect in later, your entire mix will change and you might have to EQ or compress each track all over again. If needed, review how to set up inserts and effects sends in chapter 8.

Utilizing Effects Processors and Automation in Your Mixes

Hardware effects processors and software effects programs ("plug-ins") are essential components to mixing. They provide the means to sonically alter your tracks and create "better" or unique sounds, as well as construct natural and unnatural sonic landscapes. Experiment and become familiar with the different sound possibilities in your hardware and software effects units; that way, you'll know what types of sonic alterations are available to you while mixing.

Many recording systems offer automation capabilities to make mixing an easier process. Automation allows you to save mixing "moves" like volume changes, panning adjustments, and track muting and soloing. It also allows you to make dynamic modifications to your effects parameters. It will be very beneficial for you to learn and become efficient in using any automation available on your recording system . . . this knowledge will allow you to be more creative and add a new level of dynamics into your mixes.

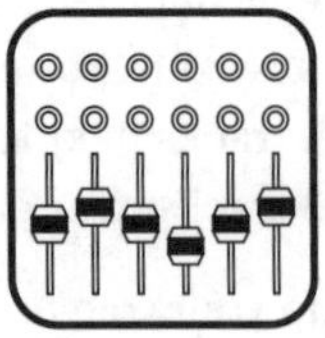

THE MIXING PROCESS

Now that we've discussed what to do before starting a mix, let's get into the mixing process. The mixing process is really an exercise in arranging . . . arranging sounds in the stereo field, arranging the sonic relationships between instruments, arranging each track's entrance and departure, and deciding which tracks (if not all) make it to the final mix. Some mix engineers like to put every instrument in its own space, and some like to

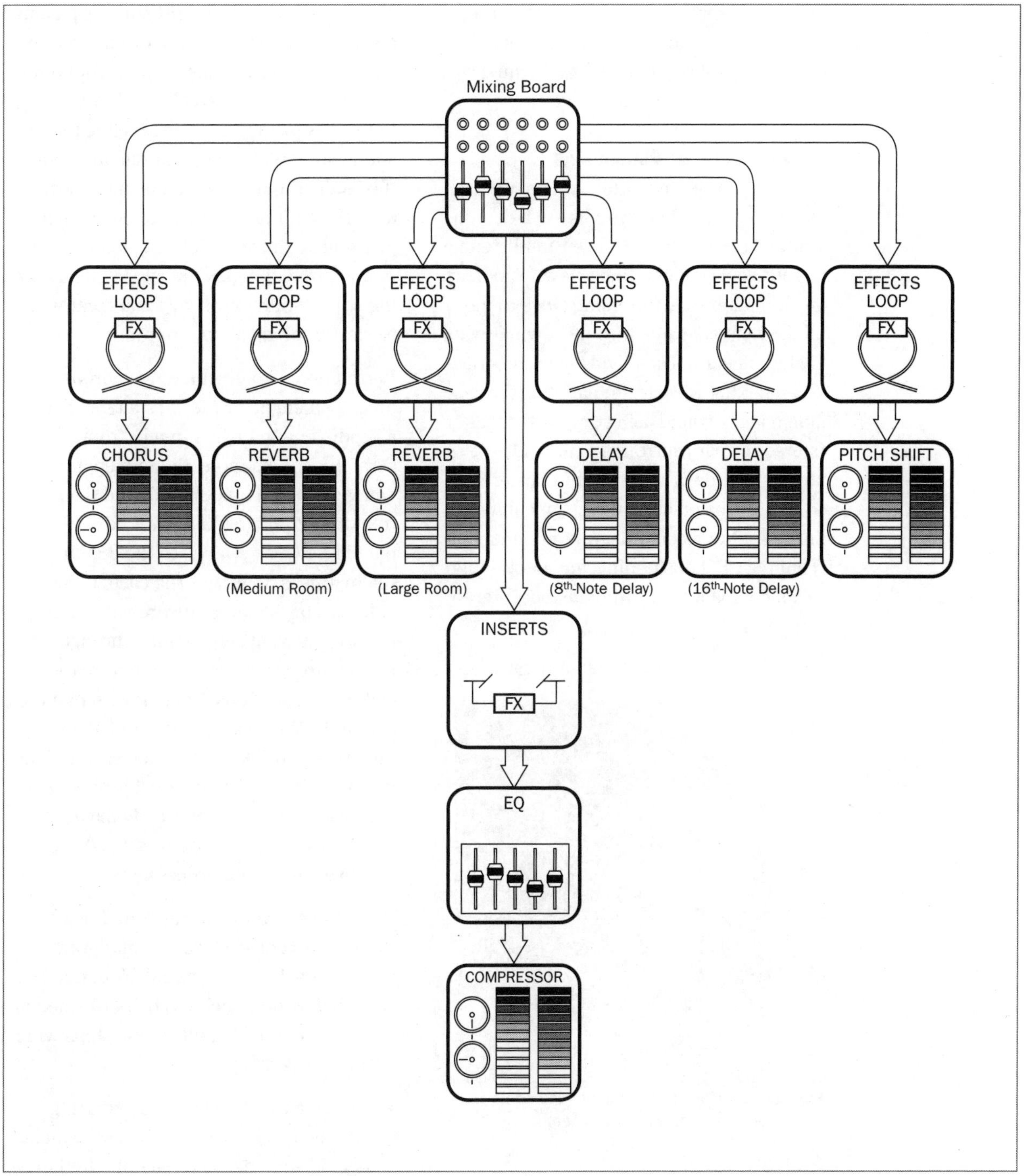
Mixing Board
EFFECTS LOOP
FX
EFFECTS LOOP
FX
EFFECTS LOOP
FX
EFFECTS LOOP
FX
EFFECTS LOOP
FX
EFFECTS LOOP
FX
CHORUS
REVERB
(Medium Room)
REVERB
(Large Room)
DELAY
(8th-Note Delay)
DELAY
(16th-Note Delay)
PITCH SHIFT
INSERTS
FX
EQ
COMPRESSOR

Fig. 12.1. Common effects used in many mixes.

create one space for the listener to enter into. Regardless of the exact technique, consider all of the sounds in your mixes as part of a three-dimensional picture.

Hearing in Three Dimensions

Humans hear in three dimensions; we can localize sounds all around us. As a demonstration, try closing your eyes and listening to your environment. Right now I can hear my computer's fan humming close to me on the right side and, through a window on my left, I hear a plane flying over my house. When mixing we can simulate this three-dimensional sound using only two speakers (stereo) or with surround sound. Most mixes these days are still done in stereo so we'll focus on creating an appealing 3D image for the listener using stereo imaging (panning), EQ positioning, and depth. I like to conceptualize three-dimensional stereo sound, as shown in fig. 12.2.

Far
Near
Hi
|
EQ
|
Lo
L — panning — R

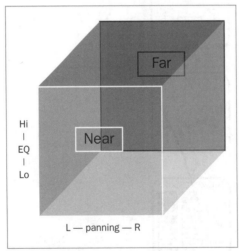

Fig. 12.2. Think of 3D stereo sound as having three planes: height, width, and depth.

Panning (**width**) is used to place sound sources on the left side, right side, or anywhere between two speakers (see the discussion on phantom image in chapter 2). EQ positioning (**height**) means placing a sound source within one or multiple frequency ranges to separate it from other sound sources. Some call this "carving EQ holes." **Depth** refers to the feeling that a sound source is close to or distant from the listener and is created using reverbs and delays. It is beneficial to envision a physical layout when placing instruments in this three-dimensional space. Balancing the sound sources visually is a great way to start thinking about your mix.

In traditional analog mixing environments, an engineer receives a tape from a producer and begins to mix from scratch—for example, the mix engineer will get a rough mix on DAT and the raw tracks on 2" analog tape with no set levels, panning, EQ, or effects. In the digital realm, this is no longer the case. Using software or digital hardware with mixing memory, mixing can be done throughout the recording process, even before the official mixing sessions. Track levels, panning, EQ, and effects can be adjusted at any time during tracking and then saved. Thus, when mixing in digital, you'll probably start each mix session already having a rough mix, allowing you to get right to the creative part of the process.

Regardless of the recording medium, there's still a procedure you may want to follow loosely when mixing. Note that the steps below don't need to be performed in this particular order, and some steps will probably overlap.

- Create a rough balance: set starting volume levels and panning assignments, decide what needs to be done to the mix.
- Write mute and panning automation.
- Apply equalization and carve EQ holes.

- Add dynamic processing: compression, limiting, gates, expansion.

- Add depth and special effects: reverb, delay, chorus, flange.

- Set final volume levels: add automation on tracks, inserts, and sends.

- Record/"Bounce" mix to tape or disk in one or more mix passes.

- Check mix(es) on different speakers, at different times, etc., and compare different passes.

- Fix any problems . . . lather, rinse, repeat as needed.

- Create more mix passes for different mix versions (e.g., vocals up mix, bass up mix, etc.).

I'll cover most of these steps here, but please note the next two chapters are only loosely organized according to the list above. Just like real-life mixing, sometimes things get moved around to improve the flow!

The Producer's Role During the Mix Process

If you're mixing with a producer and/or an artist who's producing, they are essentially the directors for the mix session(s). Although the mix engineer has a lot of creative input, the producers and artists are ultimately responsible for the project, so they're the ones who make the final decisions. It's the engineer's job to create the sound the producer or artist wants—this is true even when you're producing your own tracks. Listen to the producer inside of you. Detach yourself from all the hard work you've put into your mix and listen like you're hearing it for the first time.

Producers and artists tend to use non-technical terms for describing the sound of a mix. (In fact, some even use colors, like "orange," to describe sound.) You should try to learn this vocabulary so you can interpret what they mean. For example, if a producer says, "I think the mix should be warmer," this usually means they want you to boost the low end. Likewise, if they want it "fatter" and "more spacious," you might want to add chorus and reverb, respectively. To help you learn the vocabulary, some of these terms are listed in the EQ section later in this chapter. (And a hint for working with color-sensitive producers: "orange" is sometimes used to describe the low-mid frequencies.)

CREATING A ROUGH BALANCE

There are basically two different methods to use when beginning a mix: You can start with the rough mix from the tracking session(s) and build on that. Or, you can use the rough mix as a guide, but essentially start over by building a mix around either the drums and bass or the lead vocal or instrument track. Regardless of how you want to start, you need a solid foundation with the rhythm section; the drums and bass must be mixed well in relation to each other. Also, the lead vocal or lead instrument should be prominent—not covered by other instruments—without sounding detached from the rest of the music.

Allow some headroom for these main instruments! Don't start your mix with them too high or else you'll have no room to raise their levels if required. Once you've found comfortable levels for the main instruments you can add the rest of the instruments piece by piece, in order of importance. And while you're adding instruments and building a good general balance among everything, pan the tracks to fill out the stereo image. Think of the tracks visually along a line from left to right . . . .

The kick drum, snare drum, bass, and lead vocal/instrument tracks are usually centered in the stereo image. Toms and

> *Take Note!*
> It's not uncommon to start EQing while building the rough mix. EQ techniques are covered later in this chapter.

Far Left
Mid Left
Center
Mid Right
Far Right
Gtr L
Cymbals L
Keys L
Kick/Snare
Vocal/Bass
Keys R
Cymbals R
Gtr R

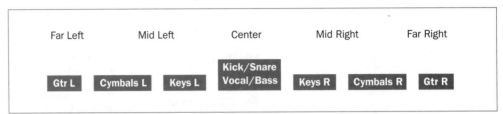

Fig. 12.3. Visual placement of instruments in the stereo image.

cymbals are usually panned, but not totally hard left and right, because that doesn't sound very realistic. Also, when panning drums think about whether you want them panned from the audience's perspective or the drummer's. Keyboards are often panned left and right for a stereo spread and guitar tracks are often doubled, with each track panned to create a wide stereo image. Stereo pairs are also common on horns, strings, and even percussion to provide expanded sonic width and balance. It's also cool to have particular instruments only on one side of the stereo spectrum. However, don't take my word for it. Experiment. Each song will most likely call for different panning schemes, so keep an open mind and try new techniques. Also, once you get further into the mix you can automate the panning of your tracks (and effects) to create more interesting stereo movement.

At this point in the mix procedure, ask yourself some questions: What kind of acoustical space do I want to put the listener in? Who is this mix for? What kind of overall sound do I want to create? What specific effects do I want to use? Are there any special arrangement issues to consider (long fades, big mutes, etc.)? Try to plan some of these things out before you continue the session.

Monitor Level During a Mix

Although you should test your mixes at different volumes, it's a good idea to keep your monitor level fairly consistent while mixing. That way you'll have a fixed reference level against which to measure any changes that you make. Some people like to mix at loud volumes. This often makes your mix sound impressive, but can be very fatiguing to your ears. Take breaks to rest your ears if you mix at high volumes! Mixing at lower volumes won't tire your ears as much, but it may not be as exciting. However, if you mix at a lower volume, crank things up at the end of the session and reward yourself with how cool your mix sounds loud. Check out the "Permissable Exposure to Noise Levels" graphic in chapter 8 for more information on monitor levels.

Note: People will listen to your songs loudly in their cars while they're speeding down the interstate, or softly while they're working in their offices. Your mixes must convey the music at all volume levels so, near the end of your mix session, listen at many different levels and make sure you hear what you need to.

WRITING MUTE AND PANNING AUTOMATION

Once I've got a rough mix, I usually record or draw mute automation on any track that needs it, if I haven't already done this in the editing stage. For example, I sometimes mute tom tracks between drum fills so I don't have to use gates on the toms or ride their levels. I'll do the same on guitar tracks to eliminate amp hum. In fact, I might even completely erase a

Take Note!

Signal flow is just as important in mixing as it is in recording. Pay attention to your levels at all gain stages in your signal path so that you're not clipping any of the inserts, effects busses, sends, aux tracks, track outputs, and master fader.

section of the track if I know it contains no useful audio, just to clean things up and make the mix easier. If you find that your mix appears cluttered with too many parts, you may decide to leave some tracks out during parts, or even for the entire song. Muting tracks is an effective way to unclutter a mix or create interesting contrast between different sections of a song.

The Danger in Muting

To write mute automation, I like to draw it in. In a case such as the one illustrated below, I can see when and where the toms are hit, and unmute the tracks.

Tom 1
blocks
waveform
volume
Tom 2
✓ mute
pan
(snd c) Bus 1-2
Tom 3

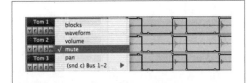

Writing mute automation makes it easy to silence unneeded portions of tracks.

However, be careful when using mute automation . . . sometimes an obvious mute can sound strange. For example, when muting toms, you take away some of the ambience provided by the tom mics, only to add it back in when unmuting the toms for a fill. Depending on how the track was recorded, muting may not sound good, so you may want to use volume rides or gates instead. Even though you can use your eyes when working with digital tracks, as always, let your ears be the true guide.

Let's discuss this example. The goal here is to unmute the toms for a drum fill at the end of a musical phrase and then mute them again after the fill—but we need to keep it musical. If we mute the toms right after the fill, the cymbal leakage on the tom mics will cut out and possibly sound strange. Thus, we need to place our mutes in strategic locations so as to make them unnoticeable. My advice is to wait until the next big snare hit (on beat 2 after the fill) or even the second big snare hit (on beat 4 after the fill) to mute the toms. That way, the decay of the cymbal crash will have faded and the loud snare hit will mask the disappearance of the tom tracks when they become muted. Paying attention to details like this really tightens up your mixes and helps to avoid unwanted audio artifacts.

Using automation is a powerful mixing technique, but riding the faders with your fingers in real time adds an energy to the mix that can't be measured, only felt. It makes mixing into a performance art. Consider combining automation with live fader riding to make your mixes sound more alive.

EQ

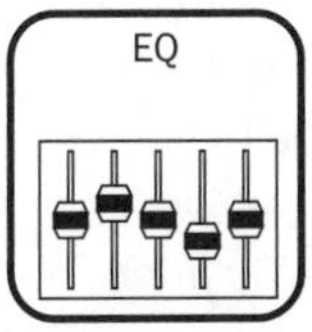

APPLYING EQUALIZATION

Originally used to help recorded sounds match the original sound source, equalizers (EQs) are frequency-specific amplitude changers. They are frequency filters that can boost or cut selected frequency bandwidths within a signal. In other words, an equalizer is used to adjust the frequency content of an audio signal. There are several reasons to apply EQ:

- To improve the tone quality (timbre) of an instrument
- To create a special effect (like a telephone vocal sound)
- To help a track stand out
- To fix mic choice and placement problems (like frequency, leakage, or noise issues)
- To make up for inadequacies in the recording equipment
- To create a better blend of instruments
- To improve the sound of the overall mix (if applied to the master output)

Most home and car stereos have some form of equalizers, ranging from individual knobs for bass and treble to small graphic equalizers with three to five vertical faders. Their purpose is the same as the EQ plug-ins and outboard EQ hardware that professional mix engineers use. However, our home and professional mixing EQ tools are usually more advanced and give us more control over the EQ parameters, allowing us to alter specific and controllable frequency ranges. When we apply EQ to a track, we're changing its timbre.

Timbre

All musical instruments create sounds with multiple frequencies, even if only playing one note. Depending on the particular note played, an instrument will produce the specific pitch for that note (known as the fundamental pitch) plus additional pitches with lower amplitudes (known as harmonics and overtones) that color the overall sound. For example, an A4 on the piano has a fundamental frequency of 440 Hz. Harmonics are exact multiples of the fundamental frequency. In this case, that includes 880 Hz (2 * 440), 1760 Hz (4 * 440), etc. Overtones are not exact multiples of the fundamental but they also color the sound. The fundamental added in with its harmonics and overtones give a note its timbre. So, when we apply EQ to a sound, we are actually adjusting its overall timbre—the fundamental pitch plus the harmonics and overtones.

Humans are able to hear frequencies from roughly 20 Hz to 20 kHz. The chart in fig. 12.4 shows the major frequency ranges and words that describe the sound of frequencies within those ranges.

With practice you can learn to identify frequencies and effectively apply EQ to improve your mixes. To help you, I've included a chart (fig. 12.5) that shows the major frequency ranges for many instruments.

To adjust certain frequencies and the timbre of a track, we have a choice between four basic types of EQs: parametric, semi-parametric, graphic, and program. The most advanced type that gives you the most control over your sonic sculpting is a parametric EQ. Parametric EQs allow you to control three parameters: the central frequency (Freq), the boost/cut (Gain), and the width of the affected frequency range (Q).

The Parameters of a Parametric EQ

The **central frequency** is the frequency that you want to adjust. For example, say you want to add some lows to a rock guitar part. Choose 100 Hz as the central frequency. The **Gain** is the amount (in

Take Note!

Often used to test and calibrate analog tape recorders, sine waves are pure tones. They have no harmonics or overtones. All other sounds have harmonics and overtones. Each sound has a unique harmonic structure that differentiates it from every other sound. This difference defines each sound's timbre or tone color.

For example, even if you have a cello and a bass guitar play the same note at the same loudness and duration, the sounds will still be different. We can easily tell them apart. Why? The way the fundamental frequency interacts with the instrument to create a unique mix of harmonics and overtones defines the timbre of the instrument. Our brains are smart enough to interpret these harmonic differences and assign them meaning.

Bass
Mid Bass
Mid Range
Upper Mids
Highs
20 Hz
100 Hz
500 Hz
2 kHz
8 kHz
20 kHz
•Depth •Power •Thump
•Warmth •Body •Fullness
•Bang •Nasality •Horn-like •Fullness of high notes
•Presence •Edge •Punch •Brightness •Definition •Excitement
•Brilliance •Sizzle •Treble •Crispiness •Airiness •Breathiness

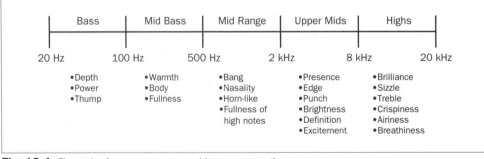

Fig. 12.4. The major frequency ranges and human perception.

> **Take Note!**
> Q actually refers to a ratio: the center frequency divided by the bandwidth, where the bandwidth is the frequency region on either side of the center frequency (expressed in octaves) that is within three decibels up/down from the center frequency's cut/boost.

Snare drum
Bass drum
Cymbals
Guitar
Bass
Keys/Piano
VOICE:
Soprano
Alto
Tenor
Bass
Trumpet
Trumpet
Saxophones
Strings
Frequency (in Hz)
27.5
55
110
220
(A440)
880
1760
3520
7040
14080
A_0
A_1
A_2
A_3
A_4
A_5
A_6
A_7

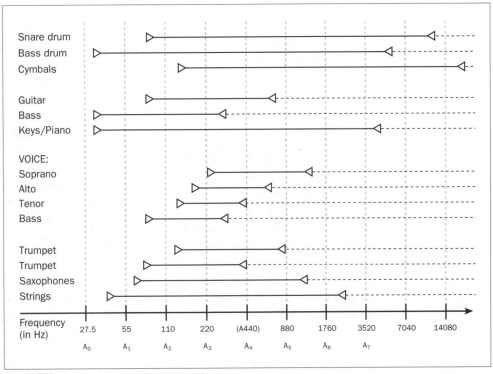

Fig. 12.5. Frequency ranges for common instruments.

decibels or dB) of increase or decrease in amplitude you want to apply at the center frequency. If you want a slight low boost in your guitar part, add 1–3 dB. For a more drastic change, add 8–9 dB. The third parameter, Q, is the width of the boost or cut region around the center frequency. The Q determines the degree to which frequencies near the center frequency are boosted or cut. High Q values yield narrow widths (for affecting a small range of frequencies) while low Q values provide expanded widths to encompass a large range of frequencies.

For example, the 4-band parametric EQ in fig. 12.6 shows a particular frequency curve of strategically placed boosts and cuts. Note the parameter numbers, particularly the Q values, and check out how the values affect the EQ curve.

12
6
0
6
12
31
125
500
2K
8K
Gain
Frq
Q
2.3
-5.5
-4.3
4.9
80
304
1531
6124
3.26
6.13
2.08
4.33

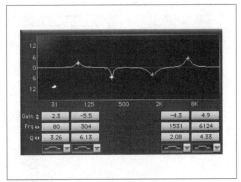

Fig. 12.6. A 4-band parametric EQ with various boosts and cuts in frequency.

The Other Types of Equalizers

Semi-parametric EQs are the same as parametric EQs except that they don't allow you to alter the Q value. With even fewer parameters to control, **program** EQs (like the treble and bass knobs on a car stereo) only allow you to boost or cut the gain of a predetermined center frequency and Q. Like program EQs, **graphic EQs** have fixed center frequencies and Q values, allowing you to only change the boost/cut amount. However, they often have a large number of bands (sometimes up to 31 bands) making them rather powerful and relatively intuitive to use.

A more limited version of a parametric EQ is a **peak equalizer**, which creates one localized boost or cut at a particular frequency. The bandwidth of the boost or cut depends on the Q value—a higher Q value means the boost or cut is applied to a narrow frequency range; a low Q means the boost/cut affects a wide range. Fig. 12.8 shows a filter with a high Q value (narrow bandwidth), then one with a low Q (wide bandwidth).

Filters

Filters, including hi-pass filters, low-pass filters, hi-shelf filters, and low-shelf filters, are a subset of equalizers. As the name indicates, hi-pass filters allow high frequencies to pass through but cut off the low frequencies. Low-pass filters do the opposite—they allow low frequencies to pass through but cut off the high frequencies. For hi- and low-pass filters, the Q value determines how steep the cutoff curve is. Fig. 12.9 shows a hi-pass filter with a low Q value and a low-pass filter with a high Q value. Shelving filters boost or cut all frequencies above a certain threshold frequency evenly, as is fig. 12.10.

As you can see in these diagrams, the gain does not immediately change from one level to another. The gain change is progressive. Truth be told, the cutoff frequency that you set on the filter is actu-

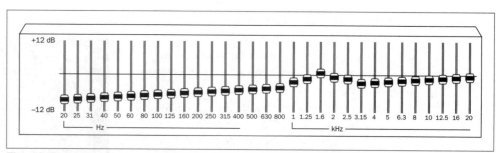

Fig. 12.7. Graphic EQs are powerful and easy to use, yet are not as flexible as parametric EQs.

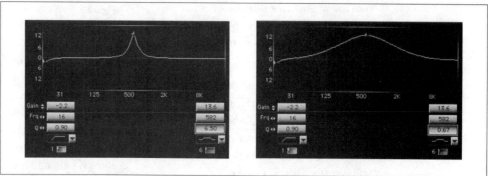

Fig. 12.8. Frequency boost with high Q value (6.50), then low Q value (0.67).

12
6
0
6
12
31
125
500
2K
8K
Gain
Frq
Q
0.0
92
0.71
-1.0
21357
0.71
1
6
-0.1
16
0.71
-7.2
5076
1.41

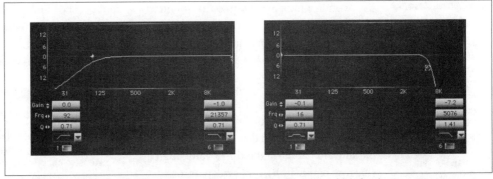

Fig. 12.9. Hi-pass filter with a low Q value, then a low-pass filter with a high Q value.

12
6
0
6
12
31
125
500
2K
8K
Gain
Frq
Q
-0.1
16
0.60
-11.2
4757
1.41
1
6
11.8
85
0.71
0.1
21357
1.41

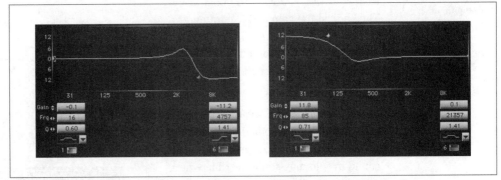

Fig. 12.10. Hi-shelf filter (cut) with a high Q, then a low-shelf filter (boost) with a low Q.

ally the point where the gain reduction is 3 dB below the original signal. Some call this the 3 dB Down Point.

There are also several modifications of the hi- and low-pass filters. Band pass filters are essentially a combination of a low-pass and a hi-pass filter, allowing only a certain bandwidth around a chosen frequency to pass, while filtering out the lows and highs. Notch filters are the opposite of band-pass filters. They cut a certain bandwidth around a chosen frequency, while allowing the low and highs to pass freely through the filter.

Hi-pass, low-pass, and shelf filters are useful for rolling off unnecessary frequencies on individual tracks. For example, high frequencies on bass instrument tracks (above 12 kHz) are typically useless, and rumbly low frequencies on hi-hat or cymbal tracks rarely add anything useful. When trying to clean up a track, the use of these filters should be unnoticeable except that they make the track sound more clear. Filters can also be used to create some interesting effects. Try setting up a low- and a hi-pass filter on some of your drum tracks. Experiment. There are many cool EQ tricks you can create, especially once you learn to automate these filter parameters.

Applying EQing—The Technique

The main idea behind applying EQ is to adjust the frequency content of a sound (its timbre) so that the sound is more subjectively appealing in the overall mix. Yet, before applying EQ, you should (1) know the frequency ranges of the instrument or sound involved, (2) have a basic idea of how each frequency range affects

Take Note!

Try to work quickly when EQing. Once you think you've found the right frequency, tweak the sound to your liking then toggle the Bypass button on the EQ and compare the original sound to the EQ'd sound. Did you achieve what you wanted? If not, tweak some more.

the overall sound, (3) listen to the sound in context (while all other tracks are playing), and (4) try to develop a clear idea of the sound you want before you start tweaking.

When looking for the frequency that you want to adjust, try this technique: Insert an EQ on a track, increase the gain significantly (like +12 dB) on one of the parametric bands, make the Q value high (narrow bandwidth), and sweep across the frequency range until you find the frequency that you want to boost or cut. Then adjust the gain and Q parameters accordingly to sculpt the modified sound. Listen to the sound soloed and with the rest of the mix. Some call this technique the "boost and twist."

However, don't EQ in a vacuum—don't keep a single track soloed very long (*if at all*) while EQing it. A great snare drum sound in solo may sound terrible when mixed with rest of the drum set or with the entire rest of the tracks. In fact, don't be afraid to make any track sound "bad" while in solo, if it sounds great in the mix. For example, boosting the vocal in the 1–4 kHz range may make the vocal track by itself sound unpleasant. However, vocal intelligibility is mainly found in the 1–4 kHz frequency range. Thus, boosting the vocals in that range and attenuating that range in the rest of the tracks can really make the vocals stand out, while maintaining a natural overall blend.

If you can articulate the sound you're looking for, use the chart in fig. 12.4 to help find the frequency range more quickly. For example, say you want to give the guitar track more of an "edgy" sound. Fig. 12.4 shows that "edge" is found in the upper mid range between 2 kHz and 8 kHz. So, increase the gain to +12 dB on your guitar track and adjust the central frequency and Q accordingly within the upper mid frequency range. When you find the right central frequency, adjust the Q and lessen the gain to right level for your tweak.

The Semantics of EQ

There are positive and negative ways to express frequency ranges. Here I'll list a more extensive chart showing both sides. Learning these will help to increase your audio engineering vocabulary as well as help you better describe what you hear. It will increase your efficiency when looking for frequencies to alter and ultimately improve your mixes.

Low Frequency Boost (below 500 Hz)	
Positive	**Negative**
Powerful	Muddy
Fat	Tubby
Warm	Woody
Robust	Barrel-like
Full	Boomy
Low Frequency Rolloff	
Positive	**Negative**
Clean	Thin, Cold, Tinny
Flat, Extended Low Frequencies	
Positive	**Negative**
Natural, Full-bodied	Rumbly
Rich, Solid	Boomy
Low-Mid Frequency Boost (500 Hz – 1 kHz)	
Positive	**Negative**
Thick	Cardboard
Punchy	
Full, "Orange"	Empty
Low-Mid Frequency Cut	
Positive	**Negative**
Distinct	Disembodied
Clean	Colorless, Hollow
Upper-Mid Frequency Boost (around 2 kHz for bass instruments and 5kHz for most others)	
Positive	**Negative**
Present	Tinny
Punchy	Muffled
Edgy	Nasally
Clear	Hollow
Defined	Harsh, Strident, Sibilant

Upper-Mid Frequency Cut	
Positive	**Negative**
Mellow	Muddy
Round	Muffled, Washed out

Flat Mid Frequencies	
Positive	**Negative**
Natural, Neutral	Blah
Smooth, Musical	No Punch

High Frequency Boost (above 7 kHz)	
Positive	**Negative**
Bright	Trebly
Crisp	Sizzly
Hot	Cutting
Articulate	Sibilant

High Frequency Rolloff	
Positive	**Negative**
Smooth	Veiled
Easy-on-the-ears	Muffled, blurred
Mellow	Dull

Flat, Extended High Frequency	
Positive	**Negative**
Open, Transparent	Too detailed
Airy, Clear, Smooth	Too close

EQ TECHNIQUES

Carving EQ Holes

Now that you know the many different ways you can affect the frequency ranges of instruments, it's time to think about how that relates to mixing. It is a common practice to carve EQ holes for specific tracks. For example, if you want to boost the kick drum and bass tracks, boost different frequencies within each of their ranges. In this case you may want to boost 60 Hz on the kick and 100 Hz on the bass. Then cut the kick at 100 Hz and cut the bass (or another instrument like guitar) at 60 Hz. Doing this will add clarity. (Note: I am not saying that each instrument should have its own dedicated frequency range in a mix. Instruments will share frequencies,

but clearing a path for the predominant frequencies of certain instruments can open up a mix.)

Also be aware that any EQ settings you change on a particular instrument will affect not only its sound, but also how the sound of that instrument interacts with all of the others in the mix. When altering EQ don't listen to the track only in solo. You might make the track sound great on its own, but it might not work with the rest of the instruments.

Let's talk about applying equalization to individual instruments. Here I'm going to present suggestions for frequency tweaking. I will present ranges of frequency values that may work for a given application. These are generally agreed-upon values that mix engineers have been using for decades, yet they do not provide all the answers and will not ensure a good sounds or an amazing overall mix. You need to use your own ears and decide what tweaks sound best to you. I'm just going to help you get into the right neighborhood.

Two of the most difficult instruments to EQ are drums and guitars. I'll start with those, then get into other specific applications of EQ tweaking. *Note: All these EQ comments apply to real instruments as well as sampled sounds and loops.*

EQing Drums

One of the first things to do when starting a mix is work on the drum sounds. That usually means EQing the kick and snare first.

Kick Drum

The kick drum (a.k.a. the bass drum) provides the rhythmic foundation. There are two basic parts to its sound: the *thud* and the *click*. The *thud* is the low-end beef

. . . the part that you feel in your chest. The *click* is the sound of the beater attack on the drum's head. As with any instrument, the kick drum creates multiple frequencies when struck. In most cases, the *thud* lives between 40 Hz and 80 Hz, while the *click* lives between 1 kHz to 5 kHz. And, on a kick drum, *mud* usually lives between 220 to 340 Hz!

The Dirt on Mud

As you read in the "Semantics of EQ" section earlier, the frequencies between 200 and 350 Hz are often associated with descriptions such as muddy, tubby, woody, boomy, thumpy, or even barrel-like. Some just call that frequency range *mud*, as in the gooey concoction of water and dirt. And who wants *mud* in their mix? By reducing the frequency content of this area in some bass instruments (like a kick drum), you can take out the *mud*, to clarify the sound of that instrument. However, as with all EQing suggestions, always listen to your EQ adjustments. Don't just cut these frequencies because of my recommendation. Reducing too much of this frequency range can cause your overall mix to lose power.

So, as a general technique for EQing a kick drum, try boosting between 40 and 80 Hz for more *thud*, cutting around 300 Hz for less *mud*, and boosting/cutting between 1 and 5 kHz for more/less *click*.

Snare Drum

Snare drums can be very tricky to EQ. Each drum sounds completely unique and thus each requires its own EQ treatment. To make it more complicated, the sound of every drum is very dependent on its tuning as well as the drummer's style and ability. Despite all these factors, most snare drums share some sonic similarities. The bottom range for a snare is around 100 to 160 Hz. The fattest part of its sound usually occurs in the 220–240 Hz range, while the

crispness of the attack is found in the 4–5 kHz range. 300–700 Hz is the boxy range; cut some of this, if needed. EQing higher frequencies (around 8 kHz and above) on the snare can sometimes add a nice sizzle to the track, but if there's any leakage from the hi-hat on the snare track, the boost may significantly boost the hi-hat as well.

Toms

The primary fullness of floor toms can usually be found between 80 and 120 Hz, while the fullness of higher pitched toms is usually found between 200 and 250 Hz. The brightness and attack for these drums, as with every drum, is in the 4–5 kHz range. And watch out for boxiness in the 300–700 Hz range.

Cymbals

Usually, cymbals don't need too much EQ help, especially if you have high quality ones. If you find they are a little dull, try boosting a little bit at 8–10 kHz. You can also roll off the low end of your cymbal tracks. The dullness (like the "gong" part of the cymbal's frequency range) occurs around 200–240 Hz. So, if you want to add more definition to your cymbal sound, roll off some of the low frequencies (even up to 600 Hz) using a high pass filter. Additionally, if you want to take away some of the clanginess of hi-hats, cut a little bit from the 1–4 kHz range.

EQ Settings for Drums

Here's a chart that summarizes some common drum EQ settings. All of these suggestions depend on the individual drum sound as well as how you want it to sit in the mix. Use your ears to choose the best specific frequency from the frequency ranges listed for each outcome.

	For this outcome...	Adjust this frequency
Kick Drum	More bottom end	Boost 60–100 Hz
	Less muddiness	Cut 220–350 Hz
	Less boxiness	Cut 500–700 Hz
	More attack	Boost 1–3 kHz
	More click	Boost 4–5 kHz
	High-end rolloff	Roll off above 8 kHz
Snare Drum	More bottom end	Boost 100 Hz
Toms	Less muddiness	Cut 220–350 Hz
	Less boxiness	Cut 500–700 Hz
	More punch	Boost 5 kHz
	More brightness	Boost 8 kHz
	More crispness	Boost 10 kHz
Cymbals	Low-end rolloff	Cut 100 Hz and below
	Less dullness (gong sound)	Cut 200–600 Hz
	Less clanginess	Cut 1–4 kHz
	More punch	Boost 5 kHz
	More brightness	Boost 8–10 kHz
	More crispness	Boost 10 kHz and above

Common EQ Treatments on Guitar

Guitars can produce a very wide range of frequencies. Without fail, some of these frequencies will overlap the frequency ranges of other instruments in a mix.

Here are some common EQ treatments that I use on guitars:

1. *Bass Frequencies*—Depending on the song, I might cut a good chunk of the low bass frequencies (below 100 Hz) to let the bass instruments have free reign over that range. Other times, I might boost a little 100 Hz to warm up a track and give it more power.

2. *Mid Bass*—As you know, "mud" lives at around 300–350 Hz, so I might cut some

here, too. However, on both acoustic and electric guitars, much of the full-ness and body reside between 210 and 260 Hz, so make your boosts or cuts very narrow.

3. *Midrange*—I often boost a little here to give the guitar its own space, safely between the bass and the vocals, and make it more beefy.

4. *Upper Mids*—This is the most important area to get right. Guitars and vocals occupy a good chunk of this frequency range, so I sometimes try to cut some of the guitar between 1–4 kHz to open up a hole for the vocals. Then I might boost the 4–5 kHz range to fit the guitar around the vocals and give it some more presence in the mix. 3 kHz is a good frequency to give electric guitars more bite, if it doesn't interfere with the über-important vocals. Note that the upper midrange is the prime area for acoustic guitar clarity, as well.

5. *Highs*—If needed, I might add some brightness to the guitars at around 8 kHz or 10 kHz. This is particularly useful on acoustic guitars for adding sparkle.

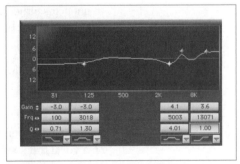

Fig. 12.11. Here's one EQ setting that demonstrates some of these guitar EQing techniques.

Take Note!

Sibilance refers to the hissing effect, usually found between 6 kHz and 8 kHz, produced when a vocalist speaks or sings an "ess" sound. With some vocalists this "ess" sound is very prominent (and irritating) and needs to be reduced to improve the overall vocal. De-essers are specific effects processors that reduce sibilance. In chapter 13, we'll cover de-essing.

Bass Guitar: The lowest frequencies on most bass guitars are around 60 to 80 Hz. Just as with drums and guitars, cutting the mud frequencies in the bass guitar track can add clarity. The attack frequencies of the bass are around 650 Hz to 1.2 kHz, and string noise, sometimes a cool sound to accentuate, is around 2.5 to 3.5 kHz.

EQing Vocals

Because everyone has a different sounding voice, vocals are one of the most challenging "instruments" to EQ. Vocal range and gender affect the recorded track most, but EQing at the frequencies in the following table will really improve the sound of a vocal performance.

To change this sound...	Adjust this frequency range...
Fullness	140–440 Hz
Intelligibility	1–2.5 kHz
Presence	4–5 kHz
Sibilance	6–10 kHz

For some additional tweaks, try these:

- To increase the brightness and open up the vocal sound, apply a small boost above 6 kHz, as long as it doesn't affect the sibilance of the track.
- Treat harsh vocals by cutting some frequencies either in the 1–2 kHz range or the 2.5–4 kHz range to smooth out the performance.
- Fatten up the sound by accentuating the bass frequencies between 200 and 600 Hz range.
- Rolloff the frequencies below 60 Hz on a vocal track using a hi-pass filter. This range rarely contains any useful information and can increase the track's noise if not eliminated.
- Create an AM radio or telephone vocal effect by cutting both high frequencies and below 700 Hz while dramatically boosting around 1.5 kHz.
- Add airiness to a vocal track by gently boosting 13–14 kHz.

You can also use the vocalist's formant frequencies to your advantage to help a vocal part stand out. A **formant** is an area of special resonance within a vibrating body. In this case, that vibrating body is the vocal tract of a singer. Because every singer has a slightly different structure to their vocal tract (vocal cords, mouth, nose, tongue, lips), the formant of a person's voice is completely individualistic. Yet, even when pitch changes, formant stays the same, giving the person's voice its own characteristic sound for every at any pitch. (The same goes for instruments, not just voices.)

For men, the main formant is around 2.5–3.0 kHz, and in women, the range is roughly 3.0 to 3.5 kHz. There are also low formant ranges: 500 Hz for men and 1 kHz for women. With these formant values in mind, try adjusting the EQ of the vocal track around these frequencies, and see what results you can get. It's another tool for your mixing belt.

EQing Piano and Strings

Concert grand pianos produce the most rich and full-bodied sound, with baby grands and then upright pianos being less robust. However, the frequency ranges for each are roughly similar.

Piano:

To change this sound...	Adjust this frequency range...
Fullness	65–130 Hz
Bass	80–120 Hz
Presence	2–5 kHz

With strings (violin, viola, cello, and acoustic bass), the sound from the bridge is brighter than from the f-hole, where you get more body. Similarly, if the string player bows the instrument closer to the bridge, the resulting sound is brighter than if bowed farther from the bridge. In general, for fullness, adjust 220–240 Hz, and for more or less edge, adjust 7–10 kHz.

EQing Brass and Woodwinds

For brass and woodwind instruments, here's a reference chart:

Trumpet

Main characteristic frequencies	1–3 kHz
Fullness	160–220 Hz
Edge	1.5–5 kHz
Straight mute (acts as a hi-pass filter)	Filters out 1.7 kHz and below
Cup mute (acts as a band-pass filter)	Mainly allows 800 to 1,200 Hz through and lessens higher frequencies

Trombone

Main characteristic frequencies	480–600 Hz and around 1.2 kHz
Fullness	100–220 Hz
Edge	2–5 kHz

French Horn

Main characteristic frequencies	340 Hz, 700–2,000 Hz and around 3.5 kHz
Fullness	120–240 kHz
Edge	2–4.5 kHz

Flute

Main characteristic frequencies	240 Hz–2.1 kHz
Mellowness	250–400 Hz
Brightness	1–2 kHz

Clarinet

Main characteristic frequencies	800 Hz–3kHz
Mellowness	150–320 Hz
Throatiness	400–440
Brightness	2–3 kHz

Saxophone

Main characteristic frequencies	130–800Hz
Main characteristic frequencies (tenor)	100–165 Hz
Main characteristic frequencies (bari)	65–650 Hz

For saxophones, the lower end of their main characteristic frequencies has the body, the middle has the fullness, and brightness is above these frequencies.

For more information, consult Stanley R. Alten's *Sound in Media*, 4th Edition (Belmont, Calif.: Wadsworth Publishing Company, 1994.)

SOME FINAL THOUGHTS ON EQ

- Not many people can hear a frequency boost or cut of 1 dB or less, on a conscious level. In fact, most people won't even notice a 2–3 dB change (except people like us). However, subtle changes like these are often very effective on a subconscious level. Large changes in EQ (boosts/cuts of 9 dB or more) should be avoided in many cases, unless extreme sound manipulation is needed.

- Instead of automatically boosting a frequency to make it stand out, always consider attenuating a different frequency to help the intended frequency stand out. That is, try "cutting" a frequency on another track.

- Be careful not to increase (or decrease) the same frequency on several different instruments. For example, if you give 3 dB boosts to three different tracks at 4 kHz, these add up and may unbalance the overall sound.

- Be careful not to boost the bass on too many tracks. Low frequencies can add and subtract (phasing) relatively easily, producing unwanted prominence or cancellation in the overall bass content of your mix.

- Cutting frequencies in the 400–800 Hz range helps add clarity to the bass, while cuts in the 1–4 kHz range will dramatically help other tracks in that range, such as vocals, stand out.

- Watch out when boosting mid and high frequencies. You may inadvertently increase the noise on a track and in the whole mix.

- Consider filtering out frequencies above and below the frequency range of a particular instrument or sound. Do your best to eliminate unwanted low-frequency rumbles (like from heating and air conditioning systems), hiss, and radio interference. This can increase the overall clarity of your mixes by eliminating unnecessary buildup of unwanted frequency content. Be careful not to eliminate frequencies that are essential to natural timbre of a sound; there will be harmonics and overtones up there to be aware of.

Pay Attention to EQ When Adding Effects

Be aware that every EQ adjustment you make to a track will alter your entire mix in some way. If you EQ a track then add other processing to that track later (like sending it to a reverb), the overall EQ on that track and your total mix will change. If you find your mixes are getting cluttered (losing definition) in some frequency ranges even though you feel you carved nice EQ holes for each track, you may have to re-EQ them later after you've added your effects—or EQ the effects to combat any unwanted frequency buildups.

In the next chapter, we'll move on to all the other mixing effects you can add to your mix. . . . ∎

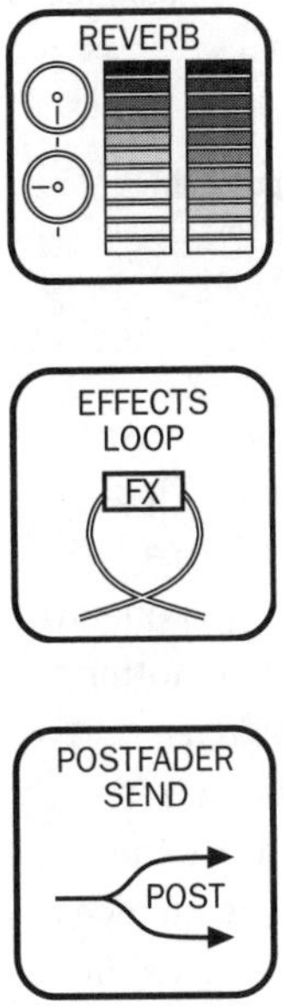
REVERB
EFFECTS LOOP
FX
POSTFADER SEND
POST

CHAPTER 13
Mixing, Part II

In this chapter:

- Adding dynamic processing
- Utilizing delays and reverbs
- Evaluating the characteristics of a good mix
- Remixing and surround mixing techniques
- Preparing your mixes to be mastered

In addition to EQ, depth processing (reverb and delay) and dynamic processing (compression, limiting, gating, and expansion) are primary tools in mixing music. Depth processing utilizes sound reflections and repeats to add spaciousness to your tracks. Dynamic processing adjusts the dynamic range of your tracks by altering the volume relationship between the loudest and softest parts of the tracks, and helping them combine better.

COMPRESSORS

Compressors reduce the dynamic range of signals that exceed a selected threshold (volume level). In other words, they turn down the loudest parts of a track, which helps to manage instruments with wide dynamic ranges, like vocals and bass. Using the controls on a compressor, you can tell it how fast to react to a loud signal (attack), at what volume level to start compressing the signal (threshold), how much to compress the signal (ratio), when to let go of the compression (release), how fast the signal reaches full compression once it passes the threshold (knee), and how much level to boost the signal by as it leaves the compressor (gain).

The Usual Suspects (Compressor Parameters)

There are five or six main parameters on most compressors: **threshold**, **ratio**, **attack time**, **release time**, **knee**, and **gain**.

- The **threshold** is the volume level at which the compressor starts compressing.
- The **attack time** is how fast the compressor reacts once a signal is over the threshold.
- The **knee** is how fast the signal reaches full compression once it's over the threshold.
- The **ratio** is how much compression is applied to the signal.
- The **release time** is how long the compressor stays on after the signal has fallen below the threshold.

Knee
Ratio = 2:1
Attack
Release
Threshold
■ = Compressed Signal
■ = Uncompressed Signal

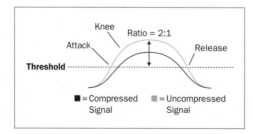

- Compressors also have **output gain** adjusters to make up for the "lost" gain from the act of compressing.

The main purpose of a compressor is to adjust the volume of a signal. What happens when a signal comes into a compressor? If a signal comes in beneath the threshold of the compressor, nothing is done to it. Lower volume signals are not touched, except by the output gain adjuster. If a signal surpasses the threshold, it is compressed. The nuances remain, but the compressor reduces the dynamic range between the loudest and softest parts of the track. Compression makes the quietest bits in your track become easier to hear, and the loudest notes less obtrusive. For example, your emotional and inspiring guitar performance will sit better in the mix, and you won't have to ride the volume fader on each expressive note. Let's look at how the compressor parameters actually affect a signal that's above the threshold.

If the signal crosses the threshold, the compressor reacts according to the attack speed parameter (measured in milliseconds). It then begins to reduce the volume of the signal according to the ratio and knee parameters. The ratio dictates how much the signal is compressed. For example, a compression ratio of 4:1 means that an input 8 dB above the threshold will come out of the compressor at 2 dB. A "hard" knee setting (low number) means compression will take effect very quickly (inflicting the maximum amount allowed), while a "soft" knee means the compressor will ease into the maximum amount.

The signal will stay compressed until it falls below the volume threshold. Once the signal is below the threshold, it's still compressed until being let go at the release time, and is then allowed to return to its regular, uncompressed volume. The compressor's gain will be applied to the output level of the signal, regardless of whether the signal is compressed or not. That means the uncompressed softer parts of the track are increased in relation to the compressed louder parts, creating a track with a more uniform volume level. So compression is not only beneficial for controlling loud transient sounds; it's also useful for bringing out softer passages on a track.

Applying Compression—The Technique

Compression is one of the most frequently used processors in mixing. Often, it is used on almost every track. However, compression is not always necessary, and can make a track sound worse if it's applied incorrectly! So, how do you correctly apply a compressor while recording or mixing? Here's what I do. First, I'll listen to the track and decide if it would benefit from compression. Then, I'll find the threshold at which I want the compressor to kick in. I usually set the threshold in one of two ways:

1. *High threshold*—This will only lower the peaks. With this setting, the compressor kicks in just on the loudest parts of the track.

2. *Low threshold*—With this setting, the signal is almost constantly compressed.

I might go back and tweak the threshold later, but first I'll dial in an approximate compression ratio that might be appropriate for the track. I decide by listening to the track and determining how much I want the lower-volume notes to become more present in the track. If it's just a little bit, I'll use a ratio of 2:1 or 3:1, so that the loud notes only come down a little, too. For tracks that need more note leveling, I'll

use 4:1 to 6:1 . . . even up to 10:1 to really squash the track and make the volume level very uniform. (You'll see examples of these settings in fig. 13.2.)

Next, set the attack and release times. This takes some thought and some listening. The attack time determines how quickly the compressor reacts to a signal that's over the threshold, so consider the type of instrument and part you're compressing, and whether or not you want to compress the initial transient that the instrument produces. The initial transient on a drum track is always *very* fast, so if you want to compress the initial transients on a drum, the compressor's attack time has to be extremely short—just a fraction of a millisecond. However, if you want the drum's initial transient to come through, set the attack time to allow enough time for the initial drum transient pass through before the signal is compressed.

Let's consider guitars. A short attack time can compress the beginning of a picked or plucked note, which often is the loudest part of a guitar note. But sometimes you'll want the beginning of the note to cut through, so it might work better to set the attack time at around 10–20 milliseconds. The same logic applies to bass guitars, as well.

You'll also want to adjust the knee. A "soft" knee means the compressor takes its time to get to full compression (think "smooth curve"), whereas a "hard" knee setting makes the compressor reach full compression quickly (think "right angle"). Use your judgment in setting this parameter by listening to what type of sound is needed for the specific track.

The release is just as important as the attack, because it determines how long the compressor stays active once a signal falls

Take Note!

If you set very short attack *and* release times, you may create rapid gain changes in your track, causing an effect called "pumping" or "breathing." Also, bass frequencies might be distorted due to the rapid gain changes. Instead of being a subtle enhancement to the track, compression is then an audible effect. In most cases, you should avoid these effects.

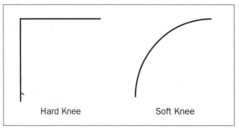

Hard Knee
Soft Knee

Fig. 13.1. Hard-knee and soft-knee compression. Hard-knee compression is useful for controlling the overall level but may make heavy compression too obvious on main instruments in your mix. Smoother compression is achieved by using soft-knee compression. In compressors without knee controls, it is often this unique knee parameter that gives the compressor its signature sound.

below the compressor's threshold. Short release times let the compressor cut out more quickly on notes that fall below the threshold. To make the compressor really work, set the release time to 20 ms or less. For a smoother sound, use values over 100 ms.

Often called "makeup" gain, the output gain on a compressor is used to make up for the gain that has been compressed out of the loudest parts of the signal. That is, if a signal comes into the compressor and is reduced by 5 dB, you can increase the output gain to add 5 dB back to the signal without the loudest parts clipping.

Common Compression Treatments

The graphics in fig. 3.2 show actual waveforms with three common compression settings: just peaks, light constant compression, and squashing.

Because there are so many things you can do with compression, it is often used as a special effect. For instance, you can use the squash technique (as shown in fig. 13.2(d)) to really mess with the sound of a track. Another popular technique is to add a compressed copy of a track to the original, to increase the *punch* of the overall sound. It's common to do this with vocals and drums.

Also consider using compressors and limiters together to enjoy the benefits of both constant compression and peak limiting.

Add a Compressed Copy of the Drum Track to the Mix

A popular mixing technique is to add an effected copy of a track in with the original track. For example, let's say you want to beef up an original track by adding in a heavily compressed version of your drum tracks into the mix. Here's a good way to do it that will make sure the two signals are in phase with each other.

Route all your drum tracks to two stereo aux tracks. If you're mixing with plug-ins, add a compressor plug-in to each stereo aux track. Be sure to use the same type of compressor plug-in on each aux track so that the processing delay is the same on each track. Press the "bypass" button on the compressor on the uncompressed track. Having the compressor in the signal path, even though it's bypassed, maintains the same processing delay on both aux tracks and ensures phase coherence between the uncompressed and compressed signals. (If you're mixing in analog, you won't need to worry about computer processing delay, and thus only need an analog compressor on the compressed track, not both.) Then, choose your compression settings and find a good balance between the compressed and uncompressed signal. That's all there is to it!

LIMITERS

Limiters are essentially compressors with ratios of 10:1 or higher. These large ratios set an absolute ceiling on the dynamic range of a signal and are applied to prevent transient signal peaks from exceeding a chosen level. Because of this, limiters (like compressors) allow you to increase the overall track level while avoiding clipping.

Limiters are useful on many types of tracks and are used most often on the

Fig. 13.2(a) An uncompressed wah-wah guitar signal.

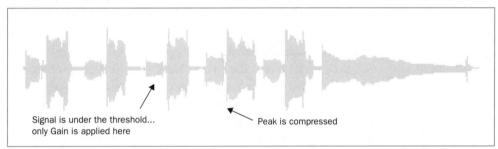

Signal is under the threshold...
only Gain is applied here

Peak is compressed

Fig. 13.2(b) Just peaks—high threshold, low ratio, fast attack, quick release, hard knee, low gain.

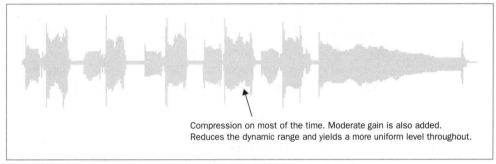

Compression on most of the time. Moderate gain is also added.
Reduces the dynamic range and yields a more uniform level throughout.

Fig. 13.2(c) Light constant compression—lower threshold, low ratio, semi-quick attack, medium release, medium knee, moderate gain.

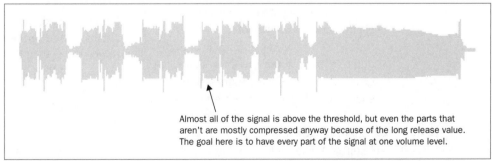

Almost all of the signal is above the threshold, but even the parts that aren't are mostly compressed anyway because of the long release value. The goal here is to have every part of the signal at one volume level.

Fig. 13.2(d) Squashing—very low threshold, high ratio, fast attack, long release, hard knee, high gain.

Threshold
dB
Time
= Uncompressed Signal
= Compressed Signal
= Limited Signal (Maximized)

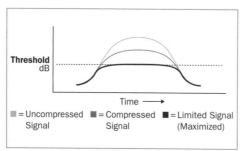

Fig. 13.3. With higher compression ratios, limiters affect the output level of a signal more drastically than compressors.

same types of dynamic tracks as compressors are, such as vocals and electric bass. Limiters are also used on submixes and in mastering to make sure tracks don't peak and cause unwanted distortion. They can be used creatively in a mix to really squash a signal and are useful for combining a squashed copy of the original signal in with the original to create a fuller overall track. Additionally, limiters can be used in cooperation with compressors to take care of the peaks, while the compressor performs the main compression duties on the rest of the non-peak signal.

SIDECHAINS AND KEY INPUTS

In addition to their main inputs, many compressors allow you to tap into their sidechain input. Usually, the sidechain simply receives the same input that the compressor's main input receives. However, routing a signal into the sidechain input allows the compressor to "listen" to the varying amplitude of a different audio source, and use that sidechain source to trigger compression. The source used to trigger compression is called the external key input. To activate the key input you often have to press the External Key or Sidechain button. If you want to listen to the key source audio and fine-tune the compressor's settings to the key input, press the Key Listen button, if available. Here are two common applications of sidechains.

De-essers

Sidechains are useful for creating de-essers. De-essing can be described as compression on specific frequencies, useful for controlling sibilance on vocals, hi-hats, cymbals, and other instruments that sometimes produce "annoying" frequency boosts between 2 kHz and 8 kHz. Most often, sibilance refers to the hissing effect produced when a vocalist speaks or sings an "ess" sound. With some vocalists, this "ess" sound is very prominent (and irritating) and needs to be reduced to improve the overall vocal. Sibilance can also refer to a strong "ess" sound on hi-hats and other cymbals.

Although there are standalone de-esser units, you can make your own de-esser with a compressor and an EQ. Here's how:

Patch a compressor onto a track where you want to reduce the sibilance. Use a send to route a copy of the sibilant track to an EQ on a separate aux track. Patch the EQ out to the sidechain (key input) on the compressor. If your compressor has a sidechain monitor button, press it. If it doesn't, monitor the EQ output in solo. Search for the offending frequency by boosting and sweeping through the 2 kHz to 8 kHz range. (Use the standard EQ frequency location technique.) After finding the main annoying frequency, keep it boosted to accentuate the nasty sound that you want to compress. This signal only goes to the sidechain, not the main output; it's not audio that anyone wants to actually listen to.

Then, unpress the sidechain button and set the compressor parameters, using settings like ratio = 4:1, medium attack, knee, and release, and threshold. That creates about 4–6 dB of compression (a.k.a, "gain reduction"). The compressor will focus its attention on those boosted annoying frequencies and de-ess the track for you. The compressor will trigger a reduction in the original track based on the strength of the nasty EQ'd signal.

(Sibilant)
AUDIO TRACK
Split the Signal ("MULT")
EQ
Filter out all frequencies except for sibilance between 4–10kHz
COMPRESSOR
Sidechain
Key Input
DE-ESSED TRACK

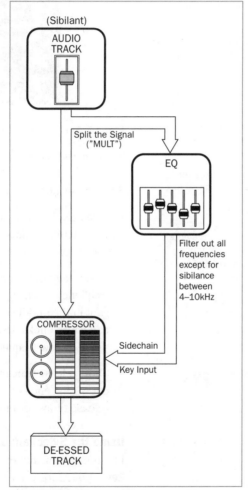

Fig. 13.4. Build yourself a de-esser with a compressor and EQ like this.

Ducking

Another common use for sidechains on compressors is creating an effect called **ducking**. For example, if a radio DJ wants the music to automatically go down when she speaks, assign the DJ's voice as the trigger (the key input) into the sidechain of the compressor on the music track. As soon as the compressor receives a signal from the DJ's voice, the music is compressed. When mixing music, consider triggering light compression on a snare drum with the vocalist's voice, to slightly reduce the snare when the vocalist is singing.

Gates

Gates allow signal to pass through them if the signal is above a specified threshold. When the signal is below the threshold, the gate closes, attenuating the signal partially or fully. Gates are utilized to allow the desired (louder) signal to pass through to the output while denying unwanted (softer) signals. Like compressors and limiters, gates can be keyed by a side-chain input. They're useful for eliminating unwanted noise on tracks (like guitar amp hum or hi-hat bleed on a snare drum track), for creating cool effects like cutting off reverb tails and making click-triggered pulses (described later in this section), and many other applications.

What happens when a signal comes into a gate? First, the gate inspects the signal and decides if it's above the specified threshold level. If the threshold hasn't been crossed, the gate remains closed and blocks the signal from going to the output. However, if the signal crosses the threshold, the gate opens up according to the attack speed parameter. The gate stays open for a specified amount of time (the hold time) and then closes after the signal has fallen below the threshold volume, at the speed selected in the decay parameter. The range parameter on a gate determines how much the volume is reduced on a signal that moves below the threshold. The lower the range value (e.g., –80 dB), the less volume the gate allows to pass through on signals below the threshold.

The Usual Suspects (Gate Parameters)

There are five main parameters on most gates: **threshold**, **attack time**, **hold time**, **decay time**, and **range**.

- The **threshold** is the volume level at which the gate allows a signal to pass through the gate.
- The **attack time** is how fast the gate fully opens once a signal is over the threshold.
- The **hold time** is the minimum amount of time that the gate stays open once a signal is over the threshold.
- The **decay time** is how long it takes for the gate to fully close after the signal has fallen below the threshold.
- The **range** is the volume level of below-threshold signal coming through the gate. This parameter allows some bleed from the original signal (if you want it), even when the gate is fully closed.

Threshold
Range
dB
Hold
Decay
Gate Closed
Gate Open
Gate Closed
Gate opens at set attack speed

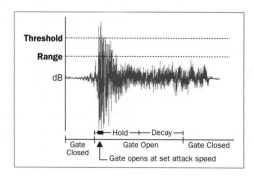

If you want the gate to allow *some* of the volume below the threshold to pass through, increase the range parameter (e.g., –16 dB). Gates with medium range values work well when applied to snare drums or toms. A good example is when you want some drum kit leakage on those tracks (below threshold), but want to emphasize the snare hits or tom fills when they're played (above threshold), as shown in fig. 13.5. Gates with medium to high range values (–40 to 0 dB) are called "expanders," as you'll read about in the next section.

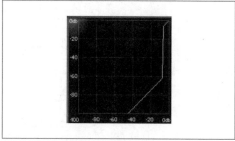

Fig. 13.5. Parameter settings for a gated snare drum. Notice the high threshold, fast attack, short hold time, quick decay, and medium range value.

Some notes about gates:

- Fast attack times are usually necessary when gating drums so that the initial transients aren't gated.
- Fast attack times might distort low-frequency tracks by quickly raising the gain in the middle of a wavelength. This can cause clicks. Use slower attack times on low-frequency instruments.
- Short release times may unintentionally cut off the ends of notes. Use longer release times for more gradual fades.

Using the Sidechain on a Gate

Limiters, gates, and expanders often have key inputs, too. You can use sidechain inputs to achieve some pretty interesting outcomes if you learn the technique and experiment with it. Here's an example where I've set up a sidechain using a click track to trigger a gate that opens and closes on a synth pad track to create a sixteenth-note pulsing effect.

(Click)
AUDIO TRACK
(SYNTH)
AUDIO TRACK
PREFADER SEND
PRE
GATE
Bus Sidechain
Key Input
CLICK TRACK AUDIO
GATED SYNTH TRACK TRIGGERED BY CLICK TRACK

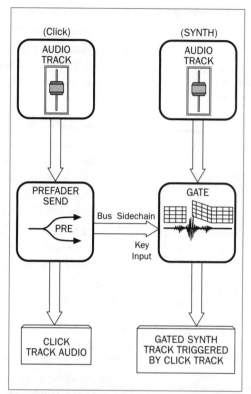

Fig. 13.6. Here's the setup for the synth/gate/click sidechain example.

What's happening here is:

1. The sixteenth-note click track output feeds the "key input" for the gate.
2. The gate on the synth track receives the click at its Key input.
3. The gate opens and closes as it receives the click.
4. The synth pad sound pulses to the beat of the sixteenth-note click track.

If you press the Key Listen button, you'll hear the click. If you bypass the gate (make the gate inactive), the synth pad doesn't pulse to the click anymore; the output is just the original synth pad sound.

EXPANDERS

Where gates are useful for eliminating unwanted noise between musical sections on a track, downward expanders are good for simply lowering but not entirely eliminating the noise. Expanders and gates often have the similar parameters, except that expanders may also have a ratio parameter. The ratio works in the opposite way as a compressor's ratio. Once a signal falls below the threshold, the ratio pushes the signal lower than it would be without expansion. (This may sound like an oxymoron, but, if you think about it, expanders actually "expand" the dynamic range of track by pushing the signal level lower.)

0db
-20
-40
-60
-80
-100
-80
-60
-40
-20
0db

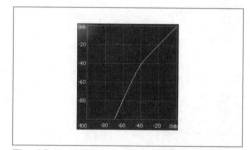

Fig. 13.7. When a signal falls below an expander's threshold, the signal level is decreased in proportion to the original signal level, based on the ratio setting.

Many times, I prefer using downward expanders to gates in most noise-reducing applications, because the level changes aren't as drastic, making the level changes sound more musical. Expanders are also useful for restoring dynamic range to severely compressed tracks. Yet, because of their function, expanders aren't usually as effective as gates for creating special effects.

Take Note!

Downward expanders turn softer parts down, while upward expanders turn louder parts up. The applications for upward expanders are rare, so I'll only focus on downward expanders here.

Take Note!

Some compressors have expanders built into them, because they can't differentiate between low level signals and unwanted low-level noise, like amp hum between guitar phrases or noise between vocal lines.

The Usual Suspects (Expander Parameters)

There are six main parameters on most expanders: **threshold**, **attack time**, **hold time**, **decay time**, **range**, and **ratio**.

- The **threshold** is the volume level below which the expander begins to reduce the gain of the signal.
- The **attack time** is how fast the expander fully reduces the signal's level once it falls below the threshold.
- The **hold time** is the minimum amount of time that the expander stays active once a signal is under the threshold.
- The **decay time** is how long it takes for the expander to fully reduce the level of the signal after it has fallen below the threshold.
- The **range** is the volume level of below-threshold signal that comes through the expander. This parameter allows some bleed from the original signal (if you want it), even at full expansion.

Threshold
Range
dB
Hold
Decay
Gate Closed Expander On
Gate Open Expander Off
Gate Closed Expander On
Gate opens and expander turn off at set attack speed

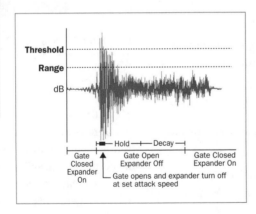

Experiment with dynamic processors by shaping your sounds in natural *and* extreme ways. Tweak all of the controls so you hear the processor working, and try using the processors on all types of tracks, from individual vocals to your overall stereo mix. Concentrate on understanding how to use compression, limiters, gates, and expanders. Applying these dynamic processing tools can provide power and punch to your tracks while improving the clarity of your mixes.

ADDING DEPTH AND SPECIAL EFFECTS

In a three-dimensional mix, we use delay to create the illusion of depth. Delay tricks our brains into thinking that we're in a larger and more interesting listening environment by creating repeats (reflections from the surrounding environment) that combine with the original sound. Short delay times characterize small acoustical spaces, while long delays give the aural illusion of largeness.

Reverb, echo, and chorus effects all revolve around delay. Echo, slapback delay, and doubling are the simplest forms of delay, utilizing a single repeat or several repeats of an audio signal. Chorus (and its brothers, the phase shifter and flanger) are short delays slightly varied in time using modulation. Reverb is a complex combination of blended delays that can be used to simulate an acoustical environment (like a sports arena or jazz club).

Echo, Slapback Delay, and Doubling

Basically, delay units record a signal then play it back at a user-selected time delay called "delay time" or "delay length." (A list of effect parameter definitions is included later in this chapter.) A single delay of less than 35 ms is called a double, because this effect makes the track sound like there are two of the same parts being played or sung at basically the same time. A **slapback delay** is a single repeat with a delay time over 35 ms. Slapback delay times of more than 35–75 ms are good for thickening vocal or instrumental tracks, while delays of 125–350 ms are useful for making a vocal or guitar track sound "large."

It is usually a good idea to set the slapback delay time in relation to the beat and tempo of the song (e.g., eighth note, eighth-note triplet, sixteenth note, etc.). The rhythm you create with the delay can add a nice groove element. To determine a delay time for your song based on a quarter-note beat, use the following equation:

60,000 ÷ song tempo·(in beats per minute) = D (delay time per quarter note in milliseconds)

For example, say the tempo of your song is 120 BPM. Well, 60,000 ÷ 120 = 500 ms. So if you want a sixteenth-note delay on the beat, divide 500 ms by four (because there are four sixteenth notes in a quarter note) and you'll have a 125 ms delay.

Adding feedback to a slapback delay can smooth out the sound of a track. The feedback control sends the delayed signal back into the delay input, creating a delay of the delayed signal. The higher the feedback level, the more delays are created.

Chorus, Phase Shifter, and Flanger

Adding modulation to a delay creates slight pitch variations in the delayed signal. **Modulation**, the varying of delay time, is created using an LFO (low-frequency oscillator) and is essential for creating chorus, phase shifter, and flange effects. The LFO speeds up or slows down to alter the playback of the delayed signal, making its pitch rise and fall. These slight variations can actually smooth out pitch problems on a vocal or instrument track.

Remember in chapter 6 when I discussed acoustical phase addition and cancellation? Modulation makes use of these acoustical phasing phenomena. As you recall, total phase cancellation occurs when two entirely out-of-phase waveforms are combined; they cancel each other out to complete silence. Likewise, combining two in-phase waveforms creates a new waveform with twice the amplitude of the original two waveforms; they add together. It follows, then, that when two waveforms are only slightly out-of-phase with each other so that there is some minor cancellation, they partially reduce the amplitudes of varying frequencies. Slightly additive out-of-phase waveforms partially increase the amplitudes of varying frequencies.

When delayed and slightly pitch-shifted (modulated) signals are combined with each other and the source sound, there is a constantly changing phase relationship between the waveforms. They sum and cancel at varying frequencies. The interaction between the source sound and the modulated delay produces a sound similar to that of several different singers or instrumentalists performing together, and this effect is appropriately called chorus. Depth (of modulation) and rate (of modulation) parameters alter the sound of the chorus effect by controlling the amount and speed of the pitch changes. Chorus effects usually have delay times of 20–35 ms.

Depth and rate parameters react differently to delay times. If you set the delay

Tempo (in BPM)	Quarter Note	Eighth Note	Sixteenth Note	Quarter-Note Triplet	Eighth-Note Triplet
D = Delay	D	D ÷ 2	D ÷ 4	D ÷ 3/2	D ÷ 3
120 BPM	500 ms	250 ms	125 ms	333.33 ms	166.67 ms

Fig. 13.8. Delay time calculations with a tempo of 120 BPM.

time to around 1–3 ms, you can create a phase shifter effect by creating waveforms that are subtly moving in and out of phase. This effect sounds like a mid- and high-frequency EQ sweep and creates an illusion of swooshing motion. Flanging is similar to phase shifting, except that it's more dramatic. The delay time for a flange effect is around 10–20 ms, and the rate and depth can be at a variety of settings according to your taste. Both phase shifters and flangers are useful on guitars, keyboards, and, at times, drums, bass, and vocals. Play with the parameters of the delay effects just to hear the wacky sounds you can make!

Delay Effect	Phase Shifter	Flange	Chorus
Delay Time	1–3 ms	10–20 ms	20–35 ms

Fig. 13.9. Phase shifter, flange, and chorus delay times.

DELAY MIX TECHNIQUES

Putting your delay effects in stereo can really make your mixes sound wide and deep. You can pan your source track to one side and a delayed signal to the other side. Or you can put the source in the middle and pan delayed copies of the source to each side. For this to be effective, select different delay times for each side of the stereo field. A good technique for thickening a part is tripling the original track by using a delay with single delays panned left and right with delay times of 16 ms and 32 ms.

You can apply the same technique for chorus, phase shift, and flange. Also, try EQing the delayed signals differently than the source to add more frequency separation, stereo imaging, and character to your mix.

Using Delay to Double

One of the simplest things you can do to fatten a track is to double the track, either by recording another track of the same part or by electronically doubling the original track. Pan one track to the left and the other to the right, and you've instantly increased the apparent size of the track.

Double-tracking (two distinct tracks): Having two similar recordings of the same part panned out sounds good; it's the slight differences between the two performances that make this technique sound so appealing. These two almost-identical tracks, when both panned to the center (mono), will often cancel each other out with massive phasing and can sound even smaller than one track. Yet when panned out, the two tracks can sound gloriously large through your speakers, while adding distinctive little nuances in each ear in your headphones.

One track, electronically-doubled: For a tighter (i.e., totally rhythmically aligned) sound, use a delayed copy of the original track as the panned "double" track. On your mono track, set up a mono send (with a mono bus) to a new mono aux track. Make sure it's being sent pre-fader on the send, so the volume fader on the original track doesn't affect the send level. Set the input of the new aux track to the same mono bus as the send output. Pan the audio track to the left and the aux track to the right. At this point, it won't sound any fatter. Why? Because the audio track and the aux track are playing back at almost the exact same time, yielding essentially a mono signal.

To fatten the sound, add a short delay to the Aux track and set the delay length to around 16 milliseconds. 16 ms is a good number because it's enough time to separate the tracks to avoid noticeable phasing, but not really enough time for our ears to separate the rhythmic timing differences between the two tracks.

This technique is also particularly useful when recording a band with multiple guitar players who are playing similar parts. Not only is it easier and faster than recording and editing four tracks, it's often tighter rhythmically to use two electronically doubled parts than to align two double-tracked parts.

The Down Side to Using Delay

Although delay can add much to your mix, *too* much can make your music lose its punch. Also, when adding stereo delay effects, sometimes the delayed and original signals can cancel each other out when the mix is summed from stereo to mono. Try routing the tracks with delay through a mono output and listen for any cancellation. If the sound is strange or cancelled out in some way, alter the delay times until the effect sounds right in mono.

Effect Parameter Definitions

Knowing what the parameters on your effects processors do will help you create the sounds you're looking for.

Wet/dry mix: The mix of the source signal with the effected signal.

Predelay: The time delay before reverb is heard.

Decay time: The time it takes for a sound to disappear (i.e., the total effect time).

Diffusion: The space between reflections/repeats.

Density: The initial buildup of short delay times (reflections).

Feedback: The amount of regenerated signal that's fed back into the processor.

Depth: The amount of pitch variation (in modulation).

Rate: The speed of modulation—how fast the pitch rises and falls.

Room size: The size of the acoustical space.

Plug-ins and outboard effects units may have alternate names for these parameters and/or additional parameters. Consult the manuals for explanations and applications.

REVERB AND REVERB MIX TECHNIQUES

All acoustical spaces (rooms, halls, etc.) have their own sound. The unique sound of a space is created by the combination of reflections (and absorption) from its surfaces: walls, floor, ceiling, and objects. Each individual reflection is a delayed and slightly altered copy of the source sound. When a large number of these reflections are added together, we can't distinguish between the individual signals, and they blend together to form reverb (reverberation). Some reverbs are created to imitate acoustical spaces, like halls and rooms, and others simulate earlier forms of reverb, such as plate and spring reverbs, both of which were originally intended to imitate halls and rooms, but eventually took on a sound of their own.

When a sound is made, we hear the direct sound waves, early reflections, and reverberation (a.k.a. "after reflections" or "dense reflections"), in that order. The direct sound reaches our ears without bouncing off any surface. Early reflections reach our ears around 10–30 ms later than the direct sound, after they have bounced off of one or more surfaces. Because these reflections arrive so quickly, they are perceived as part of the direct sound. Reverberation actually occurs when a sound reflects off of many surfaces and is mixed with other reflections, creating a denser blend of reflected sound. These reflections begin to fade away (decay) as they're absorbed into

Amount of Reverb	Decay Time	Environments
A lot	long	large church, castle, gymnasium, concert hall
A lot	short	tiled bathroom, open office
A little	medium	living room with carpeting, cocktail lounge
None		a wide open field or an anechoic (reverb-free) chamber

Fig. 13.10. The amount of reverb and the decay time of the reverb and their effects.

the material of the acoustical space. The longer a sound takes to decay, the larger and more hard-surfaced the acoustic environment is perceived to be, and the farther from the sound source the listener is (or seems to be).

On reverb effects units, we can control the parameters that determine what a reverb will sound like throughout its progression, from the first to the last reflection. We can set predelay, decay time, diffusion, density, size (of the space) and type (room, hall, plate, etc.). Check out the definitions for these parameters in the "Effect Parameter Definitions" box earlier in this chapter.

Like delay, reverb is used in mixing to create a sense of depth. When applying reverb to tracks, the wet/dry mix parameter sets the overall amount of depth—how far away a sound is from the listener. In addition to the decay time, the longer the predelay time (the time before reverb is heard), the larger the perceived size of the acoustical space.

DEPTH
Reverb and Delay
Distant
Close
100% Wet / 0% Dry
0% Wet / 100% Dry

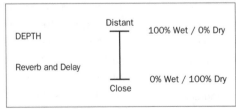

Fig. 13.11. How the wet/dry percentage affects distance perception.

Some common uses for reverb are on snare drums, guitars, piano, any group of instruments (horn section, string section, choir, etc.), any lead or backing vocal, and any lead instrument—basically, everything except bass. Like delay, reverb often sounds more impressive if used in stereo. Many plug-ins and outboard effects processors allow mono in/stereo out reverb processing; simply pan out the reverb returns. But be careful! Too much reverb can make your mix less defined and powerful, especially if you apply it to low-frequency instruments like kick drum and bass (which I rarely recommend). Consider using low-pass and/or high pass filters on your reverbs to tighten up the frequency range of the reverb output. Doing this can help to clarify your mix significantly, avoiding unwanted frequency buildups.

One of the goals of mixing is to put the listener in some sort of acoustical space. That said, try using a combination of different reverb types (like a hall and a room) to add depth and character to your tracks. If you overuse one type of reverb on many different instruments, your mix will most likely be less engaging. Backwards reverb also has its place and can sound appropriate for some applications. Slightly EQing the reverb can be a nice effect, as well, differentiating the reverb from the source sound.

Reverb

Reverb, short for reverberation, is a sonic effect that occurs when many random reflections of a sound blend together and reach the listener more than 10 milliseconds after the direct sound from the sound source. As an effect, reverb gives character to a direct dry sound by placing it in some sort of acoustical environment (e.g., a church, a gymnasium, a tiled bathroom, etc.).

Trends in the music industry tend to influence the amount of reverb that gets used on popular music. If you're trying to make your mixes sound like what's on the radio, do some serious listening to the amount and types of reverb that mix engineers are using. Also, listen carefully to your favorite mixes and figure out what types of acoustical spaces the mix engineers put the listener into. Along with listening, study the reverb parameter definitions presented earlier in the chapter by physically tweaking some tracks through different reverb settings. This kind of research is very valuable and can lead to developing your own mixing style, helping you combine techniques from the current trends and all your old favorites in with your own knowledge of reverb.

SOME FINAL COMMENTS ON SIGNAL PROCESSING WHILE MIXING

There are innumerable techniques for processing your mixes. I recommend experimenting with all of the parameters of each processor. Also, see how the processors interact with each other when they're used in series (e.g., EQ > reverb > compression vs. compression > EQ > reverb). You'll notice differences that could be very significant to the overall sound of your mix.

Keep your mind open to the infinite possibilities of effects processing, practice time-tested techniques, and come up with your own. Your mixes will drastically improve the more you practice and experiment.

Techniques to Conserve Computer Resources While Mixing

When you mix a song with many tracks and plug-ins on a digital audio workstation, you may reach the limits of your computer processing power. If this happens, try these techniques:

- Combine tracks (submix): The fewer tracks your software has to deal with, the better.

- Consolidate edits: Create brand new consolidated copies of your edited tracks, thereby reducing the edit-point processing requirements.

- Use sends, busses, and aux tracks (effects sends) instead of inserts on each track. For example, instead of putting the same delay plug-in as an insert on multiple tracks, use one delay and create an effects loop.

- Apply non-real-time plug-ins instead of real-time plug-ins.

- Reduce automation data: Each automation breakpoint requires additional processing power, so once you're done creating automation data, thin it out.

LAYERING SOUNDS

One of the best things that you can do to increase the impact of your tracks is to layer sounds. For instance, say your kick drum just isn't cutting it in the mix, even though you've applied some serious EQ, compression, and a gate. There are several ways to thicken the track using additional sounds.

First, you can duplicate the track and add different effects to the duplicate track. That is, make a copy of the original track and put it on its own track. Then, add different EQ, compression, a distorted amp model, or other effects to make the sound totally different than the original. Then, add the original and the processed copy together, and notice that the resulting track has a much better presence in the track.

This technique is also effective for any other type of track. For instance, consider thickening up the sound of your electric guitar track. Like miking an amp with multiple microphones to capture and highlight specific frequencies, you can also multiply your guitar tracks and put different effects on each track, emphasizing certain specific sounds in each one.

Another alternative is to add another sample (or a few layered samples) to the existing track. Make sure to get the timing of the samples lined up with original track so that the transients are aligned. Applying layering techniques like these can take you closer to finding a signature sound—something completely unique that will help your recordings stand out.

SETTING FINAL VOLUME LEVELS AND EQ

Once you've added the effects and layers you want, begin working on the volume levels of your final mix, fixing any EQ problems that might have been created after adding effects. You've already got a rough mix with decent levels to work from; now it's time to tweak things and create a final blend in which all tracks are heard or felt—but are not stepping on each other.

When creating your final mix balance, it's a good idea to ride the fader, manually adjusting particular tracks to even out the volume of a performance or emphasize a specific section. Spend a good amount of time on the vocal track especially, to ensure that every word comes across the way you want it to.

This may require such detailed work as boosting particular syllables *within* words

to ensure that the vocal line captures the listener's attention. I recommend using automation for this task. Also, boost and cut specific tracks when you want to emphasize certain sections (e.g., a bass fill, or a guitar note that's too low in a solo). Subtle volume changes can make all the difference in the effectiveness of your songs.

I'm Beginning to Fade

Fade-outs are often used at the end of a song as a tool to keep an album flowing and make it appear that the song goes on forever. When creating the fade-out, spend some time to get it right. A short fade-out can sound too abrupt, whereas a long fade loses its effect after a while. Good fade-out lengths are typically 6–16 seconds, depending on the type of music and what's being played at the end.

Fades usually start just after the beginning of a musical section, like when a chorus repeats. When fading out, try not to cut a lyric in half. Allow it to conclude before fading, and if there's a jam at the end, try to include one last cool lick, sound effect, or vocal phrase as it's fading out. This will make the listener wonder what's happening at the end and turn it up. (For a good example listen to the fade-out of "Every Little Thing She Does Is Magic" by the Police.)

TESTING YOUR MIX

Once you're close to having your final mix levels, panning, EQ settings, and effects, test your mix at different overall volumes and on different speakers, if you have multiple pairs. Check to see if your mix is effective at low, medium, and high volumes. You might find that the bass disappears at low levels or that the vocal is piercing at high levels. Also, people will hear your mixes through all types of speakers, from high-end professional speakers to tiny boomboxes. You might find that the high frequencies really jump out on cheap speakers or that low frequencies are muddy on others. It can be a challenge to make your mixes translate well to all types of speakers.

Often radios have one mono speaker, so be sure to give your stereo mix the "mono compatibility" test. Sometimes, stereo signals cancel each other out when summed to mono, obeying the same acoustical phasing principles as discussed in chapters 6. As mentioned previously, this cancellation occurs primarily when using stereo delay effects. Before you print your final mix, assign all of your tracks to a mono output and listen for cancellation. In its worst form, cancellation can make entire stereo tracks disappear, or it can simply make your mix sound a little weird.

When you're happy with your mix, bounce down a stereo version and don't listen to it for a while. Try listening again the morning after, in your car, through your friend's home stereo, or at a home audio or music store. Listen to it with your eyes closed and from outside your room. Take some notes on how it sounds in each different listening environment. Also, play it for other people to get their response. Then come back to it and adjust the mix, if necessary.

Keep in mind that all the decisions you make while you're mixing are subjective. There is no one perfect mix. Every person has their own preferences on levels, panning, EQ, and effects. Beware: you can mix and remix (and *remix*) the same songs forever and never complete them! Once you get to a certain point with your mix, you need to let it go. If the song is good, a decent mix will get the message across to the listener—you can always improve it later if absolutely necessary.

A producer friend of mine says with a wink, "You never finish a record—you just stop working on it."

Characteristics of a Good Mix

Although everyone hears music differently, there are some common thoughts on what a good mix sounds like. A good stereo mix has:

- An even balance and nice spread of left and right musical information. The best way to test this is to listen to the mix with headphones.

- Evenly distributed equalization. That means the lows are powerful but controlled, the mids are dispersed well among the different instruments, and the highs are strong yet easy to listen to. EQ holes are carved for each instrument and the overall mix is clean and clear.

- Depth. As we know, delay effects create a sense of three-dimensional space. This means that at least one instrument has to define the close character and one has to define the distant quality.

- Momentum. The song has a flow that the mix enhances by building from the beginning to the end. The intensity and texture of the mix change during the song so the mix isn't stagnant, but rather alive. This helps to keep the listener's attention all the way through the song.

- Consistency. That is, it sounds good on all speakers, in mono, and at all volume levels.

Mix with these characteristics in mind from the beginning, and use the techniques presented here to improve your mixes and create your own sounds. With practice, experimentation, and more practice, you'll begin to create mixes that are exciting, artistic, powerful, and imaginative.

MIXING IN SURROUND, REMIXING, AND PREMASTERING

Mix Techniques in Surround Sound

Mixing audio in surround sound is a fairly new art. The film industry has logged a good amount of time mixing in surround, and the techniques for mixing music in surround (not to picture) are still being developed. When mixing in stereo, mix engineers use effects processing to create a pseudo 3D space for each track in the mix, using reverbs, delays, etc. However, engineers mixing in surround often find they need much less effects processing because there's much more space to work with—that is, you can distribute the tracks to more than two speakers. Even with songs that have high track counts and that are musically busy, there's room for all of the parts to be heard more easily.

I've mixed in 5.1 surround multiple times. In several of my surround mixes the only processing I used was EQ—I chose to use no other effects. Because the tracks were recorded well and were panned in interesting ways, I didn't need effects to make a great mix. In this case, the room mics were very effective at providing natural reverb when panned to the back. Multiple stereo guitar and vocal harmony tracks filled out the spread of the mix.

Sound effects (as in film) provided additional aural appeal when panned in interesting ways, like circling around the listener or moving back and forth from front to back. (Try not to make the listener sick, though!) Creative use of effects in surround mixing can also be one of the most captivating aspects to this new art. Experimentation with delays, reverbs,

Doppler effects, and flange/phase effects in surround will leave you speechless with a big smile the first few times you try it. It can be absolutely thrilling.

The only other solid technique I've come across for mixing in surround sound is for mixing live concerts. Essentially, the idea is to put the listener in a particular seat at the show (e.g., center stage, row 6), giving them the perspective of actually being at the concert with killer seats. Combined with video footage of the concert, this mix technique becomes even more effective.

Note: Although my home studio is set up for mixing in stereo and surround simultaneously, I don't recommend mixing in both formats at the same time. A surround mix does not easily translate into a stereo mix and vice versa. I recommend having separate mix sessions (on different days) for your stereo and surround mixes.

Surround mixing is still in its early stages of development. If you have the facility to try it, experiment with mixing in surround sound. Trust me, you'll be amazed by the results.

Remixing

A remix is a new mix of a song. An ever-growing aspect of the music production business, remixing is often used to create dance mixes or other singles based on the original mix (like remixed radio singles).

Remixes for singles are common in the recording industry. Sometimes record labels or producers aren't happy with the original mix of a particular song that's going to be released from an album to radio as a single. So, they'll hire a new mix engineer to remix the song in a way that they feel is more appropriate. This involves sonic adjustments (like helping the vocal stand out more) and might also

Take Note!

Recording a final mix pass, sometimes called "printing" a track, is also often called "bouncing down" the track in the digital audio realm.

include edits to make the song move along faster (like eliminating part of a verse so that the song reaches the chorus faster, or removing an instrumental solo). Longer and/or slower songs might even be sped up slightly from the original recording. The whole point of remixing a single is to make the song have the greatest impact on radio listeners.

Dance/electronica remixes are a different breed. These types of remixes usually focus on the vocal line and the beat, while often editing or sometimes stripping the other instruments out of the original mix and adding new parts. They are often longer than the original song and usually allow for a much greater amount of creative freedom. There are many varieties of remixes in this vein because of the wide variety of dance/electronica music that's being made today. Let's talk about how to create one . . .

Making a Dance/Electronica Remix

A common technique to start a dance/electronica type of remix is to first figure out what kind of tempo you want the remix to be. Are you making a down-tempo chilled version, or an uptempo house version? Once you've chosen the tempo, capture the solo vocal track, slice it into phrases, and time expand or compress those phrases, and make sure they work in the chosen tempo.

Next, move on to create the new beat and bass line, possibly based on a loop of the original drum and bass tracks or parts that you completely reworked using samples, loops, or newly recorded tracks.

Then, decide if you want to use any of the supporting tracks, such as guitars, keys, strings, or horns that were used in the original mix. Create loops from those tracks.

Also, you can create synth lines, added percussion, or other additional tracks to make the remix more unique.

Finally, work out the arrangement of the song, cutting and pasting parts together so that the song has a good flow and the right energy for what you're trying to achieve with the remix.

Remixing tracks can be a blast, whether just to try out some new mixing techniques or to completely restructure and essentially reinvent a song. I encourage you to experiment with remixing. You'll learn some new production techniques that you can apply to your next production project.

Premastering: Preparing Your Mixes for Mastering

As the final step in the mixing process, let's discuss how to get your final mixes ready for the mastering process.

For each final mix that you want to master, first make sure that the output levels on the final mix don't peak or clip when playing back. In fact, it's a good idea to record ("print" or "bounce down") the final mix a couple dB lower than the digital 0 dB or analog 0 VU mark (so that the highest peak in the track is around –3 or –2 dB or VU). By doing this, you'll leave the mastering engineer with enough headroom to operate on your material and boost it up to competitive level using their mastering processors, which are specifically designed for that purpose.

Also, I recommend not using any effects or plug-ins on your master fader while printing your final mixes. If there is an effect that you must have on the master fader in the final mix, just make sure it doesn't inadvertently disguise an overload on the master fader track. In most cases, any effects that you want to use over the entire mix can be added during the mastering process.

This also goes for dither (discussed in the next chapter) on digital recordings. There's no need to add dither to a digital final mix that you'll be handing off for mastering, because you should bounce the tracks at the same bit depth and sampling rate to retain the highest resolution for mastering. For example, if you recorded at 24-bit and 96 kHz, bounce each mix at that same bit depth and sampling rate *without dither*. Use dither only on the final mastered bounce.

It's a really smart idea to create multiple slightly altered mixes of each song. For instance, create several "final" mixes with the vocal up 1 dB, up 2 dB, down 1 dB, and down 2 dB from the original final mix. Getting the vocal levels correct is one of the most important tasks of the mix engineer. With all of these different mixes, you

can choose which one ultimately works the best and you'll even have the option of editing parts of each mix together (if necessary) to get the optimal vocal level throughout the entire song. These edits can take place before or during the mastering process. Also seriously consider making mixes with higher and lower bass levels and an instrumental mix. These extra mixes can be huge time savers as well as great comparison tools while mastering.

I also recommend bouncing your final mixes without volume automation on the master fader (e.g., fade outs) so that you retain the flexibility to create that automation in the mastering session.

With your tracks mixed and premastered, you're ready to move on to the last stage in the production process—mastering. ■

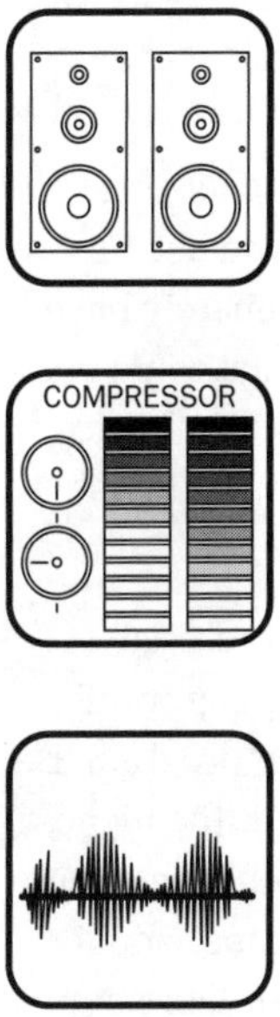
COMPRESSOR

CHAPTER 14
Mastering

In this chapter:

- What is mastering?
- The mastering process
- EQ, compression, limiting, dither, and noise shaping
- Bouncing down and burning CDs
- The steps after mastering

Okay, so you've got your songs mixed and they sound great. You've reached the final step: mastering. Like mixing, mastering is an elusive art form to many. In this chapter, I'll try to demystify the process and steer you down the path toward mastering your own recordings.

WHAT IS MASTERING?

Mastering is the last stage in the production process and takes place after you are all done mixing your entire project. Mastering can take your project studio recordings to the next level, transforming your final mixes into professional recordings. The main purpose of mastering is to sonically treat your final mixes so that (1) the recording's frequency spectrum works well on all types of playback systems, from one-speaker clock radios to hi-fi home stereos, (2) the overall volume level is competitive with other mastered recordings, and (3) that the overall EQ and volume of each song creates a cohesive final product. Other considerations in mastering are (4) checking and/or adjusting the left/right balance, phasing, and stereo imaging of the tracks, (5) listening for and fixing dropouts, glitches, and other unwanted noises, (6) possibly adding real or simulated tube/analog gear into the signal path (if working with digital recordings), (7) dithering and noise shaping, and (8) recording your final tracks to a recording medium, such as bouncing down and burning the final masters with the correct track order, timing, and fades to a CD.

NOTE: Professional mastering facilities, CD duplication houses, and project/home studios alike use digital mastering software programs. Regardless of the recording medium or analog gear that you use on your projects, your songs ultimately have to end up in some digital format to be put on CDs, DVDs, SACDs, MP3s, etc. Hence, this chapter will focus mainly on digital mastering techniques.

Once you've bounced all of your final mixes for your entire project, import all the mixes into your mastering program. Be sure to keep your audio files at the highest resolution possible. Place each song on its own track if each song needs individual attention (e.g., its own EQ, etc.), or simply place the audio files on two stereo tracks with the songs juxtaposed, as in fig. 14.1, if you're only tweaking your final mixes with effects on the master fader track.

Place the songs in the right order and with the approximate spacing to simulate the entire project. This will give you a sense of the cohesiveness of the project when you play it all back. When assembling the final order of songs for your CD, consider the song flow and placement of fades. Make it easy to listen to all the way through by placing songs so they lead smoothly into each other. Also provide contrast that holds the listener's interest using different tempos, keys, rhythms, lyrical content, and sound texture. Despite the contrast

JE voxup hhpan maste r.L
JE voxup hhpan maste r.R
Pho kickupsndn master2.L
Pho kickupsndn master2.R
GF voxup1dB master.L
GF voxup1dB master.R
BE voxup1 master.L
BE voxup1 master.R
LT voxupdrdown master.L
LT voxupdrdown master.R

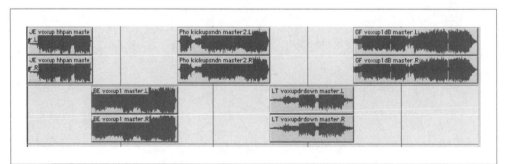

Fig. 14.1. Position each of your final mixes alternately on two stereo tracks for painless timing and crossfade management.

> *Take Note!*
> Allowing someone else to master your tracks can be a good idea if you have the money. Professional mastering engineers have great outboard gear, amazing speaker systems, and well-trained ears that can really help identify and fix problems or inconsistencies with your mixes, as well as provide high-quality, error-free master recordings that are ready for duplication.

between songs, however, the whole CD should sound like it's one piece of work, rather than a hodgepodge of different music. If the songs' volumes and EQ levels are similar and the order is right, your CD will sound professional and the audience will embrace the music more readily.

Once you've got all the tracks set up for a mastering session, set aside some time and create the right environment for super-critical listening. Then, listen to all of the tracks. Compare the overall sound from track to track. You'll probably find that some songs are louder or have more distinct EQ curves than others. Some stereo images may be different, as well (which isn't necessarily a bad thing). Take notes! Write down everything you notice about the sonic differences and similarities between the songs, including which ones sound best from the get-go and may need the least amount of tweaking. Consider comparing your unmastered songs to some of your favorite mastered songs to give you a goal. Once you've listened carefully to the tracks, compared them to each other, compared them to your reference songs, and made notes, you're ready to start tweaking.

THE MASTERING PROCESS

The usual signal path for mastering a track is through EQ, compression, peak limiting, and dither/noise shaping. There can be multiple EQs, compressors, and limiters along the way. You might also include stereo image expanders and analog/tube emulation units to further process your final mixes. To begin tweaking, set up hardware or software inserts to perform these sonic adjustments on your master fader and/or individual tracks.

AUDIO TRACK
EQ
COMPRESSOR
MASTER FADER
EQ
COMPRESSOR
LIMITER
DITHER
QUANT NOISE
NOISE SHAPING
MASTERED SONG

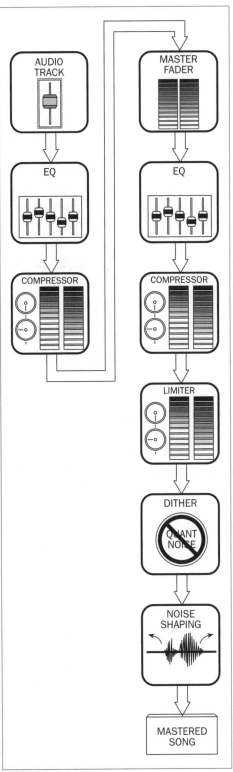

Fig. 14.2. A common mastering signal flow.

Equalization (EQ)

Use EQ plug-ins or outboard EQ hardware for general EQing and/or honing in on specific frequencies to boost or cut. Applying a broadband EQ on the master fader track in your mastering session can help all the tracks fit into a more cohesive sonic picture. However, I'm not suggesting that you use the same overall EQ setting on all songs. You'll usually want to tweak the overall EQ on each song, and I recommend saving each EQ setting with the name of the song in the setting title, if possible.

For specific track EQ, add a plug-in to the individual audio track instead of the master fader. Just don't overload the track with a massive boost. Boosting a frequency that peaks out your EQ plug-in can cause digital distortion—a definite no-no in the mastering process. Remember, cutting frequencies is part of good EQing technique, too.

A tried-and-true way to determine what frequencies to boost or cut while mastering is to listen to the frequency content of mastered recordings that you really like. Listen to how they sound on your speakers, then try to emulate the frequency curve. There are some visual tools, like frequency, phase, and stereo image analyzers, that can help you do this in the mastering process, but rely on your ears more than your eyes.

Besides creating an overall sonic picture, EQ in the mastering process is often used to further define the bass sound, add energy to or cut the crispiness of the high end, tighten up the middle frequencies, and sometimes even make the vocal track (or another lead track) stand out more. However, there are no hard and fast rules for applying EQ in a mastering session.

Apply the EQ techniques you learned in chapter 12 to bring out or cut certain frequencies, so that your mixes are clear and are comparable in frequency content to your reference master songs.

Normalizing

Some people normalize their tracks during the mastering process before compressing and limiting. Applying normalization to a track raises its overall volume level while ensuring that the inherent dynamics of the material remain unchanged. It is useful in cases when an audio file has been recorded with too little amplitude, or where volume is inconsistent for the duration of the file. However, you shouldn't need to normalize your tracks if you recorded and bounced them at good levels. In fact, most professional mastering engineers rarely normalize tracks, unless absolutely necessary. They usually receive tracks that have high levels anyway, so they use compression or limiting to bring tracks up to competitive levels.

Compression

As you know from chapter 13, compression reduces the dynamic range of your tracks by making the loudest parts softer and the softer parts louder. By making the loudest parts softer, you can increase the gain of the overall track without causing digital clipping. For instance, if you apply a compressor to your master fader track and see 3 dB of gain reduction, you can boost the gain in the compressor by up to 3 dB without clipping the signal. Hardware and software compressors and limiters provide the volume boost that raise your final mixes to competitive (i.e., radio-ready) levels.

In mastering applications, you can use broadband compression that compresses any frequency that's above the compressor's threshold, or you can use frequency-based "multi-band" compression to compress certain frequencies more or

Take Note!

Compressors and limiters often have their own "sound." Be mindful of this fact when mastering, because you'll often want your compressors to sound "transparent" . . . that is, not affecting the overall sound of the final mix too much.

less than others. Multi-band compressors enable you to divide the frequency range into several sections and compress/limit each one differently. They are often used to adjust the sound of the extreme ends of the spectrum—the lows and the highs—to get them under control and tighten up the mix. Be gentle, though. As each frequency band is compressed, the different band levels change in relation to each other. This means you could really mess up your mix if you're not careful. However, if used correctly, multi-band compression can produce a more consistently powerful master recording—something most of us aspire to create!

One of the most obvious indicators of incorrect compression settings is if your mix has a "pumping" sound. The softer parts are loud but the loud parts are compressed too much, making your music actually *lose* power and energy. Less obvious than the pumping compression, simply over-compressing and over-limiting can make your mixes sound thin and lifeless. That's because the volume level of your song will become constant throughout the song and any dynamic contrast you built into your music in the first place will be lost.

Instead of overcompressing or causing compression pumping, try to set your compressors and limiters so that your songs are more powerful yet still have a little room to breathe. That is, respect the dynamics in the song by using compression settings (threshold, ratio, attack, release, gain, etc.) that enhance the musicality of the song.

As with EQ, there are no hard and fast rules to compression settings in mastering. Usually lighter compression is used in the earlier stages of the mastering signal flow,

whether through one compressor or a few, boosting the gain some but not all of the way to the max. Peak limiting takes care of the final gain boost in the mastering signal flow.

Peak Limiting

Limiting is the same process as compression, just a lot stronger, with compression ratios of at least 10:1. In mastering, peak limiting is usually the last step in controlling the dynamics and boosting the overall volume of a track, while avoiding digital clipping. Some digital limiting tools can even look ahead at the digital audio signal coming into it and react by reshaping the signal peaks so that they never output a digitally clipped signal.

When using limiters, it's usually a good idea to have your mastered signal peak at around –0.1 dB instead of 0.0 dB. This is because actually having a signal strength of 0.0 dB could clip some CD players.

A/B-ing

A well-known practice in audio engineering, from recording to mixing to mastering, is called "A/B-ing." A/B-ing in the audio sense means comparing the quality of two or more sounds, such as the quality of vocal sound from one mic versus another, or the sound of several different reverb settings on a snare or several overall EQ curves on your master fader track in your mastering session. As you perform the mastering process, it's a really good idea to get in the habit of A/B-ing your EQ, compression, and limiting settings so that you really know how you're affecting the overall sound. Use the bypass button on the individual processors or plug-ins to check the sound against the uneffected final mix, or flip back and forth between saved settings to hear different sonic options. Also, A/B tracks that you've already mastered with tracks that you're currently mastering to get a sense of how they sound together.

Take Note!
When bouncing down to a 16-bit/44.1 kHz CD, dither and noise shaping should be applied (with a resolution of 16 bits), regardless of whether you're working with 16- or 24-bit files, to ensure quantization noise is minimized.

Final Mix.L
Final Mix.R

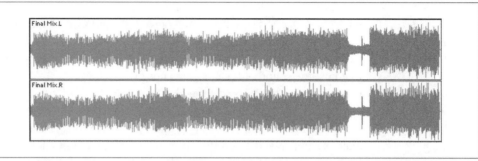

Fig. 14.3(a). The final mix waveform (premaster). Notice that there is headroom available for mastering compression and peak limiting to raise the overall level of the track.

Master.L
Master.R

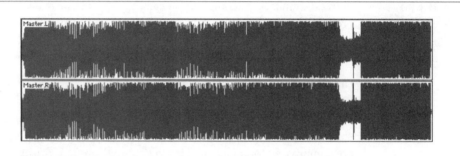

Fig. 14.3(b). The mastered mix waveform. Notice the overall signal level is higher, yet there is no clipping.

Dither and Noise Shaping

At the end of the mastering process, all audio files usually have to end up as 16-bit/44.1 kHz tracks so they work on audio CDs. Bouncing audio from a higher bit depth to a lower one creates unwanted quantization noise that occurs at low volume levels (e.g., on fade outs). It just so happens that digital audio's poorest representation of sound exists at the quiet end of the dynamic range. Recall the discussion on bit depth in chapter 2: Remember that high bit depths yield a more accurate digital representation of audio signals? Well, low-level audio signals use only a fraction of the possible 16 or 24 bits, meaning that they don't get accurately represented. This inaccuracy creates a kind of distortion called quantization noise.

Dither and noise shaping reduce quantization noise. In short, *dither* reduces the bit depth of an audio file by truncating the digital information (usually from 24-bit to 16-bit) and adds a small amount of noise to an audio signal, making quantization noise less obvious. Noise shaping utilizes digital filtering to move noise that dither adds from frequencies that our ears are most sensitive to (such as around 4 kHz) to frequencies we're less sensitive to—making the noise more difficult for us to hear.

Though there's a trade-off between signal-to-noise performance and less apparent distortion, proper use of dither allows you to squeeze better subjective performance out of a 16-bit data format (as on CDs). Together, dither and noise shaping should

> *Take Note!*
>
> If creating higher resolution recordings for DVD, SACD, or some other format, keep your recordings at the highest resolution possible. Don't bounce them down to 16-bit/44.1 unless completely necessary. In fact, when making your master mixes, you might just want to make two versions—a standard 16/44.1 version for CD and another one at the highest resolution possible (if higher than 16/44.1). Having this hi-res version is helpful archive purposes and could be very useful in the future if we move away from the 16/44.1 CD standard.

be the last processor on your master fader track for your mastered bounces.

BOUNCING DOWN AND BURNING YOUR MASTERED TRACKS

Once you've added your mastering plug-ins or hardware inserts, tweaked each individual song to create a cohesive-sounding final product, put the songs in order, adjusted the timing between the tracks, added all volume rides for fade outs, etc., then you're ready to bounce the final mastered tracks so you can burn them to a CD, DVD, SACD, or create MP3s. Bounce each song one at a time. Select the exact amount of the track that you want to bounce and save them as the appropriate file type (format: stereo files; file type: WAV or AIFF; resolution: 16-bit; sample rate: 44.1 kHz).

After you've bounced your tracks, listen to them critically in many environments and through many speaker systems. Check out how your mastering tweaks work on these different systems. If you're not satisfied, tweak the songs some more and bounce them down again until you're happy with them.

Once all of your songs are bounced, import them into the software that came with your CD burner or a more advanced mastering software or hardware system to create a CD. Assemble the tracks in the right order and make sure all the timing and crossfade information is correct. Then burn your master CD at the lowest speed to lessen the chance of errors in the burning process.

Mastering Software/Hardware, PQ Subcode, and Red Book–Compatible CDs

With many more features than simple CD burning software, specialized mastering software and hardware allows you to adjust song spacing, add/subtract gain where necessary, find volume peaks, add crossfades, create PQ subcode data, and make your CD Red Book–compatible. Because it gives you complete control of your master CD, this software is extremely useful for making your home-produced recordings look and sound like they were mastered by pros.

All audio CDs have eight channels of subcode data interleaved with the digital audio data. These channels are named P, Q, R, S, T, U, V, and W. On audio CDs, only channels P and Q are used by the CD player. (Channels R–W are used to store video information in CD+G discs, and MIDI information in CD+MIDI discs.) PQ subcode editing is the process of defining the information that is encoded into the P and Q subcode channels on a Red Book–compatible CD.

The information on the P channel tells the CD player when a track is or is not playing. The information on the Q channel is more comprehensive, describing track and disc running times, disc catalog codes, and many other parameters. You can edit any of the parameters within the PQ subcode, such as the CD track numbers, index numbers, and track start and end times.

Red Book is the name of the CD-DA (CD-Digital Audio) standard as originally defined by Sony and Phillips. It defines the format a CD must have in order to be played on an audio CD player, and what that CD player must do in order to properly play audio CDs. Any CD that's Red Book–compatible should work with any commercial audio CD player.

After you burn the master CD, listen to it carefully before you duplicate it. Listen for clicks, false starts, incorrect fades, and the overall sound and order of the songs. Obviously, go back and fix anything before you take it to be duplicated. And remember to check the master that the duplicating company makes to be sure it's as good as what you gave them.

There's an interesting side effect to mastering your own projects: as you gain experience you'll apply what you learn to earlier steps in the recording process (recording, mixing, and even writing and arranging). And because you see the final big musical picture, your songs will need less and less mastering as your production skills improve.

THE STEPS AFTER MASTERING

What? There's more? Well . . . yeah, if you want to take your music to the next level. You can create MP3 and RealAudio files to post on the Web. You should also copyright your songs—go to the Library of Congress Web site at *www.loc.gov/copyright* to download copyright forms. If you're part of a band, trademark your band name at *www.uspto.gov.*

Create some art for your CD. Disc Makers has CD jewel box templates you can download for free at www.discmakers.com. If you want to sell your music in record stores you'll need a UPC bar code to put on your CD case—go to *www.uc-council.org* to get one. Finally, put together a press kit including your CD, a bio, and a picture of yourself or your band. Send it off to clubs and record labels if you're interested in gigging or getting a record contract.

Congratulations! You made it . . . you've learned how to produce, record, edit, mix, and master in your studio. I wish you all the best with your future musical projects, and thank you for reading. Now get back to what you really love doing: making music! ∎

APPENDIX A
Range Charts

Knowing the ranges of instruments you're writing for is imperative, both for making the parts playable on real instruments and for achieving real-sounding MIDI parts. This chart shows the ranges of instruments relative to a keyboard. The ranges presented here are a little narrower than each instrument's actual limits, but keeping within these boundaries will ensure that your parts sound more authentic.

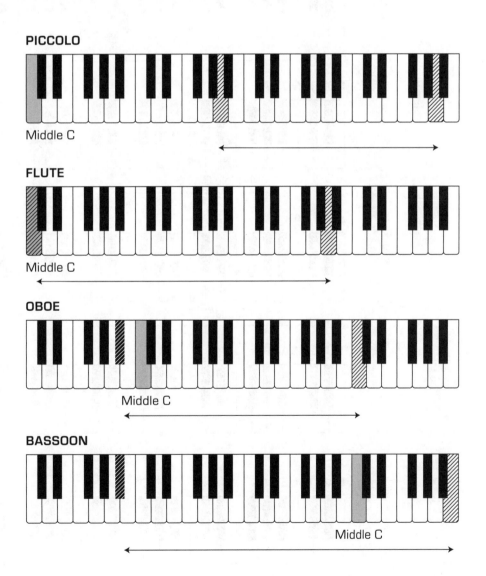

PICCOLO

Middle C

FLUTE

Middle C

OBOE

Middle C

BASSOON

Middle C

CLARINET

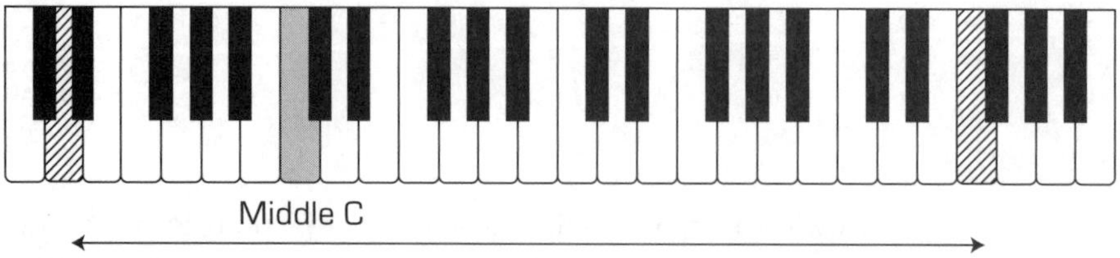
Middle C

BASS CLARINET

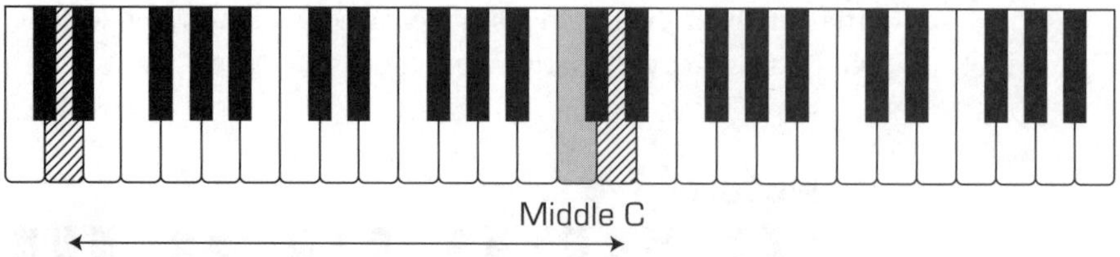
Middle C

SOPRANO SAX

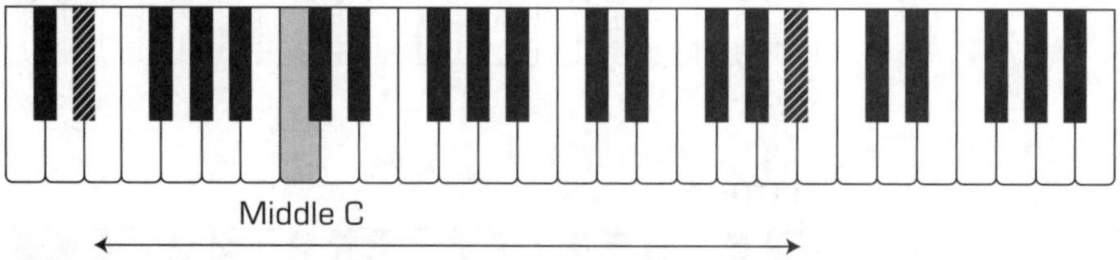
Middle C

ALTO SAX

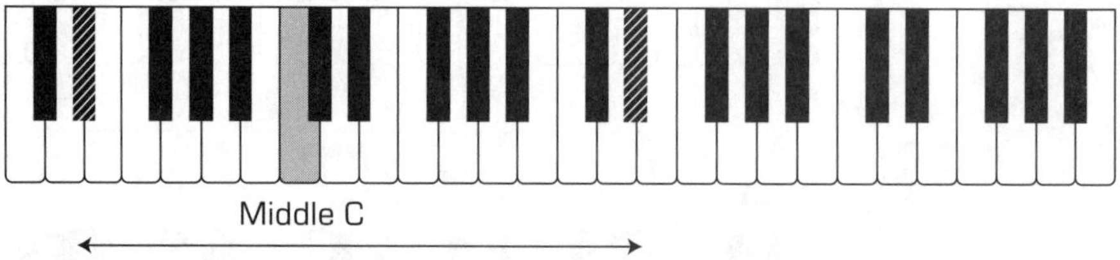
Middle C

TENOR SAX

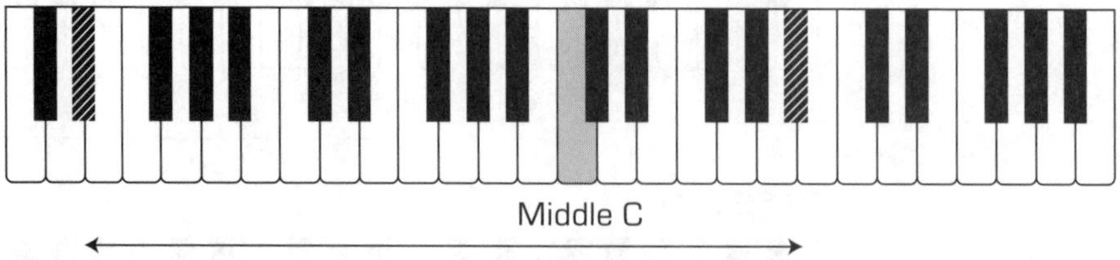
Middle C

BARITONE SAX

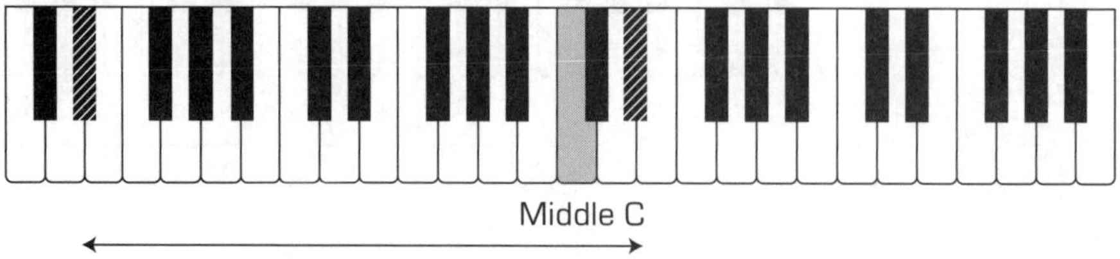
Middle C

TRUMPET

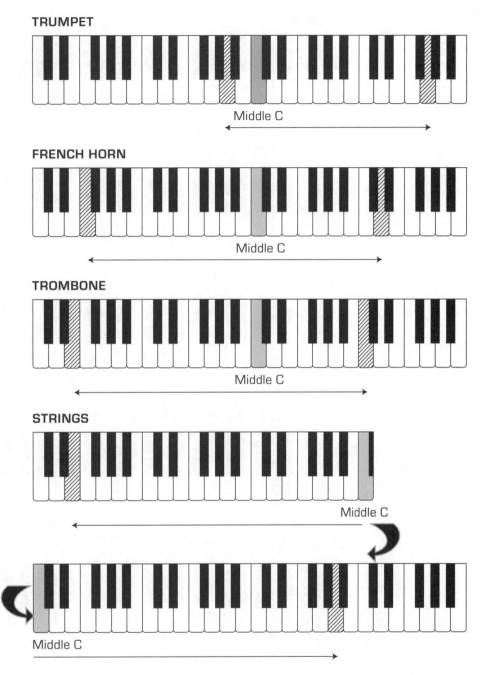

Middle C

FRENCH HORN

Middle C

TROMBONE

Middle C

STRINGS

Middle C

Middle C

HARP

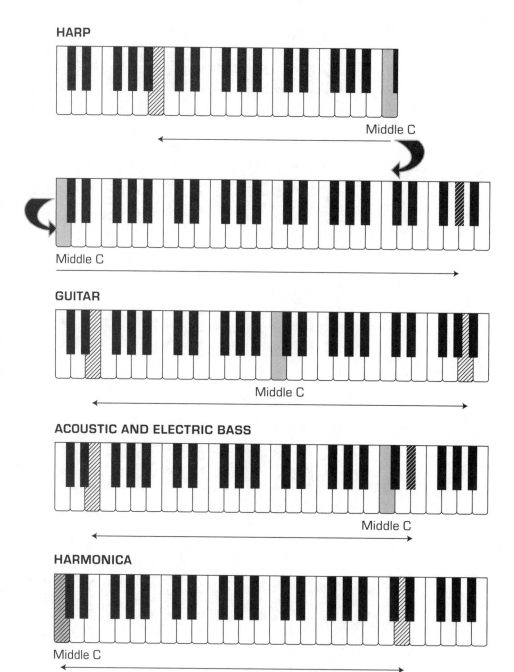

Middle C

GUITAR

Middle C

ACOUSTIC AND ELECTRIC BASS

Middle C

HARMONICA

Middle C

APPENDIX B
Web Sites to Find Musicians

Here's a list of Web sites to help you find musicians for your projects.

Berkleemusic (www.berkleemusic.com)

Berklee College of Music has created a comprehensive online training and career networking site for musicians. The site offers musicians instruction and resources to launch, advance, and sustain thriving music careers. The site is divided into four areas: an online music school, a store, a career center, and a musician's network. At Berkleemusic, musicians can find jobs and gigs, network with other musicians, promote themselves, develop their careers, and purchase music books, videos, and other educational products.

Cadenza Musicians' Directory (www.cadenza.org/musicians)

A collection of short biographies and contact details designed to put performers, composers, and teachers in touch with those organizing concerts, those commissioning new works, and those wanting music tuition. The site has information on arrangers, composers, writers, publishers, conductors, soloists, managers, ensembles, orchestras, choirs, bands, instrument makers, musicologists, music theorists and scholars, players, singers, teachers, accompanists, and music typesetters.

Coalition for Disabled Musicians (www.disabled-musicians.org)

The Coalition for Disabled Musicians, Inc. (CDM) is a voluntary, non-profit organization dedicated to enabling physically disabled musicians to pursue their musical dreams. Their Web site facilitates networking opportunities by setting up collaborative projects (bands, recording sessions, etc.) for disabled musicians.

Digidesign Production Network (www.digipronet.com)

This site is Digidesign's online directory for audio professionals.

Fastdog (www.fastdog.com)

A great source to check for available musicians, or post your own ad for free!

GigFinder (www.gigfinder.com)

A comprehensive musician's service on the Web offering free classifieds, music industry links, and much more.

Harmony Central (www.harmony-central.com)

Harmony Central is the leading Internet resource for musicians, supplying valuable information from news and product reviews, to classified ads and chat rooms.

The International Musicians Trading Post (www.musicians-classifieds.com)

This site has over 10,000 listings for musicians wanted, musicians available, equipment, and other musical services.

Musicians Available (www.musiciansavailable.com)

Musicians Available is the free place to instantly find new members for your band, find a band to join, or simply find other musicians to jam with. All musicians wanted and musicians available listings are completely free and all countries are covered.

Musician's Connection (www.musiciansconnection.com)

This site can help you find musicians, clubs/venues, recording studios, producers, and instrument manufacturers.

MusiciansContact.com (www.musicianscontact.com)

The original musicians' contact service that thousands of bands, managers, employers, and agents have used for 30 years.

Musician's Gallery (www.musiciansgallery.com)

This Web site has profiles of musicians and related musical services from all around the world.

Musicians Network (www.musiciansnetwork.com)

A central networking point for the connection of musicians and members of the music industry.

Music-Tech/Free Musicians' Classifieds (www.freemusiciansclassifieds.com)

With Free Musicians' Classifieds you can post ads in a wide variety of categories, including Musicians Seeking Placement, Employment Opportunities, Booking Agents and Managers, Songwriter Opportunities, and even Investors Wanted/Available.

Musician's Web (www.musicians-web.co.uk)

Musician's Web is a great place to find amateur musicians in the UK.

The Music Yellow Pages (www.musicyellowpages.com)

A comprehensive industry trade directory for the music, pro audio, lighting, and entertainment industries.

PrivateLessons.com (www.privatelessons.com)

Use this site to find a teacher, player, arranger, or composer for any instrument.

Taxi (www.taxi.com)

Find and be found by like-minded musicians using Taxi's easily searchable international database. Need a lyricist for your music? A bassist for your band? A studio to record your demo? A producer to produce? A singer to sing? Enter yourself into this database so people can find you, or search the people already entered to find who you're looking for.

The Mode (www.themode.com)

A database of free classifieds for musicians to get gigs, buy and sell equipment, and network with other musicians in their local areas.

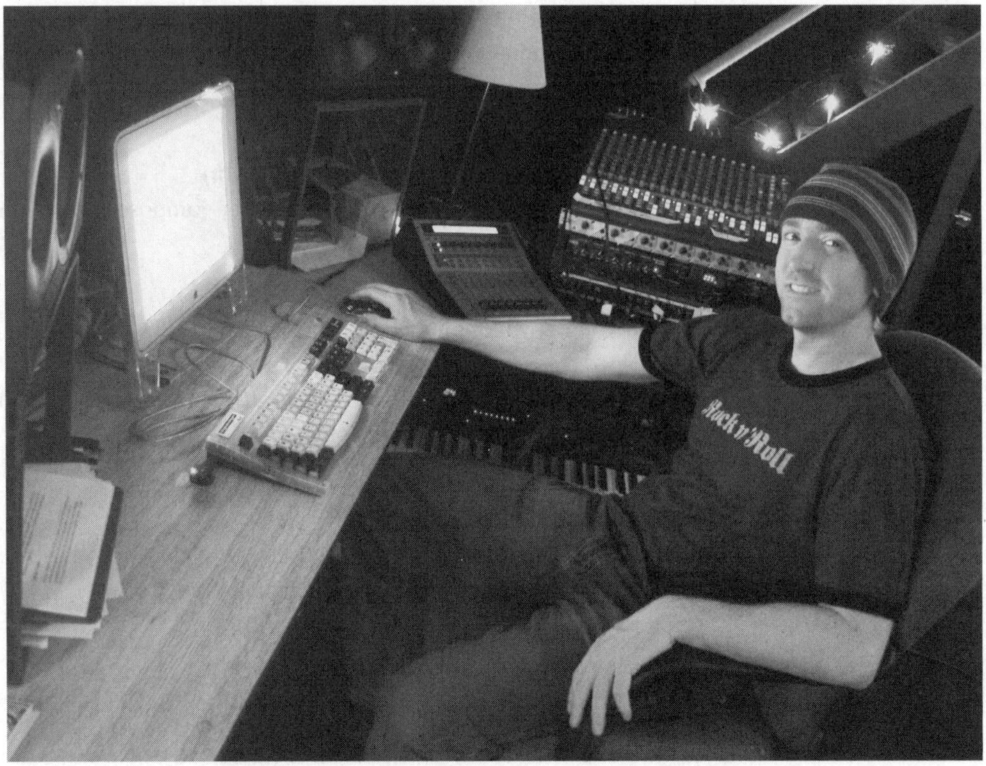
Rock'n'Roll

ABOUT THE AUTHOR

David Franz is a songwriter, record producer, engineer, multi-instrumentalist, arranger, performing artist, studio musician, author, and instructor. After earning a bachelor's and master's degree in Industrial and Systems Engineering from Virginia Tech, he attended Berklee College of Music and studied music production and engineering.

A musician since the age of five, David has been writing and producing music in home and professional studios for more than twelve years. Humbly beginning with 4-track cassette recorders and early sequencing software, he now uses state-of-the-art analog and digital recording equipment. Currently, David runs his own studio and production company, produces/records/mixes/masters records for bands and solo artists, and writes and records his own music for artistic and commercial distribution. He plays drums, bass, and guitar as well as does sequencing/programming for studio projects and live performances with his band. He is also the author and instructor of an online Pro Tools production course available through Berklee Media (*www.berkleemusic.com*) and writes a column for Digidesign's online magazine (DigiZine). He is also the author of the best-selling *Producing in the Home Studio with Pro Tools* (Boston: Berklee Press, 2003).

Visit David's Web site at *www.davidfranz.com* and his studio Web site at *www.undergroundsun.com* for information on David, his projects, his rates, and Underground Sun Studio. Feel free to contact David at *dfranz@berkleemusic.com* or *df@undergroundsun.com*.

Index

F

G

N

O

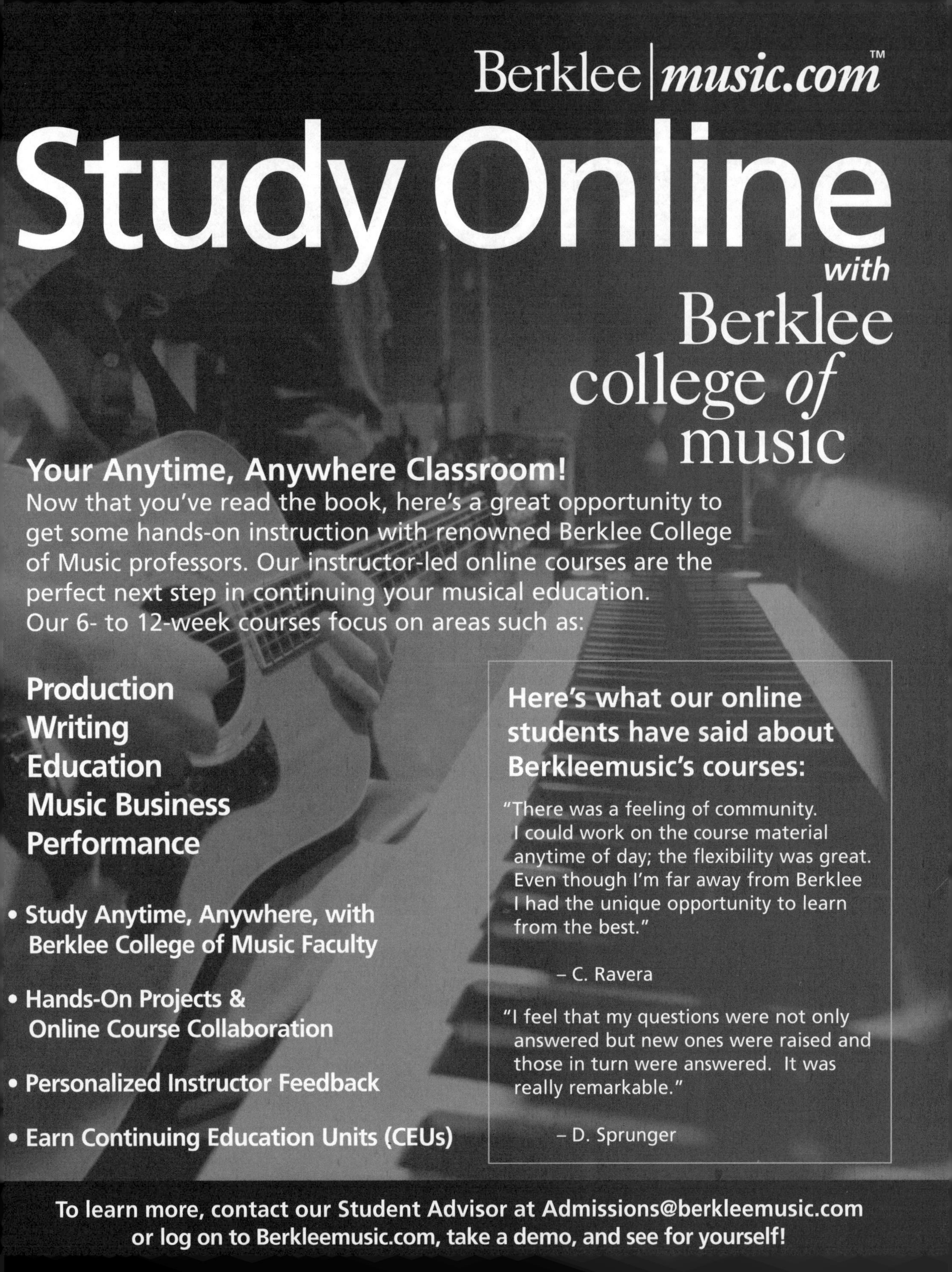

Berklee | music.com™
Study Online
with
Berklee college of music
Your Anytime, Anywhere Classroom!
Now that you've read the book, here's a great opportunity to get some hands-on instruction with renowned Berklee College of Music professors. Our instructor-led online courses are the perfect next step in continuing your musical education. Our 6- to 12-week courses focus on areas such as:
Production
Writing
Education
Music Business
Performance
• Study Anytime, Anywhere, with Berklee College of Music Faculty
• Hands-On Projects & Online Course Collaboration
• Personalized Instructor Feedback
• Earn Continuing Education Units (CEUs)
Here's what our online students have said about Berkleemusic's courses:
"There was a feeling of community. I could work on the course material anytime of day; the flexibility was great. Even though I'm far away from Berklee I had the unique opportunity to learn from the best."
– C. Ravera
"I feel that my questions were not only answered but new ones were raised and those in turn were answered. It was really remarkable."
– D. Sprunger
To learn more, contact our Student Advisor at Admissions@berkleemusic.com
or log on to Berkleemusic.com, take a demo, and see for yourself!

Berklee Press DVDs:
Just Press PLAY

berklee press

AS SERIOUS ABOUT MUSIC AS YOU ARE

Kenwood Dennard: The Studio/ Touring Drummer

| ISBN: 0-87639-022-X | HL: 50448034 | DVD $19.95 |

Up Close with Patti Austin: Auditioning and Making it in the Music Business

| ISBN: 0-87639-041-6 | HL: 50448031 | DVD $19.95 |

The Ultimate Practice Guide for Vocalists

| ISBN: 0-87639-035-1 | HL: 50448017 | DVD $19.95 |

Featuring Donna McElroy

Real-Life Career Guide for the Professional Musician

| ISBN: 0-87639-031-9 | HL: 50448013 | DVD $19.95 |

Featuring David Rosenthal

Essential Rock Grooves for Bass

| ISBN: 0-87639-037-8 | HL: 50448019 | DVD $19.95 |

Featuring Danny Morris

Jazz Guitar Techniques: Modal Voicings

| ISBN: 0-87639-034-3 | HL: 50448016 | DVD $19.95 |

Featuring Rick Peckham

Jim Kelly's Guitar Workshop

| ISBN: 0-634-00865-X | HL: 00320168 | DVD $19.95 |

Basic Afro-Cuban Rhythms for Drum Set and Hand Percussion

| ISBN: 0-87639-030-0 | HL: 50448012 | DVD $19.95 |

Featuring Ricardo Monzón

Vocal Technique: Developing Your Voice for Performance

| ISBN: 0-87639-026-2 | HL: 50448038 | DVD $19.95 |

Featuring Anne Peckham

Preparing for Your Concert

| ISBN: 0-87639-036-X | HL: 50448018 | DVD $19.95 |

Featuring JoAnne Brackeen

Jazz Improvisation: Starting Out with Motivic Development

| ISBN: 0-87639-032-7 | HL: 50448014 | DVD $19.95 |

Featuring Ed Tomassi

Chop Builder for Rock Guitar

| ISBN: 0-87639-033-5 | HL: 50448015 | DVD $19.95 |

Featuring "Shred Lord" Joe Stump

Turntable Technique: The Art of the DJ

| ISBN: 0-87639-038-6 | HL: 50448025 | DVD $24.95 |

Featuring Stephen Webber

Jazz Improvisation: A Personal Approach with Joe Lovano

| ISBN: 0-87639-021-1 | HL: 50448033 | DVD $19.95 |

Harmonic Ear Training

| ISBN: 0-87639-027-0 | HL: 50448039 | DVD $19.95 |

Featuring Roberta Radley

DISTRIBUTED BY

HAL•LEONARD

berklee press

Berklee Press books and DVDs are available wherever music books are sold.
Go to www.berkleepress.com or call 866-BERKLEE for a complete catalog of Berklee Press products.

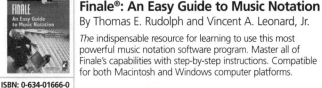